PENGUIN BOOKS

THE SPEAKING LAND

Ronald M. Berndt and Catherine H. Berndt have worked for more than four decades among Australian Aborigines mainly in the Western Desert, Arnhem Land, west-central Northern Territory and the Kimberleys, with two periods in the eastern highlands of Papua New Guinea in 1951–53. They studied together at the University of Sydney and later at the London School of Economics, University of London, where they each obtained a Ph.D. Since 1941, when they began their research together, they have specialised in Aboriginal traditional life and in the changes that have affected it. They each have an honorary degree of D.Litt. (University of W.A.), are foundation members of the Australian Institute of Aboriginal Studies and Fellows of the Academy of the Social Sciences in Australia. Ronald Berndt is Emeritus Professor of Anthropology at the University of W.A., where both he and Catherine Berndt are Honorary Research Fellows in Anthropology. They have written many books, both together and separately, including one of the classics in the field, *The World of the First Australians* (1964/1988). They live in Perth.

Front cover illustration: 'Rain Dreaming at Galibinyba'. The broad meandering lines represent the movement of Rain across the land. Smaller connecting lines are streams of water, and other patches scrub and spinifex clumps. Artist: Walter Djambidjinba, Bindubi language, Papunya, 1976, Gift from the Aboriginal Arts Board of the Australia Council to the Anthropology Research Museum of the University of Western Australia. Photography: Dr John Stanton, Curator of that Museum.

GW00673015

THE

SPEAKING LAND

Myth and Story in Aboriginal Australia

Ronald M. Berndt
Catherine H. Berndt

PENGUIN BOOKS
ASSISTED BY THE LITERATURE BOARD
OF THE AUSTRALIA COUNCIL

Penguin Books
Penguin Books Australia Ltd,
487 Maroondah Highway, P.O. Box 257
Ringwood, Victoria, 3134, Australia
Penguin Books Ltd,
Harmondsworth, Middlesex, England
Viking Penguin Inc.,
40 West 23rd Street, New York, N.Y. 10010, U.S.A.
Penguin Books Canada Limited,
2801 John Street, Markham, Ontario, Canada L3R 1B4
Penguin Books (N.Z.) Ltd,
182-190 Wairau Road, Auckland 10, New Zealand

First published by Penguin Books Australia, 1989
Reprinted 1989
Copyright © R. M. Berndt and C. H. Berndt 1988. Maps by Diana Wells

*The original illustrations reproduced in this book are in the collections of
the Anthropology Research Museum of the University of Western Australia.
All, except for the paintings in Plates 2 and 24, were obtained in the course of
anthropological
field work by R. M. and C. H. Berndt.*

All Rights Reserved. Without limiting the rights under copyright
reserved above, no part of this publication may be reproduced,
stored in or introduced into a retrieval system, or transmitted
in any form or by any means, (electronic, mechanical, photocopying,
recording or otherwise), without the prior written permission
of both the copyright owner and the above publisher of this
book.

Typeset in 10/12 Baskerville Light by Singapore National Printers Ltd
Made and printed in Australia by
Australian Print Group, Maryborough, Victoria
Designed by Lee Marquette

CIP

National Library of Australia
Cataloguing-in-Publication data
Berndt, Ronald M. (Ronald Murray), 1916–
The speaking land : myth and story in Aboriginal Australia.

Bibliography.
Includes index.
ISBN 014 012027 6

[1.]. Aborigines, Australian - Legends. [2.]. Aborigines,
Australian - Folklore, I. Berndt, Catherine H. (Catherine Helen),
1918-   . II. Title.

398.2'049915

Creative writing program assisted by the Literary Arts Board of the
Australia Council, the Federal Government's arts funding and advisory body.

CONTENTS

LIST OF MYTHS AND STORIES

LIST OF ILLUSTRATIONS

MAIN STORY-TELLERS

Myth	Personal Name(s)	Language affiliation(s)
1.	Fred Wadedi	Gagadju (Djimbura-woidbu dialect)
2.	Fred Wadedi	Gagadju
3.	Fred Wadedi	Gagadju
4.	Peter Namiyadjad	Maung
5.	Nipper Maragar	Manger(dji)
6.	Nipper Maragar	Manger(dji)
	Fred Wadedi	Gagadju
	John Bull, 'Mandjar'	Yiwadja
7.	Fred Wadedi	Gagadju
8.	Long Paddy, Djamargula	(eastern) Gunwinggu
9.	'Sugar Billy' Rindjana	Antingari
	Wogari	Yanggundjara
10.	Ganawula	Gunwinggu
	Joshua Wurungulngul	Gunwinggu
11.	Peter Namiyadjad	Maung
12.	Moara	Dadiwi dialect
13.	John Burewi	Walmadjeri
14.	Paddy Ridge, Malgada	Andingari
15.	Mushabin	Bidjandjara
	Harry Niyen	Antingari
	Marabidi	Ngalia-Andingari
16.	'Sugar Billy' Rindjana	Andingari
	Jimmy Moore, Win-gari	(southern) Andingari
	Tommy Nedabi	Wiranggu-Kokata affiliations
17.	Joe Mungu	Mara (south of Mandjindji)
	Baba-baba	Bidjandjara
18.	Joe Mungu	Mara (south of Mandjindji)
19.	Fred Mararig	Madngala
	Jimmy Leimiri	Madngala
20.	Joe Mungu	Mara (south of Mandjindji)

Myth	Personal Name(s)	Language affiliation(s)
21.	Nipper Maragar	Manger(dji)
22.	Nganalgindja	Gunwinggu
23.	Nganalgindja	Gunwinggu
24.	Long Paddy, Djamargula	(eastern) Gunwinggu
25.	Nipper Maragar	Manger(dji)
26.	Gararu	Gunwinggu
27.	Nipper Maragar	Manger(dji)
28.	Joshua Wurungulngul	Gunwinggu
29.	Nawararang 'Ngiwulg'	Gunwinggu
30.	Fred Wadedi	Gagadju
31.	Gadjibunba	Gunwinggu
32.	Mangurug	(northern) Gunwinggu
33.	Joe Mungu Paddy Ridge, Malgada	Mara (south of Mandjindji) Andingari
34.	Joe Mungu Imalang	Mara (south of Mandjindji) Ngalia-Andingari
35.	Daniel Bindi-bindi	Gugadja
36.	Danggoubwi Dundir	Djambarbingu dialect Walamangu dialect
37.	Ngaiiwul	Gunwinggu
38.	Guningbal (Guninbal) Joshua Wurungulngul	(eastern) Gunwinggu Gunwinggu
39.	Fred Wadedi	Gagadju
40.	Nipper Maragar Fred Wadedi	Manger(dji) Gagadju
41.	'Wogiman Paddy', Walgiri	Nanggiomiri
42.	Nganalgindja	Gunwinggu
43.	Mangurug	(northern) Gunwinggu
44.	Mangurug	(northern) Gunwinggu
45.	Nipper Maragar	Manger(dji)
46.	Minyaiwi Gadjibunba	Gunwinggu Gunwinggu
47.	Ngaiiwul	Gunwinggu
48.	Wurgamara	Gunwinggu
49.	Gararu	Gunwinggu
50.	Minyaiwi Gadjibunba	Gunwinggu Gunwinggu

Myth	Personal Name(s)	Language affiliation(s)
51.	Medeg	Gunwinggu
52.	Gararu	Gunwinggu
53.	Fred Wadedi	Gagadju
54.	Minyaiwi Gadjibunba	Gunwinggu Gunwinggu
55.	Nipper Maragar Jimmy Midjau-midjau	Manger(dji) (northern) Gunwinggu
56.	Mangurug Julie Djulungurr	(northern) Gunwinggu (northern) Gunwinggu
57.	Big Nolaman (Ngolaman)	Maung
58.	'Wogiman Paddy', Walgiri Mathew Maluwau'wau	Nanggiomiri Ngulugwongga
59.	Wimidji	Gugadja
60.	Gugaman ('cook-man'), Liliyara	Gugadja
61.	'Donkey-man' Lugu Fred Imyau	Gugadja Gugadja
62.	'Donkey-man' Lugu Yalwaluru	Gugadja Gugadja
63.	George Maning	Wiranggu
64.	Joe Mungu	Mara (south of Mandjindji)
65.	George Maning	Wiranggu
66.	Joe Mungu Harry Niyen	Mara (south of Mandjindji) Andingari
67.	Joe Mungu Baba-baba	Mara (south of Mandjindji) Andingari
68.	Joe Mungu	Mara (south of Mandjindji)
69.	Wimidji Wilpilara	Gugadja Gugadja
70.	'Dosi' (milang section)	Andingari
71.	Nganalgindja	Gunwinggu
72.	Samuel Mangguldja	Gunwinggu
73.	Mangurug	(northern) Gunwinggu
74.	Nganalgindja	Gunwinggu
75.	Nganalgindja	Gunwinggu
76.	Gararu Medeg	Gunwinggu Gunwinggu
77.	Danggoubwi	Djambarbingu dialect
78.	Danggoubwi	Djambarbingu dialect

Myth	Personal Name(s)	Language affiliation(s)
79.	Danggoubwi	Djambarbingu dialect
80.	Winungoidj	Maung
81.	Nalowid	Walang
82.	Mangurug	(northern) Gunwinggu
83.	Ngaiiwul	Gunwinggu
84.	Fred Wadedi	Gagadju
	Jimmy Midjau-midjau	(northern) Gunwinggu
85.	Nipper Maragar	Manger(dji)
86.	Fred Wadedi	Gagadju
87.	Nganalgindja	Gunwinggu
88.	Winungoidj	Maung
89.	Nganalgindja	Gunwinggu
90.	Mangurug	(northern) Gunwinggu
91.	Nipper Maragar	Manger(dji)
92.	Nganalgindja	Gunwinggu
93.	Jimmy Midjau-midjau	(northern) Gunwinggu
94.	George Maning	Wiranggu
95.	'Donkey-man' Lugu	Gugadja
	Djilari	Walmadjeri
96.	Doug Murray, Manmari	Mandjindji
	Peter Yagi	Mandjindji
97.	Joe Mungu	Mara (south of Mandjindji)
98.	Liyagarang	Dalwongu dialect
99.	Peter Namiyadjad	Maung
100.	Nipper Maragar	Manger(dji)
101.	Joe Mungu	Mara (south of Mandjindji)
102.	Marabidi	Ngalia-Andingari
	Harry Niyen	Andingari
103.	Marabidi	Ngalia-Andingari
	Harry Niyen	Andingari
104.	Joe Mungu	Mara (south of Mandjindji)
105.	Wimidji	Gugadja
	'Donkey-man' Lugu	Gugadja
106.	Imalang	Ngalia-Andingari
	Mushabin	Bidjandjara
	Harry Niyen	Andingari
107.	Munggarawi	Gumaidj dialect
	(Mun-gurawi)	

Myth	Personal Name(s)	Language affiliation(s)
108.	Fred Wadedi	Gagadju
109.	Gadjibunba	Gunwinggu
110.	Winungoidj	Maung
111.	Joe Mungu	Mara (south of Mandjindji)
112.	Big Guwodbad (Guwadbug)	Maung
113.	Joe Mungu Tommy Nedabi	Mara (south of Mandjindji) Wiranggu-Kokata affiliations
114.	Mangurug	(northern) Gunwinggu
115.	'Dosi' (milang section)	Andingari
116.	Minyaiwi Gadjibunba	Gunwinggu Gunwinggu
117.	Long Paddy, Djamargula	(eastern) Gunwinggu
118.	Tom Namagarainmag	Maung
119.	Mawulan Wandjug	Riradjingu dialect Riradjingu dialect
120.	Gadjibunba	Gunwinggu
121.	Jack Fish, Gadar Mathew Maluwau'wau	Madngala Ngulugwongga
122.	Minyaiwi	Gunwinggu
123.	Joshua Wurungulngul Samuel Mangguldja	Gunwinggu Gunwinggu
124.	Larry Lodi	Gugadja
125.	Long Harry, Milili Mushabin	Mandjindji Bidjandjara
126.	Fred Wadedi	Gagadju
127.	Joe Mungu Harry Niyen	Mara (south of Mandjindji) Andingari
128.	Joe Mungu	Mara (south of Mandjindji)
129.	Nipper Maragar	Manger(dji)
130.	Fred Mararig	Madngala
131.	Mangurug	(northern) Gunwinggu
132.	Mangurug	(northern) Gunwinggu
133.	Mangurug	(northern) Gunwinggu
134.	Mick Djandudjugur	Gugadja
135.	'Sandfly' Yalpayu	Gugadja

Myth	Personal Name(s)	Language affiliation(s)
136.	Daniel Bindi-bindi Mick Gabuninggu	Gugadja Gugadja
137.	'Sandfly' Yalpayu Djilari	Gugadja Walmadjeri
138.	Gararu	Gunwinggu
139.	Mangurug	(northern) Gunwinggu
140.	Nganalgindja	Gunwinggu
141.	Joe Mungu	Mara (south of Mandjindji)
142.	Joe Mungu 'Sunny Jim' Yandud	Mara (south of Mandjindji) Man-gunda (north west of Ooldea)
143.	Samuel Mangguldja Nipper Maragar	Gunwinggu Manger(dji)
144.	Old Wurungulngul	Maung
145.	Peter Namiyadjad	Maung
146.	Winungoidj	Maung
147.	Joshua Wurungulngul	Gunwinggu
148.	Ganawula Joshua Wurungulngul	Gunwinggu Gunwinggu
149.	Nawararang 'Ngiwulg'	Gunwinggu
150.	'Sugar Billy' Rindjana Tommy Nedabi	Andingari Wiranggu-Kokata affiliations
151.	Joe Mungu	Mara (south of Mandjindji)
152.	Mathew Maluwau'wau	Ngulugwongga
153.	Mathew Maluwau'wau	Ngulugwongga
154.	Joe Mungu	Mara (south of Mandjindji)
155.	Nganalgindja	Gunwinggu
156.	Guningbal (Guninbal)	(eastern) Gunwinggu
157.	Mangurug	(northern) Gunwinggu
158.	Mangurug	(northern) Gunwinggu
159.	'Donkey-man' Lugu Wimidji	Gugadja Gugadja
160.	George Maning	Wiranggu
161.	Melbourne Waldjangadolbu	Mara, with Alawa affinities
162.	Wimidji 'Donkey-man' Lugu	Gugadja Gugadja
163.	Munggaraui (Mun-gurawi)	Gumaidj dialect
164.	Bununggu	Gumaidj dialect

Myth	Personal Name(s)	Language affiliation(s)
165.	Naradjin	Manggalili dialect
166.	George Maning Tommy Nedabi	Wiranggu Wiranggu-Kokata affiliations
167.	Joe Mungu Paddy Ridge, Malgada George Maning	Mara (south of Mandjindji) Andingari Wiranggu
168.	Joe Mungu	Mara (south of Mandjindji)
169.	Joe Mungu Imalang	Mara (south of Mandjindji) Ngalia-Andingari
170.	Jimmy Moore, Win-gari Tommy Nedabi	Man-gunda (northwest of Ooldea) Wiranggu-Kokata affiliations
171.	Jubilee Bambadu (or Bagubagu)	Gugadja
172.	Joe Mungu	Mara (south of Mandjindji)
173.	Imalang Harry Niyen	Ngalia-Andingari Andingari
174.	Mathew Maluwau'wau	Ngulugwongga
175.	Mathew Maluwau'wau	Ngulugwongga
176.	Fred Wadedi Nipper Maragar	Gagadju Manger(dji)
177.	Nganalgindja	Gungwinggu
178.	Ganawula	Gunwinggu
179.	Nganalgindja	Gunwinggu
180.	'Old Nim' Dungalg Mathew Maluwau'wau	Ngulugwongga Ngulugwongga
181.	Jimmy Midjau-midjau	Gunwinggu
182.	Mangurug	(northern) Gunwinggu
183.	Mawulan Wandjug	Riradjingu dialect Riradjingu dialect
184.	Joe Mungu	Mara (south of Mandjindji)
185.	'Donkey-man' Lugu	Gugadja
186.	John Fish Gadar 'Wogiman Paddy', Walgiri Mathew Maluwau'wau	Madngala Nanggiomiri Ngulugwongga
187.	Wimidji 'Donkey-man' Lugu	Gugadja Gugadja
188.	Ngalmidul	Maung
189.	Peter Namiyadjad	Maung
190.	Mawulan	Riradjingu dialect

Myth	Personal Name(s)	Language affiliation(s)
191.	Danggoubwi	Djambarbingu dialect
192.	Meyaweidba	Maung
193.	Meyaweidba	Maung
194.	Danggoubwi	Djambarbingu dialect
195.	Danggoubwi	Djambarbingu dialect

Other Story-Tellers Involved

Ngalgindali	Gunwinggu
Lazarus Lamilami	Maung
Mondalmi	Maung
Ngalwalun	Maung
Waibuma	Gunwinggu
Mamulaid	Maung
Guwadu	Gunwinggu
Daphne Nimanydja	Ngeimil dialect

Some places mentioned in this book

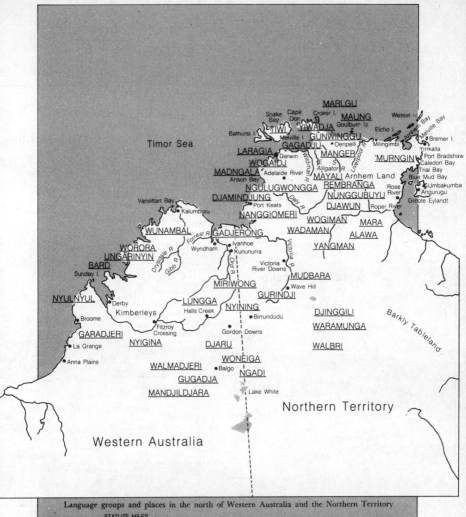

Language groups and places in the north of Western Australia and the Northern Territory

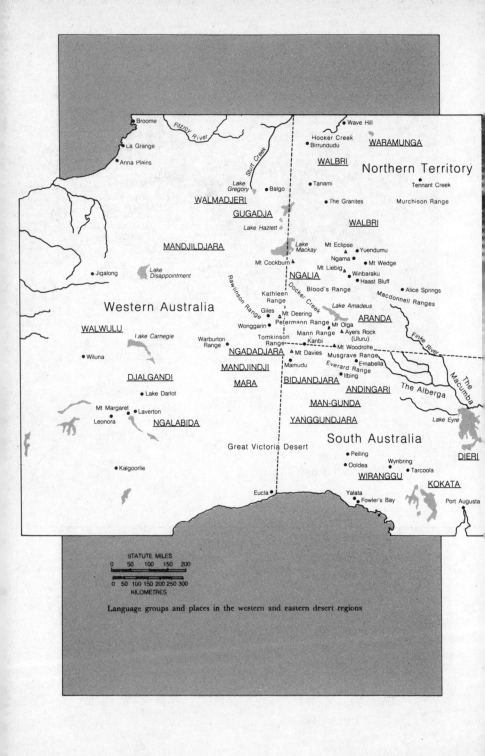

Language groups and places in the western and eastern desert regions

FOREWORD

This book has been designed specifically for general readers as well as for those especially interested in Australian Aboriginal oral literature. It consists of a wide range of myths and stories traditionally told in Aboriginal Australia. However, we have not attempted to cover the whole range of Aboriginal cultures, or the whole field of Aboriginal literature. To do that we would have needed a much larger book, or series of books.

The themes we treat are almost commonplace. They should strike a familiar cord for any reader, from any culture. In one sense the myths speak in a universal idiom that can readily be identified. In another sense, some contain an opaque or shifting screen effect that tends to obscure meaning, or at least make it more difficult to get at, and to provide a degree of exoticism.

The myths we include, in so far as their areas of origin are concerned, will be known to all members of particular Aboriginal communities where traditional beliefs still retain their element of reality and their relevance to everyday activities. Many of them have a religious component; but none is secret-sacred, from the point of view of either men or women. Moreover, none is esoteric. Nevertheless there is, of course, much symbolism associated with them.

From almost the time of first European settlement in this country, various people have written down fragments of myths told to them, in various circumstances, by Aborigines. Many of these were indifferently recorded, their content considerably anglicised in the process, and often drastically censored. In contrast to that approach, the myths we present are unexpurgated. It is only in recent years that Aboriginal oral literature has been taken seriously by people other than Aborigines — mainly, but not entirely, by anthropologists. Historians focusing on social history have been looking in this direction. So have writers concerned with Australian literature in general terms, and many others as well. Where anthropologists and linguists have been involved, such myths and stories have, ideally, been set down systematically in their own language, carefully translated and analysed, and usually looked at in their socio-cultural context. Aborigines, too, where they are literate or, if not, in conjunction with someone who is, have been recording their own myths and stories.

In spite of all this activity, professional or otherwise, no attempt has been made up to now to compile an anthology of Aboriginal mythology to enable us to see it in perspective and to gauge what impact it could conceivably make on non-Aborigines — not simply as having a story value but, more significantly, having an intellectual component that can be identified. Stories of the kind presented here provide insights into Aboriginal thinking and doing things, in relation to other human beings (kin, friends and strangers), various creatures, species and elements in the environment and, in particular, to the ultimate arbiters of the destinies of men and women, the deities of the Dreaming.

The attitudes and actions manifested in this mythology are not only of a traditional Aboriginal past — a past that is relentlessly being pushed into obscurity, and not only by non-Aborigines. On the contrary, the mythology is a vibrant and ready source of messages about a past-in-the-present — messages that are for the most part as significant as they ever were to Aboriginal contemporary socio-cultural situations. To use the imagery particularly appropriate to mythology, we may see this book as reflecting a wide range of different Aboriginal mythic actors, rapidly changing their roles from one scene to the next, but never losing their time-honoured positions within a precisely-defined topographical perspective. The land is their ultimate determinant.

All the myth-stories presented here were told to us and recorded in writing (and more recently on tape) in the language used by the story-tellers. Only a very few of them were told to us in Aboriginal-English. The fact that they were told in the speakers' own languages enabled us to render a reasonably straightforward translation in standard English (or what approximates this), unimpaired by an intermediate medium. An important consideration in making these translations was to retain, as far as was possible in the circumstances, something of the indigenous structure and organisation of the myths. In any translation of materials from one language to another, one culture to another, something is inevitably lost in the process. That aside, in preparing a book of this kind there is the primary consideration of communicating with non-Aboriginal language-speakers, of conveying both an atmosphere and sense of the original spoken versions, and at the same time managing to make it readable.

We wrote this book together. All of the myth-stories recorded by C. Berndt were told to her by women; by R. Berndt, by men. In a few cases, we include both male and female versions of a particular myth. It is likely that differences between our renderings are discernible in regard to the translation of original materials. Personally, we recognise that C. Berndt's translations approximate more closely to the structure of the original texts, although that is difficult to gauge. However, we should emphasise that each myth is, we hope, a reasonable translation into English, and that in all cases we have separated the recorded myth from our discussion of it.

It has been necessary occasionally to include some Aboriginal words. The orthography used in this respect is relatively simple. For instance, we have preferred to use the voiced consonants *b*, *d* and *g*, except in a few cases where unvoiced consonants are used, when a particular word is commonly recognised in that spelling. *Dj* is equivalent to the English *j; u* is pronounced as in *put; ng* is a single sound as in 'sing'; and a hyphen between *n-g* and/or *ng-g* indicates that these are two separate sounds. All Aboriginal words are in italics except for place, language and personal names.

We have located myths mostly by referring to language-identifications, as well as the places associated with them. The term 'tribe' can be misleading, so we have tried to avoid it. Many myths, for example in western Arnhem Land, relate how particular mythic characters travelled across large stretches of country and through the territories of different language groups. In north-eastern Arnhem Land the reference points are dialect groups, which together make up an overall language unit; traditional marriage rules forbid marriage between members of the same dialect group. That does not apply in the case of what has been called the Western Desert, where people speaking the same dialect can marry, if they are eligible according to other rules.

Some mythic beings are said to belong to specific social categories, just as human beings do — and almost all aspects of nature are classified under those headings too. Social categories are a kind of scaffolding, a framework for social relationships in everyday life as well as in religious contexts. They varied throughout the continent. Even where there are similarities between regions in this respect, there were also differences: in the names attached to the categories, or in the total patterning, or in the rules associated with them. People in any one area telling stories, or listening to them, would know about such arrangements, as a backdrop to what was being said, or sometimes as a focus of episodes in them. A story-teller might mention particular categories in referring to the characters, or someone might ask about them. We have mentioned a few, in the course of the stories, but not to any extent. Even an outline of one or two systems would call for too many names and details, and an account of how they work out in practice could become quite complicated.

One very widespread type of classification is called in English a 'moiety' division, where all members of a society belong to one or other of two moieties ('halves'). In north-eastern Arnhem Land the system is primarily patrilineal: that is, you would belong to the same moiety as your father, and his father, and so on. You would belong secondarily to your mother's moiety, and have other rights in regard to that. The names in this area are *dua* and *yiridja*. Marriage or sweetheart relationships within the same moiety were strictly forbidden, and there were other rules as well (see R. and C. Berndt 1985: 61–66). The *dua-yiridja* division has been spreading into western Arnhem Land over the last fifty years or so. But in western Arnhem Land the traditional moiety division is primarily matrilineal: you would belong to the same moiety as your mother, and her mother, and so on. The names are *madgu* and *ngaraidgu* (for masculine forms, add the prefix *na-*, and for feminine forms, the prefix *ngal-*.) Each of these is divided again into two, called semi-moieties; the Maung add a prefix to female forms, but the Gunwinggu do not. In each of the two regions there are also sub-sections — a division into eight categories that fits into the moiety system. The names are different in each case, just as they are everywhere the sub-section system has spread. In western Arnhem Land, for instance, the masculine and feminine forms *nabulan* and *ngalbulan* are an example of one sub-section. (see R. and C. Berndt 1970: 60–75). For the Western Desert, sub-sections have been introduced within recent years: *djambidjin* and *nambidjin* are an example of a male and female sibling pair. In many Desert myths, however, no sub-section term is mentioned in relation to a particular mythic character. This is mainly because in organising their activities these people traditionally emphasised alternating generation levels (see C. and R. Berndt 1983: 33–35). They did have what are called sections (that is, four male and female sibling pairs). All such patterns for all the areas mentioned were arranged to take into account appropriate inter-marrying pairs of persons. We mention these points in passing, since anthropologically they provide interesting and vital clues to questions of social positioning and relationships between specific mythic characters. The general reader should not worry about them. Ignoring them should not interfere with enjoyment of the stories.

Finally, we acknowledge the great help we have received over many years from many Aborigines who told us these myths and stories. Not only did this require considerable patience — on their part and ours; but the major point that should be emphasised was the enthusiasm they displayed, and their recognition that such material should not be lost to them and to others. They were actively concerned that non-Aborigines should know more about these stories, in which they themselves had, and have, a deep-felt interest. They constitute a repertoire of knowledge considered by them to be important, not only in understanding themselves as people but in appreciating the living environment — the land and all within it, to which, traditionally, they were so intimately linked.

Many of the Aboriginal men and women were outstanding raconteurs, having a tremendous aptitude for dramatic effect. Many, too, went to great pains to ensure that we understood the myths and stories — *almost* as well as they did themselves. We can only hope that we have done justice to their efforts and expectations. This is, essentially, a collaborative work between the many Aboriginal story-tellers and ourselves. So many Aborigines have participated in it that the only way of acknowledging this is to set out a list of their names and language affiliations immediately preceding this Foreword. Many of them are no longer living, but we trust that their descendants will find pleasure as well as interest in their contributions.

This book was completed during the course of our holding, jointly, an Australian Research Grant Scheme Award within the Department of Anthropology of the University of Western Australia. We would also like to record our appreciation of the help given by Dr John Stanton, Curator of the Anthropology Museum of the University of Western Australia for preparing the photographic material that accompanies this book; and by Ms Julie Tyers, who typed not only a couple of versions of the manuscript, but also the interleaved texts from which the translations were compiled.

Ronald M. Berndt
Catherine H. Berndt
Department of Anthropology,
University of Western Australia,
July 1987.

CHAPTER ONE

INTO A WORLD OF MYTH AND STORY

Myth is a word that can be taken in at least two ways. In the popular sense it stands for 'false belief' — something that is believed to be true but is actually false. In the other, less negative sense, the emphasis is on belief, and assessment of true-or-false is seen as a separate issue. People who use the term 'myth' in the first way are most often referring to someone else's beliefs and not their own. For the same reason, they avoid applying it to anything that they themselves believe to be true. But substituting another label will not alter that perspective or make that problem go away. Myth continues to be the most useful and most widely understood term for what we will be concentrating on here: narrative material in story form that is regarded as important and significant even when it is not directly religious or actively linked with religious ritual.

MYTHIC SCENES

The myth-stories in this book come from a number of different Aboriginal traditional cultural backgrounds and local scenes across the Australian continent. Each regional repertoire has its own particular style or flavour. Nevertheless, all of them have much in common. We can identify an Aboriginal distinctiveness that ensures for them a unique niche within the world of oral literatures.

The actors in the social events and situations portrayed here are deities and spirits who intermingle and interact with the human beings and various natural species, in a kaleidoscopic shifting time-span. The backdrop to their activities is an Australian environment that mirrors the vivid contrasts and similarities of the continent itself, its prodigality and its harshness.

All these myths were told by adult men and women. Sometimes children were present, but essentially they were for adult listeners. We have chosen to present them as closely as possible to the way in which they were told, without deleting or modifying any of the attitudes and sentiments expressed in them. These days, they are not likely to offend the sensitivities of anyone who reads them. Too often, the publicly-presented image of Aboriginal mythology has been an unreal, almost inhuman one, of heroic and unassailable characters intent on shaping a world and a code of law in which and by which new generations of human beings might live peacably and happily, the Golden Age they established lasting until it was irretrievably shattered by European invasion. (In one sense, the European intruders were counterparts of the malignant spirits and monsters against which human beings pit their strength and ingenuity — with the difference that in the story context it is the Aborigines who mostly triumph.)

That particular myth-picture is not common in the anthropological literature, and even in popular accounts there are notable exceptions. But it is a blend of mythology that has fairly general currency, especially where myths and stories are arranged in books or radio or television programmes intended for children. The assumption is that Aboriginal mythology is simple and childish; that such tales are more suitable for children than for adults. To achieve that simplicity, original myth versions have been 'watered down' to meet the supposed demands of a non-Aboriginal market. Only in rare cases are they made available for intelligent adult appreciation, or as a contribution to serious literature. This task has mostly been left to anthropologists. What happens then is that they are usually prepared for specialist readers or specialist audiences, set within theoretical frameworks designed to explain social-personal relations, reveal ideas and values, and substantiate ritual behaviour. Here we try to steer a middle course.

The myths are presented in their stark reality, not dramatised nor romanticised. Some are tinged with fantasy; others are almost bizarre. Among them are scenes of travel, of mythic beings in animal or human guise, shape-changing at will, moving over large stretches of countryside — exploring, hunting, shaping the land, perhaps paying scant attention to others already settled there. Among them too are scenes of quiet contentment, punctuated by occasional highlights of ceremony and ritual, gift exchange and trade, permeated with the satisfaction of having sufficient food and opportunities to make love. These scenes, however, are often counterbalanced or upset by acts of treachery and theft, jealousy and lust, greed, antagonism, or the flaring of anger resulting in injury and death. Violence was close to the surface of mythic living — if the myths are any guide in these respects. Not much provocation was needed for conflicts to develop. It was not that men and women were violent in themselves. That violence came from the natural forces of the elements, and was felt directly, because the protective screens between human beings and nature were quite fragile. There were also malignant or potentially hostile spirits and other creatures to cope with. All of this contributed to an aura of inevitability or unpredictability which, as the myths note, was often beyond the reach or powers of the mythic beings themselves — and certainly beyond the powers of ordinary human beings. It is this kind of story, this kind of theme, that so many Aboriginal myths convey: conflict as a normal feature of social living, a familiar natural environment never quite harnessed to the service of human beings, and a countryside that could on occasion become terrifying.

It is open to question how far these disrupting influences manifested in Aboriginal mythology should be emphasised at the expense of, or as contrasted with, the relatively peaceful and smooth-flowing tenor of ordinary existence. There are scenes of people living happily, industriously intent on gaining a livelihood from the land, relaxing, or anticipating the excitement of ceremony and the serious business of ritual on which, in an ultimate sense, their well-being depended. Aboriginal mythology is often silent on moral issues. In most cases the myths avoid evaluating and spelling out the rights and wrongs of particular situations or condemning the actions of the weak or the vicious. By implication, or in the way that a story is framed and told, it is sometimes made plain that particular actions are condemned.

As a rule, Aborigines seemingly preferred their mythology not to be *directly* censorious. They took the stand that good and bad, moral and immoral, co-exist in human interaction. In that respect, deities and other mythic characters react more or less in the same way as their human counterparts — except that, in the case of mythic beings, their supernatural qualities enter the picture. The moral and the immoral constitute a kind of continuum, with one blurring into the other, and the boundaries between them not at all clear. There are exceptions. For instance, when 'good' characters are upset or hurt or killed, a myth may go on to show, or to suggest, that whoever was responsible will eventually pay the penalty in one way or another, that disaster or death will befall them. In Aboriginal mythology the good does not necessarily have to be underlined or to be spelt out, because bad actions are likely to bring their own deserts. But, as the myths often show, that sequence of social events does not always follow.

Many of the great myths, most notably those of a religious nature, attribute to their main characters actions that in ordinary everyday life would be regarded as reprehensible. There is no difficulty about providing an explanation for myths of this kind. But the matter is not resolved merely by considering them as guides to right and wrong behaviour. Many of them were, of course, just that. On the other hand, to explore their meanings we need to consider them in another dimension. That leads primarily into an interpretation of their symbolism. There are varying levels of meaning, recognised by Aborigines themselves. This is particularly the case with some myths, for example in western Arnhem

Land, where particular mythic characters are fated to 'go wrong'. Because of some unforeseen circumstance, they are impelled to do so and there is nothing they can do to avoid it: such events, drawing to their inevitable conclusion, can have momentous results.

LIVING MYTHS

One of the major points we make in this book is that all the myths we consider are 'living myths'. They are not simply of the past, as in the case of Robert Graves' *The Greek Myths;* nor are they quasi-historical tales or folklore, the food of legend, as were the Brothers Grimm's *Deutsche Sagen.* They were believed in by the people who told them and those who listened to them. In traditional Aboriginal terms they embody 'truth', purporting to depict what actually happened. Many of them belong to the Dreaming and relate to Dreaming characters. What such characters did had an everlasting effect on human beings. These myths are regarded as having an eternal quality, relevant to people of the past, those of the present, and those who will come into being in the future. Traditionally, their veracity was not doubted.

Aboriginal mythology, for any particular group of Aboriginal people, was and is, like a huge mirror that reflected — sometimes dimly, sometimes in an exaggerated way, sometimes phantasmagorically — what was familiar to them, something they expected to see and something that they could identify. It was not necessarily a mirror reflecting reality, in the sense in which we normally use that word. But in many cases it was very close indeed to that. Much of Aboriginal mythology focused on conflict situations, and on providing explanations of how social and natural phenomena came about. This was a powerful literary device which took much of ordinary, everyday social living for granted. It did this because the intent was, apparently, to emphasise that aspect by under-playing it, by highlighting violence, lust, treachery and so on. It capital-ised on happenings of that kind in order to clarify danger areas of social living, and perhaps as a deterrent to complacency. Yet as some of the myths demonstrate, often inexplicably, out of wrong-doing, out of some overwhelming disaster, a social benefit may accrue.

Mythology is an intellectual vehicle, whether or not it appears to be directly religious. Through it basic truths and values are articulated and interpreted in varying ways and within differing socio-cultural contexts. With Aboriginal mythology we are not dealing with social documents or historical statements in a straightforward conventional sense. However, it must be recognised that from a traditional Aboriginal standpoint these myths *are* regarded as being all of these, and more. Also, from an Aboriginal point of view, such myths were considered to be fundamentally unchanging statements, valid for all time: 'as it was in the beginning, so it is now, and ever shall be'. Anthropological approaches, as such, are different: mythology is a highly receptive vehicle, flexible and incorporative, responsive to changing social circumstances, able to permit varying interpretations of its content, as occasions demand.

Over and above what myths have to say to the people who believe in them and who consider them to be their own particular brand of wisdom, as well as constituting explanations of natural and social events, they always have different layers of meaning. These were, and in many cases still are, dependent on the age, sex, social and religious status and circumstance of the people who told them or were in a position to hear and understand them. There is an overwhelming imperative which has to do with their veracity, something that serves to establish them in the minds of their possessors as being absolutely true, whatever other evidence there might be to the contrary. It is this idea that is embodied in the title of this book, *The Speaking Land*.

THE *PARTICIPATING* LAND

No traditional Aboriginal myth was told without reference to the land, or to a specific stretch of country where the incidents it narrates were believed to have taken place. No myth is free-floating, without some local identification. Without their anchorages, they could be regarded as being simply 'just so' stories. In other words, the land and all within it was irrevocably tied up with the content of a myth or story, just as were (and are) the people themselves.

'Where did he/she/they come from? What did they do? Where did they do it? And where did they go? These questions do not need to be asked, because answers are always included as an integral part of the myth-telling, sometimes in considerable detail. Also, there is information on what language various mythic characters spoke (or would speak); where their home country was located (or would be located); or what language would be imposed on, or given to the future generations of people who would inhabit that place. This kind of information about the land over which such characters moved as the tangible evidence of their presence was crucial. It served, and continues to serve, as a charter for contemporary land-ownership: a set of statements identifying and locating people and groups who are assumed to have been descended from, or otherwise associated with, the particular mythic beings who made these pronouncements in the beginning.

Mythic or Dreaming people in human or animal or other form moved across the countryside. In so doing they left signs of themselves or their spiritual presence at particular places. Many of them 'made themselves' or 'turned themselves' into an aspect of the physical environment and thus imbued it with social relevance. The whole land is full of signs: a land humanised so that it could be used and read by Aborigines who were/are intimately familiar with it, and read as clearly as if it were bristling with notice-boards.

It is, then, the land which is really speaking — offering, to those who can understand its language, an explanative discourse about how it came to be as it is now, which beings were responsible for its becoming like that, and who is or should be responsible for it now. The physiographic sites and places are like the chapter headings of a book, and each one has much to say. *The Speaking Land* must be heard. But what it says may be understood only if we know its language. The intention in this book is to provide an opportunity for its readers to learn something more about that language.

RANGE AND SELECTION

The myths we present and discuss are drawn from the very large repertoire we have assembled during our many field research periods. They come from a wide range of traditionally-oriented Aborigines, both men and women. In time-span they range from 1941 to quite recently. The primary sources we use come from western and north-eastern Arnhem Land; the Goulburn Islands; the buffalo plains east of Darwin; the Daly River; the central-western part of the Northern Territory; Balgo in the south-eastern Kimberley; and Ooldea at the southern edge of the desert in western South Australia. They are supplemented by myths and stories from others areas, including south-eastern Australia. We also include, for comparison, references to myths from other regions of Aboriginal Australia that have been recorded by other people.

The myths and stories we heard were virtually all written down in long-hand, in phonetic script, and translated in the presence of the narrators. It was not until 1958 that we had access to tape recorders. In all cases we discussed the content of each myth with the Aborigines involved. However, for the purpose of this book we give reasonably close renderings in English. In a few instances we note where a translation reflects even more clearly the local or personal style of the speaker. Because most of them were told to us in the local language of the narrators, not in English, we would have liked the original texts to be published along with our general translations, and with a discussion of stylistic and other features of the texts themselves, but that would have expanded this volume far beyond what any publisher today would be willing or able to agree to. In any case, such a format would limit it to a small, specialist or localised set of readers.

This book is a vehicle through which we hope we can help the land to speak, to permit the myths to convey their messages as they were designed to do, to give readers an opportunity to hear these 'voices' with a minimum of effort on their part. The myths are from a number of different Aboriginal cultures about which most readers will probably know little or nothing. The majority of urban Aborigines will be unfamiliar with both the content and context of these particular myths and stories. The people from whose socio-cultural regions they come will recognise their own, but will probably know little about those from other areas. We have, therefore, an anthology of traditional Aboriginal prose of considerable importance to all Australians, because, while it presents a picture of Australia and Australians which is unfamiliar to many of us, it gives us an opportunity to assess, from a different angle, the nature of the country that we all should know. This applies also to readers outside Australia, and not only to those who are especially interested in myth. More generally, in relation to the actors in the myths, this anthology provides, or should provide, us with an insight into the essential frailty of men and women, and the kinds of problems which faced them, just as they face people the world over. What we identify are images on a mythic screen, indelibly imprinted on to an Australian landscape.

We have emphasised myths from two regions: the northern Australian coast and hinterland, and one of the largest so-called arid zones, or deserts. We have done this deliberately, to point up differences and similarities between them. Additionally, by concentrating on these we are able to provide a more detailed coverage of myths than would have been possible if we had widened the range.

This is the first occasion on which an anthology of Australian Aboriginal myths and stories has been assembled in this particular way. It is a contribution toward the development of an Aboriginal traditional literature which can stand in its own right. The comments on various myths are actually an ongoing part of them, or an extension of them, suggesting lines of approach that can help if we are to appreciate them over and above their impact as stories. At one level they are quite easy to follow and to enjoy as dramatic stories. At another level they can be made even more absorbing and exciting by adding this extra dimension of enquiry: breaking through the crust of unfamiliarity in order to understand what they mean and meant to the original narrators, and what they might mean to people of a different cultural background. Narrative story-type myths can have a more immediate effect on listeners (and on readers) than their sung counterparts are likely to have in a cross-cultural context or for people hearing or reading them for the first time. A story-line is not always a medium of instant communication, but it can sometimes seem to be. Up to a point, there is an analogy with visual art forms such as painting, or auditory experiences such as non-verbal music. A person looking at, or listening to, a particular item might respond to it fairly quickly with a feeling of recognition or empathy, apprehending rather than comprehending — with or without realising the complexities (of meaning or structure or performance) that could underlie its appearance or sound. Sung myths, like song-poetry generally, call for separate treatment and analysis, and we focus here on narrative myths. Some of these contain short songs, but in such cases we do not go into details of translation and meaning.

Story-telling is an important part of human experience everywhere. It can take the form of traditional accounts where the emphasis is on continuity — the kind of material we are considering in this anthology; or it can consist of individual statements about personal happenings and personal perspectives. All of this is often included under the heading of oral literature, one that is in some respects more broadly embracing than specific labels are.

SPEAKING AND LISTENING

'Oral literature' is useful as a signpost, a guide to a constellation of interconnecting interests, some explicit and some not. 'Oral' points to a mode of transmission: 'word of mouth', spoken utterances or speech. (Its counterpart, 'aural', specifying hearing and listening, the role of ears, is used more rarely.) 'Literature' implies another mode of transmission. The emphasis in that case is usually on literacy, on material designed to be read, on written or printed words, whether or not they are also spoken or heard. Over and above that, conventional definitions of literature still call for some kind of assessment or evaluation, some criteria of quality, in regard to form and aesthetic impact, to single out works of literary merit from those that do not come up to these standards. This raises the question of canons of style in verbal and other contexts in different cultural settings, even where material was available in some kind of script (e.g. on rock surfaces) if not actually in document form. Material that rested on oral transmission alone was for a long time not categorised as literature, whatever its content, and regardless of how it was viewed in its home environment. Oral literature was claimed to be a contradiction in terms, an attempt to combine two concepts that did not belong together. The pioneering work of the Chadwicks in the 1930s has effectively disposed of the arguments against it, however, although there are still a few pockets of resistance. It has become almost fashionable, except that there is a greater tendency now to refer to oral history or oral traditions, almost evading the term literature except in its popular and most general sense as comprising the entire range of published or widely-circulated verbal material.

In 'literature' and 'oral literature' the focus is on words, not on any actions or paraphernalia that might be associated with them. Written or printed forms of plays, for instance, may be classified as literature, but their dramatic performance brings in a different dimension. As far as Aboriginal Australia is concerned, myth-stories could be told in narrative or in song; but they could also be told through visual art forms and a variety of objects (rock art, ground and body paintings, emblems, string figures and so on), as well as through the medium of religious ritual; and they could be alluded to, perhaps added to or even partly reframed, in ordinary ceremonies or song-compositions or dreams. The closer any of these were to the secret-sacred aspects of religion, the fewer were such opportunities for deliberate modification or change Conversely, the less directly or obviously sacred fields of activity and belief allowed more scope for flexibility and innovation. But all of these features, including myth-stories, were ingredients in a total pattern, not separate or isolated elements that could be understood by themselves.

The stories we have included here are set out in the form in which they were told on particular occasions. However, this is not the only way in which stories were transmitted. Quite often, fragments would be told, referring to places or to characters without expanding on the actions or following through the story-line. A child travelling through the country of some close relative (mother, father, grandparent, for instance) might be told the name of a special site and of its spirit-presence, or a wife might be given such information on her first visit to her husband's country. These items would probably be expanded later into more complete accounts. They are a vital part of the overall process of teaching and learning and knowing about myth-stories and their context in any given region.

In Aboriginal Australia there were no professional story-tellers who made a living from the task. Everyone was a potential if not an actual story-teller. Nor were there people who composed stories in the fictional sense, as contrasted with those who gave accounts of their own and other people's actual experiences. There were song-composers in some regions, although they did not always acknowledge their own role in such composition: in western Arnhem Land, for instance, they attributed such songs to characters they met in dreams. Myth-stories could be told or exchanged during ceremonial gatherings, or on informal occasions such as leisure-time gatherings around camp-fires. In any such situation the most knowledgeable story-tellers were those who had direct links with the places where the stories they told were located, and were old enough or experienced enough to know these stories well. Of course, some were more articulate and more competent — and acknowledged as better story-tellers. The aspect of creativity and the 'personal touch' was always present in any sphere of individual performance, although less noticeable in religious ritual affairs, and the actual telling of stories provided one medium for this kind of expression.

Aboriginal populations were fairly small, and their semi-nomadic life-style meant that they concentrated on particular areas where they had traditionally acknowledged rights and responsibilties in regard to land and resources. On the one hand they had outward-looking perspectives in trade and religious inter-connections with neighbouring groups. On the other, their main attention was centred on their own local and regional interests, among people who were linked in kin relationships, shared the same language or dialects, the same marriage rules, and the same broad range of assumptions and values. That did not mean there were no arguments, a point that the myths dramatise quite frankly. But it did mean that within such communities people 'spoke the same language' in the sense of understanding *un*spoken comments: they did not need to have everything spelt out, either in ordinary conversation, in myth-stories or in other circumstances. Oral communication in such a situation involved more than the physical presence or potential presence of other people listening to what was said or sung. It also involved knowing or inferring what was not said: a level of communication that is possible in small-scale communities but much harder to achieve in larger ones except within specialist groups or on limited topics.

This kind of oral transmission, in this kind of social context with its taken-for-granted primary, face-to-face relationships, we call 'traditional oral'. It contrasts sharply with forms of oral communication that depend on non-personal media — radio, television, films, video. We call these 'mechanical or electronic oral'. The new media have not entirely supplanted the person-centred, more transient forms. They continue to use speaking and listening and looking; but, like the print media, they can continue to transmit their content without the active co-operation or even the knowledge of the human beings who were originally concerned. Such changes are one facet of the larger universe of changes that has overwhelmed Aboriginal people and their traditional cultures in the last few years.

A LAND FULL OF MYTHIC VOICES

Myth can be considered as a subject in itself, just as stories can. Or it can be included under other headings: oral literature, or written literature, or literature transmitted through the mass media, the print or electronic media of large-scale communications. It is also an integral part of any study of religion.

Not all myths are in story form; and even when they are, they may be transmitted through other forms as well. A story can be spelt out more or less explicitly in the shape of a narrative, while a parallel song-series focuses on specific points or on a range of meanings, taking the related story as a 'given'. In traditional Aboriginal Australia, where religion had such a pervasive influence, even material that seemed to be on the outer fringes of the sacred dimension was not entirely outside it.

Even stories used mainly for children, or for lightweight entertainment, had their place in the overall scheme of things. In the Western Desert, for instance, they are often referred to casually as *yumu,* 'nothing', or 'of no consequence', but that is not to say they are of no importance, only that they are of less importance than others: they do not have the portentous significance of stories that are more obviously characterised as sacred. Nevertheless, all stories, no matter how slight they may appear to be, have some 'meaning' — and not only for outside observers. Some Aboriginal women have said that children need stories to help them in understanding the world around them. That does not apply only to content, although even the simplest 'just so' stories convey messages or can be used to convey them in the course of discussion or extra comments. They also have a practical meaning as demonstrations in the art, or craft, of handling words and ideas, and the dramatic skills that go with them. The most elementary story, provided it is competently told, can be an introduction to a more complex world of stories and the kinds of meaning they can reveal, or conceal.

We can, assuredly, speak of degrees of sacredness. Generally, the most sacred myths are likely to be linked with the most sacred rituals. Nevertheless, the term 'myth' can cover a very wide spectrum, with implications that are not shared by such terms as 'folktales'. We use it here in the form 'myth-stories' or in combination as 'myths and stories' to indicate the kind of material we are dealing with — focusing on the aspect of story, within a framework of something more serious than ephemeral tales.

Tonkinson (1974: 73–74) suggests that in the Jigalong area of the Western Desert myths 'can be divided into two types': one, 'the descriptive narrative', deals with major mythic characters, while in the other, 'the emphasis is on situation and character interaction', and the location is not noted or not specifically relevant. His example of this second kind is the Emu and Turkey (Bustard) story (see Chapter 9).

Earlier writers who gave accounts of Aboriginal myths, stories and so on were usually quite inconsistent in the labels they attached to these accounts: 'myths', 'legends', 'traditions', 'beliefs', 'stories', 'folklore', 'tales' were used almost interchangeably (see C.H. Berndt 1978: 57–59). Issues of translation, style and interpretation mostly received very little attention. That applies also to the majority of writers who have published popular versions of Aboriginal myths and stories. The exceptions, past and present, are the few scholarly works which include vernacular renderings with careful annotations, but they are almost inaccessible to the majority of readers, if only *because* they are so detailed and demand such patient attention: T.G.H. Strehlow's Aranda studies, for example (1971), building on the work of his missionary father Carl Strehlow; and Heath's painstaking presentation (1980) of Nunggubuyu myths and texts. The number of such contributions is increasing. At the same time, there are strong current pressures toward teaching 'Aboriginal culture' in schools and helping non-Aboriginal Australians in general to reach a better understanding of it.

The bridges in between, necessary to make such understanding possible, must be flexible enough to allow for divergent approaches, without compromising the integrity of the cultural 'territories' on either side. Even in dealing with seemingly simple stories, this is difficult, because the actual story-line, the surface meaning, is only a small part of their 'reason for being'. The nearest equivalents to these in English-language publications are the books for very young children, mainly about north Queensland, prepared by the successful team of Trezise and Roughsey, and including *Banana Bird and the Snake Men* (1980). But they are equivalent only in the sense of being a very brief introduction to a new experience — an introduction that has to be followed through if it is to make much of an impact. In a traditional Aboriginal situation, beginning-stories lead to more complex ones, and all of them are set in an ongoing pattern of happenings and relationships that reinforce and elucidate the story messages. In book or video form, they are barely even an introduction to 'Aboriginal culture'. But others, designed for older children, have greater problems when it comes to the translation-of-culture issue, or they merely ignore that issue and concentrate on imaginative and often distorted renderings of images and story-lines.

Almost every published work that includes comments on Aboriginal culture contains some references to stories, myths, legends and the like. There is certainly enough to demonstrate what a wealth of such material was available in the past and up to quite recent times. We have mentioned only a few examples, because preparing even a rough overview would have been a major task. Add to that the immense amount of unpublished, unwritten or unrecorded story material, some of it still a vital part of living oral traditions, and only an encyclopaedia of Aboriginal myth-story could do justice to it.

The general problem of transposing from an oral to a written tradition is one impediment to communication, especially within the larger spectrum of cultural differences. In a socio-cultural environment where, as in the traditional Aboriginal case, the use of time is approached in a less tense or speed-oriented way than in a highly industrialised setting, stories (for instance) can be treated more seriously, with lingering appreciation and expansive comments. Repetition is a device that can be judiciously employed for emphasis and for rhythmic balance, as well as to ensure that the main points receive proper attention. In a clock-oriented society such repetition is likely to be viewed negatively, at least in a story-telling context. It has been labelled 'redundancy', a term that Leach (1967: 2) attributes to 'the language of communication engineers'; 'a high level of redundancy makes it easy to correct errors introduced by noise'. In popular speech, of course, redundancy has a much more negative meaning — which accords with the negative attitudes toward repetition in the telling of stories, even in speech.

Over much of the continent, in the north as well as in the south, an incalculable number of myth-stories is passively available (that is, available if 'tapped') at the level of memory culture. Tulo Gordon from Cape York Peninsula in north Queensland has produced a vividly-illustrated children's book of Guugu Yimidhirr stories. His collaborator and translator, John Haviland, observed (Gordon and Haviland 1979: 55) that the stories of that region 'represent a striking intellectual and aesthetic effort to bring natural facts into harmony with a human order'. He added that Tulo Gordon's work 'represents another sort of an effort at reconciliation' in that he 'has recalled tales from an era of Aboriginal life long-since vanished, and. . .has recast them in words and pictures that derive from a life still current', 'in a drastically altered world'.

That attempt at a dual perspective, at capturing or re-capturing voices from the past so that they can be heard in the present, has many parallels among people of Aboriginal descent today. Joe Nangan, for example, the last full-Nyigena man, living in the Broome-Beagle Bay area of Western Australia, has been working on the recording and illustrating of stories that he himself remembers, but only a few have been published so far (as in *Joe Nangan's Dreaming*, 1976). The greater number, recorded by a missionary who undertook to put them into written form some years ago, still await the collaboration of someone who can translate from the Nyigena texts into what Nangan himself prefers as their published medium — standard English — to reach a larger range of readers than could the Aboriginal English employed by his friend Paddy Roe (1983).

In south-east Australia, Roland Robinson is one writer who showed concern for the surviving myth-stories remembered by people who no longer had a living, distinctively Aboriginal culture to sustain them. As he puts it (1965: 6), he wanted to hear 'the sacred voice of the country I called my home', but the 'voice. . .was inarticulate, locked up in its landscapes', until people of Aboriginal descent 'unlocked' it through their stories, which inevitably drew upon and were influenced by, their non-Aboriginal surroundings and experiences. In a different vein, and a more conspicuously 'creative' and individual type of composition, the poet and playwright Jack Davis (1982) has written plays which dramatically document and dramatise some of the experiences of Aboriginal people in their relations with Europeans in the south-west of Western Australia.

Such 'new' voices, growing in number, do not supersede the 'older', more deeply-rooted voices of the land, but add an extra dimension to them.

CHAPTER TWO

SHAPING THE
ABORIGINAL WORLD

In the beginning there were only the land, the waters and the elements: nature itself, untamed, empty of human beings. There were, however, some forms of natural species. There were spirits too, varying in shape and size, and some monstrous creatures, as we shall see. All this was really *before* 'the beginning', before what has been called 'the Dreaming'. It was a world latent in its potentialities, waiting to be awakened. That awakening was to come with the appearance of mythic beings, the deities and characters of the Dreaming, who were the forerunners of human beings as we know them today. Their role was essentially that of humanising the whole of the natural environment, harnessing everything within it, for the progenitors of traditionally-oriented Aborigines. There was always something there in that world, on that earth, before mythic beings came; something that they could shape and mould for the occupation of that land by themselves and, eventually, by their non-mythic counterparts who were to come. And the intention was to provide a congenial physical and social context for living.

These Dreaming characters who were responsible for the development of humanity were of many kinds and had widely differing personalities. They also came from many directions. Some came out of the unknown, whether or not it was named, some from the sky, and others out of the earth itself, emerging through an act of self-creation. And they came at different times, not all at once. There were many of them, all operating within the Dreaming; and they moved over the land, within particular areas, leaving tangible signs of their own physical presence there, becoming metamorphosed, turning into something else. Others disappeared out of the known into the unknown.

Wherever they went, or whatever they left, the physical reminders of their living selves are imbued with a spiritual essence which can be drawn upon for particular purposes by human beings. While death stalked their criss-crossing tracks over the landscape, they were of the Dreaming, immortals, possessed of a life-everlasting that was and is spiritually indestructible. What happened before their coming was more or less irrelevant. Everything that took place at their coming, *and* afterward, was vitally significant. Moreover, it was a Dreaming relevance, that was eternal.

One of the major consequences of their advent was the creation of human beings. Some female deities, for example, gave birth to people. Others, either male or female, 'put them' at specific places or in designated territories. These first *human* men and women were left there so that their descendants could occupy that land and propagate their own kind through the generations, continuing to live within the aura and under the auspices of one such deity or another. Not all mythic beings, however, had this particular quality of 'making and leaving people', and the manner through which humans came into being varied.

In one of the best-known examples, the two Djanggau Sisters, Daughters of the Sun, came in their bark canoe with their Brother from the mythical land of the dead, Bralgu, somewhere in the Gulf of Carpentaria. They travelled from east to west on the path of the Sun. When they reached the Arnhem Land mainland they created special trees complete with foliage and birds. They shaped the country, named places, interacted with other mythic characters, and instituted the traditional customs of Aborigines of this cultural area. Most importantly, the Two Sisters gave birth to the first people, the 'children of Djanggau', and put them in appropriate places. Then they disappeared westward into the setting sun. In western Arnhem Land, too, the Fertility Mother Waramurung-goindji with her husband Wuragag and some other mythic beings, gave birth to large numbers of the first people. Later, her husband became Tor Rock and she herself went on eastward. Throughout much of the northern part of Australia there are similar myths (see R. and C. Berndt 1985: 252–55, 276–87).

Some contrasting accounts come from the Dieri of the Lake Eyre district in South Australia. In one, at the beginning of time the earth opened at Perigundi Lake and incomplete creatures emerged. They lay on the nearby sandhills and were strengthened by the sun. Eventually they were able to stand up 'as human beings', and then spread out 'in all directions'. In another, the Dreaming character *Muramura* Paralina saw four unformed creatures. He smoothed out their bodies, stretching their limbs, shaping mouths, noses and eyes, attaching ears and breathing into them so that they could hear, and then forming their buttocks. They too dispersed over the land (Howitt 1904: 779–81). On the other hand, an Aranda myth also underlines the male principle in the creative act. At the beginning, there was perpetual darkness. The Bandicoot ancestor Karora lay at the bottom of a soak, covered with earth. As he slept, bandicoots emerged from his navel and from his armpits. They burst through the soil and sprang into life. Karora himself emerged, and slept with his arms outstretched. A bullroarer appeared from his armpit, taking the shape of a human youth. When Karora awakened, he saw his first-born beside him (Strehlow 1947: 7–18).

Whereas the Arnhem Land Djanggau were responsible for peopling almost all of the eastern part of that area, the Aranda concern was rather for a number of independent acts of creation by different mythic beings, each related to the beginnings of the first people associated with particular local descent group territories. In the literature on Aboriginal mythology, a distinction has sometimes been drawn between the northern and southern creative principles. In the north there is an emphasis on a Mother or 'Old Woman', known by several different names, who was responsible for creating the first people through childbirth. She, or they, had a bountiful supply of them in her womb: hence the label 'Fertility Mothers'. This has been contrasted with an apparent emphasis on male creative characters in the southern parts of the continent. While there are certainly examples that can be used to demonstrate this point, and to suggest and support that contrast, there is not a clear-cut demarcation, and the overall picture is more complex than that. Also, there is the issue of complementarity in regard to male and female principles — an aspect that will come up again later. One point, however, needs to be mentioned. In recent years, in the struggle for recognition of Aboriginal rights to land, a popular slogan is, 'the land is our Mother'. That relationship is not usually made explicit in the traditional mythology which serves as the basis of religious belief and action. All 'Fertility Mothers', even including the Earth Mothers of Bathurst and Melville Islands, were locally-based deities who were concerned with specific areas of country and/or sites, and not with the whole of the earth *per se*. For example, although the Djanggau Sisters gave birth to all the first people of north-eastern Arnhem Land, their acts of creation took place at specific places. Moreover, although most if not all deities travelled over the land, and some even emerged from it, the land itself was not a kind of collective Mother. Perhaps the nearest approach to that wider idea comes from the male deity Ngurunderi, who, at the beginning, stretched out his body, spiritually, along the lower River Murray in South Australia, with one leg extended along the Coorong and the other along Encounter Bay. The concept of the 'land our Mother' is a highly symbolic abstraction, having little direct correspondence in local Aboriginal mythologies. But it could well be argued in these terms, if we consider the north-eastern Arnhem Land Wawalag myth where the Two Sisters are swallowed by Yulunggul, the mythic Snake. The male principle (symbolically as rain, thunder or lightning) fertilises the female principle (symbolised by the earth and the growth in nature); the swallowing of the Wawalag by Yulunggul brought about the monsoonal season (see Myth 36).

Humankind was and is inseparable, epistemologically speaking, from what happened in the Dreaming. Men and women were originally 'conceived' and born into the creative era of the Dreaming. They emerged from the womb of a mythic being or were otherwise generated or prepared for emergence. Their coming was not a question of replacing the mythic beings. That can perhaps be argued at the physical level, but not at the spiritual. Both mythic and human beings were and are co-existent, but conceptually within different dimensions of time-span and action-frame.

Let us put it this way. In the beginning of the Dreaming, mythic characters carried out physical actions which eventually drew to an end when they became metamorphosed or otherwise transformed into something else. While that change did not impair their spiritual significance, their physical sequences were not to be repeated, neither in that way nor by themselves. However, their spiritual quality continues to exist. What they did in the beginning is non-reversible, *except* through reincarnation achieved through a human agent; and he or she may bring that about *without* impairing his/her spiritual quality, which is indeed the very essence of the whole concept of the Dreaming. On the other hand, human beings, through the nature of their origin, possessing as they do attributes similar to those of mythic beings, are limited by being the creatures they are. They do not have access to inherent power as the deities have, only to ritual power, and for that, they are dependent on the deities. It is possible for living men and women to achieve union with the deities, but only through ritual means, for example, by simulating actual events and incidents in which those deities were physically involved. The Dreaming characters themselves are bounded by a kind of circularity, by what has been called sacred time, a cyclical, constantly-recurring, essentially repetitive process which ensures their survival through time. The human beings they originally bestowed upon the earth to commemorate their initial achievements are bounded by linear or secular time, constantly interrupted or broken by death and by spiritual renewal through the medium of ritual.

Some mythic beings were shape-changing. They might appear in human form, or in the form of a natural species or element. Or the change might take place as one stage, or a final one, in a sequence. In many cases they had names that identified them as one particular creature or aspect of nature in contrast to another. Even when their shape did change, their human quality might remain dominant. It was not a case of human beings emerging from animals, even though they might be referred to by such an identifying label. What is implied is a common life-stream for all living things, including humankind; a life-force that came from the Dreaming characters themselves (or at least from some of them), and continues to be relevant. Moreover, the implied assumption is that the deities are responsible for *all* of nature, and that they hold the key to its continuation, within a world everlasting, which they themselves shaped and gave life to, and which they made habitable once and for all, along with instructions and guidelines for keeping it going.

Some mythic beings did not change their human shape and were like that, or more or less like that, at the beginning. Others were manifested as natural species or as elements of nature, or on their physical death they 'turned into', 'became', 'made themselves' something that was non-human. Various creatures and the elemental forces of nature are all symbolic of, or under the control of, specifically named mythic beings. Just in reference to elements, we have already mentioned the Wawalag epic, in which the Two Sisters, after a ritually-charged series of events, were swallowed by the Yulunggul Snake (see Chapter 3), and so set in motion the coming of the monsoonal period. There are many other such examples. The Wondjina of the north-west Kimberleys in their immense human forms symbolise, among other things, the cyclonic clouds that bring the seasonal rain-bearing depressions to that part of the country. And the mythic Fire and Rain deities of the Western Desert bring both danger and benefits to the traditional people.

Nature and its manifestations provide the basic model on which mythic beings and their human counterparts constructed their complex symbolic ideologies that served to substantiate the varying socio-cultural orders they founded, moulding them for their own purposes. Mythic beings ensured, through their re-interpretation of nature in human terms, that they would always have control over it. As mythic beings, they stood between nature and human endeavour. They bent nature to their own will. And they maintained their control through being the purveyors of a life-force through which they were able (with the ritual aid of human beings) to generate and re-generate all living forms.

The myths and stories we present here are not those of the great religious cycles. Most are not directly related to religious ritual, even though they are categorised as belonging to the Dreaming, relating to mythic characters during their physical presence on earth. Some, however, can be regarded as pseudo-historical. They have, in the course of time, been incorporated into the overall perspective of the Dreaming, and are considered to be myths in their own right.

The following two myths were recorded in 1949 at Oenpelli in western Arnhem Land by R. Berndt, but relate to the Gagadju (Kakadu) people who originally occupied part of the western side of the East Alligator River.

1. THE EMERGENCE OF MURAWULAGALA, AND THE WIVES HE COLLECTED

At Angmeridja (or Anmuridjel, on the other side of Smith's Landing by the East Alligator River) a big man named Murawulagala [*yarigarngurg*, *nangila*] emerged from the ground. His moustache was just growing. He went on to Mimungagula, where he made a *gabundji* grass hut on high ground and lived there by himself for a while. One day he was looking out from his camp when he saw smoke rising from Gunbulul, alongside East Alligator River Hill. Leaving his camp he 'followed up' that smoke until he reached a group of Gagadju people who were camped there. Murawulagala carried a stick [or club] in each hand, and when he entered their camp the people were frightened: 'Look,' they cried, 'a spirit has come!' Attempting to reassure them, he said, 'I am Murawulagala. I live there on the other side of the river. I came out of Burinbadja hole in the Angmeridja jungle.' And he continued: 'I have come: you people should give me a girl. I am a countryman of you fellows, we are of one language.'

The people talked among themselves: 'It is better we give him one. Let him take one girl!' And they gave him Geirwana [*nyindjariyaning, ngalbulan*]. He camped there with her for two days. Then he asked her, 'What about if I go out that way, Gining way, and I'll come back in the afternoon.' So Geirwana went out nearby to collect lily roots. And Murawulagala went to Gining, where another group of Gagadju people were camped. 'Ah,' they said when they saw him, 'this is a new man!' He replied, 'I'm not a spirit, so don't be frightened of me, I'm a countryman of yours. I came out of Angmeridja, I always camp in the scrub!' And he stayed there with them for a while. Then he asked them: 'What about you giving me two girls?' [Comment by narrator: 'He wanted to have plenty of children, that's why he wanted the girls: but he died 'too quick'!]

The people at Gining gave him two girls, Nukereiya and Djurulgi ['skins' unknown]. So he returned to Angmeridja, picking up his first wife Geirwana on the way. 'Now he had three girls!' Two of the girls went out to collect food each day, but one he kept back in his camp, copulating with her. He stayed there for a while and then said to the girls, 'I will go that way. You three look out for food. I might find more food!'

He saw smoke rising from camps at Baral-baral. He set out and eventually reached them. The people there had heard about Murawulagala from the Gunbulul people — about how he had emerged from the ground and that they had given him a girl. 'Ah!' they said, 'Look, it is the big man who has come.' And he replied: 'I stay at Angmeridja. Don't be frightened of me: I talk Gagadju, I am no spirit. What about you people giving me three girls?' So they agreed among themselves to give him three girls: Makerula, Galana-galeinya and Naralala ('skins' unknown). Murawulagala now had six wives. He returned with the three girls to Angmeridja. He sent five of them out for food, and kept Geirwana in his camp, copulating with her.

Now three young Gagadju men came to Murawulagala's camp, to see what kind of camp he had. Moreover, they were closely related to the girls [specific relationship not noted, but a comment was made that they were 'following up a 'sister' or a 'mother' — like that!']

Murawulagala was sitting there in his camp with a long ridge pole (which he had removed from his hut): 'he was jealous because of the girls'. The three men, named Nangaiyara, Walu-ngaidja and Mararber respectively, sat down opposite Murawulagala. 'Where have you men come from?' he asked. 'We have just followed you up from Gunbulul,' they replied. But Murawulagala thought they had come to abduct the girls. So, when it was getting dark, he got hold of his ridge pole, with the intention of killing the men. He swung the pole, hitting the three men on the nose bridge, breaking their noses. Two he killed, but the third, Walu-ngaidja, was not hurt too much.

Murawulagala told the girls to move the three dead men, so they dragged them along for a few yards to a clump of pandanus, where they dug a hole. Murawulagala did not come with them. The girls cried only a little; they were too frightened to wail properly. As they were digging, Walu-ngaidja who had been pretending to be dead looked up: 'I'm all right, I'm not dead, I'm going away now!' The girls replied, 'You go now.' And he told them: 'I'll send a message in all directions. You girls watch for five days.' Then he left them.

Walu-ngaidja went to Gagadju people living at Bindjal-bindjal, at Baral-baral, at Gunbulul and at Djanmar. He told them what had happened, and they got ready to go on a fighting expedition.

In the meantime, Murawulagala was lying down resting in his camp with those six girls. The 'fighting party' was drawing closer to Angmeridja, and as they came along shaking their spears, all painted in white clay, they cried out like cockatoos, interspersed with the sound '*um! um!*'. On reaching Murawulagala's hut, they all stood round its opening. Murawulagala emerged head first, then his arms and shoulders, and the others threw spears at him. They stuck so many in him that 'he looked like an echidna!'

'What's the matter with you lot?' Murawulagala asked. 'Why do you kill me?' But they struck his neck with a stone axe, and killed him. They took those six girls away with them, leaving the body of Murawulagala. His bones resembled milk wood (they were pinkish in colour), and were scattered about Angmeridja. [The person who told this story said his grandparents had visited this place and had seen the bones, all lying there.]

2. THE EMERGENCE OF DULUNGUN-DULUNGUL AS A CHILD

Manamaramar lived at Mowangi [on the western side of the East Alligator River] with his wife or wives, one of whom was named

Marabunganana, and his dogs. On one occasion he told his wife (wives) that he would go out to 'look round' for goannas. Leaving the camp, he walked through the bush, and hearing his dogs bark, thought they had found a goanna. As he came closer he heard a baby crying, and saw his dogs had tried to attack a child; he chased them away. A baby was lying there on the grass in a small depression. It was Dulungun-dulungul, a male child who had 'just' emerged from the ground during the night. He was really 'a proper man', although he lay there on the grass like a baby. Manamaramar picked up the child, and taking off his pubic covering put it on the ground to serve as a soft mat for the child to rest on. He broke bushes and branches and made a shelter; and he got grass and made a bed for him. He left the child there, hidden.

Having caught some goanna, he returned to his camp. But he did not tell his wife (wives), nor any of the other people who were camped there, about the child. Instead, he said to his wife: 'I went out hunting before daylight; you mustn't go food-collecting in that direction [where the baby was]; there is a nest there, and a bird may lay eggs: I will watch it.'

Next morning he went out at break of day before the birds stirred and arrived at the place where the child lay. He prepared a new sleeping place for the child and stayed with him all day. 'From the ground', the child grew rapidly: within four weeks, he was running around. Every day Manamaramar came out and looked after the child: he stayed with him until dusk and then returned to his camp. 'It was always like that!'

Dulungun-dulungul grew into a big man. And Manamaramar asked, 'What about it, my boy [son] — you've been here for two months now?' 'All right father,' he replied. 'Son, when I come back tomorrow, I'll decorate you,' said Manamaramar. Next day he prepared the materials he would use, and returned to where the youth sat. He got *wonbegi* cane from the jungle and made a bangle which he placed on Dulungun-dulungul's upper arm, as well as a *gudjudju* wristlet. He red-ochred him all over his body, put banyan fibre cross-wise on his chest (as a *guluwulu* chest-girdle) and a string of *mangmangelu* grass 'beads' round his neck. He also tied a *galamba* band around his forehead, made of banyan string painted white in the front. And he put *mageri* crane and cockatoo feathers as a head-dress, with *ngariyu* pendants of possum fur suspended from his elbows; then he placed round him a cypress pine bark *wunuru* belt, and a *ngalar* pubic tassel of wild cotton. Finally, he gave him some small *gundjugulyu* bamboo spears and a *baladi* spear-thrower. He, Manamaramar, gave all those things to that big man. Covering him with a *nyumbarabara* mat made of lily grass, he led him to the main camp.

All the people in the camp had gone out hunting and food-collecting, so Manamaramar took Dulungun-dulungul to his own camp and covered him up inside it. When Marabunganana came back, she put her basket close to where the young man was hidden. Her husband told her to move it closer to the fire and to prepare lily roots.

When all the people had returned, he called them together: 'All of you come, I've something here!' They sat down in a circle around Manama-ramar, with the mat-covered 'bundle' beside him. He then threw aside the mat, and revealed Dulungun-dulungul.

All the people exclaimed: 'What a pretty man!' The women began to argue among themselves, each wanting Dulungun-dulungul as a sweetheart. News of his appearance spread to Ganyanbulul, and some people went to tell Grudbibi (a *yariyaning, namarang* man) who was camped at Wadjunulari (at the other side of Ganyanbulul): 'A pretty one has come out of the ground; he is a big man too!' And Grudbibi replied, 'A pretty one! Well, we two men will fight.' He was jealous, so he started off for Ganyanbulul with a large group of fighting men. Arriving there, he called out: 'We two men want to fight.' He put a bamboo spear in his spear-thrower and threw it so that it hit a pandanus tree: and he said, 'I want it to be like that!' [that is, to spear him dead].

Dulungun-dulungul arrived at Ganyanbulul on the Ngararidjoridj plain nearby. It was there that the two men fought, each using a crooked, curved spear-thrower, which whipped as a spear was propelled from it. Grudbibi threw one spear in return for the one thrown by Dulungun-dulungul; then Dulungun-dulungul threw one, and this time it tipped (pierced) Grudbibi's back and he stumbled. But Grudbibi jumped up with his last spear and cried, 'You watch this!' The spear he threw struck Dulungun-dulungul right through the heart; he fell down dead.

All Dulungun-dulungul's companions from Mowangi threw spears at Grudbibi, who ran away toward the sea. Halfway he broke off part of the bamboo spear which had pierced his back; he had been dragging it along. At Gulari, at the mouth of the East Alligator River, he said: 'I will go and stay there in the sea; you can see me as a big rock.' He made himself Dreaming, turned into a big rock at that place. You can see it at the point of the river's mouth; it is a reef. At low tide you can see Grudbibi, 'along sunrise way'. He is lying there, full length, with his spears and spear-thrower which he stood up alongside himself.

As for poor Dulungun-dulungul, they brought his body back to Mowangi, where they buried him, there along the ground from which he emerged. At that place there is a high hill, now. Also, there is the grass *gubundji* hut in which he was placed by his 'father' before he was revealed to the people, and the entrance to that hut can still be seen.

These two myths have little in common with those concerning the creative abilities of the Fertility Mothers, also in the same cultural area. They demonstrate the mythic occurrence of self-creation, unaided by a female.

In both cases the emergence from the ground of a fully-grown man and of a male child who rapidly grew to adulthood, underlines a recurring theme, that of jealousy — jealousy of apparent 'perfection' which is implied to be irresistibly attractive to females, as with Dulungun-dulungul; and in the other, a deference in the face of strength and a willingness to accede to Murawulagala's requests. But he too succumbed to jealousy. In both examples, jealousy leads to death. While these themes will be taken up in other chapters, two relevant points may be made. One relates (in so far as Murawulagala was concerned) to the reason for his acquiring several wives. With Dulungun-dulungul, the reason for nurturing him and preparing him for meeting his 'father's' people is not clear; but it could well be linked to the warning that any outstanding personality is vulnerable and attracts unwelcome attentions from a man who regards himself as an actual or potential rival: his position is at stake. The second point has to do with the Dreaming aspect. The characters are mythic, and one result of their brief physical sojourn on earth is that certain things relating to them are left as eternal memorials — as, indeed, sacred sites within the landscape: the bones of Murawulagala, the remains of Grudbibi, and the emergence hut of Dulungun-dulungul.

The next two myths are from western Arnhem Land, but not of the dominant Gunwinggu culture. The first was told to R. Berndt at Oenpelli in 1949, and related to people who originally lived in the 'Buffalo Plains' area, east of Darwin. The other, from Goulburn Island, was told to R. Berndt in 1947. It concerned the country of people who lived on Croker Island and the immediate mainland.

3. DEATH OF THE PEOPLE AT MARABIBI

A lot of people were camped at Marabibi on the Wildman River, near the old Manasi reserve, in the country of the Badaya and Gurudara. It was during the Wet season: women had been out collecting lily roots and were roasting them. A small boy named Geyawan whose mother was dead was living there with his father, Dudjululu. He was preparing some of the lily roots. Having removed their skin, he gave one to his son, who found it especially sweet. However, the others he gave the boy were not so sweet, and he cried in disappointment. [A comment at the time of recording this, was that the women must have made a mistake and collected the wrong roots.] Geyawan cried from morning to sundown, until he became so hoarse he could cry no more. The people offered him different kinds of food, but he refused each in turn and would not stop crying. As a result, the Nyimibili or Yung-galya, the 'running star' [one manifestation of Indada or Numurudu; see Chapter 4] appeared. A number of them 'came down' and fell on the camp at Marabibi, burning and killing the people there: 'they burnt them, removing the skin.' It happened like this.

It was from Waran that Yung-galya heard the child Geyawan crying. He stood up. 'I'll go and look,' he said to himself. He left Waran, and came to Mandening-geramana (on the eastern side of the Wildman River, at a nearby creek). He listened; the crying was not too far away. 'I'll kill and eat him,' he thought. He came to Marabibi. Here Yung-galya made a big glow — 'He made it all light, everything was bright.' All the people called out in fear: 'Yung-galya!' He climbed up a large tree — 'He made everything very bright.' The child was still crying, although hoarsely. From the tree, Yung-galya flipped out his very long tongue and lapped up all the people, one after another, swallowing all of them and all their possessions as well. He burnt all the grass and trees from his glow, because that glow was fire. The last child he put on the tip of his tongue, then swallowed it. Yung-galya sat down, remaining at Marabibi.

Now, prior, to this, among the people living at Marabibi were Dudjululu and his child, as well as Mandjiwaga whose sister, Donggulin, had gone in marriage to a man at Goidgi. [This was the site of Red-Ochre Dreaming which is now called 'Fred Pass' stockyard, situated about three miles from 'Mountain Gap', or Manton Dam, south of Humpty Doo. Goidgi is in 'Woolner' country, and the people who lived there spoke the Murumuru language which was close to Larrakia.] Mandjiwaga spoke to his father, saying that he would like to visit his sister: they spoke Badaya. He set off westward, and eventually reached his sister's camp at Goidgi. He stayed there for a while until a dream he had began to worry him. Mandjiwaga spoke to his sister's husband, 'I have to leave: I dreamt that something wrong has happened in my country. We will have to go back to the Wildman River.' And his sister's husband replied, 'I can't follow you; you must take your sister back yourself.'

So the brother and sister left Goidgi and came to Mabalimegunu on Scot's Creek [at Manasi]: on a small 'island' in the creek there is a rock which is Faeces Dreaming. They camped at Lulugdomban, 'Corroboree Camp' [Manasi language]. They went on to Ngaidbanar, a small 'island', where they camped. Next day they crossed the Mary River [Limil language]. Near where they crossed is a swamp containing an 'island' of rocks: these are the Gobolbu-namareidju, Sun Dreaming. They made camp here. 'We'll go farther apart from each other, sister,' her brother said. And they made their camps separately, some distance away from each other. They had brought spears with them, as well as red-ochre, and so on. They continued on to Gadjalngadjara (Shady Camp), where a

Tortoise Dreaming site runs down to the Rabalya river (Mary River): there is a tortoise hole here. Then they went on to Manalidj, Lousy Camp [Manasi language]. From there they travelled to Munun, Fish Camp, on to Gunandja [Manasi language], Point Stuart area, and to Djeladjela, 'Sun Ridge', where there was a well. Eventually they reached Galwumo on the plain [Badaya language]. They walked across the plain to a 'jungle' on the point of the mainland at Manmandja [Point Stuart itself]. From there they looked across the whole country: all of it had been burnt out, all the trees and the grass. They looked up toward Marabibi Hill [on the Wildman River, at what is now called 'Sharp' Hill]: the Yung-galya had burnt all the country.

Instead of going directly to Marabibi they went on to Malwara, where they camped: 'We'll go to Marabibi tomorrow; we'll camp some distance apart from each other.' Next morning they went to Gongara-rangarara. 'We'll leave everything here,' the brother said, 'and we'll sneak up to look.' So they 'sneaked' up, coming quite close to Marabibi, where they saw Yung-galya sitting there. They saw that he had a big eye (eyes) like (a) moon(s), 'burning, alight during the day and night'. They fell back, whispering, 'He might smell us: he has eaten everyone!' They rolled back, silently, in fear, away from Yung-galya, and they returned to collect their spears and red-ochre. 'We'll go along and make camp at the springs at Banbanga (or Baranga), Flying Fox jungle.' But his sister replied, 'Let's go farther.' They crossed the running spring water to the Wildman river, and went to Neiduwalogi jungle and spring. There they made a camp. But they moved back close to the river. ['No other people were about, no one else; he walked around with his full sister!']

Since the Wet season had begun, they made a large paperbark hut. It was a big hut, and had two entrances, one for the sister and one for the brother. [The man was the older of the two, and the sister a young girl.] The place where they made their camp was Ganburug-barambar. The sister went out to collect lily roots and goanna; she brought them back to the camp, cooked them, and left some at the other side of the hut for her brother. She called out for him, and each day he would come and collect his food. He, too, would go out hunting and bring back what he had caught, leaving it at her side of the hut, calling out to her.

The two went to sleep in their respective areas within the hut. Mandjiwaga began to think to himself: 'My sister, I'll make her my wife; there are no other people here now!' The girl was asleep, tired out from all her walking; her snoring had awakened her brother. There was a fire between them, in the middle of the hut. He saw she was lying with her legs apart, through tiredness. He put some paperbark on the fire, and in the light he could see her vulva. He got up, with his penis erect and sat down between her legs. He attempted to put his penis into her, but instead missed insertion and pushed it against her stomach. [That is why this place is named Ganburug-barambar, 'miss vulva, copulate with stomach'.]

The girl jumped up. But her brother reassured her: 'It's all right now, all the people have gone. I'll make you my wife; you lie down now!' So she lay down and he copulated with her properly.

After a while she became pregnant, and a male child was born; then, a little later, she gave birth to a girl child. When they grew up, Mandjiwaga gave the girl as wife to her brother. And they had children, and so on. ['All those Wildman and Mary Rivers people came from that brother and sister, Mandjiwaga and Dong-gulin. In that country, there is brother-sister marriage; you can marry your mother or your mother's sister, because the Dreaming made it that way. But it is different on the eastern side of the Wildman. That brother and that sister made a big country, with plenty of people. There were many people there who had married their sisters. But many of them are now gone: many people died from measles — you can see their bones everywhere!']

4. THE GREAT FIRE ON GUMUL

A *yariwurig* man and his son, *yarigarngurg*, lived at Wan-garan on Malay Bay. They had originally come from Wuruldja, Grant Island (near Croker Island), which belonged to the Gari and Marlgu people. The son was a good singing man, so his father sent him to learn songs from the song-men living at Marlganga and Gunbalanya (Oenpelli). In his absence, the father took his paperbark canoe and went over to Grant Island. The son, however, on his way from Malay Bay, met his *nganung* (wife's brother), of the *mowan* (sun) semi-moiety. By this time the two men would have walked as far as Cape Cockburn, where the son became thirsty: 'I think we must go in search of water,' he told his *nganung*. So they took a stringybark canoe and began to paddle over to Grant Island. The father had already reached there.

On the way over, the son told his *nganung* that he was so thirsty he could not wait; they would have to return to the mainland. His wife's brother tried to reason with him, since they were already halfway over to Grant Island. But the son insisted, and they turned back. However, instead they went northward, and on seeing an island [named Gumul, or Poison Island — no people are there, 'no one goes there', it is a dangerous place] the son jumped from the canoe and swam to its beach. He had with him a short *wimulul* club used for killing turtles. [There is a dense jungle on this island, and when people do go to Gumul they collect turtle eggs as rapidly as they can and leave.] The son ran along the beach and seeing a turtle hit it on the back: it was a poison turtle! He threw the stick to one side and ran down to where his *nganung* was waiting for him; sweat was running down his body. Quickly, he jumped into the canoe.

'What did you do?' his *nganung* asked him. 'I had a good drink,' the other replied [but of course he had not]. 'I think we had better go back,' his *nganung* said. When they had gone about halfway to the mainland, they saw a big fire rising from the middle of the island. 'What have you been doing?' his *nganung* asked. 'I think we'll all be killed!' So he got a bit of bark and gripped it between his teeth, using it as a fighting bag, and taking up a stick hit his companion across the bridge of the nose and eyes and threw him overboard. Then he paddled on to where the father was camping on Grant Island.

When all the people there saw the fire coming out of the island, they began to fall ill and die; all the children first, then the older men and women, and at last the old people. The *nganung* died as well. The island became very hot all over. Of all the people on Grant Island, only two children survived — a boy and a girl, who stood in relationship to each other as *mamam* [one term for eligible spouse: Maung]. When they saw all the people dying they were frightened, and hid themselves in the long prickly *muru* grass. Each morning the boy went out to see whether it was becoming cooler, and he would return to tell the girl, 'It's still hot!' Among the grass they found *yiwag*, *wun-garul* and *luldji* long yams and lived on these. They stayed there for a long time [comment: 'for six to seven months']; gradually the ground became cooler. At last it was quite cool. They left that place, and lived in the open.

As time went on, the girl became a woman and the boy a man. And he asked her: 'I think I'll take you to be my wife?' She agreed, and they copulated together, and had two children. The first was a girl, *nyindjari-garngurg*, *ngalmadgu*, and the second, a boy, *yarigarngurg*, *namadgu*. They stayed on Grant Island: they did not want to leave because it was still hot elsewhere, and they thought they might die.

When the children grew to adulthood, their father agreed to let the brother and sister marry, and they had a number of children. But eventually they crossed to the mainland, and there they married 'straight' — that is, with appropriate partners.

These two myths have a common theme, although the contexts differ, and not only because they relate to different cultural areas. The basic approach is that a wrong action will be followed by some misfortune. The crying child who attracts a malevolent being (in this case, the Yung-galya) is a sure signal in many myths. The same is the case with the son who, in an irresponsible way (which can only indicate his demented state of mind through extreme thirst, although the reason for that is unclear), violates the tabooed turtle place on Gumul Island. In both cases, although the perpetrators of these acts are killed, they also involve the deaths of all members of the local populations.

However, in each case, there are two survivors: an adult brother and sister on the one hand, and two children on the other. In order to ensure the re-population of the areas, incest takes place, as the only possible course. With Mandjiwaga and Dong-gulin the issue of a brother and sister not sharing the same sleeping place is emphasised *before* they know about what Yung-galya has done to their people. In the case of the two children (who are noted in the myth as being potentially eligible partners), the incest takes place between *their* two children. In other words, incest is permissible only where no other appropriate person of either sex is available. But in the 'crying child' myth, there was Mandjiwaga's sister's husband, not so many walking days away — although he is not mentioned! While these myths cannot be compared with, for instance, the Djanggau of north-eastern Arnhem Land, that too involved incest. The Brother of the two Djanggau Sisters was the father of 'the children of Djanggau'.

The first of these two myths introduces a theme that will become more pervasive as we continue. On the return trip to their devastated home at Marabibi, Mandjiwaga and Dong-gulin camp at various places which are named and in some instances their Dreaming association mentioned. The implication is that they were not responsible for shaping or forming these sites — only at the place where Mandjiwaga attempted to copulate with his sister.

The next two stories are also from Oenpelli (R. Berndt 1949–50) and belong to the 'old' traditional cultures on the western and immediately adjacent sides of the East Alligator River.

5.   PEOPLING THE LAND

At Alawirwir, close to the mouth of the East Alligator River [Amurag language, but originally Urilg], Ilbad, an old *yariwurig*, *nangaridj* man was camping. He had two children, a boy named Aidjumala and a girl, Maidjuminmag. [Their mother's name was unknown.] One day he told them that he was going out to hunt for goanna, taking a dog with him. He returned with a bag full of goanna. His children exclaimed: 'Ah father, you've got plenty of goanna!' He called to them to collect wood and light a fire. When the wood had burnt down they put the goanna in the ashes and covered them up, waiting for them to cook. When the meat was ready they removed them, the three of them ate, and afterward the old man lay down to rest.

However, the children were still hungry and started to chew the goanna bones. Ilbad heard them breaking them with their teeth: 'Why do you do that?' he asked. 'We are still hungry,' they answered. 'You've eaten a lot of goanna,' he replied, and threw a stick at Maidjuminmag to stop her chewing the bones, hitting her accidentally on the arm and breaking it. She began to cry. Ilbad threw another stick at her brother and he too began yelping like a dog, but in his case his arm was not broken. As a result of this ill-treatment they ran away together. The old man was sorry for what he had done. He tried to catch them, but the brother and sister ran far away and Ilbad was unable to follow them. [They were now in the process of becoming dogs.]

The two siblings came to Alala where they found a big banyan tree, and stayed there for a while to make a large well. They dug it out like dogs, rolling about within it 'like a dog with a broken arm'. And Maidjuminmag found water there, saying to her brother, 'Let's make it deep, so that other people will come here and drink from it.' They left that water for the old man, Ilbad, and for the Nagalapan and Marng-ga people. [It was noted that they left this water for particular people, and that they left people there as well.]

Leaving this place, they went on to Wululbi. 'What about making a well here?' they asked each other. Aidjumala with the 'good arm' (uninjured) dug it out, and the girl found water and they drank there. They left here Amurag people [who speak Urilg]. Travelling on to Cooper's Creek, 'low down' where this creek enters the mouth of the East Alligator, they reached Ngalgara. 'What shall we do about this river?' [how can we get over?] they asked each other, as they stood by the bank. First Maidjuminmag jumped over and landed on the other side, but Aidjumala fell down in the middle. However, he scrambled back on to the bank quickly because he was frightened of crocodiles. He tried again, and this time jumped to the other side.

From here they crossed the Wiyul plain. In the jungle they found a shallow well which had not been completed by some other Dreaming. They dug it out, making it deep. And they spoke Amurag, and left that well for Amurag people. They crossed the plain to Maluluru, and made a well at Alad [still Amurag territory]. They drank water and went on to Arara springs; they drank water and continued to Mamuri. Close to Alad is Ibulin well, which the pair had also made. There they 'put' Djanberu, Gumulya and Inbili, three brothers, and Arawindji and Marbmu, their 'sons': they spoke Amurag. At Mamuri they 'put' Badawul, Miryu, Amundjia, Mangubari and Abirigali [comment: 'Those dogs had been breeding all the way along — they gave birth to those people.']

Aidjumala and Maidjuminmag walked along the Mamuri Plain until they reached Aramalya, where they rested among the rocks at Iyumbi. There they made a camp, and left a small puppy dog which is now a rock at this place. They continued to speak Amurag. They came along the eastern side of the East Alligator River to Ibid [low-down Landing], and went on to Mayuwongal and to Inawilgin. [From Ibid, they spoke Mangeryu.] At these two places they left Garaba, Gumudur and Ngalem, three brothers; Miga, the father of Ngalem [implying that the other two brothers were not by the same father]; and Ginmun-ngaiyer, the father of Miga, all Mangeri (Mangeryu). ['Those Dreaming Dogs "bred" them up, bringing them up, leaving those people there.']

On the Inawilgin plain, close to Oenpelli, they made a well at Udjun; and then went on to Manyuwudjugeg, near Mandjamandawag Point. Here they stood up, listening: 'What is that noise we hear?' they asked. It was old man Marawulbol fishing at Mang-gol. [This is where we — the Berndts — were camped in 1949–50. There was a big banyan tree here which Paddy Cahill cut down when Oenpelli became, first, a pastoral station: Cahill 'paid' Nipper who was the primary land-owner of this area. Immediately after it was cut very heavy rain fell, temporarily flooding the country.] Marawulbol saw Aidjumala and Maidjuminmag coming along. He asked them, 'Where are you from? Where do you want to go? What about staying here?' 'We don't want to stay here,' Aidjumala replied. 'I'll let you drink water,' said Marawulbol. 'You stay here for a little while, and later I'll let you go on to Waramadja-galib (Waterfall); but first you leave all those people here.' [That is, leave pups here and then go on; the Mangeri people were left by those Dogs.] The two Dog Dreamings stayed there for a while: the sister was heavy with pups, and all those stones by Gunbalanya billabong are her pups now!

Marawulbol had a kangaroo bone (*i-erm*) pointed spear (*manawoganam*), that he had thrown down with the fish he had caught when he had walked some little distance in order to speak with Aidjumala and Maidjuminmag. He had not looked at them closely or actually seen they were dogs, but had only spoken with them at a distance. Now they came into Mang-gol and sat with the old man. They told him their story, how the girl had been injured by Ilbad, and that they had run away and 'turned into' dogs, but before that were human!

They stayed at Mang-gol, and put puppies [people] there. Then they went on to Waramadja-galib, leaving more Mangeri people. They went directly to the Waterfall, the girl (Dog) limping on three legs, her injured arm useless. But the boy (Dog) was all right. They went along Nama-ginmedag creek to Ergerg billabong, and on to Undjiluwalg [also a billabong on the creek], then to Owulng-ing-gwiang-g [another billa-bong on the creek], and to Mandja-uwol (or Mandja-rowol), the Waterfall itself. As the two Dogs came along to the Waterfall, they went 'one way, one way', cutting the rocks to form rockholes. [They did this so that people can obtain fish in them.]

Following the creek from Mandja-uwol, they crossed the Waterfall hill and drank water at Maiyu-ngalmulg at the top. They kept on walking south to a Mangeri place named Maban-manyer-ngoyuman along the creek. Leaving that creek, they crossed another creek at Gondji, and went down from the high ground where they made a camp; this is a Winggu (Gunwinggu) place now. They went on to another creek, Gulumbir, and followed it along to the back of the hills, finding water at Ngamig. They continued farther into Ngalmanaggu country (Winggu) where they made a camp at Gudjalngari water. Here at Guwoid behind Oenpelli (or Gallery) Hill, Inyalag, they dug a well and in doing so threw out the stones it contained in every direction, within the immediate vicinity — and they made it deep. Actually, the two Dogs had followed the creek right around. They then went into the bottom of this waterhole and made themselves Ngalyod (see Chapter 3): 'We are Rainbows now, we have to stay at this place!' [This was the country of Nyernyer, a Winggu man. 'Those dogs are always there at this place.']

---

6. TWO BROTHERS PEOPLE THE LAND

Two brothers called Naberin-gei-yamana lived at Ginyinbul. They originally spoke Ngadug, but the story of their adventures passed to the Mudulg people. They had come from a long distance away, and were said to be 'yellow fellows' [that is, not full Aborigines, but possibly 'Macassans']. They went to Genin [where they spoke Gagadju]; there they left a man, named Manamaramara. They came on to Unmuridjil where they left another man, named Iliri [he spoke Gagadju]. They continued to Bindjal-bindjal, on the other side of the Mangaragulu Plain but lower down, and then went along the river. At Bindjal-bindjal they left six brothers, who were named Mureidjera, Mambulu, Maidjiang-ga, Gamarawul, Maniyelulgu and Malg-gugu. [Today people think these are pandanus palms, but they are really people: 'You look for people there, but you see only trees!'] They came up to the western side of the East Alligator River and reached Marura, where they 'made' one man, named Ngariyud. [Those Naberin-gei-yamana 'made the world' — 'wherever they walked people got up!']

The two men grew old. The elder brother was named Garudb. The younger, Wuremelingamb, said to him, 'You've long whiskers, brother!'

So Garudb pulled them out and put them into the ground: 'I'll leave them here, Dreaming, they belong to the *bunggawa!*' [That is, he left them for the elders of the group of people who were to occupy the area.] This event took place at Gwuwara, at the other side of what became Doyle's place. They came up to what they thought was a large group of people living on the plain — but they were only pandanus.

At Indjudbuwiang (Oenpelli Crossing, higher up) they sat rolling fibre on their thighs, making a fishing line. They fastened a piece of meat to it and threw it into the river, but a big cat-fish swallowed it. They tugged and tugged at the line. They could see it in the clear water, as the fish broke the line dragging a length of it as it swam into a deep part of the river. Garudb jumped into the water after it, and the cat-fish 'called out' *'um! um!'* He caught hold of the length of line. Wuremelingamb said, 'I have to follow my brother' and jumped into the river. But the cat-fish kept them down in the water, still making that sound; they could not escape. 'You, brother, stay there — lie down!' that cat-fish was saying. The two brothers lay down in the water facing each other, one with legs outstretched, the other with one leg outstretched and one held upright. Garudb spoke: 'You, Wuremelingamb, belong to the other side of the river, to the Eri or Eraminyunangg people.' The younger brother said to his brother Garudb, 'You look to the opposite side, to the Aburameyawaig people.'

They stayed there like rocks. ['If we swim here, we avoid those rocks — otherwise we'd go down there altogether. If we hit those stones a large flood would result.' They are like Narwerein, or like a Ngalyod. Those two men had one wife between them, who was named Igalangoi, and she was Eri. She is also in the water, lying alongside Garudb, the elder brother, although she is not mentioned in the myth. Narwerein were said to be Rainbow Snakes. Spencer (1914: 296–305) called them Numereiji. He mentioned the Naberin-gei-yamana brothers (his Naberayingamna) and their adventures, which differ from those referred to in our version, and he also noted the cat-fish incident.]

These two myths tell of the placing of human beings at particular named places, from which the new generations of people will come. In both examples we are dealing with shape-changing creatures. Aidjumala and his sister Maidjuminmag were human, but because their father hit them when they said they were hungry they left their human identity and became dogs. During their travels the sister gave birth to either 'their own kind' or humans; like her, they were not confined to one identity, or one shape. In this case their incestuous relationship is irrelevant since they are treated as dogs (although in mythic terms they are either Dogs or humans). In a different and very detailed account told by women, they are in dog form to begin with (as noted briefly in R. and C. Berndt 1970: 23).

The Naberin-gei-yamana brothers, too, left people at particular places. This is implied to be an act of 'spontaneous' creation. Although at the end of the story we are told that they had a wife in common, no mention is made of her role in these events. One inference could be that the pandanus palms at Bindjal-bindjal 'turned into' people, or vice versa. That aside, these mythic beings were said to have been responsible for shaping part of the local landscape, and in both examples they turned into something else — the Dog siblings into Rainbow Snakes and the two Brothers into rocks as well as Rainbow Snakes.

The next bracket of three myths notes the relation of mythic beings to the land. The first refers to the South Alligator River region, and the second to western Arnhem Land (Gunwinggu). They were told to R. Berndt at Oenpelli in 1949 and 1950. The third is a Bidjandjadjara story from Ooldea (R. Berndt 1941).

7. INMALAGARA LEAVES HIS COUNTRY

An old Dreaming man named Inmalagara came up from the plain country at Marabibi in the Wildman River area [where the Gunbudj language was spoken as far away as the South Alligator River: see Myth 3]. He sat down near a hill, thinking to himself: 'I'm tired of this country, I want to go east.' Getting his fishing net, he caught some small live bream, filled up his two bags with these, and commenced his journey. He camped at Burur [on the Wildman River, high up], then continued through the bush until he reached Buboroigu. Next day he went on through the bush and came to Gun-guruwonga Hill. He climbed this hill to see what the country was like ahead, just going up, but not camping there; instead, he went along the plain to Banawandju. As he travelled along he said to himself, 'I'll find a song now.' So he sang these two songs, relating to the Gabalgu side of the South Alligator River: Gunbudj language.

limanda yeraganei (repeated)
Quickly travelling I find [a song].

gini warlmang garyu-gumag
dadjung-guma ngarug-nuran
That water snake lying.
You lie there! I'll just walk away!

He went on singing these all the way along.

He crossed over at Djiri-djiridj, and went along Gadaidjel plain, on the eastern side of the South Alligator. He saw a goanna and jumped up, frightened: 'What is that?' 'It is *dadjuguma*!': so he named it. 'You lie down there; I'll just walk away!' he said. He continued on, singing. On the plain he also saw a goose nest, and on hearing him the goose flew away. He looked at the nest of eggs: 'What is that?' he asked. 'It is *gandun* (egg)!' He called out, 'You stay there, I won't pick you up; I'll just go away!'

He went on, singing, to Obiwabi spring [Wada language, close to Gagadju], and then on to Ngarumargwida springs [Gagadju], still east of the South Alligator River, singing all the way. As he walked through water there, he inadvertently put his foot on a long-necked *gadjalnga* tortoise. Again, as before, he told it to stay there and that he would go on. He walked on to Garara spring [Gagadju], where he camped, and later continued through the bush. It was at Garara that he saw a long *nabalu* bush goanna: he jumped in fright [but uttering his usual formula, he went on]. Eventually he arrived at Manga-ngalada spring, where he camped, Next day, still singing, he came to Madiyu [Gagadju]. He went down on to the plain, leaving the bush, still singing, and saw an *irabundjori* crocodile lying across his track. He passed around it and went on singing, and saw a *nareinma* water snake. He looked all around at the country. He was coming close to the place he had seen from Gun-guruwonga Hill. Singing, he came close to the East Alligator. He saw a *budjudu* plain goanna climbing a tree: it was frightened of him. He came to the river bank. 'I can't swim,' he said. 'What will I do?' he asked himself. 'I'll "straighten" (i.e., lengthen) my legs; I'll take a long step from here to the other side.' This was at Algagamanga. When he stepped over he was at Badiyagadei [higher up from what is now called Smith's Landing; Amurag language].

All this way he had carried his two bags of bream. Coming to Arara spring, singing as he walked along, he looked around to find a suitable 'hole' near the mouth of the East Alligator into which he could put the fish. 'I have kept these bream too long,' he said. So he untied his bags and tipped the contents into the billabong at Arara [Mangeri and Amurag languages].

'Which way will I stand? I'll look at the fish,' he said. And as he stood up there, he 'made himself'. [However, he still 'walks about' as a spirit living in the water, and he comes out to talk to 'clever men'. He stays there all the time, being frightened of tobacco and clothing.]

8. THE LONG SEARCH FOR A FINAL HOME

Lab-lab (Night Bird), a *namadgu, nawagaidj* man, came from Djalagmara in Rembranga and Burara country, high up inland, away from Milingimbi. He walked all the way through the bush, camping at Gureimi, eating wild honey and talking to himself. He went on to Gubara where he camped and then on to Gulbu, coming west to Maramara, talking away to himself in Rembranga but on reaching Gumadir, beginning to speak Gunwinggu. He travelled on to Djulgu-ganing, to Mimala, to Ivigu, to Manbin and, through the bush along a little creek, to Malgurun. He stayed here for a while, and then found another creek at Man-gundag (Black Plum): he ate plums there, but left many for the people who were to come.

He continued to Gegeg, looking around at the country. 'I had better go on farther,' he thought. He came to Nogburu and looked around, deciding which way he would go. 'I'll go that way,' he said. He found Midji-ildjil and then Wumbu. He was still talking to himself, looking around at the country, worrying about which way he would go. He went on to Mandjulg-gari, where he put in a *mandjulg* tree; he obtained string (fibre) from inside the tree's branches, and dipping a 'pad' of this into honey he sucked it. Continuing, he came to Mibulu. 'Which way shall I go?' He went to Beveg. 'I'd better go on farther, to the place where I can sit down (stay).' So he went on to Weli, where he camped. 'I'd better go to a place where I can stay.' He went on to Gwuwarang, to Bilbilman, camping at each place. He looked around. '*Dalg! dalg!*' he cried. 'I can't decide where to sit down, to remain!' He walked away along the bush to Mandigeri. 'There are stones here, many stones! Where shall I go?' He came on to Ngalburmu, where he camped. It was here that Djigirid-djigirid (Willy Wagtail) flew into the bushes and disturbed him. He went on to Gunmadbaru, where he camped: Djigirid-djigirid was there too, eating lizards and frogs. So Lab-lab moved on to Garuri-genyu, where he camped. He put his foot down, but found the ground hard. If it had been soft, he said to himself, he would have stayed there. He went on to Bulg-ngog (still speaking Gunwinggu), and then to Galaluyu, where he camped. He could not find a suitable place, and went on to Manmoyi [called after *mandudjmi*, green plums, from the Gumadir side; but the place is also called Manimgurug, after that plum; Manmoyi is in Margulidjban country]. He continued on to Manyalgudjalng, to Benbendulg and to Gunbol-bulu billabong. [This last place is 'dangerous'; no one drinks water here: Lab-lab made it taboo.] And on to Gundjambulu, following a creek all the way from the Liverpool River, but high up; he came to

Gugardag billabong and went on to Miwalaberd. Here he put a small *madjalwa* bamboo spear in the creek [the place name is derived from it]. 'I'll leave this place for the new generation!' he declared, and he went on to Guningundjuli and camped there; then on to Dilerbangg [named after a small fish]. He walked on to Gwiyadyei. He tried to decide whether he would remain there, but eventually went on to Gung-gu-wimdi and then to Mandarayu, where there is a big hill. [This too is a 'danger place' — 'you can't climb it!']

He went on to Namuld-gabolgmi [here there is white pipeclay and the place is named after it], to Deleg [where he made white faeces: 'We use that white paint now'], and to Man-gulnug-didjam, where he camped. 'This is close to where I will remain!' he thought. He looked around, camping there for two days; but not satisfied, he went to Gwoidjang-ngal. 'This is a good place!' he said. He slept here and put *deleg* (white clay) there. He also painted himself, to make himself 'look good': he painted his wings, and around his face and forehead — 'That is good for people who will come later!'

He was feeling himself [the onset of the process of transformation]; he hid among the grass; he found a place where he could stay. He made a large hill: he went up with his wings outstretched and he squatted like that, with his wings spread out. He 'made himself' into rock, with white clay on his 'body': and he also 'made himself' into the *lab-lab* bird, at Wuran-gi, in the bush, higher up on a creek which farther down became the Liverpool River [Gunwinggu language].

9. A PLACE TO DIE

Old man Wadi Banbun [sometimes named Walyi] crawled along on his knees. He had been kicked in the back by Linga Man (a small Lizard), a severe injury, making Banbun unable to stand. He came from Bundina, which is surrounded by *maii* bushes. As he went along he sang:

bundiluga ladu-ladu ralana gading
Waving bushes [as he goes along].

Leaving Bundina, he crawled along, making six camps before reaching Ngeni billabong [tracks lead into Ngeni from either side]. He sang:

badaderi djuwi-loru badaderi
Crawling along, churning up the dust.

He was following a *walidja* (a creature like a small wallaby, *gabidji*). All the way he crawled, leaving knee marks along the track. He followed the *walidja* round Ngeni, which is a large waterhole and soak (*gabi*). But he did not catch it. So he went on to *gabi* Manbi, where he sang:

> *manbi gada ilari gada manbi*
> Pigeon [moving] head, dancing.

Banban saw a wild pigeon and 'danced' on his knees.

He went to Ngalda and saw another *manbi* pigeon that had flown to this place. Here he sang the same song and 'danced'.

Finally he came to Ilbinga, where there are *ngalda* kurrajong trees [see name of last waterhole]. [Ilbinga is a well-known rockhole in the Everard Ranges: Banbun originally came from here, and he had crawled back to die in his own country.] He sang his death song:

> *degal-baganu gali leri elungu*
> Shaking [getting up], he throws his boomerang and dies.

He shook all over in the throes of death. He stood upright, throwing his boomerang, and fell back dead. He is now a large rock at Ilbinga.

In the story of Inmalagara, we see that he deliberately leaves his own country for an area not then known to him. His aim was to find an appropriate place where he could put his fish and 'make himself'. As we will see in other myths from western Arnhem Land, this is a common theme. Mythic beings explore the countryside, moving over territories which in the future will be occupied by people who speak a designated language. So that in a sense, particular areas were pre-empted for specific language speakers. However, the purpose of such travelling was to 'make oneself' at a specially chosen site. In that respect, it is interesting to compare the approaches of Inmalagara and Lab-lab. Inmalagara shows a rather timid, but measured, concern for the creatures he encounters in the course of his travels, and assures them that they will not be disturbed. Lab-lab is indecisive, not sure about where he should go, or where he should finally settle for his metamorphosis. His is almost a case of being neurotic, but he does finally settle on a place for that purpose. The other myth, although from a different culture (the Western Desert), is not so dissimilar. In Banbun's case it is not a matter of exploration. He is concerned for himself; and, in spite of his serious injury, he eventually reaches his homeland and dies there. He has achieved what he set out to do, lightening his pain by singing; he is metamorphosed as a rock, his spirit centre.

The following short myth is on a similar theme — of a lone Dreaming character, travelling across country in search of other people. It was told to R. Berndt at Oenpelli in 1950.

10. CALLING TO NO AVAIL

Gagai'yeibmi or Gagai'mi, a *yariyaning*, *nagamarang* man, came from Gubugoidj, in Gunwinggu territory, high up in the escarpment country. He was crying out there [hence the place name], but no one answered. He went on to Malbangandi waterhole, covered with lilies, and stood there, calling out. He went on to Mirong and sat there, calling out, but no one answered. 'Where are all the people?' he asked. He continued to Mabina, calling out, with the same result. 'I'll have to go on farther!' he thought. He went on to Luli — but again no one answered his cries. He walked farther and found some caves. 'I'll stay here,' he said. He called out from morning to sunset, but no one answered. He was becoming hoarse and his tongue lengthened itself, like a dog's. He tried to call out again, but found he could only whisper. He sprang up and 'jumped', making himself a rock among those caves. In one of them he put himself as a 'picture' [transformed himself as an ochred painting]. He named that country Gagai'mi, after himself, because he was calling out but no other people were there.

The following myths come from different cultural areas. The first is a Maung story from the Goulburn Islands, written down in 1947; the second from Yirrkalla, in north-eastern Arnhem Land (1946); the third (1960) is a Walmadjeri story from Balgo, south-eastern Kimberleys; and the fourth belongs to the Andingari dialectal group, some members of which were at Ooldea in 1941. They were told to R. Berndt.

11. SOUTH AND NORTH GOULBURN ISLANDS ARE SEPARATED

Blanket Lizard or Frilled Lizard, Gundamen, a *yariwurig*, *nawulan* man was living on the mainland at Wandjili, directly south of South Goulburn Island. He wanted to cross over to Waruwi (South Goulburn Island). He came running along the beach, trying to decide whether he should swim over, but was afraid of the deep water. Frog, Mularig, a *nyindjariwurga* (*marwala* 'skin') woman, whom Gundamen called *mamam* (a classificatory wife), was also there. When she saw how frightened he was, she called out '*Mubin! mubin! murbin!*' [said to refer to fear of the sea]. Then the island and the mainland joined together, and Gundamen was able to walk over. When she stopped crying out those words, the mainland and island drew apart and became as they now are.

Frog, however, came over to Waruwi in her *wilam* bark canoe, joining Gundamen, now her husband. They went to Andjumug billabong, on the north-western side of the island, where a large number of Maung people were camped. There were plenty of fish, so the two stayed there among them.

At this time of the Dreaming, only a small creek named Mandurl-mandurl divided South Goulburn Island from Wayara, the north island. People would set their *yalawoi* drum nets in the creek at night, and early next morning pull them up full of fish: they had plenty of fish to eat.

Crow, Gurragag, a *yarigarngurg* man, was sitting by himself. Every time the others got fish, they gave him only *walmuri*, the stone 'big belly' fish. Crow sat there thinking about all those good fish: every time, they gave him no-good fish! 'What am I going to do to all those people?' he asked himself. 'I think I must do something!' He looked around for his *aramangg* stone axe and began to cut down a big *waral* paperbark tree. It fell across the creek. Crow sat there on the tree, crying out '*Waag. . waag!*' As he did so the creek began to grow wider and wider. And Crow began to fly: 'he turned into a bird' and flew over all the people, who called out angrily. South Island was dividing itself from North Island, with deep sea in between. All the people were on the banks of the creek when the paperbark tree fell [it was the splash from the tree that caused the waters to rise]: the water rose and drowned all of them.

Blanket Lizard had in the meantime gone to Barclay Point on the mainland. On hearing what had happened, he began to swim toward South Goulburn Island to search for his wife. He was drowned halfway there and turned into a reef around which the sea is rough. Frog was drowned when the water rose at what was originally a creek. [A women's version told to C. Berndt is very close to this. And see also R. and C. Berndt 1985: 399–400.]

12. THE RIVER OF HONEY

This story refers to Limbaruku river, near Cape Wilberforce in north-eastern Arnhem land. It is really a honey river: 'It was never a proper river, but a large tree.'

Two Woyal-gandjalala spirit men [Gwolamala *mada*, dialect] went out to collect honey. Mungga-ranggar, or Maialwa, was a Blanket Lizard [Dadiwi *mada*]. Lizard man made a *marin* basket for holding honey, the fine-mesh variety made by men. The Woyal men cut out honey from a large tree with their stone axes. Lizard man listened to the sound: 'Perhaps those men are cutting honey. I'll go and see.' Leaving his basket behind, he hurried to meet them: 'I'm very hungry, I have come to ask you for honey.' 'Yes,' the others replied, 'take what you want.' Lizard went on eating honey, and the Woyal continued cutting it out. They looked round and saw Lizard running about in pain. They asked him, 'What's wrong with you?' 'I swallowed a splinter of wood with that honey and it's stuck in my throat!' He began to 'make himself' into a lizard: he tried to run up a tree. 'Don't make yourself into a lizard yet,' the Woyal called out. But he went on doing so. The two Woyal were running around trying to stop him from doing this. But Lizard climbed into the honey tree, the large stringybark tree they were cutting. The tree fell across the land, becoming the honey river, and the branches of the tree are the branches of that river.

13. THE WIDENING OF LAKE GREGORY

Two *djambidjin* Dreaming Dogs chased two Emus who were *djungurei*. They chased them down the Sturt Creek, from Burewi, near Sturt Creek station, to Lubu billabong. They were coming from the east, following them to Wideleg (or Walwedjaru, a large billabong), to 'Wobelan' [small billabongs, their name said to be a derivation of a European one], to Didjil, to Ngeima-ngeima [a big billabong], to 'Wulp' [Wolf Creek is the European name, Walwala the Aboriginal one], to 'Ken' billabong [European name: Yana, Aboriginal name], to Maiara, to Linggi-linggi, to Bolabiaru, and to Wonmandara billabongs, and then on to Won-gu, old Billiluna station. Still chasing the Emus, the two Dogs came to Galwalari billabong and then to Gurabanda billabong. At this place, another creek 'came around' at Wiriyani or Wirarara. Here the two Emus took separate tracks, each followed by a Dog. From Wiriyani one followed Emu to Inagudjara (two billabongs); on to Djindjayeri, Maiwan, Ngali (Billiluna stockyard); Nganadjara; Djurulung-gadjara (billabong); Gudu (soak); to Bulbai creek where there is also a Lake (Nyingabidi); to Yunbu; and to Gulgulruldjara, where it joins up again with Wiriyani [see above; apparently rejoining Sturt Creek].

In the meantime the other Dog, on leaving Gurabanda [see above] went directly down the Sturt Creek to Gulamara and on to Gura (Gross Soak) to Billiluna yard (Dawal) chasing his Emu. He went on to Lamanbragu creek; to Ngul-ngul; to Langan yard [billabong, beside the Sturt]; to Bandjanbragu (deep water here); to Ngalgu, Gidji and Boingadjilal; and then on to Gilwar (salty water); to Djalwi (salt lake; creek) and Yadjalanu; close to Mundagwi-ngadjada (big 'open' water: Lake Gregory); and back again to Wiriyani, where he killed the Emu, and where the other Dog started chasing, and later killed, his Emu.

The two Dogs cooked the meat and ate it. After that, exhausted, they breathed heavily and the strength of their breathing widened Lake Gregory. 'That is why it is so large!' They went on to Gundaguda, and to Banggubidi [where there is a windmill] and on to Malan [now an Aboriginal community settlement, on 'Comet' creek]. They went inside the waterhole there, which is salty from their sweat.

---

14. HOW OOLDEA SOAK WAS MADE

Gabidji, Little Wallaby, came from the west to Ooldea Soak. He came across the large western sand-ridge, close to a black desert-oak tree. He was carrying a *malu-meri* (kangaroo skin bag) or *buda* skin waterbag, which was full. He crossed the ridge and came to Yuldi (Ooldea). There he put his *buda* at the base of a large sand dune to the south, and urinated in a depression which became the present-day Ooldea Soak. ['That's the water we drink now!' said the people in 1941.] He stayed there for a while, and then went on to another large sandhill to the north; from there he looked out toward the east. That sandhill was named Bimbali. He returned to Ooldea to pick up his *buda*, and then travelled east to Yuldibina; there he spilt a little water, and that became the lake. However, he was not sure whether he should go farther and finally decided to return to Ooldea. He left his *buda* there and it was metamorphosed as the large southern sandhill. 'That's why there is always water there.' He camped for a while, then decided to go east again. He reached Dagula (Tarcoola), and there he made a large hut.

In the meantime Djunbunbin, Thunder or Storm man, had been following Gabidji. He had come from the north; he was a great *gingin*

(clever man). As he travelled during the night, he chanted his song [called *djimun*; Djunbunbin was also said to be a 'big rain man'.]

rulga-rulga ngang-gali wonggang-gu
badadara ngang-gali rulga-rulga
Rolling thunder, clouds speaking,
Angry clouds, rolling thunder.

As Djunbunbin moved across the country dark clouds sheltered him and thunder [his voice] was his chant. As he approached Dagula, where Gabidji was camped, his chant grew stronger and with it during the night came a deluge of rain which swept away his hut.

With Gabidji were some other Dreaming men. They too were washed away and carried to the place at Tarcoola where gold had been found. [The European miners were said to have found a lot of human bones when they dug for gold. Those, said Aboriginal people at Ooldea, were the bones of Gabidji and the other Dreaming men.]

These four myths describe how particular physiographical features of the countryside came to be as they are now. The first two were a result of greed: Crow was denied the good food which he could rightly expect as a visitor, while Blanket Lizard accepted the generosity of the Woyal but abused it, and consequently a splinter of wood stuck in his throat. However, these myths can be interpreted differently. Mythically, Crow himself had a reputation for being greedy, and that could have been why he was given only 'bad' fish. The Woyal may have resented giving honey to someone who had nothing to offer in return, and they were undoubtedly responsible for leaving chips of wood in the honey they had chopped out of the tree. Woyal, or Wudal, are important mythic beings in north-eastern Arnhem Land, and are indirectly associated with the two Wawalag Sisters (see C. Berndt 1970: 1,306–26). The widening of Lake Gregory has a straightforward mythic explanation. So have the waters at Ooldea and Yuldi-bina; but the reason given for the drowning of Gabidji and other Dreaming characters was that Djunbunbin was angry because of the water Gabidji had. In each case the primary mythic being responsible for what took place in the story turned into something else: Crow became a bird, Blanket Lizard a lizard, the two Dogs went down into a waterhole, where they remained, while Gabidji and the others left their bones for Europeans to dig up!

Two versions from Ooldea (R. Berndt 1941) tell how the Southern Ocean came about.

15.   THE PIERCED WATERBAG

Two brothers, one a tall man named Marlgaru and the other a short man named Alruna, came from the west. Marlgaru carried an empty *malu-meri* [kangaroo skin waterbag]. On arrival at Baki waterhole they filled the bag. They camped there for a while. Then they went south-eastward to Marlgaru waterhole, named after one of the brothers, because it was here that he dug a hole in the sand and sat in it as protection against the hot sun. Going on, they came to Alruna waterhole, where there are two rock-holes formed from the indentation of their bodies as they sat in their camp.

They continued south to Won-genya, toward Fowler's Bay, where they made camp. Alruna, who was lazy, stayed back in camp. His brother went out hunting but first he hid the waterbag some distance from their camp. However, while Marlgaru was away, Alruna followed his tracks to the hiding place and drank some water from the bag. Then he returned to the camp and made a club. Going back to the waterbag, he struck it with his club, piercing the skin so that all the water spread across the countryside and flowed down to the coast to become the Southern Ocean. As a result, the two brothers were drowned. But their spirits went into the sky to become two stars on the western side of the Milky Way. [No reason is given for what either of the brothers did. But see the next story.]

16.   STEMMING THE FLOOD WATERS

Marlgaru and Yaul were two brothers, Yaul being the younger. Marlgaru had a kangaroo skin bag full of water and two fire-sticks. They travelled toward the south coast from the northern desert. Yaul was thirsty, but Marlgaru refused his repeated requests for water. They came to Biran-bura, west of Fowler's Bay. Yaul had become thin and his throat was parched. Marlgaru left his waterbag hidden under some rocks [over which the sea now swells].

Yaul grew very angry, and when his brother returned, the two quarrelled. Marlgaru went out hunting again. When he was out of sight, Yaul went in search of the bag. Finding it, he jabbed at it with a club, breaking the skin. The water poured out. Marlgaru ran back and tried to save his bag, but the water continued to flow and spread and eventually drowned them both. It also formed the sea.

The water was spreading inland too, but the country was saved from inundation by the action of various Bird Women. When they learnt what had happened, they all came down from the north- and south-east. Minma Ngeni (a small red-breasted bird) came running. Minma Wada-wada (a species of laughing jackass), hearing the noise of water, left the kurrajong roots from which she was collecting water, and slept at six waterholes before reaching Biranbura. Minma Bulin (like a *wada-wada*), Minma Djinda-djinda (willy wagtail), Minma Didarara (a yellow bird with the cry *dira-ter*), Minma Idji-didjidi (bird like a wagtail), Minma Djinbun (a small brown bird), Minma Djil-djil (a red-breasted black or blue bird), Minma Balbaı (a parrot), Minma Badal-badal (another kind of parrot), Minma Gil-gilga (a red parrot), Minma Ban-ban (blue and red bell bird), and Dudu (a large blue bird), all flew down to Biranbura, bringing with them the roots of the *ngalda* kurrajong tree. They placed these all along the coast, making a barrier, restraining the oncoming waters that threatened to cover (what became) the mainland. [This explains why *ngalda* roots contain fresh water and the kurrajong is the 'water tree': the water soaked into the roots. It also explains why this coastline is rocky, with tall cliffs — they are the metamorphosed *ngalda* roots.]

After making this barrier, all the Dreaming women flew away to their home territory. They are the Minmara women who appear in the Nyirana-Yulana myths: they were also responsible for 'cutting' (circumcising) the mythic being Nyirana.

These two versions of the one myth, with an extension in the second, concern mythic beings who came from different parts of the Western Desert, the first from the west and the second from the north. Both reach different places in the vicinity of Fowler's Bay. There is also a name change in so far as the second brother is concerned. No reason is given for one withholding water from the other.

In the second myth, it is not only that the spilt water forms the Southern Ocean. There is the much more serious matter of the water eroding the mainland. That catastrophe is avoided through the prompt action of the Bird Women, the religiously important Minmara or Gungga-runggara, who are associated with the sacred Nyirana-Yulana mytho-ritual cycle. Further, in the first myth, the Two Brothers are said to become two stars near the Milky Way; while in the sacred myth, not given here, the Gungga-runggara become stars which constitute the Seven Sisters (see Myth 127).

In the next two myths we have examples which are reminiscent of the Dieri, telling how certain human physical features came into being. Many stories in Aboriginal Australia deal with differing human features and how they were formed. These, from Ooldea, were told to R. Berndt in

1941. The first comes from the Mandjindji, of the western sector of the Western Desert, the other from the Andingari to the east.

17.   THEFT OF A SACRED OBJECT

Two big men came from the west. They were Ngalda the kurrajong tree and Ngerin or Ngeri-ngeri (similar to a bell bird): and they were 'mates'. Ngalda was a young man who knew little about the religious life. Ngerin was fully-initiated, and a religious leader. He had placed his sacred materials in a storehouse, hidden away in the bush.

Every second day Ngerin went out to his storehouse and meditated. Afterward, he went out to catch goanna, but he always returned without telling Ngalda what he had been doing. [One of the basic rules is not to discuss secret-sacred matters with an uninitiated person.] Ngalda also went out hunting for goanna, and returning to the camp cooked what he had caught. As he ate he wondered why his 'mate' always went out alone: 'He must have something out there in the bush!'

Soon afterward Ngerin went out again to his storehouse. Ngalda, leaving a little later, went in a different direction, but then made a detour and came out on the opposite side, which enabled him to pick up Ngerin's tracks. He followed them, and when Ngerin left his storehouse he came up and looked at what was there [that is, at the sacred objects: details omitted]. Ngalda removed the most important of the objects, smoothed over his tracks to allay suspicion, walked on for about fifty miles and then flew a further distance. It was at that unnamed place that he hid what he had taken, and returned to his camp before Ngerin arrived. They talked about their hunting, and ate. Then Ngalda said, 'I think I'll walk about for a while.' Ngerin was suspicious, so he went out to his storehouse. There he found that one object had been taken. He looked all around for tracks, but saw none. He returned to the camp, but Ngalda had not come back. Ngerin sat there brooding, getting his spears ready. Then he went out, following Ngalda's tracks, and saw him sitting there. Ngerin threw a spear, but the other dodged it. He threw another, and missed him again. 'Why are you chasing me?' Ngalda asked. But Ngerin refused to reply; he came back to his camp, planning to go away on his own.

Ngerin cried in sorrow for the lost object. He turned again to follow Ngalda, saw him, threw his spear, and missed. When Ngerin asked whether he had been along his special track, Ngalda did not answer. That night, when Ngerin was asleep, Ngalda flew to where he had hidden the object he had stolen; he picked it up and hid it much farther away. Then he came to Budaling waterhole. Ngerin had followed him. He threw another spear, but missed again. Turning, Ngalda said, 'I'm only a young man, I have done nothing wrong!' He walked away: but when he was out of sight of Ngerin, he flew to Mount Margaret. Ngerin tracked him for a while, only to find that the tracks disappeared where he had flown. Then he, too, came to Mount Margaret. He saw Ngalda, threw a spear, but missed. In sorrow and frustration he returned to his 'own' camp, where he sat down in the middle of a lake [clay pan?] called Keri (Lake Carey), south of Mount Margaret. A large rock at the centre of this lake is Ngerin — his spirit remains there.

Ngalda, meanwhile, went on to Ralga where he camped, and then on to Guma and to Bandam and Bilgi. There he sat down, and heard a 'big mob' of Ngin-gadi men singing at Garal waterhole. He listened, and next morning came into Garal. He 'made himself' look like a *djilbi* (elder), and walked into the middle of the group. Some of the men said, '*Guda ngalabida*' [Brother, come on!]; others '*kamuru ngalabida!*' [Mother's brother]: they welcomed him. Pretending that he would perform a special rite, Ngalda dug a hole in the middle of the dancing ground, and the people surrounded him, waiting expectantly. But all he did was to defecate there, and the stench killed every one of them except himself.

He collected all the bodies together. Now, these Ngin-gadi men had no fingers or toes. Ngalda got a stick, or *yiladi* skewer which he put through the hands of each dead person. [He wanted the skewer to serve as a hook that would enable him to drag the bodies along.] He began to pull, but the skewer did not hold; instead, it tore the flesh, leaving the finger divisions. He did this four times to each of the bodies' hands and feet, but the skewer would not hold: when he pulled, it merely tore the flesh. ['Before that, people did not have toes or fingers — this is how they got them!'] At last Ngalda put the *yiladi* through their penes, and found that then the flesh did not tear. He dragged the bodies along, one after another, on his skewer. He came into Winbal, where a deep depression was formed by the dragging bodies. [It is now a long pool of water.] He went on to Nanari, where he cooked the bodies and ate their meat.

He travelled on, a long way, to a place [name unknown] where he met a 'big mob' of Manbi (Pigeon Men). They, too, were singing. Ngalda did as before, coming into the midst of the men, and defecating. But the Manbi did not die: they all sat around, looking at him. As they sat there, looking, Djilbi (old man, elder) Walyi came into the camp. He, too, defecated, but in this case the stench killed Ngalda *and* all the Manbi. Walyi gathered together their bodies and cooked and ate them.

18. THE TEDIOUS STORY-TELLER

Djilbi (old man, elder) Mamu (see Chapter 4) had a special stone knife which he kept hidden in his anus. He came to a particular waterhole where an old man [human, not a *mamu*] was sitting. They began to tell each other Dreaming stories. When it was his turn, Mamu smoothed out the sand before him. He drew the waterhole, and the place where they sat, and the travelling 'lines' of a number of Dreaming beings who came to that place: all their tracks, in fact, led in that direction. He told about the Bunda-gadingga (Fly people), the Bunda-minga (Ant people), the Gunma-mila (the March fly people), the Gwering (Mosquito people), the Mumbu (Mice people), and so on, one after the other. The old Mamu was only making up these stories. He went on, mentioning one lot of people after another until the old man fell asleep.

Djilbi Mamu was watching him, and seeing him fall asleep, removed his knife and cut a horizontal line across his eye sockets, from cheek bone to cheek bone. Then he killed him, cooked him and ate him. But the cut across the face left a brow ridge on the faces of *all* human beings who came afterward: a depression in which the eyes are set, the nose bridge with its horizontal indent and creases at the corner of the eyes: 'These were done by the Mamu's hand: and that is why everyone has this deep ridge under the brow.'

The crucial issue of 'completing' the shape of a human being is set within the context of a myth which has a number of other unrelated implications. We need not go into these here, except to note who was responsible. In the first case it was an uninitiated youth who violated a secret-sacred storehouse, successfully evaded punishment, and went on to deceive, kill and eat a group of 'strangers', but who was himself finally killed and eaten. In the other myth, too, it is through death, at the hands of a hostile killer that human beings 'received' their characteristic brow formation. In north-eastern Arnhem Land, when the Djanggau gave birth to the first people, female children were placed on soft grass and covered with mats to ensure they had feminine qualities of smoothness; male children, on the other hand, were placed on coarse grass, and that is why they have facial hair and are generally rough in comparison with females. While in that instance no physical act took place, it did stipulate an external condition which explained the differing appearance of males and females. And there are other examples, too.

The following three stories relate to particular plant species for which mythic beings are responsible. They come from the Ngulugwongga (or 'Mulluk-Mulluk') of the Daly River (1946), the Mandjindji (from Ooldea in 1941), and the Gunwinggu-Maung of western Arnhem Land (Oenpelli in 1949), and were told to R. Berndt.

19. YILIG THE LILY ROOT PLANTER

Yilig-moi-indji, Red Lily woman (designated 'old'), came from another country carrying a basket full of lily roots suspended from her head by a fibre cord. She came to *wag*-Bamayag, where she put in a lily root. At *deg*-Dugailyil she put another, and then several at *deg*-Nangad. Carrying her basket on her head she came to a river. She put a log across it and began to walk over, but it broke. 'Ah,' she said, 'A man should walk over it,' and she swam across at Mulya-gulmin [near Canoe Camp]. She then came to Banggala swamp where a woman, Braulum, and other women, were roasting *bundjaranggi* swamp bulbs. They asked Yilig which way she was going. She answered, 'I'm going to *deg*-Ginga, to put lily roots there!' The bulbs the women were cooking were not ready: they covered them over with stones. [They didn't give her any.]

Yilig went on to *deg*-Ngulang-bandirang, on the other side of Brown Creek. Here she threw some lily 'seeds' around, cooked some for herself, and ate. Later she picked up her basket of lily roots and went over to the grass, cleaned an area and put some lily roots there, covering them with a little mud, just a little way below the surface of the ground. However, Braulum and the other women had followed her, and Braulum asked why she had not put them deeper into the ground. Yilig replied, 'No, not deep, but near the surface.' When Yilig had gone, Braulum put some of them deep into the ground ['so that today you have to dig deeply to get these roots'], but she also collected some for eating.

Yilig picked up her basket and went on to Bundjarang-ginya on the other side of the Creek, where she sat down.

Braulum and the other women were meanwhile roasting the lily roots at Bandirang. 'Come, the roots are roasted,' they called. 'They are ready to take out.' They began to remove them, and were amazed to find that there was nothing there — only stones! All the roots had gone underground to *wag*-Bundjarang-ginya, near the river where Yilig was sitting. There she remains, Dreaming, with her basket as rock. [Comment: Mick Ga-rub from *deg*-Dilg, brother of 'Cheeky Charlie', broke this rock basket in order to increase the supply of red lilies.]

20. PEOPLE TURNING INTO PLANTS AND CREATURES

The Wadi Gudjara (Two Men), Yungga (Black Goanna) and Djimbi (White Goanna), travelling from west to south-east, saw the tracks of many men and women and followed them. [There are no place names associated with this area, because they were walking through the spinifex country.] The Wadi Gudjara camped, and that night they saw camp fires and heard the voices of people.

In the morning, they also heard people talking, but could not see anybody. They moved nearer, and saw many tracks leading into a large *danbi* or *bila* spinifex thicket and closely-growing tall *garagara* grass. They looked around in this area but could see no-one. The tracks were fresh, and they were puzzled. They lit fires at each side of the thicket, and when all the grass had burnt down they searched among the ashes and found a number of dead *bigulru* 'bob-tailed' lizards. [These lizards are brown and red in colour, and about a foot long, with a club-shaped tail. When the Wadi Gudjara burnt them, they were all hidden in the grass. The fire burnt off their tails and the remaining part curled round. Moreover, they are now the colour of ashes from that fire. 'That is how they became lizards. Before, they were people.']

The Wadi Gudjara moved on westward until they heard the sounds of a large group of people, men, women and children, singing and playing. They camped near where they heard the noise. Again, they saw many tracks leading to that particular place, and next morning they made ready to enter the camp. From a little distance they saw people sitting under trees in the shade, and heard them talking. As they approached, the people disappeared; only their fires and spears remained. The Wadi Gudjara walked all round the camp, searching under the trees, looking for them — but there was no one!

Then the Wadi Gudjara stamped on the ground where the disappearing people had sat. Immediately, *wada* plants (sweet potato or yam) grew up from between clumps of grass, twisting their tendrils round the *galgula* wild pear trees. [These 'potatoes' are six to twelve inches in diameter and in appearance resemble rockmelons: their creepers extend up the tree trunks. Aborigines hit the ground with their hands and can hear the potatoes rattling underneath. A digging stick is used to wedge them out.] These vegetables were once men, women, girls and boys — until the Wadi Gudjara came along. 'Before, there were no potatoes: they are Dreaming people.' When Yungga the Black Goanna stamped, black *wada* grew; when Djimbi the White Goanna stamped, white *wada* grew.

The Wadi Gudjara went on until they could hear another group of people. They camped nearby, and heard them singing a *milgu inma* (song, ceremony) all night long. In the morning they came closer and saw people sitting around, each family in its own camp, but when the Wadi Gudjara entered, they all turned into crows and flew away. Before, they were people!

The Wadi Gudjara continued walking until they heard the voices of many people singing an *inma*, and talking. The Two Men made camp. Next morning, they came nearer and saw people sitting before their fires, near their shelters. As the two came closer, the people disappeared. [These people were camping along the banks of a creek, some on one side, some on the other. The Wadi Gudjara came along the middle, between the two groups.] The Wadi Gudjara stamped on the ground and the disappearing people turned into *djilgali* bushes; these grow long tubers, which were formerly the people. [These tubers are sweet and eaten like apples. They are dug up, being broken from the roots of the tree, and although they are mostly eaten raw, they can also be dried.]

When the Wadi Gudjara stamped, they said: 'You stay as *djilgali djugur* (Dreaming) now.' Where Yungga stamped there are dark-flesh *djilgali*; where Djimbi stamped, white-flesh *djilgali*.

21. NGALWOIDBUG LEAVES HIS BAMBOOS

Ngalwoidbug, a Dreaming man, grew bamboos at Mang-gulyuwul on the northern side of Cooper's Creek, in the bush where there is a spring [Gunwinggu and Maung languages]. He sat there for a long time. Then he came southward toward Oenpelli, with his bamboos rolled up into bundles. He came to Angu billabong, where he washed and drank water, and continued to Magalia [where Cooper's Creek flows into another creek, at the junction of which is Malwundag]. He crossed the creek, came to Wunggudbi [close to the mouth of the East Alligator River], and went through the bush, where he found a large waterhole, Warulg (Winggu).

He then went on to Aringbener [Gunwinggu and Mangeri languages], and climbed a little hill named Manbalggur. From there he looked at the country ahead of him and saw a plain at the other side. He came on to Djaran-djarein (Mangeri-Gunwinggu creek) and drank water, then went down onto the plain, to Ranbal. [He wanted to go to Gunbalanya (Oenpelli), but he was an old man.] At Maralwudbul he hit the water with his hands (*bud! bud!*) to attract and catch fish. He thought of staying there, but went instead round by the jungle behind the 1949 Oenpelli Aboriginal camp, on the other side of the 'landing field' [for planes]. He drank water at Maraian. He still had his bundles of bamboos. He walked on to Mandjuleingoi shade place [near the airstrip], but did not drink there because *maraian* (sacred objects) were hidden there. He came along to Mandjamandawag, a small 'point' of land, and went down along the plain to Ermamb waterhole [Mangeri language]. Not staying there, nor at Yarwenbelangg, he left the plain behind him and entered the bush, going down along Umaranang-gwoyeng, and entering dry country which continued until he came to Alele-geleg springs and well. He stayed for a while, then went down to the plain to look for water and came to Manamandag-gar, where there was a billabong.

From there he went along through the large trees to a long billabong named Unaweleg, close to the Landing. He sat there until the evening, then walked on farther, carrying his bamboos, to the East Alligator River at the Landing, Indji-ngawamug: 'What am I going to do?' he asked himself. He swam over to the western bank, still with his bamboos, and sat down to rest [Weni and Mangeri languages]. Getting up, he walked over to a hill with big rocks: 'I'll go and sit there.' he decided. At Indjawanddjau he lay down, after making his camp. He unrolled his bundles of bamboos and left some of them there. 'I have to grow these for them, for those Aramang-guwel!': he spoke of those people, those Weni people. He held up the rest of his bamboos and threw them to Aramang-guwel. He threw them 'high up the river', and they landed at Ari-angangg, at Red Lily lagoon, for those Eri people. He grew a bamboo 'garden', and he threw those 'seeds' (shoots). Then he lay down and slept.

But something frightened him. He jumped up and ran into the billabong — *Bong!* He washed himself, and got up, and stood there looking back. 'I wonder what frightened me,' he thought to himself. 'It is better for me to stay here.' So he made himself into a rock, standing there, high up. He remained there in that billabong at Warayangarl [the Eri, Weni and Mangeri name for this place, which is called in Gagadju Bareyungada. 'And there are plenty of crocodiles in that billabong!']

These three myths have a common theme that appears here more clearly than before, and will become more apparent as we proceed. It concerns the introduction into the Aboriginal environment of what can be regarded as 'human resources'. Yilig came with *her* basket of red lilies, Ngalwoidbug with *his* bamboos: they brought them from somewhere else. They 'planted' or 'left' their plants to grow, to be there for the use of human beings. Where Red Lily woman remained with her basket as a rock, became a renewal centre. Ngalwoidbug left his bamboos so they would always be available to future generations of people without any effort on their part. The Wadi Gudjara, on the other hand, through a particular action on their part, 'caused' goanna and crows as well as two varieties of root foods to appear, although these had previously been something else. With the Red Lily woman and Ngalwoidbug, *plants remained plants*; with the Wadi Gudjara, *people became plants*. In the case of the latter, however, their transformation is indicated through a quality inherent in the origin of the two shape-changing mythic men, the Black and White Goanna.

The following two myths are about Cycad Man and Cycad Woman, Dreaming characters who became *djang*. They were told in Gunwinggu by women, to C. Berndt at Oenpelli in 1950.

22. CYCAD MAN

Long ago, when we were not here, when only those first people were preparing the land, a man started off in the east, heading this way. He was bringing bitter *man-daneg* yams and white clay and already-cooked cycad palm food, in separate baskets. He was coming, camping along the way, and saying to himself, 'Where am I going, where I'm to become *djang*, Dreaming?' He was talking as he came along, in his own language, camping where he saw plenty of vegetable foods and meats. He always did that. He would camp, sleeping when it grew dark, and starting off again early in the morning. He came to a large jungle, and tried to transform himself. No, he could not. But he was putting *djang* there — vegetable foods, and a bird, a rain-pheasant. He came on, still talking his own language.

He went on, and came to some Dangbun people. They saw him coming, and at last he sat down outside their camps, waiting politely while they called out to him. Then he told them all about the places he had come from. Time went on. At last he left his own language and began talking in theirs. They camped together there for a long time. The people asked him about that food he was bringing, his own food. They asked; he refused to tell them.

He went running away, and climbed up another hill, a big rock. They followed him again, and again he jumped away, across to another rock. He went on doing that. He was making himself ready, where he was lying on the rock. Still they kept asking him, as he was biting and eating the food of his, finishing what he had with him. Then they came again, doing the same, asking him; and he went on eating and finishing it. He held a little piece, and he gave it to them, a small piece. But the other piece he kept, and he buried it by the water. When he gave them that little bit, they grumbled. They said, 'What shall we do about him, this man who gave us such a little piece?'

Then, one little boy began to cry. He went on crying — sunset, early morning, still he kept crying. They tried to make him happy. No. He saw that food they had, that strong, dangerous food they were keeping from him. At last they saw water coming running, big water. That man, Cycad Man, was beating the food on a rock, it was like red-ochre, like really soft clay. He went on, and soaked it in the billabong. He was still beating it, he was making himself wrong. Now he stands underneath the water.

Those others, they all drowned. She ate them, that Snake. Cycad Man, afterward was beating that food, and then went under the water, that man from the east. By beating it he made red-ochre; he stands beating it there at his place beneath the water. As for the others, the Snake vomited them outside the water, on dry land. They stand like rocks, in the country where he came into Dreaming, and where he refused them that food. And as for that little boy, he made them wrong, so that the Snake ate them there, at Man-djawunbela (Gun-djawunbela), and they remain in that country. [Cycad Man's name was Nagun-gilmi. The crying child was an orphan; his name was Nagal'mia.]

23.   CYCAD WOMAN

Long ago, a woman set off from far in the south where the cycad palm grows, bearing food that the people there eat. She set out, coming this way, and carrying only that one food. She did not know about the kinds of vegetable food that we eat, only that cycad palm of hers. She was travelling for a long time, camping on the way, and eating that food she was bringing. She was always doing that. When she saw a good place she would settle down, and camp there. Early next morning she would set off again. She would see those goannas and possums, but she just left them, she would not kill and eat them. She just came along, always talking in her own language. She was still going through rocky country. Going along she saw fish, but she did not kill them, or catch them in the fish net she was carrying, because she knew nothing about the taste of fish. Only honey she knew about, but not in our way. She would chop out a comb — but then she would not eat the actual honey, only the wax. When she camped, at sunset, she took out that cycad food she was carrying and ate a little bit. It was already cooked, so she just heated it in the coals. Next day she would set off again.

At last she saw the tracks of those people who lived there, in the country she had been looking for. They were fresh tracks. She followed them easily, where they went up among the rocks. And she came up to them, the men and women who were gathered there. They called out to her, where she sat politely outside their camping place, and they questioned her. At last they brought vegetable foods and honey, and tried to give them to her. But she said, in her own language, 'I don't want them: I don't eat them, those foods you are holding.' They were trying to give her various creatures, and kangaroo, but she would just leave them. The only thing she would eat was the cycad palm food she had brought and was keeping for herself. The other foods she just left, and next day the others would eat them. She just stayed in camp when the others went hunting, eating that cycad palm food. At last she finished it, but still she stayed in that camp.

Sometimes if she felt like it she would go with the women when they went hunting. When they were chopping out honey combs, they would give her the yellow wax. She would put some into her long basket, and some she would eat there. It was always like that. She would go when she felt very hungry. By this time she had learnt their language, in that country where they were talking Dangbun. They told her, 'It's good that you are talking our language, because you are touching the ground of this country, in our Dangbun place.'

Time went on. The woman became weak and thin: only her bones were holding her together. They were giving her things, trying again to make her well. But no: she stopped them. She lay down. At last she collapsed, sick and dying from hunger. She would not eat any of their vegetable foods: she abstained. They tried to soften her, to change her attitude, but she totally resisted them. So, they just left her. She was very sick, dying. They all slept. The next-day-but-one, her breath cut out. They took her body and put her up on a mortuary platform.

They just stayed there for a while. Then one man went as death-messenger to the south-east, where she had started from. He went and told about her death. They just struck him down from close up, those people. He fell down, dead. Then, the next-day-but-one, they set off toward the country where those Dangbun people were living, to fight them on account of that woman who died. They just came running, they came up, and when they saw those people, they painted themselves with white clay and red ochre, and patterned their faces and noses in red and white. Then they came up talking, shouting *'Algug-waaa!'*, and speared them, killing them all, and leaving them lying dead. Then they went back to their own country, and stayed there. They settled down, but after a while they 'made themselves wrong', from a *djang*. It was a vegetable food that they handled wrongly, one like cycad palm food. They died; their bones were lying about when that Snake 'ate their noses', ate their bodies in the billabong. They themselves became *djang*. And they remain there forever. And those others, they themselves became like rocks for ever, where they had been living, in Dangbun country. [Cycad woman's name was Ngalbo-balar, and she first spoke Rembranga. She was 'old', with white hair. And the scene of the attack was at Gunbambug, in Mayali-Dangbun country.]

These two myths tell of the introduction of cycad palm food into western Arnhem Land. The 'fruit' of this tree is usually prepared in a special way; after soaking and drying it is ground and made into dampers. Both the Cycad man and woman refused to eat local foods, except that she sometimes ate honey wax. Both became *djang* (Dreaming), even though she was placed on a mortuary platform. All those associated with them also became rocks, and *djang*.

The next bracket of stories continues the previous theme, but from a different angle. Unless otherwise stated, they were told to R. Berndt at Oenpelli in 1949–50, and are mainly of Gunwinggu origin. The second Biriwilg myth (26) was told in Gunwinggu by women to C. Berndt in 1950. It is included here to provided a male and a female version, for comparison.

24.   BECOMING PANDANUS

Namalbi and his wife, Ngalmadbi, came from Banamba [east of the Liverpool River, high up from Milingimbi on the mainland: that area was associated with the Burera side, Wulagi and Yanulag languages]. They left their camp to go out into the bush, and carried lengths of pandanus. [The text mentioned that they were using *birabiri* fighting sticks, and had hurt themselves.] Raramin, his wife Djuwulgid and their female child Ngar, remained behind. [The suggestion is that there had been an argument in which Namalbi and his wife were hurt. For that reason, they had gone out by themselves.] They awaited the return of the other two. 'But those two had gone out hunting for good, they didn't return!' The three in the camp counted the days and waited. At last they decided to go in search of them and followed their tracks, but heard no sound. They returned to Banamba. Later they went out again to look. They camped at Nenigeri, then went on to Djalubunba creek, but still could not find the other two. They called out constantly as they travelled all round the area, looking. 'We tried to find those two, but haven't done so yet!'

Namalbi and Ngalmadbi, however, had gone 'to make themselves something!' The other three did not know this; they thought the two had gone hunting or to visit another part of the country. They went on to Mala-balgmen, a big creek, and camped there alongside the deep well.

Then they walked all around again, calling out: 'We don't know where they are!' Soon afterward, they found the tracks of the other two and followed them, and saw where they had camped, and the fire and the depression in which they had slept at Ngalagadjun. They followed these tracks. 'We might find them soon!' Then they came to a little creek, and saw them. The two were getting ready 'to make themselves', with 'horns' rising from their heads, and stood there, looking back at the country from which they had come. When they saw the others they began to run. Raramin and Djuwulgid and the child tried to catch up with them, to bring them back. But the other two said: 'It's too late! We have made ourselves pandanus; we can't come back now.' The 'horns', as pandanus shoots, rose from their heads, and they became pandanus trees.

The other three asked themselves, 'What shall we do?' The wife asked her husband, and the child asked her mother. 'We had better stay here.' They 'made themselves' *gungilbin* termite mounds. 'We can't go back to our country,' they said. So they are all there now, at Djalwarawara.

25. BIRIWILG BECOMES A PAINTING (TOLD BY MEN)

An old woman named Biriwilg was camped at Gwoyurbir on the western side of Red Lily Lagoon, near Oenpelli [Weni language]. She went walking around, to Bandalgwoyu and to the long billabong of Inawelag (close to the Landing), looking for lily roots to roast. She became tired of doing this. 'It is better that I go to that long 'pocket', that corner, at Magagur,' she thought. So she camped at Walg, Red Lily (*wurumanin*) billabong. After a while she went to Indju-mandagag, a large rock nearby; and then on to Umer-ngam, another hill outside the plain where there is a billabong of red lilies. There she collected roots and roasted them for eating. Continuing, she came to Mandjalan, where she made a 'road' [a dry place] across the middle of Mandjalan billabong. She walked to another billabong.

At Yalwunbenen, where she found more lily roots, she camped and slept. Next morning she went on to Ridjewad (Uridjawad) on the plain: there is a large rock here, with a cave. She climbed up to this place, Won-ganengg, and cleaned out the cave. She put her belongings inside it, including her lily root collecting bag, and she brought up soft paperbark to make a bed and to cover herself. She sat down there for a long time. She left the cave from time to time to catch tortoises and snakes in the nearby billabongs, but returned to her home to cook and eat them. She also went to the Yarugiwag hills, but she always returned to Won-ganengg.

One day, however, from her cave entrance she saw two 'men', one chasing the other: Dingo chasing long-tailed Rock Goanna, Malawamb. 'Ah', she thought, 'Men are coming!' She went farther back into her cave. Rock Goanna came in, and she went back still farther. [The two men had intended to go past her cave!] Biriwilg then 'made herself' a picture on the cave wall. 'No human being drew that picture. She turned herself into a spirit on the wall of the rock. She is there now!'

Today, men and women come to this cave and 'feel' that drawing — they touch her there. She is standing up like an ordinary drawing. And when they touch it she sends out plenty of children [spirit children] to enter women everywhere.

26.   BIRIWILG (TOLD BY WOMEN)

Biriwilg set off, coming and camping on the way, looking for honey and meats and vegetable foods. She came to Wiridjeng, where she met Ngalmoban, who was carrying *man-gindjeg*, bitter yams, and asked her, 'Where shall we go?' Ngalmoban said, 'We'll go this way, north, in search of a place.' So they came on together. They camped at Gun-roidbi-boro, a red-ochre place name, and talked together. Ngalmoban told her, 'I'm going higher up, and you go this way. We'll go separately. I'm taking *man-gindjeg* yams.' Biriwilg agreed: 'I'm going to the Garigen area, I'm not going that way.' Ngalmoban went off with her yams. She was throwing them about at different places so they would grow there, and naming the places as she did so.

Biriwilg went on by herself. At Gara-morug on the plain, eating *man-gulaid* nuts, she said, 'I'll go north and look for a place to put myself!' She came on, crossing the fresh water at Mula, and settling down for a while at Ngaraid-wodi-daidgeng where White Cockatoo had cut the rock with a boomerang. Still she came on. 'I'm looking for a house where I can put myself and stay always.' On the way she was eating long yams. 'I'll stay here for a while, at Inyalbiri, eating these yams.' Then she went on again. At Gun-ngad-bo she gave the place its name, because 'here I dug a soak, and I drank water'. She came on, climbing up, camping on the way, and crossing the water at Yawagara. She said, 'I'll go this way, where there is a big stretch of water, and I'll cross over.' She crossed a big creek at Wolgal, went on, looked at the place, and said, 'Here I'll put myself, where the place is good and the cave-house is good, where I'll stay always.' She went on, and was digging for soak water. As she dug the ground, she saw that it was only a little hole. She got up, and dug in another place. This time she was digging a big hole. Then she went, and was swimming about in it. When she had finished swimming, she climbed up out of the water and went to the cave. She said, 'Here I put myself. I am Biriwilg. I came a long way. Ngalmoban and I came together, then we said farewell to each other. She went on. I came this way, and here I'll stay for ever: I put myself. I stand outside, like a drawing [painting] I stand. But I am a woman. I started off far away. Here the name of the place is Gun-gangin, where I put myself. I stand like a person, and I keep on standing here for ever.'

27. THE OVENS OF DEAD FISH

They sat down at Malangan-gin, on the East Alligator River, high up in Eri country, at what is now known as 'Mountain Gap'. They were Mandjulewil, *yarigarngurg*, *nagudjug*, and his three sons named Wuru-melengemb, In-malaga and Garudb, all *yariwurig*, *nangaridj*, Mandjule-wil's wife Igalangoi, the mother of the three sons, and their wives, Nalwarewa, Alwelur and Manbalg-gur. [These were the names of the Dreaming people, and also the names of the 'new' generation of Eri people.] They all came to a large billabong, where there was a tall rock at Nara-nindje-wamb. They camped there for a long time, but they got tired of the place and went on to Urbir, 'Mountain Gap' where they also camped. Later they went to a cave in the rocks, at Iwilir-wilir, where creek water ran. After a while they decided to walk on to the Nadab plain; they named this place, as they did the others. Continuing, they came to the hills, and camped in a big cave at Wulan-gwiand. Rain had come, so they moved into a larger cave at Walgar. From there they went down toward the salt water [Eri country, near Doyle's camp], and on the bank of the river they saw large numbers of dead fish floating. 'Plenty of fish everywhere. What's wrong? My boys, you bring them up.' The father lay down in his cave at Walgar. His sons collected fish and made an oven, placing hot stones in the ashes with leaves on them, and the fish on these; they covered them with paperbark and mud, and left them. 'No good taking them out, leave them there,' Mandjulewil said.

They went out with their dilly bags to get more fish. There were plenty of them, all along the river bank. They brought them back and built an oven in the same way as before, a high oven, as large as a hut. They left them roasting, and went for more fish. 'What about removing the fish?' the sons asked their father, But he replied, 'Later on.' 'They might burn,' persisted the sons. 'No, they're all right,' Mandjulewil said. 'They might spoil the new people!' the sons answered. 'No, you get more fish,' their father insisted. So the sons went out again. They collected more fish, brought them back, and put them in an oven. The father came from his camp and looked at those ovens. 'What about all these fish, father?' said the sons. 'We'll leave them here; we make them Dreaming!' the father said. The sons understood.

They left this place and went on to Margarawalei (Eri) and camped there. 'We'll go that way, to Gwuwaian,' they decided. 'We have to return to our country.' They were carrying all their bamboo spears, and they put some of these at Gwuwaian, making a 'garden' of bamboos. They lived there for a while, and then walked on to Namburugwoi billabong, where they drank water and camped at a small 'island', Ilinangg. They went out collecting a lot of fish and also put bamboos. After spending a little time there, they continued, walking high up along a creek, returning from the low area, coming back from the other side of the Landing. Eventually they came to soft ground and low rocks at Manamandagal: 'It is best to make our camp here, for us to remain.' They made fires and collected fish. They brought up their lengths of bamboo, straightening the shafts in the fire and bending them with their teeth. They all sat there for a long time.

[It was at this juncture that Barramundi Dreaming made the East Alligator River. As a result of the actions of the huge Barramundi, water flooded the country.] Mandjulewil and the others heard the sound of water. 'Father, get up, the water is jumping.' The water rose. 'What are we going to do?' they asked. Surging flood water pushed them down. They are all sitting there; they made themselves into rocks, they became Dreaming. [The rocks are still there, grooved at the top to form stone heads.]

28. THE DADBI PUT THEMSELVES

Dadbi (Brown Snake), a *yariyaning*, *nabulan* man, was at Bob-bong-gi. [This is the place where Crow put a *djang*, and was responsible for 'sending up' this Dadbi.] Dadbi was with a large number of other mythic *dadbi*. They left Bob-bong-gi and walked higher up, leaving behind the Barramundi *djang* stone standing upright in the middle of the creek; its name was Bilmu-gageb-djiriri. They walked on to Manguram billabong, which the Dadbi made; to Gereibalgbulg [the 'big name' for this country], and on to Mabirigulb. The Dadbi went past all this country without putting any *djang*: they had only one *djang* left. They walked along the creek and put their last *djang* at Balaid-gadjang (Leech Dreaming) as an upright stone. [If the head of this *djang* stone is touched, large numbers of leeches appear.]

The Dadbi left to go east toward Gumadir in Gunwinggu territory. They went to Ngaldjibarara, high up. 'What are we going to do?' they asked each other. They went on farther and put a hill, which they named Namandi-gubolg-mini; they also left long *garbara* yams. Leaving the hill, they went 'bottom-side' down the same creek to Ilibulg-gul billabong. All the Dadbi 'stood up' here, 'touching their tails': and they looked round at that country. 'Which way shall we go, to make ourselves into something?' They followed the creek further but did not put any place names. They left this creek, to follow up another, to go to the place they had seen when they looked across the country. They went in that direction but put no names; they just walked quickly along and found a billabong. Again, they all stood there, looking in every direction, looking for a place where they could remain. 'We can't see any farther, we will have to stay here!' So they polished a big round stone and put themselves on it, criss-crossing each other, one on top of another, all in different colours. There they put themselves as a 'picture' on top of that polished round stone; then they 'turned round', and their bodies went into the bottom of that stone hill.

[Comment: 'No human being is to climb those rocks. There is a creek alongside where we can drink, and get lily roots — but if we do, we must call out to those Dadbi, asking their permission, making sure they are quiet first. It's our country, the narrators noted, so we can drink that water and get those roots that grow nearby. The Dadbi won't come up to us, but they will to other people, and they will kill them!']

When the Dadbi 'turned themselves', they put the name of that place: it is Guren-dadbi, their Dreaming place.

29. COUGH DREAMING

Manada, a *ngaraidgu* man, and his sons, known collectively as the Waranoidjagu, *namadgu*, came from 'Bottle Rock' [called Nanggulug in Gunwinggu, Nang-numinali in Maung] near country called Anyimunyali in Gunwinggu [Andjumu in Maung] on South Goulburn Island. Manada decided and told his sons that, 'Because we have been here for such a long time, we'll go east.' They went over by canoe to Waindjeli (Barclay Point) on the mainland and walked on to Namangar: there they put some 'things' [sacred objects]. [There is a stone on the cliff at this place that is dangerous: if anyone touches it, a big storm will come up.]

Travelling on to Womirunmu [from which the eastern corner of Goulburn Island can be seen] they continued east, reaching Yilgban-gad, [a long point on the mainland at the mouth of the King River]. Going round this point, they came to Mangaradigi [still in Maung country]. Now, the 'canoe' they had was really a baler shell. So they crossed the strip of water which took them to the top of the King River's mouth.

Manada was an old man, unable to walk far: 'My sons', he said, 'I have to stay here. You go and find the places and come back and tell me about them.' He sat down there and made himself like a long yam: 'He just sat there for such a long time that he became a long yam.'

Manada had two brothers, Bidjilg (salt-water Bream) and Dadbi (Brown Snake). Although not mentioned before, they came with Manada and his Waranoidjagu sons. The sons said, 'Father, wait here till we return.' With their father's two brothers, they went on to Magalg. They stayed there for a while, but then went on making a plain all the way to Malaidj-balwal (salt pan) and eastward to Gw'rela [Maung]. One of the sons had a bad cold, so they left him there. He just lay down and died, and turned into a hill. [If anyone touches that hill, he or she will get a bad cold.] The others went on to Abudjareid, where they stayed for a short time, and then on to Udjurulg. Here they left another son. He too got a bad cold and died, and turned into cough Dreaming. [There is a hill at this place, 'like a *djang*. You can't touch it.']

Leaving that place they went on to Ilawidu, then to Guri-ngalwilgbil and on to Mauwudjimi [still in Maung territory]. No longer following the river, they went into bush country, eventually reaching Mandibin. Four of the sons became sick here: they 'turned to' cough *djang*, becoming *mabara* trees, similar to paperbark. [No-one may touch these.]

The remaining men went on to Mangaranggi. 'It is better for us to stay here,' they agreed. They made a ceremony. The Waranoidjagu sons were all song-men, and they danced while their father's two brothers sang the Waranoidjagu cycle. A large group of people from the east, the south and the west came into Mangaranggi for this big ceremony. All those people were camping there. Everyone became sick. Only the father's two brothers were all right. They all prepared to rest. But they fell into a heavy sleep, and as they slept they died. All of them 'turned into' a hill with jungle trees.

The father's two brothers remained alive. That place is called 'cough'. No one can touch that jungle or the trees in it, because these are the people who died. Anyone who touches them will die too. The name of that place is Mangaral-rindji [in both Maung and Gunwinggu territories]. And the father's two brothers spoke, 'No one can cut these trees — this is a danger place!' They too stayed here. 'They were human; they were frightened. They remain there alive, as spirits.'

30. THE LUMINOUS ONES

Two Nalwarabara Dreaming men, elder and younger brothers, came out of the sea at Mamaradimadjila, a long sandy beach in the Manasi Reserve area [Badaya language]. They walked on to Mumbungu point, on the western side of the mouth of the West Alligator River. From there they looked eastward and saw an island [also in Badaya territory]. They went across by canoe to Gudjulugu (Barron Island), which had large stands of *garar* cypress pine. [Chinese from their timber camp on the South Alligator River would cut wood at this place.] An old man named Ganedi lived there: he had very long fingers, and would catch fish with them. [A whirlpool in the sea nearby was associated with him.]

The Nalwarabara brothers left the island and came to Ilgargu [Wada language], inside the mouth of the South Alligator. 'What about crossing this river?' they asked, and decided to do so. They jumped across to Ilgal (Wada). [There was little water in the river at that time.] Looking over to Field Island they saw only jungle, while to the east and south-east a large plain stretched out before them. From Gumboyu, nearby, one of the Nalwarabara went to look round. He found what is now a bitter yam *galoidjarbu*. He pulled out the yam root and cut it: 'It looks good food', he said. 'We won't eat it, we'll leave it for the people!'

The two men continued on to Ganerandjul, a large billabong [Wada], and on to Manmalari billabong [Wada] on the eastern side of the South Alligator plain. These two men 'came like light, the same as fire'. They were luminous, 'like sun shining on them, like a rainbow'. When they touched anything — grass, leaves, anything — it died.

They followed a small creek. The elder brother said, 'Go on the top side, leave room for the people [who will come]!' They climbed up a small hill: 'It is good country here, brother, shall we live here?' they asked each other. There is a dark jungle and it is a long way from water. They made a cleared place, and stood up some distance apart from each other. 'Not close together, we don't want people to smell us. If they do, they might die!' This was at Garaidjul (Wada). ['If you go close to them you *will* die. They stand there like stone. You can't go near them. If you do, your legs will stiffen and your body shiver. Buffalo don't go there either.']

Moving across the country, various mythic characters explore, name and shape it, forming hills, creeks, plains, billabongs, and so on. Particularly, they place themselves in strategic positions. There is a kind of restlessness, something which impels them to seek out a suitable site where they may remain physiographically and spiritually anchored, a particular place that they themselves form or adapt for their own purpose. Usually, it is of their own choice, the culmination of their travels and adventures. But their 'turning' can be precipitated by an event outside their control. For instance, in the above myths, the actions of Barramundi when he made (or shaped) the East Alligator River resulted in the Mandjulewil group being drowned; a coughing sickness befell the Manada group and all those associated with them; and Biriwilg's desire to be inconspicuous led her to merge herself into a painting. The mytho-physical identification-markers help to provide definitions for specific language groups. More particularly, they bestow upon the countryside a range of meanings about the land and its significance to human beings. It is not only that the land 'speaks for' itself, through the appropriate languages of its occupiers, but that those who 'read' its signs must be in a position to do so.

Mythic beings, as we have mentioned, are responsible for various food resources, and that point will be made again in many of the myths we will present. However, the resources of the land are not simply defined in relation to what may or may not be eaten. That word, 'resources', has a much wider coverage. For instance, there are the danger signals, as in the case of the Nalwarabara luminous ones, and the Cough, Dadbi and Leech *djang*; other myths will amplify this point. They are left in the land to provide reasons for misfortunes always being present, and explaining the vulnerability of human beings.

While mythic beings are commonly metamorphosed, some 'turn' directly into a particular resource: that is, the resource itself *is* the mythic being himself or herself. The transformation of Namalbi and his wife, from being 'human' to becoming pandanus, is an excellent example, witnessed by Raramin, his wife and child, who in turn became termite mounds. Old Manada just sat at a particular place for such a long time that he turned into a long yam site. Biriwilg, however, in her painting became a spirit child centre, upon which potential mothers were dependent for the spiritual animation of their unborn children.

The following two stories were told in Gunwinggu by women to C. Berndt at Oenpelli in 1950. Both concern the creation of important sites.

31.   MAN-AND-KANGAROO ROCK

He was going along, he was camping. He went on, and saw a crowd of geese. He killed them and ate them all. He started off, went on, and saw honey. He ate it all. Well, he said, 'I want to cut some bamboo for spears.' He went, he went farther, he saw a stand of little bamboos. He said, 'I don't like them. I don't want to cut these. I'll go and cut those that Bugbug Pheasant planted, that's what I'll cut.' He went, he kept on going, then he settled down and put down his belongings, and went to cut bamboos for spears. 'I won't go and cut many,' he said, 'only two. Big ones, one for kangaroos and one for fish.'

He went on. On the way he speared a kangaroo, and ate it all. Still he kept going. He went, crossed a plain there, went on a bit farther, and camped. He looked at the place and said, 'I don't like *this* way, I'll go *that* way, north!' He went on, he camped, he went on, a long way.

Well then, still going on, he came to where a big sea was running. He began to swim. And after him came a kangaroo he had been trying to kill. It came running. He was swimming, swimming, but he was an old man. He kept on swimming, but the kangaroo and a dog came chasing after him where he was swimming and swimming. The dog came running close to the water's edge, and the kangaroo still went on running near where that man was swimming. The kangaroo kept running, climbed up on to the man's head, and made him sink down under the water. That man still stands there, below the surface of the sea, with the kangaroo on top of his head.

The name of the place is Neya-raingu, Wildman River. They stand there together, man and kangaroo. Let nobody go near them, where they 'made themselves wrong', because it is a taboo, dangerous place always. If any new, living person goes paddling near them, a great wave might sink the canoe and everyone in it so that they drown, because it is always a taboo, dangerous place. So, people are afraid, they do not go near there, where those two 'made themselves wrong'. It is always taboo and dangerous. [At that place a rock stands in the open sea, in the middle of the water, with strong currents flowing around it.]

32. TRAPPED BY CLAMS

Long ago two young men, brothers, went looking for fish on the north coast at Warawag. The tide was out. They waded into the water, following the fish, spearing them, and threading them on their long carrying sticks. They saw crabs crawling and speared them too. Still they kept going, moving toward the open sea, so intent on catching fish that they just went straight on.

Then a great clam shell caught their feet. They tried to get up. They pulled with their hands, trying to open the shell. No, they could not. They tried to run, to get to the shore. No, they could not. At last the sea came: the tide was turning for them. They were weeping, thinking of their mother and father. Still they kept weeping as the sea came spreading out all around them. They spoke sorrowfully to each other. 'What will become of us, younger brother? Already the sea is taking us both.' They broke their spears into pieces, their spear-throwers too, and tossed them into the water. As the sea took the pieces away, they said, 'Go up on to the beach! Then they will come, they will see you, but by the time they look for us the sea will have swallowed us completely.' As they spoke they were embracing each other. The sea was already up to their throats. Then it took them under together, at the same time. They remained beneath the water. At last they became transformed into rock, rising through the water. When people came and looked at the place they saw that a rock had made itself there, where those two had been submerged. They put themselves as *djang*, where that creature bit their feet, and there they are still standing, those two young men who came into Dreaming.

Wondidjag and his younger brother Ga-nirringgal spoke the coastal languages of Wurugu and Ngadawulu, mixed with Yiwadja. As coast dwellers and fish-hunters, they should have been on their guard against such dangers as these that lie hidden among the seaweed. And that is what this story is about: it is a warning to anyone who ventures into the sea, even at low tide, without taking proper precautions. The story is compact, neatly balanced, and all the more poignant for its deliberate use of restrained understatement. The brothers' last Gunwinggu statement, 'Then they will come . . .', has a rhythm of its own: '*Galug gabirim-rei, gabiri-nan, bu gandi-yawan ngargu gan-geb-ngun.*'

The last three stories in this chapter are from the Western Desert. The first is Andingari, the second Ngalia and Mandjindji: both are from Ooldea, and told in 1941. The other is Gugadja, from Balgo in 1960. They were told to R. Berndt.

33.   MINGARI AND HER DOGS

An old Mingari (Mountain Devil) Woman came from the west with her daughter and a pack of dogs, to Yilu waterhole. The dogs smelt something and ran away in search of it. Joining another lot of dogs, they tracked down and killed a *malu* kangaroo. Mingari's daughter, Neri, followed them. She heard the dogs fighting over the meat, came among them, took the kangaroo, and skinned it. Then she cut up the meat, cooked it, and carried it back to her mother, accompanied by her dogs. The other dogs took away the discarded skin.

Mingari and her daughter walked some little distance from Yilu and came upon the tracks of an old woman, Galaya (Emu) Woman. They followed these until they saw her. As Galaya walked along she bumped into a tree at Ngalbu, and walking in another direction bumped into another tree. The two Mingari talked together and decided that she must be blind. So they followed her and found her seated before a fire. The Mingari dogs rushed up and tried to catch her; but, although she was blind, she defended herself with a digging stick. Mingari told the dogs to keep away from her. With her daughter, Mingari helped the blind woman to stand up and wiped the *yuna* (matter) from her eyes, enabling her to see. They led her to her own track and showed her the way to go. Galaya went on her way.

However, when the Mingari returned to their home camp at Yilu, their dogs did not accompany them. Instead, they had run after Galaya, bringing her down at Badil and killing her. They tore up the meat and ate it all. From Yilu, Mingari and her daughter called out for their dogs. They could see them coming: the dogs entered Yilu, each taking a different track, and each going to her own puppies ('children'). They had a lot of meat inside their stomachs; they disgorged this but Mingari took away the fat and the best meat, leaving the rest for the puppies. They cooked and ate it. As result Mingari became ill. She was unable to walk, and eventually died — the meat was not good. Her daughter, however, survived, and later travelled to the east with her dogs.

[Yilu has a deep *ngama* rock hole, as well as fresh water. Alongside is a granite rock into which Mingari was metamorphosed. Around it is a large salt lake, at the bottom of which are deep ridges or indentations which are the different track marks made by the returning dogs.]

34. LITTLE WALLABY AS A DECOY (1)

Eaglehawk (Waldja) Man and Woman were at Wogamuru waterhole, where they had a nest with two eaglets. Each day they went out to collect meat. One afternoon they heard a noise, as if something were moving about in the undergrowth at the foot of their tree. Waldja Man saw Gabidji (Little Wallaby) Man, also called Daramuda, and tried to catch him, but missed. Gabidji jumped away just in time. He tried again, but Gabidji ran away. As it was becoming dark, Waldja Man returned to the tree. During the night he heard Gabidji running about. In the morning, Waldja Man saw him again, and went after him: he swooped down but missed him. Waldja Woman also tried to 'spear' Gabidji with her claws — but she missed too. All day they chased him, until they reached Gabarin. Here Gabidji went into a burrow. They tried to dig him out, but were unsuccessful. So they sat waiting in some nearby trees. They saw Gabidji run from his burrow, and, immediately, they went after him. They swooped down but he escaped and ran into another hole at Narada. The Waldja tried to dig him out, but could not find him. It became dark, and they went into a tree to sleep. They were now some distance from their home where they had left their children.

At daybreak they continued to hunt Gabidji, but on each occasion they missed him. They reached Daleya, and Gabidji went into a hole. Waldja Man tried to dig him out, but could not find him. Again they slept in a tree, and next morning saw Gabidji come out of his hole. They tried to catch him, but he disappeared into a hole at Madul. This theme was repeated again and again: each time, when they were not looking, Gabidji escaped. [Waldja Man, it was said, was digging properly, but too far down: Gabidji was sheltering just below the surface.]

Next day when they were out hunting Gabidji they sang:

daianba munga-rundu wili buldara
dagu-wondinu dayanba
Spinifex tree in darkness, feathers fluffed out,
Swooping past.

They chased Gabidji to Rana. When he went into a hole, they sang:

dan-garung-gu bunu dalbilba
dila-diladi dan-garung-gu
[Man] with his broken stick;
[Woman] with [her] sharp claws.

The Waldja were determined to catch Gabidji. They continued digging for several days. They also constructed another nest of bushes around Rana. [This is now metamorphosed at this place as an oval depression at the apex of a large granite rock; within it are two oval-shaped stones, their eggs; these are immovable; around the edge of the nest are stones which 'are' the leaves of the bushes. This is an Eaglehawk renewal site. Where Gabidji jumped out of his burrow is a small *ngama* hole where he hid himself.]

Gabidji escaped and the Waldja followed his tracks. However, there was another group of Waldja in front of them. [This was all a ruse on the part of the other Waldja: they had sent out Gabidji to bring the two Waldja from the north-west to attend a ceremony.] These other Waldja were camped north of Loongana [on the trans-continental rail track] at a place named Bildina, where there is a soak of almost-salty water. The Gabidji ran directly to Bildina, with the two Waldja following. They swooped down to catch him, but missed. The others killed Gabidji and prepared to cook him. The two Waldja, who had spent all this time in hunting Gabidji, were aggrieved. Waldja Man complained, 'I only wanted to eat his liver', and his wife added, 'I only wanted to eat his lungs and heart.' [These organs of Gabidji are used magically, so it is said, in the north-west.] The other Waldja divided up the meat and held their ceremony. Afterwards, they returned to their home at Wogamuru: the others remained at Bildina.

Waldja Man and Woman had confidently expected to find their two children at Wogamuru. However, they had gone; their nest ('camp') had been scattered by the wind. They looked around for their children. After a while they found their faeces near some feathers. Later they saw broken spears, then some tracks and more faeces, and then they came upon new tracks. Following these, they found their two children sitting. They had grown and were now able to fly. Their parents were pleased, and continued their travels.

35. THE UNSUCCESSFUL KANGAROO HUNT

At Bulgu, west of Yabuna (Lake Mackay), lived two young *djabangari* brothers named Baribadu. They made *djirilbadja* potatoes from the roots of various trees, especially from the *djarari* white gum. [We are not told how they made these, only that they quarrelled because one had made too many, so they fought. One implication is that they were actually *djirilbadja* people who could manifest themselves as bush potatoes.]

They left Bulgu and walked on to Nginman-gundja rockhole, where they again hit each other [the place name refers to their crying]. One of them went out hunting a kangaroo in the vicinity of Buralyibungu creek. This particular Kangaroo was a *djabangadi* man, and on seeing him the boy was frightened. He returned to his brother, who asked him what was wrong. He refused to answer, and his brother knew something was really wrong. 'What have you seen?' he asked. And he listed various animals. The other did not reply. At last he mentioned 'Kangaroo!' The boy got up and embraced his brother — they 'got heavy' with strength. They each made a club, and sneaked up to where Kangaroo had been lying in the shade. There was nothing there; Kangaroo had gone. They returned to their camp.

In the meantime Kangaroo had moved round to the boys' camp. He made rain, 'to trick them'. At Mang-giri rockhole, close by, lightning struck [caused by Kangaroo]. Next morning, after the rain, Kangaroo's tracks were clearly seen, and the two brothers followed them to Walga-djara soak [where on the rocks there are ochred paintings]. They went on to Baldja rockhole where there is a big creek: they continued to follow Kangaroo to Bubadi, where they saw him lying down. They did nothing. Instead they flew through the sky, 'landing at' Yalwaran-gu [a rockhole 'behind' Yabuna]; then they flew back to Bulgu, their home. There they remained, diving down into the waterhole. [They had recognised Kangaroo as a Dreaming man.]

Malu (Kangaroo) Man left Bubadi and went on to Bundjungu claypan, where he made a wind-break and slept. Then he travelled on southward to Ril soak, where he camped. He continued to Gilgilmalu soak and camped, to Yalwilamalu [where his camp shelter fell down], to Bandadja soak [where he slept, resting his head on a shield], and to Djurawalyi and Boira claypans. Still going southward, making camp at each place, he came to Yadarudja soak, and then to Dalberu [there is a soak here, but the ground is swampy and Kangaroo got bogged in the mud], and then on to Djunuwading soak. Continuing, he came to Dalwanyina claypan where he met a small Wallaby, Wamaru Man. Together they went to Yanara claypan, and on to Yundadjungu claypan. There the two sat together in a wind-break they constructed from sacred boards. [The place name refers to putting up the wind-break.] They went on to Wadarudja claypan, Ngalmalmalu, Wandumadadji, and Wanaridja soaks, to Djudalbi claypan, Duding-gadjara soak, Baragali and Wilbidi rockholes. They made camps at each of these places, but at Wilbidi they dug a hole in which they sheltered from the heat.

They went on to Guril rockhole, where a group of mythic Gadjari women was living. Kangaroo copulated with all the women. Later he left Wamaru with them and continued on by himself. He went to Dalberu soak [duplication of place name mentioned above] and on to Yamalngi claypan, and then to Ganaladja rockhole [where he again became bogged and had to crawl along to get out of the mud]. Eventually he reached Gulia rockhole. From there he heard Dreaming Dog cry out, and became frightened.

[From this point the myth goes into its secret-sacred version. It concerns the dog(s) chasing Kangaroo and is part of an initiation sequence. The waterholes and soaks beyond this point were unknown to the men telling this myth.]

These myths, although differing in content, have a number of points in common. Except for Mingari, they depict *purposeful* travelling across the countryside on the part of mythic beings: not haphazard but, as we might say, aim-directed, in order that something may be fulfilled. They move from place to place, each linked one to the other, to constitute his/her or their track, as contrasted with the tracks of other mythic beings. Mingari, for instance, after helping 'blind' Galaya, sets her on her way, along her own track. The tracks, of course, are not inviolate; they may be and are utilised by other mythic beings, but not the whole track of any particular character. The purposeful nature of such movements is demonstrated by Waldja Man and Woman being drawn by the decoy Gabidji to a ceremony. This is also the case in the Malu myth, which is really [as presented here] in two parts. If the whole mythic sequence had been given, the Kangaroo track would have led to an initiation sequence involving the two youths who are mentioned in the first part. A clue to that is their fear of Kangaroo as a potential initiator, and the reference to the Gadjari women, who are significant in this context, supports that theme. In the Mingari myth, her movements are limited, but in others relating to her and her dogs they are extensive.

Each mythic character is responsible for having left or done something significant in or to, the environment: the metamorphosis of Mingari and the tracks of her dogs; the Waldja renewal centre, consisting of a nest, eggs and leafy bushes which are now granite; and the 'making' of bush potatoes by the two brothers, who quarrel about this. They mythic fact that the places where Kangaroo camped have names that are associated with his travels implies that he left there something tangible relating to himself: the impression of where he lay down or where he was bogged, the depression where he and Wamaru rested from the heat, their shelter of sacred boards, and so on. All these are important religious sites, and all of them, collectively, make up his distinctive and extensive track.

In this chapter we see something of the Aboriginal genesis, a genesis that is projected from the present into the past, as a basis for the development of the natural order. It is a past that is constantly vivified since it is imbued with the aura of the Dreaming.

The mythic characters who come upon their particular scenes, within the initially unknown environments, carry out actions that we might well categorise as being programmed. They have tasks to perform, and in doing so they produce coherent patterns which imprint themselves upon the landscape, providing it with a special kind of life of its own, but one that is dependent on the mythic beings. They are the implementors and the activators, the 'shapers', the 'markers' and reformulators, who not only utilised the 'primordial' substance that was there before they came, but contributed appreciably to the forms of life within it. In fact, they did more than this — they put themselves into that environment, as spiritually living memorials of their accomplishments.

The progenitors of present-day Aborigines come, in varying ways, from these mythic beings. The myths thus provide, according to their believers, incontrovertible evidence of those occurrences. But these beings did more than that. Traditionally, they bestowed upon the progenitors and their descendants a basic identity, by allocating language and territory, sustenance and purpose to their lives. This process placed them within the context of nature, as one aspect of it, not a 'merging' because each element had its own personal characteristics, but, in general, something that constituted an interdependent patterning.

It has been said that, in considering the active side of mythic endeavours, we are really dealing with a 'Divine Plan'. More precisely, however, the myths both illuminate and demonstrate that there were, and are, many different plans — different plans in regard to the peopling of specific territories, the shaping of particular places, and the fitting of individual mythic responses into a broad pattern. The myths do not support a co-ordinated approach on the part of different mythic beings in their dealings with nature, and with humans.

While we can conceptualise Aboriginal religion(s) as polytheistic, it was not a matter of the members of any one socio-cultural group recognising and acknowledging all those mythic beings relevant to their own territory. The situation was, in fact, highly personalised, compartmentalised, and consisted of many different religious perspectives, which were often the concern of members of quite small local groups whose ownership of such knowledge was defined in socio-personal terms. Some of the great religious myth-cycles do have wide-ranging relevance for large numbers of social groups; but even then, sections of such myths remain the traditional property of members of local descent groups — in a traditional sense, framed in terms of the descendants of particular progenitors who were brought into being by certain mythic characters. Again, the myths demonstrate that principle. This is especially exemplified in the mythic tracks that extend over wide areas of country, where certain sections are designated as belonging to one language group as contrasted with another.

Deities had their own plans that were responsible for humanising the land and nature. And these made it possible for people to occupy that land and to use adequately the resources available to them.

Moreover, as we will see in the next chapter, the deities were not the only characters involved in this transformation of the land.

CHAPTER THREE

SNAKES
AND RAINBOWS

Among the thousands of mythic paths that criss-cross the continent are tracks commemorating the journeys of giant snakes. Myths tell of their exploits, the sites associated with them, and their continuing presence. They were in the land from the very beginning, from the creative era, playing their part in shaping the natural and the human scene. Many of them were invariably in great snake form. Others had the potential to develop along those lines and eventually did so.

Of course, there were other snakes too, as well as other reptiles. Australia has a richly diverse snake population, ranging from quite small species such as death (or deaf) adders to quite large ones such as pythons, from snakes that are quiet or harmless (to people) to more aggressive or defensive ones. Of course, in some cases attack by a snake is a tactic in self-defence or a reaction to danger.

Traditional Aboriginal perspectives on snakes and other aspects of the natural world did not, and do not, coincide with those of non-Aboriginal scientists. Up to a point, however, they did overlap. Because of their early training and continuing everyday experiences, traditional Aborigines were well-informed about the appearance and the habits of creatures in their particular regions. They knew, not only the natural environments but also the action contexts in which various kinds of snakes lived: what they did in relation to other natural species, for instance. The unwritten books containing such information, in any given region, were much more complete than what was being written about snakes (and so on) by non-Aboriginal specialists, who have only in recent years begun systematically to take Aboriginal knowledge into account.

But this practical, classifying level of observation was only one side of the traditional Aboriginal approach. The other side was intermeshed with it, but extended beyond it, into a broader frame of culturally-prescribed belief and action. A 'snake map' or 'book of snakes' in any one area would have to be more than a simple description of snakes-in-nature. It would need to include a dimension that was less visible but even more 'real' — the dimension of the non-empirical, of symbolism and myth. A separate snake map, or snake book, would have to be reserved for secret-sacred material. (In some areas there would be two such sets, one for men and one for women.) The habits and behaviour and attributes of snakes provide a background to mythic events and their interpretation, but not as a guide to be followed exactly. In that sense, myths are larger than life. But they are also *true* to life, in the wider understanding of the phrase that goes beyond the here-and-now 'appearance of things seen'.

In assessing the relative importance of snakes, in regions where traditional myths are still a vital force, size is certainly one consideration. The notion of a huge snake is something to be reckoned with. Being defined as dangerous does not depend *only* on size, but a combination of great size and danger is seen as truly formidable. However, real importance hinges on identification within the religious sphere. As regards snakes, the crucial point is linkage with religious ritual, for instance, having a significant bearing on such vital issues as seasonal fertility, and the renewal or maintenance of life-sustaining resources in nature.

One such snake has become quite widely known in the non-Aboriginal world outside his home area of north-central Arnhem Land, because he is a prominent figure in bark paintings. This reflects in a small way his importance at home, where he has a major role in an outstanding myth-ritual complex. ('His' because, although there are also female manifestations, or counterparts, the myth usually implies, or refers to, a male. In the local dialects, personal pronouns are not gender-specific. But, apart from discussions and comments outside the actual telling or singing of the myth, there are clues in the content of the myth itself. For instance, in some versions the Snake has offspring who call him 'father' and he responds with the appropriate kin term, which is not the same as a female uses toward anyone who calls her 'mother'.) This version is only a skeleton-outline of his story — or, rather, the story he shares with two sisters in human shape whose names are now even better known than his. He is often called Yulunggul; other names, alluding to his various attributes and associations, are mostly mentioned in songs.

The following is a summary, from versions told to C. Berndt by women at various times and in various places: for example, at Milingimbi in 1950 and at Galiwin'ku, Elcho Island, in 1964.

36. YULUNGGUL AND THE WAWALAG SISTERS

The great python, Yulunggul, had been living from the beginning of time in the waters of Mirara-minar, Muruwul [and other names], toward the north-central Arnhem Land coast. It was his base, his home territory. But two young sisters were travelling in his direction from the Wawalag country, a long way inland to the south. The elder girl had a small child and in some versions was pregnant. As they went along they camped at various places, and their dogs helped them to get a number of small creatures. At last they reached the shady waterhole, built a stringybark hut, and sat down to cook a meal. But, one after another all the creatures and vegetable foods jumped out of the cooking fire and ran into the waterhole. The sisters knew that something was wrong. 'Oh, sister, maybe a Snake?' The elder sister had given birth to a child, and afterbirth blood fell into the waterhole [or menstrual blood from the younger sister, or both]. The sky was growing dark, and not only because it would soon be night. The sisters lit a fire in their little hut and tried to sleep, but a great storm broke around them: wind, rain, thunder and lightning. They took it in turns to dance, singing special ritual songs [such as Kunapipi songs] to deflect the storm. But eventually Yulunggul raised himself up, then coiled himself around the hut and swallowed them all, dogs too. An ant bit him, so he vomited them out; he swallowed the sisters again, but in some versions not the child(ren). Later he lifted up his body, head toward the sky, and spoke with other great snakes of the same moiety as himself (*dua*) from other areas in north-eastern Arnhem Land about their differing dialects, and about what they had been eating. Yulunggul at first hid the truth about what he had done, then admitted it. He was ashamed [but in other versions boastful] and sank back into his waterhole.

The myth is enormously detailed in its content and symbolism and interpretation, and most versions do not stop at this point. Also, it is the basis for the *djunggawon* circumcision rituals. Not least, the combination of Yulunggul and the Wawalag sisters was responsible for the coming of the north-west monsoon which brings the fertilising rains of the Wet season. There are other storm-bringing snakes in north-eastern Arnhem Land, including the great Lightning Snake, but the monsoon is the expected and hoped-for annual event on which seasonal growth and species-renewal are especially dependent.

Yulunggul has sometimes been called a Rainbow Snake, a snake in the water reflecting a rainbow in the sky and being itself a rainbow in the water. The Rainbow label has become attached to many other great snakes that are associated with water in some form or other. Examples of Rainbow and quasi-Rainbow snakes are plentiful all over the continent, from Cape York in the north-east to the south-west corner of Western Australia, and from the south-east corner across to the north-west Kimberley coast. In the case of Yulunggul, there is not, and was not, local-regional consensus as to whether the term Rainbow is appropriate to him. It was not usually applied to the great mythic snakes of north-eastern Arnhem Land, located at their individual sites on land or as rocks out at sea.

The north-central Arnhem Land coast west of Milingimbi, around Cape Stewart, is in one sense a transition or meeting ground for two broad cultural blocs that have much in common, but also acknowledge, traditionally, some very pervasive differences: in language; in marriage rules and practices; in initiation forms; in song styles; and in social behaviour and values over a fairly wide spectrum. So it was not for nothing (as Aboriginal story-tellers would say) that Yulunggul spoke with his great snake colleagues in north-eastern Arnhem Land, and they responded from their home sites: from the Wessel Islands to the east coast facing the Gulf of Carpentaria. Significantly, he did not talk to any of the western Arnhem Land snakes: in fact (mythic fact), he turned his back on them. His main religious ritual and mythic linkages were, and still are, with the groups to the east of Milingimbi, despite some ties with the west and an increasing number of similarities there.

The coastal islands and the mainland of western Arnhem Land, and the country stretching westward almost as far as Darwin and the north-south road, were traditionally the scene of hundreds of Rainbow myths. The Rainbow Snake is known by various names but is often referred to only obliquely: uttering the name of any powerful and dangerous character can attract the attention of that character, even from a great distance. And as for gender, some manifestations are referred to as male (especially in coastal areas), others as female (especially in inland areas). This seems to be in at least some cases a matter of grammatical gender-indicators rather than of identification as specifically female. In other cases the female allusions are clear: for example, when a snake or other victim of a hunter is discovered to be the Rainbow's own offspring and mother-child kin terms are used. Also, in one version of a creation myth, Gunwinggu-speaking women insisted that the Rainbow was the creative Mother who gave birth to the first human beings: the myth describes the process. In choosing myths about Rainbow Snakes we have included a larger number from western Arnhem Land and its western outliers, to show the Snake 'in action', so to speak, and some of the perspectives that contribute to the overall picture. From western Arnhem Land we move south, after a brief Daly River excursion, to a climatically and culturally different environment: the Western Desert.

This selection of western Arnhem Land Rainbow myths begins with characters who are already identified as Rainbows. The first story, told to R. Berndt at Oenpelli in 1950, makes it clear that there is more than one Rainbow — or, as other accounts demonstrate, more than one manifestation.

37. NGALYOD IN SEARCH OF A HOME

A Ngalyod, Rainbow, was camped at Magaribul, out east, high up on Mada creek [near Gumadir creek, but higher up, where there is a big billabong]. However, another Ngalyod was already there. 'Go away!' she said, 'I don't want you to be here. I want to stay here by myself.' So the first Ngalyod [they were both female] left and went east to Djuri where she camped for a while, looking for deep water. She followed a small creek and camped at Gandalbang [Gunwinggu]. Continuing, she came to a small waterhole, Gugoilobad, where she camped, and then on to Gugudji waterfall. But another Ngalyod named Duberg (Snail) lived there. She made a noise, and the newcomer was frightened; she could not sleep properly and moved about all night. Duberg said to her, 'You go and find another place. This is mine!' The first one went on, travelling during the day. She came to Gabolgminguleg-yongin [which refers to her resting at this place — she was tired]. 'She couldn't find any water.' Then she came to a big creek. [She was now coming back, high up along a creek on the 'back way' to Gumadir creek.] At Mabumla was a big river, but another Ngalyod was there. The first one looked at the old Ngalyod lying there: 'That new one [the newcomer] didn't like to stay with her.' And the old one said: 'You had better go on. I stay here by myself!'

The first Ngalyod went up the river, on the high side, to Gayirgeid-jobmi. She camped there, but the water was not deep enough, so she went on the high track to Ilob-bol, where she camped at a little creek. Then she went on to Benidj-gani, where she camped. Another Ngalyod was also already camped there. 'I have to live here by myself. There is no room for you; you have to go,' she told the new arrival.

So the traveller continued further, to Ngubolg-ngalgam billabong. She tried to stay there, but the billabong was too shallow. She went on to Mam-midmid, putting the names of the country, and on to Djarawala where water was surging up from springs. Coming higher up, she said, 'This might be a good place. I've walked a long way. I'll stay here in the deep water. There is plenty of room where I can sleep!' This was at Gadjandjiwul. However, there was already a Ngalyod there — an old one. She asked, 'Is there enough room for me to live here?' And the old Ngalyod replied, 'There is plenty of room for us both.' Then the newcomer put a jungle there for flying foxes, so the people who were to come could hunt them. As for herself, she is still there.

It is clear that it is not a matter of 'one place, one Dreaming character'. The story suggests, and finally confirms, that more than one can occupy a single site, or different parts of the same site. Other myths in this region, and elsewhere, also speak of multiple occupation, not necessarily by characters of the same kind, as in this case.

In the next story the two characters are called Rainbows from the start, but it seems that they were in human form throughout their journey. Their more-than-human abilities are revealed, not only in their making of places and trees, for instance, but in their association with the *ubar*, a ritual object. The story was told to R. Berndt at Oenpelli in 1950.

38. LOOKING FOR
A HOME, THEY QUARRELLED

Two Rainbow, Ngalyod, women ['or might be man and woman, we don't know'] came from Banambar, 'high up' on the mainland from Milingimbi [Yarlma language]. They walked along, finding different places — to Giwid-djir, to Gwiyuyur. They came from sunrise way, widening the small creek. They went farther on, along the creek, to Mumulu-ngoyurul where they put an *ubar*. They also put *mandin-gu* cycad palms there. At this place they stopped speaking the Yarlma language and spoke Gudjalibi. They went on to another creek, Guba-guba, and got some wild honey. They found another creek and went farther up to Gubangu. 'We'll camp here!' they thought. They tried to perform an *ubar* ritual, but the place was rough. They came on to Namarangala. [Leaving Gudjalibi, they now spoke Gurugoni.] Camping here, they made an *ubar*, sweeping the place clean for dancing. They moved their camp to another site where there was a *man-gundal* black plum tree; 'the two Rainbows put that tree there, at Man-gundal'. [This is at the other side of Guwadjeri country, on the eastern side of the Liverpool, where there is a big creek.]

They walked along. 'All right, sister, we'll put country,' and they named Ina-mandjalg. [It now appears that the Rainbows were two sisters.] At this place they made an *ubar* [and they spoke Gunwinggu]. They also made a well and camped there. They moved camp again, to Mubari, where they made a waterhole within an area they swept, which formed a billabong. They spoke to each other, 'Sister, we must find more places.' At Dainbam they made two waterholes and billabongs side by side. All the way, they walked along using *gun-ganing* yam sticks as walking sticks. Next day, they went on, poking the ground with their yam sticks to find soft places: they found only hard ground, so they went on. They came to a plain and went up to Namurgan-gani [Gunwinggu], where they made a good place, with white ochre. They dug a trench. They 'tried to stop here' because there was spring water, but the ground was hard. They continued to Nabalag-gurudi, where they put *man-gulaidj* grass nuts. They went on, following and then crossing a creek, going along it for a while. Then they left it and went into the bush, where they made a jungle — at Mang-gulugol, a Flying Fox Dreaming place. They roasted *mudji* big grass nuts. At Gadjilg-mirgani the two sisters put a paperbark tree.

They walked all along to find more country, and came to Gugunidji. Then they left the creek again and went into the bush. They were crying out '*Gaidba! gaidba!*' They made an *ubar*, and named the place Golng-geri, where the *ubar* is. They made a clear place and danced. They asked each other, 'Shall we stay here?' They argued over whether or not to leave the *ubar*, and threatened each other with bamboo spears. The elder sister threw her spear at the younger sister, hitting her in the middle of the breast. Then the younger sister threw a spear at her. They dived down into the big waterhole at this place and 'made themselves' Ngalyod.

A fight between two sisters is not unusual, but the choice of weapons is: spears, even of the bamboo variety, were not traditionally women's weapons in that area. Spearing-to-kill, also, was not expected between women, let alone between sisters. The point that it was a fight over an *ubar* is interesting in itself. It is in women's accounts, more often than in men's, that women are credited with mythic control in *ubar* matters: the Ubar Woman as a universal Mother figures prominently in these. In this connection the two sisters' use of yam sticks as walking sticks is reminiscent of the travels of the Djanggau Sisters, and the fact that they came from the direction of Milingimbi and moved westward, in itself draws attention to north-eastern Arnhem Land.

The next story also begins with a human-appearing woman who becomes a Rainbow after she is involved in a social-relations problem — in this case, a question of sexual relations. It was told to R. Berndt at Oenpelli in 1950.

39. WIND BLEW PENES THROUGH THE ENTRANCE

A Dreaming woman named Nyung-guleru-bumbu [Gagadju] was at Gabalabala, on the eastern side of the South Alligator River. 'I'm tired of this place,' she said, 'I will look around.' She went up to Nalweraba hill and looked across at the country and decided to go south. So she began her journey. She came to a creek which was full of grass, and named it

Gulamunmudi [from that special kind of grass]. 'Which way is water?' she asked herself. Walking on, she came to a billabong where there was a spring. She called it Iluburuwi. She went over to the spring and saw a deep hole: 'Ah, a large fish there! I'll kill it!' she said. But Barramundi spoke: 'I stay here, in this country. You go farther on!' She saw it was a Dreaming Barramundi, and so she followed a creek east, looking for another waterhole. Finding one, she decided to camp there for a short while; she called it Magera-mageri. Then she went on and camped at Galabiri. She was walking along during the Wet season, and the geese were making their nests in the bush. So she made a spear-thrower, and coming along Galabiri creek, built a grass hut at Rulbudji hole. Still following the creek, she travelled south-west, turning back to the South Alligator. She came to a waterhole where she sat down to wash herself; she called this place Djanaleda [after *djani*, sitting down]. Continuing, she went through scrub country and saw a large number of geese and ducks, with their nests in great profusion. She tried to spear them with a bamboo spear propelled with the spear-thrower she had made earlier on. But her intention was to frighten them. She said to them: 'You go to Magaragulu [on the plain, at the other side of Doyle's camp]. It's not good for you to stay here, a dingo will get you! You go to Yinerer [a plain, near Cooper's Creek]. You go to Yalngoi-yalngoi [South Alligator swamp plain]. . .' And she sent these geese and ducks to different places.

She went on. She looked at herself in the water, and saw that her labia majora were large. 'They are too fat, I shall split them.' Using a digging stick she 'split' her labia majora, 'cutting them at the sides', and what she removed she stood up like (as) a big stone at Minanabereneda. She built a grass house and camped there.

Three young men [names unknown] came, and seeing her there asked each other whether they would copulate with her. Nyun-guleru-bumbu had gone into her hut and was lying there resting. The three men came to the entrance and talked to her about copulation. They tried to open the entrance barrier, but could not. She became angry. She opened the hut a little at the top. Taking up her *maga* stick, she put out her head, and drawing up her *maga* swung it round, pulling the three men into her hut. She placed them lying side by side. She called this place Minanabereneda, which meant 'the wind blew those erect penes through the entrance.' With erect penes, the three men were ready to copulate with her, but she was too quick, she 'whipped herself' and made herself into a Namareidjul (Ngalyod). This place is in the dry bush, away from any creek or spring, at a rocky place. The three men became rocks; the woman became a Ngalyod.

This woman was 'a-typical' too, in her use of a spear, even a bamboo one, and a spear-thrower, although she did not intend to wound or kill with it.

As for cutting her labia majora, there is no record or recollection of such an operation being performed in this region, apart from the mythic reference to it. Also, there is no explanation of her action in pulling the three men into her hut and then killing them, instead of killing them while they were still outside it, This final episode in her story obviously needs more discussion.

'Becoming a Ngalyod' in the next story brings in a theme often associated with Rainbow Snakes in other regions. It was told to R. Berndt at Oenpelli in 1950.

40. JOURNEY ON NGALYOD'S BACK

At Alamin (or Walamin) on the other side of Smith's Landing, on the East Alligator River, there is a wet season billabong. 'I'll go and collect some lily stalks,' said Gurulmulya, a *yariwurig, nawamud* man. [This was in Amurag country.] He went down to the billabong and began to pull out lily stalks with flowers attached. [These are eaten, once the leaves are removed.] He was holding one stalk, but a Ngalyod was there, underneath, at the bottom of the lily plant. He pulled it, and the Ngalyod tipped him over. He spoke to that Ngalyod: 'Don't go fast, you go slow. I want to sit down straight on your back; don't go quickly, you might kill me.' And he climbed on to Ngalyod's back, leaving his lilies.

Now, that Ngalyod had stingray 'nails' behind her head, protruding from her earholes and tail. ['A clever one, that Ngalyod!'] Gurulmulya held on to the nails on her head; the Ngalyod's body was slippery and cold.

Ngalyod carried Gurulmulya to Madaru. It was night-time now. They went on to Imurudj (Amurag), to Alalwandjalwan, to Wiyul [low down the East Alligator, near the sea]. They went flying along over the scrub. Ngalyod was still carrying him, flying along — to Nganaya, to Idjamangul, to Wuran-melgerirl, to Woraidbag country. Flying through the darkness, following Cooper's Creek, carrying that man through the night. To Woyambal: they did not camp; they were just going along: they were going right around and coming back to the same place. Gurulmulya said to Ngalyod: 'We had better go back to my country.' So they went on to Walmidj billabong (Amurag), to Mayimbalg spring. 'We'll just see those places — we won't stop,' — and on to Malwarug and to Waramudul spring. 'Go slowly, don't go too quickly, my legs are stiff,' Gurulmulya said. Then they went to Galgal spring. All the way round 'they cut the ground'. [That is, they came close to the ground at each place and made a mark there.]

They came back to Walamin, where they had started, to Red Lily. The Ngalyod came down. 'I'll get off,' said the young man. Ngalyod said 'Yes.' Gurulmulya made ready to wash off all the *geing-gi* [the slippery stuff from the Ngalyod's body]. But Ngalyod said, 'Don't wash it off. If you do, you will stay with me. Your father will warm you, and red-ochre you.'

Gurulmulya returned to his camp. His father and mother and his brothers were all there. There were Djeinburu, Meryu and Badawer, his brothers; Gayewara, his father; and his 'classificatory' brothers from different mothers (Amundjia, Aberigali, Inbili, Gan-gudbi and Minyimag). And Indja-belangayar, his mother. They were all Amurag. When Gurulmulya returned, they all cried for him. They made a fire to warm him. Gurulmulya told his father, 'The Rainbow told me not to wash in water.' But the father did not take heed. He washed Gurulmulya to remove the smell (*manyilg*). All of them washed.

Next day Gurulmulya was gasping for breath; the beat of this heart slowed down, and he died: he became a Ngalyod. All the others remained alive — those 'old' Amurag. That Ngalyod remained in the billabong: 'We don't get red lilies there; only white ones, because of that Ngalyod down in the bottom.'

So now there were two Ngalyod in that billabong, though the ending mentions only the new arrival. The climax illustrates a motif that is found almost universally in myth and folktale repertoires: a warning from a supernatural figure ('Don't do this or that'), along with a threat ('If you do, then this or that will happen'); then rejection or ignoring of the warning, for reasons that are often unexplained; and, finally, dénouement, when the warning 'comes true'.

A human problem, jealousy this time, leads to the next transformation; the story was told to R. Berndt at the Daly River in 1946.

41. FLYING FOX AND RAINBOW

Flying Fox (Djinimin or Wudjara), a *djanama* man, had two *nangari* wives, 'Little Rainbows' (Djaguld). [That is, theirs was a 'wrong' marriage.] He was jealous of their sweetheart Rainbow, Djaguld, *djangala*. [This, too, was a 'wrong' union: Rainbow was not an eligible sweetheart for these two girls.] The story takes place in Djamindjung country.

Djinimin went out to hunt kangaroos. He got one and brought it back to his camp. However, his two wives were not there. They had climbed a steep hill and were looking down at him. He called out for them, and then saw them at the top of the hill. 'Why did you go up there? I can't come up, it is too rough!' he said. But the two 'Little Rainbows' looking down at him did not like him. They wanted to go to their sweetheart Rainbow, who lived at Gimul on the sea coast. So they had made a long rope.

They let the rope fall to the ground, after attaching it firmly to the rocks above, and told Djinimin to climb up. Carrying kangaroo meat on his shoulders, he pulled himself up by his hands. When he had almost reached the top, the two girls cut the rope and he fell to the ground 'broken to pieces'. The two girls climbed down and ran to join Rainbow at Gimul.

Flying Fox picked up his eyes, his nose and fingers and all the other pieces, and remade himself. He was a clever doctor. He sewed his limbs up with sinew and made himself whole by singing. Picking up his stone-bladed spear, he sat down, alive. After a while he followed the tracks of the two girls to Rainbow's camp, and heard them talking together. He came into the camp. Rainbow, who did not know Flying Fox had a spear, said 'Ah, my mate!' Flying Fox said nothing. He just threw his spear and hit Rainbow in the back. Rainbow fell into the water at Gimul, where he is now — a Rainbow.

The area concerned is on the salt-water side, near Bradshaw, near, but east of the Fitzmaurice River. The cause of the dislike of the two girls for Flying Fox is contained in the secret-sacred version of this myth, where he is a primary character: he was not subincised. Later, Flying Fox was responsible for introducing this ritual to the Djamindjung people.

With the next story we come to a theme that is especially common in western Arnhem Land: not 'becoming a Rainbow', but becoming what could be called a victim of the Rainbow, although it is rarely described in quite that way. It was told to C. Berndt at Oenpelli in 1950.

42. GULBIN'S STORY

Long ago she set off, one woman, coming from far away in Dangbun territory. She was coming down among the rocks, looking for the place where she would put herself as *djang*. She was bringing plant foods and creatures, looking about for a good place to put them. Then she would pour them out, those fish and those plant foods. She was still coming, talking in her own language, stumbling as she moved among the rough rocks. But then she was going downhill among good, smooth rocks, and at last she came to scrub and bush country. She went on, and camped in country where she called out, called out many times and her call kept coming back as an echo. And she said to herself, 'Here the name of the place is Gadjiman-gai'mi!' an echo name, where she put her word. Well, she slept. Early in the morning she started off again. She came running, and on the way she poured out creatures and plants as *djang,* making them come alive and grow there.

She went straight on, and came to where she saw a big expanse of water — water here, water there. It was a good place, all around. She settled down for a while, camped and slept. She listened, getting the feeling of the place. No, no leeches bit her there. Next morning early she planted brown *man-godbi* potato roots, and put the spirit of the *man-godbi* there as *djang.* It made itself like rock. She went on. And her children: she put the spirits of her two dead children, so they stand like paintings; they made themselves like rocks. She put the place name, Wud-geyi-yimiran, 'crying children'. She called the name. She went on, running, and settled down where she saw a billabong. She dug in the ground and made water come up, a big expanse of water. She was carrying raw roots of the *mandem* waterlily, and at last she poured some out into the water. It became like real plant food. Well, she slept. Early next morning she started off again. She put the place name there. She said, 'The name of this country is Maba-ngandi,' a waterlily name.

She came running on from there, still following through the scrub country. She came on, and settled down where she saw great rocks. She was searching about for a cave to live in. She saw cave-houses at Yibin-yibin, and camped there, eating plant foods and meat and honey. She camped for a while, then she finished with that place and moved away to a new one. She went on, and settled down in country where she put the place name, Djoon. She was getting stringybark. She put it there. And she made a house for herself there, made a home and stayed there. She went off now and then, getting plant foods, making scrub and bushland, killing creatures for meat, chopping out honey, and coming back to sleep. The next morning she would do the same, going hunting.

Then one day she killed a *maindjururlg* snake and brought it home to cook. She put its body down in her basket while she was getting firewood, making a heap of wood and building up a big fire. She waited for the flames to burn down to coals, eating little bits of meat and some plant food as a snack. She went and broke up the coals, heaped them up, and put the snake in among them to cook. The snake was burning, burning. She left it and lay down to sleep. She was sleeping, and that creature was burning, burning. It kept on sizzling. Well, She heard that voice, She who lives underneath the ground, that mother Snake, because it was her daughter that the woman was cooking. Gulbin thought it was a real, ordinary creature. And so she just kept sleeping; she did not wake up.

At last, water was coming, big water: she was getting wet. She got up, saw the water. Already the coals were soaking wet. She said, 'It's my own fault, I did wrong. I'll be drowned!' Everything was wet. The water was up to her waist. She couldn't do anything. At last that Snake, that mother, came rising up and 'ate' her body. She was leaning sideways on one arm, that woman. Time went on. There in that country where she had been living, the Snake vomited her bones, and they became like rock. She stands leaning to one side, where she became *djang*. Well, she was talking Gunwinggu when she got to that place, in Winggu country. She put herself as *djang*, and she remains there for ever, that old woman who came from the south.

Gulbin's story starts off as an almost routine report of a mythic journey. The daily round of getting food and finding shelter is punctuated with episodes of making and planting foods, and so on. Even when she put the spirits of her dead children as rock paintings, that was a minor event, compared with the mistaken identification that led to her final transformation. Mythic characters, like ordinary human beings, must take care not to let goannas and snakes and other smallish creatures sizzle while they are cooking: that is one way of attracting a Rainbow Snake. But it is almost impossible to know in advance whether any such creatures have a special relationship with the Rainbow. The final scene, where Gulbin's bones are vomited and become rocks, is an example of the most common pattern, explaining the multitude of rocky shapes in the the escarpment country.

The next story is similar in its broad approach, and like the last it conforms very closely to the style of the Gunwinggu-speaking narrator. It was told to C. Berndt at Oenpelli in 1950.

43. JOURNEY TO MANGURLGAN

Long ago a woman was travelling with her three children, a girl and two boys. She was bringing them by herself, coming from far away, looking for a place. They came following the beach, pausing for a while at Wongaram where they put the place-name, but only for one night; then they set off again. They were eating fish, and getting turtle eggs and crabs. They camped for three nights at Wondmug. But then they turned over those turtles and ate them, so it was finally four days they spent there. The mother herself and the older boy were killing small creatures; the others were getting firewood, and cooking turtle and grilling eggs on the beach.

When their days of camping there were finished, they started off again. At last they came to a place where there was a point, a 'nose' of land going into the sea. They stood on the beach and said, 'Here the name of this country is Wawoyi. We'll go on, because it's getting dark. Already the sun has gone down.' They went on, with mother getting food for them on the way. They kept on doing the same thing.

They went on, and got to Nganggu-lali. There they planted paperbark trees, and made fish. They were still going along, there in the country where they were looking for a place. They settled down, listening to each other. 'Where are we going, mother?' They were asking, talking together. Their mother said, 'Well, children, this isn't the right place, it's different. Where we are going the red lily grows, and there in that big expanse of water we will be transformed.'

They were coming along, killing small creatures, getting plant foods, chopping out honey and filling up their palm-leaf baskets, bringing them back full of honey. As they came they saw a plain, that Marganala (Murgenella) plain, and they said, 'At last, mother, we are close to that country. Perhaps we'll get there tomorrow, to that place we promised ourselves!' As they were coming they were still crying for their father, when their mother was 'pushing' them to cry by crying herself — crying for them. They kept on, crying, travelling, getting various foods, filling up their baskets, going back to their camping place. Then at midday they got to that country, Mangurlgan, that great stretch of water.

They went and settled down in the shade. One brother had already made a small fishing-spear. They ate, he and his mother — but not his sister. She was eating goanna that her mother gave her, because she could not eat food from her full brother. They camped there for a long time. They got stringybark and paperbark to make a hut for themselves with a bark roof. Then their mother left them in camp while she took her dog and her baskets and her axe, to get honey and other foods for her children — because they had no father to care for them, only herself. So she got honey and plant foods, and her dog killed small creatures. She filled up her baskets.

The baby was crying for milk. His older brother and his sister were calling to their mother, watching for her, and at last they saw her coming. The little girl ran to get firewood, and lit a fire so it would burn down to coals. Their mother got the baby and breast-fed him. Then she took some food from the baskets and gave it to the two children to eat as a snack, because they had got hungry while they were minding their little brother. She put the baby to sleep, and cooked the meat and the plant foods. That is what they always did. Then she took it from the coals and shared it out, dividing the goanna between them. They ate a little, and slept.

Then water came running from underneath the ground. They heard that Snake, coming up for them. Wind, too. They heard it coming, and they became frightened. Maybe they thought it was the Snake. But that fire they had made was 'talking' loudly, making a noise as the wood was crackling and breaking up. 'We can't do anything, my dear children,' she told them. Well, the fire was already close to them; it came right up to them. At last they started to jump into the water, into the billabong. The Snake took them. They remain there, Dreaming, in that country, Mangurlgan. They said, 'We make ourselves here, in our country, Mangurlgan, because at last they set fire to us, to burn us in this place. So then we went into the water, we put ourselves Dreaming here, in our Yiwadja country, we fatherless children. We came because already our father had left us, only our mother was looking after us,' they said. 'None of you made trouble for her while she was still alive. And now we go, we have just become Dreaming. Like a fish that goes swimming in the billabong, that's how we made ourselves,' they said. They went for ever, they put themselves *djang,* and there they are still, at Mangurlgan — not rocks, or fish, but spirit beings in the big trees by the water.

Many mythic travellers are very different from their ordinary human counterparts in regard to the range of their travelling companions. Some, as in Myth 42 are 'loners'. Some go about in same-sex pairs, such as siblings. Others again, as in the last case, and the Wawalag Sisters (Myth 36), constitute single-parent families. For the fatherless, husbandless group bound for Mangurlgan, this was not a matter of choice. The assumption is that their father/husband was dead, and that was why they wept. At the same time there is a suggestion that some people thought they should not have left the far-away place where he died, that his widow did wrong in taking the children away. This could be implicit in the children's comment. 'None of you made trouble for her while she was still alive.' She knew the place they were trying to reach; the children did not — although in the final scene it has already become 'our country'. In any case, we are told that she did her best, in a difficult situation, to compensate for their fatherless state. From the way the narrator carefully incorporates some of the domestic details and conversations between mother and children, it may be evident that she herself was a woman. So was the narrator of Gulbin's story.

No reason is given for the rising water and the coming of the Snake, except perhaps that the fire was too noisy in the first place, and became more so under the Snake's influence. This is where the hint of 'someone may have been responsible' comes in: 'they set fire to us.' The travellers accepted what had already been foreshadowed as their destiny: they jumped into the water, and were drowned ('eaten by the Snake'). The futility of trying to escape the power and ruthlessness of the Snake is dramatically portrayed in this next mythic event, set in the waters off the north coast near Cape Don. It was told to C. Berndt at Oenpelli in 1950.

44. DANGER AT ARAGALÁDI

Those first people were living there in what is now the middle of the sea, various men and women, really first people, living there in their own country.

They probably did not know, when some young men went to a creek looking for fish, that long ago a *maar* rock had put itself there: it was a *djang*, a dangerous Dreaming rock, and the Snake was there watching over it. Well, those young men went there, and in their ignorance they did wrong: they knocked it, that rock. They were eating cockles, in that country where the *maar* rock stood as *djang*. They brought back those sea creatures and fish. They came home, and slept.

Rain fell for a long time there in the middle of the sea, that was then dry land, where people were camping. Still it kept falling, that rain. At last fresh water was coming running in search of them, those people talking Yiwadja and Marrgu and Wurrugu as their own languages in that country where they were born.

Then that place went under water, when fresh water came up from the sea for them. Children and women were swimming about, trying to get to the rock, in that country where the rock stands, Aragaládi. They had settled down in that country long ago, when we were not here. The sea was coming: it swallowed them up. There was nowhere they could go, except for that one rock, rising up in the middle of the sea, Aragaládi country. But it was not a real rock. That Snake made it rise up for them.

Those who were still living had no canoe to enable them to cross over in this direction, to the mainland at Djamalingi (Cape Don). The sea was all around them. Some of them were alive, but hungry. Others drowned in the sea, and they remain there under the water. When those living people saw salt water rising high up all around them, they wept. 'What can we do for ourselves? We did wrong, it was our fault, when some of you were always going after those sea creatures and fish. That's why the sea is rising everywhere for us!' they said to one another. They were still trying to climb up the rock. There was nothing else they could do, because that Snake was looking for them, wanting to eat them, because they had made themselves wrong — they had done wrong to that *maar* rock. The Snake was still moving about, while water was rising everywhere as she was urinating salt water. She was making everything wet. Trees and ground, creatures, kangaroos, they all drowned when the sea covered them. Those people were sorry for themselves; they were weeping. They were searching for bodies, of their mothers and fathers and grandparents. They were weeping all the time. 'What can we do about ourselves? The Snake might eat us up too. If only we could get to dry land!' they were saying in their minds, looking at the sea coming, high up, toward them. It was frightening them. They could not stop weeping.

That Snake heard their words. She was already coming to make trouble for them, heading toward them, there where they were trying to climb up the rock. They looked about, toward the mainland, and saw a man putting a canoe in the water. He was trying to come across for them, trying to get them. He managed to come a little way, but there in the middle of the sea he drowned. His canoe lies deep under the water. They tried to see it, but no, they could not. That Snake came rising up and swallowed them, in that country of Aragaládi. She went on. Then afterward she vomited their bones. And she made that water very deep, when she filled the place up with sea water where it strikes against the rock there in the middle sea.

So, people do not go in any kind of canoe or boat, where the Snake ate those who lived there before. They became rocks, those first people. She ate them all. They tried to run away in fear, but the sea just threw them back. They stand there as Dreaming, where they put themselves as *djang*, those very first people. They were putting the place name. They said, 'Here in the middle sea, where we put ourselves as *djang*, is Aragaládi, where nobody goes — no canoe, or boat — or that Snake might take them under the water, she who ate us!' They stand there, Snake and people, there in the middle sea.

Forcefully and poignantly told by Mangurug, the Gunwinggu version of this human disaster came to life with the help of all the non-verbal techniques in which she excelled: pauses, gestures, body and facial movements, vocal changes and emotional involvement, making it a memorable experience for the listeners.

Next, a different story returns to the theme of 'becoming a Ngalyod', but introduces another, very common motif: the crying child. It was told to R. Berndt at Oenpelli in 1950.

45. DEATH IN A FISH TRAP

Ngayulyul, a Hawk Dreaming *yariyaning* man, sat down at Mamul Hill [Eri, Gagadju] near Doyle's camp. He had a cane basket fish trap, a *milil*. [Fish can go into this kind of trap but cannot come out.] He also had a wife. They were camping there. Now Ngayulyul, although he was really an Idud (Hawk) was also a Ngalyod: he was human in the camp, but when he went flying about he was a Ngalyod. They had a small son [also Idud]. They lived near the billabong; his fish trap was not completed yet.

They came on to Wulen-gwiandj and walked down to catch fish. They camped there, cooked their fish, and next morning went to Namburuwoi, close to the East Alligator River. They crossed over to Mang-gagur and looked for fish at Ugengg billabong. 'You wait for me here, I'll go and look for fish that have died.' He had seen a large number of birds eating fish at the billabong. He filled up his bag, and saw a hill at the other side of the Red Lily lagoon: that hill is named Indjumandagub, and the billabong (lagoon) Indjuwunewei. Among the rocks by the lagoon he found a cave and sat down there.

His wife [unnamed] came down to collect red lily roots. By this time Ngayulyul had almost finished making his fish trap. The place where he sat down among the rocks, in his cave, was Indjumug-gundewol. His wife was roasting the roots she had collected at Ugengg. Ngayulyul went down to that camp, leaving his trap in the cave, and got a bag full of the roots. They ate there, and slept in a protected hole. Next morning he returned to his cave and completed his fish trap. He 'shut it up': 'If a fish wants to come out, it will poke out its eyes,' he thought. He left it there, and they went to collect lilies. The child sat on the bank of the billabong and began to cry for milk. His mother, however, did not hear him. ['No one came back to the child!']

Ngayulyul became angry; 'I'll have to put him into my basket trap,' he said. So he put the child inside the trap, 'Why are you putting me here?' the boy asked. 'We are just trying you to see how the fish go in,' he replied. 'I'll throw him into the water,' his father thought. He did that. He threw the child, in the trap, into the water. ['You can see that rock sticking up now — it's that boy in the trap.'] The boy struggled to get out. He came close to the bank, but his father threw him back into the water. He watched him trying to get out. That child was always crying! The father dived down to make sure the child was drowned. He was sorry. 'You stand up there [as a rock]. I'll leave you there. The Eri people will call you *Ngawamun* [*Idud*, in Mangeri, Hawk Dreaming].'

Then Ngayulyul went back to his camp at Ugengg and lay down, pretending to be asleep. The boy's mother returned. She 'awakened' him, and he jumped up. 'Which way did the child go?' she asked. 'I don't know, I've been sound asleep. I haven't seen him,' he replied. They sat down waiting. At last he told her, 'I threw him into the water!' 'Why did you do that? He was our boy!' She was crying. Ngayulyul became angry and hit her on the head. But she hit back, and they fought.

He caught hold of her bag of red lily roots and he caught hold of her. He held them. 'We will go down to wash, and there we will stay. I am sorry!'

She tried to move, but she could not. They went down into the billabong together. Now they stand there as rocks, in the middle of the water, very deep; they are close together. 'They are sorry for that child and they cry and cry. They sit down there to help that child; and the child is alongside them, as a rock. They turned into Ngalyod. All that country is Eri-muyunangg, Eri country.'

The next story is included because it bears a rather curious resemblance to the last one. We have left in the short account of a woman becoming an emu because that is how it was told. The teller, Minyaiwi, insisted that this was how it should be, and other women present agreed with her. They did not explicitly condemn the man for throwing his son into the water: these were 'first people', the women said, and some of their actions were inexplicable from the point of view of present-day men and women. They story was told to C. Berndt at Oenpelli in 1950.

---

46. ORPHAN, EMU, AND *MANBADARI* NUTS

Two women were chopping at a *manbaderi* tree where people were knocking down nuts. A little motherless boy was sitting nearby. The women knocking down nuts would call out to him, saying 'Come here and get some!' But when he started to come, they would tell him, '*We're* eating!' They ate them all. He would go back, crying, 'Oh, what am I to do?' They were calling to him, knocking down nuts, saying, 'Come here, you eat them!' But when he tried to go there *they* were eating the nuts. They were just teasing him, tricking him all the time, and he would go away crying.

[There now comes a short interlude or diversion in the story, relating to one of the women.] 'What am I going to do?' said one woman, of the *ngalgangila* sub-section — Emu Woman. She re-arranged her feet. She got some termite mound and ate big chunks of it. That's how she was making eggs. She said, 'I ate termite mound because I want to make eggs. I re-shape my feet. Is this the way I do it? Is this the way I run with my feet?' Her feet became like emu feet. She got feathers and put them on her back, and she made herself a long neck. She said, 'I'm a creature, a bird, I'm a real emu. At first I was a person, but now I'm a bird!'

[Now back to the little boy sitting near the nut tree.] The little motherless boy was sitting down, crying. Water was coming running, running, making the ground wet where he was sitting. 'Oh, what am I to do?' he said. His father came, picked him up and threw him into the water. He asked, 'What is the name of this place? The place name is Namalaid-djabo-delmeng, because that's where I threw that motherless child into the water!' This made a creek flow, with water swirling round. He asked, 'What is the name of *this* place?' 'Oh,' said the others, 'This is a *different* place!'

The child's father ran and began to make a *milil* fish net of twine and sticks, and when it was finished he put it in the water. But the little boy had upset the place with his crying. That father was hoping fish would go into the net, but they did not. The water took away the net. He got it again, then ran and put it outside. They all slept until morning. He went and got it, threw away the tail of the net and put the head outside. And fish went in, for him: barramundi, various little fish, and long big-eyed fish — they went in until the net was full of fish.

He said to the women, 'You, first, stopped my son from eating *manbaderi* nuts, and *you* were eating them! Ah! And endless amounts of water came pouring out, and fish came pouring for me! And now this place is taboo, dangerous!' He struck himself on the nose several times, and he said, 'Dangerous, taboo! You are not to eat here. Women are not to eat at this place, because it's taboo. Only men are to eat here. Afterward, at burning-grass time, women can eat. That's because he made it dangerous, taboo to you.' Then he said, '*I'm* dangerous, taboo, because you first refused to share with my son those *manbaderi* nuts you were eating!'

The child in Myth 45 was put into the fish trap and thrown into the water by his father, but not simply because the crying annoyed him, or that the child cried so consistently that the father could stand the noise no longer; nor was it an attempt to punish his wife indirectly for neglecting the child. Other examples of the child crying motif indicate clearly that the cries attract Ngalyod, and that not only the child will be swallowed, but the whole camp of people. While that did not occur in this myth, the father, mother *and* child became Ngalyod, which amounts to the same thing. In the second myth, 46, there is also a crying child — because food is withheld from him, just as milk was withheld in Myth 43. The fish net appears, but not as a vehicle of death: the child is thrown into the water. While Ngalyod is not referred to in this context, the child's father becomes dangerous — a Ngalyod quality. Compare it with Myths 174 and 176 for the fish trap or basket being used as a death vehicle: in the case of Crocodile on one hand, and the drowning of a sister's husband; in the latter case, the fish trap became, or was, a manifestation of Ngalyod.

The crying child leads us into a bracket of stories dealing with the Nyalaidj dancing, a travelling ceremony associated with gift exchange or trade between different groups. The first story emphasises an elder

brother's concern, and everyone else's neglect of the child. It was told to
R. Berndt at Oenpelli in 1950, and is Gunwinggu.

47. THE BREAKING OF RAINBOW'S EGGS

People came from different places, from Junction Bay, King River, and
Goulburn Islands, from the sea coast and from Tor Rock and Barclay
Point. They all set off from these places for Gabari, for rituals.

At Gabari, Rembranga and Dangbun men painted themselves in ochre,
decorated with wild cotton. They were awaiting the Maung, Yiwadja,
Marlgu and Walang people who were sending them a young boy from
Port Essington for initiation. It was the first time a boy had come from this
area for circumcision. [Western Arnhem Land was traditionally a non-
circumcising area.] The Rembranga and Dangbun made a big ring place,
and while they waited for the others, they sang:

galbara bareya mural-muruli

[The meaning of these words was unknown to the men who were present
during the telling of this story, although Galbara, or Gaalbaraya, can be a
place name.]

On their way to Gabari, a small boy was crying: his mother had
recently died. But the people were singing and dancing the *wirbu*. They
reached Gun-ngulugi, where they camped. The boy's elder brother went
out hunting. Some women tried to stop the boy from crying, but he would
not. Then the women were diverted by the singing and dancing.

The *nyalaidj* group at Gabari could see the camp fires of those people at
Gun-ngulugi close by; they had seen them coming up, dancing and singing
the *wirbu* (*wurbu*), bringing the novice with them, calling out as they came
closer. The *nyalaidj* group said: 'They are coming, bringing that young
Port Essington novice.' The people at Gun-ngulugi sent a messenger to
Gabari to say they were ready, and began to paint the novice (*walg*). After
a while, the *nyalaidj* and *wirbu* dancers came together at Gun-ngulugi. In
the meantime, the brother of the little boy who was crying returned from
hunting. He went directly to the camp where he had left him. He did not
see the *nyalaidj* and *wirbu* dancers but went straight to his little brother. He
thought the others were still in the bush. He had made a basket and had
hung it, with an unfinished basket, from a tree above his little brother's
head. When he had left to go out hunting, he had told the boy he would be
a long time, and not to cry.

Then the *nyalaidj* group got ready to circumcise the novice. All of them kept dancing. The elder brother came up to the child and saw that he had became very thin — he had not eaten anything at all! The others had eaten 'bitter' yams and had tried to give the child some, but he would not accept any. He went on crying all the time.

That elder brother knew about those Rainbow eggs; but the other people did not. All of them were dancing. He told them: 'I'm sorry you didn't give food to my brother; he's very thin, he'll die soon.' Those Rembranga and Dangbun people had to continue dancing the *nyalaidj* — they were all decorated.

That elder brother said, 'I'll finish all of you!' He took his stone axe. By now all the people were sitting down. 'You listen to me. See what I have in my hand. I'm very sorry for my little brother. You see me! I'm going to break the Rainbow eggs, and water will "jump". You don't know where they are.' He took those Rainbow eggs out of the ground, and held them up for all to see.

All the grey-haired men cried out; they tried to stop him. He knocked those eggs together; the water 'jumped out' and spread. That man went back to get his little brother. 'We had better go and find our place.' They went sideways along the hill at Gun-ngulugi: 'You had better stay here; you are sick. You stay here, small brother.'

The little boy became rock, at the side of the hill, near the billabong. The elder brother went farther up the hill, with his two baskets. He climbed up until he saw an entrance to some caves. 'I'll put both baskets here. I can't make them into rocks. I'll put them as a picture.' Ochred paintings of those baskets are there in those caves. The elder brother went further up and made himself into a rock at Ngiwulban, where he is sitting with his two baskets below him in the caves, and the child down by the billabong.

In this story, as in the one preceding it, it is women who are blamed for their failure to look after the little boy — not only for being unable to stop him from crying, but also for not ensuring that he had enough to eat. And the reason is underlined: they were preoccupied with the dancing, at the expense of their social commitments. The Rainbow Snake's eggs are a potentially dangerous weapon. They appear in several other cases, including one in the 1940s when a Rainbow egg stone near Oenpelli was reported to have been stolen, and people became anxious and upset. In this particular story, the Snake does not appear personally to avenge the breaking of the eggs, but sends water instead. The implication is that all the people except the two brothers are drowned.

The next version is one of three, all told to C. Berndt, by women at Oenpelli in 1950.

48. THE *NYALAIDJ* DANCERS (1)

Those people were coming, setting off from the south, taking a ceremony to those who were living in Gurudjmug country. Already word had gone out to them, and they all came. They were coming, camping, still going on, travelling among the rocks. They went straight to the place that he had arranged with them, that man who had taken the message to them and led them to the right place. They were coming, camping as they went along, getting kangaroos and honey to eat on the way. That's what they kept doing. When it grew dark they slept, and next morning they set off again. At last they got to the creek that runs in Gurudjmug. There they got plant foods on the way. They climbed up the rocks, and heard people calling out — men and women, and children. There, for a while they painted themselves.

The man who was travelling with them, the man who had brought the message, went running to the people living there and told them that the visitors were getting ready. So they painted themselves and painted their spears and spear-throwers. Then that man went back to where he had left them, those visitors. At last they were beginning to move off, dancing and singing as they went, bringing that *nyalaidj*. At last they reached the camp where those people were living, where they were welcoming the dancers. The name of the place where they were painting themselves is Gun-ngulugi, where they put the name and then went on from there. So they were coming, dancing and singing, and those men and women were calling out to welcome them. Then they slept.

But a little boy, an orphan, a motherless child, was crying for *mandaneg* roots that they had withheld from him. For a long time, he kept wanting it badly, that *mandaneg* food of theirs. Morning, afternoon, and at break of day he could not stop wanting it — taboo food, that they had already put aside for the *mareiin* ritual! They made as if to hit him, trying to quieten him. He just went on crying. At last she drowned them, that Snake he brought for them; she ate them all, those who were living there. They all drowned: they are all inside the billabong. As for those who brought the *nyalaidj*, they climbed up among the rocks, climbing high up. They went on, and they became like rocks, and there they remain. So their name is Nyalaidj *djang*, only that name they had for all of them, one name. And that one who made the others go wrong, that child, he was drowned along with them. They remain underneath the water. They became like rocks for ever: they remain there. They first showed him that food, so then he kept thinking about it, and he kept crying for it, and so the Snake ate them all.

Maidjuni is where the *nyalaidj* dancers are, up among the rocks. The others are all at Gabari, inside the billabong, a 'wide creek, a big sandy place', where the creeks meet. The messenger is there too. Nabalagaidj was his name, a Gunwinggu-speaking man from that country.

Here, some blame is attached to the child: he should not have demanded taboo food, so he was the one who brought the Snake and spoiled the dancing for everyone. But the real blame rests with the adults: they should not have let him see the food if they were not going to allow him to have it. That theme comes up in other stories, and in everyday life. 'If you don't want a child to have something, the only course is to conceal it from him!' The ending in this case is the conventional drowning and swallowing and turning into rocks, which happens in the next version too.

49. THE *NYALAIDJ* DANCERS (2)

They came from the north, from the salt-water coast. They were making for the place where the *nyalaidj* ceremony would be, and there they would stay. They went on, camping along the way at Gadjabeg where there is a creek. They went on, up into the scrub, still going, camping along the way, still looking for the place where they would take the *nyalaidj*. They would stay there, where they proposed to dance. They crossed a little creek on the way, and they said, 'Where are we going, taking this *nyalaidj*, where we can dance?' They said, 'Still we keep going, still we're searching for a place where we can stay.' They came on, and crossed the creek at Balali. They said, 'Here we'll stay, and you can dance the *nyalaidj*!' They camped; they danced; they saw that it was good. They said, 'We'll go on, because you all danced so well!'

They went on. They climbed up a rocky hill and looked all around. They were asking one another, 'What about giving some thought to where we are going?' And they said, 'We've come from far away, let's still keep going!' They went on, camping along the way, climbing up again into the scrub. They were still going, because it was a big stretch of scrub and bush country. So they went on, camping along the way. Then at last they came to where those people were living.

The people had been looking out for them. They said, 'That lot, they're coming! They called out, they've come, they're dancing the *nyalaidj* for us!' So they called back to them. They said 'Come here, where we made the place ready for you, where you are to dance, and where the ceremonial ground is the one that we prepared before! We cleared it ready for you!' They all slept. Next morning they got up. Still they were dancing: they kept dancing for a long time. One girl climbed a pandanus palm. She got hold of it and climbed up, right to the top, and she was calling out, calling out to them. They were still dancing, and she was still calling out from up there, and a little orphan boy was crying and crying.

Still they kept going. They were dancing, she was calling out, and that little boy was crying. Nobody thought of saying, 'Don't let's upset the place, or something might eat our noses!' They did not think of saying that: they just kept dancing and calling out and crying. So, from underneath, water was coming out for them, where they were gathered there dancing, and that orphan boy was crying and crying. Water was coming up from underneath. They were keeping on dancing. Well, they began to look at the ground. It was getting soft; it was getting very wet. They were calling out, 'Why is this ground getting wet for us? And getting soft for us? We can't do anything about running away, because the ground is so soft that we can't run — *where* can we go?' That's what those others were saying. But that orphan boy and that girl who had climbed up the palm tree, those two just went on calling out. They did not hear the others crying out in fear. Those two alone went on upsetting the place. Nothing made them think about it. Then afterward the two of them saw water flowing, they saw water 'tearing' along. They said, 'What has come out for us? What is going to eat us here? We ourselves, we all did wrong, we were upsetting the place, and the orphan boy kept crying!' They were all calling out. They said, '*Wouu!* Where are we to go? Because here water has come up for us, water getting bigger for us. We can't run anywhere, because we just made ourselves wrong, when that orphan was crying and that girl was calling out and we were dancing!'

Well, already that water was getting bigger and bigger, where they were crying out in fear. They kept saying, '*Wouu!* What are we going to become? Water has come up for us, now it is covering us, and Ngalyod is eating us!' She ate them first, those who were calling out, and the orphan boy who kept crying. They went underneath the water, and there they came into Dreaming. They said, 'Here the name of the place is Gaalbaraya, where we were dancing and water came up for us, and where we made ourselves wrong.' It is still a taboo, dangerous place. 'People are not to go there, or they might go underneath the water if they set foot in that place, because it is a taboo, dangerous place always, where we made ourselves wrong, where water came up for us, and where we remain as Dreaming. A taboo, dangerous place always!' Nobody is to pass by, near that place, because it is always a taboo, dangerous place, where they remain, and where they made themselves wrong.

[The *nyalaidj* dancers in this version came from Gunbalang (Walang) language country. Now they live on in spirit at Gudjegbin, in Gabari, the 'mother country', a 'big creek, and big waterhole among the rocks'.]

Here, the child's crying is combined with the calls of the young woman who has climbed a pandanus palm. She is calling invocations to the country, arousing the Dreaming spirits and this is also an important role traditionally adopted by particular women in, for example, *ubar* religious rituals. The *nyalaidj*, although secular, has some associations with the Kunapipi (see R. Berndt 1951: 170–71). In such circumstances, the cries of the child on one hand and the invocations of the woman (girl) provide an almost ideal situation for attracting the Rainbow Snake.

The following *nyalaidj*-dancing version includes frightened children, but not children who cry loudly and can't be consoled. In this case it is the sound of bees that upsets the festivities.

50. THE *NYALAIDJ* DANCERS (3)

He went along — he started from Bo-delmeng, one of the first people. He went along, to Mangga-marlgamarl, he came out there and went round, went on and went round, and came to the place of the *nyalaidj* dancers. They were gathered there, at that one creek. Women and men were painting themselves with white clay, and they were dancing. *Nyalaidj*, that is the name of the song they were dancing to. They spoke Woraidbag, those people who were dancing.

But at last the ground was shaking ['turning around'], Ngalyod was coming! They heard her talking, just like the sound of bees. They said, 'What's that, talking here? Listen, all of you! Would you all listen? Maybe some taboo thing has made us go wrong! Maybe some *djang* has made us go wrong! Maybe water will drown our children and us ['eat our noses'], that Creature will eat us, she who lies beneath us, under the ground.' The children were frightened. They were saying, 'Get me, mother and father, get me, because I'm frightened!' They could hear Ngalyod coming, Ngalyod and water both coming, together, Ngalyod herself going along underneath the ground, and water coming running on top. Well, water just came running and covered them all up, rocks as well. Underneath, at last, they remain. They went under the surface, they 'ate water', and there they stay. So then they said, 'Ga-nyalaidj-gendi, the place of the *nyalaidj* dancers, is the name of this place, because before we were dancing, and now we remain underneath. Something got us!' Well, there underneath, they became taboo, dangerous.

That character was talking, talking, he kept saying, '*Nguuu. . .!*', like the sound of bees, for the first time. So then it was here that the water 'ate their noses', and he himself went on, still talking, and put himself as a rock a little distance away. He became rock. But he was a real honey-bee, and so that is now a taboo, dangerous place. If people see real honey, and bees coming out, nobody is to eat it: it is truly taboo, and dangerous. And if people go there and dig out that honey from the ground, then water will come out and 'eat our noses', all of us, and we will 'go wrong', as they did before. So then it stays taboo. Nobody is to go there and touch it, or Ngalyod might eat us up. She put herself a long way off, while they, those who were dancing, remain there together in one place. They became like rock, like the white clay they were painting themselves with: their life as people was over.

But among the people at that *nyalaidj* ceremony was the man who had thrown his motherless child into the water because the boy would not stop crying. (See also Myth 46.) They were standing together on a little hill like an island among the sand. The father took his son by his two legs and flung him into the air so that he landed on top of a big rock. The boy sat there, and his father covered him with hard grass; and he became *djang*, taboo and dangerous. The father himself went away, following the same creek. He went on and stood at a place where the rocks were full of holes. 'What is the name of this place?' And he answered himself, 'The name is Galdjarlgdum, but the big mother name of the country is Gabari!'

He went on, and stood there high up where water came pouring down. Then he came back. 'Where shall I go, to put myself?' He came running to the top [of the rocks] and looked about at the country. It was not a good place. So he ran back. 'Shall I stay here?' He came running on and put himself there. 'Shall I stay here, at Niwoban?' So then he turned into pandanus-palm threads, round leaves: 'I'm pandanus threads!' he said. And there he is now, a round rock, up on the rocks above the water.

The unnamed character at the beginning of this story turns out to be a honey-bee, a Honey *djang* man. We are not told why he went deliberately to that place and made a noise that he knew would attract the Snake. Minyaiwi, who told the story, said she did not know: he was a *djang* character, and had to do what he did.

We continue with honey-bees and Ngalyod. The following two stories, in a way, belong together, as two versions of one story. They were both told to C. Berndt at Oenpelli in 1950.

51. THE *MANYALG* HONEY *DJANG*

A man was lying asleep, and a honey *djang* on a tree was talking [the sound of bees]. The man went on sleeping, still listening to it talking, and that Snake was sleeping, dreaming and listening. Not good! He was listening, it was still talking. He said, 'What *is* that, still going on talking? It should be stopped, it shouldn't go on like that!'One more time he lay down to sleep. He listened. Not good! Time went on. She came out, Ngalyod. She rose up, Ngalyod. 'There she is, she who makes things wrong, the Rainbow!' She rose up. He tried to look but already she had emerged, already she had risen up. Water came out: Ngalyod was 'cutting him off' at the neck. 'What can I do? Well, no matter. She's eating me!' That's what he said when water 'cut' him, up to his throat. He just died. [This happened at Bi-lerrmi-djam, east of Oenpelli.]

---

52.   A HONEY *DJANG*

He was sleeping. He got up, saying, 'I'll go and look for honey.' So he did. He was chopping out a honeycomb, looking at it. No good. He chopped out another. No good. Still he kept searching, and looking at what he found. Still it was no good. He moved camp to a different place — searching, chopping, looking. No good. '*Why* is it no good, so I can't eat it?' he said. 'I'm dying of hunger!' He went back; he slept. Early in the morning he went searching again, in a different place, moving his camp again. 'What if I search here, and see a bees' nest and chop it out?' He did that: he saw a nest and chopped it out. No good. '*Why?*' he kept saying. 'What is spoiling it? What's wrong?'

Well, he went on. He came to a creek, and as he went along he came to a palm tree [or trees]. He cut it [or them], and was going back. The one he cut first, he ate. As he was preparing to go back he heard a noise, something talking. '*Gu-gu!*' it said [meaning, 'water']. It was the sound of bees talking. 'What did I do wrong?' he asked. 'Was that a *djang* palm tree? I'd better follow those others and let them know about it, if I did wrong to a *djang*. But I did it unknowingly, when I cut it!' He ran, and came to where the others were staying. 'Let's go!' he told them, 'Because I did wrong to something or other, perhaps to a *djang!*' 'And what was the name of the place where you cut it? Djalarr-main-bugbi?' 'That's the one. I cut it, I did wrong to a *djang*. So, all of you run and burn that piece I cut!' 'And I'll run and call out,' said one little girl.

They went and lit a fire, and she was calling out, 'What did you do, cutting that thing and making us go wrong?' They were cooking that piece of palm tree in the fire, trying to burn it, but water was rising from it. Soon it was full of water. They climbed up a big *manbaderi* tree, a high tree that grows close to the water. And that girl was climbing up the rocks, calling out. They climbed the *manbaderi* tree, but water was rising from underneath it. It fell, taking them with it, down into the water. The girl saw them, from high up on the rocks. The tree was already submerged, along with them, while she was still calling. They all drowned, those who had climbed that tree. '*Aaaap!*' they said, making the sound of swallowing water. It 'ate their noses', and they disappeared from her sight. She herself, up on the rocks, just went hard and became like a rock. 'What is the name of this place? Gudju-mandi!' Nobody goes there, in case he takes them, too, under the water, that Honey *djang* man!

These two Honey *djang* stories were told on the same day, the first in the morning, the second in the afternoon. The first story-teller was a young woman, Medeg, and the translation keeps very close to her Gunwinggu rendering. She had no extra comments on it: the sound of the bees brought Ngalyod, who 'ate' (drowned) the man, in a straightforward sequence. While she was telling it, Gararu (the sister of Medeg's long-dead mother) was present, and so was Gararu's own daughter. That afternoon Gararu told the second story, in her usual rather compressed personal style, but with an air of expanding on the first story. She included some repetition for dramatic effect in the actual telling; but much of what she had to say depended on discussion, helped along by her daughter Gadjibunba. For instance, the fact that the main character is himself a Honey *djang* man is not revealed until the end of the story. He was a westerner, from Woralga in Wuningag-language country. His unsuccessful search for good, edible honey is not explained. Nor is the connection with the *marun* palm tree he cut. Even his own fate is left vague. The implication is that he was drowned with the others, but this is not certain. As for the girl, while her body turned to rock, her spirit was transformed into a smallish brown bird living among the rocks with a cry resembling its name ('*Djin-di! Djin-di!*') In this sequence of events there is no reference to the Rainbow Snake. The flooding-and-drowning follows automatically from the damage to a *djang*, and in other stories too, *marun* palm trees have a significant role in this respect. The 'not good' (or 'no good') comment in the first story has its equivalent in the second, but the first points to the general situation (something was wrong), whereas the second relates directly to the honey. The place names are referred to as being separate. And these were said to be two distinct, though very similar, stories.

Honey comes into the next story, too, as one item that attracts the attention of Ngalyod. It belongs to a cultural tradition west of the East Alligator River and was told to R. Berndt at Oenpelli in 1950.

53. THE WATERSPOUT

Two Dreaming brothers named Nangurlbur were camped at Maburarari [Ngadug language] close to the mouth of the East Alligator River. They heard the sound of a woman, Medgadba, Wild Bee ['sugarbag']. This was her Dreaming place. 'We'd better leave here,' the brothers agreed. They went on to Meyayung-nung-guli, where they dug out yellow (ochre) clay or mud. Leaving there, they walked on to a jungle and spring at Andjari. 'Not many fish here. We'll go to the other side,' they said. They moved to Gedung-gu springs; these run to the South Alligator River. The two men went that way, finding a lot of fish. They went up to the other side, on to the plain, through *malu* bamboo grass to Gareigi. 'Brother, I want to get some bamboo lengths to throw.' They made a spear-thrower and broke off bamboos; and they threw their spears back to Nyumbarbir [Gagadju; the other side of Angmeridja springs].

They walked across the plain to Yeri, on the other side [Ngadug language], and camped there. Later on they came back to a hill, an 'island', and followed up Mandula creek. They came along the mouth of the South Alligator. There was only a little water there, but gradually the water came up. Water Dreaming had smelt the two men, because they carried ironwood and wild honey wax, and these had got wet. Ngalyod smelt them too. A big wind came and 'shut the two men up like smoke'. 'Brother,' one said to the other: 'Look at the waterspout (*wariwuwon*)!' Water started flowing across the land. That Ngalyod was looking: the wind came, and the waterspout, and they encompassed the two men, spinning them around; they could not sit down. [There is a reference to their heads being blown off — but that is not clear.] The elder brother said, 'My foot is stuck in the ground.' The other tried to drag him out, but could not move him. 'We have to stand up here; we have to stay here.' At Ginbineri, at the river's mouth, they stand near Ilgargu Point, on the sea coast, where there is a large sandbank, with Barron Island at the other side [Ngadug language].

Ironwood is used more often as a means of averting 'supernatural' danger than an item which could attract it. Getting wet is an unusual way of neutralising its power; and wet honey wax seems to be equivalent to the sound of bees in drawing Ngalyod's attention.

Next, an unsuccessful attempt to keep the Rainbow at bay, and a closer look at the Rainbow herself. The story was told to C. Berndt at Oenpelli in 1950.

54. IN GOGALAG.
NABERG-GAIDMI

Man-labal-gimug. [So the story begins.] A big, round billabong in Gogalag. She came, she went into the water: Ngalyod, the Rainbow Snake, she who lives underneath the ground. She was urinating, that Ngalyod, she made the place deep, and the water became large and wide.

One man was working there. He was going about, lighting fires. He was saying, 'Ngalyod might eat me!' He was afraid. He was lighting fires on each side, very big ones, and lighting fires from his head around to his feet, because he was so afraid she might eat him. He was putting fish-poison leaves in the water so that the fish would die, then he would get them and eat them.

Ngalyod rose up, ran [moved fast], got up, ran, settled down and put herself as *djang*. She said, 'What is the name of this place? Yilobel! She settled down. Her back is flat, stretching out this way and that way. 'I am Yilobel!' she said, 'And here at Mamara-wiri I put the place name.' Then, 'I leave that place,' she said. It is a taboo, dangerous place where a *djang* put itself! She went on, looking for the place where Mudfish rose up — rose up, making a hole in the rock. He rose up, making a hole as he went down into the water, at another place. He was running, lighting fires in this direction, underneath the water. He rose up, making a hole in the rock. People were looking at the place, thinking it was Mudfish, but it was Ngalyod. She rose up, from Mamara-wiri. And that man who kept on eating fish before, and many other people, women and men, they all sank down there and remain as Dreaming. They became taboo, dangerous, for ever. Nobody is to try to look at that place, or they might make themselves wrong too if they go there. So then it is still a taboo, dangerous place, where before they went wrong.

She went on a bit farther, that Ngalyod. On the way she rose up, still going along. She rose up, then she went high on the rocks and kept rising up there, making a lot of holes. Then she went on and 'put herself'. She made a cave-house, and she still lies there, where she put herself. 'What is the name of the place?' she said. 'Gabo-ngur-gumdo-gumdongi is the name of the place, where already I made myself wrong, came into Dreaming.' So then Mudfish came. He got up from Mamara-wiri. He went on, and put himself close by, where he made the place and put the name Gabo-ngur-gumdo-gumdongi. At the Mudfish place in Mamara-wiri, water is underneath and rock on top. The Gunwinggu name for Gabo-ngur-gumdo-gumdongi is Magali-gumdo-gumdongi, 'where Mudfish kept getting up'. Ngalyod and Mudfish are there together, Ngalyod underneath and Mudfish on top. ['If people want to get fish now, they light fires all around that billabong to stop Ngalyod, as Naberg-gaidmi did before.']

This is one of a constellation of locality-centred stories and sketches, putting an assortment of characters in perspective in relation to one another. Naberg-gaidmi had been spending much of his time catching fish, using a special fish-poison. He tried to protect himself from Ngalyod by lighting a ring of fires around himself — as used to be done, traditionally, in other circumstances in everyday life. (At childbirth and during menstrual seclusion, fires were believed to discourage the Rainbow from coming too close.) This device did not save him. The story then turns to Mudfish, and the partial identification of that fish with Ngalyod.

Next we return to the crying child theme, but with a difference. The difference lies in the ending — resistance to the Rainbow, foreshadowed in the last story. It was told to R. Berndt at Oenpelli in 1949.

55. THE KILLING OF NGALYOD AND THE RESCUE OF THE VICTIMS

A small orphan boy was being looked after by Inimbu (*nyindjariwurig, ngalgamarang*), his mother's sister. The child was crying. Inimbu gave him a lily root to eat. He tasted it, but threw it aside. 'No', he said, 'I want something sweet!' He continued to cry. She gave him goanna tail fat; she gave him snake; he tasted each, and threw it aside, asking for something sweet. He went on crying. She kept trying to persuade him, but he just reacted in the same way. They were living at Ilngir, a high point on the plain, low down on Cooper's Creek, near the mouth of the East Alligator River, in Amurag country.

Now Ngalyod, Rainbow, from his/her camp at Waiara (North Goulburn Island) heard the boy crying, He/she was lying in the water when he heard the crying. He listened, got up and swam in the direction of the sound, across the sea and up Sandy Creek, Gandinman [where Maung, Yiwadja and Gunwinggu people camped]. He listened again and heard the crying, and went right up Sandy Creek and came out in the bush at Wudin-nyambid. Leaving the creek, he flew through the sky to Ngawindjin billabong. Then he flew on to Iluwa, and was lying there for a while before climbing up the rocks to listen again to the child crying: 'I have to go a long way yet,' he thought. He flew again, coming down ('falling') at Andimari-en, where on landing, he made a small billabong. He stretched up his neck and listened to the crying: 'Still a long way!' From there he went along Mabur Creek, and at Unbarang-yunig [a Yiwadja place] he found spring water. Continuing, he came to Murmi springs (Yiwadja), and then came up and lay in Mia billabong. Next morning he went on to Umalyi billabong, where he slept the night. He coiled himself, 'trying it out' to see whether his coils would encompass a large group of people. He listened again to the child, who by this time was hoarse. Then he went on to Muridj billabong [mainly Amurag, with Yiwadja sharing].

From here he went across Ngalmar plain [at the other side, the sea-side, of Cooper's Creek] and crawled all the way along Ulgolbir [a salt-water creek running to Cooper's Creek]. He swam to the other side, lay down on the bank, and looked up and listened [at Wuwaraidj, which refers to 'listening']. By now, it was dark and very cold. At Ilngir camp, where the child cried, a cold and heavy fog or mist (*gun-gandum*) blanketed the camp and put out all the fires; everyone was lying down and shivering. Ngalyod had sent that cold wind.

Ngalyod went down along the mud and into it. Then he came up from the ground and, seeing the camp, coiled his body around the whole of it. He made a great noise like thunder and swallowed the child. Everyone began to run; but as each did, Ngalyod caught him or her on his backbone, tossed him into the air and caught him in his mouth, swallowing all of them in that way — everyone, and everything: the cold fires, the huts, food, digging sticks and spears, everything!

One small girl, Gominyamunya, *nyindjariwurig, ngalgamarang*, escaped. She climbed into a tree by herself and was very quiet, so Ngalyod did not see her. But after a while a mosquito bit her; she hit it very quietly so Ngalyod would not hear. He *did* hear, however, and swallowed her *and* the tree. All of this happened at Ilngir.

Ngalyod lay down there. He could not move properly: he had swallowed so much. He could only drag himself slowly along the ground, 'like a snake'. He went down along Wiul, close to the East Alligator River mouth [Amurag], and swam across. He jumped up at Ganyanbulul, his body stretched out behind him ['it was still coming']. He went into the jungle. He was too heavy and could not walk, so he lay down at Milyeri [Gagadju and Ngadug languages, mixed].

A large group of people [Ngadug, Amurag and Gagadju] were camped at Ngarulroidjuradj, on the western bank of the East Alligator. Among them were two young Ngadug men, Gawilub, and his mother's brother Mugulul: the first man was *nagamarang*, the other *nabulain*. They were throwing spears while out hunting. They came closer to Ngalyod. 'What's that white thing there?' they asked each other. 'All the different birds have come to look at it. What is it?' They ran back to their camp to get some 'clever men' and others. 'Come on! Come on! You want to look at this big one; it might be a Ngalyod. It is red and white, and all the birds are looking at it!' They felt the cold wind. The big men knew. 'He might be a Rainbow; he has eaten too many people, that way.' And the young men

said, 'You clever men, come and look this way!' All of them came to where
that Rainbow was: 'Might be a Rainbow!' The clever men went in front,
the young men behind. No women came with them. The clever men
looked: 'Yes, he has eaten too much, too many people.'

They all stood around that Ngalyod. 'Where do you come from?' they
asked, 'Mabur?' Ngalyod said nothing. 'Where do you come from?' they
asked again, 'Manggulalgudj?' [That is, a place at Croker Island, Marlgu
people.] But Ngalyod lay quietly, saying nothing. They asked him
whether he had come from the Marganala plain; they asked where he
had got the people to eat. Still he would not answer. Then they asked
whether he came from Waiara. He replied, '*Um*'.

They continued to question him about where he had swallowed the
people. They called out a long list of place names, and as they called each
name Ngalyod answered '*Um*'. But they did not believe him. At last they
called out 'Ilngir'. On hearing the name, he vomited them all out, at
Ngarulroidjuradj. [When the Snake vomited out all the people, most of
them were said to be still alive. No further reference was made to them.]
Then the people speared him and began cutting him up with axes. They
tried to eat some of the meat, but it was too salty and could be eaten only
by the old men. [It was said to have tasted like very salty fish.] They burnt
all of Ngalyod's bones.

However, a little piece of the Ngalyod's tail went off by itself. It went
into the ground and came out at Mang-gararawa springs, near Ganyanbulul point [a 'pocket' at the top, with a river running to the mouth of the
East Alligator; it is Gagadju and Ngadug country, as well as Wurilg, or
Uralg, close to Amurag]. That tail made itself into a long Ngalyod, and
lived there at those springs. ['You can hear him calling out. He no longer
seeks out people to swallow. He had enough! There is running water and
plenty of fish, and he eats those.']

This starts off as a conventional search-and-destroy mission on Ngalyod's
part, provoked by a crying child. The desperate attempts by the child's
half-mother are mentioned in other versions too; but are always unsuccessful. And mosquitoes foil people's efforts to escape in other stories as
well. But the main feature here is the assertion that Ngalyod is not
invulnerable. In this instance he has allowed himself to be *visibly*
vulnerable, through being greedy. But killing a Rainbow is a coastal, not
an inland theme.

The next example is also about killing a Rainbow Snake, and dealing
with the victims. Mangurug adopted a rather different style from her
usual story-telling procedure. We have included it very much as she told
it, without adding extra linkages or bridges. It was told to C. Berndt at

Oenpelli in 1950, and the main character, unnamed, is the Rainbow
Snake, Ngalyod, or Ngalmudj.

56. A DEFEATED RAINBOW STORY

She was coming along. [She reached] Margirru. She came to a small
creek. She was coming along. She came to a large creek. [She was making
places, and putting the place-names.] Ngudin-baidbi, Gainmud-djag,
Aaru, Maliiga, Mara-gurnba·, Yimin-djunin-dju, In-yarn-bain, Malar-
garlg. Wudi-nyambidj, there she slept. Yin-ganarr, Nawindjin. It was
there that she fell, at Nawindjin [and left a mark on the ground]. She got
up. She got up; at Yiluwa she fell down. Then she came through the
middle of some rocks. Ngandi-mariyin [she slept there for a long time],
Yuunidj [she slept there]. Wudi-nyambidj, again, Malwarug. She went
on. At Miya she fell down, when she heard a baby crying. [She slept at]
Aaldaa-ngidj, Moridj, Did-dorlgang ('Moon-got-up'). At Ngarda-walar
she ate them.

[The narrator, Mangurug, had already noted what she saw as the two
main points in this part of the story. She commented briefly on them in
discussion. The crying baby was a motherless 'orphan', and the Snake ate
him first. Then she ate all the other people in that camp. Mangurug
simply repeated the word *nguneng* (roughly, 'she ate') a couple of dozen
times.]

Two men came, two who called each other cross-cousins. They were
coming. They came. She was lying down, that Snake. They saw her, lying.
'Cross-cousin, that, lying down, Rainbow Snake! (Ngalmudj). Did she eat
them?' They were all camping at Mawolwid, those other people. The two
men went back to get them, and came up to them. 'She ate them, Ngalmudj!
She's lying there, we saw her! Supposing we go and kill her?' 'We'll give
those others time to get their breath. They went after goannas. There they
are, just coming.' 'Come on, all of you! We'll go and see [that creature
who] ate them!' 'Yes, let's go!'

They came and got their spears, and went to find her. They went, and
saw her lying down. 'She's dangerous, she might eat us!' they said. 'We'll
spear her [but maybe we'll miss] because she's dangerous! No matter,
we'll kill her!' Here, on her back, they were spearing her. 'There are
people in her belly! We might spear them!' They speared her [many
times] on the other side: they killed her. She lay quite dead. 'We'll cook
her and eat her, perhaps.' They looked her over. They emptied out her
inside organs completely, into the billabong, and there they were bathing,

those people who were strong, still living. Those who had died, they 'threw them away' [buried them]. Still they were bathing, those who were still living, and they were burying the others. The living, they were still washing them — still! Another five days went by, then another five days, when they did not go looking for honey or meat, but just lay down sleeping. They went, and after a long time they [some of them] climbed up [out of the water] on to the western bank. But still they were washing them, all the time, [Mangurug repeated the last phrase, in her Gun-winggu narrative, five more times.] They did not go after goannas or bandicoots, they just stayed in camp, stayed in camp.

Herself, that Snake who had eaten them, they chopped her up, and cooked her in an oven with pieces of hot termite mound. Men, women, children were eating, eating, that dangerous Snake. [But] those who were living, that she had eaten, they were just lying down — still, still, still [or, for a long, long time]. The sun was standing low in the sky, when they were still burying those who had died. They just stopped for a meal — all the time, all the time! For a short time they sat down, stayed sitting. . . Then they got up and were burying them, still emptying them out from the Snake, and burying them. They slept. Then they continued to empty them out and were burying them. They went on. When they had finished their meal they had a 'breather', sitting down. In the afternoon when the sun grew weaker, they were burying them. At sunset they stopped. For a while afterward, many of them lay dead, others were sleeping. Early in the morning they went, they were digging the ground, they were burying them; themselves they were burying them [the last part repeated seven times]; still they were burying them. Here, afternoon. They sat down. They were digging the ground. They went, they were burying them, there where they were eating that Snake, where she ate them [those others]. The sun grew weaker; they sat down. They were digging the ground, they were burying them. [The last part was repeated three times.] Sunset, they slept. Early next morning they were digging the ground. Afternoon, they sat down, they had a 'breather'. They were burying them. They went; the sun grew weaker; they slept. Early next morning they were digging the ground; they sat down; they were burying them. . .

Mangurug continued in this vein for quite a long time, in the same words. This was, she said, because the whole procedure took a very, very long time, and so many of the people the Snake had swallowed were dead and had to be buried. The ordinary process of putting dead bodies on mortuary platforms would not have worked in this case. There is no reference to the usual mortuary rites.

The next story, in the same vein, is more succinct, with a neater narrative line. It was told to R. Berndt at Goulburn Island in 1947.

57. THE FATE OF THE CANOE PADDLERS

This happened at North Goulburn Island a long time ago. Three men went out hunting turtle. A large Snake [called here Iwadbeid) appeared, swimming underneath the canoe and then like a waterspout — 'but different, like smoke'. It came up at Inag, east point (Ainag Point). The Snake began to ask for one of the three men: 'You give me one man to eat, because I'm hungry!' 'What are we going to do?' the men asked each other. They were very frightened. One man in the middle of the canoe said, 'Let us give him our turtle rope, turtle spear, paddles and baler shell — let us try this!' But the others said, 'If we do that, how will we be able to to get back to the shore?' The other man replied, 'We'll give those things to him, then we'll try to float back to that corner of the point, Ilyaru (Yilyaru).' So they agreed to do this. They gave that Snake all those things, and asked him, 'Is that enough?' The Snake shook his head: 'Not enough!' One of the men said, 'We'll give him the canoe, because it's not far to the shore and we can swim there.' 'Would you like the canoe?' they asked. But the Snake replied, 'No.' 'You want the canoe with the three of us?' they asked. And the Snake replied, 'Yes.' And he swallowed the lot.

The people on North Goulburn Island were waiting for the three men, and when the men did not return they thought they had come ashore elsewhere. So they waited another day. Then a man from Inag went across to Wulagbiridj on South Goulburn Island in a bark canoe, looking for them. There was no drifting canoe, no sign of the men, and the water was calm. He returned to Inag: 'Maybe something has happened!'

In the meantime the Snake went to Maliwur [No. 2 Sandy Creek]. He followed the creek [which is the Snake's track] to Sandy Creek Hill, Inganar, where the Snake was living. From there he could listen to people living on the Marganala plain, near Cooper's Creek, Gabal [plain]; he was listening for the cry of a child. He stood up to listen. 'Someone's crying there! I'll go to see those people, because I'm hungry!' He went toward the camps, stood up, and listened; went on a bit further, then stood up and listened again.

In the main camp, a child was crying. His parents were unable to stop him. He just went on crying. The Snake came closer and saw all the people. He coiled right round the camp, making a big ring with all the people inside. One of the men stood up: 'Look, there is a big thing here!' All the people were frightened. The man killed the child, afraid that its crying would attract the Snake, and that they would all be swallowed. He asked the Snake: 'Why do you want to come here?' The Snake listened for the child's cry, but heard nothing. He said: 'I heard a child crying — from Sandy Creek, I heard it. I want some of you.' They gave him the dead child. He swallowed the child. 'Is that all?' they asked. The Snake replied, 'No.' They gave him a live child. 'Is that all?' they asked. 'No.' They gave the Snake another, and then another. 'Enough,' they said. 'No,' said the Snake, 'I want all of you!' And the Snake swallowed all of them at that place, on the plain at Andalmulu.

Some of the people who were outside the encircling coils of the Snake escaped. One man climbed a tree and watched what happened. The Snake was 'full up inside' with people, and vomited up the canoe that he had first swallowed with the three men. The man saw the canoe, and he asked himself, 'Where has it come from?' So he brought the news from Andalmulu to Ross Point (Wamili), where he built huge fires that could be seen at Andjumu billabong on South Goulburn Island. The people there signalled to those living at Inag, and they came to Andjumu. The man who had seen the Snake vomit the canoe came over from Wamili, and told the story of what had happened at Andalmulu. And the man who had gone in search of the canoe and the three lost men said, 'That canoe may be from us. We were looking for it, but couldn't find it.' The man from Andalmulu said that the Snake had also vomited bones, rope, spears, paddles and a baler shell. On hearing this, the North Goulburn Island people came over from Madbalabigbin (Mawadbalabigbin) [Fletcher's Point, to Ross Point on the mainland] and they held a meeting. 'What are we going to do?' 'Is the Snake still there?' And the Andalmulu man replied: 'Yes, he is full of people: he can't move.'

They sent word by two men to Oenpelli. Another two messengers went to the South Alligator River, to the Gunandjan people. Another two went to Cape Don, and another two to Croker Island. They brought all the people together, and they all went to Andalmulu, where they killed that Snake. They cut him down the middle. All those people he had swallowed at Andalmulu were alive: they had not been digested, except for the first three.

Not so long ago there were enough accounts of canoes being lost at sea along the north Arnhem Land coast to make the danger seem only too real. In some cases, mythical and otherwise, one person loses the paddles or behaves in a way that threatens to overturn the canoe and cause the death of everyone in it. Then sorcery accusations are likely. (As in the case of the girl killed by a crocodile, in Myth 133, a sorcery victim is a danger to others in any situation. But sharks and crocodiles and other such creatures supposedly do not kill people unless they are *already* sorcery victims.) When there are no survivors of a canoe trip, other explanations are available. The travellers went too near such places as Poison Island, for instance. Or, the most likely cause of disaster, on the basis of such mythic precedents as the Aragaládi story (Myth 44), is the Rainbow.

In this story, the Rainbow behaves like a ruthless sea pirate, and refuses to accept any compromise. The crying child motif is approached in the same blunt fashion. It is not that the Snake is irritated by the sound of crying. He uses the sound to track down something he wants to eat because he is hungry. In that respect he resembles such malignant characters as Wirindji (Myths 91 and 92), and Biyubiyu (Myths 89 and 90). But the child's own relatives are in their own way just as ruthless. They are so afraid of the Snake that they are prepared to sacrifice the child to save their own lives. In short, the Snake is shown to be so malevolent that people are justified in killing him. And he turns out to be not only greedy, but as vulnerable as they are.

The next example of a Rainbow who plans to eat a crying child comes from a region some distance away from western Arnhem Land, south-west of Darwin on the Daly River. It was told to R. Berndt in 1946.

58. RAINBOW OUT-MANOEUVRED

Bulaloyi (Rainbow) lived at Anson Bay (Banagaya) in Wogaidj country, into which the Daly River flows. He/she heard a baby crying at *deg*-Dilg in Ngulugwong-ga territory. That Rainbow thought, 'I'll go and I'll eat that child.' So Rainbow started off, going through Wogaidj country on the western side of the Daly, attracted by the cries of the baby. As he went along, Rainbow made a creek.

At *deg*-Dilg, two women were making dilly bags. They had in front of them upright sticks on which the twine was rolled and drawn out as they plaited. The baby went on crying. The name of one of the women was Gabad, and it was her child.

Rainbow moved toward *deg*-Dilg and came out at a little billabong. He listened and heard the crying. He came down into country which was half Wogaidj and Maranunggu. He went farther down to a large round billabong, Galbu; he walked through the water, making that billabong. He continued to Magad-Galbu billabong. Then he climbed up a *djirami* Leichhardt fig tree and looked around. Looking in the direction of Dilg, he said, 'Ah, the baby is crying there!' He climbed down, and going underneath the grass came out at Bang-geri-magad billabong. Again he climbed a Leichhardt fig tree [now dead], and heard the child crying. He climbed down and made a long billabong at Banggeri [in Maranunggu country]. Then he went under the ground, came up half-way, and heard the cries from Dilg, which was now nearby. He went underneath again and came out, making a long zig-zag indentation [about three to four feet wide], 'like a creek'. He could hear the sound of the crying, and of voices.

There in the camp was Gabad sitting before her entwined stick, making her bag, with the child behind her. The other woman was kneeling before her stick, plaiting, while Wulgul [see Myth 186b] was copulating with her from behind.

Rainbow came near the hill at *deg*-Dilg and broke a road through it. He was close now, and lifted his head to survey the domestic scene. He was ready to swallow that baby.

'Ah, Rainbow is here!' said Gabad. As Rainbow bent his head forward, Gabad pulled out her dilly bag stick and, using it as a club, struck Rainbow on the head, breaking his neck. He lay there dead.

That Rainbow is still there as a rock. Gabad is there with her dilly bag, her stick and her child, as rocks; and the other woman and Wulgul are also there, as rocks, at *deg*-Dilg.

There are some interesting contrasts here. Most of the short myth is taken up with Rainbow's journey, over and under and through various kinds of vegetation and terrain and water-places, some of which he made. The small camp he was heading for, however, was almost static, focusing on the tranquil task of dilly bag making; Wulgul's action in enlivening the scene was so arranged as not to interfere with that task. It was a noisy place, however, with the sound of the child's crying audible over a great distance, and the more muted noise of voices. Gabad is implied to be a neglectful mother in this respect — not trying to quieten the child, and even turning her back on it. Unlike the women in Myths 46–49, she is preoccupied, not with dancing and singing, but with her bag-making.

But no comments were made about her being neglectful. And when the Rainbow actually arrives and prepares to eat the child, the tenor of events changes. It is Gabad who is alert enough to recognise the intruder and, in a burst of activity, to kill him single-handed. We are not told how large the Rainbow was, but he was aggressive and determined, not lethargic after eating other victims; yet it took only one woman to kill him, and not a crowd of armed men. Of course, he is said to have appeared *as* a Rainbow, not as an impersonal storm or flood, and was at least visible and accessible. Nevertheless, the final outcome was the same for the human beings concerned. They did not need to be drowned or swallowed. Perhaps their contact with the Rainbow was enough in itself to turn them into rocks.

In spite of the big rivers and more permanent sources of fresh water across the north of the continent, there are also sizeable dry stretches: scrub and bush, and rocks. Mythic characters who travel through the escarpment country of central Arnhem Land, or even along the edges of it, complain about being thirsty, and about hurting their feet on the sharp rocks. They do that too in parts of the Kimberley region of Western

Australia. Throughout the centre of the continent, however, the arid expanses are larger and likely to stay that way for much longer periods, waterholes tend to dry up more quickly, and soak-water supplies are correspondingly more crucial. Also, there are salt lakes that can look deceptively fresh, and some underground water is so highly mineralised, or salty, that it is virtually undrinkable.

Still following the Rainbow, we look at myths from a couple of regions that are away from the direct influence of the north-west monsoon, the rain-bearing force of the north and west. The first comes from Balgo, in the south-east of the Kimberleys and on the edge of the Great Sandy Desert sector of the Western Desert. It was told to R. Berndt in 1960.

59. RAIN-FALLING-DOWN

Wadi Waral, Rain-falling-down, a *djuburula* man, came from Nganggali [meaning clouds] out east, toward Yabuna side [Lake Mackay]. He went to Mundubanga soak [rain travelling, clouds only], and on to Balandjiri soak. Here rain commenced to fall and rivulets formed on the ground. He went on to Gimoyi soak. He was just lying there. He put his sacred *daragu* objects under his head to serve as a pillow, and rested.

After a time he went on to Nabagulang, where rain fell. Here, there was a soak. As a man, he was carrying all his *daragu*; he collected all the soak water and 'turned into' a cloud. As a cloud, he went on to Yaliyalu claypan. Then, travelling through the sky, he continued on and came down at Nganggali. Rain fell and formed a soak and water ran in every direction. Then he went on to Winba soak, where his lightning struck trees. On to Nabagulang [same place name as above, but a different site] — where rain was still falling. Then on to Bararibaru soak. Here lived a Guleyi or Rainbow Snake (*Woneyera*). Wadi Waral put rain there. Then he went to Djimari [second place of that name], where water from the rain flowed underground. Then on to Gura soak, where he slept, and then spread out all his *daragu* to dry. He stayed there for a long time. Then he recommenced his travels — to Giribaru soak and to Wanubulgu soak. Once more he turned into clouds and came to Ngalibi soak — where he remained.

The principal character here was not a snake, or a Rainbow, but he is identified even more closely with rain and lightning than are some of the Rainbow Snakes in this region. He went so far as to put rain at the place where a Rainbow Snake lived, but there is no record of the Rainbow's response. The assumption is that the sacred objects he was carrying were connected with rain and storm. But although he fluctuated between being a man (in human shape) and being a cloud, he himself did not turn into a Rainbow.

In the next myth there is an echo of a western Arnhem Land mythic sequence, where a great snake, hearing people dancing and singing, goes to look for them and swallows them. It was told to R. Berndt at Balgo in 1960.

60. WONEYERA SWALLOWS THE INITIATION GROUP

A Dreaming *djabaldjari* Water-Snake or Rainbow (Galbidu or Woneyera) lived at Gangunung, near Manggai and Luwana (Lake Lucas), where there was a large hill with spring water, running along Didjeral creek. He crawled to Gira, where there was a big cave with a spring. Then he turned back, and at Gundu he made holes with his tail; there is no water at this place.

At Gunabaru (or Gunabaureru), a large group of people were dancing for *malulu* initiation novices. The Snake heard them and went into a cave at that place, but before going into his hole he released wind from his anus [hence the name of the place]. He crawled from there to Wogarung rockhole, erected his head and looked over at the people assembled at Gunabaru. He went on a little farther, and at Nundiwiriwiri 'he made himself ready' by coiling himself and began to roll along ['like a tyre'] to Gulu. There was a big tree there. He stretched out his 'neck' — there was no water. Using the tree as 'a spring' he propelled himself, landing at Labilabi rockhole. The people had come there from Gunabaru. He seized them all, 'covering them up', and swallowed them.

All the people moved about inside the Snake's stomach. The Snake went back to one of his places and attempted to vomit them there. However, he vomited only their whiskers and body hair: and because of that, this place is named Djananga or Djanganga (whiskers): there is fresh spring, as well as salt, water here.

The Snake went on to Wogilbi creek, where he camped. Then he continued to Djimari [the place name refers to 'fat'; the fat 'fell off' inside the Snake] and then to Balgar [in salt country, no fresh water], and it was here that his stomach burst because he had swallowed too many people. But they remained inside the Snake, encased by his ribs. He continued to

Ngandu. There he vomited out some of the people and gave them to Daidjal [a non-poisonous Black Snake, with a distinctive mark on its back]. He went on to Gudugudu [where there is spring and salt water] and to Maidjaral swamp: here he lay down with stomach pains. He dragged himself into Rabi (Lake White); the rest of the people were still inside him. He went into the lake, where he remains to this day. The people emerged from the Snake, and they too are still there. They drink salt water: 'We can see their tracks, and the marks of their bodies; they don't come out into our country, they remain there!'

The snake did not say he was hungry as a reason for hunting down the initiation camp, or that he was annoyed by the sound of dancing or the singing that must have gone with it. It must have been an 'attraction of likeness'. In many initiation rites, the novices are said to have been swallowed by a great snake — as in the initiation rituals associated with Yulunggul (see Myth 36). The swallowing and vomiting in such cases symbolise death, or partial death, followed by rebirth to a new life. Here, as in the northern examples, the victims live on in spirit — except that this is not spelt out in regard to Daidjal. But it was facial and body hair, not bones, that the Rainbow vomited out at first — no rocky escarpment here!

Next, another myth from the same region (Balgo), where the Snake does not eat the people he is coming in search of. But there is a hint that, because the *maban* men could see him coming, they may have taken some magical action to avoid it. The myth was told to R. Berndt in 1960.

61. THE DEATH OF GULEYI

At Woneyera Hill near Old Balgo settlement [about seven to eight miles away], a Guleyi Snake emerged from his cave in the *djumanggani,* the Creative Era. [The crack through which he came may still be seen.]

The Guleyi came crawling along, coiling himself, erecting his head, and flying. He carried water in his coils. He went to Gagurudindja claypan, near Yabuna. All the *malulu* initiation group were singing there. They were Gugadja-speakers. Among them were 'clever' men (doctors), who could 'see' with the help of their *maban* 'pearlshells' that the Snake was coming [actually, at this stage, there appear to be two. Sons belonging to this *malulu* group were still alive in 1960; for example Fred Imyau, a *djabaldjari* man at Sturt Creek, whose father was Lolgu, a *djungurei* man: probably a mythic projection into the present.]

Guleyi was coming toward them: some of the *malulu* novices were sleeping, and some were singing. He (or they) came close, and one Guleyi fell on top of the people. They all jumped up and climbed on to him, and 'rode' him. Guleyi took them into the sky; *bulidra* hail fell from him. The *maban* men were also riding the snake; they were cutting open his belly, and his bones fell to the ground. The rest of his body fell back in coils onto the ground: the coils extended to their hole. The men remained on the snake all night. In the morning he 'settled down' dead. His bones were scattered all over this area. His ribs, head and hide [skin] are all there and may be seen — they are hard, 'like stone'. [Donkey Man said he visited this place as a child and played with the hide — hard skin, 'like a motor tyre' and bones heaped up like a hill.] None of the *malulu* was killed; they continued afterward with their singing.

The main features here are the association with an initiation camp and with *maban* men; the fact that ordinary people as well as *maban* men were riding the snake, or snakes; and the snake's death, killed by the *maban* men. The people concerned were not killed, nor even hurt. They just went on with their ritual. In one sense, the episode itself appears to be part of the initiation proceedings, and the esoteric interpretations of that do not come into this version. The snake's carelessness (or deliberate action?) in falling on the initiation camp is unusual too. But at one level the myth accounts for the strange material to be found at this site, which was not a closed or secluded place: the man telling the story recalled playing there as a child among the snake's 'remains'.

Next we return to the theme of 'snake swallows man', but with a difference. It is complicated by a fight between snakes. It was told to R. Berndt in 1960.

62. TWO KINDS OF SWALLOWING

A *djabanangga* man named Gadabana went out in search of a dog, taking his spears and spear-thrower. He tracked the dog to Milga. At this place lived a *djagamara* Rainbow Snake who had come from Yirandal claypan, near Yabuna. This snake was also shape-changing. For instance, he decorated his body with emu feathers and turned into a *mingadu* bandicoot, then turned back again into a snake. He was a quiet snake. On his way to Milga he came to Wilgibaganu where there is a large tree under which he rested. Looking back, he saw a man walking quickly along near Walarindja claypan. He followed the man all the way to Milga, and the tracks the two of them made formed a creek. This 'quiet' snake went into his hole at Milga, and nearby is a red-seed *wirdjirgi* tree that is his shade.

[Back to the main story.] The dog reached Milga, drank water, and rested under the *wirdjirgi* tree. The man who was being followed by the Rainbow was Gadabana. He came into Milga and speared the dog. The dog cried out, disturbing another Snake who was far from being 'quiet'. He emerged angrily from his hole, seized the man and swallowed him.

The big 'quiet' Snake felt that something was wrong. He, too, emerged, and saw the other Snake swallowing the man. Then he became angry. The two snakes fought for Gadabana. Other dangerous snakes joined the one which had swallowed him. The fight went on for a long time. At last the quiet snake defeated all the others. The snake that had swallowed the man lay on the ground, exhausted. The quiet snake 'pulled out' the man and took him away to Walarindja [see above], and placed him on the creek bank. He wanted to revive the man. To do that he swallowed him and then vomited him 'alive', so that he fell at Walarindja claypan.

In that vicinity lived the Manggugrada people who 'ride this snake', as *maban* men or traditional Aboriginal doctors do. These people found Gadabana, and because they were *maban* men and healers they looked after him. He had been for a long time inside the snake's belly, and was 'too wet'. They arranged fires all around him, and massaged his body with warm ashes, so that he became well again. Then the Manggugrada people took him to his own relatives at Landa-landa claypan, close to Walarindja. The quiet snake went back to his home at Milga.

One interesting point here is that it is the Rainbow Snake who is 'quiet', friendly and helpful to a human being, as contrasted with another great snake who actually swallows the man. But the quiet snake succeeds in overcoming the swallowing snake and his supporters. And he uses the swallowing device as a means of reviving, not killing him; for that to succeed, the snake must vomit him out alive. However, that was not enough by itself. There had to be help from *maban* men; and the snake dropped him at the right point for that. The men telling the story added that Gadabana became white in colour from being too long inside the snake's body — 'his skin was burnt': it was only after a couple of months that he returned to his normal dark colouring.

Next, it is only at the end of their story that two Wonambi, sometimes called Rainbow Snakes, reveal their power to give or withhold water. In swallowing people, their concern was with producing a different kind of liquid — turning people into nectar. This story comes from the Great Victoria Desert sector of the Western Desert, and was told to R. Berndt in 1941 at Ooldea, near the transcontinental railway line and north of the Great Australian Bight.

63. SHAPE-CHANGING WONAMBI

Two Wonambi (*ganba*, snake, Djidara), father and son, slept at Dabidi waterhole. During the night the young man walked away while his father was asleep, to collect *ngilwer* wild honey. [Both of them were powerful men, *gingin*. When they came to Dabidi they changed themselves into Wonambi, because that monstrous snake is associated with *gingin*.]

While he was getting wild honey, the son came upon a group of men and women. Next morning he 'drove' them toward his father, who was sitting in his camp at another place, also called Dabidi, close to the Dabidi where he had slept. He swallowed all the people, one by one. Then his son moved down a creek to another small waterhole, where he himself swallowed a number of people.

Later, after the two Wonambi had masticated the people, they vomited them here and there, so that the resulting substance fell on all the flowers of the *wabudi* bush. Now, in the mornings, after the *wabudi* flowers have been filled with dew, their nectar (the *ngilwer*) can be collected in wooden dishes.

The two Wonambi went up and down the creek bed collecting *ngilwer* — and the creek bed itself is their track. They remained in the country as Wonambi, and did not change back to *gingin*. When they smell strangers coming to Dabidi, they drain the waterholes dry, but when their own 'countrymen' come to this place, there is always water for them.

Men, occasionally women, with special powers were believed to have shape-changing abilities, but for this father-son pair the change seems to have been more than a task-oriented effort or a ritual exercise. It was more like the realisation of a deep-seated potential — and it was permanent. The change in itself did not explain why they ate people who do not seem to have done anything to provoke them. Rather, the suggestion is that it was the destiny of these particular people to become nectar, and, as in western Arnhem Land, the Rainbow helped them to achieve that destiny. They did not actually eat their human victims, but used them (so to speak) for 'juice-extraction'. The sweet nectar that resulted from the mixture of human remains and *wabudi* flowers was a welcome part of a traditional Desert diet. There is no further reference to these Wonambi as eating people, merely as depriving strangers of water, which could of course in certain conditions amount to the same thing — death. And they now protect the people of their own country in regard to that vital resource.

The two Wonambi in the next story are quite passive until the final scene. Then, instead of remaining in the place to which they were taken, they shape the course of a river as they make their way to the sea. The story was told to R. Berndt at Ooldea in 1941.

64. TWO WONAMBI ARE STOLEN

A large group of Geniga (spotted native Cat) were camped at Beril-beril waterhole; nearby was a lake in which lived two Wonambi. One day Minma Murulu, Marsupial Rat Woman, came from the north to this place. She was carrying on her head a very large wooden fish containing water. When she saw the Geniga camp, she hid her dish in the bush so the Geniga women would not see it. Coming into the camp, she found that they were all out hunting except for one old Geniga woman. Murulu sat down with her, and offered to delouse her. The old Geniga woman agreed, and lay down on her stomach with her head in Murulu's lap. As Murulu set to work, the Geniga woman began to feel drowsy, and fell asleep. Gently Murulu moved her head aside and got up. Walking over to the bush she picked up her dish and carried it to the swamp's edge: the dish was empty, because she had drunk the remaining water in it before coming into Beril-beril. She put the dish at the edge of the lake, filling it with all the water and everything else, including the two Wonambi, the ducks and the other creatures that were there. She emptied it completely leaving only wet mud. She left the place and headed back to the north.

The other Geniga returned to find their lake empty. It was nothing more than a swamp. Crying in rage, they found Murulu's tracks and went after her. She kept going, carrying the dish, coming eventually to Murulu country where the nests of these creatures are. She placed her dish on top of a clump of spinifex, instead of firmly on the ground. But she was diverted by the *goga-murulu* nests, and started to hunt. The dish with its contents capsized, the water flowed out, and one of the Wonambi swallowed her.

This water is said to have formed the Fitzroy River in the Kimberleys. One especially interesting point is that this myth was told at Ooldea, by men who had heard of the area but had not seen it for themselves. The Wonambi swam toward the sea, forming the river's banks, and as they swished their tails they caused the curves in the river so that today it meanders like the track of a snake. So, all the lake water from Beril-beril eventually found its way into the sea, as did the Wonambi. The Geniga who chased Murulu were also drowned, and those who remained at Beril-beril died of thirst.

The country of the *murulu* nests was said to be located at the source of the Fitzroy River in Wayungari country. (Tindale 1940: 211, places the so-called Waiangara 'tribe' near Lake Hazlett: however, the story reference is probably to Malan, Lake Gregory.) There are also details not included here, about the people who lived in Wayungari country.

Large wooden dishes for carrying water and other things were traditionally a feature of Desert domestic life, and this story does not account for their introduction — on the contrary, strangely enough. It was evidently an enormous dish, in true mythic style, but (again, in true mythic style) not too much for her to carry over a long distance, the two Wonambi and ducks and water included. The Wonambi, however, did not swallow her when she was removing or transporting the water, only when she reached the appropriate mythic site. There is no reference to her being vomited, or surviving in any other specific form as an individual being, although perhaps the implication is that her spirit remained with the other Murulu characters (suggested by the nests) in that country. She herself and the Geniga people were in human shape to begin with, though the myth does not spell that out; the Wonambi were not. And this is one of the relatively few myths which end with people dying of thirst, a fate which overtook some traditional Desert dwellers from time to time in seasons of drought.

As one sequence in a large saga, two mythic men make a Wonambi snake and also, separately, his 'vocal' equipment. They themselves also make rain. The myth was told to R. Berndt at Ooldea in 1941.

65. MAKING OF A WONAMBI

The Two Men, the Wadi Gudjara, Yungga [in this case called Ngindjiri] and Djimbi, came from the west to Borli, where there was a Wonambi. They had killed a possum (*waiuda*). They pulled out its entrails and put them to one side while they cooked and ate the meat. Then they made a young *djidara* Wonambi out of the coiled entrails and put it into Borli rockhole. They also kept the bladder, which they cleaned and blew up, tying it at both ends. They put this in the rockhole too, keeping it in place with a shield.

They left these things at Borli and went to a place in the bush, where they sat down, and each of them made a *walina* returning boomerang out of mulga wood. They returned to Borli, looked into the rockhole, and saw that their shield had been 'thrown' aside. They looked around for the *djidara* Wonambi. At last they saw tracks, and followed them. By this time the young *djidara* had grown into a large Wonambi.

Coming to a particular place [unnamed], they made rain and wind so they could see the Wonambi's tracks clearly. [The wind had smoothed over the surface of the ground, while the rain made it clean and damp so that new tracks were easily visible. Moreover, the rain filled two claypans, which are now lakes.] They went on a bit farther and saw the Wonambi's tracks. Then they came to a place where the snake had been lying, eating mallee-birds (*djinbun*). This place is now a long, straight sandhill, Dali-indjil. They followed the tracks to another sandhill. Djimbi walked by himself to the right, while Ngindjiri danced and sang:

djunda djiberi manman-manu
Legs (thighs) dancing backward.

And he threw his boomerang toward a mallee tree (*mindel*).

The Wonambi was just disappearing into a rockhole. He was half-way in when Ngindjiri threw a boomerang at him, not to kill, but only to frighten him. Djimbi, however, was greedy — he wanted to kill and eat the snake. He threw his boomerang, but missed. By this time, the Wonambi was completely in the hole. Djimbi tried to dig him out, but as fast as he dug, Ngindjiri covered up the hole. There is a big rockhole at this place, Wandumaruri, where the Wonambi lives: he is in a deep cave, and cannot emerge. Near this place there is a *golgu* mulga tree, and Djimbi sang:

golgu lalal bungu djindjindji gadarara
Hitting the tall mulga, singing.

They went on, encircling the area, to reach Gadala, a place with small holes and *gudana* grass. Through these holes one can look down to the deep cave with water where the Wonambi lives; the cave connects with Wandumaruri. The Two Men returned to Borli, and sang:

gadadanga dabi wonggana gadadanga dabi
Roaring, talking sound from the cave.

This refers to the Wonambi at Borli, roaring. The Wonambi was made out of the entrails by the Two Men, and it is the bladder they left that makes the sound.

As they came nearer they heard scraping sounds. It was Wonambi in his cave underneath, with his scales scraping its sides. Ngindjiri sang:

gudana budanudanu bun-gana birun-gadi
Among the grass, [Wonambi] scraping himself.

[At Wandumaruri, the water level never varies. The water is evidently mineralised; the word *maruri,* as part of the place name, refers to its purgative qualities.]

At Borli, the Two Men sang:

> *gudidji yalwuludu linmuru linmurudju gudidji yalwuludu*
> Shield, holding it down.

The reference is to the shield they had placed earlier, handle upward, on the bladder.

When they could not find the tracks of the Wonambi, they sang:

> *djina-ngalangu lidia-lidia djina-ngalangu*
> Looking for his [Wonambi's] tracks.

And when they made rain in order to see the Wonambi's tracks, they sang:

> *djindjira wibuwibulu djindjira wanda-nadi*
> Lakes filling with water.

The Two Men are widely known throughout the Western Desert and in other areas as well, under a variety of names. Some of their exploits and attributes are secret-sacred. Other myths where they are central figures are 'open', as this one is. An unusual feature here is that they actually made a Rainbow Snake. Because the snake had grown from the entrails of an edible creature, a possum, Djimbi may have felt justified in wanting to kill and eat him, but the comment in the myth is that Djimbi was 'greedy'. Possums are mythically important in other ways too, as reported in other stories about them. The disagreement between the Two Men is especially interesting if they are regarded as two parts or two manifestations of *one* man.

After the telling of this myth, the narrator said that this Wonambi does not hurt his own 'countrymen'. An example was said to be the case of Billy Mandjina and another man from Fowler's Bay, who went down to Borli with buckets to get water. They reported that Wonambi's head appeared and almost swallowed them: they dropped their buckets and ran away. Later, countrymen of this Wonambi retrieved the buckets without harm to themselves.

Beliefs and traditions about Rainbow Snakes are not always spelt out in story form. In some circumstances, a few words are enough. 'That place is dangerous. Rainbow is there!' Or, 'Something is there, might be a Rainbow!' Or, 'That's where a snake (or, 'that snake') ate some people!' Or, 'If that ground is disturbed (as in mining), something terrible might happen to us all!' The story, or some of it, might be filled out in other settings — told as a story. In any case, statements that have some bearing on it are likely to be made in other ways: through bark paintings, or rock art, or ground paintings, or ochred body designs; in dramatic actions as in ritual, or songs, or reports of personal experience. None of these media, including myths and stories, could tell 'the whole story' by themselves. The total picture, on this as on other topics, has to be drawn from all of them. The information that was available traditionally in any one region was open to changes from within, but it was also open to changes from outside, through the interchange of songs and stories and ideas (for instance) between neighbouring groups, or during larger gatherings on ritual occasions.

It would be hard to pin down the Rainbow Snake as a mythic character bounded by any one locality or region. This is not a matter of there being varying perspectives on a specific mythic personage. Rather, in one sense there are many Rainbow Snakes. Even those few who have personal names (other than place names) are not distinctively identifiable to the extent that most other characters are.

As for appearance, there is basic agreement that a great snake is involved, but other features vary. In western Arnhem Land, for instance, reference is often made to 'horns', one at each side of the snake's head, to 'whiskers' (when it is a male), and to the dazzling light from the snake's eyes. But mostly it is the sound of the snake's approach, rather than the sight, that is mentioned in stories. The victims are so overcome by what is happening to them that they have only a vague vision of 'who' might be doing it. Apart from the sight and the feel of rising waters, trees falling and their belongings being washed away, they hear the noise of rushing flood-streams or tides, and the roar of the wind like the combined 'voices' of many bees, or like a huge bush-fire speeding toward them. That noise is sometimes contrasted, in myths, with the stillness and quietness later on when all is over, when the bones have turned into rock. At some sites a pool of clear water reveals, deep down and unmoving, rocks that were once the domestic belongings of the people who had lived there. On the other hand, in bark paintings from and around western Arnhem Land, the Rainbow Snake is a favourite subject, and artists 'telling a story' in ochres through that medium present a wider assortment of shapes and of details than is revealed in the word-pictures of myth.

In a different physical environment, people who came to Ooldea from the Great Victoria Desert in the late 1930s and early 1940s spoke about Wonambi, the great snake of those regions. One manifestation, at Wandu waterhole in spinifex-grass country north of Ooldea, was said to have a huge mouth with sharp teeth, big 'shoulders', and a mushroom-shaped head, and to swallow children whole. He was multi-coloured, and the noise he made was a loud blowing sound, sometimes like the clapping of hands. In general, as well as being associated with water, Wonambi was held responsible for whirlwinds. He also lives in the sky. Two stars are his eyes, thunder is his voice, the rainbow is his reflection, and he sends rain. The rainbow beginning in one direction is Wonambi starting his journey across the sky, until his whole track is bright, like the full rainbow. But on earth Wonambi can be dangerous. Two people with withered legs were said to be survivors of Wonambi attacks — bitten, but not killed. When new arrivals from the central ranges came south to Ooldea they were alarmed by what they thought was a giant snake with blazing eyes advancing toward them across the Nullarbor Plain: by night, the trans-continental train was visible for many hours as it approached along the almost-straight railway line. But in more conventional and more familiar circumstances as well as new ones Wonambi, under his various regional names, continues to be a force throughout the Western Desert area, as far as the fringe of the Kimberleys in Western Australia. And there he links up, or merges, with other counterparts or Rainbow manifestations.

Across the sub-tropical north of the continent the connection between snakes and storms is expressed more vigorously and consistently, if only because of the nature of the weather patterns in these regions. On the north-west coast the powerful Wondjina mythic characters, variously depicted on the rocky walls of their sites, are very closely linked with the Rainbow Snake. They share a common concern for the replenishing of water supplies through rain, the movement of tides, and the cyclonic storms of the Wet season; with spirit children, and the general fertility of the land and its inhabitants. The same concern extends to east and north-eastern Kimberley where the Rainbow Snake has rain-and-flood-making powers, pearlshells, and fertility within his orbit, but was traditionally also regarded as a law-giver. In the Port Keats area south-west of Darwin, the Rainbow has water and spirit children and fertility associations, though the Snake Woman also has spring-water responsibilities. In north Queensland, in his destructive involvement with cyclonic storms and floods, the Rainbow is actively linked with the taipan and other deadly or dangerous snakes. We have seen something of the Rainbow's ubiquitous presence in western Arnhem Land, and something of the Yulunggul connection. But a journey in search of Rainbows would take us Australia-wide.

The impact and force of the Rainbow Snake image have extended its range to include, at least partially, other great snakes who in the past had their own local domains. They need not be called Rainbows to be included within that ambience. Yulunggul and his individually distinct north-eastern colleagues are not the only ones. Even, for instance, the great northern Aranda serpent of Emianga can be perceived to have something in common: in his case, not storms, but a deep pool from which he emerged and in which he now lies coiled eternally. But his exploits included the swallowing of people and material things on a scale not matched by most Rainbow Snakes, and his final vomiting-out sequence produced something much more unusual and sacred than bones or nectar (Strehlow 1971: 158–65).

The swallowing-and-vomiting theme is, obviously, not confined to Rainbows. The snake-in-nature behaviour of pythons, however, is only a starting point for considering such accounts. What matters is the way the theme is handled and interpreted in the myths of various regions, and in the religious rituals that include it. We have used the term 'vomit' rather than the more important-sounding 'regurgitation', because regurgitation implies the return of what was swallowed in the same or almost the same form: in many, if not most, cases that is not what happens. In one instance there was, supposedly, no prior swallowing. In the account of the Rainbow as creator, noted at the beginning of this chapter, the Rainbow gave birth to the first people by vomiting them out, and then licked them dry with her tongue.

Rainbow Snake stories, and others like them, allow scope for their narrators to expand on the images they conjure up: the fury of cyclonic winds or violent seas and the terror and the helplessness of the victims, even where they initially attempt to defy the Rainbow or refuse to accept their fate; or the mystery of deep pools, even those that do not reflect the rainbow or are not explicitly associated with it. Rainbow Snakes, more consistently than others, symbolise the destructive *and* beneficent forces of nature, not quite unpredictable but potentially so. Almost primeval, territorially mobile in their various manifestations, they have a special place in the mythic list of 'who's who'. We have met some of these manifestations in other chapters, and there is still much more to be said about them.

CHAPTER FOUR

ALSO THERE FROM THE BEGINNING

So, even at the beginning of the creative era the land was already alive. Different beings were moving about, or in the process of settling down at sites that were to become specifically associated with them. Transformations were going on; new life-forms were emerging. The great creative beings were adjusting their own physical shapes, and setting in train the first human populations as well as many of the natural species. Some of the natural species were there to begin with, in non-human forms, and the great mythic characters encountered them or observed them or used them on their travels. As we saw in Chapter 3, most of the huge mythic snakes were invariably in snake form, or underwent that transformation early in the creative era. But numerous other characters were there too, in human or partly human shape, although not identified as truly human.

These are the characters often labelled in English as 'spirits', a term that is too vague and too wide in scope to have much meaning — but then, both of those features (vagueness, wide scope) can be attributed to some of these characters themselves. They can be invisible, can be there and yet not there, can appear to be like ordinary human beings until something happens to unmask them, and the terms used for them even within one region may be loosely defined or interchangeable.

It is such characters that we are concerned with in this chapter: not monsters in the shape of giant dingoes or other creatures, but those who in at least some respects resemble human beings and interact in various ways with them. Even those who treat people as a food resource seem to be regarded more as predatory cannibals than as non-human carnivores, even though the dividing line between these is blurred. Specific labels aside, they range from Dreaming or 'little-bit Dreaming' beings who have 'always been there' at their particular sites, to the ghosts of dead humans. In a number of regions the ghost aspect of a dead person is believed to remain in and around his or her old haunts for an unspecified period, perhaps achieving a sort of immortality in that form. Some spirits have 'power'. Some ghosts, as in western Arnhem Land, also have 'power', which they can pass on, individually, to living relatives who can thus become healers or doctors, or acquire their own personal little Rainbow Snakes that they can use in sorcery.

The multitude of spirit characters (to stay with this general label) throughout the continent show the same mixture of similarities and divergences that mark other aspects of Aboriginal culture. Out of the thousands of possibilities in this respect, we have selected a few from the same areas that we have been looking at in other chapters. One noticeable point is that none of our examples is whimsical or playful. That is not to say that, traditionally, there were no such characters. But perhaps they have become more popular or appropriate in the more recent past — for example, where Aboriginal people have been under greater pressure from outsiders, and children grow up learning about fairies or goblins or 'little people'. Potentially frightening characters can persist in such circumstances too, of course, and it is not only missionaries who have chosen the label 'devil' or 'debil-debil' to refer to them.

In the Western Desert, *mamu* is one of the most widespread names for an assortment of non-human and potentially hostile, or at least unpredictable, spirit beings. There are other words in some areas, and also other named spirit characters, but *mamu* figure prominently in many stories and songs, anecdotes, and reports of personal experiences. Their roots in the land go back to the creative era, and they are said to have had direct dealings with major as well as minor mythic personages.

The following four stories concern the Western Desert *mamu*; the first three are Andingari, told to R. Berndt in 1941, and the fourth, Gugadja, is from Balgo (1960). Note the special *mamu* characteristic of killing their victims by biting them.

66. A BOY OUTWITS A *MAMU*

A Dreaming Didji [meaning child, in this case a boy] went out into rocky country, east of the Warburton Range, where he saw the tracks of a *ngindagu*, varanus lizard. To the west of that range a large group of *mamu* was camping with their headman Djindjindji.

The boy was hunting kangaroo, and walking along he saw a fire from the *mamu's* camp, but he did not know they were *mamu*. He came into their camp and saw that they, too, had caught kangaroos. They gave him some meat as a sign of friendship, and he reciprocated.

Later, Djindjindji directed some *mamu* men to go out kangaroo hunting and to take the boy along. He expected the boy to be killed during the hunt. One *mamu* went with the boy. Each of them carried two spears. They went a long way, until they saw two kangaroos sitting in the shade. The *mamu* told the boy to sit down and wait for him. The boy gave him his spears, but the *mamu* did not take them. The boy watched the *mamu* go sneaking along, and saw first one kangaroo, then the other jump and fall down dead, but he could not see how they were killed because the dust from their struggle obscured his vision. When he came up to them, he saw the *mamu* rubbing his teeth trying to remove blood from them. [He had been biting the kangaroos.] The boy noticed that both kangaroos had been bitten on the throat. He realised then that he was in the company of a *mamu*.

The *mamu* built a large fire, and while they were waiting for it to burn down to coals, they sat quietly together. When it was ready for cooking, the *mamu* dug out a hole among the coals and threw in the kangaroo guts. Then he told the boy to throw in the big kangaroo, so that it would fill the hole he had dug. He planned to push the boy into the fire. The boy replied that the animal was too heavy and he could not throw it. So the *mamu* stood up to throw it in. But the boy was close behind him, and as he lifted it up to throw, the boy pushed him on to the fire instead. Then the boy raked the hot coals over the *mamu's* body, killing him. Later on he removed the body from the fire and placed it alongside the two kangaroos, after cutting off the kangaroo tails. Then he hurried away.

From a distance, Djindjindji saw the smoke from the fire and waited for the return of the *mamu* who had gone with the boy. But no-one came. At last, most of the *mamu* set off in search of him. They followed the tracks of the *mamu* and the boy to the fire. They saw their friend's body and mourned over him. Then they cooked him and the two kangaroos and ate them all.

In the meantime, other *mamu* from the same group had gone in search of the boy. They followed his tracks but could not catch him, so they returned home. But Djindjindji continued on by himself. The boy had already got to his own camp, where his own people were. The next morning Djindjindji arrived, but sat to one side. The people saw him, and built a large fire at the centre of their camp. He looked about for the boy; the others did nothing. At last Djindjindji located the boy, and chased him around the camp. The other men arranged themselves to form two double parallel lines, leaving a path to the fire. They had placed themselves in such a way that Djindjindji could not see the fire. As the boy reached the men, with the *mamu* following close behind him, they opened their ranks. The boy ran through toward the fire, then dodged aside, but Djindjindji fell into the fire and was burnt to death.

Two features here provide clues to the relations between *mamu* and human beings. One is that superficially they *can* look very similar: the boy was unable at first to distinguish between them and ordinary men and women. The other is that they are basically different. The identifying signs can be in appearance, for instance, or in some form of behaviour. It was not until the boy saw the blood on the *mamu's* teeth and the bitten throat of the kangaroo that he knew what he was up against. Also, although *mamu* do on occasion outwit human beings (mythic characters) they are sometimes portrayed as being rather gullible, as in this case.

67.　THE WALLABY DECOY (2)

Native Cat Man, Wadi Geniga [white-spotted, bushy tail], came from Beiling waterhole north of Ooldea, travelling north-west to Mamudu waterhole. He arrived quietly, not showing himself. When he saw an old *mamu* woman camping there, he retraced his steps and made a detour around Mamudu. The old woman went out to collect *wandiri* grass seeds in her wooden dish, and returned to her camp. She warmed the seeds over a fire, at the same time winnowing them with quick movements. Then she began to grind them on a wooden platter, preparing flour to make damper. She camped there all the time doing just that — collecting seeds and making damper.

In the meantime, Geniga had walked to a small rockhole where he speared a female *gabidji* [a small wallaby]. Cutting her up, he found a young one in her pouch. He put the young *gabidji* at the back of his head, using it as a hair pad and binding it up like a bun. [That is, similar to the hair-bun usually worn by initiated men in the Western Desert.] It was completely hidden. Then he went on toward the west where a large group of Geniga was camped. He told them to wait there until he returned with another group of them. Their idea was to set off on a 'war' *wanmala* expedition, to kill the *mamu* woman. Geniga went on to the other group and told them about this plan. They set off to meet the first group. When they were half-way there they camped and decorated themselves with feathers in their hair, and white clay and red-ochre body patterning. They left that place and joined the others, who had also decorated themselves. [Then they performed a series of *wanmala* rites, not outlined here.]

The men set off on their *wanmala*, while all the women remained in the camp. When they were about two miles away from Mamudu they sat down together. They sang all night. They re-ochred themselves and straightened their spears, sharpening and replacing the single barbs. About twenty older men carried bundles of spears; the young men took only their spear-throwers and clubs. They camped close to Mamadu and sent the first Geniga, the leader, to see whether the old woman was still there. She was. He went back and told the men to get ready. Then he returned to Mamudu. Sitting down, he unwound his hair-bun, took out the small *gabidji*, and put it inside the woman's wind-break.

As she was grinding her seed, she heard the sound of a *gabidji*, and looked round to see where it was coming from. She got up, saw it, and threw her grinding stone at it, but missed. She tried several times, without success. At about sundown she went into the nearby bush to camp without a fire, afraid that something was wrong. But the *gabidji* continued to make a noise. She got up and chased it around the waterhole.

Wadi Geniga was watching. He waved his spear-thrower from side to side, attracting the attention of the *gabidji*; it came toward the *wanmala* group, with the *mamu* woman following it. The *wanmala* party surrounded her, all throwing their spears, from every direction. The spears struck her in the back, but she did not fall, just went on chasing the *gabidji*. At last, however, she fell, and died. She was metamorphosed as a rock.

Wadi Geniga picked up the *gabidji* and replaced it in his hair-bun. The other Geniga smelt the blood that poured from her spear wounds, but that blood was poisonous and they all died. They can be seen today as a number of granite rocks, with the *mamu* rock nearby. Wadi Geniga went to the south-east, where he met Moon Man (Wadi Bera) and fought with him. [See Myth 170.]

The instinctive reaction on the part of Geniga was to kill the *mamu* woman, who was potentially dangerous to all human (mythic) beings. (Even after she was dead, the fumes of her poisonous blood affected all the other Geniga.) To defeat her, the aid of other Geniga was needed. (The ritual they performed is noted in R. and C. Berndt 1943: 62–66.) The *gabidji* decoy distracted the *mamu* and made her less cautious than she normally would have been, even though she feared that something was wrong. The next myth concerns the death of the *mamu* leader, Djindjindji.

68. THE DEATH OF DJINDJINDJI AND THE *MAMU*

The Two Men, known generally as the Wadi Gudjara, Yungga and Djimbi, both Goannas, were travelling north when they came to a large tree containing an eaglehawk *(waldja)* nest. They leaned their spears against the tree and climbed up. As they were about to remove the two eaglets from the nest they heard a man's voice: 'Leave them, they're mine!' Astonished, they looked around: 'Where did the voice come from?' And they saw a *mamu* man, Djindjindji, the leader of all the *mamu*. He said that, although the eaglets were his, he would help them to get the birds. So they became friends. The *mamu* said he wanted the feathers to use in a ceremony (an *inma*), which he would show them, and they could have the meat.

Djindjindji took the Two Men to Gadjara waterhole, where many *mamu* were camping. He left them nearby, asking them to wait. In the camp, he told the other *mamu* that he had brought two fat men whose meat would make good eating. But first, he said, before they killed the Two Men, they would 'make an *inma*' that night. During the ceremony and while the visitors were off their guard, then the *mamu* would 'bite' them.

The Two Men remained in the bush outside the camp while the *mamu* prepared for the *inma*. Djindjindji decorated himself with the eaglehawk feathers and down. When it was dark, the Two Men were brought in. They sat a little apart from the singing men on the *inma* ground. All the *mamu* were there: men, women and children. Then the *mamu* sang:

> *Djindjindji guyarulu*
> *walga-dunu buyarureri*
> Djindjindji [and the *mamu*]
> Decorating with green marking.

And then:

> *wara-nangu bilbu-bilbu*
> *bidjangu wara-nangu*
> [He] saw them first,
> Saw them [being dragged along]

The *mamu* all danced the *ganduni* dance around a large fire in the middle of the ground. When the Two Men heard the second song, they became apprehensive. Moreover, the *mamu* were beginning to close in on them. The Two Men, sitting by themselves, untied their *garalba* pearlshells, and each bit off a small piece from his and spat it out [Pearlshells are traditionally associated with rain and with Rainbow Snakes. Ritually spitting out little pieces of pearlshell is, in some areas, believed to bring rain.] As they did so, rain began to fall. Immediately the *mamu* stopped dancing and rushed into a big cave nearby, their usual sleeping place.

The rain continued to fall heavily. When all the *mamu* were asleep, the Two Men went out to the bush nearby and used their stone axes to cut a large supply of mulga branches. They tied these together, making five bunches, and 'warmed' them over a fire they had built in a sheltered place. Then they brought the fire over to the mouth of the *mamu* cave and placed the leafy bunches on top. Soon billows of smoke emerged and the Two Men, with the aid of mulga branches, 'blew' or directed the smoke into the cave. The could hear the *mamu* inside the cave calling and trying to escape. The smoke surged along the roof of the cave until it reached the back where Djindjindji was sleeping. In the uproar he awoke and shouted to the others to get out of the cave. But they could not: the smoke was becoming dense and they were suffocating. Djindjindji rushed forward, knocking aside the other *mamu*, biting them and throwing them from one side to the other, making a track through them for himself. By the time he reached the cave entrance, he was having difficulty in breathing. But as he came rushing out through the fire the Two Men were ready for him. They beat him about the head repeatedly with their clubs, and killed him. All the other *mamu* died in the cave, where they remain. The Two Men continued on their travels.

The story underlines the treachery of the *mamu*. They are not to be trusted on any account, however amiable they may, superficially, appear to be. And that is the point made when Djindjindji violently pushes aside his own people in an attempt to escape. This story concerns the death of the same *mamu* leader already mentioned in Myth 67.

69. THE DESTRUCTION OF THE *MAMU*

The Two Men (the Wadi Gudjara) came in the course of their travels to Yunbu, south of Balgo, north of Manggai, out west. Yunbungau, who was a cannibal, and a 'little bit *mamu*', met them there and invited them to attend a ceremony. They accompanied him and sat down while Yunbungau and his group began their singing and dancing. After a while, Yunbungau prepared his sticks ready to kill the Two Men. However, they were 'clever', suspecting Yunbungau's intention. All the *mamu* had put white feather down on their bodies. The Two Men made themselves grow taller, and caused a whirlwind to materialise. But the *mamu* built a high, strong wind-break to keep off the wind and just went on singing. Then they went back to their camps. They sent two girls to the Two Men, who had camped nearby. Yunbungau had told the two girls to hold the men while they were copulating so he could kill them. But when he came to kill them they had slipped away from the girls, because they thought something like that might happen, and were hiding.

Next morning the Two Men came close to the main camp but did not show themselves. The *mamu* brought food for them, pretending to be friendly, but could not find them. They called out, 'Where are you camped?' They called back, 'We are camping here!' Those Two Men 'threw' their voices in various directions.

In the late afternoon the *mamu* painted their bodies in red-ochre; but two of them, including Yunbungau, sneaked away in search of the Two Men, who knew about this, and were ready. Some of the *mamu* began singing their death song. In the meantime, all the others were clustered together around a tree: 'they were sitting down in one heap', some in the tree. The Two Men had made a deep pit, and covered it with branches: they sat waiting. Following their tracks, Yunbungau and the other *mamu* came dancing along, sticks in their hands, ready to kill them. But the Two Men made a big whirlwind that picked up all the *mamu* sitting together, including their tree, and deposited them in the hole. The other two *mamu* also fell into the pit. The Two Men threw all the *mamu* possessions in there on top of them, including their fires: nothing was left. Then they covered up the hole.

All this happened at Yunbu. [The place-name refers to Yunbungau.] 'The Two Men are there still! And there are plenty of *mamu* down the Canning Stock Route way!'

Although the situation differs, the theme is the same as in the other three stories. The incident where the *mamu* cluster around a tree, some within its branches, has a parallel in the story of 'The *mamu* tree' told to C. Berndt by women at Ooldea in 1941 (R. and C. Berndt 1944: 341–43). However, the *mamu* in that case were 'just living there' and using it as a place in which to keep their meat, and the tree and those *mamu* were not, in that case, lifted up by a whirlwind and deposited in a hole.

Hostile actions between *mamu* and human beings did not need to be justified: the enmity between them was fundamental. It was tantamount to a kind of endemic warfare on a small scale, involving only a few combatants at any one time. Any tactics would do, but subterfuge and deceit were said to be especially characteristic of *mamu* — as in this story told to C. Berndt at Ooldea in 1941.

70. THE *MAMU* MEAT-TRAP

A young man with the hair-bun of an initiate was sitting by himself at the top of a sandhill when he saw an old man coming. The young man said, 'I'm alone here. There's no-one near to tell Dreaming stories to, no-one to listen.' And he told the old man, 'There's some kangaroo meat over there. Help yourself.' The old man went over to where the meat was hanging up in the leafy wind-break, ate some, and lay down to sleep. It was afternoon. At sunrise the young man went to look for him, but nobody was there: 'Is he dead?'

He went off to another place, sat down and looked about. Another old man was coming. But this old man saw that it was a *mamu* sitting there, a deceiver. The young man with the hair-bun, that *mamu*, came up and sat down, asking, 'Where are you from? Will you tell me Dreaming stories?' Later on, when it was getting dark, he said, 'Have some meat, over there!' The old man took the meat, put it down in the wind-break and saw that it wasn't real meat. He could see teeth in it, *mamu* teeth! He lay down in the wind-break. (He didn't eat any of the meat, just pretended to do so.) After a while he got up and built a big fire. When the young man wasn't looking, he threw him and the meat on to the fire and burned them up.

The so-called meat was really the young man's older wife, in disguise. Any man who ate that 'meat' would die. When he swallowed it, it would pull at his heart; the teeth would get into his heart and bite him, and the old woman would laugh, saying, 'I'm not meat!' Then the young man would eat him, before going away to watch for his next victim. But the second old man in the story was a 'clever man'. He knew that the young man and the meat were not what they appeared to be.

This is typical of the short *mamu* stories that were told to children, as well as for light entertainment among small groups of adults. An old *mamu* woman could take the shape of a stone spear-blade lying among the sandhills, and cut the throat of a man who unsuspectingly picked it up. Or she might turn into a little girl playing alone by a shallow pool of water, but the man who took pity on her, picked her up, and took her home to his camp would be her next victim. Young men could take the shape of old men, and vice versa, or indeed whatever other disguise seemed most appropriate. Stories of this sort were neat and compact, not elaborating in words; they could be told dramatically with maximum effect around desert camp-fires on moonless nights. One message they conveyed was, 'Can you be sure that the person you are talking to is *really* that person?' The question reverberated from the scene of the story into the ordinary, everyday world. The way some women put it was: 'You might be sitting by the fire, and think you saw me coming to sit beside you. But it wouldn't be me, because I would be far away. It would be a *mamu*, *looking* like me!'

In the next bracket of six stories the main characters are *maam* from western Arnhem Land. The first and the third to the sixth were told to C. Berndt at Oenpelli in 1950; the second to R. Berndt, also at Oenpelli, in 1949.

71. HE ATE HIS OWN BABIES

Long ago, that *maam* was one of the very first inhabitants. He was always 'eating' his wife, and so after a while they found a child. It entered her belly, that child, and one afternoon it was born: it was a boy. The father went running, pierced a hole in the baby's nasal cartilege and put a kangaroo bone through it. Then both of them, mother and father, put the baby into a paperbark carrier and went hunting.

The father was chopping a tree branch for honey. The mother left the baby there with him while she went to find honey in the ground among the rocks. Well, he was chopping the tree, and the branch bearing the honeycomb fell down. He left it, took the axe, and came running to eat the baby. He cut off the top part, ate it and finished it. He was full. Only the bottom part with the two legs was lying there. The mother came back, saw him, and cried out, 'Who's been eating my baby?' He said, 'A dingo ate the baby.' Well, they filled their baskets with honey and went back to where they had made their camp.

She kept carrying the baby's bottom and legs. Time went by, and she found another child. He came again, that child; he was there again in her belly. Another day came, he was born, he was lying outside. The same thing kept happening. The two of them went, as before, and he ate the baby. Well, that mother was getting angry: 'What am I to do with him, when he keeps eating my babies?'

They were camping there in a cave. She set about gathering dry grass, putting it near his sleeping place. Next day they went hunting, came back, and lay down to sleep. In the middle of the night when she saw he was sound asleep, she ran and got a lot of grass. Her own husband! She stood outside the cave, and she closed up the whole entrance with grass. Then she set it alight — there, where her husband was sleeping! She said, 'It's good that I cooked you, because you were always eating my babies!' He was still burning, in there. She sealed up the cave entirely — she, his wife, sealed him up in there! He turned into rock there, where she sealed him up. She herself went away, and at last met another man, a true *maam*. Well, the two of them camped together. He was good, he did not eat her babies. So she said to him, 'You and I, we can be married. You're good. But as for him, he used to eat my babies. So then I cooked him with fire, and I sealed him up in the rocks!' He is still there at Gudjaran-dongi [meaning 'spirit character banging on the rocks']. He remains there for ever.

The *maam* of western Arnhem Land are not all that different from the Western Desert *mamu*, especially when — as in this case — the *maam* is a cannibal and eats the children he and his wife have produced. 'Eating' (except in relation to the child) is in this context a synonym for copulating. However, the wife, who is presumably also a *maam*, draws a distinction between (from her point of view) 'good' and 'bad' *maam*.

72. HIS FRIEND THE *MAAM*

A *maam* spirit named Gulgulg-gwagin lived in the ground, in a hole resembling a grave, with an entrance that could be opened or closed. His mother and father lived with him, but while the mother and her son were 'like' human beings, the father had no flesh on his bones. They were at Mabubu, at one corner of the Plain [Amurag language. The names of the father and mother were unknown.]

A 'real man' named Inmalegara, *yariyaning*, Amurag, went out in his canoe to collect goose eggs. The *maam* son also went in his canoe to collect goose eggs. Inmalegara saw the other canoe from a distance and said to himself, 'Something is there, perhaps a man, or perhaps a spirit. I'll go and look.' The *maam* also paddled toward him. As they came close to each other, the man saw that the other's face and body were different from his own. He became frightened: 'That's a spirit now!' he thought. But the *maam* said, 'I'm a man, I'm like you. Don't be frightened. Come close to me.' And the man came nearer. The sun was going down.

'Where are you going to camp?' the *maam* asked. The man replied, 'I don't know. I'd better go back home. I'll travel during the night.' 'You'd better come back with me, to my home, where my mother and father are,' the *maam* said. And he added [as an inducement], 'You'll hear the sound of my father's bones rattling — and then you can tell all the others about it!' Thus persuaded, the man accompanied him. They left their canoes at the swamp, and carried with them some of the goose eggs, water snakes and geese they had caught.

After they had gone a little way, the *maam* asked, 'What about cooking the food here?' The man agreed, and looked round for a firestick [to find the appropriate wood to use in making fire]. 'What are you looking for?' asked the *maam*. 'A fire-stick.' 'No,' said the *maam*, 'I've got fire here.' He put some dry grass among a pile of wood and blew on it, and a fire flared up. They cooked the food they had brought; some they had left in their canoes. After eating, they went on walking. It was getting dark: 'A snake might bite us, if we walk in the night!'

As they drew near his home, the *maam* said that the man must 'walk level' with him, placing his foot down on the ground at the same time: they must be in step, so the *maam's* mother did not hear that anyone else was with him. 'She's a dangerous woman, that's why we must walk level,' he said. They came to Mabubu creek, and washed themselves, because 'My mother and father might smell you,' the *maam* said. He told the man to hang up his cooked food on a tree, so that in the early morning when he left the *maam's* home, he could pick it up and take it back to his own camp.

When they reached his home, the *maam* told the man to watch carefully when they came to the entrance. The 'door' was at the side of a little hill. 'I will just blow on it, and it will open,' said the *maam*. As they entered the *maam's* home, they heard his mother calling out, 'Son, you have gone a long way. Are you dead? Has somebody killed you?' [She was frightened; he had been away for some time.] The *maam* had told his visitor, 'You have to follow me, do the same as ᵈo.' He said that when his mother gave him yams to eat, the man must ᵣeak them and chew them at the same time.

They sat down together. 'Son, are you home?' the mother called when she heard a sound: 'Yes, mother, I'm home.' 'Come close, so I can see you. I want you to tell me if you have met any humans,' she said. 'No, mother, they don't know us, we are under the ground,' he replied. 'Well, son, you had better come and get some cooked yams. You must be hungry.' 'I'm very tired', answered the *maam*. 'I'll come later on, after I've rested in this cool place. It's too hot where you are. Then I'll have the yams.' When he had rested, he took the eggs he had collected, and other things to his mother and father. He did not speak to the man, just pinched him to indicate where to sit — otherwise his mother would hear that he was not alone. He accepted the yam from his mother and told her, 'Mother, I want to have a rest, I've eaten plenty of goose eggs.' 'All right, son. If you see or hear any human being, you tell me!' 'No one is here; they don't like us,' the son replied. He returned and sat where the man was and gave him some yam, but did not speak to him. They broke the yam at the same time and put it into their mouths at the same time. They camped there.

'If you want to urinate, you tell me, and we'll go out at the same time and do that, otherwise mother will hear you,' the *maam* said: 'She doesn't sleep; she is always listening for human beings.'

They slept. When the *maam* smelt daybreak he nudged his companion, letting him know it was time to get up. They left the *maam's* home, the *maam* blowing on the door to open it. 'Come on,' he said, 'we'll run, before my mother smells you.' The man collected the food that was hanging in the tree, took it to the canoe and pushed it away.

The *maam's* mother had meanwhile come out of her home. The wind had brought the smell of a human being, her son's companion; she had jumped from her bed. [The inference is that she smelt the human being while he was *in* the cave.] She came angrily toward her son, holding her fighting stick (*mabil*, the long fighting club). 'Why did you bring a man here, son? I want to kill and eat him.' 'Why do we want to kill him? We've got plenty of goanna: my father can't get up. There are only the three of us here, and there are plenty of human beings. Why do we want to kill them?' the son asked.

The man had gone now, and was back in his camp, where his relatives were. His father had been out looking for him, and was happy to see him coming. 'What has happened? You must tell me.' 'Father, I met a spirit and he took me to his camp. He lives in that Aranga hole. He took me in, his gave me this yam. If you don't believe me, you can see the yam.' 'Where did you leave the yam?' asked his father. 'Hanging in that tree.' They went to look at it: it was a very big yam, 'just like a tree' [in size]. Everybody in the camp ate some of it — there was so much of it!

When the man left, the *maam* had said to him, 'Some time, when you look for goose eggs, perhaps we could meet?' The man had replied that he would, but he was frightened because he had heard what the *maam's* mother had said.

Next morning he went out in his canoe to collect goose eggs and met that *maam* again, also in his canoe. They talked together, and exchanged food, as friends do. 'We'll go ashore,' the *maam* said, 'we'll make fire and cook some of our food, since I'm hungry!' They sat down to eat, and his *maam* friend said, 'While we are here, I want to tell you, friend, I can't take you to my camp. My mother will smell you; she will get wild. She wants to eat you. This time she will know, if I take you to my camp.' The man's fear increased: he got his canoe, and returned home. He told his father, 'I met that *maam* again, but he told me he wouldn't take me back to his home, as his mother would smell me!' His father said, 'I can't let you go back. She might kill you. You can get goose eggs nearby and come home before dark.' So he did not go far from his own camp. He never met that *maam* again.

This story provides us with some details of the appearance of *maam*. Apart from the *maam* father who is almost a skeleton, the son is distinguished as being different from a human being, and the 'ordinary' man recognises this at their first meeting. Nevertheless he is willing to make friends with the *maam* son, and accompanies him to his home. It is the cannibal mother who spoils the relationship between them. Her son tries to persuade her to live at peace with human beings, but is unsuccessful. As in the first myth, some *maam* are 'good', and in this case the *maam* son is friendly and unwilling to hurt a human being — but friendship between them is impossible. The reference to Aranga, when the man tells his father where the *maam* live, is to a malignant spirit with an abnormally long penis (see R. and C. Berndt 1951: 171–74). There are several variants of this story; in some the non-human friend is a *marlwa*; in others a *namandi*. (See

C.H. Berndt 1979: 65–67.) In one, from women, the non-human boy goes off with his friend and does not return to his parents until after they are dead.

73. A YOUNG WOMAN MEETS A *MAAM*

A woman set off in the west, coming this way, talking a Gunbargid language. She was carrying her baskets for plant foods, her digging stick, and a fire-stick, travelling along, looking for a Woraidbag-language place. She was coming, camping, setting off again. As she went along she was looking about her, and when she saw plenty of small creatures and plant foods, there she would camp, eating various foods. At sunset she would settle down and sleep, and early in the morning she would set off again. She kept doing the same thing, getting various foods, and still talking Gunbargid, her own language.

Going on, she saw the salt-water tide had come up at the place where she hoped to go across. So she camped there. She made a sleeping platform up on a tree, because so many mosquitoes were biting her. When at last early morning came she made a paperbark canoe, paddling with her hands to cross to the other side. Then she started off again, with her belongings. She went on, and at last she reached the place she was looking for, in Woraidbag country.

A *maam* was living there, in a cave house, and when he saw her coming he was excited. 'My woman has come! My body's no good, but today we two will sleep together!' [They met.] She gave him vegetable foods, and he reciprocated with fish. At last they 'took each other', married each other, and they slept together. But as time went on that woman did not like it. 'Whatever can I do?' she said to herself, in her mind. Well, they went on sleeping together. At last she sharpened a stone axe. They were lying there, sleeping. He lifted his head, preparing to stretch himself to get up and 'eat' her. But she was already reaching for the axe, and she slashed his neck. Then she looked around, got fire, and 'cooked' his body.

Perhaps he just tossed away the flames, that *maam*? Anyway, he came out alive again. 'You, woman, why did you kill me? And I didn't 'eat' you! I'll just go, then, and cover you up with my wings,' he said to her. 'And I'll seal you up, so you become like rock!' She tried to hide herself, but he found her. He sealed her up, in the cave where she was lying. The cave remained for her, the dark cave. She kept on talking in there, abusing him. But he was congratulating himself, that *maam*. At last she became like rock.

He went back to where his mother and father were and his various relatives. They all praised him, so that he swelled up with pride. But as for her, she was transformed into rock for ever, in the country where that *maam* first put the place-name — Yinyalanj, where he sealed her up. The *maam* won. She stands there as rock, forever.

The woman in this story was an adolescent girl, named Ngarlmo. It was after two days with him that she decided she would try to kill him. The *maam*, named Na-wurlgala, was a young man with body hair, very thin, with a 'crooked' body and also, apparently, he had bat wings. The story-teller, Mangurug, said in discussion that she had first heard the story from her father, before she reached puberty.

Different facets of a *maam's* character are revealed. In this case, he is avid for sexual intercourse. However, the girl dislikes him, probably because of his appearance since the *maam* himself says that 'his body's "no good" '. Some *maam* are invulnerable, as this one was. After his revival, he not only gets his revenge, but by sealing up his 'murderer' in a cave, he achieves a victory over a human being.

74. PAY-BACK AT LIGINMU

Long ago those two, that man and woman, were married, and after a time they found a daughter. They were carrying her about, she was growing, and then she was talking. That husband would go after kangaroo, and the other two would go after vegetable foods and honey, filling their honey baskets. That's how it always was. Those two would take their baskets back to camp and wait, looking out for him, when he was coming back with kangaroo for them. They would all eat, and then they would sleep. Next day, if he felt like it they would all go hunting together, and come back in the late afternoon. They would sleep, and next day he might go hunting alone while mother and daughter went by themselves, coming home later with food to the same place. That's what they always did.

But a *maam* was coming from far away, making for that place where they were living. He was hunting about, a long way off, but he was coming that way. And he heard them both, that girl and her mother, chopping out honey. They were by themselves, because that father had gone looking for kangaroo. Well, the *maam* heard them chopping. He came running and stood on the other side of a big stretch of water, and called out, 'Who are you, you two chopping there?' The girl called back, 'We're chopping here, my mother and I!' 'Are you alone, you and your mother?' he asked. 'Then

I'll go and get her for my wife, that mother of yours!' But the girl said, 'My father is here with us!' She was trying to deceive him. They still kept on chopping. He said to them, 'I'm coming, because I'm dying for it, I want to get your mother!' Well, those two sneaked away. They filled their containers with honey, took all their baskets, and hurried off. The *maam* was coming, running. They ran too, and hid inside a deep cave among the rocks. He came running, and saw the empty bees' nest. Too late!

He tried to follow their tracks, but no. He was just jumping about among the rocks, near where they had gone into the cave. They sat quietly because they could see him going round and round, searching. He was talking as he went, scolding them. He tried hard to find them, but at last he went back to his own place. They were listening as he went away, talking. Then they just ran, back to where they were living. They saw that the girl's father had made a fire and cooked the kangaroo: it was ready for them. As they came up to him, he saw that they were out of breath. 'What's been eating you,' he asked, 'that you came running, out of breath?' So the girl told him what had happened. 'Father, a *maam* was following my mother and me. He would have taken my mother as his wife! He wanted my mother!' He said, 'Leave it to me, daughter. In the morning I'll go looking, and I'll find him and kill him!' They all slept. In the morning he left them both in camp. They had told him exactly where they had been hunting.

That man had special power. He went on and on, searching, and heard the *maam* chopping out honey: he was eating honey, then he went back to his own place among the smooth rocks. The man changed his body appearance to look like smoke, and at last he sealed the *maam* up. That man had won. He listened to the *maam* making a loud banging noise in the cave and talking away in there. Then he went back, and said to his wife and daughter, 'Let's go, so you can see where I sealed up that *maam*!' They set off, and went straight to the place. But there waiting for them was another *maam*, the other one's elder brother. They were about to go; they were looking around, then they sat down in a cave. But the brother blew on the rock, crushing them underneath. They came into Dreaming there, together. The *maam* sealed them up, because that man had first sealed up his brother. He stood listening and talking beside the cave. He said, 'They are the ones who sealed up my brother. So it's my turn to show them another trick, those three, daughter and father and mother!' He sealed them up; they remain there. As for him, he flew up into the sky; he went for ever. But there at Liginmu they remain, those three people and that *maam*. They went into Dreaming, like rocks, for ever.

In this story the tables are, to some extent, turned: the *maam* is killed but his elder brother avenges his death. The lesson is 'to leave well alone' —

kill a *maam* by all means, but do not return to where the deed took place! As in the last myth, the elder brother *maam* has wings: he flew away from the cave in which he had sealed the family group. Also to be noted is a third use of the word 'eating' — in this case, it refers to something having 'upset' or 'excited' a person.

75. THE SINGING *MAAM'S* REVENGE

Long ago, a husband and wife set off from their home camp. They were coming this way, crossing over the water, going far from home to get the right wood for mosquito fires. They put down their things, went on and got the wood and brought it back. It was *manlargwi* wood, [meaning 'empty'] because it was so light. Well, they came on, picking up their things on the way, and kept going until they reached their home camp. Then at last they put down their things and their firewood and were cooking meat and plant foods and big fish they had caught. They slept. When that special wood was finished they set off again to the same place. They tied up their bundles of wood, and each of them carried one lot. They came back, resting for a while on the track because they had so much wood. At last they reached their rocky home, among the long caves, where they stayed for a while.

Early in the morning they went for fish. They were carrying a fish trap, and the wife was carrying fire. They ate some of the fish close to the water, and some they wrapped in paperbark and took back to cook at home. They had water peanuts too, some cooked and some raw. Next day they stayed home, using food they had already cooked, because they were tired. That is what they used to do. When they wanted meat, they would take their dogs and their long baskets into bush country, cook their meat on the coals there, and go home in the late afternoon. When their firewood was finished they set off for more. When their cave got dirty with old charcoal from their fires, they moved to another place, cleared the ground and hung up their things there, and in the late afternoon they cooked some meat.

Well. That *maam* was coming, tracking the smell, looking for them. He was singing to himself, a happy hunting song:

Mu, mu mu! I can smell fish and meat for me!
I'll kill those two to get that fish and meat!

He was coming from a long way, talking as he came. Those two put out their fire, went outside the cave, and put some fish there. They said in their minds, 'That *maam* is coming to get fish to eat, but we'll kill him!' They put the fish on a smooth rock at the place where they first had their home. They were listening to the *maam* threatening them as he came along, singing '*mu, mu*', tracking the smell of meat and fish. They heard him coming close, there where they were camping. He was coming, tracking the smell to where they had put the fish. They each had a piece of unused firewood ready, and as he came along, they struck him. The *maam* caught one stick and threw it back, striking the wife. Her husband ran and got a glowing piece of firewood. He kept hitting that *maam*, killing him. Then the two of them climbed up the rocks, into a deep cave.

But the *maam's* father came and healed him: he gave him life. That man and woman were sleeping, along with their dog, when both of the *maam* came after them to kill them. The dog began to bark, but already those *maam* had covered them up with their wings so that they turned into rock, sealed up in the cave. The *maam* son talked, while his father was fixing the cave, 'Shame on you both! You killed me! I lay dead and you thought you had won — you were congratulating yourselves! But my father came and sealed you both up, you and your dog!' They were talking angrily inside the cave, that man and woman, both abusing the *maam* father. Too late. He had already sealed them up. Firewood, baskets, fish, plant foods were all spread out there: all became like rock. Spears, spear-throwers, her digging stick, became like rock, there at Bamburli, where they came into Dreaming. Those two and their dog and their belongings all remain there. Those two remain there in spirit, in that country, forever.

Again the *maam* triumph, despite the *maam* son's temporary death. His father's power made him invulnerable. When he appeared on the scene, the *maam* son proclaimed his intention of killing the husband and wife, so they were justified in trying to defend themselves. It is not really possible to placate a *maam*: such creatures are never satisfied. And offering him fish would simply have led to further demands.

75. A *MAAM* STORY: TWO INTO ONE

'I'm going!' he said. He kept on going, alone. He kept going. He went, he was climbing up the rocks and looking around at the place. No. [He didn't want that place.] 'So, where am I going?' He kept moving, climbing up the rocks. He was going, he was feeling his hair falling down from his head. He still kept going. But then he looked closely at himself, at his hair, and saw that his hair was falling down, and he thought in his mind, 'Perhaps someone has been following me, he's going to catch up with me!' Well, it was true. That other was coming up close to him where that hair was. In that one place the other came up close to him, and mixed his body with his. He blended his own body with his for a long time: those two blended their bodies together. Then they could not separate themselves, so they still remain joined together [that happened at Bagbari, in Djurlga].

This unusual story tells about the merging of two *maam* — as separate persons, but co-joined. The narrator said she did not know the reason for this: it happened at the very beginning of things, and only the characters themselves would know. However, in some of the traditional western Arnhem Land bark paintings, there are occasional representations of Siamese twins. We were told that some actual cases had occurred in the past, and they would almost certainly have been regarded as having *maam*-like qualities.

The next three myths are from Milingimbi and were told to C. Berndt in 1950. They concern north-eastern Arnhem Land *mogwoi*.

77. MISFORTUNE ON A HUNTING TRIP

A man set off on a hunting trip. He got three different kinds of possum, several kinds of goannas and lizards, including blanket lizard and blue-tongue, and a flying squirrel. He got plenty. In the afternoon he went back to his hunting camp, got all of them together, and sat down. He made a big fire, and covered them all up to cook. He ate two of them. But he took out the intestines and threw them away. Then he climbed up on to a tree branch that was wide like a platform. It was already dark by then, and he sat down up there.

A *mogwoi* was moving about, sniffing around, speaking in his own language. '*Mamama!*' he was saying. He could smell meat. 'Whose meat is that? A human person's?' He was moving along, getting close. He came to the dead fire of old coals and was searching about in it. Then he looked up and saw a penis hanging down, just over the edge of the branch where the man was sitting. 'There's my animal!' said the *mogwoi*. He climbed up, and pulled at it with his hands and teeth. He pulled it right out, pubic hair too. *'Yakai!'* the man cried out. 'Pubic hair, penis, all gone, finished! The only one I had, pulled out from me!'

The *mogwoi* was going along eating the penis, mixed with other meat. *'Yakai!* My penis! You, you *mogwoi*, your nose rotten with sores!' All the *mogwoi* said was *'Winya-winya-winyi'* in his own language. 'You're no good!' said the man. He got together his stone spears, and the animals he had killed, and picked them up, ready to go. But, 'How am I to go? Now I have no penis, only testes, because he pulled it out! *Yei!* They'll scold me when I get back, all my wives! No more coitus or children for them!' He went on talking like that, to himself. 'Oh, he was wicked, that *mogwoi!'*

It was night-time: everything was dark. He came to a tree with soft leaves, broke some off, and wrapped them up with twine to cover the sore. He was ashamed. He hurried along, carrying the animals in his long basket-bag. His children were playing. The little boys called out, *'Ya,* here's father! He's been spoilt!', as they could not see his penis. He sat down quietly, and put down the meat. Then he lay down. His wives asked, 'What's the matter? How did it happen?' 'A *mogwoi* cut off my nose-for-coitus!' 'Oh, husband! Stand up!' Then all his wives wept.

The name of the man was Lumburgmiri, and his country was Djiliwiri. He had three wives, all named in discussion. The *mogwoi* had a human body, but no tongue — he could not talk properly. He wore a *ritar* hard-grass spear on his head, falling down in front of his face. The story records the kind of fortuitous incident which could occur where a *mogwoi* is concerned. The real issue, however, is the man's careless treatment of food, in throwing away the intestines of the creatures he had killed when normally they would have been eaten. On the other hand, the *mogwoi*, attracted by the intestines, callously treats the human being's penis as meat.

78.   THE *MOGWOI'S* BABY

A *mogwoi* woman set off, carrying her baby under one arm in a paperbark container. She was going to collect some bush foods. As she went along, she called out to her husband, 'You go and get fish for us both! I'll get plant food.' She chose a good place to leave the baby, and set to work. She got some food and put it down. She got more and put it down. Got more, put it down... The baby was crying. 'Ah, my baby's crying! I'll give her milk. There she is, over there.' She set off, sat down, and breast-fed the baby. Then she left her and went to get more food. This time she was farther away among the grasses, too far to hear.

A human man called Laarnmirndja set off with his dog, to go hunting. The dog smelt something. He sniffed about, smelling, looking around. He kept on looking about. 'What's this I'm smelling, something for me? An animal? A *djanda* goanna, maybe?' He went digging about, digging in a great hurry, around the baby. The man, going along, saw the baby. 'Here's a nice baby for me. I'll take it!' 'He picked it up, and went running off. He ran — and *brrr!* He got there. The people living at that place said, 'A baby for us, a nice one!' 'Yes, for us! What is it? A girl? That's good!' they said. 'For me, give it here to me!' 'No, I've got it, I'm holding it!' 'No, for me! Give it to me! I'll give it milk, breast-milk!'

The *mogwoi* woman was talking to herself. 'I'll eat some food first: it's still early morning.' She went to where she had left the baby, and saw it was gone. She began to abuse whoever had taken it. 'Oh, my baby! Some deformed creature snatched you away, someone with a damaged nose and a twisted-up mouth! Oh, my dear child! Oh, who snatched you away from me?' She hurried about, searching. She found the man's tracks and followed them. Human children were talking and calling out. She heard them, and went running in their direction.

They heard her coming. 'She's on the way!' they said. She was waving a long, thick stick, ready, as she hurried along. 'She's the baby's mother, she's hurrying,' they said. 'She's on the way, looking for her baby!' She was going along. Hurry, hurry, hurry! Getting close! 'Where's my baby?' They picked up another baby, one of theirs. 'This is your baby!' 'No. This is yours. It's no good!' They gave her another baby. 'No. This is yours: it's covered with sores!' She threw it away. They gave her another baby. She left it, did not pick it up. 'This one's no good, no good at all. Ugly face!' They gave her more, but she did not want them. Then she lifted up the corner of a paperbark cover. 'This is my baby, this truly good one!' She picked it up, and ran off. Then they attacked her. They hit her, many of them; they struck her with stone axes and fighting sticks; they threw spears at her. She ran away. She dived into the jungle. 'Husband! Come here!' 'What?' 'They were all hitting me, they took my "eye", my baby!' 'Come on, wife!' he said. 'Let's go to that lot, those people!' They hurried together, the husband carrying his spears, holding them ready to throw. He flung spears at those people. They flung spears back at him. He jumped aside. And again! Men came at them with stone axes. And again! They fought. Then those two rushed off into the jungle, into the jungle of dense trees like banana plants.

The *mogwoi* woman's name was Wornggil-boi, and her home was at Wornggil-ngu, a *mogwoi* place. Her husband was Bibala-gala. They had clan and language affiliations, like human people, and they were married according to ordinary marriage rules. The baby's name was Banbalara: her hair was moderately long, but she was not yet at the walking stage.

It is not so much the old story of inherent enmity between *mogwoi* and human beings, as in the case of *mamu* and *maam*. Possibly this was because many *mogwoi* are spirits of the dead, although they can also be antagonistic. Some, too, are Dreaming, associated with particular places from the beginning of time. As in the last myth, this is an example of thoughtless cruelty. A human man takes away a child he finds, without considering what its mother may feel: *mogwoi* and human beings behave more or less in the same way. The interesting point is that the human beings regard the *mogwoi* baby as acceptable in their own terms, even to the extent of considering it more attractive than their own children. The *mogwoi* mother is more discriminating: she finds the babies they offer her ugly in comparison with her own. It is only when she runs away with her child that they attack her. In general terms, however, to all appearances the human beings in the myth do not draw a distinction between themselves and the woman and her child.

In the third *mogwoi* example a lone *mogwoi* is at first the aggressor but ends up as a victim. It was told to C. Berndt at Milingimbi in 1950.

79. A RUNAWAY WIFE
MEETS A *MOGWOI*

A lot of people had made bark houses at Gugumir, an inland place, and among them were two sisters married to the same man. Boaliri was a *wirgul*, just adolescent. Gadjabawi was a little older, but had as yet no children. Boaliri had adorned herself with cane bracelets, on this arm and that arm. Her husband saw them. 'What's the matter with you? Are you looking for a sweetheart? Or have you already got someone else for a sweetheart?' 'No! I'm wearing these because I'm only a young girl yet! And I'll get more, because you're scolding me!' 'No,' her sister told her. 'Just pull them off, like this!' And her husband said, 'Yes, *I'm* the one who looks into your eyes as a sweetheart, a sweetheart for both of you!' Night came. They slept.

Early morning! Boaliri was getting ready to leave. She wanted to see her father and mother and her younger brothers. 'Come on, let's go!' said the others. Her husband and her sister were setting off to get tortoises and water-lily roots and bulrush corms. But Boaliri was cutting cane for more bracelets. 'I'll run away to my own people, my own place!' she said. She ran, ran, ran, ran, ran — and came to some thick bush, a little valley among the trees. Going through the valley she saw a fresh-water stream. She saw some light, barbed spears going past [not explained in the story]. But she also saw many *gulaga* yams, and filled two baskets with them. Then she said, 'I'll get some *djidama* roots!' [These are inedible until specially treated.] She dug some, arranging her other baskets to carry them. 'I'll get plenty of ant-bed' (termite mound). She broke some firewood, heaped it up and let it burn down while she got plenty of paperbark; some she used as a container to carry fresh water and water weed. Then she moved aside the firewood, flattened the ant-bed and spread the weed on it, and covered it all with paperbark. She put the 'bitter' *djidama* roots inside, and the *gulaga* yams on top where they would cook quickly; then she covered the whole thing with earth. 'I'll get some more, while I'm waiting.' She got plenty, put them down; got plenty, put them down. She cooked five baskets-full.

The fire was burning, the food was cooking. She ate some of the *gulaga* yams. She ate; she was full. 'Now I'll look at the oven.' She took out the ant-bed, heaped up the *gulaga* yams, and heaped up the *djidama* separately. She peeled the *djidama*, threw away the skin, and arranged a sharp stick at an angle in the ground to slice them. Slice, slice, slice! Then she filled two baskets with them, and suspended them in the running water of the stream. She was hurrying. She sat down, ate some more of the *gulaga* yams, and tied up the rest with string. 'I'll get paperbark!' She got some, brought it back, and used it to make a small house. And she built up a fire.

A *mogwoi* smell that fire. '*Mamama,*' he was saying. 'My wife, my son!' [He was calling out the words for these.] He was clapping his hands together, greedily; he was stretching out his penis. He was carrying a stringybark container full of goose eggs, with more goose eggs in a long dillybag. '*Mamama!*' He was moving quickly. 'My wife, my son! My wife, my son!' Hurry, hurry, hurry, hurry, hurry! Getting close! He took the dilly bag from his shoulder, kept going, and copulated with the hot ant-bed... Hurry, hurry, hurry! He was listening.. A big fly [near Boaliri's house] was saying '*Nyi-nyi-nyi-nyi!*' It was saying, 'Woman here, come on! *Mogwoi*, come here! This is your outside fire burning!' [The fire burning outside the girl's house.] He said, 'I'll play with you! I'll sleep with you! Nice vulva!' That's what the *mogwoi* said. 'Nice vulva! Wife!'

He got into the house; he came right inside. His big head came breaking in through the wall. '*Wai!*' cried the girl. She jumped up, seized a long stick and threw hot coals at him. But that *mogwoi* put a finger into her vagina — finger-coitus! He kept copulating: she couldn't stop him! Daylight came, sunrise: from early morning through until dark he was copulating, for a long time he was copulating, until the sun was overhead again at midday. Then the girl said, 'You stay here, I'll get those *djidama* from the water. 'Yes! Quick! Hurry, wife! Hurry, my wife, my son! I want to copulate with you when you come back!' She took one basket of *djidama* from the water, but left the other basket there. Then she hurried back. He was sitting waiting, ready. He used his finger. Then he pushed her over and copulated properly. Finished. He started again! She was eating yams, that girl. He was copulating, copulating, she was kneading the sliced *djidama* into a cake. '*Wai!* Let's eat some food first, some *djidama* yams!' 'I want to copulate with you for a long time first, because I've been without a woman — only a man by myself!' he said. 'First I'll get leaves for a house, and make a fence for it.' Then he sat down, and copulated... He got up, hurry, hurry, hurry, making a path. Sat down, copulated.... finished! Hurry, hurry. Then he kissed her mouth, and set off, running, to get a goose he had killed. She finished making the house, and put a log of wood in her place and covered it with paperbark. Then she ran and got the bag of *djidama* from the stream, and the *gulaga* yams. As for the goose, she said (talking to herself), 'You wait there, *mogwoi*. I'm going to see my father and mother, my uncles and aunts and cousins and grandparents!' [She listed the proper kin terms for these.]

She hurried off, came to a stream, and swam across. It was getting dark. She got to the other side. Hurry, hurry! Pre-birth fluid was emerging. A baby came out, a boy. She cut the navel cord, then struck him on the chest and left him there. Hurry, hurry, hurry! She went on, came to a dry waterhole, came to a tree-post. A girl baby came out. She cut the navel cord. Then she got some paperbark, folded it to make a baby-carrier, wrapped the baby in it and held it under one arm. Hurry, hurry! She got to the place, saw that people were there. 'This is father's big house,' she said. 'I'll sleep inside it. First I'll leave the *djidama* and *gulaga* in here, and then I'll see father, mother, elder sister, younger brothers, everyone!'

She set off, and saw them all: they were getting water-lily roots, bulrush corms, tortoises. Her elder sister saw her. '*Ya!* Younger sister, my younger sister!' Her mother was weeping for her. Her elder sister asked, 'Whose child is this?' She answered, '*Mogwoi's!*' 'Come, bring it here to me! I want to look at it.' Hurry, hurry! She took the child to her. 'Here, sister, this is my baby.' Her sister took it by the legs: 'It's got a big head!' Bang! She dashed it against a tree, then again, and threw it away.

The *mogwoi* was carrying the goose on his head, in three baskets. Hurry, hurry, hurry, hurry, hurry! He sat down. 'Just wait a while, I'll cook this goose for you!' He moved away the hot coals, scraped them away... And he took it out, cooked! He wrapped it in paperbark, held it in his hands, hurrying, and put it down. '*Wai!* Wake up! Here is the goose, it's cooked!' he said. No answer. He spoke again. She didn't answer. Then he lifted up the paperbark and saw the log of wood lying there.

He went running, sniffing out her tracks ['like a dog'], running. He came to the stream, crossed over, got there. 'Sweet vulva! My wife! My son!' Running, running. 'Guru-djudjur!' A brown, white-necked bird hunting fish was talking. 'I saw her here, at this place!' The *mogwoi* looked about. A baby boy was lying there. 'This is my son!' He ate it — his child! Then, afterbirth blood. He ate it! Soon he came to a place where a lot of people were living, but when he got there the camp was empty. He broke through the paperbark walls of one house, then another: he broke into all the houses. 'Maybe this is her father's place!' He went through the camp. His eyes were like lights, like moonlight. 'Quick, quick!' people were saying. 'This is like afternoon for us, let's go back to camp!' Hurry, hurry! Got there!

She got there first, that girl, that *mogwoi's* sweetheart [his 'eye']. She went inside. He put out his tongue at her. '*Wai! Mogwoi!* This is a *mogwoi* here, he put out his tongue at me!' They got ready their fighting sticks, their barbed spears, their big 'crowbars', and they attacked him, that *mogwoi*. They attacked him, struck him. He was sitting down. He tried to get away, running crookedly. They struck him. No blood! On his head — no blood! On his belly — no blood! On his back — no blood! They burnt him with fire — no sores (wounds)! They cut his penis — no sores! He was like a *wongar* (Dreaming being), standing on this side, that side! He ran off, into the bush, to his place. He didn't eat the goose. He died there, died in the jungle. He went in, lay down, and in the middle of the night he died. That's all!

The names and social affiliations of the main people in the story were all known to the story-teller. The two girls belonged to the Djambarbingu dialect unit and Galwayunggu clan *(mala)*, like their father and brothers and the third sister, Manawan, who killed Boaliri's baby. Manawan's husband Wudungu, and the two girls' husband Deinganngu, were both of the Gobubingu dialect, Daiwurur clan. The girls' father's name was Bunuwal, their mother's Biyei'ngu (her dialect was Djinnang), and their brothers were Malambi and Buridnga. As against this, according to the story-teller, the *mogwoi* had 'no name, no dialect, no clan!' Yet the *mogwoi* used the right word for wife, and the correct term for a man to use in addressing his son or daughter (their mother would use a different term for them). He excused his behaviour on the grounds that he had been alone for too long, considerately letting the girl sleep, as he thought, while he prepared a goose for her dinner. Otherwise, his appearance and his actions marked him off as a *mogwoi*, not a human being. The baby girl's unnaturally large head and the reference to a *mogwoi* father were enough to justify killing her. The short gestation period is a feature, not so much of mythic time as of *mogwoi* time. But although the *mogwoi* appeared to be invulnerable (hence the *wongar*, Dreaming, allusion), he was mortal after all.

As for Boaliri, her husband's accusations at the beginning of the story foreshadowed what actually happened to her. If she had not paused on the way, there would have been no encounter with the *mogwoi*. But the delay was not related to her earlier, defiant cutting of more cane bangles for her arms. It was a consequence of her sudden interest in ordinary domestic tasks — getting yams, spending time in preparing the otherwise inedible *djidama*, and making a paperbark house, with the implication that she planned to spend more than one night there. To the story-teller and to the other women discussing all this, the girl's involvement in such matters was excessive, not in keeping with the need for a quick snack at that stage of her journey, and almost parallelling the *mogwoi's* immoderate behaviour in other respects. Her *mogwoi* experience *was* her punishment, the only one noted in the story, but for her it was not lethal, and the Boaliri who emerges in the course of events is not the same almost carefree adolescent girl we met in the quarrel about bangles. The story itself is like a warning to girls, but of course it is more than that, too.

On the western side of Arnhem Land, we have already mentioned the *maam* spirits. However, in that area there are also other spirits, among them the *mimi*. They are non-human, stick-like creatures who are said to live among the rocks of the escarpment country and are often depicted in what are regarded as ancient cave and rock shelter paintings. We present two stories about them, from Goulburn Island, told to R. Berndt in 1947.

80.   FRIENDSHIP AND DECEIT

A *yariwurig* man, speaking Woraidbag, living near Tor Rock in Gunwinggu country, went out each day to hunt geese. He was a good hunter. He used to climb a tree, and as the geese flew by he would hit them with a long stick, breaking their wings so that they fell to the ground.

Mainya, a *mimi* spirit, came along when the man was in the tree. He would hide, and when he saw a goose fall to the ground, he would steal it. He did this every morning, but the man did not know. Now, Mainya had a mother and father, who were *mimi* who lived among the rocks, and he took the geese to them. They were just like the paintings on the rock shelters — all skin and bones, naked stick-like creatures with big heads and hair. You can see right through them. They don't like wind, and leave their caves only in calm weather. To come out of their caves, they would speak to the stone covering and it would open. Once they were outside they would speak to it again, and it would close.

So, every morning Mainya would follow the hunter, steal a goose and go back to his parents. 'Son,' they said, 'You are a good hunter!' But one morning they followed him — and as they walked their bones 'would talk' [rattle], because there was no flesh on them. The human hunter saw them with their son. 'Ah!' he thought. 'That's the one who has taken my geese!' Then he said to himself, 'I think I should take him home to my place.' He followed Mainya and they talked together. He tried to persuade him to come back to his camp. But Mainya refused. 'It is better for us to cook the geese here.' So they cooked the geese, and the human hunter persuaded Mainya to eat it whole: 'Don't cut it up, just eat it whole!' He did so. 'Now, stand up!' said the human hunter. 'No, I think I'd better stay seated. After all, I've eaten the whole goose!' He had swallowed it whole, just letting it slide down into his stomach; first, he had broken a small branch off a tree, flicked it over his body and then thrown it away: then he has swallowed that goose whole. [The reason for this is not clear.]

After that, the human hunter said they would go back to his camp, but at first Mainya refused. 'If we go there, your mother and father might see me and kill me!' Finally the human hunter persuaded him. 'Come on, let's go!' But when they got to his camp, the man hid Mainya a little distance away. 'You wait for me here.'

He went to his mother and father and gave them the geese. They cooked and ate some. At night the man went to where Mainya was, and brought him back to where they were living, among the big caves. He did not tell his parents. Next morning, he and Mainya set off together. But as they were going, his father saw them and called out, and his mother asked, 'Why did you bring that spirit here?' She began to hit the ground and the rocks, threatening the *mimi* and trying to get hold of him. But at last they became reconciled to him. They made a big fire around him, and he sat in the middle with all the smoke enveloping him. He got used to them too, and stayed with them, and the pair would go out hunting each day. Every now and then the man let Mainya go out by himself, to see whether he would return to his own family. [And that was what led to trouble between them.]

After a while, when Mainya went out alone he would kill geese and eat them himself. He cooked them out there, in the bush, and ate them. He brought nothing back! They would say to him, 'We can see lots of blood on your arms, your legs and your body. What happened?' But he would reply, 'Bad luck, I couldn't find anything.' Every evening he would return empty-handed.

So the son asked his father and mother, 'What shall we do? It's probably better for us to kill him. He doesn't bring anything back for us.' So they got together a lot of grass and heaped it up by the entrance to the cave, and put more heaps inside. Mainya was sleeping soundly [after having eaten so much without sharing it]. The man tried to awaken him [to give him a last chance]: 'Come on, let's go out hunting!' But Mainya would not wake up. The man told his parents to leave the cave. Then he set fire to the heaps of grass. Mainya just went on sleeping, but he awakened as the fire began to spread. The others, outside the cave, could hear Mainya calling, 'Why did you light all these fires? Let me out! Let me out!' But the man continued to pile up grass at the entrance to the cave, and Mainya was burnt to death.

This story is in part structurally similar to Myth 72 where the human man accompanies his *maam* friend to his home. In this case the *mimi* is persuaded to return to the man's home, even though he had consistently stolen his geese. In both cases, the reaction on the part of their parents is the same. In the first example, the friendship between the *maam* and the man is broken because of fear of what might happen: the situation was too dangerous. In this case, the friendship between the *mimi* and the human beings appears to have run smoothly until the *mimi* kept for himself whatever food he obtained: this was sufficient to cause his death by burning.

81. HUMAN MEAT FOR *MIMI*

A Gunwinggu-speaking man from inland went looking for wallaby and kangaroo, but could not find any. He went directly to some rocky hills near Oenpelli where *mimi* lived. As he was walking over the rocks, he accidentally knocked some of them together so that they made a noise. This attracted the attention of a *mimi*, who emerged from one of the cracks and caught hold of the man's leg and pulled him down. The man struggled to get away, but the *mimi* held him tightly until he was exhausted. While he was still alive, the *mimi* cut flesh from one of his cheeks and left him there, guarded by another *mimi*. The first *mimi* went in search of others who lived in caves in the area. He showed them the flesh he had cut, and they were pleased: 'Now we will have a feast!' He told them they had better hurry, in case the man ran away.

So all the *mimi* came down from their caves, dancing and singing:

manburi manburi manburi manburi anbuloglog

[The word *manburi*, repeated, was said to refer to a rock yam, like cassava; the meaning of the last word was unknown.]

In the meantime, the *mimi* who had been looking after the man had cut off all his flesh until only the bones were left, and had eaten all the flesh. When he heard the others coming, he ran away, so the others arrived to find only the bones. They were very angry. They began to hit that rock, but could not find the *mimi* who had eaten him. They went back hungry to their cave homes.

This cruel story gives another side of the character of *mimi*. In Myths 72 and 80 friendship was possible between a human being and a *mimi* or a *maam*, even though it was short-lived. There are other such accounts, too. Here, however, the sole intent is to treat human beings as a source of food. In this respect, apart from their differing appearance, they resemble the Western Desert *mamu*; and, like the *mamu*, *mimi* are untrustworthy as far as their own colleagues are concerned. In R. Berndt (1964/68) two plates (36 and 37) illustrate these events, while on pages 88–89 a slightly different version of this myth is given.

The next two myths concern a variety of spirits named Daadubi, who were separately categorised by the Gunwinggu The first was told to C. Berndt and the second to R. Berndt, at Oenpelli in 1950.

Some people say that Daadubi, who could be one person or a group of them, have no direct dealings with *mimi*, only trading relationships where each of them would leave goods at specified places but did not meet. But in this story a Daadubi had a *mimi* wife.

82. A DAADUBI SHOULDN'T MARRY A *MIMI*

When the land was young, that Daadubi had a wife. She was a young girl, a *mimi*. Well, for a long time she had had a sweetheart, a *mimi* sweetheart, who brought her wild potato (*manburi*) leaves, as if they were hand-kerchiefs! Still she kept on living with her husband. When she went hunting for plant foods that young *mimi* man would go too and meet her, and they would lie down to sleep together. He would give her a lot of food, filling her baskets with wild potatoes. And he would tell her, 'When that Daadubi dies, I'll take you, we'll go away together!' They would fight playfully together among the grasses, clasping each other's necks.

That Daadubi felt his heart hurting him. He said in his mind, 'Perhaps someone has been meeting my wife, because I'm sick, dying in my heart!' When she came home he asked her, 'You tell me straight. A man met you! Because I'm sick, ever since my heart began to hurt me!' But she was still hiding the truth. He struck her. She ran away to her mother and father, but they brought her back to him, back to her husband. He told her, 'If you run away again, just one more time, I'll spear you — and you could die from that!' At last, when night came, they both slept. But he didn't let her go hunting by herself again, because he knew in his mind that she would meet that man. He asked her again, talking strongly, 'Why are you afraid of me? Why don't you tell me the truth?'

After that, she would sneak away from him at night and not come back until early morning. He would ask her, 'Where were you, when I looked for you in the night? Did you go where the young men were sleeping?' At last he hit her, he was so jealous of her. So then she left him altogether: she never came back to see him again. They called out to one another, those *mimi* and Daadubi; they were spearing one another on account of her. They speared one another — but they became hard while they were still living. They go about just as people do, but they don't die like we do. Our bodies die, only our spirits go on living. But they stay alive in their own bodies. They 'made themselves' like that, long ago, those *mimi* and Daadubi. They go on living there among the rocks in their own country, they live there in the middle of the rocky country for ever.

The story-teller, Mangurug, said she first heard this as a young girl from her paternal grandmother, who came from the rocky country near Nimbuwa. Sweethearts (*mararaidj* in Gunwinggu) in ordinary life, as in this story, were expected to exchange gifts and tokens to show their affection, but they always ran the risk of being attacked by jealous husbands — or jealous wives.

83.   EVADING DAADUBI

At Gumarinbang, near Gugur at the junction of the Gudjolduru river, on the eastern side of the Liverpool River, higher up than Margulidjban in Gunwinggu country, a Dreaming man called Djurubir, *yariwurig*, *nangaraidgu*, was looking for *garbara* yams. Still searching, he walked on to Migulid, where he found some. He camped there for two nights and then went on, following Gudjolduru 'creek' along until he came to Gunugdi, where he collected and ate more yams. Travelling farther, he decided to climb some rocks, then came down and went along a creek that ran to the head of Gabari [lower down from Gumadir]. At Bamgalamai, there was a big jungle with plenty of these yams. He camped there. 'I have to sit down here,' he said. He cooked the yams, and ate them. Each day he went out collecting them.

A Daadubi smelt the yams cooking. 'Ah, someone there. I'll go and find him,' he thought to himself. He came toward the place where Djurubir had his fire. Djurubir was cooking yams and crushing them with stones to soften them, because he was an old man and had no teeth. Daadubi could smell those yams: he came close and saw large heaps of them, cooked and uncooked. He entered Djurubir's camp. 'I smelt those yams. You should give me some,' he said. Djurubir looked up: 'Ah, a *namandi* or a *maam* has come.' Daadubi sat down, 'Don't be frightened of me, brother.' But he was deceiving Djurubir, who said, 'Why do you come here and ask me for yams? I don't know you. You are a *maam*, not a human!'

Djurubir had flying fox wings, big ones, 'just like a tent'. He threw them over Daadubi, covering him entirely. Then Djurubir quickly collected his yams, filling his bags with them, and ran to Mountain Gap. Looking back, he saw that Daadubi had thrown aside his covering and was beginning to search for him; but he couldn't find him because Djurubir went into a cave and made himself *djang*. Daadubi went away to another rock, where he remained as a spirit. [The cave in which the *djang* Djurubir lives is a big hole, a 'danger place'. But yams can be obtained outside the hole (cave), not from inside. 'If you go in, the *djang* spirit will kill you!']

Djurubir is not deceived by Daadubi, who greets him as a 'brother' and expects to share his food. Djurubir identifies him as a malevolent spirit who could do him harm and copes with the situation accordingly — but at the cost of Djurubir becoming *djang*, and the metamorphosis of Daadubi. When Djurubir looked up and saw Daadubi, he was unsure whether it was a *namandi* or a *maam*. In some accounts the spirit characters are called *namandi*, rather than *maam*. In others, *namandi* is more likely to mean the body or ghost of a dead person. But 'real *namandi*, from the beginning', are a 'little bit Dreaming'. In Gogalag, for example, a number of small place names relate to them. Gadjiman-gai'mi is an echo-name, 'Gadjiman is calling out', and within that is a smaller place, *Namandi-djiga-rawun*, 'Namandi breast-feeding (her son)'. In the Gunwinggu language, *na* is usually a masculine prefix; for a female, the prefix is *ngal*; so it is interesting that the word *namandi* does not change its form even in cases like this. In a conversation with other *namandi* they agree that they and their homes are smelly, 'stinking', 'like dead bodies'. A smaller place name, in Girdoldol, puts it bluntly: *Namandi-gunud-budji-bebmeng*, 'Namandi-stinking-body-smell-came-out'. At Nyibin-nyibin in Maganyir, in the same broad region, another *namandi* and his family have their Dreaming site. And as they all exchange greetings with one another, their voices echo like thunder among the rocks.

Spirit characters living among the rocks (at Gunugdi) are *mimi*, *woramaam* (spirits of dead people), *marlwa*, Daadubi and Namurudu. Daadubi, an old man with white hair, lives mainly on fish, and is always accompanied by his dog, Miribongbong (Bat). His home is in the coldness of the deep caves; he doesn't like the heat. (But, as above, there *can* be more than one Daadubi.) Namurudu is his younger brother from the same father, but they live separately. Their father, Gwiyamarung, speaks Woraidbag. Their mothers were half sisters from one mother, speaking Gunwinggu. Namurudu was a *maam*, but he 'makes himself frightened' and takes on the identity of Namurudu. He eats mainly meat. And he says, 'I take fire to people who are dying. I take their breath. I'm always dangerous! I carry my fighting-stick to break their necks, those new spirits! I always wear my dancing-feathers and carry my fighting-stick, with my hair belt tied around me. And if people see my light, they say, "He's that dangerous man, carrying fire," and they call my name — Namurudu!'

The following three myths relate to this dangerous spirit, named Namurudu among the Gunwinggu, but also called Indada and Yung-galya by Gagadju and associated groups: often he/she is depicted as a giant. They were told to R. Berndt at Oenpelli in 1949.

84. STEALING NAMURUDU'S FISH

A number of Gagadju people were camped at Ginyanbulu point: among them were Ngadug, Ngarug and Amurag speakers. Some Yung-galya [Gagadju equivalent to Namurudu] came from Angmeridja but were living at Yuwaga hill, close to the East Alligator River, near Smith's Landing. These Yung-galya were fishing. As they caught each fish they threaded a string through its mouth. When they were ready to leave, they pulled the long line of fish behind them. The fish were still dragging along when they reached their camp at Yuwaga; they continued to pull in the string.

However, some people from Ginyanbulu were out hunting and passed the long line of fish: 'Look, a lot of fish here, belonging to the Yung-galya!' They cut the string with a mussel shell knife, collected the fish and took them back to Ginyanbulu.

[It is not clear at first whether more than one Yung-galya was involved, but the story now focuses on a single Yung-galya, regarded as the leader.] The Yung-galya pulled in his line of fish and counted them: 'What's happened?' he thought. 'Has my line broken? I've lost some of my fish! I'll go back and look.' In the meantime the people had been cooking the fish. They had made a number of fires, and Yung-galya saw these. 'Ah, those people have taken *our* fish. I can smell the cooking of fish, being carried on the wind.' He returned to Yuwaga and told the other Yung-galya.

The people ate the fish, but swarms of mosquitoes disturbed them and they went into the caves, shutting up the entrance with grass to keep them out. They all slept, snoring after having eaten so many fish. The Yung-galya 'boss' got a small stone and took it to the caves. He flattened it out 'just like wax', and put it over the entrance, sealing all the people inside. In the morning, all the people awakened when they heard the birds calling. They went to the caves' entrance and tried to push it away, but it would not open! They remained there.

Their relatives came from Ginin. They followed their tracks to the caves, and saw where the Yung-galya had blocked them in with stone. They sent messages to various camps, telling them what happened. And they said, 'If we see a long line of fish being dragged along, we can take one fish. If we cut a line holding many fish, the Yung-galya will seal up our huts or our caves, wherever we are living!'

Stealing a Namurudu's fish results in the incarceration of the human beings responsible. The main point made in the myth is that to take one fish from the long line of fish is all right — but to take more, well, 'those people were asking for trouble!'

85. THE CHILD AND THE NAMURUDU

At Wimurun in the bush at the top of Cooper's Creek, on the eastern side, low down from Manyulg in Amurag country, all the women in the camp went out to collect food. They left a little boy, Aranmanubi, *yarigarngurg*, *nagudjug*, there, with his father named Arimuniga, *yariyaning, nangaridj*. They, too, were Amurag. The child was crying for his mother, Miradbug, *nyindjarigarngurg, ngalangila*. The father tried to stop him, but he just kept on crying. After a while the father got tired of this and told him, 'Go and look for your mother!'

Now, an Indada [Namurudu] heard the child crying. 'I'll catch that child,' he thought. Indada came down from his rock home. He was a giant, and took immense strides as he walked, with a foot in one place and the other foot back on the hill [his footprints can be seen today]. The child in search of his mother saw this giant towering up above him. 'Don't be frightened,' Indada said, 'I'm human. I'm a man. I'll take you to my home and make you a big man, and I'll give you lots of things.' So he picked up the child and took him back to the rocks: 'Don't you cry, I've got plenty of food in my camp.' When they arrived there he got a *mudjag* 'bitter' yam, cooked it, mashed it up and gave it to the child, who ate it. He sat down quietly and did not cry, just went on eating *mudjag*.

In the meantime, the boy's mother and the other women returned from collecting food. They could not find him. All the people began to cry, and then they all went out to look for him

Another Namurudu, called Wulubinmag, heard them from where he was sitting at Yengidj rock. 'I'll go to Manyulg to find out what has happened.' When he got there he called out, but no-one was about. He returned to Yengidj, and from there he called out to the people in the camp at Wimurun, 'Why are you crying?' They called back, 'We have lost a child. Perhaps he got lost in the bush, or a Namurudu has taken him.' 'I'll go and talk to Indada — he might have taken the child,' Wulubinmag thought. [Wulubinmag had been out fishing when the child was abducted.]

He came to where Indada was camped, and found the child there. 'I'll take him back to his people,' Wulubinmag said. But Indada wanted to keep the child: he tried to hold the boy. However, Wulubinmag took him to Wimurun. He called out to the people, 'I have brought him. Here he is, come and get him!' And he told them that he was returning to fight Indada: 'You listen to us!'

Wulubinmag went back, and the two giants began fighting. The people could hear the noise from the camp — '*Du! Du! Dududi!*' 'Don't kill me, brother — don't hurt me too much,' Indada pleaded. Wulubinmag defeated Indada. From their camp, all the people heard them — 'and you can still hear them!'

The two Namurudu, Indada and Wulubinmag, are giants. They are certainly dangerous, but ambivalent with regard to human beings. In this case one abducts the child, while the other returns him to his family. It is not so much the father who is to blame for telling the child to look for its mother, but the child's cries. This is part of the 'crying child' syndrome (see Myths 47–49). Mostly, the child's cries attract the attention of a Rainbow Snake and, consequently, bring disaster on the whole camp as well as to the child. As far as Namurudu are concerned, the effects are less drastic. Nevertheless, children who cry at night are warned that if they do not stop a Namurudu will come and take them away: 'and they stop crying immediately!'

86. INDADA'S DEATH

At Imadangun, close to Smith's Landing on the East Alligator River, lived Mugullul, a *yariwurga, nabangari* Amurag man. One day he went out hunting among the big rocks. He killed a kangaroo and hung it in a tree, intending to return and collect it when he had got another. He speared the second and brought it back, then made a large fire on which to throw it. The north wind was blowing against the big rock at Yiwa, and from a long way it brought the smell of singeing kangaroo fur to Indada [Namurudu]. Indada rose and 'put his feet three times' [that is, three paces]: one step at Almurug-gamunu; one at Idbadja [where there is a 'sharp' hill] and then he moved his legs to Amurawona Rocks, where the kangaroo was being prepared.

Indada climbed up a big stringybark tree and said: 'I have come for you! I smelt your fire.' When Mugullul looked up and saw him, he felt giddy with fear; he could not speak. It was the first time he had seen an Indada. Indada said: 'I want to take you to my place.' 'All right,' the other managed to reply. Indada came down, and told the man, 'Put your feet on mine!' In this way, with Mugullul, Indada jumped once, then again, and back to his original place at Yiwa. He took the man inside his home. Mugullul saw a large number of Indada there. He could not speak. Indada told his brother, 'Brother, I have a man now! My son, my daughter, I have brought a man!' But the brother was angry, 'Why have you brought him?' And the other replied: 'He belongs to this country, like his father and his mother. He only wants to look at this country; he wanted to come. Tomorrow, any time, he'll go back.'

In the middle of the night the first Indada went out after telling his brother to look after the man while he was fishing with his sons. The man, in the cave, heard the Indada dragging along his fishing line [see Myth 84].

The other brother asked the man: 'Do you want to go back to your father and mother, to all your relatives? 'Yes,' the man replied. So Indada opened the rock entrance [which was like a lid]: 'Come on, you put your foot on mine, and I'll let you down from the rocks easily.' He put the man down on the ground. The man ran to the place where the first Indada had found him and picked up his spears and spear-thrower. And he thought, 'I'll get more wallaby and kangaroo.' He killed a large one, made a fire and threw the kangaroo on the fire. Again the north wind blew.

Indada returned from fishing and, finding the man gone, quarrelled with his brother: 'Where's that man?' he asked. 'He may have followed you,' said the other. The first Indada smelt the singeing fur: 'I had better go and look.' So he flew like a djabiru bird, looking for him.

Now, that man had two stone-bladed spears. He pulled out the blades and threw aside the bamboo shafts. Indada brought wind and Mugullul became giddy. Indada flew on to a limb of a big tree and spoke to him. 'I have just followed you.' But the man did not answer: his kangaroo meat was cooking in the coals. Indada sat down by the tree: 'I'm hungry,' he said: 'I want that meat.' Mugullul threw the head of the kangaroo at him, and as the other was eating, he re-connected the stone blades to their shafts. Then he gave Indada the rest of the meat. As Indada's head was bending over the meat, Mugullul threw his spears and killed him 'through the heart'. With a loud cry, he fell down. Mugullul left him lying there and returned to Imadangun. His father and mother asked him where he had been. He replied, 'I have been camping out in the bush.'

Mugullul went to sleep — but no daylight came. [When an Indada was killed, this caused a long night.] The father asked his son: 'What have you done? Perhaps you have killed something.' [Indada can stop the sun: no more daylight.] 'My son, you get your spear-thrower and spears, the ones you used: warm them in the fire and swing them around.' He did this, calling, *'Gubulbul djabang-ga!'* [Sun come out (let it)!] And it opened then; the daylight came.

As in Myth 85, the conflict between the Namurudu brothers over abducting a human being is repeated here — but in this case over a man and not a child. On being returned to the place where he had been hunting, the man purposely re-attracts Indada and succeeds in killing him. Now, although Namurudu are giants and are dangerous, they are also said not to be really like spirits: 'They are like men, and sit under the shade of banyan trees during the day and camp in the rocks and caves at night.'

The following is a brief version of the Thunder and Lightning man who is categorised within this group of spirits. It was told to C. Berndt at Oenpelli in 1950.

87. NAMARGUN

Long ago Namargun came from the north, from where he parted company with Wuragag, Tor Rock. He was looking for a place to 'make himself *djang*', travelling alone because he was very dangerous. He carried a fighting stick, an axe and a lighted torch. People could see from far away the grass and scrub fires he was lighting. When he came to the right place, he made himself taboo. He practised making fires, like lightning flashes, tearing apart trees and rocks, and his voice was like thunder. He speared a kangaroo, brought it back, singed off its fur, cut it open and fastened its arms and legs, and was waiting for it to cook in the hot coals when its guts burst open, breaking the skin. So he 'made himself wrong'. He became truly Namargun. He made two wings for himself, took his axe and flew up into the sky. He burns and flashes like fire up there. His bones became rock, where he stands holding his axe at his *djang* site, Ngugurumu. But his spirit is up in the sky, where he follows the rain, for ever.

This myth has many parallels in other parts of Aboriginal Australia: for instance, in north-eastern Arnhem Land where Bodngu, the Thunder Man, has a carved spear which he throws to make lightning; he urinates to make rain.

We turn back to another giant who lived on Goulburn Island. This story was told to R. Berndt in 1947. Mayangaidj, his antagonist, orginally came from Bumara, Hall Point, on the mainland. The people there, called Mananggari, spoke Maung but are said to have repeated their words, saying each word twice: all the Mananggari are now dead.

88. MAYANGAIDJ AND THE GIANT

Mayangaidj (Maya-ngaidj) lived at Mamalang, a camp on the eastern side of North Goulburn Island. With his empty *wula-nguna* dilly bag hanging from his back, he went to Fishing Creek. There was a jungle nearby and he planned to obtain *mariwi* jungle-fibre to make an *alawi* fishing net.

But Yumbarbar, a giant, lived in that jungle. Mayangaidj went in and began to cut lengths of fibre. While he was doing that he saw two painted fighting *igana* clubs hanging there. As he was walking into the jungle, having crossed the creek, his empty dilly bag made a noise as it moved from side to side. The rattling noise awakened Yumbarbar. 'Is that you, Mayangaidj?' 'Yes', said Mayangaidj, turning round. When he did that the giant saw his dilly bag and asked him for it. 'No. I can't give it to you, it's mine!' The giant asked him again. Mayangaidj explained to the giant that the dilly bag was a present and he could not give it away. The giant replied, 'I think, then, we had better fight over it!' He gave Mayangaidj one of his clubs and picked up the other for himself.

The fight began. Yumbarbar hit Mayangaidj on the back, and he fell down. The giant thought he was dead, but Mayangaidj was only pretending. He lay there, his club in his hand, thinking, 'I'll kill this giant!' The giant was standing with legs wide apart, and his testes hung down so that they touched the ground. He was looking to see whether there were any other people around. Mayangaidj jumped up and swung his club at the giant's testes. Yumbarbar fell, in pain. When he hit the ground, both North and South Goulburn Islands shook, and so did the whole area from Cape Don to the Liverpool River.

Mayangaidj returned to his camp at Mamalang and told the people there what he had done, and they went with him to look at the giant. They walked into the jungle to find the giant's home, called Gaidjili. 'It was [a big place] like a mission house.' They praised Mayangaidj for having killed the giant. Then they all went home. Later, when the giant's body had decomposed they came back and removed his eyes. These were carried from one place to another and shown whenever this story was told.

The eyes of the giant did not return to Goulburn Island, as far as is known. Mayangaidj is said to have died when the first Macassan visitors arrived on the north Australian coast. The story suggests that the epic fight between the giant and Mayangaidj was already planned: consider the two clubs hanging in the tree from which the man was to cut his fibre, and Yumbarbar addressing Mayangaidj by his personal name. The fall of the giant with the consequent shaking of the local area could well serve to account for an earth tremor. The next two giant stories were told by women to C. Berndt at Oenpelli in 1950.

89. BIYU-BIYU: A MALIGNANT GIANT (1)

Before, those old people were talking about the first inhabitants of this country. When we were small they told us. They said: There was a man who was enormously big, like a rock. And he was dangerous. He was killing us, he was finishing us altogether. He said that he was the only man, the rest of us were just meat for him, for him to kill and cook and eat. So it is good that they killed him, those people: they speared him so that he died.

One girl was pregnant, the other had just reached puberty, and they had taken their baskets to look for plums because they were hungry. The younger sister was carrying the baskets for them both. They were up in a tree eating plums — but those were Biyu-biyu's plums. From far away he heard them biting the hard skin of the plums and crunching the nutty seed inside. 'That's my meat,' he said to himself as he came, 'those two biting my plums!' And he sang a happy song:

Mo-ngerg mo-ngerg, mandjuli-biriri, mowani,
Di'diri-di'diri!

Mo-ngerg is the name of the song, *mandjuli* might mean 'shade', and when he sang *'Di'diri'*, he was throwing his faeces about, throwing them a long way. But he was singing in his own tongue, and we don't really know what he was saying — only that he was happy to think of killing those girls when he heard them eating. He kept singing as he came, then he stopped and bent forward, defecating in excitement, 'My meat, those two up in the tree!' He was carrying his long crooked stick, with a big dilly bag like a fish net over his shoulder. He was looking through the leaves, and saw the two girls high up, filling their baskets. So he hid in the grass, that Biyu-biyu, and came crawling along until he was close to the tree. Then he threw his stick. It struck the older girl on the nose. Both girls fell from the tree, but the younger one was not injured. Biyu-biyu put them in his bag, tied it tightly at the top and checked it carefully for holes. He was grumbling to himself, because he was hungry for good meat and was afraid it would spoil: 'I have to eat it all, by myself.' He had already eaten the blood that had flowed from the elder sister's nose when he struck her. Now he took the bag with the two girls in it back to his camp, and ran to dig the ground for an oven. He put bark inside, and a large straight stick, and got some ant-bed ready.

The younger girl had been taking stock of her situation. She nudged her sister, but the girl didn't move: she was dead. The younger girl tore apart the side of the bag with her teeth when she saw Biyu-biyu had gone some distance away. When he came back she held the hole shut, hiding it. He threw down some ant-bed beside the oven and said to his *djabo*, the spotted cat who was his dog, 'You watch over our meat. I'm going a long way off to get some paperbark so we can cook it in the oven.'

The younger sister got up and ran. The 'dog' tried to catch her, but she was young and she ran too fast. The older girl lay dead in the bag. The younger one went running across a stretch of shining sand, so dazzling that no-one could see her.

When Biyu-biyu came back with the paperbark, he asked his dog what had happened. The dog said 'Yes, one meat ran away, but the other is still here!' Biyu-biyu scolded him, beat him up, and sent him off into the long grass. He didn't give that dog any of the guts or liver or heart, just ate them himself, as a punishment for letting the girl escape. So for one day the dog slept hungry.

Biyu-biyu skinned the elder sister and cut her up like a kangaroo ready for cooking. While he was waiting, he ate her liver and heart as a snack. He had taken out the baby from inside her and cooked it separately on the coals, and ate that as a snack too. At last, when his dog came back, he took the paperbark from the oven and put the joints of the meat into a bag. He carried it back to the cave-house where he was living, and he and his dog sat down together and ate it: both legs, breasts, both arms, head: they finished it all.

The younger sister had taken the message about the dead girl to their husband, and he was pressing her uncles and her father and mother to set out on a revenge expedition. They were all weeping for that girl, and sending the death-message to her relatives. They were getting axes to gash themselves in grief, sharpening sticks and spear blades, preparing a range of different spears as they cried for that girl. They were gathering together many bunches of spears and fighting sticks. And those two uncles, the girls' mother's brothers, were both clever men, powerful men.

In the meantime Biyu-biyu was still singing, there in his cave-house. He was happy. He had eaten that girl, and he was full. But the two uncles had killed all the flies around them and put them inside their bodies so that Biyu-biyu wouldn't see them (and realise they were approaching him), because he was truly dangerous. Then the two men went crawling under the ground to where he was singing. He had an echidna blowing the didjeridu, and his 'dog' was dancing. And he was singing his song,

Mo-ngerg mo-nerg, mandjuli-biriri, mowani,
Di'diri di'diri!

He thought he would be going on singing, but too late. The uncles and those other men too were aiming their spears ready to throw. They speared him in the back, all over his back, all over his body. He was trying to get up, but they struck him down with fighting sticks; they cut his head in half, they speared him, they chopped him up with axes. He was dead. They looked at him. 'Shall we bury him?' 'No, burn him up!' They got firewood and made a huge blaze, to destroy him. As for the 'dog' and the echidna, they ran away, far away, in fear.

The dead girl's legs, already cooked, had been dropped in the cave. The men took them [the bones?] back to their own country, where they joined all the pieces together and put them on a meat ants' nest. After a while she became like a baby: she got up, she was alive. Those two uncles had made that girl alive again. When her mother and father saw her, they stopped crying. They were happy again. She was alive. But that dangerous man was dead, dead for ever. If he had stayed alive he would have gone on killing people — us dark people and those pale people, he would have killed us all, because for a long time he had been eating our people. He thought that he alone was a person and the rest of us were just meat for him, that's what he called us. So it's good that they killed him, or he would have done away with us all.

Biyu-biyu came from the west of the East Alligator River, from the Mangerdji (Mangeri) language area. His subsection was *nagangila*, his semi-moiety Djoned, March fly. The two girls were of the same subsection, *ngalgangila*, but *yariwurga* semi-moiety, and they came from the south-east of Oenpelli, where the Gunwinggu language overlaps with Dangbun. The elder's sister name was Ngalmiraya; the younger, Djurl-gidj. The two uncles were Gigid and Wolarg. Another version of this story appears in R. and C. Berndt (1985: 402–03). A variant (Myth 90) which starts with a different setting was told by another woman a few weeks later.

90.   BIYU-BIYU: A MALIGNANT GIANT (2)

Long ago, when those first people were making all the places, that big man came into being. He had a big penis. At last those winged creatures, those geese, were making eggs on the plain. And he himself, that Biyu-biyu, made a paperbark house and hung up his belongings inside it. He went and cut down a stringybark tree and made a canoe for himself. He would go and collect eggs, fill up the canoe, come back with a load of eggs, and put them in his house. He kept on doing that, going a long way in search of more eggs.

Two women, two girls, were coming in that direction, looking for a man to be a sweetheart or a husband. One girl had breasts. The other was younger: no breasts yet. Well, they came to the house — Biyu-biyu's house — and went inside it. They said to each other, 'Sister, this is a good house that we've found. Come on in, we'll sleep here, and then maybe a man will come and get us!' They ate some of the goose meat and goose eggs that were in the house. But Biyu-biyu had gone, as he always did, to look for more. He had gone a long way and hadn't come back yet. He just kept going, and didn't come back until the middle of the night.

The two girls were lying there waiting for that man, but when darkness came they fell asleep. He was getting closer, coming back with his load of eggs that made a rustling sound as they moved in the canoe. He went into his house and made a big fire, and in its light he saw the girls lying there. He said to himself, 'My women! They've come here to me, so now they'll be my sweethearts, my wives!' He felt their bodies, touching them all over. He felt the older sister, with breasts, and the younger one with none. He took the older girl, and tried her: he put in his penis and tried to 'eat' her, but he just tore her body open, from her vagina to her throat. He got up, and saw that she had stopped breathing. She was dead.

The younger sister had already escaped. She ran away, hiding from him. He tried to catch her, but she was too quick. She kept going, to where her mother and father were living, and told them what had happened. 'My elder sister and I, we met that man with a dangerous penis and he tried to eat us! He tore my elder sister apart! So then I ran away, I was frightened!' She told her mother and father and all her relatives there.

Meanwhile, the older girl's body was starting to decompose, so Biyu-biyu took her out and buried her. But the younger girl had gone to get all her relatives to come and spear him, to kill him. They were cutting themselves in grief for that elder sister who had been killed. They rose up: they prepared their spears and spear-throwers and their fighting sticks and promised to use these weapons to avenge her. They set off and came to where he was living. He gave them a lot of goose eggs, and they camped there with him. They lay down to sleep. When they saw that he was sound asleep, they got their spears and spear-throwers and speared him to death. They killed his three dogs as well, finished them off. Then they burned him up, in a great fire, and set fire to his house.

After that they went back to where they were living, but they didn't live there for long. They came into Dreaming, they became *djang,* and they remain there as rocks in the place to which they gave the name, Yarrgu. They became *djang* when they killed that man with the dangerous penis — dangerous like a knife, tearing up those two girls [i.e., he *would* have torn both of them, if one hadn't escaped.] They were camping among the rocks, eating honey and plant foods, in that country they had been looking for, where they put the name Yarrgu, and where they found that dangerous man and killed him.

In this account Biyu-biyu was living at Nawalbin, a Woraidbag-language place on the plain a little to the east of the East Alligator River. The girls also spoke Woraidbag: Maldrinma the elder sister and Abudji the younger. Their sub-section was *ngalbangari,* their semi-moiety *yariwurga.* Mangurug, who told the story, said she heard it for the first time when she had just reached puberty, before she was married. In a number of her stories girls who go looking for sweethearts meet with disaster, or at least one of them does. In this case, unlike the preceding account, Biyi-biyu did not have murderous intentions: he was conforming with the girls' expectations, although they did not realise how unsuitable (ineligible) he was. The end result was the same for him, however: his death was inevitable.

The last two myths in this chapter concern the Wirindji spirit women. The first was told to R. Berndt, the second to C. Berndt, both at Oenpelli in 1950.

91. WIRINDJI (A MEN'S VERSION)

Two sisters and their five daughters, all called Wirindji, came from a long way, from Banambar along the Goyder River [Yanulagi and Wulagi languages]. They came dancing along, singing:

wirindji wirindji gaidba gaidba gurlb gurlb (repeated)

They came to a big billabong, Lugu-lugu, where they camped. They danced and sang all day until evening, when they slept.

They went on dancing to Ninigeri (Yanulagi), where they drank water from the billabong on the top side of the hill, going south-west. They came to Burugulg, a billabong with red lilies, where they agreed to camp. They continued dancing and singing, and from their dancing feet dust rose like a whirlwind, a *ngaidjerawul*. They went on to Gu-bolgbarbin, to a creek in the Liverpool River area, high up in Gunwinggu country, and then on to Gudjalduru creek. 'We'll camp here,' they decided. The younger sister went out to collect food with the five daughters, while the elder sister continued dancing and singing all day. They brought back food. 'Will you eat some food, elder sister?' 'No,' she replied, 'I'll go on dancing and singing, and I'll eat at night.'

Eventually they came to Mandaidj-gadjang, where they drank water. They climbed up the rocks, then walked through the bush to Manbidugari and camped there. As usual, the elder sister danced the *wirindji* dance, while the others went out to hunt. Then they all went on to Malgarwul, high up on the eastern side of Gumadir. Leaving that place, they went to Djinbiri, where they camped. While the elder sister danced, the others went out and obtained plenty of honey and 'bitter' yams. Next morning they went on to Maguru-maldjarang. They were looking around to find a good place. 'We have to sit down here, at Ganara.' They looked all around, and decided that Ganara was good country. They were dancing and singing, and dust was rising.

Now, there were two young Dreaming men from Walarai, farther down the river. They saw the rising dust. They thought that some of their countrymen were burning off grass and causing the smoke, and decided to go and look. They came to an open plain, and sneaked up to the Wirindji camp. They saw the elder sister dancing, and the younger sister preparing food. The two women saw the two men, and discussed whether they should invite them to come to their camp. On the other hand, the two men were a little frightened: 'They might be Wirindji!' Eventually they came into the camp and the two sisters gave their young daughters to the two men; they slept with them.

The two sisters carried stones on their backs — they used these to kill men, and roast and eat them. The younger sister asked the elder what she wanted to do. She replied, 'I want to kill them!' 'Better not kill them; they might kill us,' said the younger. But the elder sister told her sister to go away. She got her round rock and threw it at one of the men as he ran away, breaking his neck. Then she threw her stone at the other man, hitting his head, and he fell.

The two sisters quarrelled. The younger one did not want to eat them. The elder sister told her to collect wood, but she refused. 'You get it yourself!' She added, 'You roast them yourself!' The elder sister prepared the fire and cut up the two bodies, opening up the stomach and removing the entrails and internal organs. She cut off the arms, shoulders, legs and feet and cooked them in the hot coals and on stones covered with coals and earth. When they were ready, she removed them from the oven and allowed them to cool. 'Come on,' she called to her sister. 'No, I can't eat human beings. I'd vomit. Other people will hear about this, and they will come and kill me!' So the elder sister ate all the meat herself.

The father of those two men had also seen the dust which they had thought was smoke from a fire. He had actually sent them to see whether any people were there. [The father had a dream, and in it the presence of the Wirindji was revealed to him.] He sneaked up to the Wirindji camp; he smelt the cooking human flesh. 'They have killed my boys!' he cried. He returned to collect members of a revenge party. He brought together people from Bunggul [or Bawun-gul, close to Bamboo Creek, near the South Alligator River]; from Nalwelandja [a creek running into the South Alligator, near Timber Creek]; from Walarai [higher up from the last place]; from Wanbi [near the East Alligator River, on the other side of Doyle's place, at a swamp]; and from Gwundulg [lower down from the last place]. He brought them all together, and 'they walked like grass, like ants — there were so many people'. They went to Walarai, and the father 'put a rope around' them all, to assess whether there were enough people. There were enough. He went down to check whether the Wirindji were still there, at Ganara. Returning to Walarai, he got the men together and they sneaked down to Ganara, completely surrounding the Wirindji, 'ring after ring', surrounding them.

They heard the elder sister singing and dancing; they saw the other sister and the daughters, and they threw their spears. The daughters saw them and cried out to their mothers, warning them. The elder sister turned in every direction, dodging the spears as they were thrown. She threw her stones which they, in turn, dodged. But the spears began to pierce her until she looked like an echidna. Then they speared her in the heart, killing her. She fell down: she remains sitting there at Ganara. They took hold of the younger sister and the daughters. The father of the two men wanted to save them, but the other men killed them — 'They might breed more dangerous women like the Wirindji!' They burnt them, but the elder sister turned to rock. There is also a hole at this place, which is now a billabong. That was the place where the fire was, and where the other Wirindji were burnt to death.

These are, in a sense, the wild, dangerous women feared by men, who are irresistibly drawn to them — and killed. In some versions the men themselves join the dancing women: but the singing continues for so long that they fall exhausted to the ground and are killed.

92. WIRINDJI (A WOMEN'S VERSION)

Long ago, when we were not here, long before we were born, an old woman set off from far in the east, coming this way. She was dangerous, she would have killed us all. She was coming in search of Gunwinggu country, following along the edges of tidal creeks and along the sandy beaches. Nobody came with her, because she was so dangerous: she always carried a very long, flat, smooth pounding stone, to knock people on the head so that they died straight away, and a fighting stick sharpened at the point and on two sides to break their noses. She came, making country in what they call the Bulgai, the Middle place, near Maningrida, and coming to Margulidjban, she made country there too. And she put plant foods and fish, and planted *man-gulaid* nuts and *man-gindjeg* yams. But she herself did not eat them, or kangaroo either, because she had a rage inside her: she kept wanting to kill people. So, all she ate was a few *man-gulaid* nuts.

She set off from far away, coming to our country, but at last she dropped her own language and spoke Gunwinggu because she had reached our Gunwinggu place. There she was dancing, as she made her camp, all by herself. Dust rose from her feet as she danced, rising like a whirlwind. Early in the morning she was still dancing, and she kept dancing along all the paths she took as she came looking for a home. This was her song:

Wirindji Wirindji Wirindji!
garba garba,
durb-durb-durb-durb!

I'm Wirindji!
[My feet hit the ground
Making this noise, *durb-durb. . .!*]

She came to a jungle at Gundjumburng, in Gumadir, where there were many flying foxes. She went into it and made a stringybark house for herself, and there she waited in hiding for people, real people like us, to come along the path, 'so that when they come', she said, 'I'll kill them straight away!' She was still dancing, hiding near the path, but nobody came. Those people had seen the dust rising from her dancing. At last two men came, two young initiates. The others [who had been involved in the *ubar* ritual] had said to them, 'How about you two going to see that fire? Maybe it's your father and mother who lit it, for us, for you two young men!' They thought they were telling the truth, that it was a fire burning, because the mother and father of those two young men had sent a firm message about it [to guide them to where their parents would be].

Well, those two were coming from a long way distant, so they were still travelling when night fell. They went on in the darkness, looking ahead to the light of that fire — she had lit the fire, that dangerous woman. They thought they were coming to meet their father and mother, but already they were getting close to where that woman, that Wirindji, was living. She was lying there in her camp. They came and sat down beside her fire, but by then she was sound asleep and did not hear them even though they were treading on dry leaves. Those two didn't know about her. They fell asleep on one side of the fire, while she was asleep on the other. During the night she felt cold. She got up and built up the fire to warm herself, but she did not see them properly because the fire was so big [and she didn't see past the flames]. At last she got up from sleep when the first birds began to call. She got her sharp fighting stick and her long pounding stone and began singing and dancing, she was so happy to see the two men. As she sang she threw the stick at the elder brother, breaking his nose in the middle. The younger brother tried to get up and run away, but she had her long stone pounder ready. She struck him on the head and he stopped breathing. Younger brother and elder brother, they lay dead together, lying there uncovered while she danced. Dust from her feet rose up like a whirlwind, like the smoke from her fire.

The mother of those two young men, the mother who bore them, felt sick, dying: her breasts were hurting her. Their father was the same: before they heard the news, when their sons died, he felt sick, dying, he felt pain in his shoulders. They both wept, talking and crying, trying to find their two sons through words. They hoped the two were still alive, but they were already dead. The mother and father set off in search of them. They went on, camped one night, and next day they saw great clouds of dust rising from where Wirindji was dancing. They thought it was smoke from a fire. Then they heard her voice, as she danced. She didn't bury the young men's bodies; she was just waiting for them to decay.

The boys' parents came quietly, hiding, and listened to Wirindji's dancing song. They said to each other, 'Perhaps *she* killed our two sons!' They didn't go any closer to where she was dancing. They sneaked away, going back to take the message to their relatives and gather men to fight her. When they got to that place, they wept as they told what had happened. 'Why do you all look at us?' they said. 'We have lost our two children. We threw away their bodies when we let them go to that *ubar* ritual. We thought they would go and look at it and come back quietly. So now, you want to get your weapons together quickly!' They told men of the various semi-moieties, *yariburig* and *yariyaning, yariwurga* and *yarigarn-gurg,* and *djoned;* men from every side, and all their countrymen, and men from their mothers' countries. Men were preparing big bundles of spears: men of the *namadgu* moiety were sharing their bundles of spears and their spear-throwers, and men of the *ngaraidgu* moiety were doing the same.

Spears, spears-throwers, stone axes, metal-bladed axes (*galiwon*) from the east, they were sharpening ready for her, that Wirindji, promising to kill her.

She herself was still dancing. She danced so hard that she made a hole in the ground. So she moved to a new place and went on dancing there. She was looking for more men to kill: that's what she wanted. When she saw all those men coming she was very happy, and danced harder at the thought of killing them. But they put down their bundles of spears; they were quickly fitting spears into their throwers and flinging them at her. She was big like a rock, with a big skin, so she didn't die for a long time. They filled her with spears, all over, and at last she stopped breathing: she died for ever. They chopped her body into pieces with axes, while others were getting wood for a fire. They said to one another, 'We won't bury her because she's dangerous, we must burn her with fire.' 'Yes, that's good, break open her belly, or she might kill us and finish us all!' That's what they did: they burnt her. They put the bones of the two young men into baskets and took them back to the east where they came from, their own country. They had killed that Wirindji, and it was good, because if she had remained alive she would have finished all of us. She was alone, nobody mixed with her to share the same paths, she had no relatives. So then she was dangerous, because she was alone from the very beginning; and she was alone because she was dangerous. People saw the dust from her dancing and thought it was smoke from a fire circling upward. But that avenging party went after her, and killed her for ever.

The story-teller said she heard this first from her mother, before she reached puberty and before she was married. Wirindji was of the *ngalgangila* sub-section, *yarigarngurg* semi-moiety, and her language was Djinba. The place where the *ubar* ritual was held was Demed, by a fresh water creek in Gumadir. The two young men were of the *nabangari* sub-section, *yariwurga* semi-moiety: their *gunmugugur* was Djurolam. Their names were not known, but they came from the Dangbun side, 'properly Dangbun but half Mayali'.

One of the pervasive themes of this chapter is potential or actual conflict — between spirit characters and human beings, and among the spirit characters themselves. In this setting, conflict or acts of aggression help to make the supposed behaviour of such spirits explicable to ordinary people. Spirits are expected to behave in much the same way as they do in the myths. Simultaneously, the stories themselves expose for scrutiny particular areas of danger for spirits *and* human beings. It is important to recognise that these myths and stories are 'saying things' about the nature of intra-human associations, as well as about interaction between humans and non-humans. In other words, it is not stretching interpretation too far to suggest that humans themselves are presented in the guise of spirit actors in the exploits and tragedies that are being played out. Moreover, the behaviour of human characters is not strikingly different from that of their spirit counterparts. And in many respects people would not expect it to be so.

But the situation in relation to such myths and stories is not as simple as that. People, in this case Aborigines, are often frightened, anxious and suspicious in particular contexts — frightened of other people, disturbed at unfamiliar actions, fearful of the manifestations of natural phenomena and of the destructive forces of the elements in the world around them. That is certainly not to say that fear stalked traditional Aboriginal societies all the time. But, as in all societies, it was present in one way or another, and is easily activated. A major issue is *how* or through what media, a real or imagined fear or anxiety is projected. In the context of myth it is cloaked in a particular way in order to sharpen public awareness and to serve as an explanation of *why* it occurs; that is, to place it within the realm of ordinary understanding. Fear is to a large extent a measure of learning how to cope with social living. Fears and anxieties need to be accounted for, and in the process must be brought into the open. For that to be possible they must be dealt with in a socially acceptable fashion, however aberrant its content may be.

The spirit beings mentioned here are located within the landscape as part of its very shape from the beginning of time, as that is conceived in Aboriginal belief. Some were present when the Dreaming characters (discussed in Chapter 2) initially came on the scene. They were, and are, contemporaneous with the Rainbow and Wonambi and other great snakes (of Chapter 3); and they were there too when the first people, human men and women, made their appearance. Many of these spirits were and are of the Dreaming. They were *there,* and they did not necessarily 'turn into' something else. For most, the process of transformation was different from the way it was for other Dreaming characters: their destiny was to be as they were and as they are — *not* to be something else.

From the stories in this chapter, we can distinguish two dimensions of spirits co-existing with human beings. First, there are the *mamu, maam* and *mogwoi.* They can be conceptualised as having originally been associated with spirits of dead human beings, as ghosts. Often, but not in all cases, the spirit or 'soul' of a person on death is divisible. For example, for the Western Desert, there are the *gordi* and *mamu* manifestations; for western Arnhem Land, the *gunworal* and the *maam* or *namandi;* and for north-eastern Arnhem Land, the *birimbir* and the *mogwoi.* In the first case of each, generally speaking, the spirit in that form is conceptually re-cycled in human terms, being re-channelled through the Dreaming to enable it to re-enter the human sphere. In the second case of each (that is, the *mamu, maam* and *mogwoi*) the spirit is, in a sense, 'earth-bound'. Each constitutes a reservoir of both 'new' and 'old' spirits (or parts thereof) of the dead which, over the passage of time, lose their human characteristics although not necessarily or not entirely their human-like appearance, becoming malevolent, untrustworthy, dangerous and unpredictable. Having the ability to change their shape as occasion demands, they are enemies of living human beings. It is true that there are exceptions, and not only among *namandi* or *maam*. Some *mogwoi* can provide services for a close living relative, warning of impending danger. Such expectations are dependent specifically on the recognition (by both parties) that a *mogwoi's* living-name and at least some kin-linkages are remembered. When that kind of personal identification cannot be made, the spirit's *mogwoi* qualities become dominant.

Mimi do not belong to this general category. Like all spirit types, they have their own characteristic shape and appearance, distinguishing them from other spirits as well as from human beings. While the human-non-human antipathy is appropriate for all spirits, there are exceptions. Take the case of a *maam* on one hand and a *mimi* on the other, or a *marlwa* (in another version) who strike up a friendly relationship with a human being — although (as in Myths 72 and 80) that friendship is short-lived. *Mimi* are dangerous characters and are usually separate from other spirits. For example, Daadubi had a *mimi* wife (Myth 82); but he should not have married her, because they are substantially different. A significant point made in that particular myth is that *mimi* 'became hard while they were still living'; they did not die; they were like that from the beginning; 'they stay alive in their own bodies'. And in that respect they are virtually unique. (Even Moon changes his body each time he comes up new again.) In Myth 80, however, a *mimi* is burnt to death! (But maybe he revived in another instalment of the story.)

The second dimension relates to most of the other spirits whose shapes or behavioural patterns are equally un-human, perhaps bizarre. They are mythic characters who represent, symbolically, although sometimes indirectly, the dangerous aspects of nature. In a sense, the Rainbow-Wonambi Snake complexes (of Chapter 3) are the primary exponents in that direction, although for purposes of discussion we have placed them separately. Daadubi, Namurudu, Namargun and Yambarbar, among many others we have not mentioned here, are related in differing ways to physical manifestations of nature. We are not suggesting, however, that the Wirindji female/females (Myths 92 and 93) are of that kind. They have the 'normal' characteristics of malevolent spirits, and are also antagonistic to members of the opposite sex. They are more closely drawn in the conventional image of the European sirens who attract men to their ultimate destruction, but are much less romanticised than their Daly River counterparts (see Myth 153).

In this chapter, as in the two that have preceded it, we have introduced the principal characters, or kinds of characters, who make up the *dramatis personae* of the myths. Of course, it is not simply the actors we introduce but also the roles they play, what they do, and what they are saying. These mythic and spirit beings interact among themselves, as they do from time to time with human men and women. In doing so, they are among the many voices of, and in, the Speaking Land.

CHAPTER FIVE

SHAPES IN NATURE

The stories presented here, as in Chapter 2, are about how the natural environment took shape, how various aspects of nature were humanised or, to put it another way, how they were subjugated to human demands — although it is never quite like that. Mythic characters are likely to turn into something other than what they appeared to be before. But if that was to happen, something else had to happen first. The situation had to be congenial, and the pattern had to be designed, or worked out, before it could be completed. Whether the transformation was simply a rapid change-over from one character to another, *or* the soul-searching of a mythic being who was looking for a particular place where he or she could feel ready to be transmuted into *djang* form, the process involved was not necessarily different. So that, in relation to some myths in other chapters, these stories provide a further range of contexts and perspectives. And the focus is not so much on the human element, but on how natural species came to be as they are now. One implication, however, is that they are not always what they seem to be.

Not all mythic characters in the natural world started off as human beings, or seemingly human beings. Many snakes, for instance, did not (see Chapter 3). Nor did the characters in two western Arnhem Land myths. In one, two young sisters from North Goulburn Island 'came up as fish from inside the water and made themselves into people'. (They left a Dreaming didjeridu at one place in their travels, but were later swallowed by the Rainbow.) In the second myth, being human was an intermediate stage in the main character's earthly existence. She started life as a *man-gindjeg* root, but as she emerged above the ground she took the shape of an old woman. She ate only *man-gindjeg*, and part of her story tells how to prepare these roots to make them edible. Then she was involved in a fight with a malignant spirit who was stealing her roots, and to escape him she flew up into the sky as a cicada. (The cry of the cicada, now, tells people whether the *man-gindjeg* roots are ready.)

However, in the case of many mythic characters, one significant point is their assumed quality of initial humanity: the point of their *having been* human, and then being transmuted into something else — because of something they themselves did, or one of them did, or because they were driven by an urge to fulfil their destiny, or through a concatenation of events outside their control. From a state of being or appearing to be human (even though perhaps already bearing the name of a particular creature, which is a kind of pre-emption on their part), they become natural species: not merely *like* the species whose shape they take, but that species' archetypal form, from which all species of that kind are derived or replicated. While in physical terms their initial human quality is put aside, their spiritual quality is seemingly unchanged. They are depicted as thinking and behaving in human ways even though their physical shape is not human.

It is this one-way process, mythically non-reversible *after* the actual 'turning' in formal terms has occurred, which is interesting. *After*, because such 'turnings' are different from the shape-changing propensities of certain mythic beings mentioned in Chapter 2. This process, the movement from being human to being animal, vegetable or something else, can be seen as enlarging or widening the range of natural species, as well as a definition of particular shapes in terms of their human origins. A contrast can be drawn (as has so often been done) between people *in* nature and people *apart* from nature. While Aborigines may well contend that there is a spiritual *and* physical affinity between human beings and other shapes in nature, it is true that the situation cannot be so simplistically stated, although contrasts of this kind are made in Aboriginal mythology as in everyday life.

Shapes in nature are those that are relevant to human beings. It is not only that Aborigines lived, traditionally, in close and even intimate association with all aspects of nature, while the buffers that protected them from the inroads of nature were minimal. Rather, what is significant is the social relevance of particular natural aspects that hinge on the kind of mythic transformations that have taken place. An *a priori* reason that links a particular person or social group to a particular natural species depicted as a Dreaming character (in whatever form) provides a key to understanding the traditional concept of the Dreaming. That reason is the special quality they have in common, a human quality. Mostly, although their physical shapes may look utterly dissimilar, their reactions to particular situations and their general behaviour are believed not to be so distinct, even though some aspects may be emphasised as against others. The actions of natural species are identified as familiar human or almost-human ones, perfectly explicable when given the premises on which the myths themselves are designed.

The stories in this chapter are usually succinct and straightforward, although they are in some cases ambiguous. They are not intended to be more than simple statements, within the frame of myth; and they provide non-empirical answers to questions that demand a response. While they are not arranged as dramatic presentations, that is not to say they are devoid of dramatic impact. However, the principal drama lies in their momentous implications, rather than in the details of their stories.

The following story was told to R. Berndt at Oenpelli in 1949. It is of Gunwinggu origin.

93. KANGAROO'S DECEIT

Dog, Durug and big red Kangaroo, Gulubar, were men at Adbaldi. Kangaroo said, 'You try to paint my body, to make me look attractive.' So Dog got his ochres and clay and painted him to look like a kangaroo.

When he had finished, he said it was Kangaroo's turn to paint him. 'I have drawn you well. Now make me look as pretty as I have made you.' So Kangaroo set to work and began painting Dog. But he did it in a different way, and made him look like a dog. When Kangaroo had finished, Dog looked at himself in the water and thought how ugly he looked. He was angry: 'I drew you well, made you pretty; but you have made me like a dog, ugly!' And he continued, 'Now you've made me like this, I will bite you: it's your own doing, you made me like that — with a long nose, a long tongue and long teeth. I've got to chase you and bite you!' And Dog began to bark. He chased Kangaroo. But since he had four legs and Kangaroo only two, Dog soon caught up with him and bit him. Kangaroo ran on, but Dog caught up with him again and bit him. All the way along Dog was chasing Kangaroo and biting him, until they fought together. To escape, Kangaroo ran into a cave in the rocks at Biwulg-wulgmang on this [Oenpelli] side of Tor Rock. Dog waited for him outside; later Kangaroo emerged and Dog chased him to Iniwanang waterhole, where they fought again. Dog had a *mandubang* ironwood fighting club that he put into the rocks here and made it like a tree. Kangaroo and Dog turned into rocks. Dog said, 'I have to kill kangaroo because I am a dog, and I have to eat raw meat.' Kangaroos walk about now, but dogs always chase them.

As a result of Kangaroo's mythic deceit, these two creatures became enemies. That theme is a common one in Aboriginal mythology over a wide area, especially in the Western Desert. (See R. and C. Berndt 1985: 248–49.) There are two points of interest here. Each made the other in the shape he would eventually take as an animal. And both were metamorphosed as rocks, but continued as enemies in their spirit form, and this state of affairs is transferred to all animals of their particular kind.

The next story concerns Kangaroo and his two companions. It was told to R. Berndt at Ooldea in 1941.

94. THE MARCH FLIES

Wadi Malu, Kangaroo Man, and Wadi Ganyala, Euro Man, were brothers; their 'uncle' (*gamaru*) was Djudju (a small night bird that lives in hollow trees). They travelled until they reached Maba(n) waterhole. There March flies, *mila*, bit the testes of the two brothers, who brushed away the *mila* with their tails. Djudju sang:

djurung-ga djurung-ga alu beriberi
Djudju brushing away [the *mila*].

And Malu sang:

malu djururu malu djururu
Kangaroo dancing.

[The last song refers to the movements of Kangaroo as he tries to get rid of the flies.]

Maba waterhole is connected by a system of caves leading to two other waterholes close by — Gundjilbi, where Djudju went, and Inala, where Malu went; Ganyala remained at Maba. [Radiating out at one side of Maba are long depressions or grooves in the ground which may be seen today, formed by the two brothers moving their tails. Similar radiating depressions are at Inala, made by Malu moving his tail.] From Maba, Ganyala saw a large group of Gabidji (Little Wallaby), Dalwaba (Wallaby) and Mala (Kangaroo Rat) coming into Maba. Because it was very hot, all the incoming people sheltered from the sun in a cave at Maba; but they were also sheltering from the *mila* which were attracted to the waterhole in hot weather.

The cave in which the visitors took shelter was large, but there were smaller openings at the other two waterholes. Ganyala, Malu and Djudju built fires at the mouth of each of these caves, piling on green boughs to smoke out those inside. The three men sang as the smoke poured into the holes:

buyun-buyun gan-gangu djandu lerileri buyun gan-gang
Smoke rising, entering [the caves] suffocating [them].

Then, again:

guru mung-gara buyuru bungu guru mung-gara
Eyes, smoke getting into their eyes.

As they sang this, the three men ran away: ['Over there' (in the song) refers to them looking back toward Maba. They ran away because the smoke might get in their nostrils.] Running, Ganyala sang:

saru nguluri wani djindu
mira-mirara nalwed-nuringu
waru-nguluri
Frightened of fire, leaving in the heat (sun)
Dying, in swirling smoke.
Frightened of fire.

Then Malu sang:

miridja wongga-wongga
balgaguyanu
Sounds of dying in the cave.
(Run quickly.)

Finally Djudju sang:

ilgari guldu-guldu djulbal agani
djanba binali walaring
Clear sky, sounds of dying.
Sun moving, legs running.

This story episode in a long myth is about the angry reaction of Kangaroo, Euro and Djudju to being bitten by March flies. This part of the myth does not explain why they attack the visitors instead of the March flies. However, they are important Dreaming characters who are shape-changing, and later in this version they turn into their respective non-human forms. Before that they leave their imprint on the natural environment, in this case at Maba, as they do at many other places in the course of their travels.

In the next four myths the focus is on Emu. They came from three different areas: the first from Balgo (1958), the next two from Ooldea (1941) and the fourth from Yirrkalla (1946): all were told to R. Berndt.

95. THE KILLING OF THE TWO EMUS

Two Emus, Galaya Gudjara, have been killing a number of people, among them members of a *dingari* ritual group of men and women. The

Emus cooked and ate those they caught. The people decided that something had to be done: too many of their group had been killed. The two Emus had been putting kidney fat (*gaberadji-djira*) on their heads [the reference is to sorcery]. The others saw this fat. The Emus always killed 'strangers', and passed on the meat they had caught to their relatives.

The *dingari* people [those who had suffered these depredations] were Gargain (Chicken Hawk people). They decided to hold a ceremony to which they invited the two Emus and their relatives ('countrymen'). They arrived in large numbers. The Gargain danced as did the two Emus, with their arms spread out. And the Gargain were thinking, 'We must do something; there are too many of them!'

When the ceremony stopped, the two Emus went out hunting. Two Gargain men prepared themselves by sharpening an axe. In the afternoon the two Emu returned; they sat among the Gargain and the ceremony continued. While they were so engaged, the two Gargain (Right hand and Left hand men) who were related to each other as *wapadju* [daughter's husband-wife's father], and were said to be old men, sneaked up behind the two Emu men. As they spread out their arms [wings], each Gargain struck one Emu, splitting him down the middle, killing him. This took place at Gunalbungu or Gunalwulbul, at the other side of Bishop's Dell, west of Djaliwan. The two Emus turned into two big river gums at that place, while the Gargain went into the soak at Gunalbungu. All the others left the place.

96. EMU ESCAPES

Minma Mingari, Mountain Devil Woman, heard the approach of Emu Man, Galaya, at Ilungu, in Mandjindji country. She sent three of her dogs after him, telling them to follow and kill him. And she called out again and again, '*Balwal!*' urging them on. Then she went back to her camp and slept. By sunrise the dogs had not returned. She lay down again and waited. By midnight she could hear them panting in exhaustion as they came back, one by one, to her camp to lie down behind her. She knew they had not killed Emu.

Next morning she got up early and, calling her dogs, travelled on to a particular place [name not mentioned]. There she made fire, kindling it with bark in which she had kept some of the live coals carried from her last camp. As she was doing this she heard Emu talking not far away. She sent her dogs after him, urging them on: 'Go after him, don't let him escape!' She followed him for a while, then camped at another place, lay down and waited. During the night the dogs returned panting and crept behind her. She knew they had not been successful.

Next morning she heard Emu talking again. But she also heard a 'big mob' of Emu having a ceremony: they were *nurinidja* 'stranger' Emu people. Again she sent her dogs after the first Emu, who ran through the ceremony where the others were dancing and singing. But the dogs made a mistake. They caught and killed one of the strangers, while the first Emu escaped. The dogs returned to Mingari with emu fat.

97. EMU IS KILLED

Wadi Galaya, Emu Man, came from Ilungu [near 'Lindon']; he was blind. However, Minma Mingari, Mountain Devil Woman, lived there with her husband Wadi Bunyu, Kangaroo Rat Man. Mingari, on hearing Emu coming, sent one of her dogs after him. The dog chased Emu to Budil waterhole, and killed him; the dog ate half the meat and brought the rest back to Mingari. Bunyu immediately got hold of the meat, cooked it and ate it. As a result he became ill and died. Mingari buried him in a hole which became the deep rockhole called Gadal at Ilungu ('death place').

Minma Mingari travelled on to Babungu, where she camped; then on to Midaga, or Miriga ('die'), where she herself died. Here there is a large rockhole. Before she died, she sang:

mingari wi-yalguna mingarila wi-yalguna
Mingari coming to an end [throwing up her legs in the throes of death].

The next story is about a large sandbank near Ga'reiga, at Arnhem Bay. It refers to the metamorphosed body of Gandji, Crane, *dua* moiety.

98. EMU AND CRANE'S SPEAR-BEAK

Malwia (or Wurban) Emu was making a carved spear; Gandji was cooking a *won-gura*, bandicoot. Malwia told him, 'Don't cook close to me, because I'm making a spear.' ['In the old times, cooking food near where people were making spears was not allowed.' It would counteract their power and their efficacy.] Gandji got angry. At Ganumbeli he made a big fire, and when the flames burnt down, he removed a live coal and threw it at Malwia. Gandji made himself into a bird and flew away. [In another version of this myth they had also fought at Blue Mud Bay.]

Malwia immediately picked up his *djimbai-djimba* spear and made as if to throw it, but Gandji had flown too far up into the sky. So he got his spear-thrower, hooked on his spear and tried to point it at Gandji, who by this time was almost in the clouds. He tried his spear alone but it was too long. He began to cut it, making it shorter, speaking to it as he did so: '*baiangu-ngi ngarana baialaga-laga rangardja!* ['I have nothing to say, but forgive me for doing this cutting.'] He tried it, then threw the spear straight toward Gandji. It hit him, entering his anus and going through his body and neck, coming out of his mouth. Gandji fell to the sandbank; he tried to withdraw that carved, barbed spear, but he could not. He said, 'I'll leave that spear for my children; this spear they can have and fly with.' And Gandji's beak is the carved point of the spear which cranes now use to catch fish.

There are many Emu myths associated with different traditional Aboriginal culture areas. Usually he or she is depicted as being timid, easily frightened, and responding aggressively only when there is no alternative. However, the Balgo and Yirrkalla examples are among those where Emu is not shown in that light, although in the Yirrkalla one he was not the first to start a fight. In an East Kimberley (Djaru) story, people are afraid of Emu, but manage to shorten his long wings so that he cannot use them for flying. The Western Desert versions conform more to the general pattern. In the first, the *dingari* ritual group respond to the aggression of two Emus who are also regarded as sorcerers. In the death scene each is split, and the reference to the Emus spreading out their wings also implies they were foreshortened to the size they are today. It is in the act of killing that they 'turn' (become something else) not into Emus, but as River Gums. In two Desert myths, it is Mingari and her dogs who are the aggressors — in search of Emu as food. However, it is not until the next myth that (as a Blind Emu) he is killed, an event that brings about the death of Mingari's husband (Kangaroo Rat) and Mingari herself. In the fourth version, the focus is on Crane *vis-à-vis* Emu, who is responsible for the shape of Crane's beak. It was Crane who turned into a bird, not, in this case, Emu. Incidentally, the men who told this last story said that 'it is a funny story, for laughing'.

Next, Crane re-appears in a different cultural context, on the mainland opposite the Goulburn Islands, in a story told to R. Berndt in 1947.

99. THE SELFISHNESS OF CRANE

Gawagawa, Crane, *yariyaning*, came from Manalwugan, on the Liverpool River [Gunividji language]. He was walking to Yiwadja country.

Eventually he came to Waag ('Crow'), a large creek near Malay Bay. He decided to fish there. First he made a *yalawoi* drum net. He took it out into the water and left it there. Next morning he found it full of fish. He untied the string that held it and removed the fish.

There were a lot of people, mainly Yiwadja, camped at Waag. When he tipped out his drum net, there were all kinds of fresh-water fish. Instead of giving some to the other people, he ate them all himself. Every evening he put out his drum net, and every morning he collected the fish it held; and he kept all the fish for himself. Crow was there — but Crane gave him no fish. The people were angry. They decided to go out hunting themselves, and to give him no meat.

Crow reminded them that this was the time for goose eggs. The people went out and collected eggs on Marganala plain. They filled their net dilly bags and returned to Waag. In the meantime, Crane had obtained a lot of fish. Crow and the other people ate the goose eggs and gave none to Crane: Crane ate only his fish. This situation continued: the other people went out for goose eggs and wild honey, and gave him nothing.

The fishing man (Crane) said, 'I think I had better move my drum net to Iloyag creek' [which jutted out from the other]. He continued to get fish, while the others brought home food for themselves and Crane ate his fish. However, his catch at Iloyag was becoming smaller, so he went to another creek at Marmari [another small tributary of the main creek at Waag]. Goose eggs and wild honey were being brought into the camp in large quantities, but Crane was getting only a few fish. Leaving his drum net, he went in search of a big creek and found one at Wongaran [on Malay Bay]. Here he met Waramurung-goindji, the great Mother, who was also catching fish. [She was on her way east.]

Crane, seeing all the fish she had got, told her, 'It's better for you to go on east, because you are taking too many of our fish.' So Waramurung-goindji went on. Crane went back to get his drum net. He took it up to Waldanggu waterhole, a little inland from Mountnorris Bay, and put the net into the water — but only *ngalmangiyi* fresh-water tortoise and *baramid* prawns went into it: there were no fish! So he went down to the beach at Wurgi and 'cutting across', came to the other side [where Reuben Cooper had his mill, later] at Malyilogu: there he put his drum net and got plenty of fish. Something made him stay here and he could go no further — he liked the place. So he 'turned himself' and his net into rocks, and remained there. The other people at Waag left that place and went on in the direction of Tor Rock.

Crane broke the rules of reciprocity when he would not give any of his large supply of fish to the people he was camping with. So they applied the appropriate sanction. They had their chance to treat him in the same way

when the goose egg season began. When Crane's supply of fish ran out, he
was forced to find new fishing grounds. The magnitude of his selfishness
was exemplified in his arbitrary treatment of Waramurung-goindji.
Eventually, he found a suitable place and 'turned himself,' not into a bird
but into a rock.

Crow appears again in the following story, told to R. Berndt at Oenpelli
in 1949.

---

100. CROW'S REVENGE

Gagud (or Guruwagwag), Crow, a *yarigarngurg*, *nabangari* Dreaming man,
was camped at Arguluk Hill beside the billabong at Oenpelli, Gunbalanya (Onbalan). He lived at the top of this hill, and when it rained he
went into a cave. He kept his canoe down at the billabong. His usual
practice was to collect wild honey, and for that purpose he usually carried
an axe; but when goose eggs were in season he would get these. He would
fill up his canoe with eggs and return to his mooring place; he would leave
some in the canoe, and carry up a banyan-string dilly bag full of eggs to
his camp. All the other Crow people lived there too; and usually he would
make a number of trips from his canoe to the camp, bringing up the bags
of eggs.

Two other men, one named Nandjamalamal, Native Companion or
Djabiru, *yariwurga*, *nangila*, and Wunyagaul, Shag, *yarigarngurg*,
nabangari, both *namadgu*, were camped at Red Lily, Indjamandagab.
They had made a *mangawarn-nyangg* fish catchment or trap constructed of
cane. Crow decided to visit them because he wanted fish; the two men
always had plenty. He took some eggs along with him.

Djabiru and Shag removed the fish from their trap, leaving it in the
water, and went along the cliff to cook them; after cooking the fish they
placed them on flat stones around the cooking place. In the meantime, on
his way there, Crow had found wild honey in a tree. As he was getting the
honey, some green ants that were in the tree stuck in his hair — he did not
know they were there. He continued on his way and came close to the two
men's camp. They saw him coming, and through his net bag they saw,
too, the eggs he carried. They called out to him, 'Come this way, sit down
here!' And Crow replied, 'I am bringing goose eggs for you two!' He gave
them the eggs, and in exchange they gave him fish. Crow got ready to eat
the fish, his head bent forward. However, the two men saw that green ants
had fallen on to the fish. [There is a taboo on eating fish with green ants
on it, because the spirits of the ants would prevent fish from entering a fish
trap.] They grabbed Crow's head and pulled him back, stopping him

from eating: 'If you do that, no fish will go into our trap!' And they asked him, 'Have you been eating green ants?' 'No,' he replied, 'They must have fallen into my hair when I was getting wild honey. But what does it matter?' He was offended and went to sit by himself. He was angry. He got up and took back his eggs, saying, 'You men stopped me from eating fish!' In turn, the two men grew angry. However, Crow walked away. 'I have to go back to my camp,' he said.

The two men called out, 'Old man, you come back!' 'No, I must go,' replied Crow. 'If you are angry,' the two men said, 'You come back and the three of us will fight.' Crow came back, and they got their clubs and they fought. Crow defeated them, but said 'We will fight again!' He left them, and went to his mother's country on the Mang-goralgul plain, on the western side of the East Alligator, in Gagadju country. When he came to his mother's camp, all the people cried for him — it was such a long time since they had seen him. 'My son (*nainmaba*)!' his mother cried; 'My son (*nanawumbiri*)!' cried his father. Crow sent two of the men in the camp to 'muster' the other men. They were Burdekin Duck, Ambarigambar, *yariyaning, namarang*, and Diving Duck, Mandjerigin, *yarigarngurg, nagudjug*. They brought together all the Gagadju and Ngadug people. But those first two men, Djabiru and Shag, 'mustered' the Mangeri, Eri, Weni, Wuningag and Ing-gu [Neinggu; close to Gunbalanya] men, and they made for the camp at Mang-goralgul. Crow saw them and was angry. He sat at Mang-goralgul waterhole beside a large banyan tree and watched them all coming. His father, his mother, his mother's brothers and other relatives, said, 'Don't quarrel any more, don't be angry. This is your own country you have come to. Let these two men (Djabiru and Shag) come up here and we will have a big ceremony, singing and dancing. Let them come up clear!'

Crow had a pandanus basket full of honey, and he had his axe. All the people, including the visitors, sat under the branches of that large banyan tree. Crow's mother's people commenced singing, and Goose, Manimunag, *yarigarngurg, nawagaidj, namadgu*, was playing the didjeridu. Diving Duck [see above] was singing and clapping his sticks. Crow said he would just walk around. 'But keep on singing,' he told them. He was standing there. 'Keep singing,' he repeated. They went on singing until some fell asleep, while others lay down ready to sleep. Crow said, 'All right now: I'll keep watch while all of you sleep.' He called out again, 'You hear me?' He called out twice, but no-one answered. They were all sound asleep.

Crow took his axe, slung his bag of honey round his neck and shoulder, and climbed into the banyan tree. He chopped off a branch, which fell on Djabiru and Shag, killing them. All the others awakened, asking each other what had happened. Crow chopped off another branch and tipped out all his honey from the bag, and it fell like rain. 'I am Crow now!' he called. [He had 'turned into' that bird.]

The honey rain came down so heavily that it flooded the whole area, making a billabong. All the people there turned into birds and flew away, because 'Crow made water come out: he spoilt it all. He made the rain we now have, like honey. [The reference is to the heavy rain we had at the time of recording this story.] Crow made it, and flooded a great deal of the surrounding country.'

The myth provides a 'classic' example of how easily a major catastrophe can come about through trivial beginnings — in this case, from an unintentional slight when Djabiru and Shag are concerned that the fish they had should not be contaminated by green ants.

Crow is avowedly a difficult mythic character, a point brought out in many myths, but probably no more so than many others, He is, however, ready to take offence. And, as the myth tells us, he would not even take the advice of his close kin that he should not fight on his home ground. The final act of destruction meant not only his own transformation but also that of all the people present. In that respect he is an agent or an intermediary in the mythic process of evolution — the changing and diversification of physical forms.

The following are three short versions of a story about Willy Wagtail, told to R. Berndt at Ooldea in 1941.

---

101. A DISASTROUS ARGUMENT

Several groups of Dreaming women came to Daralguda water. Among them was Djinta-djinta (Willy Wagtail, also called Djidi-djidilba) who came with the Djalbu-djalbul (Blue Pigeon) group. They were followed by the Mula group (a species of Pigeon). All went out hunting; the Mula women caught fat *gabidji*, little wallabies; Djinta-djinta caught only two skinny ones. They built a large fire, burned off the fur and threw the animals onto the coals. Djinta-djinta was looking after the fire and, with a long stick, moving the cooking meat to ensure it was not burnt. In doing this, she moved her two skinny animals to one side, replacing them with two good ones.

A Mula woman saw her doing this and called out, 'Those are mine!' Djinta-djinta replied, 'No, yours are over there!' They began to argue and then to fight. The Mula woman hit Djinta-djinta over the head, and she returned the blows. It was not long before they were joined by other women from both groups and the fighting extended. Another Mula group, hearing the noise, hurried to Daralguda and joined in the fray. They fought on until all had been killed — they all 'finished up' at this place. Their fallen bodies were metamorphosed as rocks, and the blood that flowed from their wounds formed a red-ochre deposit. All the trees round this waterhole are covered with red-ochre dust, which is the blood of those Dreaming women.

102. HAILSTONE OF DEATH

Djinta-djinta, Willy Wagtail's Dreaming place, was at Djindilgara waterhole, north-west of Ooldea, and he usually stayed there. However, on one occasion he was out gossiping some distance away from his own camp when he heard thunder. The sky darkened, with heavy clouds. He set off, running, back to Djindilgara, but rain began to fall heavily, and as he reached his home a hailstone fell and killed him.

As he ran for shelter he sang:

> *djinta-djinta waru gudjala*
> *gabi bala ilaringani*
> Wagtail [with his] fire-stick.
> Water, coming close [to his home].

103. WILLY WAGTAIL

Djinta-djinta was living at the same place as in the last story. He saw heavy rain approaching. Quickly he built a strong hut, in which he sheltered. The rain fell for several days, damaging his hut. Still the rain kept falling. He repaired his hut, but the rain damaged it again. This happened several times. At last, one morning the sky became very dark, and a heavy deluge of rain swept him and his hut into Djindilgara waterhole. There he remains.

In the first version Djinta-djinta is a woman, in the other two, a man. In neither case does she/he turn into the bird of that name. In the mythology, Djinta-djinta is usually characterised as being a gossiper, or rather devious in his/her social relationships.

Still following the birds, but introducing other mythic creatures, we turn to a further story from Ooldea, told to R. Berndt in 1941.

104. THE IMMOLATION OF OWL

Wadi Gumba (Night Owl or Mopoke Man) came to Yaramara water, where he saw a large group of Teal Ducks, Gogugara. The men among them were wearing *garalba* or *lingila* pearlshells [also called *daguli* or *djaguli* and used for 'making rain'; usually worn as a neck pendant, or from a hair waist-band, as a pubic covering]. Gumba particularly wanted one of these shells for rain-making. So, on seeing Gogugara, he moved a little way out of sight and made a club. Returning to Yaramara, he found the Ducks in a cave where there was water. He threw his club, but instead of hitting a Duck, it fell against the top of the cave entrance and dislodged a rock that disturbed the Ducks inside. They all rose, and fled. Gumba called after them, 'Give me, give me one shell!' They paused and dropped one shell, which Gumba picked up and carried away to Dandjan rockhole. Here he saw a *djimbi-bedi* goanna's hole. He dug this out and collected all the eggs, made a fire, and cooked them in the ashes. As he pulled them out with a stick, one egg burst and its contents spurted over his thighs and pubes, burning them.

He walked away in pain and came to Walga water where a big group of Waru, Rock Wallabies, were camped. Among them was Minma Gumba, his sister. He went a little way from the encampment, and behind some bushes painted himself with red and white ochres; and from his waist-band he hung the *garalba* he had obtained from the Ducks. When he was ready, he appeared before all the people, so that they could all see he was a *gabi badalbalal bidina*, rain-maker. That night he made heavy rain by biting his shell and spitting out a little of it.

All the Waru had good shelters: they could warm themselves and keep dry. But Gumba lay in the open without a fire; no-one asked him to share a shelter.

Next morning he rose early, feeling very cold. He walked over to the Waru thinking he could get warm, but they chased him away and refused to let him warm himself at their fires. He went to each in turn, but all refused. He was very cold indeed. He returned to where he had slept in the open. There he found an old, long, lower leg bone of a kangaroo [a *miri-darlga*, a dead bone], and sharpened it at one end to form a point; at the other end he attached gum, in which he embedded a few white feathers. When the object was ready, he put it into his hair-bun. Then he moved toward the camp, crying '*Dr. . . dr. . . dr. . .*' [his *derin* cry]. Running backward, he took out his *miri-darlga* from his hair, crying. He stood upright before all the people, his dagger held upward; then he plunged it into both his eyes. Immediately, hailstones fell. His sister rushed toward him, and sheltered behind him in a nearby cave. The hailstones were so large that they killed all the Waru, as well as Gumba: only his sister escaped. She still lives there in the cave, but she cannot see during daytime.

A large round rock at Walga is the body of Gumba. This is to be seen on open ground not far from the waterhole, while all the other rocks clustered together are individual members of the Waru group who have been metamorphosed. The small stones and *kandi* flakes are metamorphosed hailstones.

An overwhelming desire to impress the Wallaby people was Owl's reason for wanting a rain-making pearlshell. In spite of causing rain to fall, he was not appreciated; in fact, he was ignored. It was because he was deeply humiliated that he plunged his kangaroo bone dagger into both eyes, blinding himself (an explanation of why owls cannot see during daytime). As a result, hailstones (as in the case of Djinta-djinta in the previous myth) kill not only Owl (in a kind of suicide) but all of the people there, except his sister.

The next myth, from Balgo, was told to R. Berndt in 1960.

105. THE TWO BOYS AND EAGLE

Two *djabanangga* boys were living at Djan-ga, east of Nandabiri [within the Luwana, Lake Lucas area). As they played there, an Eagle dived down, trying to catch them, but they ran toward the bushes nearby and hid in a cave. Eagle watched, waiting for them to emerge. He was Duru, a *djabangadi* man.

Eventually Eagle got tired of watching, and left to go in search of *mala* kangaroo rats. He encircled Warimbilingi soak and hill and then returned to Djan-ga. He sat watching for a while. Then he went out again, encircling Wogura soak and looking for *mala*: he ate the entrails of a dead *mala* at this place, then returned to Djan-ga to watch the cave where the two boys were hidden. Going out again, he encircled Warara claypan, where he 'ripped the flesh' of a *mala* [the place name refers to this], and returned to Djan-ga. Then he went to Djuludjulu claypan and killed another *mala*. He continued, encircling Yalwalurubanda soak, where he killed another; to Gulagibanda, where he killed one more, and on to Marur where he killed yet another. He returned to Djan-ga, and saw one of the boys who had come out of the cave: he swooped down and killed him. [Eagle has a nest at Djan-ga containing his two Eaglets, Gudun-gudjara, *djabanangga*. The implication is that the two boys had been attempting to kill Eagle's children.] Finally, Eagle went into the hole where the other boy was hiding. Both are still there at Djan-ga soak.

The story is straightforward, if not commonplace. Eagle is ferocious, especially in his bird form, and that attribute is emphasised in his encircling the country but always returning for the kill. He does not turn into a bird, because he is already one in this context. In this story of death (for one boy, as well as for the *mala*) and metamorphosis, he and one of his victims remain at the soak.

The Eagle theme is continued in a story from Ooldea told to R. Berndt in 1941.

106. DEATH OF NIGHT BIRD

Wadi Gun-garu, Night Bird Man, came to Babil (or Baba, Dog) water south of Bilgi water in spinifex country [where Mingari's dogs tore out the stomach of Gunabilgi, Small Wallaby, leaving it lying in pieces]. Gun-garu found a dingo pup there, but leaving it untouched went on to Biril waterhole. In the meantime, Wadi Waldja, Eagle Man, came to Babil and killed and ate the pup. Gun-garu returned to find only blood lying there: Waldja had left.

Gun-garu went angrily in search of Waldja, following his tracks until he saw him. He threw a spear, but missed him. Then he used his club to break Waldja's legs. Leaving him lying there, he continued to Golbilidja ('club' place). But Waldja tied up his legs with sinew, making them strong, and set off in search of Gun-garu. Arriving at Golbilidja, he made a club. Gun-garu had gone on to Narbrada water, where he met a number of Walbidi [long-nosed ant-eaters, striped body, long tail] and they held a ceremony, singing and dancing all night. Waldja arrived in the darkness and sat on the outer edge of the dancing ground; he was not seen, and he held his club at the back like a tail.

When the Walbidi finished dancing, it was Gun-garu's turn. As he danced, Waldja moved forward and threw his club, breaking off Gun-garu's head. The headless body is metamorphosed as rock at Narbrada, the force of the club causing the head to fall about four miles from there. Waldja followed the head in order to recover his club; the head too had turned to rock. All the Walbidi left Narbrada and continued on their travels.

In spite of Eagle's injury from which he recovers by healing himself, he succeeds in killing Night Bird. Rarely, in Aboriginal mythology, does Eagle suffer defeat — although he comes close to it in this story.

The following story, from Yirrkalla, was told to R. Berndt in 1946. It is one of several versions.

107. BECOMING BIRDS

Djirid, Fishing Hawk, lived at Gulin-mirawi. He went out line-fishing in his canoe and caught a *lalu*, parrot fish. His young son was pleased and helped his mother, Damala, white-breasted Seahawk, to make a dilly bag. Then he asked his father for some fish: 'Give me a little piece of liver or guts from that big fish?' His father refused. 'No, you can't have any of this.' However, the boy stole some of it. When his father discovered this, he took it back.

At that the boy began to cry, and would not be quietened. His father offered him some of the fish, but he pushed it away and went on crying. Whiskers began to appear on his face, and feathers began to grow. The boy looked at himself in the water and saw that he was almost ready to fly away. He tried to fly, but fell down. His father encouraged him to try again: he fell down, but then flew into the sky. He had made himself into a bird! His father was looking: 'Where has he gone?' He made himself into a *djirid* and flew away. Damala did not know where they had gone. Looking into the sky, she saw them swooping far away. Then she too made herself into a bird. She climbed into a tree, and leaving her dilly bag behind she called out to the other two, '*Ngag! Ngag!*' Her feathers grew quickly and she flew away after them.

The reason Fishing Hawk refused to give his son any of the fish he caught was that it had been reserved for religious (*mareiin*) purposes, obliquely implied by the making of a spirit dilly bag.

When the self-willed boy stole some, this could have precipitated a crying-child-and-Rainbow-Snake sequence; but his father's offer seems to have averted that and encouraged him to realise his potential for becoming a bird. His transformation was therefore automatic, and the transformation of his parents into Fishing Hawk and Seahawk followed as necessary events in that sequence. The narrators added that this was a story told to children who didn't take notice of their parents — that it made them laugh while at the same time they were learning.

The following story could well appear in the conclusion of Chapter 8. However, it is included here because of Guragura's transformation as a bird. It was told to R. Berndt in 1950 at Oenpelli but was associated with a culture located on the western side of the South Alligator River.

108. THE SPIRIT-TAKER

A Dreaming woman named Guragura [a long-tailed, sharp-nosed bird, possibly a Hawk] was at Djamayin on the western side of the South Alligator River [Wada language]. Guragura was eating bitter yams at Djamayin, but she crossed to the eastern side of the river and, camping at Wa-erandju, put these yams in the jungle. Then she paused at Ganer-aindju billabong [where the two men named Nalwarabara went past her: see Myth 30]. She moved on, to Eringu-budju-bumbu swamps: she was pregnant. She came down along the plain and went to Ngaramagida spring, where she spoke Gagadju. There she ate fish. Going on to Beli-ingada, she camped for two days: her belly was now too heavy to go far. She made a big hole to serve as a 'nest', but too much water seeped up and she went on. Her baby was almost ready to be born. She came to Garara, and there she made a depression, crushing the earth to make it soft. Before she could squat down [in the approved child-bearing posture] her baby quickly 'slipped out'. She cut the umbilical cord with a stone flake, and placed the child in the depression she had prepared. She thought, 'I'll go and find goose feathers and make myself into a bird!' She picked up those feathers and put them on her body, on her back, arms and feet. Then she spoke. 'I'm no longer a human being, I'm a bird now! I have to kill men and women when they're sick.' ['That bird is like a doctor; she is clever, *malguna*. Even when a camp is large, she sits nearby, waiting to take the 'shade' (*yewiwayu*) or spirit of a sick person. When she calls *Garlg! Garlg!* she carries a person's 'shade' on her shoulders; when she shakes herself, the 'shade' falls off and the person dies.' Her child also turned into a bird.]

This is an unusual story, without many parallels in Aboriginal mythology. Why she made herself into a bird is not noted, but it was said to have been a deliberate act. Apart from waiting to take the spirit of a dying person, it was also said that Guragura would 'climb on his (or her) head and kill him'.

However, an interesting counterpart of the Guragura bird appears in a story told to C. Berndt at Oenpelli in 1950; it comes from the eastern side of the East Alligator River.

109. THE WURAAL BIRD

Those two were going along eating nuts, *man-gulaid* nuts. They set off, going to another place. They looked around as they went and saw geese, sitting high up [on the trees], many of them. They said, 'We'll camp here, so we can kill and eat geese.' When afternoon came they went to cut sticks, little throwing sticks. They said, 'We'll go and kill them when afternoon comes, because that's when the geese get up, and we can kill them!' They went, and saw a flock of geese coming. They were killing them, those geese, high up on top of the trees. They got plenty. They said, 'We'll go back and cook them, and eat.' Well, they went back, cooked them all, and ate. Then they said, 'What shall we do? Shall we go?' They said, 'Yes, we'll go to another place.' They went.

They went, they camped, they were eating plant foods and meat and fish; they were eating honey. They were going on, they were camping, they were looking about at the place, they were saying, 'Well, we'll go on, because it's a long way!' They were going on, they were camping. Then afterward that other one felt sick, felt he was dying.

Well, then it came up, it climbed a tree, it was talking, talking, it kept saying, '*Gu-ngaag! Gu-ngaag! Gu-ngaag!*' He heard it talking, that other one, and he said, 'Maybe that creature talking means, perhaps, we're making ourselves wrong, coming into Dreaming!' They slept. In the middle of the night it came running, close to them, it climbed a tree. It was still saying the same thing. '*Gu-ngaag! Gu-ngaag!*' it kept saying. Well, one of them was afraid. He said, 'Now, we're making ourselves wrong, coming into Dreaming!' But the other one was not afraid, because he was dying. Well, when they were lying asleep, it came down close, that bird: it was striking the dying man with its claws. It kept striking him, it killed him. Then, afterward water was coming up, where it was striking him. They both went under the water together, man and bird.

He was trying to run, that other one. He was looking at the rising water. He tried to run, he was looking, looking about at the water running. The water kept on running. Then afterward he just ran and fell into a hole in the ground. The three of them went under the water together as *djang*, all three became *djang*. The name of the place is Wuraal, because those three came into Dreaming there.

This myth requires little explanation, except to point out that in both cases, the Guragura and Wuraal birds were attracted to a sick person, and both 'killed' their victims, taking their spirits. The rather abrupt style is very close to the Gunwinggu original, and in the actual telling was dramatically very effective.

Seahawk appears again, this time from South Goulburn Island, where R. Berndt recorded it in 1947.

110. THE DOUBLE-SIDED REVENGE

Djuddjud, Seahawk, a *yarigarngurg* man and Walanguru [brown and white-breasted Gull], a *yariyaning* man, were living on Manggulalgudj, Croker Island. Their language was Marlgu. They went out turtle hunting at Maruruni near Cape Croker. They caught two or three turtles and brought them back to their camp. After the turtles were cooked, the other people in the camp gave Walanguru only the *yurulg* turtle shell, but no meat. This went on for some time. Each time they went out hunting and brought back turtle, Walanguru received nothing.

Walanguru decided that something had to be done about this. 'I'll gather together a lot of men,' he thought. So he went to Muruwanyan, Jap Creek. [At a well here, named Adburug, there is a deposit of white clay.] At that time all the birds were people. He called on them to join him, and at Adburug they painted their bodies with white clay. Walanguru led the party back to Maruruni, and when they saw Djuddjud they threw spears at him. He dodged them all. However, he saw that he was outnumbered. 'What am I going to do?' he asked himself: 'I think I'll turn myself into a bird.' So he flew up as Seahawk, holding a piece of turtle meat. Talking to himself, he asked again, 'What am I going to do with myself?'

All those birds [people] went to Mindjilang [Mission Bay, near Jap Creek]. Djuddjud, from the air, saw that they had all gone down to the beach to collect *gwubiya* cockles. He decided to turn himself into a *Wamba* shark. When the birds [men] were diving for cockles, Djuddjud in his shark form began to kill them. Some tried to escape, but Shark killed them all. Then he turned himself properly into a shark, so that he could continue to kill people. Walanguru turned himself into a gull.

Getting food is one thing; sharing it is another. The problems involve social relations even more than economic issues. Myths and stories have a lot to say about these. Withholding food that a person considers he or she should have received usually leads to trouble. In this example, Gull's revenge misfires, because to escape defeat Seahawk turns himself into a bird, and then into a shark to make sure he succeeds in achieving *his* revenge.

Next we return to Ooldea, where Curlew withholds food, but in very different circumstances. Told to R. Berndt in 1941, it was said to have been originally a Ngalia myth.

111.   THE STRANGE BEHAVIOUR
OF CURLEW

Wadi Wilu, Curlew Man, made a large hut (a *maia-maiara*), of a kind that was commonly used north-west of Ooldea. It was an enclosed structure built round four upright posts and horizontal poles, with an aperture [door]. Wilu lived here. A woman came to that place and camped with him.

Soon afterward, Wilu sharpened his two spears and told the woman to go out to hunt rats, while he would go after kangaroos. He left his camp and, tracking down a kangaroo, killed it. He removed its entrails and trussed it up with sinew, ready to carry back to his camp. He put it aside and went on to spear another kangaroo, which he also trussed up. Picking it up, he collected the first one and returned to his camp. He placed them out of sight within the framework and boughs of his hut: he did not want the woman to see them. He drank water, and waited for her to return. When she came back, she saw no meat, but only blood on Wilu's spears. She asked about this, but he replied that he had only wounded a kangaroo. They slept together.

Next morning he went out hunting again while the woman looked for goannas. As before, he returned, bringing two more kangaroos that he hid in the same way. The woman came back, and they cooked and ate some of the goanna meat she had collected. The next day he went out again and so did she. But she was growing suspicious. She returned early to see what he did: she had caught two goannas. She sat down inside the hut out of sight. Wilu, who had killed two kangaroos, returned carrying them. Hearing him, she emerged from the hut and called out, 'How pleased (*yiyi-yiyi*) I am: there is meat for us both!'

Immediately, at the sound of her voice Wilu dropped his kangaroos and his spears. Feathers began to appear all over his body, and he cried out in a mournful way — *Wilu! Wilu!* [He cried because the woman had seen his kangaroo meat.] He turned into a curlew bird.

The woman pleaded with him: 'Friend, stop being a bird! Come back, friend!' [She wanted that man.] But he went on being a curlew. She returned sadly to their camp. Looking in the hut's covering she found the now-decomposing kangaroo flesh which he had placed there uneaten. She picked up the recently-killed kangaroo meat, cooked it, ate some and then offered some to the bird Wilu, asking him to return to her. She offered him the meat many times but he would not return; he remained a bird.

The strange behaviour of Curlew is not explained — to us, or to the woman concerned. In much of Aboriginal mythology, Curlew is a taciturn and gloomy fellow. As a bird, his cries echo mournfully and are often taken as presaging death. The suddenness of his transformation has a dramatic quality tinged with pathos.

The next story concerns a different sort of bird, paired with a Blanket Lizard. It comes from the Goulburn Islands and was told to R. Berndt in 1947.

112. THE DECEIT OF BLANKET LIZARD

Wudbud, Pheasant, of the 'fire' [*yariburig* semi-moiety] was a woman who lived at the top of the King River [Maung language]. Also camped nearby was Gundamen, Blanket Lizard. She asked him if he would give her white clay to paint her spears, but he replied, 'No I haven't any.' But Wudbud persisted, asking him again and again. 'I think you've got clay but you won't give me any!' He held up his hand to show he had none — but he raised only four fingers, holding his lump of clay with his thumb. She kept on repeating that he did have some clay. That conversation continued, with Gundamen denying he had any and Wudbud pleading for some: 'I must paint my spear with it!' At last she said, 'I think you haven't any clay.' And Gundamen replied, 'No, I haven't any.'

Turning around, Wudbud showed him the bundle of bamboo spears she carried under her arm. She flew up into the sky, making herself into a bird, all the spears sticking out from behind her. ['All her tail feathers are her bamboo spears'.] Gundamen was afraid she would throw them at him. He called out: 'Yes, I have some clay!' But she went on flying and saying '*Pud! Pud!*'

Before she flew up, she had had a large paperbark tree. She had taken this with her, and as she passed over Gundamen she threw it down on top of him. The tree went right round his head, and stayed there. ['That is why we now see Gundamen with those big ears.'] He turned into a lizard. The place where this happened is Alwun-djiling-wudbud-gundamen ['having fought over clay, pheasant and blanket lizard'].

This is another story on the theme of not sharing, but it is also about how two natural species came to be as they are now. Various explanations are offered, and this is one of many. In telling how Pheasant got her tail feathers, it does not comment on the unusual circumstances of a woman having spears (there are other mythic cases, but they are rare), or the

possibility that this is why Gundamen refused to supply her with clay —
or to suggest that she should get some for herself.

The following story is about a different kind of lizard. It was told to
R. Berndt at Ooldea in 1941.

---

113.   THE RUSE OF BERN

Wadi Bern, 'Barking lizard' Man was a big old man [a flat-tailed, black
and white sand lizard, large-eyed]. He was walking along with his club
and fire-stick when he saw from a distance a number of camp fires. He
knew there were people there, and camped not too far from them. He sang
to himself:

darang-ga waia-waia ringani wadi bambu-nga
lolgari baia barina-nana darang-ga
Old man standing, seeing [them], frightening [them],
Because of his face, seeing [them].

[Bern is dangerous. He sang this while lying on his back, 'practising' it,
because he planned to sing it when he reached that camp.]

Next morning, he came toward the camp to find the people were
already moving away: the men had gone and the women were picking up
their bundles of possessions and their babies. They were all leaving. Wadi
Bern entered the camp 'behind them'. He stood in the centre of the now
deserted camp, turned himself into the shape of a small boy, and waited.

A woman returned to look for something she had forgotten, and saw
him there. She walked over to him and tried to catch hold of his arm,
saying: 'Come on, child! Who are you? Come on!' But the child Bern did
not answer; he moved back, away from her. Again she tried to catch hold
of him, but he moved farther back. She called out to the other women,
'You there, whose boy is this little one?' All the people returned and
looked at the child Bern. They talked among themselves, each saying he
or she did not know him. 'He must be a stranger child!' they decided. The
boy retreated a little, but in turning round he fell over a stick. He got up,
and walked a little, but he was hurt. He clutched a tree branch, and as he
stood by the tree he grew — from a child he became a young man, from a
young man he became a big man, he became himself, Bern! His eyes had
grown large, like those of a lizard. As he chanted his song [as above], all
the people became frightened. He ejected a poisonous stream of *nayinbu*
liquid from his anus [just as the Bern lizard does 'from the end of his tail'].
The *nayinbu* was inhaled by all the terror-stricken people. One by one, they
fell down dead.

Wadi Bern then made a big fire, cooked all the people and ate a number of them; the rest of the 'meat' he bundled up and carried away.

The myth of Bern is an interesting one. No explanation is offered for his actions and, moreover, he turns out to be a 'people-eater'. Apart from that, there is a moral attached to this story: a 'stranger' child is always viewed with suspicion and, in Western Desert mythology, Dreaming children are self-willed and their behaviour is not predictable. In this case Bern, as a child, is be-friended at first, when the people try to find out who his parents are. But they become frightened, with due reason, when he sings his song and shows himself in his real shape.

The next myth concerns Loglog. One of his other exploits is given in Myth 177. This story was told to C. Berndt at Oenpelli in 1950.

114.　THE TRANSFORMATION OF LOGLOG

Long ago, that Loglog lizard was a man. He came from the north, and was speaking Yiwadja. He came, he camped, he was eating vegetable foods and meats and kangaroo, and chopping out honey, and then he would go back to his camp to sleep. He kept on doing that. He was looking for a place, a country that he had been promising himself he would find. He was still going along, still speaking Yiwadja. As he came, he made a lot of fresh-water places. He would look to see where there was plenty of honey and would pause for a while, eating and camping about, for two days. After that, early in the morning he would get up and keep going.

He went on and saw a big expanse of water. 'Well,' he said, 'Supposing I plant *mandem* water lilies here: then they will grow roots.' He planted them, and he made fish and put them there. He was still following the water, that big water. He went off in another direction, but then he came back and found his old tracks and went straight on. He was killing creatures and cutting out honey, and as he went along he was filling up his honey-baskets, with some grass to keep the honey from spilling. He went on to another place, where he dug a deep hole in the red soil. He saw water come rising up for him, and tasted it: it was a little bit salty. He went on, and dug again. He said, 'Maybe I'll go to another place and dig there.' He went, he dug, and he saw water coming up. He tasted it. 'I've found fresh water!' He drank it all. And he planted a palm tree that is still standing.

He went climbing higher to a good place, on top, where he made places and built a stringybark hut for himself. He said, 'Maybe I'll leave the language I'm speaking, Yiwadja, because here I've come to Gunwinggu country, and Maung country.' So he left Yiwadja and was speaking Maung and Gunwinggu. He was still camping where he was making places. He would go hunting, and come back again. He always did that: he was preparing to transform himself. 'I suppose, before, I was a man,' he said. He went hunting one more time, that Loglog. He went and named the place in that country where he planted big paperbark trees. 'Here the place-name is Manbulluyu,' he said, giving it that name. He went on and named various little places. Then he came back along a small creek. He was making places while he was following the stream, and making foliage for various plant foods, and he was making lizards and honey. He kept following that creek, and for three days he was camping at Mardan, where he put the name, eating honey and meats and plant foods, and kangaroos too, when he speared them. When his days there were finished he set off again. As he went along, he was speaking Maung. He camped for a long time at Indjumal. For a while he was eating fish, when he went to the great water at Mangarubu, Cooper's Creek, and caught fish to bring back to his camp. He would go there when he had finished all the fish he had brought home. He would go hunting too, looking for small creatures. And he would paint himself with white clay, to disguise his human smell, when he went after kangaroos. He would cook them and eat them there. He settled down, when afternoon came, in that country where he had made his camp. He still went along speaking Maung, and Gunwinggu too. He made creeks, and went after long-nosed fresh-water crocodiles, killing and eating them.

Time went on. At last he was 'listening to himself', contemplating what he should do. 'Already they are all gone, all my relatives. They have all put themselves as *djang*. Well, I myself, in my turn, I should follow them, and do what they did first.' He went, and at last he transformed himself into a creature. He made himself a tail, and he stopped speaking in human speech as he had before. He made two legs and tried to crawl. He said to himself, in his mind, 'Yes, it's good when I try to go along like a creature: I'm transforming myself, when I crawl along. So then, those people don't eat me. I'm a real creature, and I just go about like that very small *bundjing* lizard does. All we eat is flies,' he said. He went on, and at last made himself completely into a little creature. Everything was all right when he went crawling about, and he had made a proper tail and legs. He just went for ever like those various creatures that go crawling about, such as *bundjing* and *galg-galg*. 'But then, myself, I'm just a different kind of body,' he said to himself. So now he was really transformed. When he wanted to find his relatives, as living people, they had already become creatures. So then he just followed them and tried to do the same. That's what they all did, those first people, so that's what he did too. We see him, crawling about. He does not speak — no words, no language. Long ago he talked like a man, but now he has gone like a creature for ever, crawling on trees and among the grasses, and we see him as he goes about all over the place.

This myth parallels a number of others that concern the gradual progression of a particular character toward finding a suitable place for his or her transformation. Loglog in carrying out this compelling act leaves things within the landscape as well as making places, and he does all this along with his everyday pursuits. This story is especially interesting in revealing Loglog's reasons for his transformation, and we will come back to these at the end of this chapter.

The following Western Desert story was told to C. Berndt at Ooldea in 1941.

115. THE SINGING FROGS

A man was walking along. He was listening. He saw tracks where a frog had been getting green grass. He made a fire and lay down to sleep, still listening. A *mamu* frog came up singing, and lay down in the sand. The man covered up the fire, and when the sun rose he got up and went away, looking at the tracks going inside the sand. He got the frog. Then he went off and made a fire, took out the guts, cooked it and ate it: finished it. He got up and went away. Next day he set off, and saw tracks where a frog had been getting green grass. He made a fire by the grass, and lay down, listening. A second frog came up singing, and lay down. When the sun rose the man got up. He went along, kicked out two frogs with his foot, cooked them, and ate all the meat; finished it. Next day at sunrise he went along, and saw tracks where three frogs had been eating grass. He made a fire and a brush shelter and lay down to sleep, listening to that *mamu*-meat. Next day he got three frogs, cooked them and ate them.

The following day he got up and saw tracks. He made a fire and a brush shelter and lay down. Those *mamu* frogs: there were ten of them singing. He got up. Moving his feet in the sand, he got [four], brought them back to his camp, cooked them and ate them: finished them. He got up, went, and saw five tracks. He made a fire and a brush shelter and lay down. Then he got up and went. Moving his feet in the sand, he got five. He brought them back, cooked and ate them; finished them. Next he saw the tracks of six frogs. The following day he killed them and brought them back to camp, carrying them on his head. He cooked them and ate them. That night he heard the singing of many frogs [ten]. Next morning he was listening as he went along, he was looking all around. He saw large tracks. ['He had gone the wrong way'.] He killed one frog, got up, and saw a crowd of them. One frog told him, 'You killed my friend!' Then they all bit that man until he died. The frogs were singing:

> *djindu galala diwaling bungu*
> *djindu galala diwaling bungu*
> *dugur-dugurdu*

> Sun comes up. Far away, hitting, killing.
> Sun comes up. Far away, hitting, killing,
> Dreaming [this].

['There you are, dreaming that first thing in the morning you're going to kill us!']

This peculiar story is structurally interesting. Arranged round the common theme of food-collection, it is made exceptional since in reality the frogs are *mamu* frogs (see Chapter 4), in a position to avenge themselves for having been caught and eaten. The song of the frogs is saying that the man has dreams about killing frogs: 'far away' (in the middle of the night) he is dreaming about this. When he awakens, he actually kills them. Eventually, the frogs bite him in the conventional *mamu* fashion and he dies.

The next story is a segment of what happened in Gogalag: see Myths 54, 122 and 157. It was told to C. Berndt at Oenpelli in 1950.

116. AN ASSORTMENT OF *DJANG*

[To begin with, three characters are talking together about their plans for the future. Then Honey Man goes away and meets others.] 'Where are you going?' asked Honey Man. [Namurudu answered] 'I'm going this way. I'm Namurudu. Where are you going?' [Honey Man replied] 'I'm going to find the place where I saw rocks, and I'll stay there. It's a good place, where I saw rocks, so I'm going there.' 'The place name is Ganimi-loglog, I'm going there,' [Na-gidgid] said. [And] the other one [asked], 'Are you going to stay there?' 'Yes! I'll stay there. I'm Ganimi-loglog, I'm dangerous. I might kill them, I might kill anybody!' [Na-gidgid answered]. 'I'm dangerous. I'm Namurudu!' [the other replied]. He stays there. He made himself *djang*. He made himself like a rock.

'What are we going to eat, perhaps?' 'Ah!' said Na-gidgid. 'Maybe you lot are going to eat fish. We eat kangaroos, and yams.' They were asking each other. Na-gidgid asked again, 'You, what do you lot eat?' 'We eat fish,' said Namurudu. [Then Honey Man goes on, meeting others.]

Well, the Honey Man said as he walked away, talking, to look for the place he wanted, 'Maybe you can all go after kangaroos! But I'm going for honey,' he was saying. 'I'm doing this, I'm making places.' He was going along, talking and walking. He was saying, '*Nguuuuu!*', humming like a bee, as he went along. 'I'm making a big honeycomb,' he was saying to himself. He wasn't travelling with anyone else, only himself.

Two women were eating *mandjudmong*, little brownish berries, a *djang*, Dreaming food. One of them made a heap of berries, and it became *djang*. The Honey Man was still making honey as he went along. He had not yet reached the place he was seeking, where honey is, his own honey-place. He went along, and showed Brown Berry Woman the proper place for her. 'You stay here,' he told her. He went on a bit farther and spoke to Man-baram Woman [a yam-like root]. 'You stay here,' he said. 'You're a *djang*, Dreaming food.' He showed them both where to go.

He went on farther and saw another woman. 'You, you other one, where are you going?' She said, 'I'm Man-godbi, a *djang*, Dreaming food!' [a bitter root]. 'I'm staying here, I'm making myself a *djang* food.' 'Yes,' said Honey Man, 'And I'm going this way, this is my road, I'm following this little creek.' 'Where are you going to stay?' she asked. 'I'll stay at Man-gung-Gawogiyo' [Honey Bee is Talking there.]

Man-godbi Woman was going on talking. She said to Djarbal Woman [a long, hairy root, *man-ngabeg-dubbei*, covered in (enclosed with) hairs, very hairy, like the *garbara* root], 'Where are you going to camp?' 'I'm taking this way, it's a good place!' She went on, Djarbal Woman, and was 'putting herself': 'I'm going here, this way. I'm a *djang*, Dreaming food. I'm always a good, sweet food. If people like, they can eat me any time!' But Man-godbi Woman said, 'I'm going to be the same as *garbara*, long yams: I'm always good and sweet to eat — not like some of those *man-godbi* roots. I always taste good!' [This concerns a sandy place in Gogalag: see Myths 54, 122 and 157.]

The three characters in the first part of this myth-sequence are Honey Man, Namurudu and Na-gidgid, the last two being malignant spirits (see Chapter 4) who turn into *djang*. In the second part, Honey Man goes on by himself and meets three food-bearing *djang*; each is allocated her *djang* place, the first two women being directed by Honey Man, while the third had already decided for herself. In the last part, two *djang* women talk about their transformation.

The following Gunwinggu story was told to R. Berndt at Oenpelli in 1950.

117. THE CHILDREN AND TORTOISE

High up, at the top of the Liverpool River, at Maban-gan in Gunwinggu country, a lot of Wud-wud [children] went down to swim, having first asked their mother(s). They made a ring with one boy in the middle, and they hit the water with their hands, making it splash. The 'middle' boy dived down under the ring of children and came up behind them. He was hiding himself — he came up at another place. The other children looked for him: 'There he is!' they said. But he slipped through their legs. 'There he comes now!' They tried to grab him, but missed; then another child tried, but also missed. Again he dived and went between their legs, or slid through them. 'You need to catch him quickly!' they called out to each other. This went on for some time. 'We are little boys; we can't catch him!' they agreed.

Now Ngalmangiyi, Long-necked Tortoise Woman, *nyindjariga̓rngurg*, *ngalmadgu*, was also in the water. She was pretending to help those children to catch that boy. She came sneaking along; the children did not know she was there. She stole that boy. She emerged from the water, and so did the other children. They saw her: 'That's the one who's stolen him!' However, the boy escaped. Ngalmangiyi pretended to help the children to catch him, but he escaped from her.

Ganawaiwai, Diving Duck Woman, *nyindjarigarngurg*, *ngalmadgu*, saw where the boy was, and tried to catch him. They were all looking for him. The name of that boy was Nanyam-balabala [the name of the water game the children were playing]. All of them came to another small billabong, where they continued to play. That boy jumped over their heads. They cried to catch him, but he jumped again. 'We must catch that boy!' they said.

'What about you, Tortoise?' they asked, 'You catch him.' 'I'm not much good at this,' she replied. 'What about you, Duck?' they asked. 'You might be good.' 'All right, I'll try,' she answered. They all splashed that water; the boy jumped. Tortoise said, 'It's my turn now, I want to catch that boy.' Both Tortoise and Duck jumped, as well as the other children: but Tortoise got hold of the boy. She took him inside the water. The others tried to bring him back, but Tortoise jumped to another place with the boy. And as she did so, she sang:

gabun-garagara (repeat) bir bir yul
Sweeping along, leaving tracks along the bank, into the water.

And she said, 'I won't give you back to those boys.' She was singing. She held her head up and looked at the big water. 'Better I dive down here,' she said. 'Big water now, I'll dive down!' She was singing again. She came close to the big waterhole and then to its bank, and she dived down into that billabong with the boy.

All Tortoise's children were waiting for her. They saw the boy she had brought. 'What have you got, mother?' they asked: 'My daughters, my sons djeidjei, this one is no good,' she replied. All her children watched to see what she had brought: and then they speared that boy and ate him. They told their mother, 'You gave us something not much good!' And they all vomited. 'We'll all stay here at Negerid-djal!' They turned into rocks; one is the mother Tortoise, the others her children. The spirit of that boy, and all the other children and Duck, turned into rocks at Maban-gan.

There is no reason for the abduction of the child by Tortoise, except that she wanted food for her 'children'. 'Human beings hunt for tortoises, but tortoises don't hunt for human beings!' What is the proper relationship between human beings and tortoises? And the point made is that human meat is not suitable for them. We might well ask why the relationship between them needs to be spelt out. While it is fairly clear that the children are human, it is not clear whether Diving Duck and Tortoise are in their human or animal forms. Nevertheless, all are metamorphosed as rocks and do not turn into some animal, or in the case of Duck and Tortoise, their identified form.

Tortoise is mentioned again with two other Dreaming characters, in the next myth, told to R. Berndt at Goulburn Islands in 1947.

118. TURTLE, TORTOISE AND BLACK BIRD

Mangili, fresh water Tortoise, yariwurig, and Manbiyi, green-backed Salt Water Turtle, yarigarngurg, spoke both Maung and Yiwadja. They were arguing about the fat that Manbiyi had within him; Mangili had only a little. He said, 'You had better give me half of the fat you have, as I have so little.' But Manbiyi refused. He said, 'If you want my fat, I'll draw you first.' Manbiyi had a goose feather quill: 'You lie quietly and I'll draw on you; when I've finished I'll give you some of my fat.' When he had completed this task, he gave him the fat. But Manbiyi told the other, 'You won't be like me, I'll be different; you will have a long neck and I'll have a short one!'

They went down to the water together and both jumped in. Green Turtle came up to the surface of the water, but long-necked Tortoise stayed underneath. Manbiyi got a big stone and put it on the back of Mangili to keep him under the water: 'You're not going to come up out of the water like me. Don't follow me!' And he added, 'I've given you half my fat; now I'm going to the salt water, while you will go to the fresh water'. They both went on to the beach. Manbiyi said, 'You stand there and watch me: I'm going into the deep water, when the tide goes out.' He went into the deep water, going down and then coming up; 'but you will hold your breath and stay under the water'.

Now, Diwul-diwul, Black Bird, a *yariwurig* man, was watching those two. When Manbiyi went down, Diwul-diwul noticed that he could not see. So he picked up a stone and threw it at Manbiyi, hitting him on the eyes. The pain after the blow gradually disappeared and Manbiyi, looking up, could see the sea and the land. Manbiyi said: 'Now I have my sight back so I can look properly. If anyone comes near me I can see them. I can dive down to make it hard for people to get me!' He remained in the sea, while Mangili remained in the fresh water.

The events noted in this myth took place at Didi on Croker Island. It was there that Turtle and Tortoise argued over their respective shapes and eventually fought. At Didi there are heaps of rock which resulted from that mythic fight, and presumably it was at that time that Turtle partially lost his eyesight. In this version, the place is the same. Each partially re-shapes the other, and this constitutes their 'making themselves' and adopting their own animal characteristics.

The turtle theme is continued in the next myth from Yirrkalla, told to R. Berndt in 1946. It concerns the Dreaming site of the two Marlban (or Dalwaidba) green-back Turtle: they are metamorphosed at Djarlboyi rock. The two Turtles are husband and wife, cojoined in coitus. This is the 'beginning' place for all turtles of this kind: 'All of them come from here.'

119. MARLBAN AND THE TWO TURTLE HUNTERS

Two Riradjingu dialect men, Minyaba and Wulewal, were living on Bremer Island. They had caught two *marlban* and were preparing coals for cooking them. Two young uncircumcised boys, named Gageral, came and sat with them as the two men were engaged in this task. [Only mature men are allowed to cut turtle, and 'un-cut' boys are not permitted to come close to where this is being done.] But those two 'old' men said nothing to the Gageral boys. They just threw them on the coals and left them to burn to death. The two men loaded their canoe with the two turtles and paddled over to Djarlboyi where the two Turtles are now [as rocks].

Later those two men went out again by canoe. They 'killed' [injured] a young turtle with a harpoon or turtle spear, but it sank down into the water and did not come to the surface. Instead, it travelled underneath the water until it came up and crawled round the reef which was really the bodies of the two large turtles. It came to that father and mother Marlban rock and woke them. It told them what had happened. The mother Turtle lifted her flipper and caused a large wave that capsized the two men's canoe. They did not know that big Turtle was there. They were swimming around trying to find their canoe. Someone from the sky [that Dreaming man, spirit of the male Turtle] spoke to them: 'That big Turtle is a friend of all of us; don't be frightened or worry about him or her.' When the spirit had spoken, the large mother and father Turtles came to the surface, floating. The spirit told those two men: 'Climb onto their backs and hold their shoulders so they can't move over: if you don't do that, a big sea wind will spring up and a storm will come!'

They climbed on the Turtles, who carried them rapidly back to the island. As the Turtles turned their heads to the sea, the two men climbed off. From their camp they watched the two Turtles swimming away — watched until they disappeared. Then those two men said to each other, 'They know our language and everything! Shall we speak to them, asking them to bring back our canoe?' and they agreed to do so: 'Will you get our canoe and everything that was in it?' they called. And the Turtles dived down and collected everything, which they put in to the canoe and sent it floating back to the shore. The two men looked to see whether everything was there: paddles, baler shell, ropes, spear-thrower, spears, turtle harpoons. All there!

The father and mother Turtles went back to their rock, taking the young turtle with them to make sure the turtle hunters did not get it.

The first part of this story tells how the two Dreaming Turtles came into being as rocks at Djarlboyi. It was later that the two hunters went out turtle hunting and injured a young turtle, their 'child'. However, because of the men's earlier association with the mother and father Turtles (having 'put them there'), the Turtles were willing to rescue the two men and recover their canoe and belongings.

In the following myth, Barramundi searches for a place to make himself Dreaming. It was told to C. Berndt at Oenpelli in 1950.

120. BARRAMUNDI BECOMES DREAMING

He was going along. He started off, coming in this direction, from a different place. He was trying to 'put himself' somewhere, to find a Dreaming site for himself. When he saw that a place was not right for him, he went on, following the water, that Balawurdu creek. As he came, he was trying to 'put himself', feeling what a place was like. And he was tasting, feeling the water. When the water was no good, he just kept going. He camped at Gundjeldi, seeing what the place felt like. It wasn't good for him, so he didn't stay. There was a lot of sand, and the water was shallow. He went on, camping on the way where bamboo spear-plants were growing. He tried the water there. It wasn't right.

Still he kept going. He went to the Garigen place, stood there and 'tasted' the place. It wasn't right, and had only a little water. He came on, and there he camped. At Mayawin. He tried the water. It was deep. 'I don't want to stay here,' he said. He went, camping on the way at Djalagu-rulba. He went into the water and 'tasted' the place. Too much mud. So he was still going on; he just kept going. He stood, on the way, at Mana-burdalba. He went into the water, and tasted it. It was a little bit good. He said, 'Here I stay, always!' But he kept tasting it, trying it. 'No, I'll go on.' He was still following the water. He came on, and went into the water of a little billabong at Mumbiri. He stood there, feeling it, trying it. 'I'm still going on!' On the way he went into the water. 'I'm not going to Gamil.' He went into the water. A lot of weeds there. He moved on, still following the water. He stood, pausing, at Bindja-rangga-djawud, and camped there for two days. Then he went on.

He crossed that big creek at Miggin, went on, and put himself there among the rocks at Yirulwi. There he put himself. He made a cave-house, made a hole in the rock, and slept. He said, 'Here is my house. I made a cave-house. And I get up and go into the water of the billabong. I go for ever!' He got up then and went into the water, there at Yiyaral, with its large billabong. Then he got up and put sand, sand at Garabuli, and sand at Namangul, his own place-name, Barramundi, then more soft sand there. He went on farther, and on the way he put sand at Yarulg [Doyle's Landing, on the East Alligator River]. Still he went on. Then he got to a creek where the salt-water tide came up, and farther on to pass the Turkey *djang* site. Then further on to Ngalman-durga, and on farther, putting more sand. And there he came into Dreaming.

He became a rock. So then, when the salt-water tide comes in, he is submerged. When the tide goes back, he comes out again, Namangul, Barramundi, he stands there. He remains as a rock in the middle of the water. If people are travelling in canoes, they do not go close to where he stands, but they keep a long way off, away from him.

There are several versions of the Barramundi myth. In one, a Mangeri version told by men (in contrast with the one we present here, which was told by Gunwinggu women), Barramundi was observed by three hunters, one of whom (named Nagwungbid) speared 'him'. Barramundi broke loose and went in the direction of the coast, followed by the hunters, making the East Alligator River. Finally, he 'turned himself' into a rock at Gulari Point, at the river's mouth. His Dreaming place can be seen at low tide. The myth set out here has similarities, although no hunters, and, in any case, the focus is on Barramundi seeking a place for his metamorphosis. It was said that this was not the same Barramundi manifestation as the one who shaped (made) the East Alligator; women also told about him.

The next myth is from the Daly River and was told to R. Berndt in 1945. It comes from the Wogaidj, Wadjaging language, and is associated with Nicholas Creek on the Daly. It concerns two varieties of shark, both Dreaming women, Djeyu, the smaller, and Djindjari, the larger.

121. THE SHARK PEOPLE

The Shark people lived in the vicinity of the Daly River. The women cut string from the banyan tree, dried it in the sun and rolled it on their thighs to make long strands to form a fishing line. They also made a wallaby bone hook, threading through their line at one end. They went out to cut bamboo, and sent out the young men and adult men who were camped with them to collect mullet [the fish preferred by the shark]. On their return they cooked and ate some of the fish but kept some for bait.

Next morning they sent the men out to get shark: they themselves were human. [Calling these people 'shark' implies an association with them; they had a special aptitude for catching these creatures, but were not themselves sharks.] The men prepared their fishing lines, which ran along a bamboo rod [like a European fishing rod]. They baited their hooks, stuck the thick end of the bamboo into the mud at the river's bank, and waited. A *djeyu* shark came up, snapped at the bait, and broke the line. The men put on another hook, baited it and waited. Again, the *djeyu* came up. ['She, Shark, was curious; "just like women", she came up again.'] However, she was not caught.

The women in the camp called back to the men, 'You are no good!' [Actually, they sent two or three parties of men down to catch Shark, but each group was unsuccessful.] Next day the men went out to get mullet. On the following day the women gave them lines and they went down to the river to catch Shark, but could not. The women were impatient and said they would go out themselves. They went down to the river and tried with their lines and bamboo rods. Each time the Shark came up, it snapped off the bait. The women called out 'Sister', trying to attract it — but the *djeyu* did not listen. They called out to the men that they, too, were unsuccessful.

The men, after collecting mullet on the following day again went down to fish for shark. They put out their lines all along the river bank, and they whistled up that Shark, that big female *djindjari* shark and caught her. They called out to the women: 'The women were no good, but the men are!' They returned to the camp carrying that shark. There they prepared it, cooking it in an earth oven after cleaning and wrapping it in leaves and tying it up 'like a basket'. When it was taken from the oven, all the moisture was pressed out and the flesh moulded into a large oval ball.

[The scene changes.] Djindjari sat down in her camp with her child, Nearby, Djeyu sat in hers, with her child. Djeyu went out to obtain mullet, leaving her child behind. While she was away, Djindjari decided to change over the children. So she took the Djeyu child, leaving hers in its place, and went away. Djeyu returned and looked at the child. 'What is the matter with his forehead — it's wide and flat? Where has my boy gone?' she asked. 'This is Djindjari's child!' Taking him with her, she went in search of Djindjari. When she found her, they fought with digging sticks and Djeyu injured Djindjari's foot. They went on fighting and 'turned into' sharks, swimming down the Daly River, but they also made themselves into rock, deep in the river: it can only be felt at low tide with a long bamboo.

The format of this myth, which is in two sections, is interesting. The first concerns the Shark people using line rods originally made by Djeyu. The

Plate 1, right: Biriwilg lived near Red Lily Lagoon. She became a painting on the wall of a rock shelter and the design on her body represents her paperbark covering. See Stories 25 and 26.
Artist: Nipper Maragar, Manger(dji), Oenpelli, 1949. On bark.

Plate 2, below: Mythic Dogs chase Emus. At the end of their travels they are exhausted, and their heavy breathing widens Lake Gregory in the south-eastern Kimberleys. Nearby, on the Sturt Creek, is the home of a Rainbow Snake. See Story 13.
Artist: Desley Milner, *nangala* subsection, Djaru, Balgo, 1986. Acrylic on board.

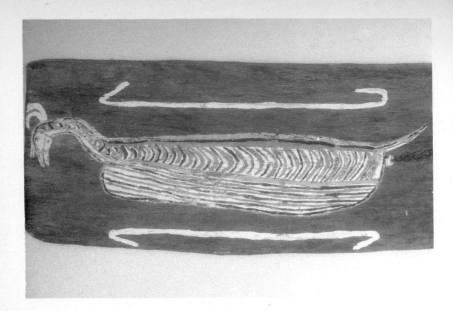

Plate 3, above: Ngalyod, the western Arnhem Land Rainbow Snake. The hooked bands, above and below, are its reflections — the actual rainbow. See Chapter 3.
Artist: Samuel Mangguldja, Gunwinggu, Oenpelli, 1947. On bark.

Plate 4, below: A husband and wife mythic pair live on the headwaters of Gumadir Creek. Their roasting wallaby bursts and the sound brings two Rainbow Snakes, who swallow them. They are now two hills at Gudjabin, and Wallaby became a painting. A young Rainbow is seen at one side. See Chapter 3.
Artist: Ngaiiwul, Gunwinggu, Oenpelli, 1950. On bark.

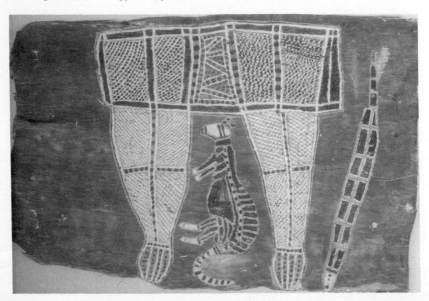

Plate 5, above: A section of the great Wawalag and Yulunggul epic. The upper panel depicts male and female Yulunggul, the Two Sisters and the child of one. The bottom panel shows where the Sisters danced, were swallowed and eventually regurgitated. See Story 36.
Artist: Mawulan and Wondjug, Riradjingu, Yirrkalla, 1946. Crayon on brown paper.

Plate 6, right: Nyung-gulerubumbu from the South Alligator River cuts some fat from her labia majora. See Story 39.
Artist: Fred Wadedi, Gagadju, Oenpelli, 1949. On bark.

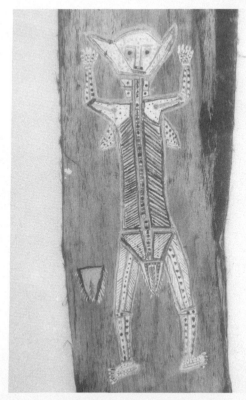

Plate 7, left: In this example, Nayugyug roasts a goanna, and when its bursts the sound brings the Rainbow Snake who encircles both him and his bag. They were metamorphosed at Igudandji Rock, on Gumadir Creek. See Chapter 3.
Artist: Ngaiiwul, Gunwinggu, Oenpelli, 1949. On bark.

Plate 8, below: The *nyalaidj* dancers. See Stories 48 to 50.
Artist: Ngaiiwul, Gunwinggu, Oenpelli, 1950. On bark.

Plate 9, right: Two myths are presented in this painting. One concerns Djuddjud, who 'turned himself' into a shark. See Story 110. The other relates to Rainbow, who swallowed people (represented by a man and a woman) after being attracted by a crying child. Some escape by canoe, but they are eventually swallowed. See Story 57.
Artist: Tom Namagarainmag, Maung, Goulburn Islands, 1947. On bark.

Plate 10, below: The Wadi Gudjara make a Wonambi from a possum's entrails. The waterhole in which it is placed is shown, as are the boomerangs made by the Two Men and their tracks. See Story 65.
Artist: George Maning, Wiranggu, Ooldea, 1941. Chalk and crayon on brown paper.

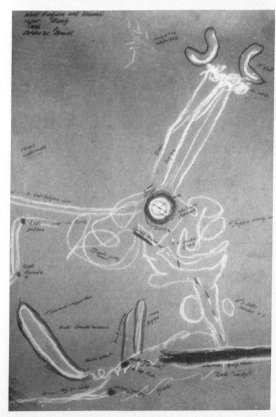

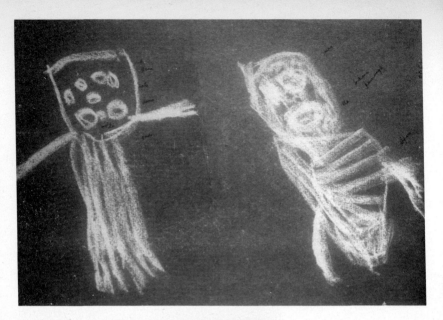

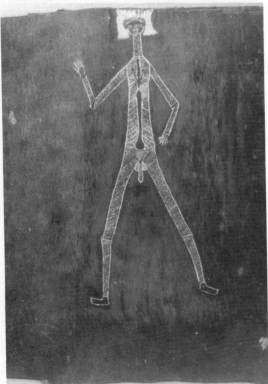

Plate 11, above: Two representations of *mamu* spirits, See Story 66.
Artist: Wiriga, Western Desert, Ooldea, 1941. Chalk on brown paper.

Plate 12, left: A *mimi* spirit, or Mainya becomes friendly with a human being and lives with him and his family. However, Mainya deceives them and is killed. See Story 80.
Artist: Tom Namagarainmag, Maung, Goulburn Islands, 1947. On bark.

Plate 13, right: Mimi spirits on the mainland opposite the Goulburn Islands. See Story 82.
Artist: Peter Namiyadjad, Maung, Goulburn Islands, 1947. On bark.

Plate 14, below: A fisherman spirit, Manadbrugur, is shown with his fishing spear, dragging a line behind him through which he has threaded fish. The hooks at his elbows may be extended to pick up his spears. This story resembles Story 84, although in that case the Yung-galya are involved.
Artist: Jimmy Midjau-midjau, Gunwinggu, Oenpelli, 1950. On bark.

Plate 15, left: A Wirindji woman dances with her potential male victim. See Stories 91 and 92.
Artist: 'Billy Compass' Namadbara, Yiwadja-Gunwinggu, Croker Island, 1968. On bark.

Plate 16, below: A northern version of a mythic woman (left) who 'turns into' an Emu (bottom right) not far from Nimbuwa, near Oenpelli. She carries a basket, has a digging stick and a flat-ended scoop for yams. Three varieties of yam are shown. See Chapter 5 and Story 46.
Artist: Long Paddy Djamargula, Gunwinggu, Oenpelli, 1949. On bark.

Plate 17, above: Dog and Kangaroo agree to paint each other in ochres, with the intention of ultimately establishing their appearance. This occurred near Tor Rock in western Arnhem Land. See Story 93.
Artist: Jimmy Midjau-midjau, Gunwinggu, Oenpelli, 1949. On bark.

Plate 18, below: A typical story explaining why particular creatures take the shape they now have. Echidna woman had two small daughters, one of whom is eaten by Tortoise woman. They fight. Echidna flattens Tortoise with a large stone (the round object in the painting); Tortoise throws her bamboo spears and they become Echidna's quills. See Chapter 5 and also an episode in Story 117.
Artist: Long Paddy Djamargula, Gunwinggu, Oenpelli, 1949. On bark.

Plate 19. A Dreaming site at Djarlboyi rock, north-eastern Arnhem Land. The mother Turtle, shown in the bottom panel, causes huge waves with the movement of her flippers. Other turtles, porpoises, sea-eggs and various fish are depicted, along with rain-bearing clouds. See Story 119.

Artist: Gungoilma, Djambarbingu, Yirrkalla, 1947. Crayon on brown paper.

Plate 20. Mináliwu, betrothed wife of Nabin-gulou. Mináliwu refuses to accept her husband and is killed. In this version she is shown suckling a child. See Story 132.
Artist: Samuel Mangguldja, Gunwinggu, Oenpelli, 1949. On bark.

Plate 21. An 'eternal triangle'. A wife has been caught with her sweetheart. Her husband is at the left, with arms upraised in anger. See Chapter 7.
Artist: Jimmy Midjau-midjau, Gunwinggu, Croker Island, 1968. On bark.

Plate 22. Bala-ngudjalg-ngudjalg sends his two wives to Balbanara to collect good *man-gulaidj* nuts. While they are there, they spend most of their time with sweethearts. See Story 147. *Artist:* Samuel Mangguldja, Gunwinggu, Oenpelli, 1958. On bark.

Plate 23, left: Cockatoo man's wives consider him too old, so they go in search of younger men. On their return, they are persuaded to climb a ladder to enter a cave. Cockatoo pushes the laddder aside. Unable to climb down, they die there. See commentary to Story 147.
Artist: Samuel Mangguldja, Gunwinggu, Oenpelli, 1947. On bark.

Plate 24, below: The Gunggaranggara sisters are chased by a mythic man. They eventually escape into the sky and become the Pleiades; and the man becomes the Morning Star. See Story 159.
Artist: Gracie Green, Walmadjeri, Balgo, 1986. Acrylic on board.

Plate 25, above: Dulina kills a *mamu* child and brings it back for his wife and children to eat. His wife discovers that it is her sister's child. Shocked, she leaves her husband and children. In the drawing Dulina and his wife are shown. He has a *maban* shell in his forehead that provides him with x-ray vision. See Story 172.
Artist: Mick Djandjureri, Andingari, Ooldea, 1941. Chalk on brown paper.

Plate 26, below: Yirawadbad in snake manifestation, within a hollow log. His mother-in-law is at one end and his betrothed wife at the other. His wife's sisters are shown below. Above are roasting potatoes and a potato plant.
Artist: Jimmy Midjau-midjau, Gunwinggu, Oenpelli, 1950. On bark.

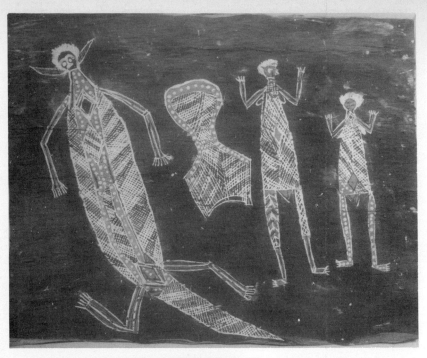

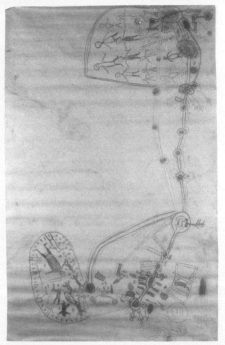

Plate 27, above: One of the myth versions of the much feared Luma-luma. On the left he is shown in his human whale form as he originally emerged at Cape Stewart, near Milingimbi, central coastal Arnhem Land. There he swallowed two girls (right) and cut a man's body in half (centre). See Story 182.
Artist: Nalowid, Gunbalang (Walang), Goulburn Islands, 1947. On bark.

Plate 28, left: The voyage of Yawalngura to the *dua* moiety Land of the Dead. See Stories 190 and 191.
Artist: Mawulan, Riradjingu, Yirrkalla, 1947. Crayon on brown paper.

people of the Shark Dreaming had special power over these creatures. If a shark bit off the bait and hook, they would whistle the shark back: it would return a second time and the men would speak to it: 'I will bite you!' And in return, the shark would bite the line and bait, and be caught.

The second section takes the perspective of the two Dreaming Shark women, Djeyu and Djindjari, who fight after one has abducted the other's child and, as a result, turn into sharks. The *djeyu* shark is said to resemble a woman: it has a smooth skin, and its two side flippers are its breasts. On its belly is a small mark, its navel, and an aperture is its vulva. A semi-circular mark at the end of its body, near the tail, is the mark made by Djindjari during their fight. The large fin on the upper middle part of the body is her basket, which she carries attached by fibre to her head or shoulders. *Djindjari*, as a fish, does not have these human characteristics: she is the hammer-headed shark, much more ferocious then *djeyu*.

In the first section there is an indication of rivalry between the men and women engaged in catching sharks. When the men are unsuccessful, the women become impatient and try their hand at it. When they fail, the men try again, and by using their special technique succeed in catching a shark. The men return to the camp, boasting they are better than the women in this respect. The point made in the myth is that the female shark (= woman) responds to men but not to women (even though they address it as 'Sister'); that relationship between the sexes had, for the Daly River people, wide implications.

The final two stories, about Leech (told to C. Berndt) and Lice (told to R. Berndt), come from Oenpelli, in 1950.

122. LEECH AT MAMARAWIRI

He started off from the billabong, the same round billabong where that man had been soaking fish-poison leaves in the water, and eating fish, at Mamarawiri, in Gogalag [see also Myth 116].

He got up, he went. He went, Leech. He looked this way, that way, as he was coming. He saw a good place. He said, 'I do this, because it's a good place. I'll settle down, I'll stay always!' That man who was eating fish, Naberg-gaidmi, asked him, 'What are you?' And he said, 'I'm turning into Leech, I'm going to stay in one place. I'm going to become a rock, a little rock, and stay here, with a flat head, a short head. I'm Leech *djang*, Leech Dreaming!' he said. 'I'm Leech!' And he said, 'Here I sit [stay]. This is my creek flowing, this is mine, where I'm sitting [staying]. I'm *djang*, Dreaming!'

123. THE INFESTATION
OF THE LICE PEOPLE

Maidadjan, Louse, *yariyaning, nangaridj*, was one of a large group of those men [people] who went along the same creek as did the Dadbi [see Myth 28]. 'We have to follow the creek,' they said. [The Dadbi and Maidadjan were of 'one company'.] However, the Dadbi went north, while the Lice went west, following that little creek and they put a hill nearby named Djirung-gam. They all camped there for a while. 'We must find a place where we can remain!' They had left the big creek and followed a smaller one to Yagaga, where they camped. 'Where are we to go?' they asked one another. 'We'd better go back to the creek that we left.' They turned back: they found the creek and went back to where they had parted company with the Dadbi at Inbanigularnga. All the Maidadjan were thinking about those Dadbi — they wanted to 'mix' with them.

All those Maidadjan did not have lice before; they started to scratch their heads. Those lice went into their moustaches, into their pubic hair, spread all over their bodies. They could not get rid of them.

They followed that little creek. Then they came to a big one with waterholes and a billabong. 'We'll stay here and kill all our lice — so that we can continue to find the country!' They all sat down at that billabong. They tried to get rid of the lice, but could not. Those lice got on to their eyelashes and closed up their eyes, closed up their mouths — they were everywhere, even under the armpits and in their pubic hair. They tried to kill them, but could not!

'We have made a mistake. We shouldn't have come to this place: there are too many lice. Maybe we will stop here or make something!' This was at the waterhole named Igurlbung. They all sat down there. One man shut his eyes; his mouth closed: he couldn't see; he couldn't talk. He dived into this water, into a cave underneath. 'One man has died!' they said. 'Maybe all of us will die! We have camped in a "stranger place".' They tried to sing out those lice, but the lice blocked their eyes and their mouths. All those Maidadjan dived into the water: 'Those things came out of their bodies!' They could do nothing! Only one man spoke: all the others were unable to do so. They all dived down into that cave under the water, at Igurlbung [alternative name for louse, *gurlbung*].

The Leech Dreaming, in talking about the shape he will take as a rock, says that he will be a small rock; 'where I sit (stay), my head is flat, and my head is short': '. . . *guri ngani, nga-goid-wola'wola ngani, dja nga-goid-djumbu.*' Leech's metamorphosis occurred in Gogalag, the scene of several other events noted in this book (see Myths, 54, 116, 122 and 157).

On the other hand, a group of Lice people, at one time associated with the Dadbi Snakes (see Myth 28), try to rid themselves of the lice which attack them, but cannot. Their only hope is to dive into the water and remain there as Lice *djang*: the lice have overcome them completely. (In a louse story from another site, a young wife gives birth to a multitude of lice instead of the human baby that she and her husband and co-wives were expecting; see R. and C. Berndt 1970: 25–26.)

The shapes of, and in, the natural environment are obviously those that can be seen and touched. They include human beings and natural species along with other visible, tangible features of the landscape. However, from an Aboriginal standpoint, such tangible shapes are made more real, and more clearly identifiable, by having meanings attached to them, and these in turn add to the concept of 'shape'. Shape in this context has a mythological meaning as well as a social relevance. So that, in addition to 'living' natural features that are subject to change, there are the 'meaning-shapes' that are relatively constant and, traditionally speaking, basically unchanging — provided the belief system remains viable.

When we come to look at the issue of 'meaning-shapes', in mythological terms, they come about (as the myths tell us) through certain activities of mythic beings that lead to their transforming themselves from what they 'started off' as being. In the thirty-one stories presented in this chapter, twenty-five of the principal characters turn themselves into (or become) a natural species which is indicated by the original name-tag that is used in identifying it. (That is, being called a Kangaroo Man, an Emu Woman, a Loglog Lizard, and so on.) But there are some variations, too. For example, Seahawk turned into the bird of that name, then into a shark and remained in that form; two Emus became river gums; Eagle went into a soak and stayed there. Also at least nine (including the Wud-wud — children — counted as one in this case) are metamorphosed as rocks. 'The singing frogs', however, are an exception.

Some of these characters who made themselves *djang* (in Gunwinggu terminology) became rocks. However, the metamorphosis of becoming *djang* does not necessarily mean that sort of manifestation, although it mostly does. It can refer to a 'turning' into a natural species, as in the case of the four food-bearing plant women who become *djang*. And, in the myth concerning 'An assortment of *djang*', Honey Man 'makes himself' *djang* but is a symbolic representation of honey bees. His two companions, Namurudu and Na-gidgid, remain as malignant spirit *djang*.

In these myths, in three cases (referring to Emus) there is no transformation; in two others (Willy Wagtail) the character is killed but is not transformed. In one other example, Wuraal was, and remained, a bird.

The issue of initial humanity, of being a human person, is not always clear, even though the incidents in which the character is involved mirror human-like behaviour. The assumption is that, where they are specifically noted as being transformed, they were previously in human shape — except for Seahawk, who became a bird, then a shark; and Wuraal, as a bird. However, the major point is the 'meaning-shape' which is imprinted upon the 'physical-shape', and those two aspects in a complementary way constitute the identification of shapes of and in the countryside.

It is worth mentioning again the illuminating comments on the process of transformation that appear in the Loglog myth. Loglog says, 'I suppose, before, I was a man.' He is preparing to transform himself. And, then, he is 'listening to himself,' thinking about what he should do. He feels that he is becoming something else: he is impelled to fulfil his destiny. All his relatives have gone; all of them have 'put themselves as *djang*'. Then, he 'made himself completely into a little creature'. Finally, comes the revealing point. 'I'm just a different kind of body' — his personality as it was as a man, is the same as it is as a creature — it is merely in a different shape! And that is significant in understanding traditional Aboriginal attitudes to their countryside and what it contains, as it is in relation to themselves.

In the myths in this chapter, transformation is triggered off mostly by a conflict situation — although there are four exceptions (the two cases of Willy Wagtail, Loglog Lizard, and in 'An assortment of *djang*'). It is on that note of conflict that we turn to the next chapter.

CHAPTER SIX

BREAKING THE RULES

In considering the myths we have been looking at so far, we may well ask what the rules are. Of course, they vary according to the particular Aboriginal cultural perspective to which the myths belong. Nevertheless the question remains, and it is not all easy to find cut-and-dried answers. What can be regarded as serious crimes, of which the myths give many examples, are generally condemned in real-life situations. That applies to some mythic instances of homicide and physical injury, rape, incest and brutality, whether or not any of the mythic characters concerned react against them. However, condemnation of violence depends on a variety of circumstances; on what took place beforehand and, for that matter, on what has taken place afterward. Moreover, violence begets violence, a point demonstrated in the myths as it is in ordinary life.

What about theft, greed and selfishness, withholding food or some object from another person who could reasonably expect to receive it, or slighting a person in other ways? The rules are often more explicitly enunciated in such matters than they are in relation to serious crimes. But they are quite explicit too in regard to incest, and to the infringement of sacred laws. With issues of sorcery, what is involved is not so much condemnation as trying to ensure that a stand is adopted against it or, alternatively, giving in to it entirely. Elopement and abduction, even without violent intent, usually raise the question of finding and punishing the persons involved. But that in itself can provoke repercussions which will almost certainly include some form of violence or threat of violence on the part of an aggrieved husband, for instance. However, one thing is clear from mythic (and other) examples: in most cases the punishment does not fit the crime. This is particularly so where trivial misdemeanours explode into serious confrontations.

More often than not there is no firm public opinion as to how a person should proceed when faced with acts of violence, potential or otherwise; and, for that matter, how to proceed against an aggressor. In small kin-based societies, as in traditional Aboriginal Australia, many persons, mythic or otherwise, were likely to escape conventionally appropriate punishment or retribution for something they had done, or not done. The outcome did not rest on an impartial assessement of whether one form of action was good or bad. In practice, the real question revolved round *who* was involved or implicated, over and above the nature of the 'crime', and how such action could affect other people. Not least, it had to take into account cases of aggressively strong persons whose personality or reputation discouraged or militated against the likelihood of reprisals. Not all such points are spelt out in the mythology, but they are often obliquely indicated. In the absence of a centralised judicial system in the traditional scene, responsibility for avenging a wrong fell fairly heavily on the person most directly concerned. In other words, the focus is not so much on social justice as on achieving personal satisfaction through revenge, or what has usually been called self-help, even though physical injury or death could be the result. In traditional Aboriginal society, the social good did not necessarily coincide with the personal good.

Mythology is resonant with social nuances. Contained within it are basic assumptions, even though these are mostly wrapped up in unfamiliar forms. But even if they are, they can generally be read by those who know the language of myth. Other things being equal, myth is a guide to action — actions of all sorts. But in myths as in real life, other things are not necessarily equal, and the norm could well be one of inequality. On the other hand, rules can be identified only in the breach. Further, these rules, in a negative sense, are articulated through what takes place as a result of one being broken. And if mythology is any indication, it can be difficult even then to distinguish what the rules are. Moreover, when we compare the mythic situations with real life, the differences are negligible. We are not saying that mythology is a mirror-image of real-life situations. Nevertheless, it constitutes a set of statements about the nature of reality — and, in fact, is regarded as such by traditionally-oriented Aborigines. Mythology is a kind of purposeful and deliberate presentation of varying images, purporting to convey essential truths about human existence and social living. It is a kind of social mapping of the dangers inherent in social interaction, and a spelling out of the kinds of action that could conceivably result from unleashing dangerous forces. It is a recognition of the fact that people can and do behave in unreasonable ways.

A large number of the myths reveal, either overtly or covertly, the lineaments of conflict between various mythic characters. What is mostly clear is what takes place and why, who the aggressors are and who the victims. What is not spelt out, in so many words is, who should be condemned. It is almost as if the decision rests primarily with the listener. What did the 'victim' *do* to bring about such a state of affairs? Who indeed *is* the real aggressor, and who the real victim? The myths do not always provide direct categorical answers to such questions. Clues are certainly provided — but they often depend on interpretation. In short, the answers have to be teased out. In this chapter we follow that theme a little further.

The first myth was told to R. Berndt at Balgo in 1960.

124. THE EXPLOITATION OF MUDILA

An old man, Ngadjinawuru, lived with a small boy named Mudila, at a place bearing the same name as the man: it is a big hill, with no water, west of Balgo near the Canning Stock Route.

Ngadjinawuru made a large number of boomerangs and spears and gave them to Mudila to carry. Mudila did not want to do that, because they were heavy. The old man insisted. 'Carry them or I'll hit you', he said. So the two went hunting, and the boy killed some animals. When they were cooked and ready for eating, the old man gave him none. He went out again to cut wood to make more boomerangs, leaving the boy without a fire. Then he sent the boy out to get meat, but when he brought some back, the old man would not share with him. The same thing was repeated. One day the boy went out with the boomerangs. He was angry about the way he had been treated. Coming to a large termite mound he broke up all the boomerangs on it. 'He was hungry for meat, and for fire!'

The old man returned from cutting boomerangs; the boy came back without meat. During the night the man left the camp to defecate. The boy threw a live coal so that it fell near the man, frightening him: he thought it was a falling star, and ran back to the place Ngadjinawuru and hid in a hole. The boy took some fire and ran away. The old man remained in hiding until the morning. Then, emerging from his hole, he looked around and saw the dead fire: nothing but cold ashes. He followed Mudila's tracks and came to where the boy had cooked meat: Mudila had left a little meat for him, knowing that he would follow.

From there, the boy crossed a deep creek. Seeing him on the other side, the old man began to 'swear' at him. The boy called out, 'Don't be cross, come over! It's not deep!' But Mudila tricked him! The creek *was* deep, and Ngadjinawuru was drowned. The boy went into a hole, and remained there.

The reason for withholding food that Mudila himself had obtained is not given, nor is the relationship between him and Ngadjinawuru. But it is clear who is in the wrong, and who brings disaster upon himself. However, there is the issue of Mudila taking fire when he runs away.

While that theme is only passingly referred to, it becomes a central focus in the next two myths.

The first, about fire, comes from Ooldea (Western Desert culture). The other is from Oenpelli but originally from the western tradition, beyond the East Alligator River. They were told to R. Berndt, the first in 1941, the second in 1949.

125. THE RECOVERY OF FIRE

Djilbi [meaning Old Man] remained in his camp while a number of young Yin-ga men went out hunting. With them was his own son, Yilgadidi. They returned in the late afternoon with kangaroo and possum meat, but cooked and ate it themselves without giving any to him.

Djilbi sat in his camp for many days and became increasingly hungry. When the young men had finished all their food, they went out hunting again. Djilbi remained. He was very angry. He covered up all the fires with sand, putting them out completely, except for one fire-stick that he took with him. Then he went eastward to Walangara waterhole and camped there, making a fire for himself.

When the hunters returned they found all the fires extinguished. They stirred the ashes, and wrapping coals in tinder they blew on them, trying to make a flame but without success. [They did not know how to make fire.] During the night it was very cold and they huddled together to keep warm. Next morning Yilgadidi went in search of his father, found his tracks, and followed them to Walangara. But Djilbi had already left, taking his fire with him and completely extinguishing the fire he had used overnight. He went on to Binandi, camping there, and later covered his fire and continued to Ngubal. His son was following him, but found the fires at each place covered and cold. From Ngubal, Djilbi travelled a few feet above the ground ['nearly flying'], going directly to a site near the sea at Eucla. He walked into the sea water, and by the time his son arrived he was up to his neck, holding his fire-stick above his head. His son came behind him and, just as his father began to disappear into the water, grabbed him and pulled him back to the shore. [He threw him over his shoulder back to the land, thus saving his father *and* the fire-stick.]

Yilgadidi took possession of the fire, and the father and son camped there 'for a long time'. They died there, being metamorphosed as rocks. The Yin-ga, on the other hand, remained at their first camp; and as they had no fire they died of cold.

126. TWO MOTHERS REFUSE
FIRE TO THEIR SONS

Two 'old' Dreaming women, together named Numburmanugu, lived at Gira, close to Muwangi on the western side of the East Alligator River in Gagadju country. There is a small creek there. They had two sons, Madjalbida and Manamaramar [see Myth 2].

The Numburmanugu went out looking for lily roots; their two sons went to hunt for goannas and snakes. The women came back early to their camp, cooked the food they had collected and ate it themselves. They sat there with their fire until it became dark, but their sons did not return. Rain began to fall, and it was cold. The Numburmanugu made a large fire to warm themselves. From a long way off, the sons saw that fire. 'Our mothers have a big fire. Let's go home and warm ourselves: it is too cold!' they said to each other. They came close to their camp, travelling across the plain; they were hunting for a *gerigeri*, plover. The Numburmanugu heard them coming. The two sons came closer. 'I can hear the bird they have frightened,' one woman said to the other. So they got together all of that fire and put it inside their vaginas — putting it all in there and hiding it.

The two sons came into the camp and spread out the goannas and other creatures they had caught. They looked around, but there was no smoke, no fire! 'Where's that fire, mother?' they asked. 'We looked back when we were hunting and saw it,' they said. 'Ah, sons,' they replied, 'We haven't any fire; we can't make fire.' 'But we saw that fire. Where is it?' the sons repeated. 'We don't have fire', the women insisted. So they all slept. Because there was no fire to cook what they had caught, the goanna and other meat went rotten. They questioned their mothers, 'Both of you have cooked food — where did you get the fire from?' 'Oh my boys,' they whined, 'We dried our food in the sun.'

The two sons went out hunting again: 'We'll look at what our mothers are doing,' they agreed. The Numburmanugu went out for food too, and returned to their camp. The two sons killed goanna, snake, possum and tortoise. The women called to each other: 'Sister, we'll go back to cook our food before our sons return.' They came to their camp and made fire with their fire-sticks. [The horizontal, grooved stick is *nyumeragadi*, the female; the vertical stick, the pestle, is *nyung-gunu*, the male. When a fire is being made, with the pestle twirling in the under-stick, this is symbolic of coitus.] The women made a big oven for the lily roots they had collected.

The two men, with no fire, could not cook their food. The two women ate their cooked roots and waited for their sons to return; they sat there till sundown. The sons said, 'It is cold and dark: let's go home. Perhaps our mothers have fire and we can warm ourselves.' Again, on the way back, the men hunted birds. They saw the bright firelight from their mothers' camp, and again they ran quickly to get there. As before, the two women heard the birds being disturbed. They sat down, spreading out their legs, and scooped up all the fire, hiding it in their vaginas. Then they went inside their grass hut.

Arriving at the camp, the two men threw down what they had caught. Everything was wet. They said how cold they were, and asked about the fire: 'We saw the light from it as we were coming along the track home.' The two women denied they had fire. Their sons accused them of having used it to cook their lily roots, and declared that they must have some cooked food hidden in their hut. But the women repeated that they had dried their food in the sun.

Next morning, the two sons went out hunting in the usual way. They caught various creatures, but because they had no fire the food became rotten. They decided to go to a billabong in the nearby jungle. There they got a heavy stick. One brother lay down, bending his shoulders, while the other smashed his jaw bone on both sides, making him look like an *ilbundjuri* crocodile. He had the head of a crocodile but the body of a man. 'Look at me,' he said, 'Am I all right? Have I got a long jaw?' 'Yes, brother,' the other replied. 'Now I'll lie down and you do the same to me!' And the other 'made' him a crocodile head. They got gum from the roots of an ironwood tree [see Myth 145], and each put a lump of it on his nose, making it a crocodile nose. They made each other's nostrils. The elder brother told the other to go down into the billabong to see how he could bubble [through the nostrils] as he floated. 'Ah, that is good, brother! Now we must kill our mothers!' And he added, 'You can't stand, you have to swim.' The two brothers made wind through their nostrils. 'You are no longer a man!' they said to each other. 'We will stay in the water!'

The two women were collecting lily roots in the billabong. Their two sons [crocodiles] were floating there. The elder brother said, 'I will kill your mother, you kill my mother!' And they attacked their mothers, dragging them under the water, 'cutting' their throats. Then they spoke: 'We will kill animal, man, anything!' They jumped out of the water, and broke off a mangrove stick. One brother told the other to stand up, and used the stick to break his arms and legs, making them short like a crocodile's. The other did the same to him. Then they both went down to the sea.

In the first myth the reason for the old man running away with the fire was the greed and selfishness of the youths in withholding food. The linkage is direct, and so is their eventual death from extreme cold. The old man's son was just in time to rescue the fire-brand. The implication is that he was not simply being selfish but was acting more positively, at least partly to help his father, and, through him, fire was safeguarded for future generations of human beings. The second myth is more ambiguous. Why the two mothers hid the fire from their own sons is not clear; it was obviously not a simple matter of depriving them of food. (A very similar story was told to C. Berndt at Goulburn Island in 1961 by Maung women.) But the myth was said to explain why the vaginal walls of human women are now red — from the fire that was hidden by the Numburmanagu women. Their death at the 'hands' of their own sons also explains why crocodiles became like they are now. 'They were made to be like that, because their mothers would not give them fire!'

The next myth is structurally interesting because it provides a preamble to the main story. It was told to R. Berndt at Ooldea in 1941.

127. MOON'S JOURNEY AND DEATH

[Preamble] Wadi Bira, Moon Man, also called Gidjili or Galga, came from the western sector of the Western Desert, carrying a large fighting boomerang. He reached Djunbada waterhole and threw his boomerang, watching it circling around, falling to the ground. As he did this he sang:

galigigiri yanu waru wada mungadu
Boomerang went circling, returning at night, to the fire [at the base of] the tree.

Bira walked over to pick up his boomerang, and sang:

bira biraya wadi-yara
munu biraya gadal-gadal djela bira wadi-yara
Moon man moving [to pick up his boomerang]
Moon man, a long way, across the open plain.

He threw his boomerang again and sang:

ganilba leridi waningu
Throwing [that] boomerang well.

He walked away and sat down on a sandhill. From there he saw smoke in the distance. He sang:

nimeru-nimeru boyu gorei gulbunei nimerei-nimerei
Smoke in the distance, thinking of walking.

Then he smelt the smoke and sang:

bundira nyinei winin-winindai
Sitting, smelling [the smoke].

[These songs explain the movement of Moon across the sky. Bira throws his boomerang, which falls some distance away from him; he goes in search of it. This is repeated as Bira 'walks' across the sky. Finding it, sitting on a sandhill toward the end of his journey, he sees smoke rising in the distance. He gets up and walks toward it, smelling it, and continues walking toward the camp of the Two Men, the Wadi Gudjara.]

[The story begins here.] Wadi Bira, Moon Man, walked on until he came to where the Two Men were camping. With them were the Gunggurunggura women, the 'Seven Sisters' [see Myths 16 and 159]. Bira met the Two Men, but the women were out hunting. He sat a little distance away from the men, who were behind a bush catchment designed to trap kangaroos. The women drove the kangaroos from the left toward the catchment; on reaching it, the animals jumped over the bushes and the Two Men killed them with their clubs. They told Bira to hunt kangaroos from the right-hand side. In doing so he did not see the women, who returned to the Two Men. They told the women to camp some distance away and not to let Bira see them. [Bira had a reputation for making his own rules in regard to women: if he wanted them, they were eligible and should be available to him.]

The Two Men killed a number of kangaroos, taking the best away and leaving only the thin ones [those with no fat]. Bira, however, when he was driving in the kangaroos, had branded with his fire-stick some particularly fat ones. When he came to look at those killed by the Two Men, he could not find them lying there: 'They are gone!' [They had been given to the Gunggurunggura women.] Bira asked, 'Where are mine, the marked ones? Where have they gone?'

He looked for them, thinking, 'Who could have taken them? Somebody must have!' He stayed at this place a long time. Every day he went along the same track, rounding up kangaroos for the Two Men to kill. Every day he could find no trace of his branded animals.

Each night, too, when Bira was asleep, the Two Men went and slept with the women, returning at dawn. One night, however, when the Two Men had gone, Bira awakened and found himself alone. Next morning he said nothing to them about this. He became suspicious, and noticed that every night the Two Men were absent. He said to himself, 'I'm always walking along the same track driving in the kangaroos.' So next day he took the other side, the left-hand side, without telling the Two Men. As he walked along, the women emerged from some bushes and crossed his track. He chased them.

The Two Men waited by their catchment for the women to drive in kangaroos, but none came. After a while they got up and walked around. They saw a fire in the distance, and Bira still chasing the women. They made a cleared space, removing all the bushes, and waited. Soon the group of women ran past them, with Bira following. The Two Men made another clearing, and the women came and lay down. As Bira entered the clearing, the Two Men killed him. He remained there. After that the Gunggurunggura went north, and the Two Men continued their travels.

When all the women lay in the space made by the Two men, the men sang:

gungga derara-derara walburi reri-reri
Women lying on their backs, side by side.

[At this point the myth enters its secret-sacred version, not noted here.]

The second section of this myth purports to explain the first. By night, Bira chases the Gunggurunggura women across the sky, throwing his boomerang, trying to persuade them to stay with him. During the day the women are driving kangaroos for the Two Men to kill. They are chased by Bira. When they return to the Two Men's camp it is dawn, and Bira is killed. Later he revives, at night, and the process is repeated.

The ostensible reason for killing Moon is his interest in the Gunggurunggura. But this was the fault of the Wadi Gudjara, who exacerbated the situation by giving the fat kangaroos to the women, when some of them had already been marked by Moon; 'they were deceiving him' — but they also had a reason for that!

The next myth too was told to R. Berndt at Ooldea in 1941. It was said to have originated in the Djalgandi country between Lakes Darlot and Carnegie, north-west of Ooldea.

128. HOW THE TWO WIRILBA
MET THEIR DEATH

Wadi Wirilba and his son came from Djalgandi country in the north-
west, where *wada* potatoes grew in great profusion. Wirilba resembled a
Possum; he was a big man. The two were camped at Nalabulgan
waterhole, collecting *maii-nyunbulba* mulga apples. They put them in a
bark container and took them back to their camp, where they roasted
them in the coals and ate them. They did this every day.

One morning, however, the son took up his boomerang and went out on
to the open plain, and walked around until he saw a large kangaroo. It sat
down near him. The young man pulled out his boomerang from his
waist-band and threw it, hitting the animal's head and killing it. It was
too heavy for him to carry alone, so he left it where it had fallen and
returned to get his father. They carried it back to their camp, where they
cooked it and then placed it in a nearby tree, covering the meat with green
leaves and branches.

Now it happened that old Wadi Gegi [see Myth 167] had been chasing
this particular kangaroo for a long distance, all the way down from the
north: it was *his* kangaroo! He came to the place where it had been killed,
and saw Wirilba's tracks leading from it to his camp. He followed them
and came to where old Wirilba was sitting. Gegi said at once: 'That's my
kangaroo!' Young Wirilba answered, 'I killed it myself!' To quieten Gegi,
old Wirilba gave him one rib of the kangaroo, which he ate. That was all
they gave him. They ate a great deal of it themselves and then put the rest
of it away, back in the tree.

Gegi went out by himself. Wirilba built up a big smoking fire by the tree
to keep the flies from the meat; and he did the same for the coals in which
he cooked the mulga apples. Then the father and son went to collect more
apples.

In the meantime Gegi had gone some little distance away, and from
a high ridge he saw the Wirilba had left their camp. He returned, took the
remaining meat and placed it in green branches, tying it up with fibre,
and went away with it.

The two Wirilba collected enough apples for themselves. The son told
his father that he would go ahead and remove some of the meat that was
stored in the tree. The father agreed. When the son found that all the meat
was gone he became angry. In his rage he swayed from side to side, crying
and hitting the ground, until he inadvertently fell into the fire and was
burnt to death. He father, hearing the crying, ran to see what had
happened, leaving the apples behind. Too late! He saw his son in the fire,
dead — and the meat gone! In grief he fell backward into the fire and was
burnt to death too.

Gegi continued northward, taking with him what remained of that meat.

This is a typical example of ostensibly unplanned or unintended conflict, showing how serious repercussions can follow from what could have been a misunderstanding or mistake. The Wirilba son did not know that the kangaroo he killed had already been pre-empted by Gegi. However, the matter could have been resolved, if the Wirilba had been willing to share the meat with Gegi on an equal basis. They insulted him by giving only a rib. The double tragedy was the Wirilba pair's own fault; Gegi had only reclaimed the meat he considered his own, and regarded the killing and taking of *his* kangaroo as theft.

The following story, from country between the South and the East Alligator Rivers, also concerns theft. It was told to R. Berndt at Oenpelli in 1950.

129. THE STOLEN STONE NUT-CRUSHER

Ngayulgan, a *yariwurga*, *nagudjug* man was sitting under a banyan tree at Djayubal, near the mouth of the South Alligator River [Banidja language]. He was living on nut grass, geese and fish, using a round stone to crush the nuts because he had no teeth. However, someone stole his round *gudugudulg* stone. He went from one camp to another looking for it. 'I can't find my stone!', he said. 'I'm going to leave my country!' He told his countrymen and women: 'I'm leaving you now; I'm going to my mother's country. I will stay there until I die. And I'll take my children with me.'

His sons, Mangalmir, Gamirili-urau', Ngayulgan [named after his father], Namadalagalg and Wiriridj, and his daughters Nalawadag, Magungu, Gindjarmu and Malanduganing, accompanied him. So did his two wives, Wurupanga and Gindjarmu [whose daughter, above, had the same name], both *nyindjariyaning*. They set out for Ngayulgan's mother's country near the East Alligator. They walked to Mamagala and then on to Badjulu-gagu [a long 'pocket' near the South Alligator running to a plain where geese nested; still Banidja language]. From there they went to Gabanbul spring, where they camped, and later to Naberi-idberu [Gagadju], where there is a deep hole in the bush country. Continuing eastward, they found a creek running to the East Alligator; there they camped, catching fish and tortoises for food. They went on to Ganamulg [Banidja name; the Gagadju name is Anugana], where they camped.

They caught fish, and ate the grass nuts they had brought from Djayubal. Leaving the creek, they walked through the bush and came to Manan. There was a large group of people there; they were getting near Ngayulgan's mother's country. At last they reached the place where his maternal relatives were camping. They all cried when they saw him. 'Why have you come, leaving your country?' they asked. 'Because someone stole my round stone. I looked everywhere, but couldn't find it. I worried about it. That is why I came,' Ngayulgan replied.

He stayed there with his mother's people. He went to an 'island', Imbangar, a hill rising from a plain. He stood there looking all around: 'This is good country!' he thought. So he made a hut there, and so did his sons. They also made two canoes.

He lived there until he was an old man. He, his wives, sons and daughters all got sores [*malip* = leprosy], and they all died. [The place where they died is low down from Madjeli creek, running into the East Alligator. 'No one goes near there, it is a dangerous place. If people were to go there, they would get leprosy or sores.']

The story documents a case of theft that no one would admit to. Because of that, Ngayulgan could no longer trust his own countrymen and women, and accordingly left them. It is an unusual case, since there are no repercussions. That he and his family eventually succumbed to leprosy is not necessarily linked to the stolen nut-crusher.

From the Daly River, this story of deception was told to R. Berndt in 1946.

130. THE BASKET-MAKERS

'Old man' Barramundi, Murwerag, had a hut in the waters of Djiramu billabong at Duwari, where he lived with his two wives, Malalam and Bi-ayi.

Malalam went out to collect jungle grass for basket-making: she gave it to Murwerag, who took it to Dudu where a group of people were camped. The Dudu people had agreed to undertake the task of making some baskets, because they were specialists in this craft. When Murwerag returned to Dudu later, to collect them, he was told they were not ready. So he went home again. Malalam asked whether the baskets were finished. He said no. 'They want more grass.' So Malalam went out to collect more grass, and Murwerag took it to Dudu, where the people were sitting under banyan and kapok trees plaiting baskets. He left the grass with them.

Next day Murwerag went out in his canoe to catch fish. The people at Dudu were collecting mussels and lily roots in the billabong. Malalam had gone to visit them, but found no-one in their camp. She looked round and saw many completed baskets. 'They lied to my husband!' she thought. She returned to her own camp, and then went out again to cut down a large hollow tree. She carried it into the billabong, sneaking up to where the Dudu people were collecting food. She came closer. Lifting up her hollow tree, she 'turned it round', stirring up the waters of the billabong so that they became like a whirlwind. It drowned all those Dudu people.

Malalam came back to her camp and called out to Murwerag. 'Come on, bring those fish!' He loaded his canoe with barramundi, cat-fish and other fish, and came poling back. 'What's wrong, you two?' he asked. Malalam replied, 'I worked hard collecting all that grass, but those people hid the baskets they made. They deceived us! I killed them for that!'

Murwerag, in sorrow, took up the barramundi, but he broke the *dayi* cat-fish at Nunum (or Nunung) where Goose had her banyan tree. He broke the cat-fish too at Dayiwura, where it became the White Stone Dreaming. He took the barramundi and his two wives to Ngulgul-ngulgul, the hill of the 'half-dead' [see Myth 186b], then on to Duyu and eventually to Anmel, the Land of the Dead. [The barramundi he took was *himself*; and before going to Anmel, he left himself Dreaming there at Duwari.]

The issue of conflict is muted. Barramundi's wife Malalam was too hasty in assuming that the basket-makers at Dudu were deceiving them, when she had no evidence for this except the finished baskets she saw in their absence. Murwerag recognised her 'error' and its dreadful consequences: what happened had 'spoilt their lives', as well as those of the Dudu people. Sadly, he prepared to make himself Dreaming, and for all of them to go to the Land of the Dead.

Next, a story from Oenpelli which deals with the serious issue of elopement. It was told to C. Berndt in 1950.

131. A RUNAWAY WIFE

Long ago they were living there in Wurdirag, those truly first people. We didn't see them, because none of us was here. As for them, they were talking Woraidbag, and a little bit of Yiwadja. They did not know this Gunwinggu language that we speak.

Well, one of them, a young girl, had a sweetheart, a young single man who spoke Yiwadja. The two of them thought only of each other. For a long time they had been 'talking strongly' to each other, making love among the grasses, when she went hunting by herself. He said to her, 'That man, your husband, he's very jealous. So, I'll take you right away from him and then he won't be able to spear me. He's a difficult man.' But one day her husband went hunting with her. When that young Yiwadja man came sneaking up to the place where they were to meet, it was empty. She was not there. He asked the old people who were sitting in the camp, 'Did you see those two here?' He called the name of that man: 'She and her husband, did they go hunting together?' 'Yes. They went hunting together, because he's a bad man, he's jealous. Once he let her go hunting with the women, but now every day they just go together all the time.' He said to himself, that sweetheart, 'Then I'll get her away from him, because they keep going together!' Her husband went looking for any urine they might have left, because he contemplated working sorcery on the two of them. But he could not. She was very pretty, that girl. Men wanted her — eligible or not! Men in the right categories, men in the wrong categories!

But that man, her sweetheart — well, she had been truly his from when she was small, when they played at being sweethearts together. Time went on, he grew her up, and they became real sweethearts. As for her husband, she was his proper betrothed wife — but he did not give her any kangaroo, or other meat. And that single man still kept coming back to her, because the two of them had got used to each other.

At last, when her husband was feeling very tired, she was able to go hunting with some of the other women. Already her sweetheart had pointed with his spear-thrower, showing the place where she would find him. He said, 'Get your belongings ready. I'll meet you there, and then we'll go on to my country, Warawag.' She got her things. And she got together any leavings connected with her, and covered her urine patches with fresh water, because she said in her mind. 'He might get my leavings to work sorcery on me, when I leave him and elope with my sweetheart.' So she went off with the women, and her husband went fishing. Her sweetheart pretended to go kangaroo hunting, to trick those young Woraidbag men, but instead he went to meet the girl. He saw her going along, and came up to her, but they did not linger. They just met and went straight on. Afterward the other women were calling out, looking for her. But she had already gone, and the two of them were camping together.

The other women returned in the late afternoon, talking as they came up. 'A man took her, that girl who was with us!' Her husband came running. He struck them, those women who had been with her, and left them lying about, hurt. Then he went and got his spears ready. He cut and polished fighting sticks from an ironwood tree, and fixed up his stone axe. Already he had urged those young men, his relatives, to join him. They all slept, but by morning they had already gone, a crowd of them, twenty of them. They carried spears and spear-throwers, stone clubs and polished fighting sticks. They went stealthily, after that girl.

Those two had got to the place where they were living, and were watching out for her husband. He was already on his way with all his men, but those two did not know about that. They just stayed there. The men went on. When they heard people talking, and the girl's voice, they painted themselves, getting ready to attack them. They said, 'She's talking Woraidbag, that's the girl who eloped!' They got their spears ready, they sneaked up, and at daybreak they rushed at them, shouting, *'Ngug-waaa!'* The people in the camp jumped up, and were speared. That girl took a lot of spears: she was bristling with them. They speared her sweetheart-husband until he lay dead. Those were the two who made trouble for the place, by eloping! The men left some of the old people, and speared the others. They said. 'You can bury them, those two who ran away as sweethearts — that's why we killed them.'

Those men went back after that, and settled down in the country where they first called the name, Wurdirag. They were there for a long, long time. But by then the Yiwadja men were ready to take their revenge. They sent a message stick about the country, calling men to come and fight. Yiwadja men, and Marlgu men from the coast and islands came together to Wurdirag and fell on the Woraidbag people, so that they in turn lay there as bones. All of them became like rocks, those first people: those who made trouble by eloping, those who came to kill them, and those who avenged them. They were fighting one another, and they killed themselves off. We didn't see any of them. We didn't know them. Those Yiwadja people came into Dreaming as *djang* at Warawag, where their bodies lay dead, and those Woraidbag did the same at Wurdirag. Long ago they were fighting about women, that's how they finished themselves, those first people who were making the land ready for us. They remain there as rocks. And we came out, we are here now, we new people.

In the traditionally-oriented society in which this story was current, extra-marital relations seem to have been tacitly tolerated, provided the pair concerned were discreet and in the approved kin categories. However, a major exception to this is the attitude of the girl's husband. In this case, as the story emphasises, he was inordinately jealous. It was inevitable, therefore, that tragedy would befall the eloping girl and her sweetheart. The husband had right on his side. The narrator herself condemned the elopement: 'Those two made trouble for the people with whom they camped.' Not only were they themselves killed, so were some of the people who, presumably, gave them refuge. This provoked reprisals, — to the extent of virtually wiping out members of two language groups.

The following myth, told to C. Berndt at Oenpelli in 1950, is one of several versions, and its main theme has parallels in many other accounts.

132. DEATH OF A 'FRIGHTENED BRIDE'

Long ago, a woman was pregnant. Time went on, and a girl was born, Mináliwu, there in the country of Wuragag, Tor Rock. Mináliwu's mother had promised the girl to her proper son-in-law, so she gave her to him first, as he own promised wife. He was still coming from the north. Yiwadja was his language. Her parents talked Yiwadja and Marlgu. They sent word to him, here where Wuragag stands. Her mother and father let him know, that Nabin-gulóu, 'Maybe you would like to come to your mother-in-law, where Wuragag is, so you can see her — in case perhaps she's died!'

He came then, he arrived, and at last he saw her, that Mináliwu. She was growing up, already she was an adolescent, and as pretty as could be. That is why Nabin-gulóu made a lot of trouble. When he came, his mother-in-law told him, 'Don't go back, because already your promised wife is growing up, so you two can get married. I don't want to keep on looking after her, I'm tired of it. So you yourself, you take her!'

They all settled down. He went and speared kangaroo, and was chopping out honey. He gave them to his mother-in-law, Mináliwu's mother, as a gift in their special, partly-taboo relationship. When it was getting dark, she sent her daughter to sleep with him. The girl said, 'No!' She defied her mother, because she was very much afraid of Nabin-gulóu. Well, Mináliwu and her mother and father still went hunting together. Himself, that son-in-law, he went hunting separately. She was still afraid of him. They did not sleep together.

Nabin-gulóu went on. At last he got tired of it, because he wanted her so badly. She was a young, adolescent girl. He was asking himself in his mind, talking 'inside'. He said, 'Whatever can I do to her, that girl? But I can't kill her openly, so I'll go and hide my hand about it,' he said. At last she went hunting, that Mináliwu. Well, Nabin-gulóu was making himself ready, and at last that Snake came out. He said to the Snake, 'Go and bite her head, that girl who is afraid of me!' The Snake rose up, bit the girl's head, and took her underneath the ground.

Nabin-gulóu had been thinking in his mind. He made her come out again, that girl. She was dead, just a body lying there. He went on. . . He gave her a child, to breast-feed. He was just taking her about. Then he made himself like a Snake, he became a Snake. He and that Ngalyod went along the ground, and went underneath together. Then afterward he was looking for a rock where he would put the girl as a drawing [painting]. She is there still, in a large cave. She was always afraid of him, that Nabin-gulóu. So then he 'turned his hand' for her: he made her into a drawing for ever, she remains as a drawing among the rocks.

Mangurug, who told this story, added that Mináliwu was not really afraid of Nabin-gulóu, and he was not an old man, but quite young. The girl was afraid of his other two wives, who were jealous of her because she was so young. The plot suggests some parallels with the Yirawadbad myth (see Myth 181): the betrothal, the rejection, the husband's revenge and the girl's death by snake bite. The snake in this case turns out to be Ngalyod (see Chapter 3), but Nabin-gulóu himself later assumes that identity. The reaction of the girl's parents is not noted; but Mináliwu herself is enshrined as an ochred painting on a cave wall, where her spirit remains.

The next story builds up a different sequence of events on the same theme of a betrothed girl who rejects her promised husband. It was told to C. Berndt at Oenpelli in 1950.

133. REVENGE FOR A CROCODILE-DEATH

Before, long ago, when there were only those very first people, one woman was a victim of sorcery. That man had already worked sorcery on her, taken her soul, because she would not accept him as her husband — even though her mother, his proper mother-in-law, had given her to him as his promised wife. She rejected him. So he made trouble for her. He struck her with a magic spear, and called out to that creature, that water-dweller, the salt-water crocodile.

Well, all the children went together to swim in the creek. She was the one who urged them to do that. She said to them, 'Let's go and swim, and get mussels to eat!' They talked about it among themselves, those older adolescent girls. She already had breasts, and that was why she did not want that man for her husband. ['She hadn't got used to him when she was small!'] And so he killed her: he took her soul.

They were all swimming, those adolescent girls and those children. That creature, that crocodile, was lying far away. At last it got her 'smell', the smell of a sorcery victim, a body without a soul. They saw bubbles coming running along. Maybe they thought it was a fish hitting the water. It just came running. At last the others climbed up from the water, those adolescent girls, and the little ones. She was alone, that sorcery victim. At last it got hold of her, and took her under water. The others, climbing out, asked each other, 'What about her? Where did she go?' And they said, 'A crocodile got her, and took her under the water!' The creature swung its tail, striking them. They were just dying of fright. But they ran and beat the water with their hands, asking that creature desperately, 'Show her to us, that girl you took! Perhaps there was something wrong with her, that we didn't know about!' The crocodile came floating up then, with that girl on his back, where he had put her. The other girls were crying. Then they began to recover, but for a while they lay in the sun, on the warm sand, until their bones became stronger. At last the older ones took the smaller children on their shoulders and went home to where their mothers and fathers were living. They went on, and when at last they came close, they gave them the death message. 'That girl, a crocodile got her, took her for ever, underneath the water!' And her mother and father told all about it, far and wide.

They were striking themselves with axes and sticks, grieving for that girl of theirs. Her father was cutting himself, her mother and uncles were all cutting themselves. They were talking and crying, singling out that one man who killed her, the man who was sulking because she rejected him. When he came up, and they told him about it, he said, 'I'm not the one, I didn't kill your child!' He was still hiding the truth, not telling them. Well, they all cut themselves. Then he got up, that husband, and went back to his mother and father. He went on, got there. His mother and father asked him, 'Why did you come?' At last he told them, 'A creature got them, those children, where they were swimming. That's why I came.' They said, 'Tell us straight, *which* girl?' They kept asking him. He said, 'That girl of mine, she's the one that creature took!' Those two cried; but he didn't cry.

At last her father cut marks on a message stick and sent it to people in the east, various relatives of that dead girl. The messenger went running, he came to the 'middle place' country, and reached them, those men and women who were living there. They were getting their spears together, they were making a lot of trouble — her brothers, her father, her younger brothers, all of them. At last they all came, those others, they got there, they just threw spears among all those people: that mother and father and those uncles, on account of that girl.

Then, they stayed there and 'listened' to one another. They joined in a mortuary ritual. Some of them were asking, 'Show us the girl's husband, the widower. Where did he go?' The others told them, 'He's gone back there, to his mother and father.' 'Well, perhaps he killed her, and then just hurried off!' They were making up their minds about it — because he had gone away, and because they had seen a *borid*, a sorcery clue, in that girl's hair. So they said, 'That man, he's the one. He was sulking for her because she wouldn't stay with him!'

They got ready for fighting. Only men. They put the women there, where they were camping, and they set off. They heard children calling out in play. They painted themselves there: they painted their spears and sticks and spear-throwers, painted them all, and in the late afternoon they moved in to fight. They speared those people, struck them with sticks: finished them off. Only their dogs were moving about there. Those men and women, they had speared them: finished them all. The children they threw against the rocks, cutting off their breath. They lay dead there. Nobody came to get them, for mortuary rites.

Themselves, those men went back to where their wives were living, and told them about it. They said, 'Only the country is left, nothing else. We killed them all, we finished them, because that man made things go wrong for them first, when he made trouble for her, our girl — so we, in our turn, struck them down!'

Time went on. There they became like rocks, as to their bones: their bones lie scattered about there at Mabun, where they put the place name. As for the others, they themselves lie as bones in that country they went to and where they stayed, Ngorrlwarr. It was there that the Snake came and drowned them in the sea, because they were cooking a little creature. She smelt it, she who lives in the billabongs, she took them all under the waters. Then in an 'outside' place, in the middle of the scrub, she vomited them. She made them into *djang*. She herself brought sea water there. Then she threw back that water, where the tide goes back, and she named the place, saying 'Here is Bowidu country, where I put the place name, there where the tide goes back.' Well, she went for ever, that Snake. There, high up where she put herself in spirit and where she vomited them, they became like rocks, as to their bones. They remain there as *djang* forever.

The question of sorcery in relation to 'a runaway wife' was raised in Myth 131 but discarded in lieu of direct physical action. In this story, the rejected betrothed husband decides to use sorcery, causing the girl to be vulnerable to death by a crocodile. The sequence of the story is as follows. On hearing that she has been killed in this way, her parents and relatives mourn her death; they also send word of her death to other camps. Discussion then revolves round who is responsible (who carried out the sorcery). The culprit denies he is involved. However, he returns to his own parents. They question him: he does not cry when they mourn, and so they know that he was responsible. They send a message to other relatives, who prepare for a revenge expedition, gathering together their spears. At the girl's parents' camp they throw spears conventionally without injuring anyone, to show their anger. They join in the mortuary ritual, then ask where the betrothed husband has gone, set off after him and kill all the people at his parents' camp, although there is no specific reference to this. The bodies of the slaughtered people turn to rocks, So, later, do the others, swallowed by Ngalyod (see Chapter 3).

The story underlines the danger facing a girl who rejects her promised husband — danger not only to herself but also to others. Repercussions are bound to follow a death from (supposed) sorcery. However, here it is the alleged sorcerer who is condemned, and not the girl.

The next story, about a man's failure to take someone else's wife, was told to R. Berndt at Balgo in 1960.

134. ATTEMPTED ABDUCTION

Wiranyula, a *djabaldjari* man, was living at Lulul, where he urinated. [Now there is a salt-water spring there.] He went on to Badei claypan [alongside Yabuna, Lake Mackay], and to Bingalu-badjal soak. Ants bit his testes, so he continued on to Djundi soak and camped there. He spent his time hunting *lunggar* euro that live in the surrounding rocks and holes: he tried to use fire to smoke them out, but could not catch any. He had been travelling along blind. He sang to open his eyes, and on reaching Madjud claypan found that he could see! He went on to Madjadi rockhole, where he found a small *gililbi* (or *mala*) kangaroo rat. He pulled off his *madjadi* pubic fringe and threw it at the creature, but missed. He named the place after the pubic fringe.

He went on to Naberi-naberi claypan. Two people were living near this place: Yilbril, a *djabangadi* man and his *nambidjin* wife. Seeing them, Wiranyula lighted a fire-stick, sneaked up to Yilbril and hit him with it. Then, taking his boomerang, he slashed the back of his victim's neck, severing his head. [He killed Yilbril because he wanted Yilbril's wife: he was jealous.] The place where this incident took place, Rung-gan, is now a rockhole. Wiranyula picked up his fire-stick because he was cold, but by that time the woman had escaped.

Disappointed, Wiranyula continued to Rilana soak, on the other side of Yabuna. He went into this place. 'He finished there: he had to go in, because he had killed the other man!'

This rather gloomy story details a short series of mishaps. Even when Wiranyula was able to see, he could not succeed in any of the tasks he set out to accomplish, except killing Yilbril, and that counted against him. His attempted, unsuccessful abduction of the woman was almost incidental; but because he killed her husband, he was obliged to disappear into Rilana soak to become Dreaming.

The next myth follows much the same theme. It too was told to R. Berndt at Balgo in 1960.

135. DJANBA AND THE TWO WOMEN

Galan, a small spinifex Rat Man, *djungurei*, had two wives, both *nangala*, and one son, *djabaldjari*.

Djanba [a group of malevolent beings] came from the south. [Other mythic versions speak of Djanba as resembling ordinary human beings in appearance. In one, two Djanba came to Binaragura rockhole where they killed Djangalawanu people with boomerangs, and did the same at Walangara rockhole. In return, others killed them.]

[To continue with the main myth.] The group of Djanba reached the place where Galan and his family were camping. They saw the two *nangala* women go out to collect grass seeds, and wanted them. So, first they performed *ganingura* sorcery on both Galan and his son. [This kind of sorcery involved inserting sharpened *gudima* sticks into their bodies, withdrawing them and closing up the holes; the victim was then temporarily revived.] The father and son went out hunting and brought back meat for the women. They cooked the meat and the women made a grass seed damper. They ate, and slept. The father was awakened by a severe pain. His wives offered him meat, but he refused. He drank water, but his illness increased: he died. [Nothing more is said about the son. Perhaps the sorcery was performed in earnest only on the father. In any case, the son now drops out of the story.] The two women buried their husband and left the place. The Djanba followed their tracks. However, the women met up with their relatives and the Djanba went away, returning south.

In the meantime Nyindaga, Perentie, a *djabaldjari* man appeared. He went into the ground and came to where the dead man was buried, picked him up and took him away. The women had told their relatives what had happened, and a small group of men went to see whether the body was still there. They looked, but found nothing: they thought that *mamu* had taken it away to eat. They did not look for *mamu* tracks or, for that matter, Djanba tracks. The two women eventually remarried, and remained in that country, around Binaragura rockhole.

This story is a segment of a larger one about the Djanba. They performed a special form of sorcery on Galan, and conventionally he would be expected to die on the third day after the operation. His two widows escaped the attentions of the Djanba, who do not seem to have pursued them once they had joined their relatives. Nyindaga is one of the Wadi Gudjara, the Two Men (see Myth 20). He took Galan's body to a Dreaming site. When the wives' relatives found it was gone, they blamed a malevolent and cannibal *mamu* (see Chapter 4).

The following myth also was told to R. Berndt at Balgo in 1960.

136. LINGGA CLAIMS HIS BETROTHED

Lingga, White Snake, was travelling as a *djabanangga* man from Gunadul soak, to the south-east. He came to Djamban soak, named after arm blood, went on to Bandadja rockhole, where he camped, and next day continued to Wiwul soak. Later he came to Gamiyara rockhole, where he slept with a *naburula* woman.

The Gamiyara people had promised this woman to Lingga; but another man, a *djuburula* man, had taken her. Lingga had come from Gunadul to take her away from him: 'She was the right woman for Lingga!' Because she had a *djabangadi* child from that other man, Lingga killed it [see Myth 137]. Then, taking her with him, Lingga started on his return journey. But the man she had been living with called up the other Gamiyara men to pursue Lingga and recover her. They followed Lingga's tracks. A *djangala* man saw the two of them together. The group caught up with them at Gundanyindja rockhole and spring. [The place name refers to 'cutting themselves with stone knives'.] Surrounding them, they began to fight, while the *djangala* man went to one side to block any chance of escape. In the end all of them were killed: not only Lingga and the woman, but all the members of the revenge party. They all remain there.

This story underlines the serious repercussions that can result from a woman going to a man other than her promised husband. It is compounded by the callousness of Lingga toward her child. This same aspect comes up in the next myth, also told to R. Berndt at Balgo in 1960.

137. THE BRUTALITY OF LIRU

Wadi Liru, 'white' Snake Man, *djabanangga,* abducted a *nangala* woman whom he called *banggu,* a mother's brother's daughter. Her husband Djindalbi was a *djungurei* man. She had recently given birth to a child. Her husband brought her meat, which he tossed over toward her, since a man should not come near his wife immediately after childbirth. Then he went hunting again. In the meantime, Liru came to where she was camped and took her and the baby away with him.

Djindalbi returned from hunting to find his wife and child gone. He gathered together a revenge party, and they followed Liru's tracks to a rockhole north of Djarabiri. There they found that Liru had thrown the baby on to the ground and pounded it with his feet. ['He didn't want a child from another man!'] The rockhole is called Didji-badal [child pounded into ground. It was at Didji-badal that Langanyida, a Gugadja *djangala* man, 'found' his Dreaming. Liru appeared in a dream to both his father and mother at Langanyida's 'conception'.]

The revenge party continued, following Liru's tracks. Among them was a *djangala* man who found Liru: they fought together with stone knives. The *djangala* man's knife cut horizontal marks on Liru's body. [That is why all *liru* now bear these marks.]

As a result, Liru was weak. Nevertheless he continued, with the others following his tracks. But Liru became weaker, he could hardly walk, and he still had the *nangala* woman. He made camp at Gundindi; the pair slept. The revenge party found and awakened him and then killed him [with a sacred object]; they also killed the woman. Today, they are to be seen, metamorphosed as two small mounds in the bush close to Gundindi.

The story resembles closely the one immediately preceding it. It depicts the brutality of Liru — as Lingga did, he killed the child, in Liru's case by pounding it into the ground with his feet. He did not want to be encumbered by another man's small child. The reference in the myth to Langanyida (who was living at the time this story was told to R. Berndt) notes that, in Dreaming terms, he was the original brother of the abducted woman *and* the Dreaming man who found Liru. In both myths, the abductor and the woman were killed. They became Dreaming.

In the next three stories we turn to the issue of incest on the part of a brother, a father and a grandfather. Each was told to C. Berndt at Oenpelli in 1950. The change in narrative style is especially obvious in the first.

138. HOW THE *MAN-GINDJEG* YAMS BECAME 'BITTER'

His two sisters went to get yams: *man-gindjeg*, the bitter kind that need special treatment, and long yams, *garbara*. The two of them were digging and they got plenty. They put them down in their cave-house, then brought some out and cooked them. They put the bitter yams aside for a while and went off to dig more, and more long yams. Then they came back to their camp and cooked there.

Their brother was coming. He came and asked them, 'Give me!' The older girl, the elder sister, gave to him, but the younger sister did not. He did not really like the elder sister. 'Elder sister! Give me your younger sister!' 'Not her! No, I won't give you your sister, because she's a young girl! I won't give you! Your inside might go dark! You're her full brother. It might be wrong for you to eat!' 'Don't you two refuse me when I'm asking for her! Don't go hard to me!' 'No. We won't give you. But we already gave *her* [the elder sister?] to you: you ate!' His sisters still said that. They went hard to him. 'If you refuse me,' he said, 'I'll urinate on your *man-gindjeg* yams. You won't be able to cook them in the ordinary way!'

He did urinate on the *man-gindjeg* yams. They went 'bitter'. He wouldn't accept those yams the two girls gave to him then. 'You two eat! You two quarrelled with me, you didn't give me — I don't want it! You eat! It might be a good thing for you if you leave it!' He urinated on the *man-gindjeg* yams. Then he got the long yams and threw them away among the rocks.

[At this juncture the story — or rather, in this account, the first part of the story — ends. It takes a different turn, into what is usually a separate one, the story of Biyu-biyu: see Myth 89, in which case it leads directly into a fight between two brothers and ends with the tracking down and killing of Biyu-biyu, whose song is also included.]

The story, told in the usual succinct style of this particular narrator, is slightly cryptic until we take into account that in Gunwinggu the ordinary words for 'eating' can be interpreted to mean 'copulating', according to context. The brother does not specifically ask for food — simply, 'Give me!' And the elder sister replies in a way which could refer either to food or to intercourse. The meaning becomes clearer where the younger sister is concerned: a sexual association is implied but not explicitly stated. The elder sister herself may not have resisted (did not resist?) their brother's demands — that is not spelt out. The story-teller brushed the question aside, emphasising that it was the younger girl he wanted; and both sisters were opposed to that, despite his threat. In several other stories, too, ordinary edible roots become 'bitter' after a character deliberately urinates on them, and 'that is why they have to be specially treated now before we can eat them!'

139. AN INCESTUOUS FATHER

When the land was young, a father was looking after his two daughters because their mother was dead. The elder sister was adolescent, but quite mature. She was pregnant, with a child in her belly. Well, the three of them were going along, they were camping.

'Daughter, what about bringing me some fire — you, younger daughter!' But the elder sister replied, 'She doesn't want to, my little sister, so I'll bring you some, and you can make a fire.' She came with a fire-stick for him and gave it to him, that elder sister. He got water and put out the flame. Then he called out again. 'Bring it, bring it for me, younger sister!' he kept saying, that father of theirs. 'All right, I'll ask my little sister whether she'll bring you fire,' said the older girl. She was quite young, that little sister, that is why he wanted her very much — her own father!

Well, the elder sister was urging the younger one, saying, 'Take a fire-stick to father, so he can make a fire to warm himself,' So then the younger girl came to him, and called out to wake him up. 'Father, I've got this fire-stick for you!' He was sitting in his hut, that father. He said to her, 'Daughter, bring the fire-stick inside so you can build up a fire for me, because I'm tired.' 'I don't want to,' she said, that daughter. 'I'm going away to make up a fire, so I'll put that fire-stick here.' Well, she put the fire-stick down. 'But why are you afraid, daughter?' he asked. 'I don't want to!' she said. Well, he kept on doing that, putting out the flame, that father. He was deceiving his daughter. Those two girls were scolding him. They said to him, 'Why are you talking to us like that, father? Do you want us to hit you?'

They all lay down to sleep, warming themselves at one fire, where that father had his camp. He was lying by himself, and those two sisters were lying together. They were asleep. He got up, that father. He wanted to get her, that younger sister. He would have 'eaten' her. But the elder sister was already awake. Their dog had let them both know, when he saw their father coming crawling toward them. They were angry, then. 'Father, you were coming here! You were trying to come over and get my little sister!' He denied it. 'Daughter, I don't know anything about that! I was just lying down, sleeping. But I went to build up the fire for you both, you and your little sister!' Well, his daughter kept saying, 'You say now that you are our father, but you don't think about our mother, your wife, who bore us. *Are* you really our father?' they said to him. They were all quarrelling. And then, 'We two are going away, to tell our uncles [mothers' brothers] about this! We didn't realise you would try to treat us as sweethearts! We were wrong to follow you!' They left him. He stayed, and they went back, those two sisters.

As for him, he went on. He killed a little creature there, where he was camping. While he was cooking it, that great creature, that Snake, came rising up and ate him. As for those girls, they went to the place where they were to put themselves in spirit. They went on, still in their human body form, and sat down. They could hear that Snake, the same one, following them as they went along. 'Where shall we go, little sister?' the older one was asking. They were sorry for themselves, crying all the time. They just went on, and turned into rocks. That Snake came out and ate them both there, where they 'made themselves wrong'. Those two girls said, 'This country is a Djelama place, where we put ourselves as *djang*.' And they called the name of the place, that country. They said, 'The big mother-place-name is Gurudjmug; but where we put ourselves, the little daughter-place-name is Gabari!' That's where they first were transformed. They made the place taboo, dangerous, and the water as well. Vegetable foods too: women are not to get them there, in that taboo place. They went down under the water. They went on. That Snake vomited their bones, and they became like rock. Fish and plant foods, people are not to get there, where those two went inside the water. And that unborn child of theirs still keeps crying, there in the water. They remain there in spirit. People are not to go there with fish nets, or spear fish there, or they, too, might 'make themselves wrong'. So then, people who are still living go outside the range of that place. They can see the light of the sisters' fires when they are alone there: no people. Then those girls go down again into the water, where they first put themselves as spirits. And he himself, that father, he went under the water there, where he put himself in spirit, but now he is there at the same place where those two left him when they were in human body form. He went on, he became like rock, standing in the middle of the scrub, that father of theirs. And they are there in the billabong, where they made the place taboo, dangerous for ever.

The two girls resist the approaches of their widowed father, although the older sister at one stage tries to placate him by urging the other to take fire to him. The narrator did not know who the father of the older girl's child was, but said that she had probably left her husband to look after her own father and her little sister. Their father's intention is quite clear. In this context, that intention alone is sufficient to bring about the downfall of all three of them, or four if the child is taken into account. The father is swallowed by Ngalyod who, in turn, swallows the two girls 'because they made themselves wrong'. They are caught within an essentially wrong situation and because of that their destiny is sealed; there is no escape — they all become *djang*. A parallel can be drawn with the taboo place for which the girls are responsible: anyone going there would 'make himself/herself wrong'. In other words, the concept of wrongness is pervasive and does not rest solely on someone carrying out a wrong action. Note how the kin terms ('father', 'daughter') are reiterated in the text, underlining a relationship which calls for very different behaviour and attitudes between them.

140. AN INCESTUOUS GRANDFATHER

Long ago they were travelling about, those first people. An old man was taking with him two young women and one man, their husband. That husband went away looking for small creatures and for kangaroos, while his two wives stayed in camp with the old man, their grandfather. Well, those two were sitting there, they were hungry ['dying of hunger']. They got their digging sticks and baskets and went off to dig *garbara* long yams.

That grandfather went separately, looking for *garbara* leaves [so he could dig the roots]. The two girls were looking in another jungle. They had told him, 'You go separately to get those yams. Don't come with us while we're getting them, because we're embarrassed in regard to you — because you are our own mother's father.' Well, he went by himself. He was digging a long way below the surface, getting yams from deep underneath, filling his baskets. He came up to the surface, and made a big fire ready for cooking them. When he saw it breaking up into hot coals, he moved the burning sticks to one side and arranged the coals and hot ashes. While the yams were cooking there and the fire was burning, burning, he lay down to sleep.

The two girls were coming, with their raw yams, to the same place where the old man was cooking and sleeping. In their turn, they were preparing hot coals and ashes, for small yams and for the very long *garbara*. Then they put the bitter *man-gindjeg* roots [see Myth 138] to cook in a separate fire. They finished that. All of them were lying in the shade, sleeping, waiting for the food to be cooked. And the two girls were waiting for their husband.

They were all looking out for him. When they saw him bringing back small creatures and kangaroo, they built up a fire for him, a big fire, so it would burn down to a lot of coals. Soon he was skinning the kangaroo, and the girls were getting the inside parts of a goanna and eating them as a snack. As for him, he made a hole in the kangaroo's anus and got out the guts and liver, the heart, lungs, and two kidneys, and the fat, for all of them to share. They were all waiting for the coals to be ready. He cooked the kangaroo separately. The two girls cooked the goanna. They were all taking the long yams from their fires, and eating them. The bitter *mangindjeg* yams, too: those girls scraped off the skin, filled the baskets they had ready and hung them on a tree. They took the goanna from the fire to get cool, and he threw the kangaroo out from the coals. They cut it up, and the girls tore off the stomach skin of the goanna. They ate, and some they took back to their camp. They began to set off, going back to the same place.

They settled down there. They were full. They did not eat again, but they waited. That night they ate just a little, and kept the rest until the next day. Then they ate again. They did not go hunting, because they had the left-over yams and kangaroo meat. They just stayed in their camp, resting. Night came, and they slept.

Early next morning, they decided they should go among the rocks, where there were some yam leaves. They went, and were digging among the rocks. Well, that grandfather hid the younger girl's long yams, the big ones. He did not take the elder sister's yams — no, not hers, because he didn't want her. He wanted only the younger sister, that old man! So he hid the yams, buried them where he was camping, buried them in the ground there. He did not tell her, just hid them from her.

The girl's husband went hunting and only the three of them were there: the two girls and the old man. The husband had gone a long way off, so when it grew dark he just camped there, where he was, and did not come back. They looked out for him, but in vain. 'Because he's camping where he went, a long way off!' they said. The old man was talking to those girls; he was asking for a fire-stick. 'She with the breasts standing up, grand-daughter, bring me a fire-stick!' the old man said. He was looking for her, but the girl who had borne a child was getting up and coming toward him, giving it to him, and going back. Then he crushed out the fire-stick, because he did not want the older sister who had brought it, only the younger. He would be happy if the younger one gave it to him. Well, he was calling out again, saying, 'It died, that fire, grand-daughter, so you two bring me a fire-stick!' Well, she was getting up, the one who had borne a child, the same one, she was bringing him a fire-stick and giving it to him. She was about to turn away, when that grandfather was already crushing out the firestick, extinguishing it.

She went back and said to her younger sister, 'When I give it to him he tricks me and crushes out the fire. It's you he wants, badly. You go and give him fire, so it will be all right!' At last the younger sister got fire, brought it and gave it to him, saying, 'Here, grandfather!' She gave him the fire. He told her, 'Sit down here, where I'm lying.' Then he insisted, 'You go and get those long yams of yours, that I hid!' Well, she went right inside, a long way, that girl, and got them. She was coming crawling back, trying to get outside again, when he grabbed her as she went past and threw her to the ground, to 'eat' her. Well, he tried to put his penis inside, but he could not. It was too big. So he went and got some soft green tree-fungus and painted his penis with that, and then it was all right. He 'ate' her. But he got up when he felt he was making himself hot and weak.

Well, that elder sister and her two children were just outside. When they saw what he was doing, they were clapping their hands in time with his movements and singing:

Na-wun goyeg bai!
Na-wun ga'ri bai!'
He's from the east!
He's from the west!

And they were calling out to him, 'Hey! He's eating that girl, publicly!' Then they stopped, when he pulled it out.

They were all sitting there, when they saw that husband coming up, bringing a lot of kangaroos for them. He came, and he saw blood on his wife, the younger sister, and saw that she was not able to walk properly: that old man had hurt her legs. He asked the elder sister, 'What's been eating her, to make her thighs sore and splash blood on her fur pubic apron?' The elder sister said, 'He's the one, who took her as a wife. We thought of him as our grandfather, but he was deceiving us, he was wanting her when he saw her body developing. So then he hurt her thighs, when he took her as a wife!'

They all slept. Then he went off, that husband, He saw black *man-gundal* plums lying on the ground, and he came back. He did not go far, he came back from close by, to where his wives were. He said to them, 'What about telling that grandfather of yours that I can take him to some black plums, because I've seen them lying about like anything, breaking the tree, there are so many of them!' So those two went to that old man, their grandfather, and said, 'You go with our husband, because he saw a lot of black plums lying about!' Well, he got his baskets, and his digging stick to help him in walking. The husband took his axe, and they went off. He showed the old man those plums. The old man was getting them, plenty of them, filling one basket and then another.

Then the girls' husband said to him, 'You stand here, and I'll climb up and cut the branch for us!' He climbed up, chopped the branch and it fell down for them. They were getting plums, eating them. The old man was eating separately. The husband was going to eat afterward. But already he was making his stone axe ready, sharpening the blade and tightening the string. Then he slashed the old man's neck, right across. And he said, as the old man screamed, 'It's good that I'm cutting you, because you hurt my wife's thighs, when you took her as your wife!' Then that husband, that man who killed him, dug a hole in the ground, took his body and put it in there. He picked up the baskets full of plums, and put the old man's digging stick beside him, where he was lying. He covered him with earth, buried him entirely, then left him and went back to camp where his wives were, and his children. He sat down in their own camp.

The two girls asked him, 'Where did you take the old man?' 'Well, I finally slashed his neck across: he lies dead. Because she's only a little girl, and he hurt her thighs when he took her as a wife! That's why I killed him there, where we were eating black plums. His body lies there, where I buried it!' That's what he told them.

They did not go on camping there, where they left the old man. They got their belongings together and went to another place. The two girls asked their husband, 'Where are we all going?' Standing up, he said to them, 'We can't go anywhere else except to one country, where the place name is Gumarinbang. That's the place we must go to!' They went on for a long time, and there they stayed. They were still camping there when they came into Dreaming, they turned into *djang*, at Gumarinbang, and that is where they are now.

Structurally, this myth has great merit. Its plot is well designed and followed through, with details and explanations clearly set out. In many such stories where seduction is the theme, preference is usually, but not always, given to a younger sister. The act of incest is especially serious since a mother's father, a *mamam*, is involved: a grand-daughter has reason to expect both kindness and consideration from him. An unusual aspect of the story is his having coitus while watched by his other grand-daughter and her two children. The song implies he is 'mixed up', not knowing what direction to take. Note that the myth does not specifically condemn the act of incest: it says obliquely, 'he took her as wife!' Also, as in the previous story, the older girl encourages her sister to pacify the old man by taking fire to him — fire, and herself. The explanation of why the husband killed the grandfather rests on his having hurt the girl. While the *mamam's* death is a foregone conclusion, so is that of the others, who finally became *djang*.

In the next myth the content changes. It is an Andingari, Western Desert, story told to R. Berndt at Ooldea in 1941.

141. THE DEATH OF THE DJORDJOR

Wadi and Minma Djordjor, Night Owl Man and Woman, with white eyes [the name is the same as the bird's cry], had two dogs, Wilina and a bitch named Badun. They camped at Doildoil [close to where Gumba the Owl died: see Myth 104].

The Wadi Gudjara, Two Men, also came to Doildoil and camped nearby. Leaving her husband, the woman went out into the bush with her two dogs, to hunt. She was looking for possums and caught a number, which she cooked. When they were ready she tied them up into a bundle, hiding them in the branches of a nearby tree. Then she turned herself into a possum and, carrying her two dogs under her arms, made the tracks of that creature, leading close to Doildoil. Then, with her dogs, she entered a hollow tree.

Next morning Wadi Djordjor got up and, looking around, saw the possum tracks. He told the Two Men: 'You two come, we'll get possum meat: see that track!' With the Two Men, Djordjor followed the tracks that led directly to the hollow tree (or log). Minma Djordjor held her dogs in readiness, so they could spring out at the Two Men. Wadi Djordjor climbed into the tree. The Two Men, however, were *gingin* 'clever men!': they had *maban* magical shells behind their eyes, and they could see through anything. They saw Minma Djordjor hidden inside the tree with her dogs, waiting. Realising what she intended to do, they smashed the tree with their clubs, breaking it open. The two dogs sprang out, only to be killed by the Two Men. The possum [Djordjor woman] fell out and they killed her too. Wadi Djordjor fell from the top of the tree, and they killed him. Then they continued on their travels.

This is more than a question of inhospitality. The Djordjor are taciturn, lonely Dreaming characters who dislike visitors; they prefer to be by themselves. So, Djordjor Woman plans to get rid of the Two Men (see, for example, Myths 69 and 127). When the Djordjor and their dogs fell from the tree they became rocks at Doildoil, and the shattered dead tree lies there too.

The following myth also concerns unwelcome visitors. It, too, was told to R. Berndt at Ooldea in 1941.

142. CURLEW'S 'SNAKE' SPEAR

Old man Wilu, Curlew, lived with his son at an unnamed waterhole.
Young Wilu went out hunting kangaroo while his father remained in the
camp. He speared one and brought it back; they cooked and ate it. Next
morning he went hunting and speared a kangaroo. Rather than returning
immediately to his father, he made a fire and cooked the meat. Through a
previous arrangement between them, if a stranger was approaching their
waterhole the father was to light a fire of green boughs, the smoke from
which would warn his son. As he saw the stranger coming, old Wilu made
a long-drawn-out cry: the sound of the curlew.

Wadi Dalbu-dalbu (dark grey, black-headed bird), who came from the
west, arrived at the Curlew men's camp. But old Wilu told him to make
his camp elsewhere, some distance away, and not to sit with him. On
hearing his father's cry and seeing the smoke signal, young Wilu returned
and sat with his father.

Young Wilu had a *djawal* 'snake' spear that was a real snake: it stood
upright and could be animated at will. [In appearance it was like a snake,
stretched to its full length.] Old Wilu said to Dalbu-dalbu: 'Brother, if you
sit there by yourself, he [my son] will quarrel with you and finish you. Go
and stand close to that tree.' Dalbu-dalbu, in fear, stood with his back to a
tree, facing young Wilu, who came up and speared him sideways through
the ribs, killing him. Old Wilu said to the dying man, 'We light a fire for
ourselves. You always come when you see our fire; that's why we kill you!'
In that way old Wilu and his son killed many people who came from the
west, usually one each day. However, on one occasion old Wilu saw the
Two Men coming toward his camp. Immediately he sent a smoke signal
to warn his son, and began to call out. Young Wilu saw the signal and
came quickly home. When the Two Men arrived, Wilu told them to stand
against a tree, 'Brother,' he said, — he called all the visitors 'brother' —
'stand by that tree, otherwise my son will quarrel with you and kill you,
because he hasn't seen you two for a long time!' The Two Men suspected
treachery and, instead, stood a little way apart from each other.

Young Wilu returned, but went first into the nearby bush to prepare his
snake spear [which he used only for killing people]. He sharpened it in
readiness and came running back to the tree, brandishing it in front of the
Two Men. Old Wilu felt 'no good'. [He had a presentiment that all would
not go well.] Young Wilu threw his spear, but it went between the Two
Men, missing them. Old Wilu came up. He was sorry his son had missed
them. He began to cry. The Two Men took out their magic boomerang
and, throwing it, hit the heads of both Wilu. Their heads fell off and rolled
some little distance away; when they stopped they continued to cry
mournfully. They turned into rocks. Looking round the camp the Two

Men found many bones from the victims the Curlews had killed. Then the Two Men continued on their travels.

This is another myth in which the Two Men, the Wadi Gudjara appear, although the focus is on the Curlew pair (see also Myth 141). As in the last story about the Djordjor, the Wilu do not want to entertain a visitor. The reason is that they do not want to share the meat they have caught, as they would normally be obliged to do. They accuse Dalbu-dalbu of always coming when he sees their fire, as an excuse for killing him. When the Two Men arrive, the tables are turned: the Curlews are up against a more wily pair of opponents and pay the penalty of their duplicity.

The following Gunwinggu myth was told to R. Berndt at Oenpelli in 1950.

143.   A TREACHEROUS MOTHER'S BROTHER

Nabandjul-bandjul, a *yariburig, nabulain* man and his uncle (*ngadjadj*, mother's brother) Wiri-wiriyag, also *yariburig, nawamud* [both Winggu], were camped at Gumulawuradmi, to the east of Oenpelli on the 'top side' of Gumadir. They went out to collect wild honey. Wiri-wiriyag was lame and sick, and his testes were swollen. The boy said, 'Uncle, you wait for me here, as you can't talk much. I'll look round for honey.' Leaving Wiri-wiriyag he went on, and eventually found wild *manburi* potatoes among the rocks, many of them. He began to fill up the baskets he carried, moving along, digging them up and placing them in his baskets.

When engaged in this task, he happened to look up at the top of a tree and saw a *nawaran* rock snake coiled around its branches. He called out to his uncle, 'Come and cut out honey, there's plenty of food here!' But Wiri-wiriyag was angry. 'Why can't he dig those potatoes and bring them here!' he thought. 'I can't hear,' he replied. 'There's plenty of honey and potatoes here,' the other repeated. But Wiri-wiriyag refused to hear. However, his nephew called the name of the *manyalg* honey bee, instead of mentioning the name of the snake: 'Uncle, there is a little *manyalg* here. You come and we'll chop out this honey!' By this Wiri-wiriyag knew that his nephew was referring to a snake. He came quickly, without thought of his sickness: 'What do you want me for?' he asked. 'You come, and we'll chop out some honey,' the other repeated. 'Good boy, we'll kill him! Where?' the uncle asked. 'You look up there!' Wiri-wiriyag saw the snake coiling and covering the branches. He got a long stick with grass tied at one end. He held it up: the snake bit the grass apex, and Wiri-wiriyag pulled it down, grabbing its neck and head. The snake coiled its body round him and squeezed him until urine ran from him. 'Nephew!' he called. 'Come here!' Nabandjul-bandjul hit the 'nose' of the snake with a stone and killed it, and he uncoiled the snake from the other's body.

They carried the snake along, collecting more rock potatoes. Wiri-wiriyag said he would return to their bush camp, and that he would have the snake cooked by the time the other returned. So he did cook the snake. He saw it had plenty of fat. His nephew returned carrying one basket on his back, another on his head. 'You come now and eat the fat. We'll cook the potatoes afterward,' Wiri-wiriyag called. But his uncle had eaten all the fat, and gave him only the bladder, which was encased in fat. Wiri-wiriyag told his nephew to shut his eyes and open his mouth, and he threw the bladder into his throat. Nabandjul-bandjul nearly choked because that bladder, covered as it was with fat, contained poison. He almost died. He washed out his mouth.

After Nabandjul-bandjul had recovered, he set to work to roast all the potatoes. When they were ready, he removed them and commenced pounding them to make them soft. 'Come on,' said Wiri-wiriyag, 'Throw one to me!' 'No,' said the other, 'I'll prepare all of them first.' 'No, you throw me one now!' Wiri-wiriyag sat there with his legs apart. 'If I throw one,' said his nephew, 'it might fall and hurt your testes.' 'No,' said the other, 'What's the matter, I can catch it.' So he threw it to his uncle. He tried to catch it, but it fell onto his swollen testes. Wiri-wiriyag felt the pain all over his body. 'Go on, run away, I'll kill you,' he said in anger. But his nephew continued to pound the potatoes, softening them. 'I tell you, run away!' Wiri-wiriyag said. He got a stick and tested it. It broke. He got another hardwood one and hit Nabandjul-bandjul on his chest, neck, nose, and head and killed him. He dismembered the body and put the pieces into the cracked openings of the rocks at Gunbun-ngurl-bun-nga.

Wiri-wiriyag gathered together his belongings and returned to Gumu-lawuradmi where his nephew's mother and father lived. 'Where has our son gone?' they asked. 'He's coming later,' the other replied and added, 'He said to me, "You go home first, and I'll find honey and return before dark."' They waited a long time. That mother and father were calling out for their son. 'Where did you leave him?' they asked Wiri-wiriyag. 'He's coming. It's a long way: he'll come in late.' They waited and waited; they thought Wiri-wiriyag had killed him. They went out looking for the murdered boy. They saw a hawk over the remains of his body. 'He must be there!' They saw the bones of the snake the two had eaten, and the ashes of the fire. Then they saw their dead son, and they saw the stick Wiriwiriyag had used to kill him. They said, 'He didn't speak the truth. We'll have to kill him!' And they buried their son.

They returned to their home camp. They told Wiri-wiriyag, 'We saw plenty of black plums out there.' 'I'd better go and get them,' he replied. They described where they had seen the plums. Wiri-wiriyag got his baskets and went in search of the plums.

The parents told their two sons, Nabandjul-bandjul's brothers, Gulidjag the elder and Nalangag the youngest. They took spears and went after Wiri-wiriyag. They saw him sitting beside the plum tree collecting fruit, filling his baskets. He was talking to himself: 'Somebody might kill me. I killed him! Maybe his two brothers are coming!' They were listening to him: they threw their two-pronged *mandain* spears. 'Why do you spear me?' he asked. 'Because you killed our brother!' 'Yes, I killed him!' he admitted. So they speared him to death and left him lying there beside the plum tree at Gaburu-malidja.

They returned to their own camp and told the others, 'We killed our uncle! We heard him saying he had killed our brother.' And where they left the body, they left his baskets too hanging there in the tree.

The relationship between the two main characters was obviously strained from the beginning — but no reason is given for that, except Wiri-wiriyag's illness. Nabandjul-bandjul was forbearing to the end, in spite of the attempt to poison him. Only when Wiri-wiriyag insisted did his nephew throw over a roasted potato and, moreover, it was his uncle's fault for not catching it. In the face of a crescendo of anger on Wiri-wiriyag's part, his nephew remained calm — but met his death. Wiri-wiriyag's deceit brought about his own downfall at the hands of his other two nephews. This story should be compared with one from a different narrator (Myth 179), that has some similarities but also some obvious differences.

In the next story the trail of death continues. It was told to R. Berndt at Goulburn Island in 1947.

144. MURDER OF TWO BOYS

A man, unnamed, arranged to take two of his brother's daughter's sons with him on a journey. [The mother of the two boys called him *bunyi*, father; and he called them *mamam*, daughter's sons.] The man's wife was dead. They went together up to the hills at Gumarinmag (or Gumarin-bang) in Neinggu (Gunwinggu) country, along Gumadir Creek. There they saw a *mandalgidj* kangaroo rat which disappeared among the rocks. The man told the boys to go after it. While they were searching inside a cave, he gathered dry grass and leaves into a big heap, piling it around the cave entrance. He got his firesticks and began to make fire. The two boys could hear the noise from inside: 'What is that, *mamam*?' they asked. 'It's only sticks rubbing together in the wind — that's what is making the noise,' he replied. 'You go right in,' he added. So they climbed farther in, seeking the kangaroo rat.

The man put leaves and grass around all the cracks, closing the openings. The two boys asked him, 'What are you doing? It's becoming dark inside?' He answered, 'You know, it's clouds coming up, covering the sun!' Then he set fire to all the heaps of grass and leaves. He could hear the boys crying out until after a while they were silent. They were dead. Then he went in to get the bodies, they were cooked! He ate them. When he had finished all the meat he collected their bones, putting them in a large dilly bag, and took them back to his home.

When he reached the camp, he told the boys' father and mother to get ready. 'I have brought a lot of people back with me!' he said. They passed on the message to the others to get ready to welcome the visitors. They all sat together. [The man had broken off a large branch and dragged it behind him as he entered the camp — it sounded just like a lot of people, and it was night-time.] He went out again, dragging the branch and dancing and saying to the imaginary people: 'Come up, come up! There are people here who want to see you!' He came up to where the boys' mother and father were sitting with all the other people in their camp. He stood there before them. Taking up his dilly bag, he tipped out all the bones in front of them.

The dead boys' parents began to cry. Men grabbed their spears and other weapons and went after that man. He made *magarada* dancing across the ground, dodging the spears as they were thrown. Then he ran away. He entered a small snake or rat hole. The people began to dig it out; they found him, but he escaped. They threw many spears at him, but he went into a hollow tree. They gathered grass and piled it all round the tree and set fire to it, but he jumped out and ran away, with the others after him.

He came to an upright tree with a hole beneath it, and went into that. The men chopped at the tree, making a hole: he went into that. Then he jumped out and ran away. The men came after him, throwing their spears. He went into an ironwood tree. They tried to cut it down with their stone axes but could not — all the axes they had broke! They gathered more grass and leaves, piled them around the tree and set fire to them. They could hear that man calling out from inside the tree. He couldn't get out; they had put too many heaps of burning grass around. At last he died. All the wood had burnt down: all that they saw were his bones.

The man was taking the two boys to an initiation ritual, or that is what he told his 'daughter' (brother's daughter), their mother. But before they had gone 'half way' he burned them to death in a cave. The reason given for his inexplicable (or, at least, unexplained) action is that 'he was hungry'. The narrator added that 'Liverpool River people take meat and fat from dead people to eat.' There is little evidence for this accusation as far as the traditional people of that area are concerned, but in the 1940s that rumour persisted. The implication is that the man came from the Liverpool which is not particularly far from Gumadir, since the Margulidjban district of the Gunwinggu is close to the upper reaches of the river. The brutality of his action is emphasised by his callous approach to the boys' parents. The boys' death was avenged by the same means — death by fire; and, as in their case, only his bones were left. It is interesting to compare this story with two others, told by different narrators in different circumstances (Myths 177 and 178).

The following myth also was told to R. Berndt at Goulburn Island in 1947.

145.   CROCODILE'S REVENGE

Gwunbiribiri, Crocodile, was a Maung man who camped at Gwungandba on the King River. A lot of birds [people] who came from different places arrived at Gwungandba and made a large camp. They decided to go to Wandjili, Barclay Point, and from there to cross over to South Goulburn Island. From Wandjili they began to ferry the birds [people] across by bark canoe. There were so many people that it took 'three to four weeks' to carry most of them over to the island. Only a few were left. At last Crocodile asked the two ferry men to take him over: but they replied, 'You will have to wait because you are so heavy — we'll take you at the end.'

Crocodile went back to his camp, brooding about this rebuff. He said to himself, 'I'll get some *galanyun* ironwood roots.' He collected these roots, made a big fire, threw earth over it and put the roots on top so they grew hot and lumps of gum oozed out. [This substance is poison, and is used at the top of spear-throwers to fix in the prong: it hardens rapidly.] Crocodile brought this big lump of black pitch back to his camp. There he made it hot and moulded it, putting some on his neck and on his nose. After he had done this, he called together all the goannas, who were people then: the big *marwagara*, the *gawirdji* (spotted one), the *yudi* (water goanna), the *marnganga* (that climbs trees and dives into the water, or the *maranga*), and the *wararigi* (rock goanna). They came, and Crocodile spoke to them: 'What about all of us moving down to the creek and trying to go under the water?' He asked the *marwagara* and *gawirdji* to try. They dived down and came up quickly. Crocodile told them they did not stay long enough under the water, so they had better go on dry land. Then he asked *yudi* and *marnganga*: 'What about you two going down and staying under the water?' They dived down, and came up to breathe. Crocodile said, 'I think you have a long breath (*wonduyag-gwilngag*). You and I will follow the creek.' Then Crocodile and *wararigi* went down to the creek together. They dived down together, but rock goanna did not go 'a long way'. Crocodile, however, stayed down in the water. At last Crocodile came to the surface: he looked around but could not see rock goanna. At last he saw him on the bank, and told him: 'It is better for you to go and live among the rocks, because you can't dive properly!'

The two men who were engaged in ferrying the birds [people] across to South Goulburn Island were taking the last of the group over. When Crocodile saw that canoe he dived down and followed it. He dived down and then came up to the surface, following the canoe when it was still close to the shore. Then he sprang and pulled at it, tipping it over so the people fell into the water. They tried to get away, but in doing that they 'started to fly upward' into the sky. Now they are birds.

Crocodile said to himself, 'I'll make myself crocodile. If I meet any people, I'm going to kill them; it's better for me to be a crocodile!' And he named that place Iniman-arwila [meaning 'pull the canoe back'] at the King River, 'before going over' to South Goulburn Island.

This is another myth (see Myth 126) that explains how Crocodile as a person became crocodile as a reptile. It also tells how Crocodile allocated the particular habitats of the goannas (in a sense, *how* they became goannas). The core of the myth, however, is the supposed slighting of Crocodile. He was told he would be the last to cross over to South Goulburn Island, but actually the ferry man had decided not to take him because he was too large for their fragile canoe and also because he was dangerous. Crocodile, realising that, took his revenge.

The next myth, too, was told to R. Berndt at Goulburn Island in 1947.

146. THE TWO BROTHERS

Naganmara, a *yariyaning* man [Gari language], was camped on the beach at Ngadagi-wonyan-ngi, between Port Essington and Cape Don. His elder brother Adjibin-gu, with two wives, was camped some distance away. Naganmara sent a couple of men to his brother to tell him he was sick, that he had a severe stomach ache. When the message reached Adjibin-gu he sent his two wives back with the messengers, telling them, 'Go and see my brother. If he is really sick, bring the news back to me and if he *is* sick, I'll go there.'

At last the two women came to Naganmara's camp and, after talking to them, he sent them back to his elder brother to confirm that he was really sick. They returned to their husband, Adjibin-gu, with the message. He sent them back again to make sure, but when they reached Naganmara's camp, they found he was dead.

Adjibin-gu's two wives returned home and told him of the death. He got ready to go, but sent his two wives ahead. He went afterward and hid himself near his brother's mortuary platform. When the death rituals were completed and all the people had returned to their camp, Adjibin-gu climbed up onto the platform and sat watching his brother's body. 'What is it [the body] going to do?' he asked himself. He saw that dead body moving: it started to rise. It got up from where it was lying, and it sat upright.

Adjibin-gu asked his dead brother: 'You know me? I'm talking to you!' And the dead brother answered, calling his name: 'My big brother!' At first the dead man could not articulate his words, but after trying several times he pronounced Adjibin-gu's name properly. Then Adjibin-gu told him to stand up properly, on his feet. He was alive! And Naganmara said to his brother? 'If it hadn't been for you, I wouldn't be alive! My life came back again. It's good that you came!'

Adjibin-gu gave his brother *aralwulgang* bangles, and a *bandag* ball fighting bag, and painted him with *gurud* red-ochre. He also gave him small *yanawal* bamboo spears, a *wondulg* spear-thrower, and a *maralaga* bunch of feathers mounted on a stick that was worn at the back during dancing. The two brothers came down from the platform and walked toward the camp. They could see their mother carrying a *wuluru* [a paperbark parcel of human bones] and crying: 'My son! my son! And their father was crying for his son.

Adjibin-gu told his brother that they were crying for him: 'Now you start running from here and run until you reach our father and mother!' He ran toward them and stood before them, and everyone saw him. They were all glad. Naganmara praised his elder brother for 'making him come alive again'. Adjibin-gu had *margid* power, he was a 'clever man', and all the people gave him presents.

While it is not specifically stated that there had been ill-feeling between the two brothers, by implication the neglect of a younger brother when ill is tantamount to a declaration that there is; this is especially marked when he sends his wives to his brother's camp twice, and makes a move himself only after the other's death. However, he compensates for unbrotherly behaviour by reviving the dead man and earning the gratitude of his relatives.

This story concludes the series on conflict on a more pleasant note. As it turned out, no harm was done to anyone — contrary to what happens in most stories of this kind!

Conflict is the essence of social living, according to some statements in the anthropological literature. We are not directly concerned with real-life traditional situations. Nevertheless, we contend that the kinds of myth and stories we consider here do have some bearing on contemporary ideas and attitudes. One issue is what sort of impact the reiteration of such material has, or could have, on people in varying age categories, especially young people. On the other hand, in our experience, the content of such myths was taken very much for granted as illustrating aspects of social behaviour that could easily be identified and could well occur from time to time. The generalisation that conflict situations are the essence of social living always needs to be seen in context, in Aboriginal Australia or anywhere else. It is inseparable from questions of what kinds of conflict, how much, and the likely or actual outcome. In any event, it can hardly fail to acknowledge that conflict is fraught with difficulties, not only for the people (or mythic characters) immediately involved, but also for others. It would seem more relevant to think of some types of conflict as linked with death, which looms large in many of the stories we present, and not only in this chapter.

In the myths discussed here, few of the aggressors or 'activators' and also few of the victims, escape death. In these twenty-three stories, the 'activator' escapes in only five cases. Of those five, one (Myth 129) involved the theft of a nut-crusher, but the thief was not identified. In the second (Myth 133), the culprit's death is not noted as having taken place. In the third (Myth 135), an attempted abduction turns out to be a non-event, with the two women escaping as well as the would-be seducer, *but* their husband and (probably) the child of one of them were killed. In the fourth (Myth 138), when a boy's attempt at incest with his sister is thwarted, he makes one kind of yams bitter. The fifth (Myth 146) ends happily for all concerned — the only example of this!

In all but two instances, a fatal outcome is explained or justified. In ten, the reason is sex-related. In another, interpersonal dissension leads to a boy being bullied to such an extent that he causes the death of his tormentor. Other reasons are denial of food or fire; the killing of a creature supposedly belonging to someone else; supposed theft; opposition to entertaining visitors; being slighted; probable deceit; and implied sibling rivalry. In eleven cases, mostly of a trivial nature, the resolution involves violence. And in two, both of a violent kind, no justification is given for the murders that resulted (Myths 136 and 137).

Apart from the small selection of myths discussed in this chapter, many of those in other chapters include situations of actual or potential violence. The incidence of death for both activators and victims is very high — by such means as drowning, burning, beheading, spearing or clubbing to death, or sorcery. Moreover, interpersonal conflicts can ramify to include others: for example, where a revenge party sets out in pursuit of a supposed offender. This is particularly the case in sex-related crimes, where a victim rarely escapes death. Of the four most physically violent examples (Myths 134, 135, 136 and 137), two involve the killing of the victim and her child; in the other two, the husbands of the women concerned are killed. Of these four, three of the women escape death and two are killed, while of the aggressors, two are killed, one escapes and the other comes into Dreaming.

The last outcome is one conventional way of resolving a situation of conflict within a mythic context, when one or more of the characters disappear from the living human scene by becoming Dreaming, or *djang*. That transformational disappearance is not really a disappearance at all, only a removal from that particular scene, and applies to victims as well as aggressors. Some escape through the medium or intervention of a Ngalyod (see Chapter 3), and some by turning into a non-human form. This raises an important issue that has been mentioned previously. Particular mythic characters caught up in a conflict situation, not always through their own fault, are sometimes said to have 'done wrong' because of having been involved in that particular situation. That is, the concept of 'wrongness' applies not only to people who have 'broken the rules' (although these may not necessarily have been stipulated), but to those caught up in the consequences of such an event. Examples are the story of the dilatory basket-makers (Myth 130), where the husband recognises the 'wrongness' of his wife's action; the case of the rejected husband (Myth 131); as well as Myths 139 and 140, where a father attempts to commit incest and a grandfather succeeds. In Gunwinggu society, in relation to a mythic event, references to 'going wrong' are not invariably linked with particular characters becoming *djang*. But there are enough examples to make this plain: that as a result either of personal wrong-doing or of being personally involved in a sequence of events regarded as being 'wrong', although not necessarily of that person's making, transformation is achieved; a consequence of which could be the conferring of a social benefit on future generations. In Myth 139, however, as in many others, a dangerous place (as one of the consequences) is defined as such in order to protect human beings from death or misfortune. In considering such implications, we come close to a concept of good and bad that is much more pervasive than a personal act of wrong-doing. This concept is less noticeable for the Western Desert, where broader implications of a recognised act of wrongness are not necessarily articulated. Nevertheless, there too, mythic characters come into Dreaming, whether or not they are first killed or injured.

Of the myths in this chapter, eight could conceivably pose the question of *who* is the victim, *who* the aggressor. Who is *really* responsible for triggering off the sequence of events that leads inevitably to disastrous results? In Myth 127, with reference to Moon and the Two Men, *who* is to blame for what took place? In Myth 128, is the son really responsible for having killed a kangaroo that had been pre-empted by another person? Did the basket-makers really attempt to deceive Barramundi's wife? Is a rejected husband-to-be really to blame for over-reacting to the elopement of his promised wife? Such questions are also raised in Myth 138, regarding a brother's attempt at incest; or when one person does not want to share something with another, as in Myth 142; in the slighting of Crocodile (Myth 145); and in the revival of the younger brother (Myth 146). In most such cases, Aboriginal public opinion is ambivalent.

These myths provide clues to Aboriginal attitudes toward 'breaking the rules'. But the emphasis is not so much on the rules, as on how particular mythic beings proceed in order to resolve the consequent rupture. Conflict situations are not necessarily insoluble. But in the process of achieving a resolution, considerable personal and social damage can occur — and, as we are reminded in Myths 131 and 133, such conflict can escalate to such an extent as to destroy fairly large groups of people.

CHAPTER SEVEN

EROTICISM

Eroticism as a concept usually covers the whole gamut of sexual relations and passion and is not focused solely on the sexual act. Eroticism also has to do with love in emotional and not just in physical terms, as well as sensuality where the issue of sexual enjoyment is obtrusive (see R. Berndt 1976: 4). While some of these features are apparent in Aboriginal mythology, they are more directly referred to in the song-poetry — in, for example, the great love song-cycles of north-eastern Arnhem Land, the 'Gossip' songs of western Arnhem Land, the *djarada* and *ududju* of the central-western part of the Northern Territory, and the *ilbindji* of the Western Desert. Many of these songs explore in considerable detail facets of erotic activity. Among some of them is an element of magic, intensifying the sexual feelings of the persons involved, or designed to attract desired partners. Many others are associated with religious ritual. The 'Gossip' songs use a highly-personalised approach to report conversations and behaviour of unnamed people in a kind of 'guessing game': they range from sentimental yearning to quite explicit accounts.

In contrast, in Aboriginal mythology generally, sexual incidents are treated much more prosaically, almost as being incidental to non-erotic factors. The basic assumption was that sexual relations were a normal expectation between eligible and consenting adult men and women and did not require spelling out. What really provided story value was what can be called aberrations on that particular theme: forbidden sex, as between ineligible partners, or persons who belonged to non-inter-marrying categories; unfaithful wives who abused the credulity of their husbands; and the misdemeanours of lascivious males. Rarely, in Aboriginal mythology, was the whole of a story or a myth devoted entirely to sexual matters. Some do approach this — as in Myth 147, where two young wives, unaccompanied by their husband, pretend to go in search of a special variety of nuts but spend most of their time copulating. In that case the emphasis is on their eventual punishment. Closer to the aspect of eroticism is the incident mentioned in Myth 176, where a man is attracted to his sister and has coitus with her. Or consider Myth 180, where a father copulates repeatedly with his elder daughter when she comes down to collect the fish he has caught. That particular incident or series of incidents resulted, through the action of the girl's mother, in the formation of the Milky Way. And there are numerous other examples.

Certain Dreaming beings were reputed to have an insatiable sexual appetite. Moon man was one such personage, especially in the Western Desert. Another was Wayungari, among the Yaraldi of the lower River Murray in South Australia. More often, this sort of characteristic was attributed to some non-human spirits (see Chapter 4). Among the exceptions are the conventionalised sex-and-violence adventures of Boma-boma (Poma-poma) or Namarangini or Gwingula, whom Warner (1937/1958: 545–62, 564–65) called a trickster: we give here three of the versions that were told to us.

Most of the myths discussed here are concerned only partly with sexual aspects. The focus is usually on exploring the implications of the sexual act for the people directly involved, or on what might follow as a result of it. In other words, the sexual interlude is usually of only passing moment, almost incidental to the main thrust of the story. That is not to say that it passes without comment — rather, that it is not used specifically for an erotic purpose. It is this treatment that is of interest. In our experience, traditionally-oriented Aborigines, both men and women, have invariably been frank in talking about sexual matters, and did not hesitate to elaborate when that seemed appropriate. In the myths, however, it is the non-sexual aspects that are emphasised, so that any one myth caters for a range of interests and is not necessarily dependent on its sexual props.

The following story was told to R. Berndt at Oenpelli in 1949.

147. THE UNFAITHFUL WIVES

Bala-ngudjalg-ngudjalg, a *yariburig, nangaraidgu, nabulain* Dreaming man [Winggu] lived at Gugagawandji, on the hill side of Gumadir creek. He usually carried his stone axe and wore his *gundjarbalg* spirit bag when he went out collecting pandanus food [the *man-gudjed* seed within the pandanus brush]. He would knock these down with a stone or, with his two wives, he would chop down a pandanus tree: they would cook the green [new] ones but eat the old ones without cooking. The two young wives were sisters [their names were unknown].

Bala-ngudjalg-ngudjalg told his wives to go eastward to find good *man-gulaidj* nuts: he was tired of eating pandanus 'seeds'. So the two girls set out east for Balbanara [farther than the Liverpool River, almost to Milingimbi]. He remained by himself in his camp, living on *man-gudjed*. His wives had taken empty dilly bags. 'I don't know when they'll come back,' he said, and counted the days as they passed: they had said they would be away for about two to four weeks because it was 'a long way to go'.

On reaching Balbanara, the two girls filled up their bags with *man-gulaidj* quite quickly, but they remained there because they had many sweethearts. For each act of coitus they put a dot of semen on their bodies: their breasts and faces were soon covered with dots of semen.

At last they decided to return to their husband. They walked back from Balbanara — they had enough food in their bags and they had had enough coitus. Some distance from Gugagawandji they made a big fire on the eastern side of the Liverpool River, big enough for their husband to see it in the distance. He was pleased when he saw it: 'They have brought good food!' he said to himself. Next day he could see them walking toward him, and the sun upon their bodies showed clearly the white semen dots shining. When he saw this he said nothing, not then. They entered the camp and told him that they had brought the nuts. 'That is good,' he said, but he had not forgotten what he had seen. He went out by himself and sang for rain. Returning, he told the girls that heavy rain was coming. 'We had better find a good cave where we can sleep,' he told them. 'Yes, husband,' they replied, 'We'll find a good place and we'll leave those nuts behind.' [They left those for us, for the 'new people' to find later on.] They came to some caves in the hills near Gugagawandji. There they made a forked stick pole to serve as a ladder and placed one end on the ground, with the other resting at the cave's entrance. 'I'll hold the pole as you go up. You make that place clean,' their husband said. The two girls climbed up and cleaned out the cave. The elder sister called out, 'It's your turn to climb up for sleeping, because we haven't had coitus for such a long time.'

Bala-ngudjalg-ngudjalg was angry. 'Is it all ready, have you cleared it out and made a fire?' he asked, still holding the ladder. Then he pushed it aside so that it fell down. 'I've finished with you two women. You've been copulating with those men at Balbanara. I'm leaving you there!'

The two girls called out to him, 'Let us come down! We didn't have any boys at that place, we only want to sleep with you!' But Bala-ngudjalg-ngudjalg was not deceived. He walked away from the cave, which is at Magaldoi hill, taking no notice of their cries. He returned to his camp and picked up his bag of pandanus seeds. 'I can't eat these,' he said, 'Where shall I put them?' He looked round for a creek. At Gabari creek he tipped out his bag of pandanus seeds — and there they are today!

Bala-ngudjalg-ngudjalg came back to Magaldoi hill. He heard them speaking to each other: 'Sister, we can't get down; we have to put ourselves like a picture!' They turned into two ochred paintings on the wall of the cave — and they are still there. Below that cave, Bala-ngudjalg-ngudjalg made himself into a rock. He too is still there today.

Little explanation is required. Unfaithfulness on the part of wives is punished, if discovered, but in this case the blatant behaviour of the two sisters, by demonstrating their promiscuity through the semen dots on their breasts, made tragedy a foregone conclusion. As the story-teller commented, 'They should have known what to expect!'

C.H. Berndt first heard this story in 1946–47 from women in north-eastern Arnhem Land who knew the dramatic theme, but not the details. Aboriginal crewmen on the two mission boats that brought mail and supplies to mission stations along the Arnhem Land coast told it as an almost-humorous warning about what could happen to unfaithful wives. High rocks in the escarpment, visible from the sea, had been pointed out to them by western Arnhem Landers as the punishment site where the two girls remained in spirit for ever. Early in 1950 the story was told to C.H. Berndt at Oenpelli by a Gunwinggu speaker who said she had first heard it from her father and 'step-father' as a young girl before she reached puberty. It is very much like the version set out above, except for several points. Bala-ngudjalg-ngudjalg, in this account, was a white Cockatoo man, and he collected more pandanus food than he could eat: he used to take bags full of it to sandy ground to bury it, hiding it near his camp to get later on. [White cockatoos especially like this food.] He was an old man, and his two wives didn't like him: they wanted someone younger. That was why they went to Balbanara. They told him, 'We're going there for a while to get *man-gulaid* nuts for the three of us!'

But when they arrived there, they each found a sweetheart, and the two young men helped them to get plenty of nuts so quickly that they could spend most of their time in love-making. It was the young men who painted them with semen dots, all over, when the girls said they thought they should go back to the old man. He had been watching out for them ['dreaming them to come'], and saw them coming, with bags of nuts on their heads, and the semen paint shining. When he accused them, in a rage, they tried to 'soften' him by pleading for coitus: 'We're dying for it, starving for your penis!' But he kept on accusing them. After they had climbed up the 'ladder' to put their belongings in the cave, and their husband had pulled it away, they begged him to believe them: 'We just went there for food! Look at us, we're empty!' They tried to show him their vulvas. He turned away and left them, tipping out the nuts before he made himself rock; the girls came into Dreaming near the edge of the cave; and the nuts took root and grew, to be eaten by the people of that country.

The next myth was told to R. Berndt at Oenpelli, in 1950.

148. THE TRUSTING BETROTHED HUSBAND

At Megu, between Tor Rock and Yiriwin, where Yiwadja, Winggu, Amurag and Maung people meet, lived Maidjaninbir, a *namadgu, yariwurga, nabangari* man. His home was a cave and, since he was a *margidbu*, clever man, he was able to 'turn himself' into a dragon-fly when he came outside. His *ngalgurng* [potential wife's mother] had a camp some distance away: her name was Yiwan-guning, *yariyaning, ngalngaraidgu, ngalbulain.* She was living at Benbibum, King River Hill, with her daughter.

Maidjaninbir thought to himself, 'I'd better get my *ngalgurng* to give me her daughter.' The girl's name was Amanar, *yariyaning, ngalwamud,* and Maidjaninbir called her *ngalgobeng,* 'wife': she had been promised to him.

The mother and daughter came from the north-east, from Benbibum [the big name for the hill there was Ngalu-ngalu, with Ross Point on the coast to the west], and arrived at Megu, where she met Maidjaninbir and told him: '*Nagurng,* I want you two to get married: she has grown up now!' He replied, 'All right, *ngalgurng,* I'll get married.' The mother and daughter went in front and Maidjaninbir followed them, looking for wild honey. He camped at several places by himself, filling his pandanus baskets with honey. 'I must go now and find my *ngalgurng* and my wife,' he thought. He followed their tracks. He walked farther on and found some caves: 'I had better camp here,' he said to himself. This was at Djirui, a cave facing west. Next day he went on looking for the other two: 'I'd better find them, they may have got lost.' He went farther round this rocky area to Ing-guluyung on the eastern side where there are also caves. [Djirui and Ing-guluyung are small names within the larger area consisting of a mass of rocks, called Mang-gumu.] Maidjaninbir slept at Ing-guluyung, near a creek flowing from Ross Point to the south. He went east to Adbaggawuri spring [on the track running to Barclay Point], then on to Yiwanialabir billabong [Winggu and Gunmarung]. He heard the sound of the mother and daughter calling out, 'They may be looking for me,' he thought. He was feeling happy. He went on farther. He heard his *ngalgurng* say, 'There's my *nagurng* coming!' 'Where is he?' asked the girl. 'He's coming!' Maidjaninbir came into the camp, at Mari. They sat there eating roasted goanna.

Then they set out to return to Benbibum. It was dark by the time they got there, and they went at once into the caves. He slept with the girl; she was frightened, 'but she was a good girl!' He had found honey and wallaby meat for his *ngalgurng.* Next morning he asked his wife to let his *ngalgurng* know he had gone out to get meat. Mother and daughter sat waiting, eating the meat he had given them before.

Now, at Barclay Point, Waindjili [Maung country], Guruwilgu (Seagull), a *yariwurig*, *nabulain* man was camped. He saw Maidjaninbir's fire, and a lot of smoke. So he left his place and came down to see if people were camped there. He walked through the bush. [Guruwilgu called Maidjaninbir *ngadjadj/ganggin*, uncle/nephew, and because of that relationship he called Amanar *gagali*, potential wife.] He came at dusk to Ngalu-ngalu (Benbibum), to the camp where they were. When Amanar saw him, she laughed with pleasure; she was happy: 'My *mararaidj* (sweetheart) has come!'

But remember that Maidjaninbir was clever. He returned from hunting. They all lay down to sleep, with Guruwilgu camped some little distance from the others. Maidjaninbir and his wife lay together, but that girl would not sleep: she kept looking out toward where Guruwilgu was lying. When her husband was sound asleep she got up and went to Guruwilgu. She slept with him: they were 'talking together'. Then she returned to her husband. She did this every night; her husband did not know! [He didn't know that 'underneath', privately, she called Guruwilga by a term, *gagali*, that could imply a spouse or sweetheart relationship. He thought she called Guruwilyu *gulun*, nephew, and he called her *belu* (father's sister); but that was 'outside' publicly, and privately they were *gagali*!]

Each night she went to Guruwilgu. One night, however, Maidjaninbir awakened and saw her going to her sweetheart. He thought, 'I believed she called him *gulun*, but they are sweethearts playing together. I've got to kill someone! They didn't promise (betroth) me properly. I have to finish them off!' Early next morning he cut some arm-band tree cane and hid it in the bush. He left the cave where they were camping. He left the others inside: 'I'll lie down outside.' Amanar asked, 'Suppose I come and sleep with you outside?' 'No,' he answered. Amanar called out for him. 'No,' he replied. 'I'll come back when I feel cold. You make the bed ready for us.' He slept outside, his wife inside. Then his wife and her sweetheart slept together! He made a big fire and from its light saw the two lying there copulating. 'It's true,' he said to himself. 'I didn't know, I thought he called her *belu*!' He was very upset. His mother-in-law was in the cave too.

He got long lengths of cane with sharpened points, and he bored a hole in the side of the cave's wall, at the entrance to where they slept. He made the hole ready and threaded the cane through and brought it out of the entrance so that he held both ends. Just before daylight he decided to close up the cave. He pulled the cane and closed up the aperture, and he tied it with a knot so it would not open.

The three people inside called out. They tried to open the cave, but the rock shut them in. They stayed there. Maidjaninbir left Ngalu-ngalu and flew back to his home at Megu, where he put himself as a picture [painting] in the caves; he remains there, as a *djang*.

The girl showed no aversion to her betrothed husband, unlike the promised wife of Yirawadbad (Myth 181), who refused to sleep with him. The sweetheart relationship was almost institutionalised in this area and the girl and Seagull were not carrying on a surreptitious love affair. The reason why Maidjaninbir reacted in the way he did was because he had not been informed about their relationship *and* because he had not been consulted — or asked. He considered he had been slighted and tricked, and responded accordingly. Other stories focus on different aspects of Maidjaninbir's life, including his final transformation into a dragon-fly.

Next, another story told to R. Berndt at Oenpelli in 1950.

149. A FOOLHARDY HUSBAND

Dugan, a *namadgu, yariwurga* man and his young wife Gabilg (*ngal-ngaraidgu, yariburig*) were living at Igaradagin on the plain below Cooper's Creek, on the south side [Woraidbag language]. They lived on honey, but they were hungry for meat. 'Shall we go out hunting?' he asked his wife, and she agreed. They went to Iraraid billabong. He told her to keep watch: 'I'll dive down and find some fish or crocodile,' he said, but she replied, 'No, this water is too deep: you can't dive down, a crocodile will bite you!' 'Wife, this is a good place, plenty of people have dived down here,' he said. She insisted, 'It might bite you!' But he had made up his mind. 'I don't think so. If it's there, I'll grab it and catch it.' So he dived down and caught water snakes and tortoises, throwing them on to the bank for his wife. She asked, 'Are there plenty of tortoise and snake, husband?' 'Yes, plenty,' he answered, and dived down again, calling out to her to prepare the food while he caught more. She made a fire and put stones on top in readiness. Returning with more, he asked her, 'Have we got plenty now?' She replied, 'Enough.' Dugan emerged and they roasted the food, ate it and returned to Igaradagin and slept. Next morning they went out to get honey. They lived on that for a while and then went out to get meat. However, beforehand they made two big dilly bags, one for each of them. Carrying their bags, they came to a large billabong. Dugan said, 'This is a good place!' But Gabilg replied, after looking at the water, 'I don't think you should dive down, it is too big and too deep. There are crocodile tracks on the bank and one has come out in the middle of the water.' 'It can't bite me,' he boasted. 'I'll catch one — there'll be plenty of meat; the tortoise and snake are not enough. I'll get a crocodile for us. You make a fire, one for the crocodile and one for the tortoise and snake.'

So she set to work making the fires. He dived down and got a tortoise and threw it to the bank: 'What about you cooking that if it has plenty of fat? If not, we'll go to another billabong.' She looked at the tortoise after taking off its shell — it had plenty of fat. 'Perhaps it is too fatty and we can't eat it.' She looked at the water snake. It, too, was very fat. However, he came up to the bank and after the meat was cooked they ate it. Afterward, Dugan dived down again into the water and got more of them, filling up one of the dilly bags. When they had finished eating, Dugan said, 'I'll go down again, because what we have eaten is too fatty. I'll take the two dilly bags, yours and mine, and another bag that I'll fill with crocodile meat. You get the fires ready.' Gabilg said, 'No, husband. I saw the crocodile track: when you see him, don't try to catch him, because he'll kill you. If he kills you, there's no-one I can go away with!' But he replied, 'I can easily get it. I'm stronger than a crocodile!'

Dugan dived in again and filled up the two bags with tortoise and snake and took them to the bank. Then he got the empty bag for the crocodile. 'I'm going to dive now!' He dived in and felt all along under the water; he felt the big hole the crocodile had made; he felt that hole and it was warm. He emerged and told his wife, 'Well, wife, I feel a big hole; the crocodile is there. You prepare a fire.' Gabilg made a fire, and Dugan dived in again. He put his hands into the hole; the crocodile jumped over him and got out of the hole; it waved its body. Dugan tried to grasp its tail, but it turned round and bit him.

On the bank, Gabilg saw the swirling water: 'Ah, my husband is all right. He is a good man, he spoke truly! He has caught the crocodile; soon he will bring it out of the water.' She piled more wood on the fire. But the water continued to bubble. The crocodile bit Dugan's legs, arms and head: it ate that man!

She waited there for a long time, until she saw his basket floating on the surface of the water. 'He must be dead: the crocodile has bitten him. What I said to him was true! He didn't take notice of what I said!' She saw that basket floating, and she saw his entrails floating too. And she called out, 'My husband is dead! The crocodile has eaten him!' She collected the tortoise and snake: 'I can't take all of these. I'll leave some of them here because my husband is dead!'

She went running, crying all the way. She heard her husband's younger brother, Loglog, cutting wild honey. He heard her crying. He came down from the tree where he was getting the honey. 'Ah, that's a woman crying!' He looked from a long way off. She came closer. 'My brother's wife! Maybe my brother's dead!' He ran to her. She looked at him. 'Don't look at me,' she cried, 'Your brother has been killed by a crocodile; he lies under the water.' And Loglog cried for his brother.

When he had finished crying, he said to her, 'Ah well, I'm going to have you now because my brother is dead. It is my turn now! We'll sit down here.' They camped there for some time. Then he said, 'I want to copulate with you now. It's been a long time since he let me do it to you. It is good that he died!' His penis stood up and he attempted to insert it. But Gabilg did not want him. 'Your penis is too short. Your brother had a long one; when he put it in, I felt it; but yours only goes half-way in. It's too short!' So Loglog rubbed his penis and stretched it, making it longer. 'All right,' he said, 'You try it now, it's like my big brother's.' So Loglog went to put it into Gabilg, but didn't look properly, it went into the ground. 'You want to look properly at my vagina,' she said. So he tried again and it went in. 'Your big brother did it just like that! Try it again.' And he put it in again: 'That's the way! You're my second husband; you can take his place. I call you husband now; and you call me wife!' Then they returned to Igaradagin. He told all the people, 'I've got my brother's wife now!' On hearing of Dugan's death, all the people cried and cut themselves. Gabilg and Loglog, however, went on to Wulwun, south of the Cooper's Creek, copulating together all the time!

In the face of his wife's warnings, the foolish and boastful husband was taken by a crocodile. It is also a story of a dutiful wife who is concerned for her husband, but equally concerned for her own future without him. The erotic interlude is incidental to the main plot. The levirate provides replacement for a widow, usually a younger brother who in this case was very ready to assume his responsibilities. However, she was not prepared to accept him unless his sexual prowess approximated that of her dead husband — as, eventually, it did. Not all versions of the story include this 'interlude', and the details vary. As for the ending, in one case the dead man is re-assembled and brought back to life with the help of a nest of meat-ants. In another, his wife and child go back to their camp without lingering by the billabong. After a while they get tired of waiting and go back to their relatives. The most constant item is the wife's attempt to discourage her husband from getting more of whatever it is he is trying to catch, and his insistence on continuing.

The next story was told to R. Berndt at Ooldea in 1941, originally in Andingari dialect, but having associations with Wiranggu territory.

150.   THE SEDUCTION OF EAGLEHAWK'S SISTER

The sister of Wadi Waldja, Eaglehawk Man, was chased by Wadi Manbila, Black Duck, who wanted to seduce her. Her brother followed to defend her. She ran from Yuria, a big rockhole east of Fowler's Bay. Manbila reached there afterward and made rain with his *garalba* shell.

The wet ground enabled him to see her tracks more easily. She camped at Nananula and next morning went on to Bindi, and then on to Buri where a big rock is associated with her. Manbila, following close behind, just missed her. Eaglehawk was also following his sister but by the time she left Buri he was two nights away, back at Nananula. Meanwhile she went on to Gumburu rockhole and then to Balgana rockhole, where Black Duck Man almost caught her. Again he made rain in order to track her. Half way to the next 'water' he came up to her and they walked together into Guridji. There Black Duck dug a large hole [which may be seen today] while she sat watching: there was no water in it. They lay in the depression and copulated, then slept. She had been carrying a wooden dish of water, from which they drank; there is a creek here, near Guridji, formed by the rain Black Duck had made before leaving Balgana.

Next morning Eaglehawk's sister awakened first and began to walk away. Black Duck heard her and jumped up. As she turned to face him, he saw her vulva. His penis became erect and walking over to her he inserted it, and in that position flew with her into the sky, turning back toward the grassy flat country and camping at Mingura [no water there]. They slept together. Next morning, she again got up first. As before, Black Duck heard her and impaled her with his erect penis. They flew toward Bundina [Walbina is to the south and Bundina is between that place and Yuria.] They camped there. [The same sequence of events was repeated as they flew to Munaba, to Uldubina, to Bagudidja, to Gulila, to Gandja, to Gadjiwa and to Wadangga.]

Eaglehawk was not far behind: he was intent on killing Black Duck. While his sister and Black Duck were camped at Wadangga, Eaglehawk came in. The two men fought. Then, exhausted, they lay back and died from their wounds. They are metamorphosed at that place as two large rocks. Eaglehawk's sister died of sorrow, and she too is metamorphosed there as a large rock.

This story, with its simple structure and straightforward theme, requires no special comment. The erotic aspect is subordinated to the movement of Dreaming characters across the countryside: their travels actually extend beyond the confines of the Western Desert culture. The myth belongs to a series that concerns various adventures of Eaglehawk: see Myths 34, 68, 105, 106 and 107.

The next story was also told at Ooldea (R. Berndt, 1941) and is of Western Desert tradition.

151. AN ATTRACTIVE UNCLE, AN UGLY NEPHEW

There were two men, Nori (or Nuri, an Owl) and Gagala (white Galah or Major Mitchell). Nori called Gagala mother's brother or wife's father, and they were camped at Dulorbi waterhole, in the country of the Worda people, west of the Man-gula [north-west of Ooldea].

Leaving his uncle, Nori went out to collect *galgula* wild pears, putting them into a *banga* carrier made from the bark of a *miliri* gum tree. As he was doing this he saw two young full-breasted girls: one was Mararu [alternative names Manda-ngalgu or Bilbi, Bandicoot, a bushy-tailed, long-nosed creature] and the other Windari [or Muda, resembling a 'guinea pig', bluish-grey, with a short tail]. Nori ran after them, trying to catch them. He chased them round and round, but they were too quick for him. He called out to his uncle, 'Uncle, come and catch them! Give one to me and you have the other!' He continued to chase them.

Gagala, hearing his nephew call out, ran toward a cave in which the two girls lived. Entering the cave, he sat down and removed white feathers from his bag and put them all over himself, as well as on his head to make himself look good. He wanted those two girls to be attracted to him. They did not like Nori and ran away from him because he was so ugly: 'His feathers were sticking out all round his face' and he was said to resemble a piece of wood.

The two girls, carrying witchetty grubs in their bags, came to their cave and saw Gagala, the 'pretty man', standing there. They ran toward him and sat down with him. Nori came running after them but found his uncle already there. He asked his uncle to give him one of the girls, but Gagala refused; he took them back to his camp, where they made fires and slept together, one at each side of him. Nori sat some little distance away, and slept by himself.

Next morning Nori heard a dog barking. 'Uncle,' he said, 'I hear a dog crying!' His uncle replied, 'It's mine!' [implying that he would catch it]. The two men and two girls went out together, and came upon the dog's tracks; it had entered the girls' cave. Nori urged his uncle to enter the cave and catch the little dog. Gagala approached the cave entrance, while the girls looked on. Nori urged him again, 'Uncle, you go inside, but leave all your feathers here!' [He warned his uncle that he could damage his feathers while getting the dog.] Gagala was persuaded to do this and went into the cave, looking for the dog. Nori peered in and saw that Gagala was right at the back. He got a large rock and rolled it across to block the cave's entrance, leaving his uncle inside. He took up the feathers and decorated himself so that the two girls would not find him repulsive. They saw that he was now a 'pretty man', so they went with him to his camp and copulated with him, each in turn. Then they slept.

In the meantime Gagala was trying to escape, but he could not move the rock. So in the morning he dug a hole from inside and emerged from under the rock, found his spear and followed Nori's tracks. He came upon Nori sleeping between the two girls. They saw Gagala coming but said nothing, because they really preferred him to his nephew. Gagala speared Nori through the chest, killing him. He took the two girls and they continued on their travels, leaving Nori lying there.

This is a story of sexual jealousy between close relatives, leading to deliberate duplicity and treachery on the part of both men. While the kin relationship between them and the two girls is not noted, the relationship between the two men is significant, whether or not it is classificatory. A man should defer to his mother's brother, who may also be a potential father-in-law; moreover, they should not compete for women.

We turn now to a Daly River myth recorded by R. Berndt in 1945. Although it concerns a Wogaidj woman, the story is Ngulugwongga (Mulluk-Mulluk).

152. THE FATE OF THE *GANAWULG* GIRL

All the Wallaby (*ma*) men were attending a *wongga* ceremony held at a Wogaidj place. They sang with their clapping sticks, and danced, pounding their feet on the ground. Among the local girls were two sisters, one named Wulalu. She said, 'I'm going to get one of those boys!' Her sister replied, 'I'm going with that one!' When the ceremony was finished, the Wallaby men returned to their own place, *deg*-Baramalmal, where they camped during the Wet season.

The two sisters planned to run away in search of the two men they had chosen. [That is, they were 'going *ganawulg*', sneaking after men.] 'Where are those two girls?' the people asked. 'Which way have they gone?' 'Nothing: they have gone out *ganawulg*!'

Wulalu and her sister came to *deg*-Wongamadj. Leaving that place, they went on. 'Sister, my legs are tired, let us stay here!' But Wulalu said: 'Sister, you sit down.' Wulalu went on by herself to *deg*-Bomayag, where she washed, and to *deg*-Baramalmal where the Wallaby men were camped. She sat outside on the fringe of the camp. A boy saw her coming and called out to his friends. They all walked over to look at Wulalu: 'A *ganawulg* girl: where does she come from? She's a Wogaidj girl!'

The young men came up to talk with her: 'Which boy did you come for?' She replied obliquely, 'Yes, I've come to stay with him — no matter what his Dreaming is, no matter if he's my brother!' 'Will you take this boy?' they asked, pushing forward a small boy. She would not answer. Another young man came forward. 'Will you take him?' Again she made no answer. Then her classificatory younger brother came forward. 'Will you take him?' they asked. She nodded. 'Ah, you, young man — she comes for you!' The young Wallaby man came and sat by her and talked to her. But he told all the other men to take her into the grass and copulate with her. He just sat down by himself in the camp.

All the men lined up and copulated with her, one by one. The last was 'Old Wallaby'. He came to copulate with her, but opened her legs too wide and dislocated her hips. She could not walk: she could only sit. She sat there on the bank of the Daly River and turned into a rock. [This rock had its head broken off by Europeans, but is still there, with the broken part on the ground.]

Old Wallaby was also her classificatory brother. 'What are we going to do?' he asked. They all commenced digging holes and went into them: but they could not stay inside them. They came out and went along the banks of the Daly River. All of them were saying, 'What are we going to do?' They jumped . . .

Old Woman Djedi (long-nosed Frog) was close to the bank at the other side of the river. She sat there and spoke: 'You will become like me, a rock, and the flood-waters will cover you!' Those Wallaby men, all together [as a group], became Wallaby Rock in the Daly River, between the two river banks, near Djedi. They all jumped together into the middle of the river.

The myth purports to give the origin of the *ganawulg* institution that sanctioned unmarried women seeking a male partner who was attractive to them, but also provided opportunities for sexual promiscuity. However, the myth underlines how unpredictable the fate of a *ganawulg* girl can be if the man she has chosen rejects her advances. While group copulation in this area, in traditional times, could be expected in these circumstances, the myth gives a reason for it. The girl was 'love-sick', her judgement was impaired; she was also of the same exogamous moiety (*garlg*) as the Wallaby men, but she refused to take that into account, and said so. An injury similar to that incurred by Wulalu is also mentioned in Myth 165. Since this is an institution origin myth, specific sites are noted. The Wallaby men recognised that something had gone wrong after Wulalu turned into rock. They had to follow suit — it was their fate.

The following myth is also from the Daly River and was told to R. Berndt in 1946.

153. THE YOUNG WOMEN'S REVENGE

Nguwarilg, an old man, was said to have come from the Laragia (Larrakia) language group that occupied land near Darwin: he was uncircumcised. He decorated himself to appear as a woman; he wore a wide waist-band and arm-bands with wild cotton pendants, a necklet and cockatoo feathers in his hair so they rested on and over his forehead. ['He made himself pretty like a girl, but he was really a man.'] He accompanied, or followed, a group of young girls (*aluwa-darawura*) from Wirig to Wawul, and on to *deg*-Wirig: he had been walking along the Wirig river above Nicholas Creek. He/they went on to Malngin, to Magum, then to Yirelyi and Anaranyi, and reaching Djiramu swam in its water. He/they came through *deg*-Bondu-yarengin to *wag*-Wulngin billabong. It was while the girls were swimming that he jumped at one of them and tried to copulate with her. This was the place where he was revealed as being a man, not a woman.

They went on to Yinindjangu and to Bidjilg-djagma; he cut his way through the bush to Wageriyal, and to Magad at *deg*-Berng-ganang. All the girls were there. One had become tired, as they had all walked a long way. 'Ah, my legs are tired, I'll stay here and rest,' she said. 'Yes, you are tired; which way will you sit?' Lying down, she became a rock, Dreaming, at Magad.

While they were still at Magad, some of the girls went out to cut wood for making yam sticks, but some went down to the billabong to swim. Nguwarilg followed them down to the billabong: he planned to catch one of them, but the water was too deep. The girls caught small *biri* fish and brought them up to the bank and sat down. [This place is in the Yunggur or Nyinma language group territory.] Nguwarilg also went out to get fish but returned, sneaking along toward the girls. 'Where is he sitting down?' they asked one another. 'Ah, he is coming among us!' they cried out. He jumped at one of the girls and held her firmly. The women swore at him. [They accused him of having a long penis, and with copulating indiscriminately.] While he was copulating with her, all the girls watched: she lay on her back, with her legs apart. [The women were shocked, not at their copulating, but because he was on top of her.]

Afterward, Nguwarilg went out and cut a special kind of bark [stripped from the *mandjil* bark tree] and some grass, and wrapped the bark around this. Taking it into the creek at Ganyung billabong, he pushed it before him through the water; the *daug* 'poison' contained in the bark attracted the *biri* fish and made them easy to obtain.

The girls were angry: 'The Dreaming has spoken,' they said. 'Women should not lie with legs apart in coitus; they should lie sideways. If it's done the other way, everyone will look and be ashamed. All of us must turn to the side: that is the good way!' All of those girls said the same; all of them agreed.

They were so angry that they went out from Ganyung to get sticks, which they sharpened at each end. Then, as a group, they all sneaked up to where Nguwarilg was looking for fish, pushing along his bark pad. He pushed it up and down; then he came back and sat on the bank. All the girls came up and threw their double-pointed sticks, turning and breaking them and then thrusting them in again, breaking them off and throwing away the pieces of wood. Nguwarilg cried out, 'My sweethearts! My *avoibei* (fathers' sisters, mothers' brothers' wives, wife's mothers), my *avanbi* (sisters), my *gilangbei* (mothers), my *ariyabei* (daughters), Let me go!' ['Let me live!'] But they killed him, killed him dead, throwing him into the water.

Those girls did not stay there; they went on. But they were Dreaming girls, and so they are still there today! If, when you are out hunting and become separated from the others, you call out to them, one of those girls will answer instead. 'You come here!' she will call. So you follow that call. And you will call out again and that girl will answer. Then you will find her and copulate with her, and she will become your wife; you may have five or six wives. You won't find the others from whom you have been separated. They will look around for you, but after a while they know you have been taken by those girls, and will return to their camp. But you will stay with those girls; you can't go back!' When women go to a billabong to collect lily roots, they bring these back to their camp where their menfolk are. They leave the lily roots there and go out to collect more. While they are away, those Dreaming girls come to their camp and take away all those roots. When the women return they find the roots gone. They growl at the other people there, accusing them of taking the roots. But, of course, they haven't. Those Dreaming girls have taken them!

The man disguised as a female is soon revealed for what he really is, once his intentions are apparent. While the posture taken by Nguwarilg during coitus is said to have angered the other girls, the real reason appears in his death speech. All the girls identified by the kin terms he used were sexually taboo relatives, actual or classificatory.

The final part of the myth introduces a rare motif in Aboriginal mythology — that of the sirens who lure men, not to their doom but to separation from their own kind. Once they join the Dreaming girls, they are lost to their own people.

Turning to the Western Desert, the following myth, of Mandjindji origin, was told to R. Berndt at Ooldea in 1941.

154. AN ENORMOUS PENIS

Wadi and Minma Nurai were husband and wife. They were both 'big people' [like giants] and they came from country west of Ooldea. The man had a brother, also named Nurai and so was his wife; they were living in the north.

The first pair of Nurai went out hunting for meat. They travelled a long way. Eventually they met a group of women, uninitiated youths and children. There were no men, because the men had gone on a *wanmala* [revenge] expedition. The two Nurai came into their camp and sat down to one side, talking to the others. The Nurai expressed a wish to hold a ceremony, something belonging to themselves. They built a large fire and prepared a dancing ground. It was a long clearing. At one end were bushes, behind which performers usually decorated themselves. At the opposite end was a wind-break where the women and the others assembled to watch the Nurai's dancing. In front of them, toward the long dancing ground, sat the Nurai woman, by a fire. It was behind the wind-break [and not behind the bushes at the other end] that Wadi Nurai painted himself. As Minma Nurai sang, her husband painted himself with white-ochre bands across his chest, superimposed with eaglehawk feather-down: he had no head-dress, but instead stuck *djidan-djidan* flowers all round his head-band so they hung down over this forehead. Now Wadi Nurai was a very big man and his penis was enormous: he erected it and painted it with black, white and red-ochre bands. When he had completed this, his wife began to sing:

dindaralu-ganga naul-bidjaleyini
nadalgu ngulurinei-ni daralu-ganga
Walking with penis erect,
Holding it, frightening [the women].

Emerging from his place, Nurai danced with legs apart, stamping his feet alternately, holding his upright penis. All night he danced, up and down the long ground, making grooves in the sand. By midnight, the watching women and the others who were clustered within the wind-break became tired and fell asleep. But Minma Nurai sang on, and Wadi

Nurai continued dancing. Before daybreak, however, they stopped; and while the others slept the Nurai left the camp and went out into the bush, reaching a place where they had hidden an immense club. Carrying this back to the camp, they killed all the sleeping people. They rebuilt the large fire on the dancing ground and cooked all of the dead people. Removing the bodies from the fire, they ate the children first. The dead women, they tied up into two bundles and, each carrying one, continued on their travels.

Soon afterward, the menfolk of the murdered women returned from their *wanmala* expedition. They saw the fire and the place where they had been killed, and saw, too, the remains of their children and the youths. Immediately, they set out after the Nurai. But the Nurai were walking very quickly, taking long strides. The men ran behind them. In the distance they saw the Nurai, who had paused to dig out a goanna hole, leaving the two bundles of corpses alongside them. The men came nearer and encircled the Nurai, and threw their spears again and again. The Nurai were so big that they could not feel the spears that pierced them. They brushed them aside, took up their bundles, and continued on their way. Again and again the men attacked, piercing their bodies with spears, but they were unable to stop them. The Nurai kept on walking and the men, becoming exhausted, returned to their old camp.

Eventually, Wadi Nurai arrived alone at his brother's camp. His wife had died on the way from the spear wounds she had received. Wadi Nurai dumped his 'meat' [the bodies of the women he and his wife had killed] and lay down to rest. His brother did not know of his arrival: but Nurai was not far away from a bush catchment his brother had erected. The brother's wife was driving *mala*, kangaroo rats, toward the catchment [or trap] where her husband speared them. While doing this, she saw her husband's brother's tracks. When they had killed about ten *mala*, she told her husband, 'Your brother is there, that way!' Quickly he exclaimed, *a:o!* ['Don't talk'.] He told her to gather together all the *mala*, while he picked up his spear and followed the other's tracks. Coming upon him, he saw the large bundle of meat [the dead women]. The first Nurai, however, was digging out a honey-ant nest and was partially within it: he was weak and ill from his wounds. Nevertheless, his brother came over to him and speared him in the ribs and beat him dead with his club. Then he made a big fire and cooked and ate his dead brother; the other meat [the women] he put in a tree.

He rubbed himself all over with fat from the dead women, and smeared charcoal over his chest. When he returned to his camp his wife saw his painted chest, and she knew from that sign that he had killed his brother. Later he returned to where he had left the bundle of female corpses and ate them: he gave none of the meat to his wife.

Nurai are malignant spirits, antagonistic to human beings, and unpredictable to each other, however close the kin tie may be. They are closely associated with the Western Desert *mamu* (see Chapter 4). The so-called 'erotic interlude' provokes no sexual excitement — only fear. The unprotected women, youths and children had little choice but to watch the ceremony performed by the Nurai pair. The monotony of the repeated song by the wife and the continued dancing of the husband, sent them to sleep, and made it easy for the Nurai to kill them. Finally, the wounded Nurai's death at the hands of his brother emphasises the fearful character of these spirits.

The following story concerns *maam* spirits. It was told to C. Berndt at Oenpelli in 1950.

155. THE JEALOUS NEW SPIRIT AND THE HONEY-GATHERERS

Those two *maam*, well, they used to go hunting for wild honey. They used to sing their own song about honey when they were finding it: '*Wooroo, wooroo!*' they used to sing. They sometimes found a nest with wax, breaking its 'nose'. She would say, 'It's a little one, husband!' Then they would do it again, going along singing, finding honey. They would squeeze its 'nose' and when they saw it was a hard one they would dig in the ground to get out the comb, singing, in their own language:

Ga-bilgga-bilg, gu-daid!
Woyol, woyol, maidbad-gom!
Digging, digging, cutting paperbark for a basket!
Getting water! Got it all, now home to sleep!

Then they would go back to their camp and sleep. They always did that. Early next morning they would go on looking for honey and singing their song. They were alone, only the two of them. They would fill their baskets with honey and take it back to their camp, in a deep cave among the rocks. They lived there for a long time. Some days they just stayed at home, 'eating' each other until sunset. Then next day they would go hunting again, looking for kangaroo and vegetable foods, and carry them back to their camp.

Well, at last he came, a new *maam* spirit, newly dead. He came to their place, where they were camping. They were lighting a fire inside the cave. He said to himself, that new spirit, 'What shall I do to them, those two, that woman and man — because they are always "fighting" each other?' Well, he just blew on the rock, for them, he sealed them up for ever.

They were calling out, they were swearing at him, that one who had sealed them up. 'Your secretions come out! You copulate with your mother, and you eat her bones! Did we first make trouble for you, so that you sealed us up, my husband and me?' asked that wife. Her husband said the same. But the *maam* just went away; he flew up into the sky. Those two turned into rocks. They remain there in the cave, at Gandjirbi, where they became *djang*. They remain there for ever.

The unpredictable nature of such spirits is underlined here. As the *maam* husband and wife themselves pointed out, they were doing no harm to anyone. All they were doing, apart from food-getting, was 'eating' and 'fighting' each other (i.e., copulating). It was only because the newly-dead spirit was jealous that he incarcerated them in their own home.

Also from Oenpelli is a further *maam* story, told to R. Berndt in 1950.

156. REVIVING POOR GUWILU

Weli, black and red Parrot was a *nangaraidgu*, *yariyaning*, *namarang* man. His wife Guwilu, Curlew, was *ngalmadgu*, *yariwurga* and *ngalbangari*. They came to Gagun-gudwelbmi, and there Curlew pulled out her pubic hair and hung it up on the rocks. This was toward Wanbi creek, running to the East Alligator River [between Wanbi and the South Alligator River, on the other side of Doyle's camp]. They went to Ibadang. Weli said to his wife, 'You stay there, I'll go after kangaroo.' He went off with his spears.

Curlew was hungry. She waited a long time for Weli, and then went out to find something to eat. While she was looking for *duberg*, rock snails, her shadow fell upon the entrance to a cave in which a *maam* lived: it was his home. He saw this. 'What's here? I see a shadow!' He got up and looked around: 'What is that something, that shadow?' he asked himself. He searched all around until he saw Guwilu standing there. 'Where do you come from?' he asked her. 'I'm looking for snails,' she replied. 'Have you a husband?' he asked. 'Yes, I have one, he's gone out hunting.' 'You come with me for a while,' the *maam* said. He wanted to copulate with her. She went with him to the crack in the rock leading into his home, and into the cave: she lay down and he copulated with her. Then she left his cave and began to walk back to her camp. But the *maam* was thinking about her: 'It is better if I go and get her again!' That girl was very young. The *maam* called out to her, 'Wait for me!' She replied, 'All right.' He caught up with her: 'We'll go to these flat rocks on the outside' [near his cave]. He put her lying down: that *maam* was still hungry. He jumped on to her and copulated again.

Now, that *maam* had a sharp stone knife, and when they had finished copulating, he pulled it out and cut her in half: he took away the bottom part, leaving the 'head part' behind. 'He took her legs and the lower part of her body, and went away.' All the way, that *maam* made a special noise [song]:

dul dul ngawili-wili bereni mu mu
Dul dul [he sang] I'm carrying that [body part].

Her husband, on his way home, came past the rocks and saw the top part of her body lying there. 'What has happened to my wife? Who has cut her like that?' he cried. Then he saw the track marks of the *maam* and heard his song. 'That *maam* has taken my wife!' He got his best stone-bladed spear and began to run, calling out *din! din!* as he sharpened that spear blade [while he went along]. He heard the *maam's* song, circled around and came to stand in front of him, but the *maam* went past! Weli ran behind, following him. ['He wanted to kill that *maam*!'] Then he heard the *maam* singing from behind. Weli was in front of him now, and stood blocking his way, holding his sharp stone-bladed spear: 'I'm going to kill him with this!' [The *maam* didn't know Weli was in front of him.] Behind some bushes, Weli got ready. He hooked his spear and threw it at the *maam*, spearing him through the heart. He speared him again, then cut off his head with a stone axe and left him lying there. As he fell, the *maam* had dropped the legs and lower part of the body of Guwilu. Her husband picked them up and carried them back to their camp where the head part was. He joined the two parts together; he tied the entrails and sinews together, and the flesh; and he gathered together all her blood. Then he put her joined-up body close to a nest of meat ants. He left her there, and hid behind a tree while he sang some special songs. The meat ants bit her all over: 'She feels herself, and she shivers a little!' Weli was watching. She moved; she became alive! She called out: 'My husband!' 'I'm here, my wife,' he replied. 'What happened to you?' he asked. She told him. 'I have killed the *maam*,' he said. 'You know that *maam*?' 'Yes,' she said. 'He ran away with half your body! I killed him. I brought it back and I put the two parts together.' 'I can see no mark here,' she said, 'How did he cut me? I don't know anything about it!' 'You've got the mark inside. Now, stand up.' She stood up. [He put his feet under hers and, putting his arms under her shoulders, lifted her up.] He made a fire, and with warmed bushes he 'burnt' her ears to restore her hearing, since she had become deaf. He 'burnt' her on the buttocks and on the back. 'Try to walk. I want to see.' Then he told her to run. 'I want to see whether you are strong.' She ran toward him. She fell half-way: she wasn't strong enough. She tried again, and fell. 'I'll have to look at you again!' He pulled her to her feet, making her strong. She ran; she was all right; she ran along quickly.

They left that place. 'You go in front,' her husband said.. 'I want to see you all the way!' But she made herself into a Rainbow Snake at the Dreaming stone at Mungaring. Weli made himself into a bird, saying: 'My wife has turned into a rock. I'll make myself into a bird, and I'll fly around.'

The unsophisticated young wife was an easy prey for the treacherous *maam*. The reason given for her compliant behaviour was that 'she was a young girl who didn't know any better!' The *maam*, on the other hand, was so 'hungry for it' that he carried away with him the relevant part of Guwilu's body, leaving only the rest of it for her husband to find.

The focal point of the story is really the revival of the girl. Joining up a severed body and then using meat ants to revivify it has parallels in other Aboriginal mythology, in other areas as well as this. For instance, the Wawalag Sisters of north-eastern Arnhem Land who were swallowed and then vomited out by Yulunggul, were brought back to life in that way (see Chapter 3). In general terms, however, the erotic element is secondary, and the story emphasises once more how malignant and ruthless *maam* spirits can be.

The next story was told to C. Berndt at Oenpelli in 1950.

157. WHAT HAPPENED AT GOGALAG

Long ago, two girls were coming this way [toward Oenpelli]. They set off far in the east, camping in country where they saw plenty of honey and plant foods. After that they were travelling among rocks. They would camp, and early in the morning they would move on again, making for the place it was their destiny to reach.

But two young men were coming, looking for kangaroos. So then they were getting close to meeting each other. Those girls saw a big expanse of water running, a flooding creek. The two men were on the other side, they were on this side. The girls went on, and saw bees. Well, they heard those two men chopping out honey for themselves, and they got ready to call out. They talked about it first. 'Younger sister!' 'Yes, elder sister. Surely it doesn't matter if we call out to them, asking whether they'll give us that axe they're carrying so we can chop out some honey?' 'Yes,' said the elder girl. 'You climb up a tree and call to them from there, so they'll hear you!' She climbed up: she asked them. The girls said, 'Who are you, chopping honey? Would you mind giving us something to chop with, so we can get honey?' The two men said, 'Those two girls are calling out to us, younger brother. Let's go and stand on the bank so we can see them properly!' They stood on the bank, looking at them, and said to each other, 'Two girls for us, adolescents — look at them, little breasts standing out!'

The girls were calling out, thinking, 'Maybe they'll give us an axe.' The two men came and stood facing them, and said, 'Come quickly, you two, and copulate with us! Then, after that we'll give you something so you can chop out honey.' 'No!' said the girls. 'We don't want to. We're going, we're afraid of your penises. You two go away!' They ran off, frightened, and hid among the rocky caves.

The two men had already crossed over the creek and were picking up their tracks. The girls were still hiding, not talking, just keeping very quiet. Then the men got their tracks and followed them straight on, to where they led into the cave. The men were feeling about with the long spears they were carrying. The spear blades got caught, twisting in the girls' hair. They said, 'These are the girls, this is their hair! What shall we do to them?' The younger brother said, 'You stay here, because you have a big body, and I'll go inside so I can get both of them for us. We're lucky to have found them — although when we go back to our country we might get into trouble about them from other people!'

At last he went into the cave. First he seized one of them by the arm: the elder sister. He put her outside, where the other man was waiting. They just began to 'eat' each other, without delay. Then he himself brought out the younger sister, and they began 'eating' each other straightaway, at the mouth of the cave. All of them: their bodies felt quite worn out. As for those girls, their thighs and joints were paining them. But still they kept on doing it. Then they went to where they were camping, in a cave among the great rocks. The elder sister slept with the elder brother, the younger one with the younger brother. They all slept.

Well, already the betrothed husbands of those two girls had been singing up trouble for them, singing up fire and flames for them. The four of them had tried to light a big fire, in that cave where they were camping. But at last their paperbark 'blankets' caught alight: they were burning, and their hair was burning! They ran to the water and plunged in. And there, close by, that Snake was lying. She ate them all: finished them. She carried their bones about, then afterward she vomited them there, in that country where she put the name. 'Here, where you come into Dreaming, the place name is Gogalag,' she said, putting the name, that Snake, as she vomited them.

They went, she vomited their bones, they became like rocks. And they remain there, where they came into Dreaming, those women and men who went underneath the water. They remain in that country, Gogalag, for ever, they put themselves as *djang* there. So then, nobody is to get plant foods there when the leaves are turning yellow; they are to get only those with green leaves. Honey, too: people are not to chop it out if the bees' nest points toward the water where those others came into Dreaming, or they too might go underneath the water for ever there; that Snake might eat them too, so that they would all remain there together, as rocks, where they came into Dreaming.

A basic assumption here was that unaccompanied females, especially young ones, were 'fair game', in so far as the sexual attentions of men were concerned. Although the two girls at first said they were frightened of the men, even to the extent of fleeing from them, it was not long before they were willing participants.

Sexual relations, however, in certain circumstances and quite often in myth, can lead to tragedy. Their betrothed husbands heard of the sisters' escapade and, presumably through the use of sorcery, caused their death. That provided the girls with the opportunity to fulfil their destiny, foreshadowed at the beginning of the story: they jumped into the water and, through the agency of the Rainbow Snake (see Chapter 3) became *djang*; and so did the two men, their 'sweethearts'.

The following story was told to C. Berndt at Oenpelli in 1950.

158. AND NOW THEY ARE AT MALBAID

Long ago, far in the west two girls set off, coming this way. As they came they were making places, and always talking in their own language, 'Gunbargid'. They put foliage and roots of various foods, and they made living creatures. They would make hands and feet and heads for them. Then they put them where there was strong sunlight and red ants were running about. They would hide, and when they saw a creature's tail beginning to move they would creep up close and tap it on the head with a spear-thrower until it ran off. All the time they were sending away such creatures, some of them quite large. They were making vegetable foods, and making fish and putting them into the water.

At last they decided to leave their own language, 'because already we have set foot in Yiwadja country, so that's what we should speak now'. They tried to settle down in a cave-house, but leeches began to bite them. They moved on. They saw many stringybark trees growing on hard ground, and made a house for themselves there. They said to each other, 'Where do you think we can get a man, elder sister?' 'Yes, younger sister! Let's light a fire, a big grass fire, so that some young unmarried man will come, and then we'll get him and marry him!' They prepared a fire-stick, and collected soft stringybark and set it alight. They lit a lot of fires among the big grasses. The fires were burning, burning.

Two young Maung-speaking men were coming from the north. They set off, following the light of the fires, and ran until they were close to the flames. As for the two girls, they were lying asleep in their bark house. The two men looked about and found the house, came up to it, and saw them inside. The elder sister was lying a bit farther from the door; the younger sister in another corner. The men touched the girls' hair with their spear-throwers. They woke up, and looked around. At first the men were hiding. Then the younger brother showed himself. The girls were delighted to see that a young man had come to them. He told them, 'My elder brother is sitting over there!' The girls were happier still. They ran and got him. They gave the men plant foods and meat. After that the younger sister slept with the elder brother, and the elder sister with the younger brother. They did not go hunting. They just lay in camp all the time, talking together and embracing each other, each pair of them lying separately.

Two old men, uncles of those girls, came looking for them. They had said good-bye to them before; now they came to see where they were living. They went away satisfied. The young men had told them, 'We are lucky to have found those two girls, our wives!' And the uncles said, 'It's all right for you to sleep together, because you two men were not married before.'

But one day the four of them killed a creature where there was a *djang*. What they were trying to kill was not an ordinary creature. It was a daughter of Ngalyod, the Rainbow Snake. They killed it by mistake. That mother was crying, coming looking for her child. They saw a great rain-storm coming, in that country where they were living. They saw trees breaking and water running where the Snake was coming in search of those who had killed her daughter. They were trying to run away, looking for rocks that they could climb. But the rocks went under the water, leaving them swimming again. At last their breath failed them, and they sank beneath the water. That mother ate them. She carried their bones about for a long time. Then she vomited them, inside that same water. They became like rocks, there where she ate them. They called the name of the place, Malbaid. Only old people can look at that water, and they are the first to eat various fish there, because that water is still taboo and dangerous. Those two girls and their husbands remain there together for ever, transformed into Dreaming rocks.

The sister and brother pairs are named, but not the girls' uncles. The elder sister was Mara-barag, the younger Wobai; the older brother Namurulga, the younger Marali. There are three main parts to the story. In the first, the girls were makers and distributors of natural resources. Because they were young, only adolescents, they enjoyed the fun of shaping and animating lizards and goannas. Mangurug, a knowledgeable and vivid story-teller, emphasised this human quality in them. She went on to imply that, being so young, they became bored with their almost-routine mythic tasks. Once the girls had decided that they wanted a man — one between them, if not one each — they concentrated on this kind of relationship in the second phase of their story. Nothing more is said about their earlier role as food-resource contributors. Their uncles (mother's brothers), as senior relatives with some authority over them, bring this middle phase to a tidy conclusion by approving of the marriage arrangements. But the story has to end, in a way that locates the four characters at a named, specific *djang* site. Failure to recognise the Snake's daughter was not necessarily a youthful mistake: older characters in other myths have done the same thing. It simply provides a locally plausible climax, and in this case there is no suggestion that anyone else was responsible for what happened to them.

The following brief excerpt from a large mythic cycle was told to R. Berndt at Balgo in 1960.

159. THE GUNG-GURANGGARA 'SISTERS'

The Dreaming Djagulugulu, 'Seven Sisters', were all of the *nabaldjari* sub-section, and the language area in which this incident took place was Gugadja. Yuleyula, a *djagamara* man, was following these young women when he noticed that one of them had left the main group and gone in search of food. He went after her and found her sleeping. He awakened her, and they copulated, but his penis got stuck, and he was unable to withdraw it. The other women, coming in search of their missing sister, found the pair locked together in coitus; they tried to pull him off, but could not. They returned to their camp to think the matter over. Then they came back. Standing astride and over the two, they urinated, making them slippery so that the man was able to remove his penis.

They slept, the man alongside that woman and the others nearby. During the night those other women climbed into the sky, where they sat looking at the pair. When the woman woke up, they let down a rope and pulled her up into the sky with them.

The man awakened and turned toward her, to find her gone: he ran round looking for her. He heard all the women in the sky laughing at him, so he put a tall pole firmly into the ground and began to climb up. When he had nearly reached them they pushed back the pole so that he fell to the ground. The women moved higher into the sky, a 'rock' cloud covered them, and he was unable to see them. 'He can't climb up to them; he went another way and became the Morning Star.'

These are the same Gung-guranggara women who appear in Myths 16 and 127, where they were responsible for stemming the flood-waters that resulted from the broken water-bag. They are also important Dreaming characters in the secret-sacred mythology of the Western Desert. Here, through the act of coitus, they became the Seven Sisters (the Pleiades), while the man who seduced one of them became the Morning Star (Venus).

The next myth was told to R. Berndt at Ooldea in 1941.

160. A RECALCITRANT CHILD

Two Dreaming people, a boy and his mother's sister, were camped in spinifex country north-west of Ooldea. They were hunting together, following the tracks of a possum. It entered a hollow tree. The boy sat at the base of the fire, while the woman climbed up. He was looking at her vulva.

She caught the possum, climbed down from the tree, and cleaned the animal for cooking, sitting with her legs apart. The boy kept looking at her vulva. They cooked the meat and ate it, and then continued hunting for *djimbi* goanna. They camped. That evening the boy began to cry. She gave him some *djimbi* meat, but he brushed it aside. He went on crying and saying '*Munga-ludju*' ['Morning': in the morning I saw it.] But she did not know what he meant. She offered him different slices of meat, but he threw each aside, repeating '*Munga-ludju!*' Eventually, she understood what he meant. 'You saw my vulva?' she asked. 'Yes'. So his mother's sister made a wind-break and, stretching out behind it, prepared for coitus: she gave her sister's son her vulva all night.

At daybreak, the boy [now called Didji-guda-muril, a species of white-haired rat] left the woman and walked away. His mother's sister awakened, and looked around, but at first she could not find his tracks. At last she did, and followed the boy.

That boy travelled along by himself, singing:

> *gunagu ira nang gunagu ira nang*
> *didji-gudjara*
> Hungry for coitus, from the top he saw it!
> Those two boys.

[The reason for two boys being mentioned was not known to the story-teller.] The woman sang:

> *didji gudal-gudal mirara wonanu*
> Following the tracks of the child-Rat.

The boy was transformed into a *gudal-muril* rat. The woman who followed him also turned into a rat. She made a camp, and walking around it, saw the boy Rat and killed him with her digging stick.

> *djuringbadu walyini ya djuringbadu walyini*
> Throwing the club at him.

This incest story is followed by tragedy, the Rat boy, being killed by his mother's sister (a surrogate mother) with whom he has copulated. The story-teller interpreted the transformation of both of them as a punishment, even though this is a Dreaming myth in which shape-changing is a generally-accepted mythic characteristic. The fact that the boy turned into a rat with white hair symbolises that he has either had sexual relations with a menstruating woman or committed incest; traditionally, premature white hair was said to be caused by such an act. That point was not made in the case of women similarly placed.

A similar theme appears in an Alawa myth from the Roper River area. It was told to R. Berndt at Mataranka in 1945.

161. A THWARTED CHILD

An old blind man lived at Wabal waterhole near Hodgson Downs with his wife and small grandchild, his daughter's son. Their real home, however, was in the sky. The woman and child went out to hunt and during the day caught one large and one small goanna. When she had cooked them she handed the smaller one to the boy, but he refused it. He wanted the large one. She told him, 'I can't give you the big one: I must take that to my husband.' The boy became angry. He grabbed the large goanna and threw it onto a flat rock. 'You are a bad boy!' she scolded, and hit him. 'We'd better return to our camp, grandson,' she told him as he continued to cry.

She collected her belongings and began to climb a large stringybark tree that extended up into the sky. As she climbed, with the boy following, he was able to see her vulva. In excitement, he slipped down the tree trunk. She started to come down, to pick him up. 'I want to copulate with you before we go home to that old man,' he told her. 'What do I have to do?' he asked. 'I can't copulate with you,' she replied. 'My vulva belongs to the old man. Your penis is too small. You can't have it!' 'You come down!' he cried. 'You give it to me first before we go home.' But she would not copulate with him. When she refused him again, he bit her and she squealed out in pain, crying out to her husband: 'The little boy has bitten me. Come quickly!'

The old man, in spite of his blindness, came rushing up with his axe: but the boy had made himself 'like a rock'. The man spoke, 'I don't want either of you. You had both better go back into the *gomerindji*.' He sang:

arangindjaru dar-uradji
ngaii-nyingaya ungi-urunga
gomerindji

Daylight coming.
I don't want you two. You go into
The *gomerindji* constellation.

The spirits of the woman and the boy entered the *gomerindji* constellation [which we call the 'Seven Sisters']. There they remain, stuck together, the boy still biting his grandmother's clitoris, and fading with the coming daylight.

R. Berndt was told that the large goanna was the old man's penis, and the smaller one the immature penis of the boy who wanted to have a large one. His slipping down the tree on seeing the woman's vulva emphasised his immaturity. The myth is a non-secret version of the Wadabir Goanna Dreaming associated with *yabudurwa* ritual (see R. Berndt 1951: 185–87).

The following Gugadja myth, told to R. Berndt at Balgo in 1960, also concerns incest.

162. INCESTUOUS DANGIDJARA

Dangidjara was a *djagamara* man. From Njinyirawurul, east of Yabuna near Lake Mackay, on his way to Windal claypan, he came to Munggu-gadja rockhole where he camped. Later he went on to Bulgal rockhole and then to Yumari rockhole. Here Magindi, a *nangala* woman, was camping: she was related to Dangidjara as a mother-in-law [*yumari*, hence the place name: a taboo relationship]. 'He couldn't help it. He copulated with her!' He camped with her for some time. He walked all around the place and speared kangaroos, removing their entrails; there is a soak where he did this. He returned to Yumari now and then to supply Magindi with meat. She became pregnant, and eventually gave birth to a *djabaldjari* son.

Leaving his *yumari* and his son, Dangidjara went on to Nundjil. Here he slept in a big rockhole, but while he was sleeping, ants bit his testes so severely that they fell off and 'ran away by themselves!' He went on to Malga, where there is a big rockhole, and camped there. His testes had gone in the opposite direction. His penis too, as a result of the ant bites, had dropped off and gone in another direction. In the morning he called out for his testes and penis — but they did not return. He walked on southward, and camped — but they did not come back to him. It was not until he reached Lungulurul swamp that his testes and penis rejoined him.

Dangidjara continued to Bugudi swamp, where he camped, and tied up his hair into a *bugudi* bun. He walked on to Wila-duludjara where there is another swamp. He was tired. He turned back to Yugala, where he camped for a while to recover his strength, then went on to Baldjaga swamp and camped, and to Mandan-gunda where there is a hole, but no water. Living in the lake area nearby were Munga-munga people — 'wild' people, who were looking for him. Seeing them, he 'dived into' the hole at Mandan-gunda. The Munga-munga blocked the entrance to it. However, he came out at another place, Djindara, after having travelled under-ground. They continued looking for him at Mandan-gunda. He called out to them from Djindara, 'teasing' them, then ran away to Njiringgi soak. The Munga-munga followed him. He went on to Gunawiri soak. It was there that they found him. They encircled him. He dodged between them and escaped. He placed his sacred boards in a tree nearby and, standing on one leg, gathered together all the Munga-munga people and put them into Gunawiri soak. As he stood there on one leg, he turned himself into a rock. All of them 'finished up' at that place.

A version of this myth is contained in R. Berndt (1970: 231–32); it is part of a much larger cycle, some of which (not this) is secret-sacred. The point made in this section of the myth is that punishment inevitably follows an act of incest. What happened to the *yumari* and Dangidjara's son is not followed up. Dangidjara leaves them and the focus is on his own experiences. Apart from the loss and return of his own genitalia, he is followed by the Munga-munga (or Manga-manga). These are not 'wild' people, but are really the beautiful young daughters of the Fertility Mother, the Old Woman, Gadjari, belonging to the north-eastern tradition (that is, north-east of Yabuna) rather than to the Gugadja. However, in this context they are intent on avenging the wrong done to one of their *own* women (as Magindi was). In the final outcome, all of them become Dreaming.

The following three myths concern the adventures of Bomaboma (Namarangini or Gwingula, or other names). They were told to R. Berndt at Yirrkalla in 1946.

163. THE ABDUCTION OF BUNBA AND HER ESCAPE

Wubelu (Wobalu, or Bomaboma) went out to get crayfish and Wilagidj (Wulagidj) hunted for stingray. Wilagidj had a number of daughters and sons. On his return Wubelu offered to give crayfish to Wilagidj's children, but he was just tricking them. He called out the names of those boys and girls, one by one, but when they came up to him he refused to give the crayfish. Then he called out the name of the eldest girl, Bunba. She told her younger brother to go: 'You get the crayfish for me!' The brother went over, but Wubelu said, 'I didn't want you to come. I want Bunba to come before I distribute the food.' Each time he called her, she sent her brother; and each time the boy asked for the crayfish, Wubelu replied that Bunba would have to come first. At last she came. When she reached him he gave her the crayfish, and at the same time held her arms. He ran away with her.

When Wilagidj came back from fishing his sons told him what had happened: 'Father, he has taken our sister!' 'Who?' he asked. 'Wubelu!' 'Which way did he go?' 'That way!' So Wilagidj went after them.

Wubelu put Bunba into his hut and secured the entrance to it. He went to a nearby tree and climbed up into it and looked out for Wilagidj. He saw him coming along the track. Wilagidj went straight to Wubelu's house: he tried to get into it, but could not move the entrance closure. Wubelu was looking at him: Wilagidj was trying to open that 'door' — 'but it was too hard'. Wilagidj went back a little way and got his *gwimala* [a bunch of emu feathers waxed to a stick: the usual fly whisk] and spear-thrower. He put the emu feathers on the end of the spear-thrower, rubbing

it with his hands and waving it. In this way he sent his spirit to get the
girl. He put the spear-thrower behind him, holding it with his buttocks
'like a tail', moving it from side to side: that is, 'his spirit was walking'. At
the same time, the girl made herself into a 'butterfly'. The door of the hut
opened and she flew out. Flying round, she eventually settled on the
spear-thrower. After a while the spear-thrower became heavy: he looked
round and saw his daughter. He was very happy!

Wubelu was watching in his tree. He did nothing, but he was becoming
angry. There was nothing he could do. When Wilagidj left, Wubelu saw
that he was accompanied by a *djabiru* (native companion) bird sitting on
his spear-thrower. Wubelu did not know it was Bunba. He climbed down
from his tree and went over to his hut; the door was closed in the same
way as he had left it. He opened it and looked inside — but the hut was
empty. He looked all around: he couldn't understand it. That hut was at
Gadawida'wi, near Blue Mud Bay [Bidingal dialect, *yiridja* moiety]: he
made himself into Black Eaglehawk. Wilagidj lived at Gerangani, also
near Blue Mud Bay [Djabu dialect, *dua* moiety]. He made himself into
Long Tom fish. Bunba made herself Butterfly.

---

164. THE CYCAD NUT GRINDING STONE

Namarangini, a Ngeimil dialect, *dua* moiety, spirit man lived at Wurudjilgaru (or Ngurudjilgaru) on Arnhem Bay. This was a place where women
gathered shellfish. Among them were two sisters named Buwad [Wonguri
dialect, *yiridja* moiety]: but they had other names too, such as Yiwama,
Gureri, and 'singing names' referring to their attributes and activities.
Namarangini was unmarried.

The two sisters went out to collect shellfish among the mangrove roots;
Namarangini came up from one side looking for fish. He heard the two
sisters calling to each other. Namarangini sang up rain, with lightning and
thunder. The thunder snake 'burst' around the women and the rain
poured down upon them. They were frightened and called out the name of
Namarangini and swore at [about] him 'because they knew that rain and
thunder came from him'. They did not know he was nearby, listening to
them.

However, they went on putting shellfish into their baskets. As they were
doing this, he grabbed the younger sister by the arm. She called out,
'Elder sister, help me! Namarangini has caught me!' The elder sister
became angry and, breaking off a tree limb, began to beat Namarangini as
he tried to copulate with the younger sister. He went on trying while the

other sister was beating him, but 'he didn't put it in properly'. He took her to his camp where he had been fishing: he had plenty of food there, possum and bandicoot, and he had made a bark hut. He spoke to that girl, but she would not reply.

The elder sister returned to their husband Gurulungun [Dadiwi dialect, *dua* moiety; he was Milkwood tree, *rida* or *dalug*].

Namarangini made his house ready. He got his fire-sticks and made a fire just outside the entrance of the hut: he did not blow on the tinder, it just flared up, and billowed with smoke. But the girl still refused to speak to him, even though she was coughing with the smoke. He made more smoke. Then she called out, 'Namarangini is blowing that fire, making smoke!' and she swore at him. 'That's all right,' he replied, 'you speak to me; you're a nice girl, you can talk to me!' He grabbed her as the fire flared up; he opened her legs and put his penis in but he felt something inside. He tried and tried to have coitus — but there was a rock in her vagina. 'You can't do it,' she said, 'there's a rock inside!' 'I can do it,' he replied. He got a special stick which belonged to her, a *galadangi*, which was used to beat cycad nuts. [One of the names of these two sisters is Lialwonu, which refers to the time when cycad nuts are ready to collect and people are crying for them.] He put that stick into her vagina and loosened the stone, removing it. Having removed the stone, he copulated with her easily. When they had finished, she made herself into a fly and returned to her husband. [This event occurred at Milungura, on Arnhem Bay.]

Her husband, who was camped at Wurudjilgaru [also Wuradjunggera], was pleased to see her. 'You are back, I am pleased: there is palm nut bread there.' Afterward, when they had eaten, he told his children to play some distance away. 'I want to sleep with my wife,' he said. All his other wives [the other Buwad sister, and apparently other *buwad* and sandflies, *gaidjiri*, who were all said to be 'sisters'] had gone out into the bush to collect honey. Gurulungun made a big 'square' song stick which he put into the ashes to make hot. He called to the younger sister, asking her to delouse him, and put his head between her legs to make it easier for her to get lice from his hair. While she was doing that he looked at her vagina and saw that the stone had gone. 'He didn't want the girl for coitus; he only pretended he did because he wanted to see whether the stone had gone.' He put his penis in and then took it out. 'I'll try again,' he said. This time he got his heated stick and thrust it into her vagina; he kept on pushing, so that the stick went into her stomach and she died. She was crying out as he did this to her, and smoke came out of her mouth and nostrils. When she was dead, he covered her up with paperbark: then he lay down beside her, covered himself with bark and went to sleep.

When all the other 'sisters' returned, as well as the children, they saw a woman lying there; they didn't know who it was. [They had been out when she returned, and had not spoken to the children about her.] 'Who is there?' they asked. 'She came back,' Gurulungun replied. 'When?' 'This morning,' he said. 'She is still asleep!' The elder Buwad sister came over to awaken her; she shook her, and tried to awaken her — but the girl was dead. Buwad knew immediately that Gurulungun had done something to her. The women talked together, telling each other that she had been killed. They all cried for her. Then they got their yam sticks and cycad nut beaters and set upon Gurulungun: they beat him and stuck those sticks into him. He ran away, and as he ran he removed those sticks from his body. He went to Banbiwonga, on the Yirrkalla side of Arnhem Bay, where he died: he turned into that big milkwood tree there, the *rida*, where his spirit remains.

When Namarangini copulated with the younger sister there was no creek at Milungura, only mangroves. As soon as the Fly and Sandfly women cried for their 'sister', rain began to fall heavily, and went on falling for several weeks. They began to make bark rafts [which were used prior to the introduction of the Macassan-type canoes]. When they were doing this, spring water rushed down from the 'top' [inland]: it was so strong, they could hear the roar of the flood water. They tried to block the flow, but it was too strong, it pushed their rafts into the salt water [sea] down toward Cape Wilberforce and then out farther into the sea. All those women who cried at the death of the younger sister, and all their children, and all their possessions were swept out to sea — their string, rocks, stringybark huts and cycad nut grinding stones — to Cape Wilberforce, to Galiwinku (Elcho Island), and to Milingimbi; 'and when you go by sea now, you can still hear them crying!'

In the old times, women had this stone in their vaginas. When men copulated with them, they didn't bother about it. When a child was born, it pushed out the stone; menstruation wouldn't move it. It was Namarangini who opened up those women for the new time. That stone within them was really the cycad nut grinding stone. In the old time, women could take it out as they wished and use it. They lost it when the spring water came flooding down, washing them out to sea.

---

165. THE TRICKERY OF BOMABOMA AND HIS DEATH

A large group of people were living at Yilgala [not Yirrkalla, but situated south of Trial Bay]. There was Bugabalur, who was Bomaboma's *ngati* [father's mother's brother; his name meant fibre string from the flowering eucalypt used in making some dilly bags]. There was also Yii, White

Duck, who was Bomaboma's *gurung* [father's sister's daughter's daughter, of the same moiety, a taboo relationship]. Bugabalur was Yii's *duwei* [husband]. They were all living there, fishing for kingfish.

A message came to Bugabalur inviting his group to attend a ceremony at Waralba. The message had been sent to various camps, inviting different birds, including the djabiru, native companion. Bugabalur told Yii to accompany Bomaboma: 'You go with him. You will want to see your mother at Waralba; there will be a big ceremony there!' [Yii's mother was Gurulgu, Djabiru bird.]

Yii went with Bomaboma. They had come 'half-way' to Waralba when it became dark. This was at Bambeingoi, where they caught small *rima* fish. He went some little distance away from her and put some *rima* blood on his foot, pretending to have had an accident. He called out to Yii: 'My foot is very sore, I can't walk: we will have to camp here.' Yii replied that she wanted to go on quickly to Waralba. Bomaboma, however, sent her to get the special wood used in making a pair of fire-sticks. She brought this back. He pretended to try to hold the horizontal stick with his foot [while he propelled the vertical one, to make fire]. 'My foot is too sore, I can't hold it, you will have to.' Yii replied, 'You have to hold it, I can't.' [She refused because, if she did this, she would show her vagina.] But Bomaboma said, 'Don't feel shame, you are too young!' [As she was his *gurung*, she was sexually taboo to Bomaboma.] Since there would be no fire without her help, she agreed: 'All right, I have to put my foot on the stick.' She did so and he saw her vagina. Bomaboma sat in front of her and pretended to make fire, but every time he put the upright fire stick into the indentation of the horizontal stick, it slipped out. [He was disturbed at having seen her vagina.] Yii became frightened. Eventually, Bomaboma made fire. [Comment: Yii was only young: she didn't know how to make fire.]

Once the fire was made, Yii cooked the fish. Bomaboma lay down and said he could not walk. After they had eaten, he sent her out to get paperbark to make a shelter 'so we won't get cold!' When Yii was out, Bomaboma jumped up and collected some pandanus nuts. He put these in a hole close to where the shelter would be made and covered them. Yii returned with the bark and made a wind-break. On her return she saw track marks. She asked him, 'Do you know this track?' and added 'Look, *maralgur* [reciprocal of *gurung*], I saw those footmarks, someone must have been running about here!' 'Keep quiet,' Bomaboma replied, 'Those tracks are of your *mari's* (mother's mother's brother) spirit: they belong to my *baba* (father), who died here. Don't say too much, perhaps that *mari* is after you!' She was frightened. Bomaboma crawled round, pretending he couldn't walk: he made out he was very sorry for himself.

Eventually they settled down in their bark wind-break, with a fire between them — Yii on one side, Bomaboma on the other. The girl went heavily to sleep. Bomaboma got up and went to where his pandanus nuts were hidden, uncovered them, and took them out. He threw one, which hit the bark; that did not awaken her. He threw another and then another, but Yii did not hear them. He came closer and threw a nut. This time she did awaken and jumped up in fear, thinking it was her *mari's* spirit. When she jumped, she came close to Bomaboma; he jumped at the same time and held her. Yii cried out.

'Why is this woman crying?' he asked himself; and then said to her, 'I don't want to put it inside you, only to lie between your legs.' Thinking that he simply wanted to put his leg between hers, she was not frightened. Instead, he put his penis into her and 'broke her leg' [dislocated her thigh, since it was said that he had an abnormally large penis].

Early next morning they left for Waralba, Bomaboma carrying the injured Yii. Before reaching there, he hid her and went into Waralba by himself. Yii's two Djabiru mothers [one her own mother] were waiting for them. Bomaboma said nothing to them but rushed over to dance. They followed him, calling, 'Where is our daughter?' Bomaboma went on dancing and did not reply. 'Where is your *gurung*, our daughter?' they cried. He replied, 'Don't ask me, I haven't finished dancing yet. I want to dance first before I tell you!' And as he danced, he sang:

waidjeru-waidjeru minala-minala
daidbangu-daidbangu bagera-bagera djurulura yanganu-yangulan
Swimming, fresh water tortoise.
[Singing names of the tortoise; special names used in the song].

And as Bomaboma danced, he called out *waingg! waingg!*

The two mothers grew angry. They ran over and broke off a branch from a white flowering eucalyptus tree. Coming back, they asked him again, but he replied in the same way. They hit him across the back and on the buttocks. But Bomaboma danced on. They hit him again, and after that he told those two mothers: 'You go up there [indicating the direction], and you will find my *gurung* in a tree, where I left her.' 'What is wrong! What has happened to her?' they asked him. He answered, 'She ran after a bandicoot and broke her leg!'

The two women went into the bush and found their daughter lying by a big tree. They asked her what had happened, and she told them: 'That man did something to me, my *maralgur* made me frightened.' Those two women cried, since they knew what he had done; and they carried her back to their camp at Waralba.

Bomaboma was still dancing. When they had attended to Yii, they went over to him and commenced hitting him. They hit his head, his arms, and his neck. He went on dancing; he was so engrossed in his dancing that he took no notice of the blows. As the hitting continued, he began to feel sore.

Running quickly away, he picked up his fish spear. 'What do you think I am, a stick, or what?' he called out. He ran across and killed a dog — he didn't kill a person! Then he ran across and speared that cycad nut bread: there was a large pile of it, because of the dancing. [Comment: 'He's a funny man!' — laughter.] When Bomaboma killed that dog, that cycad bread; he cried out, speaking to that dog and to the bread: he didn't speak to any of the people. But all the people began to fight among themselves and they killed Bomaboma at Waralba. After they had done that, they made themselves into birds — different kinds: djabiru, duck, goose, and so on.

Traditionally, there were many variants of the adventures of Bomaboma, who had several alternative names. The three stories we present are typical. In each example Bomaboma is characterised as a trickster, behaving in a way an ordinary person would not. He is usually involved in nefarious pursuits relating to females.

The first is a kind of introduction to his exploits. It was said that this myth constituted validation for abductions taking place — validation, but not necessarily justification. Before Bomaboma engaged in this attempted abduction, none had taken place. In this case, Bomaboma was out-manoeuvred by Bunba's father. Although the relationship between Bomaboma and the girl is not mentioned, it is fairly certain that she was his *gurung*, a sexually taboo relative.

In the next, Namarangini engages in a ruse to secure the younger Buwad sister. Again, his kin relationship to her is not noted, but given his propensity for female *gurung*, she is probably of that categorisation. The myth takes on an even more serious note with her death at the hands of her own husband. Tragedy piles on tragedy, with the husband being killed by his wives. When the wives are mourning their dead sister, rain begins to fall and, as a result, a flood washes away all the women into the sea. Namarangini escapes unscathed: he has liberated women from the burden of having a grinding stone within their vaginas, and has made sexual intercourse easy for the 'new' generation of people. More importantly, he is responsible for the cycad nut grinding stone becoming a secret-sacred *dugururu* emblem. This and a hollow log appear in the secret-sacred version of this myth: both were taken by the flood waters into the sea. The myth we have presented is its secular version: but there are implications within it for north-eastern Arnhem Land religion.

In the third story — in spite of Bomaboma (Wubelu) having trans-formed himself into an Eaglehawk in the first story — Bomaboma reappears. Through trickery he seduces Yii, his *gurung*, and in doing so injures her. His duplicity is well-orchestrated: his pretended injury, the sexual symbolism of the fire-sticks, the fear he engenders in Yii by telling her the spirit of her dead *mari* is nearby and could harm her, and the throwing of the pandanus nuts. The reaction of Yii's mothers and Bomaboma's eccentric dancing all mark him as being a strange, unpredictable sort of person. His death and the transformation of all the people who attended the ceremony as birds, wind up these stories of his irrational behaviour.

In another version told to C.H. Berndt by women at Milingimbi in 1950, the girl's name is Rabaraba. She is a big girl, adolescent, with developed breasts and plump hips and thighs: she wears many arm-bands, a twine head-band, and a cross-over breast girdle. Gwingula (Gwi-ngula; Bomaboma), eating cycad food that women are preparing, offers to take one of the girls fishing. He tells them, each in turn, to run and then take a long jump. None of them is what he wants. He tells Rabaraba, 'Come on: your turn!' She stands up. He 'eyes' her like a sweetheart though he calls her *gurung* and should not even speak to her. He praises her; 'You do that well, my *gurung*; nice breasts, nice buttocks!' They set off to get fish. As he sits facing her in the billabong his penis grows very long and touches her. She gets her stick to hit it, thinking it is a fish, but he pulls it hastily away. Later, after she has cooked the fish they have caught and they have eaten it separately, Gwingula pretends to have a sore foot, hurt by a catfish; he has put fish blood on it, and sits by the fire holding it, unable (he says) to walk back to their home camp. She offers to go and tell the others, but he persuades her to stay with him. Next comes an episode of building two huts; then heavy rain and the bombardment of pandanus nuts on the roof of her hut so that she takes refuge with him. He copulates with her, but his penis is too big. She dies immediately. Blood comes running out of her ears, her eyes, her mouth, and from her vulva. He is upset, and hits his penis and thighs. He puts her body in a tree, and tells her relatives that a catfish hurt her foot; her mother goes searching, finds her, returns and tells the others. The girl's father throws spears at him, but he keeps jumping aside. As in Myth 165, he hits and kills a dog, and then hits and breaks up the cycad food. But they trick him into entering a large fish-trap basket to try the size, then fasten it tightly and throw it into the water. Some days later they go to look at it: they could see him through the mesh of the net. 'He's finished! Good! He's dead!' They leave him lying there in the water. The events are detailed, and the tension builds up to a series of climaxes until the final quietness of the scene where the basket-net floats just below the surface of the water.

The myths presented in this chapter have been categorised to some extent as erotic. As we have seen, this aspect is minimal. In such circumstances it is well to consider briefly the bases of our selection. Firstly, there are erotic episodes in a number of myths which appear in other chapters. Our selection has rested primarily on subject emphases. Secondly, in choosing the ones we have, we first considered several hundred myths that we ourselves have recorded over the years. We excluded from these a number of myths from western Arnhem Land and elsewhere that have already appeared in R. and C. Berndt 1951: 150–70; 1985: 392–408). Moreover, we excluded those of a secret-sacred nature. Much secret-sacred material is rendered in poetic-song and not in prose form and would have been put aside in any case, but much of it also contains aspects of a sexual kind. Our sample, then, is a fairly large one. If what we have selected is reasonably reliable in terms of its typicality, as we believe it to be, could it be said that Aboriginal story-tellers and their listeners are not particularly interested in myths that have a sexual association in an erotic sense? That seems unlikely, especially if we were to consider relevant evidence from other aspects of the socio-cultural life of the people from whom the myths are drawn — songs, for example, or case history material. It is therefore logical to seek an explanation elsewhere.

It is probably true to say that sexual activity in a mythological context is good (or can be good) for personal stimulation and pleasure, in so far as listeners are concerned. On the other hand, when the sexual content of a myth is developed to some extent, that could detract from opportunities for plot elaboration. This appears to be the case with the self-willed Wogaidj girl who brings disaster upon herself (Myth 152); the irrational reaction of the jealous *maam* (Myth 155); the seduction of two initially unwilling betrothed girls who unwittingly court tragedy (Myth 157); and the response of the Gung-guranggara women when an erring sister is caught by a lustful man (Myth 159). The most sophisticated examples on this theme are the three Bomaboma stories (Myths 163–65), where the plots are consistently carried through on the basis of a sexual act, attempted or otherwise. In other words, it is what happens before and after the sexual act that constitutes the main trappings of a story. The sexual element becomes a literary device only when other things of a non-sexual kind are introduced.

Our mythological repertoire in this chapter includes no idyllic love tales. The nearest approach to this is the widow's response to the penis of her dead husband's brother, and her pleasure at finding it to be equivalent in size to that of her dead husband (Myth 149), or where the *maam* couple, so happy together, are rudely interrupted and callously destroyed by a jealous *maam* (Myth 155). The sirens on the other hand, as a continuing Dreaming phenomenon in the contemporary scene (Myth 153), may qualify as providing 'idyllic' interludes — except that this means, for the man concerned, complete separation from his own kin and all other associations. There are myths in other chapters, and in other examples we could have selected, where romantic love or sexual attraction is noted as a powerful force, but mostly this is not highlighted except where it leads to some kind of trouble — or at least the possibility of trouble.

What emerges from these particular myths is that the sexual act is fraught with danger, and, unless this is so, it has no story value. For instance, in the myths we have given here, five of the principal female characters are killed, although one is revived; nine are transformed, involving two who were injured beforehand; four are swallowed by a Rainbow Snake; and six survive unscathed. Of the principal males involved in abduction, seduction or in some sexual adventure, nine are killed, nine are transformed, four swallowed by a Rainbow Snake, and five survive. Further, in six cases other people who are not themselves necessarily directly involved are either killed or transformed. In only one case is it possible to speak of a 'happy ending' (as in Myth 149), and that was only after the woman's husband had been taken by a crocodile. In general terms, then, a sexual episode usually brought about, or was associated with, some form of aggression — personal injury to someone involved or implicated in it. If the characters concerned were not killed, they escaped from what could be regarded as an impossible situation through the process of transformation or metamorphosis.

CHAPTER EIGHT

DRAMATIC
PERSPECTIVES

Aboriginal traditional drama is not, of course, confined to this particular chapter. Every example of Aboriginal mythology, to a greater or lesser degree, has within it ingredients that go to make up an organised story. Nevertheless, some are deliberately low-key, especially where mythic characters travel over wide stretches of country, moving from one place to the next, without a great deal happening. In our experience, stories of that kind often have a greater appeal to local listeners than those that could be regarded as being more exciting. Mostly this is because the major focus is on other aspects: particular places; the nature of the terrain; the resources available there; who was mythically involved, and how. But the context in which they are communicated is always significant.

It is on the ritual ground that we find a maximum dramatic impact. Such a ground is a natural 'stage' on which religious performances take place. Mostly these present segments of sacred myths and purport to replicate, or re-enact, events experienced by mythic beings. They are designed to achieve particular aims. Many, not all, are restricted in terms of age and sex. In general, they are not intended for entertainment. Their dramatic force depends on an emotional commitment on the part of participants, and on the atmosphere that is created, aided by music, song and dance. In contrast to religious rituals, ceremonies performed in the public domain are usually for entertainment, although they carry other messages too. As well as singing, they often include dancing or dramatic scenes. Many of the songs in religious rituals are poetic-song renderings of myths that may not be available in prose form. The structure of the story content of these songs differs markedly from their prose versions, when they have these (see Chapter 1). Moreover, in their song versions they rarely cover the whole myth-story on any one occasion.

Our focus here is on narrative versions of a series of myths that do not necessarily exist in song versions. Occasionally, as we have seen, where a song is referred to in the course of a story it is often sung as part of the overall narration. The story-teller, male or female, is concerned with telling a myth in a way that will hold the listeners' attention. To achieve the required dramatic impact, he or she must ensure that the composition is made up of a set of correlated events (or incidents) and that it leads to a dénouement. In other words, it must include at least one plot that is followed through coherently to its logical resolution.

The myths and stories presented here conform, more or less, with these criteria. However, there are two points to keep in mind.

Firstly, we are dealing with traditional myths where it *is* important that the social and topographic settings and the events themselves are unfolded so that the maximum story value is retained. The sequence and nature of events should not be appreciably altered, because when they are told within the context of a small-scale camp, many of the listeners will already have heard them many times. We can say that the listeners' interest is heightened to the degree to which the story itself is familiar to them. They often constitute a critical audience ready to comment if the story-teller strays from the point, or makes an obvious mistake in his or her rendition. Secondly, a measure of improvisation is both legitimate and expected, provided structural components of the story are not changed too radically. There is a general recognition that individual variations in story-telling are normal, and only to be expected. It rests on the fact that some story-tellers are more adept than others at communicating with members of their audience. This also has to do with knowing how much in the way of detail should be spelt out — the delicate balance between stating what is necessary and overstating to the point of boredom. That is always difficult, and it is a problem not all story-tellers have resolved to the satisfaction of their listeners. Myth 18, in Chapter 2, is a case in point, when an old *mamu* sends his sole listener to sleep in the course of telling one long story after another.

We turn to our first story, which was orginally associated with the Wirangu and Kukata language groups of the Western Desert, south-western South Australia. It was told to R. Berndt at Ooldea in 1941.

---

166. THE MAGIC BOOMERANG

Djunban came from the north-west and reached an unnamed waterhole not far from Tarcoola [on the transcontinental railway line]. He was a big man with a long beard, a rain- and thunder-maker. He had two dogs which he left at this place along with his *winda* or *yuriyura* spear. He continued eastward in search of his own group of Dreaming people who had gone ahead. They had been out hunting *dalwal* wallaby, *gabidji* little wallaby, and *mala*, kangaroo rat, and had killed a number. There was plenty of meat to eat, so Djunban joined them: he was their leader. Later, he went out to hunt. He threw his boomerang, but instead of hitting a *mala* it struck on the leg of a woman to whom he was related as a classificatory 'brother'. Immediately, she picked it up and hid it in the sand. When Djunban walked over to recover it, he could not find it. He looked all around, but it was nowhere to be found. He was worried, because it was a magical boomerang. As the people were on the move, hunting, he picked up his 'sister', named Mandjia, and carried her on his back: the boomerang had hurt her leg and she could not walk. He found her a heavy burden, and sang that he could hardly lift her:

> gana mara-da-mara budu-djali mara-da-mara gana
> man-gana mara-da-mara budu-djali
> So heavy, lifting by hand.
> Standing, holding [her] by hand.

After a while he gave Mandjia to a woman to carry, and sent his group away to hunt while he went off alone to look for his boomerang. He looked all around, turning up the sand, but could not find it. He visited various waterholes in the vicinity, asking people who were camped there to show him their boomerangs. They threw them down before him; he examined them but did not find his own among them. He visited many camps. . . .

He then came to Bandada rockhole [east of Barton] where his group had reassembled. He sat down near them, by himself, worrying about his boomerang. Now, not far from Bandada a group of people was camped: they were called the 'Budilga mob' and were 'strangers', in general terms, to the 'Bandada mob', Djunban's own group. But Djunban knew them. Members of the two 'mobs' came together to hold a ceremony. Later, he told them to disperse and go hunting toward the east. A woman carried Mandjia [who had not yet recovered from her leg injury] to where the Budilga were camped. Mandjia told her to go over to her brother's camp. Djunban, in the meantime, had been searching for his boomerang and eventually found it, and set off walking back to his camp. The woman left Mandjia and, on her way to Djunban's camp, sat down to rest and singed off her pubic hair with a fire-stick. [This was done by desert women, from time to time 'to prepare themselves for coitus'.]

On his way back, Djunban smelt the singeing hair: he quickened his step. The woman met him, and together they made camp. However, he was heavy, far too heavy to get close to the woman for intercourse. He therefore removed from under his skin a large group of men and women. He was now much lighter in weight. He placed all the people around him, and they watched as he copulated with the woman.

After that, Djunban stood upright and replaced all the people, putting them under his skin again. He walked away and came back to Bandada rockhole, where he sat down by himself awaiting the return of the others from hunting. [The teller of this story remarked that Djunban really had no need to wait, because he had plenty of people under his skin!]

While he was waiting he cleared a long stretch of ground for a ceremony, removed all the people from under his skin, and placed them at one end of the dancing ground. At the other end Djunban had built a wind-break. Going behind this, he decorated himself in white and red bands across his chest and legs, putting eaglehawk down around his face and some on his chest. He began to chant:

> galbara ngara gudju
> waru bana galbara ngara
> Getting up, one by one,
> By the fire and the sandy ground.

As Djunban began his shuffling dancing movement toward the men assembled at the other end of the ground, they took up his song. First one man knelt down, his hands and knees in the sand, while the others climbed upon him, one man kneeling on the first, then the next on him, and so on. As Djunban approached them, the human column collapsed. By this time, the people who were out hunting had returned to Bandada. They saw the ceremony in progress and mingled with the people who came from under Djunban's skin.

Next morning, Djunban gathered together 'his mob' and put them under his skin. Then he and the others walked on to Ganyan (or Gandjan) rockhole [near Barton]. They cooked and ate what they had obtained through hunting. Djunban sat a little distance from the others, at Nandjida. He called to the others at Ganyan to go to Balbangu dam. There they made camp and sang: first the song mentioned above, then another:

> nganggali bada-djara
> rurgu djuna nganggali. . .
> Stormy clouds,
> Thundering...

Djunban took out his garalba shell, bit off a small piece, and spat it out to make rain, and then there was thunder. [Comment: 'He was teaching his people how to make rain.'] He caused several showers of rain and accompanying thunder. The rain clouds passed over.

Next morning all the people went to Gulgara [south of Wynbring] and on to Binaling. After a while, they moved on south-east to Gadjina [its name relating to spears]. Before reaching this place [not a waterhole then], each man in the group threw a spear toward what became Gadjina, and where they stood, their footprints may be seen today. The women had gone on to this place by themselves. On the right-hand side of Gadjina [coming from the west] Djunban's sister, Mandjia, died from her injury caused by the magic boomerang. She was metamorphosed as a large rock. After throwing their spears, the men walked into Gadjina and pulled them from the ground: as they did so, water gushed forth, and that place became a waterhole.

They travelled 'right around', a little north beyond and between Tarcoola and Wilgena (Wilyena), where there are big rocky hills. They made camp on the side of one of the hills. Djunban sat down, scraping his *garalba* shell with a stone 'knife': he was preparing to make rain. However, he was thinking in sorrow of his dead sister and not concentrating on his task. Before he realised what he was doing, he had ground off over half the *garalba*, at the same time singing his rain song. The rain came. He went over to the main camp to warn the people. But the rain was too heavy and the resulting flood waters were rising higher and higher. It was so strong that it washed away all the main camp, all the people and all their possessions: they were washed down toward Tarcoola. This was the Munga-biladinu, 'the washaway', and all the people (Djunban among them) were drowned and covered up with silt, which formed a big hill. There they all finished up.

[The myth ends with a comment by the story-teller. This hill, he said, had recently (that is, about the time this story was told to R. Berndt) been excavated for gold. The gold that was found, as well as the bones that were uncovered, were those of the Dreaming beings and their possessions: it was their possessions that had been metamorphosed as gold. He added that the bones and the gold should never have been touched — they were of the Dreaming, but if they had been, 'the gold should be ours — all those things belonged to our ancestors!']

The myth commences with Djunban's magical boomerang inadvertently injuring his 'sister' and ultimately bringing about her death. The implications of the event are clear. All that happened can be traced back to the boomerang, even though it is not mentioned again after it has been found. The people under the skin of Djunban are revealed when his 'sister' sends him a woman, which she does as a gesture indicating that she is sorry she has hidden his boomerang. The ceremonial scene is simply a highlight; the seriousness of the situation becomes apparent when Djunban, pre-occupied with sorrow, makes too much rain, and thus causes the death of all his people, including himself. It happened because that magical boomerang hit his 'sister'.

The following story was associated with the southern Andingari language (dialect) group, and was told to R. Berndt at Ooldea in 1941.

167. DESTRUCTION OF A WATERING PLACE, AND GEGI'S REVENGE

Wadi Gegi, brown or grey Hawk Man, came from the north-west of Ooldea carrying with him water, *gogara* teal ducks and Wonambi, a Rainbow Snake. By digging a large hole [said to have been about thirty yards in diameter] he made Rerdina watering place. Here he poured into it the water, the ducks and Wonambi. At this place was a cave in which Wonambi lived. Water flowed from the waterhole through the cave, and came out at the other end to form a swamp in which ducks swam. Gegi made his camp to the right. The whole area was surrounded with spinifex.

Gegi also made a bush-catchment to the left of the waterhole, near the swamp. Since he was by himself, he could not drive in the small *gabidji* wallabies which he sought, and at the same time spear them. However, by burning the surrounding spinfex he was able to drive them toward the waterhole. They would jump over the catchment and go to the swamp; then Wonambi would poke out his head from the cave, bite each of them and place them to one side, until a heap of *gabidji* accumulated. Gegi would collect these and take them to his camp, where he would cook the meat, giving some to Wonambi. He would get water, eat and go to sleep.

At another place named Guna-lawan [about six to seven miles east of Rerdina] there lived two men, Wadi Waldja (Eaglehawk) and Wadi Djalagu or Wiranggara [similar to a Waldja but with a white under-wing and 'chest', this bird lives in hollow logs and comes out at night, making the cry '*djer djer!*']. They were mates, and were camped under a *gogulga* kurrajong tree. Guna-lawan is not really a waterhole; all water was obtained from the roots of this tree. [The root is broken off, scraped at one side and a ridge cut with a stone knife; this is chewed or sucked, and the water is sweet.] These two men also hunted for *gabidji*, bringing them back to their camp, lighting a fire, cooking and eating them. Gegi saw their fire as they saw his. Gegi did not want them to visit his camp: instead, he went over to them, taking meat and giving it to them. They reciprocated. [This is a kind of ceremonial exchange, when two groups of people meet; they make friends, *yamadji*.] They also gave Gegi a *gogulga* root, but he sucked it only a little [as he had plenty of water himself]. He slept there. Next morning the two men went hunting, but Gegi did not want to go with them. When they were out of sight, he returned to his own waterhole.

The two men thought that Gegi must have water. They came back from hunting, cooked the *gabidji* they had killed, and obtained *gogulga* roots, some of which they put aside for Gegi. Gegi stayed away all day, but returned to the two men's camp at dusk; he brought cooked food and gave it to them. He sat facing in the direction of his waterhole, with his back to the men. Looking at the back of his head, they saw that it was wet and that there were scraps of green *wandaru-wandaru* water weed in his hair. They knew from these signs that he had water to drink. [The same water weed is placed on the surface of water in a wooden dish to keep out flies.]

Gegi slept. The other two men only pretended to sleep. In the middle of the night they got up and, each taking a club and a fire-stick, walked round the camp until they found Gegi's track. They followed it to Gegi's waterhole. They came round on the windward side and, with the breeze, smelt water; they also heard the ducks splashing. Coming nearer, they saw Wonambi's head protruding from the cave. Djalagu went to the left-hand side, Waldja to the right. Waldja, on reaching the place, jumped onto the rock where the cave was, smashing it in, trying to kill Wonambi, who was inside. Djalagu jumped from his side, also smashing in part of the rock. Wonambi withdrew further into the cave, trying to escape the falling rocks. Again, Waldja jumped, and this time went right inside the cave: Djalagu did the same from his side. [The holes they made are still there, the large one made by Waldja, the smaller by Djalagu.] They killed Wonambi; the ducks flew away; and the water ran away into the sand, leaving only the swamp. [It is not clear whether the swamp was formed in this way.] The two men also drank much of the water, leaving only a little. They skinned Wonambi, throwing his flesh away. Then they returned to their own camp and lay down without disturbing Gegi.

Next morning, Gegi, not suspecting anything untoward had occurred, suggested that he go out hunting by himself. The two men said nothing, but went out in the opposite direction. Gegi lit fires all the way to his waterhole, to drive the *gabidji* toward it. He watched and saw that they went past his catchment, where Wonambi would normally have been. He chased another *gabidji* — again it went past his place. He began to think something was wrong. He tried again with the same result, then for the fourth time he tried, and watched from a high sandhill. A *gabidji* jumped right over his waterhole. Now he knew for sure that there was something wrong. He began to cry. He reached his home and saw a small trickle of water spreading over the ground from the wrecked waterhole. He mourned. He saw the dead Wonambi: he mourned. He saw the tracks of the two men: he was angry.

He drank a little water and cried for a long time. Then he collected all the *gabidji* bones that were scattered over the ground, sharpened them and gathered them into a bundle which he took away to a particular place. He collected brush and twigs and made a *gabidji* nest, putting bushes all round. In the centre of the nest he made a pit in which he placed the sharpened bones, point upright, at the bottom; he covered this with grass. Then he made *gabidji* tracks leading toward the nest. Having completed this task, he went back to where the two men were waiting for him. He had no meat; he looked very sad; he sat down with bowed head. From this, they knew he had discovered what they had done. They gave him meat. He cried to himself. The two men slept. Later, Gegi went out and since the ground was wet from recent rain, he made further *gabidji* tracks leading to and from his trap. He returned and slept.

Next morning he spoke to the two men: 'We are one company, all friends: let the three of us go out walking [hunting].' They agreed. They went out together, with Gegi in front. He pretended he saw a *gabidji* track: 'I say, come and look here, meat for us!' [He refers to tracks he has made.] They followed them. He said, 'Don't come close, go that way'. [He meant, 'make a detour, don't go too close to the *gabidji*, otherwise they will be frightened'.] They came to where the nest was. Gegi lighted fires all round the spinifex, and told the two men to jump together onto the nest in order to catch the *gabidji*. They jumped, the grass gave way, and they fell into the pit onto the sharpened bones. The bones pierced them all over their bodies: they were unable to move. Gegi ran round in joy — they were punished for destroying his camp and the creatures in it. The two men called out for help, but he replied, 'No, you stay there and die!' And running round in joy, he sang:

> *gegi-la-landi*
> *njina gada nawuldji*
> Gegi's trap,
> Staying in the pit [with] heads [above].

[The trap 'nest' turned to rock: the rocks in the depression are the sharpened bones, and the other two rocks the two men. These may be seen at this place today.]

Gegi went a little distance from the trapped men and sang:

> *gan-ga-baganu gornu-runeru*
> *gumbilubilu yanu gan-ga-baganu*
> Jumping up backward, a long way,
> Gone jumping up farther away.

Gegi walked to a sandhill, away in the distance, leaving the two men. They tried to get out, moving themselves, gradually managing to crawl, pulling out the sharpened bones from their bodies. They crawled along and, lying there, eventually revived. They moved on slowly to their kurrajong tree and rested, and with their wounds healing, they began to feel better. They got charcoal and white ochre. Waldja crushed and pounded his charcoal and, rubbing it all over his body, made himself black; he put white feathers on his wings [arms] and body. Djalagu put white-ochre all over himself. Then Djalagu spoke: 'I will stay [sit down] in a hollow log!' And Waldja said, 'I will stay [sit down] at the top of the tree!' They changed to birds. Waldja flew away, crying '*gilyal-gilyal*'! And Djalagu flew away, crying '*djer djer*'!

Gegi, however, travelled on to the north.

The tranquillity of Gegi's existence at his own watering place is disturbed by the presence of Waldja and Djalagu within the vicinity. While Gegi is willing to exchange food with them according to local etiquette, he wanted his supply of water kept secret. But water from kurrajong roots is no substitute for ordinary water, and where a basic resource is concerned, it should be shared: Gegi is remiss in not doing so. The reaction of Waldja and Djalagu, destroying Gegi's home when they found that he did have water, was excessive: they went too far. So, what happened next was almost inevitable. The two-fold metamorphosis and, then, transformation of Waldja and Djalagu, is interesting. On the one hand, they left a tangible manifestation of themselves, imbued with their spirits, as a validation of the myth and of their own punishment. On the other hand, they turned into the actual birds whose names they bear within the context of the myth, so that all the birds of their species are living representatives of themselves.

The next story is a short Andingari myth from Ooldea told to R. Berndt in 1941.

168. SYMBOLIC INITIATION

A boy, Didji Mula (species of pigeon) was chasing a small *dalanggara* sand lizard: he frightened it with his spear. He saw it again, and threw his spear, missing it. It stayed there looking at the boy, then darted off. Mula went after it, threw his spear, and missed it once more. He did this again and again, without success. By this time he had gone some distance from his camp: he followed the lizard till sundown. He returned to where his mother was camped and got a fire-stick, but left her without saying anything. While the light held he followed the lizard's tracks; when it was dark he camped. Next morning, he continued, following the tracks. Dalanggara had by this time grown bigger. Pigeon Boy camped that night, and went on next morning. The lizard had now grown as large as a goanna, and Pigeon Boy had grown too: he still chased the 'goanna'. The boy's mother went out to look for him: she followed his tracks. She believed he was lost, and cried.

The lizard had grown even larger: 'he' was like a *yilba*, larger than a varanus lizard. [He had made himself into a small lizard in order to lure the boy away from his camp.] Pigeon was now a young man. They came to a particular place [unnamed] where he saw the tracks of a large number of goanna.

Yilba went into a hole that is now Ngadjina waterhole. All the other goanna entered after him. Pigeon could see their tails protruding. He built a large fire near the hole and pulled out one goanna by the tail. He looked at it — but it was not the one he had chased. He killed it and threw it aside. He pulled out another, but it was not the one he sought; he killed it and threw it aside. He did this again and again, thinking he would find 'his' goanna. He looked at the large heap of goanna. He pulled out another, but without success. [He was seeking 'his' goanna, which had special markings of fat and red-ochre.] He looked down the hole again and thought he saw the markings: he pulled it out, but discovered that the markings on this goanna had been transferred to it by its proximity to the one he sought. There was only one left in the hole: it must be Yilba. He clasped it firmly by its tail and pulled. He pulled and pulled so that a piece of it broke off in his hand. At the same time, Pigeon's own foreskin fell off.

Yilba had brought Pigeon all that way to circumcise him; Yilba called Pigeon *maradju* [wife's brother]. Pigeon was now an initiated young man. He cooked the goanna he had caught; and he tied up his hair into a bun at the back to signify his new status, and put feathers into it. He left Ngadjina, first tying up the meat into a bundle, and returned to his mother.

There are a number of myths of this kind which, while not substantiating initiation ritual, underline the importance of circumcision. Pigeon Boy was unaware of the real intention of the goanna, who was really his initiator (being Pigeon's *maradju*, he was the appropriate person to circumcise him). The rapid growth of both the goanna and Pigeon Boy emphasises the initiatory process. In this myth the goanna is not treated as a mythic character.

The following myth is also of the Andingari group, and was told to R. Berndt in 1941 at Ooldea.

169. THE MIRACULOUS CLUBS

The Wadi Gudjara, Two Men, Yungga and Djimbi, travelled from the north-west of Ooldea and camped at a particular waterhole where they cut some *gurara* needle wood from two trees and shaped it into two clubs, one each. They left these in their camp while they went out hunting.

Returning, they saw carpet snake tracks that led from the bushes where the two clubs had been hidden. They looked for their clubs, but 'they had gone, turned into two snakes!'

The Two Men followed these tracks, and coming a little way, sang:

> *yidil-gudjara wanbularala*
> *gurei-ri nudjal-dangi yidil*
> Two carpet snake tracks,
> Swishing their tails, moving away.

They continued on and met another man, Wadi Gudara-gudara [Or Gudjara-gudjara, 'Two-two': a relative, but kin affiliation undefined.] The Wadi Gudjara asked him to follow the two snakes, while they returned to their camp. Gudara-gudara agreed, and came along 'behind' the two snakes.

In front of the snakes at Inderi waterhole were camped a group of Dreaming children (Didji Mudila-mudila). They belonged to no one; they were just wandering about. That morning they had gone out hunting: early in the afternoon, they returned to Inderi with goanna and possum. On their way back, however, two of the boys made a detour, going forward while the others came on behind. They saw the carpet snakes' tracks. Throwing down the meat they were carrying for the others to pick up, they followed the tracks, each carrying a stout stick from a nearby tree. They saw the snakes go into a burrow. The two Mudila-mudila sat down, one at each of the two openings, directly opposite each other. They began to dig. Putting in their hands and arms, they tried to grasp a snake. Each boy was on his knees with the full length of his arm extended down the hole. So close were they together in the separate holes they had made that their penises protruded into the hole and lengthened. Each grasped the other's penis, thinking they had caught a carpet snake. But then each called out, 'You've caught my penis, let go!'

They withdrew from the holes and looked around: they saw only their penises, and tracks indicating departing snakes. Following the tracks they came to a sand-ridge, and looked down across the country. They saw those two snakes 'walking along together'. They had left their sticks at the burrow. Now they picked up new sticks, and coming down from the ridge they attempted to 'round up' the snakes. They saw the snakes' heads standing upright: one boy threw a stick, but it missed them. The snakes attacked them and just 'missed' one of the boys as he stumbled after throwing the stick. He got up quickly, and both boys ran back and stood some little distance away. In the meantime, the other boys had followed the snakes' tracks; they, too, climbed the sand-ridge and from there could see the snakes and the two boys. They rushed down and encircled the snakes, throwing their sticks.

By this time, Wadi Gudara-gudara had reached the sand-ridge. He saw the children and called out: 'Children, look out for a spear, stand back!' The children moved back out of the way, while the man threw his spear from the sand-ridge. The two snakes were lying together: the spear pierced the neck of one and also that of the other, impaling both. At that moment, the snakes 'flashed' their tails so that all the children standing nearby were scattered, some being killed.

The spear fell from the snakes' bodies and the two went into a small goanna hole. Wadi Gudara-gudara strode across and picked up his spear. He saw the hole, which had two openings. He covered one of these, and at the other he piled bushes which he set alight. The smoke from this went into the hole: he could hear the fire roaring as he blew [actually breathing the smoke into the hole because of its smallness]. He kept on blowing the smoke in, but the snakes did not emerge. He looked round for their tracks but could see none. He stood up and looked in each direction. To the north, in the far distance, he could see smoke issuing from the broken branches of the original two needle wood trees from which the clubs, which had 'turned' into snakes, had been made by the Wadi Gudjara.

Wadi Gudara-gudara walked slowly back to the sand-ridge, where he sat watching the smoking trees. After a while he saw two stars, very bright, come out from the smoke, travel across the sky from south to west, and then fall: they were *bandala* or *mala* 'shooting stars' which local people say foretells a death. He knew these were the spirits (*gordi*) of the two snakes: 'they had come out, their *gordi* had gone away!' Wadi Gudara-gudara travelled west, following the stars.

When Wadi Gudara-gudara saw that smoke from the two trees at what he regarded as his 'home' waterhole, he sang:

boyoli boyoli boyu boilai
yanu baganu
Smoke emerging,
Rising, gone away.

When he went back and sat on the sand-ridge, looking across at the smoke, he sang,

gudara-gudara
lalildjara nyina
[Myself] Gudara-gudara,
A big man, sitting [there].

The stars, the *gordi* of the two carpet snakes, had fallen a long way away. Wadi Gudara-gudara eventually came to where they were at Biana waterhole, located west to north-west of Lake Darlot in the country of the

Walwulu. He killed, cooked and ate them at that place. And when he killed the snakes he sang:

bilaru-bani gadin gilganu
mai-yumbana wambada nari bilaru
Snake skins lifted high,
[There they] lie.

Wadi Gudara-gudara remained at that place.

Across the Western Desert there are many myths about the Wadi Gudjara and their miraculous deeds. Their shape-changing clubs, like their magical boomerang in other contexts, indicate their inherent power. The Mudila-mudila, on the other hand, do occasionally appear, as in this case, and have no claim to mythic parentage; while they are 'children', they are well-developed, hence the reference to their penises. The carpet snakes are Dreaming. In spite of being impaled by Gudara-gudara, they escape and transfer themselves to their 'origin' trees; their spirits become shooting stars, heralding their own death. However, their physical bodies remained for Gudara-gudara to consume.

The following myth has Andingari, Ngalia, Yanggundjara, Wirangu and Kukata associations, and was told to R. Berndt at Ooldea in 1941.

170. EVENTS CONCERNING MOON MAN

The Wadi Gudjara, Two Men, came to Wondina waterhole where Wonambi, a Rainbow Snake, lived. They looked in the water, but could not see him. Milbali (white Goanna) and Yungga (black Goanna) are the Wadi Gudjara. Milbali kept watch while Yungga returned to Guli, not very far away. There Yungga obtained some long sticks which he broke from trees and came back to Wondina. Here he dug a hole at the side of the waterhole and inserted one of his long sticks to drive Wonambi from his 'home'. [The hole he dug may still be seen at this place.] However, there was no Wonambi: he had escaped. Yungga looked through the tunnel he had made and saw light at the other end: he called out to Milbali to open it further. This opening is called Gadal-galbada. The Two Men climbed through, but there was nothing. Wonambi had gone travelling westward.

They had piled up their objects and left them near Wondina. Now they collected them: their spears, fire-sticks, spear-throwers, clubs, shields, waist-bands and magical boomerang, among other things. They went on to Guliguli [Guli is on one side of Wondina, Guliguli on the other] and held a ceremony. There is a large tree here under which they sat and sang:

> guli buruna munga
> dundju-dundju guli-guradu yilgari wu djun-gadi guli
> At Guli, pounding the ground, at night
> Under the dundju-dundju tree.

They travelled on to Wilirung-gana waterhole, where a sand-ridge was called Bira [Moon]. Wadi Bira, Moon Man, had dug a large hole in which he was resting. To his right were his fire-sticks; to his left a wili which was constructed from several spears joined together, with a bunch of dalyuru feathers at its apex. [This served as a decoy for kangaroos that were attracted by the feathers.] The large Bira sandhill spread behind Wadi Bira and served as a wind-break. At one end of it was his kangaroo djandu skin bag containing different kinds of stone 'knives'. [That is, implements such as migadu adzes; bunyuru; round bira cutting tools; wadana; mudjilina; wadinga; large gadul-walga stone knives; and an ilabi, a long flake about nine inches long.]

The Wadi Gudjara on seeing the wili struck it down with their magical boomerang. Wadi Bira, hearing this, shouted out to his dogs: 'Baianu!' (Bite them!). When he learnt who they were, however, Bira and the Wadi Gudjara became friendly, and they sang together.

> gadei-yawuru wilinbaga gadei-yawuru dali-dalinba
> wili gadei-yawuru dalinba rilidji-rilidji
> Spears together that wili at the sandhill,
> Breaking it.

The Wadi Gudjara then left Bira and travelled southward.

Wadi djilbi, old man, Bira picked up his fire-sticks and the spears he had used in making his wili and, putting his bag of stone implements on his back, went westward; but then he turned east and reached Wadinga waterhole. [There is a big hole here in which he rested; and he left a large number of wadinga stone implements which may be picked up in the sand today. Mainly, such wadinga were used for circumcision — hence their name: 'into man' wadi.] After resting he went farther east to his home camp, Duruna. [It was said at Ooldea that Bira came originally from Port Lincoln, on Eyre Peninsula.]

[The scene changes.] From Duruna he travelled north to Bulbara [probably Poochera, also on Eyre Peninsula] and then west to Bindi

['Pendis'? west of Tarcoola]. He walked on to Winbara (Wynbring), where he saw the tracks of a large number of Dreaming Wonambi. He continued on to Adilina, where he camped; then to Gadara, where he killed a carpet snake. He went on to Bira (where he met the Two Men): there he cooked and ate his meal of snake meat. While he slept, the fire 'got away' and burnt out all the surrounding countryside, forming a lake called Birana [probably Lake Bring: it was after this that the Two Men came to Bira.] Sometime afterward Bira left Birana and went on to Paling, where he killed another carpet snake, and then on to Mubana. He continued to Burina, where he saw the tracks of the Wadi Keniga, Spotted Cat Men. Bira followed their tracks, and met them not far from Duruna. They fought until they were exhausted. The Keniga went to one side and, dying, were metamorphosed as rocks; Bira went to the other side and he too died, turning to stone.

[The scene changes again.] Wadi Keniga [first noted here as one man], came from the west, from the Ngalia. As he travelled along, he sang:

gulada djin-galba waruwaru gulada
mang-gu djinu gulada
Prong of the spear, straightened over fire.
Leaving the imprint of the spear[-thrower].

nganu balan nani
dalga miru
Attaching the spear point,
Fitting it on to the spear-thrower.

lalalba muru-nara warumba ganduna
webu-webu nari mulgaru gangarara warumba ganduna webu-webu nari
Cutting up the *waru* rock wallaby;
Cutting its chest and tail with a stone knife.

Travelling along singing, Wadi Keniga had come from Mamudu-langu. On the way he saw the tracks of Minma Mila, Mosquito Woman: there were many of them. He followed them. At Miladuna, Mila began to dig the soak that had been filled in with sand. There she was, throwing out the sand behind her. Wadi Keniga watched, hidden, because Mila was a *mamu* woman. He sneaked up and killed her. He left this place, but had not gone far when he saw Moon Man, Wadi Bira, returning from the east. Keniga camped at Galdjana, while Bira stayed at Iduldu. Next morning Bira went out hunting and killed a carpet snake at Gadara. He did this in the following way. There were actually two Gadara: he poked a long stick through the first, and the carpet snake came out from the second waterhole. He put the snake into his bag and carried it to Birana [as above]. There is a deep hole here with a long rock formation. He cooked the snake, and while it was cooking, he lay down in the hole to sleep [see above]. The flames from the fire spread to some *gubaru* grass, burning out the surrounding countryside. The burnt-out country is now a large clay pan.

After meeting the Two Men, Bira left his camp and continued homeward. Keniga came up from behind: he had his magical [sorcery] stick: he wanted to fight. In the morning, he saw where Bira was camped. Bira turned back and saw him. The two men fought on an open place not far from Birana where, to the left, is a large sandhill. At first they used boomerangs as weapons. One of the boomerangs broke open Bira's skin bag and all his stone implements poured out and were scattered in the sand. They each picked up long stone knives and fought with them, cutting each other. [Today, among the many stone tools found in the sand there are some with red markings: they have been stained with the blood of these two Dreaming men. A large rock to one side is the empty kangaroo skin bag.]

After fighting in this way, the two men were exhausted. Wadi Bira lay down by a big sandhill, while Keniga lay down a little farther away behind the sandhill. Each built around himself a wind-break: there they died, each in his wind-break, and turned to stone. [See above; the story-teller remarked that Keniga was of the *garimara* section, a 'big man' from the mallee country, and a sorcerer; Bira was of the *burong* section, and he was a 'short man'.]

In the meantime, the Wadi Gudjara continued north to Inmil where they found a mallee hen's egg. Minma Nganamara, Mallee Hen Woman, had covered it up in the sand. The Two Men frightened her away, then dug out her egg and ate it. They watched her fly away. They held a ceremony about this.

Mallee Hen Woman went northward to another place, also called Inmil, where she laid another egg, covering it up. The Two Men followed her, and again stole the egg and ate it. And they made another ceremony about it.

This myth is included not simply because of its intrinsic interest, but for its structural treatment by the story-teller. It is reproduced here in exactly the way it was told: it is not set out in a chronological sequence of events, as most myths are. There are a number of clear-cut scenes (eleven all told), two of which are repeated. The story starts off (1) with the appearance of the Wadi Gudjara, the Two Men, who are seeking Wonambi. This is followed (2) by their meeting with Moon Man, including the destruction of his *wili* and, afterward, their friendship. The Two Men leave him, and Moon goes east to his home area (3). But he leaves there to go north (4), and on the way sees Wonambi tracks (the same Wonambi the Two Men were looking for). Through carelessness on Moon's part, his camp-fire spreads and burns out the local countryside, forming a claypan (5). The time dimension is now changed, since this last event took place *after* Bira had met the Two Men. Moon meets Keniga; they fight (6) and are killed, and metamorphosed as rocks.

The scene reverts to Keniga coming south. He meets the Mosquito woman and kills her (7); he also sees, but does not meet, Moon (8). However, Moon goes hunting; and his cooking fire burns out the country (9) — which introduces another time change. Moon continues homeward, followed by Keniga, and the two of them fight (10); Moon's stone implements are scattered and both die and are metamorphosed. Finally, the Two Men travel north (11) and 'steal' Mallee Hen's eggs.

The chronological sequence is as follows. (1) the appearance of the Two Men; (4) Moon comes northward; (7) Keniga comes south and kills the Mosquito woman; (8) Keniga sees Moon from a distance; (2) the Two Men meet Moon and destroy his *wili*; (11) the Two Men leave Moon and go northward; (5) and (9) Moon's fire spreads across the countryside; (3) Moon goes east; (6) and (10) Keniga catches up with Moon and they fight to the death, and are metamorphosed: end of sequence.

The problem faced by the story-teller was how to tell the story and, at the same time, cope with two primary events: firstly, the meeting of the Two Men with Moon, and secondly, the meeting of Keniga with Moon, while simultaneously treating Moon as the pivotal character. The version we present is an example of how he tackled it. However, there are two further points to keep in mind. Adherence to an exact chronology regarding the mythic events was not important, since in this context we are dealing with cyclical, Dreaming time. Also, two people were involved in assisting the narrator in the telling of the story. One man came from Mamudu, just south of the Mann Range (where Keniga killed Mosquito Woman); the other was from a little north-east of Cook, and was associated with Mubana and Paling (Peiling), north of Ooldea, but not too far. Both Mubana and Peiling were close to Birana (the Moon place). This man also had linkages with Inmil (where the Two Men 'stole' the second egg of Mallee Hen Woman). The narrator had Wirangu-Andingari affiliations. This meant that each of the three men had a special interest in at least one of the mythic characters noted in the story.

Moon is not a popular figure in Western Desert mythology, mainly because he was always chasing after women, and is associated with death. Keniga's wish to kill Moon was due to his seduction of a mythic woman; at the same time, Keniga is the 'patron' of sorcerers, and the pair were unevenly matched in their fight.

As a further contribution to the Wadi Gudjara repertoire, the next story is from Balgo, told to R. Berndt in 1960 and is related to the Ngadi and Gugadja people.

---

171. THE DISINTEGRATION OF TICK WOMAN

Two small girls named Yambeyambara, of the *nambidjin* sub-section, lived with their mother, a *nungurei* woman. They were Dreaming Dildi (Kangaroo Ticks), camped at Djamidjabu soak and spring water. The Dildi mother made a long stick with eaglehawk feathers bunched and attached to one end. She gave this to her daughters, telling them to wave it so its feathers rustled, to frighten kangaroo rats into their holes where they could easily be caught. While the children were engaged in this pursuit, their mother went to hunt in the surrounding bush. When she heard them call out, she hurried back to help them dig out the rats. In this way they had a plentiful supply of meat.

The Two Men walked round and then returned to Djamidjabu, but saw no Dildi. However, the Dildi could hear the Two Men as they sheltered within the spring: actually, from underneath, they smelled the Men. When the Men left, the Dildi emerged. Leaving her daughters at this place, the mother followed the tracks of the Two Men to Wiridji hill [so named because they tied on their waist-bands there]. Then they walked on to Nyunbalareii claypan and, going north, continued to Djuluda claypan. The Dildi followed them, lighting fires all the way along, hoping to kill them. At Djuluda the Two Men painted their bodies with ochred circular designs, and danced. Then they went on to Djabila-djabila rockhole (north of Balgo). Dildi continued to follow them to Yirilangu claypan. The Two Men were *maban* 'clever men'; they carried water in their hair, in their heads and in their moustaches ['water lived in their hair, solidified; they carried it like a "billycan"']. At Buduruduru soak, the Two Men sat down; they were frightened. Dildi had encircled them with fire, with burning spinifex. To escape this, they went under the ground and came out at Bulgadji soak, where they camped. Then they continued to Yundadjun-gu claypan, where they built wind-breaks [which may be seen today].

By this time Dildi had walked a long way; one of her shoulders dropped off. She continued travelling with one side [shoulder], but soon that fell off too. At Yugubulu soak, a leg fell off; at Weding soak, her other leg fell off. Then various parts of her body fell off — her stomach, her ribs and other parts, until only her head was following the two men. Then her eyes dropped out near Langgura-gadal and, finally, her empty head rolled away. [All along the track, from Yundadjun-gu, the various parts of Dildi's body were metamorphosed as rocks and remain there today.]

At Langgura-gadal, the Two Men cut a hook for their spears. It was here, too, that Djandu, a mythic dog, 'came out'. One of the Two Men patted Djandu, though the other warned him to be careful: 'It might bite you!' It bit Yunggamaru and, holding him in its mouth, dived down into the water of Langgura-gadal. The other immediately dived down after them to rescue his brother. He hit Djandu with a spear: it dropped Yunggamaru, only to swallow him. Nyindaga speared the dog and, as he did so, it vomited Yunggamaru. His brother carried him back to the camp and stretching him out put *maban* pearlshells into his body and waited for him to revive. They camped there for a while, and then went on to Yunbu billabong. The Two Men dived into this place, where their spirits remain.

This story enhances the reputation of the power of the Two Men. As in the myth of Gegi (No. 167) the Dildi do not want visitors, and the mother is intent on getting rid of them — in spite of their being of the same sub-section category as the two Dildi daughters. However, the Dildi mother goes too far (in her effort to take revenge, and in the distance she goes from her own home). Her final disintegration symbolises the two points. The miraculous revival of one brother, Yunggamaru, by the other, Nyindaga, emphasises the power of the Two Men as *mabanba* (doctors).

The next myth is from Ooldea, told to R. Berndt in 1941 and is Andingari.

172. THE *MAMU* REVENGE

Djilbi Dulina, 'Old man' Dulina, was a big man, 'like a *mamu*'. He and his wife, Minma Dulina, had two children, a boy and a girl, and they came from Bagalan, not far from Mandi-bagalam and Galin: it was at Bagalan that their children were born. The woman went out hunting for meat, her husband for wild dingo. He speared one and brought it back to their camp, where they cooked and ate it. Each day Dulina hunted. One day he saw the tracks of two *mamu* children. He followed them for some distance and then made camp. He constructed a *wili* decoy [see Myth 170], but left it and went to hunt rats. Then he continued to follow the tracks of the *mamu* children and found they had entered a hole. Dulina repeatedly stamped on the burrow, which collapsed: he put in his hand to drag them out. He removed one *mamu* child and strangled it, throwing it aside. He heard the other child running around inside the blocked cavity, trying to find a way out. Bending down, he put his hand in again, but moving it around could feel nothing. He dug out the cavity, cleaning the inside of it, but saw no sign of the child. He looked all around outside: he knew it could not escape, because in stamping on the hole he had broken its leg. 'It can't go far,' he thought. Leaving his search, he made a fire and cooked the dead *mamu* child. He returned to his own camp, taking the meat with him, thinking he would go after the other child on the following day. He left that cooked *mamu* by his hut.

His two children ran out and saw the meat; they broke off one of its hands at the wrist and ran back to show their mother: 'Mother, see the *mamu* hand!' [In the cooking, the fingers of the *mamu* child's hand had folded back in a particular way, with the small finger above the third. 'When a *mamu's* hand is 'cooked' it always takes this shape.'] The Dulina children held the hand up to show their mother. Immediately she identified it. In shock, she knocked the hand from their grasp; it fell some distance from her. She was upset. It was the hand of one of her sister's children: they were like her own children, and now her husband had killed one! [This implies that she, too, is a *mamu*.] She got up from where she was sitting and picking up a circular *dali* ring pad [used by a woman for balancing a wooden dish of water on her head] she threw it away, she threw away her other possessions in the direction she intended to go — her digging stick, wooden dish, and so on. Without saying anything to her husband and children, she got her fire-stick and walked quietly away. She would not see her husband again, because he had killed her sister's child!

Old man Dulina and his two children ate the *mamu* meat. Next day he left the children at the home camp and walked out to the *mamu* hole, taking his *wili*. Arriving there, he saw the hole and the ground where he had dug, and he saw where the injured *mamu* had escaped. He looked around, thinking it could not have gone far. He saw the place where the child had sat down and then got up again, limping away. Dulina continued to track him. As he strode along he saw other *mamu* tracks leading into Nundon. Altogether there were five separate tracks, and one of these belonged to the lame *mamu*. Dulina followed these and saw that they all led to one hole. He prepared his *wili*; he could hear the *mamu* knocking on the inside walls of the cavity. They were aware Dulina was there and threw out dust to annoy him. He stamped on the hole, and with his feet he could feel the *mamu* inside. He killed them one by one, the five of them, but the lame *mamu* he could not find. He dug all around; he got a long stick and poked it all over the ground. Still he could not find the *mamu* child. He cleared away the sand and earth from the remains of the hole; he sifted it through his fingers, but there was no sign of the child!

Making a fire, he gathered together the bodies of the dead *mamu* and roasted them. When they were cooked, he removed them from the coals, wrapped them and tied them up with bushes and twine. He swung the bundle over his left shoulder and returned to his camp, where he and his children ate the meat, leaving some for the next day. [There is no reference to Minma Dulina, who had gone away.] There were two camps at this waterhole. Next morning they awoke, finished the meat that had been left over, and slept again. That same day, Dulina tied up more eaglehawk feathers for his *wili* and told his children to remain there while he went out to stamp on more holes. 'I will get more meat!' he said.

Leaving them there he went to Nundon, where he had killed the five *mamu*. [The story-teller said that Nundon was about fifty miles from Bagalan and Mandi-bagalan: he covered the journey quickly and easily because he was a big man and took big strides.] He saw where he had sifted the sand and the nearby hole from which the lame *mamu* had escaped. He had emerged just where Dulina had been sitting, watching the cooking *mamu*. Seeing the tracks of the lame *mamu*, he followed them for a long way, as far as Wedrunbi. Coming into this place, he camped there for the night; he had come too far to return home. Next morning he continued tracking until he saw a larger number of *mamu*: men, women and children, their tracks crossing those of the lame *mamu:* they were out hunting. However, he went on, following the lame *mamu*. Coming along a little farther, he saw tracks of *mamu* going in every direction. He climbed a sand-ridge, where he could see the *mamu* camp — a big cave (Wedrun-bidal). He saw that his *wili* feathers were loose. He fastened them on securely, tightening the fibre, but they came undone: the feathers fell! [a sign indicating forthcoming disaster]. He felt unwell and lay full-length on his belly. He was thinking, 'What is the matter with me; why have the eaglehawk feathers become loose?' Getting up again, he retied the feathers and stood upright, holding the *wili*. Looking down toward Wedrun-bidal he saw two *mamu* running out of the cave holding shields: they came dancing along. Dulina cried out, 'You can't catch me!' He came up to them, brandishing his *wili*, trying out its effectiveness.

There were many holes at Wedrun-bidal, and he tried them all. He saw dust issuing from them, clouds of dust. He went from one hole to the next, poking them with his *wili*. By this time he was in the middle of the camp of holes (*bidi-ngura*). He stamped on them. Then, groping about with his hands, he pulled out one or two *mamu*. At that, all the *mamu* emerged and broke up Dulina's *wili*. He ran away, with *mamu* hanging on to the remaining end of the *wili*, which he continued to hold. They climbed up his arms, biting him, and gradually getting him down. They swarmed over him — 'he was a very big man!' They killed him. Then the lame *mamu* appeared: He called out, 'I want his testes and penis. Give them to me, they're mine!' The others pulled out the penis and testes and gave them to him.

The *mamu* rested, while Dulina lay there flat on his back, dead. Now, Dulina had big breasts with large nipples: the *mamu* squeezed these and found they contained milk. [The explanation given for this was that Dulina's children had not been weaned when their mother left, so Dulina had suckled them and kept them supplied with milk.] When the *mamu* saw the milk they had squeezed out, they knew he had children. They cooked Dulina and ate the meat. Next day, they assembled as a large group of *mamu* men and retraced Dulina's tracks back to his home camp: they took several days to reach it. Before coming into Bagalan they obtained feathers and put these in their hair; they also decorated themselves with ochre.

In the meantime, Dulina's two children [who had a presentiment that something had happened to their father] gathered all the animal and *mamu* bones lying around the camp. They sharpened these at one end [like *miri-darlga:* that is, *miri-djining-gari,* 'from shin-bones of dead persons'], and bundled them together to await the return of their father. The *mamu* came closer, and the Dulina children thought it was their father returning: they called out, 'Here, father!' Hearing this, the *mamu* called back, '*waul!*' The children said to each other, 'He sings out strangely: another one, father, sings out loudly!'. Standing outside their hole [cave], the children saw the *mamu* coming nearer; they knew then that these were *warmala* [revenge expedition] *mamu* because of the ochred designs on their bodies. Coming first toward the children's camp as a group, the *mamu* divided into two columns, and encircled it from each side. They threw their clubs, but missed the children, who disappeared inside their hole, taking the bundle of sharpened bones with them. The hole was S-shaped and they sat down on the inside level, away from the curved entrance. There they sat each holding a sharpened bone in each hand. The *mamu* dug all round the hole and at the opening: 'Come on, dig it out!' they said. 'Have a look inside!' One man went in.

However, among these *mamu*, in the group to which the lame *mamu* belonged [he was also related to the Dulina children as a mother's sister's son] were two of the children's mother's brothers [their uncles, *gamaru*]. ['Old man' Dulina had married a *mamu* woman from this particular group. Dulina was not really a *mamu* himself, only 'like a *mamu*'; he was a giant, his wife was small like a real *mamu*.] These two uncles were doctors: they had *maban* pearlshell discs between their eyes [a magical eye 'which enabled them to see through anybody or anything'. They could, for instance, see where the two Dulina children were hidden: 'their eyes x-rayed the ground'.] Knowing this, and because they were the children's uncles, they sat directly above the children — and the other *mamu* did not dig there.

The *mamu* dug all around. As one came near to where the two children were, they stuck a pointed bone into him. Each *mamu* who was pierced in this way thought he had been bitten by a *mandalbai* bull ant. They looked all around but could not find the children. Another lot of *mamu* began to dig: they, too, were pierced and came up from the hole, to be replaced by another lot; they went into the hole, four at a time, but each was pierced. Those *mamu* lay there sick, 'too hot'; they were tired and ill. Others continued to poke round with sticks, but they could not find those children.

All the *mamu* were now lying down. Some died from their wounds, while others went away, dying along their homeward track. None reached Wedrun-bidal. The boulders strewn along the track from Bagalan to Nundon, to Wedrunbi, to the *mamu* cave, are their metamorphosed bodies.

The two uncles waited until all the other *mamu* had gone. Then they told the children to come out and return to their mother, giving them directions as to where she would be found. The uncles spoke together: 'You two children, walk along: you take up the *mamu* spears, you take them, tie them up; go along and leave this place.' The uncles returned to their own place, Wedrun-bidal, passing the dead (metamorphosed) bodies of their relatives. The children gathered together the scattered spears of the *mamu*, tied them into bundles, and set off in the opposite direction to that taken by their uncles; they travelled east to Wadududa, where their mother was camped. They stayed with her for a long time; but one night they climbed into the sky, where they now remain as stars.

As we saw in Chapter 4, the unpredictable and often vicious *mamu* are of the Dreaming as well as being a continuing malignant presence, believed to be physically manifested in the land, inveterate enemies of human beings. In this story, however, Dulina is a giant and his wife a *mamu*: she and her children are closely related to the *mamu* children, one of whom Dulina killed while the other he hunted. In this respect the myth emphasises kin loyalty as well as revenge. But it also reveals an anomalous situation, and not only physically — a marriage between a large giant and a small *mamu*, virtually two different 'species'. Especially, he sets out to kill some of his wife's relatives, and brings one back for her and her children to eat. Did he *know* they were her relatives? If not, why not? If he did know, this in itself raises some interesting questions. Another unusual point is that the father was able to breast-feed his children after their mother left them.

A further story from Ooldea told to R. Berndt in 1941 is Mandjindji and Yanggundjara.

173.   THE REVENGE OF DJIDILBA

'Old man' Djidilba (Kangaroo Flea) came from somewhere to the west of Ooldea where he had been married, after which his wife had been abducted. He reached Yunidju [north of Ooldea] where he met and camped with his *narumba* (a mother's brother's daughter). She was Minma Teiru, a sister of Wadi Teiru (Tiger snake Man). He told her about his trouble. He drank a great deal of water there and, leaving her, went back west in search of his wife. He came to Walbudjara where a large group of people was camped, among whom was his stolen wife. He sneaked up to the edge of the encampment and worked magic so that all of them — men, women and children, the old and the young — went out hunting and food collecting. From behind some bushes he watched them take a special track, then he hid himself and went to sleep until the late afternoon. He was awakened by their noisy return: he saw his wife among them. They all went to their camps to cook the meat and other things they had got, and rested.

Djidilba broke off a couple of leafy branches from a tree. Holding one in each hand he began to rustle them and wave them from side to side. A strong wind began to blow. It swept across the camp, gathering up all the people's belongings and taking them skyward. When Djidilba stopped waving his branches, all the things fell back into their right positions. The people were very frightened. Again he made wind, and each time he did this their possessions were taken into the sky and then returned to their correct places. By this time the people were terrified; they huddled around their fires, eating their meat. By this time, too, the sun had set and it was becoming dark. Again Djidilba rustled his branches, waving them strenuously. A great wind arose and, as it swept across the camp, caught up all the people and all their things. It carried them skyward, forming a mass which then fell earthward, entering the ground and forming Walbudjara waterhole. All the people were killed, including Djidilba's wife. Their spears, spear-throwers and other objects turned into snakes of different varieties but the mass which constituted all the people and their huts and wind-breaks formed a monstrous snake — the great Wonambi. [Now nobody, no human being, may drink the water at Walbudjara, because Wonambi would swallow them. But various creatures may drink there. Around Walbudjara the country is bare, because everything disappeared in the great wind. And in the distance the cry of Wonambi may be heard, like rumbling thunder.]

Old man Djidilba returned to Yunidju. On the way there he stayed for a while with some *malu* (Kangaroo) men, then he went on. Approaching Yunidju he smelled something quite horrible. On reaching there he found Tiger snake Woman, his *narumba*, dead: it was the stench from her rotting body that he had smelled. In sorrow, he lay down at some little distance from the corpse, and he, too, died. And at that place are two large stones, which are the bodies of Djidilba and his *narumba*.

This story lends itself to dramatic presentation. It was told to R.M. Berndt in a high-pitched voice. The men who were listening were silent. Old Mushabin, as he told it, drew the waterholes and tracks of Djidilba in the sand, and acted out the movements of Djidilba as he made the wind, stretching his arms outward and upward, then bringing them down to the sand and pushing his hands into it, all the while making a whistling sound resembling the wind. It was a momentous performance.

The story itself is compact, succinct, and to the point. Djidilba has wreaked vengeance on the group of people responsible for the abduction of his wife. But behind that was his attachment to his *narumba*, a matri-cross-cousin, who in some Western Desert dialects may be called *guri* (a spouse): much depends on the closeness of the relationship.

We turn now to a Daly River myth associated with several contiguous language groups, but mainly the Ngulugwongga (Mulluk-Mulluk or Malag-Malag). It was told to R. Berndt in 1946.

174. THE DEATH OF CROCODILE

Yingi, 'old man' Crocodile, lived with his two wives, Djin and Berid (Pigmy Geese), in the jungle at Barei-wulgidj, near Bangeran billabong. At Mudanggi on Yinayariginga billabong, members of a *djaboi* ceremonial group were encamped around a small hollow which was their dancing ground. [Mudanggi later became known as 'Wilkinson's place'.] From his jungle, Crocodile saw the *djaboi* men go out hunting ducks [various kinds noted] at the top of the Yinayariginga billabong along the plain. These ducks had sores and were unable to use their wings. [Comment: 'they were as if *mururu*', that is, sorcerised, but this probably refers to their moulting.] When the *djaboi* people returned, Crocodile went over to join them, but although they had plenty of ducks, they would not give him any to eat. Nevertheless he joined in the *djaboi* dancing, and when it was dark he returned to his jungle home. His two wives did not leave the jungle.

Next morning he saw the *djaboi* group go out again for ducks, and on their return he went over to Mudanggi to join them. However, they didn't give him any ducks. He sat talking with them, and when they began to sing, he danced. Then he returned home.

He told his wives that the *djaboi* people had given him nothing: he was angry. Next morning he went out to cut blood-wood to make a *wara-wara* club or throwing stick; he painted it white, with red-ochre at the top. While the *djaboi* men were out hunting, he went to Mudanggi with his club and then returned to the jungle. He watched them come back, and again went over to them, taking his spear-thrower but no spears. On the way he smeared himself with horizontal bands of mud. Arriving at the *djaboi* camp, he talked with them, and when they sang he danced by himself. When he had finished, they all cried out for him to dance once more. 'Then you can go back to your camp early,' they said. He danced once more, then stopped, and suddenly pulled out his *wara-wara* from where he had hidden it. All the *djaboi* people looked at him in fear, and tried to run away. Going after them, Yingi threw his club, hitting two to three of them; then ran on again, and killed another three or four. He placed his *wara-wara* upright in the ground at Mudanggi, where it became a *bungu* bloodwood tree [which is now dead]. He returned to his two wives, and told them what had happened. They said, 'Why didn't you kill them all? Some have run away!' But he replied, 'I killed them all!'

Next morning his two wives went by themselves to Charley's Creek, which runs into the Daly River at Djinan-derara. A large group of Malagmalag men were camped there fishing. The two women had a message from Yingi, that he would visit them next day. The Malag-malag people gave the women cat-fish and barramundi and other fish to take back to him, and they returned to their husband. 'Ah,' he said, 'You bring fish.' 'Yes,' they replied, 'they want to see you tomorrow.' 'All right, I'll wash myself, I haven't been there before.'

Next morning he went to Djinan-derara. 'Old man has come!' they said. 'I haven't been to your country before,' Yingi replied. 'There are plenty of fish here. I haven't walked about in this place. I'll leave the jungle, I like it here. I'd like to stay here; it's no good my living in the jungle.'

These people were camped on one side of the creek near its mouth at Djinan-derara as well as on the other side of the Daly River, opposite, at Djadi-ramdjed. At the mouth of the creek [at Djinan-derara] they had placed their *biyarig* [an oval drum fish basket made from jungle-grass twine, with a one-way entrance for fish]. 'There's a *biyarig* there,' they told him. 'That belongs to you, and it is full of fish!' [This is the Dreaming site of Biyarig, which is a hollow tree trunk.] Yingi went down to the bank and waded out and pulled in the *biyarig*. He opened it up and pulled out the cat-fish, tossing them into a heap. Then he crawled inside to get the rest of the fish. As he did so, all the surrounding people, who were sitting looking, jumped up and lifted the *biyarig* and began rolling it up and down until the barbs of the cat-fish still left inside wounded Yingi; then they rolled it into the Daly River. The people were frightened. 'Suppose he stays there as a rock, as a Dreaming!' they said.

Those people at Djadi-ramdjed [on the other side of the river] were looking, and they saw what had happened. Wonggid (Dog) 'made himself' into a dog and began howling when he saw that basket, with Yingi inside, rolling into the middle of the Daly. He ran away, but the people called him back. He jumped into the water and swam. The people watched Dog swimming over the place where the basket had sunk down, and saw Yingi appear as a crocodile — no longer a man. He caught Dog and held him under the water until he was dead. Then that Crocodile emerged with Dog and spoke: 'Why did you throw me into the water? I don't sit down as a rock or go Dreaming. I go another way! Nobody can come swimming in this river. Look out for me! You people, dogs, wallabies, and other creatures, be careful! You will all be frightened of me!'

This myth explains how Yingi became a crocodile, and why he is so dangerous. Even though he danced with the *djaboi* men, they were frightened of him and that is why they did not give him any ducks. On the other hand, Yingi was angry because although he had danced they did not recompense him, as was customary. When he told his two wives what he had done, they warned him that he should have killed all the *djaboi*. As it turned out, those who escaped let the people at Djinan-derara know what had happened. When Yingi expressed his wish to remain with them, they decided to set a trap for him.

The following myth is really a sequel to the last; it tells what happened to Crocodile's two wives. It too is Ngulugwongga, and was told to R. Berndt in 1946.

175. YINMALA CHANGES OVER CANOES

The Dreaming spirit Yinmala came from a long way: he spoke Djauan, Yangman, Wogiman and Merel [a dialect close to that spoken by people at *deg*-Bolid, near Wogiman territory: when he came across the plain to Wunalan (Fish) billabong, he spoke Malag-malag.] Yinmala was a big man who was associated with a group of Goanna people [not followed up here]. In this section of 'his' myth, he was poling (with a large bamboo pole) a long ironwood canoe which was very heavy. While at Fish billabong he left his canoe to defecate and, as as result, formed four 'islands', Gunagberu, Merad-djara, Wunyunyu and Melmid. In the meantime the canoe drifted away, but he was able to reclaim it.

As Yinmala was poling along, the two wives [now widows] of Crocodile [see Myth 174] saw him. They asked him to wait and take them to Gayil billabong. On the way he took them to Bundag-waulwerul billabong, which is below Gayil. It was here that they saw a Dreaming woman, Midingan, walking through the water. The two women asked her, 'Sister, which way are you going?' 'I'm not going very far,' she replied. She was gathering lily and other roots. Yinmala left the canoe and followed her: he wanted to copulate with her. They lay together in the sharp-edged grass [named after her, *midingan*]: he lifted her leg for coitus, but the grass had scratched it as well as the other leg and blood was running. When he saw the blood, he let her go. This occurred at Djedurug.

The two widows of Crocodile continued in Yinmala's canoe to Gayil. Here Yinmala again got out of his canoe to defecate and, as a result, formed a good 'island' camp. Now, these two women, Berid and Djin (Pigmy Geese), got out of the canoe. Berid jumped into the middle of the water at Gayil, where she remained; Djin jumped near the billabong bank, where she, too, remained.

Yinmala was angry when he saw they had left him, because he had wanted to copulate with them. He took up his bamboo pole and went on in his canoe. He came on Yunduru (Small Duck) in his *djulngulu*, kapok wood, canoe, and saw that this was a good canoe, better than his own heavy one of ironwood. While Yunduru was washing himself and collecting lily roots and mussels, Yinmala sneaked up. He damaged his own bamboo pole, by breaking it with his teeth all along its length, left it in his canoe and took Yunduru's kapok canoe and good pole. He left his own ironwood canoe and the broken pole. Yunduru, returning, saw that his canoe was gone: 'Which way has it gone? It's gone a long way now!' He climbed into the one Yinmala had left and tried to pole, but the bamboo broke. So he left that canoe there. Yinmala went on, away from Gayil, to his own place named after him, between the high ground at Melbalyi and the Djabiru (native companion) Dreaming place. Yunduru remained near Gayil.

Old Mathew, who told this story, said that he had seen this Dreaming canoe as a boy. Women out collecting lily roots had found it under the leaf-covered surface of the billabong, and had brought it up to the bank. They used it to get roots, and Mathew often 'rode' in it. At dusk they would bring it to the bank near where they were camping. But next morning, it would be back at its Dreaming place at Gayil. The women would go after it and feel about in the water with their toes until they found it. They would lift it up, take out the water, and use it. But at night it would always go back to its Dreaming place. Now, it has gone!

Primarily, the story is about the introduction of a more utilitarian canoe and the creation of billabong islands, through Yinmala's defecation, and of other Dreaming places. The statement about grass scratching Midingan's legs is an oblique reference to menstruation, regarded as being dangerous to males. Midingan and the two widows of Crocodile all escaped the sexual attentions of Yinmala — although, being unaccompanied by a husband or male relative, they could expect such overtures.

The following story belonged to the people who occupied the area of country from the Mary to the East Alligator Rivers, and was told to R. Berndt at Oenpelli in 1949.

---

176. THE TRAVELLING CANNIBALS

There were three of them: Ngamanmulg, a *yarigarngurg*, *djabangari* Dreaming man and his 'brother' Mubering-geyemuna [said to have had 'no skin'] who changed his name to Wiyn (Win) when he came to Mangeri country, and a woman, Igalangai [also 'no skin'] who was the wife of the elder 'brother' [presumably the second man]. They came into Bilyenggi [high up on the Mary River, near Mt Bundy station], and the language spoken in this area was Ngalwenmil. They went on to Geimunggu springs [Numbugala language], where they camped. Then they followed the South Alligator River to the high reaches where there was fresh water, and where Waramurunggoindji [the great Fertility Mother] had left bamboos. Continuing along Gergergrogidj creek [where Ambugala was spoken], they eventually came to Gun-gumewulu, a big billabong, and on past Marara billabong and a small one named Yireri. They reached Gun-gundjung, a long billabong with an abundant supply of lily roots. 'Brother,' one of the men said to the other, 'There are plenty of lily roots here. Let us wait until the woman collects them.'

Now, these two men had eaten many people at the Daly River (Wuril), and after that they had come east. Both men had big bellies, as did Igalangai — big, 'with all those people inside!' The woman obtained lily roots and returned to the bank of the billabong, to Gangala-nalarugidj where they were camping; they had carried a fire-stick all the way. Feeling uncomfortable because they had eaten so much, they rolled round on the ground, and the bones of the people inside them hurt their stomachs. They stood up. First the elder brother vomited up human skin, bones and hair, and so on, and then the younger brother and the woman did the same. They drank water, washing out their mouths. [A large mound of bones may still be seen at this place; Ambugala language.] They 'put' two brothers here, Muroyil and Man-galgir (*yarigarngurg*).

They came to the 'head' of the plain, Ganababalwul. [Another Red Lily billabong, on the South Alligator; Numbu language, said to be like Gagadju.] They named four brothers, Maralgalg, Gulumog, Ilari and Mayimalbul, who were *yariyaning*, *nangaridj*. Ngamanmulg, Mubering-geyemuna and Igalangai said to them, 'You people remain here. This is your country, you'll speak Numbu!'

They went on until they reached the arm of a salt water creek, and crossed over and continued eastward, reaching Djurugol (Numbu). They climbed along a point of a hill and saw Numbu men digging a hole in order to bury a corpse [Dreaming 'Dead Body' here]. These people, seeing the three travellers, asked where they had come from. 'We come from the Daly River. We are human, like you are!' Waramurunggoindji was also there — 'she had come first!' The Numbu people said they intended burying a dead man [a brother of a man named Mayimalbul, mentioned above]. They covered him up, and the three travellers continued on. However, before they left, the people asked where they were going, and they replied. 'We are going that way [pointing east] to look for good country.' They had wanted to go up to where Waramurunggoindji was camped. But she said, 'You go low down, along the plain.' 'She hunted those three back from where she was,' at Garamulg billabong where there is a jungle and slightly higher ground. From this point, people spoke Widjelg.

The three went on to Manggerini, a big billabong where they put a large banyan tree [which was still there in 1949]. From there is a big plain, and at Nyanggalga, a swamp. [Nudu, a dialect of Widjelg, was said to be close to Gagadju, which was spoken along this plain.] They drank water at the swamp and went on to Gulurbu where there was a spring and swamp, with water running to the South Alligator. Going on to Naberiboidjburi, they found a deep hole full of fish. One brother said to the other, 'Let us catch fish.' They caught a lot, but then found they had no bag. However, the woman had three, so they filled these up with fish and a long-necked tortoise. This was Bandjal (*yarigarngurg, nawagaidj*) who was a young Dreaming man: he remained at this place. [That is, the long-necked tortoise was a manifestation of Bandjal and remained in spirit form.] The two men and the woman decided to find a place where they could cook what they had caught. But there was too much rain. Bandjae materialised in human form [that is, the tortoise they had caught transformed himself into a young man], and going before them said, 'I'll show you a large camp where all the Gagadju people are singing and dancing.' However, the two brothers asked Tortoise, 'What about you, young man, going to that camp and getting fire so we can cook the fish?' He replied, 'All right, I'll go.' He did not go into the camp but stole some fire and carried it back to them. But because of the rain, the fire 'died'. When Tortoise came to where the others were waiting, he told them the fire had gone out. They replied, 'You had better go back and get more. We are hungry!' So Tortoise went along Anagana creek to the camp to get more fire; he returned with it, but it, too, went out. 'Too much rain,' he told them. 'No matter,' the others replied, 'You go in front, and we'll follow you to the camp.' Tortoise as he walked along 'cut the ground' and made it slippery, 'made it open'.

At this camp there was a woman's hut where Murulgu (*yariyaning*, Gagadju) was segregated during her first menstruation. Another girl was with her: Madeniya [also *yariyaning*], who was pregnant for the first time. The two brothers said to each other, 'It's better we eat these people, brother: will we?' And they agreed to do so. The two men came along inside the ground, along the grooves Tortoise had cut. The people in the camp were sitting in their stringybark huts sheltering from the heavy rain. The two men came up from underneath and tipped up the huts, one by one, so the people could not escape, and they swallowed all the people, including the two women in their segregation hut. 'They swallowed everything!'

The two men [and presumably the woman, although she is not mentioned here] came to Djanilda to catch fish, although they were 'full up with people'. While Tortoise and the elder brother went down to the billabong to wash, the younger brother sat on the bank. 'Brother' he said, 'you have lice!' And they both said, 'We'll stamp them in here at this place, leaving them for Ilbaru and Galararu, two Gagadju *yarigarngurg* men. [No further reference was made to Tortoise.]

Following Anagana creek they came to Galabiri. 'Come, brother, you and I will vomit here. We can't carry all of this inside us!' They vomited at this place, and camped there. They had brought from the Daly River an old basket made of *magana* rush or knife grass. 'You and I will sit here brother.' By rolling the fibre on their thighs, they made a long string which they soaked in water and then wove a fine-meshed *djuboyu* fish trap.

Now a woman, Gureneneri (Black Crane), *yarigarngurg, ngalwagaidj*, Gagadju, was a 'sister' to the two brothers. [The wife disappears from the story at this juncture and the sister appears]. She was at this place. 'Sister,' they told her, 'Go and bring Manumoguruguru' [that is, her husband who was at Manmalari on the South Alligator; Wada language].

One of the brothers, who was in the billabong, was standing with his legs apart, throwing water to attract fish to his net. As he did this semen spurted from his penis. 'What's the matter?' he asked himself, 'Why is it coming out?' And more spurted out. 'Something is wrong!' he thought. Then he saw Gureneneri on the bank. His penis stood erect as he looked at her, and more semen spurted. 'Ah, that's the matter: that's why I did it!' And he stepped out of the water and went to her. 'I had better copulate with her now,' he thought. But she said, 'Your brother said we'll go to my husband.' He replied, 'I want to copulate with you a little: my penis is hard!' So she lay down and they copulated. Afterward, when the semen ran from her, she cleaned herself with grass and placed it on a forked stick with a stone on top. They walked up to the other brother: a big *ngudji* jungle fly, a blue one, had taken a message to the younger brother informing him of what had happened. That fly hit the elder brother again and again on the eye. And Gureneneri set off for Manmalari to get her husband. 'We shouldn't have sent her to get him,' the younger brother said. 'Let him come,' the other replied.

Gureneneri and her husband came to the two brothers' camp. Nothing was said about the elder brother copulating with his sister. But the two brothers took up a length of string they had made, in order to measure the depth of the Daly River bag they had brought with them. They asked Manumoguruguru to climb into it; it covered him completely. They told him it was just for gauging its size — but the two brothers squeezed and choked him. Before he died, he called out from inside the basket '*Karlg! Karlg!*' He 'turned into' a salt-water Black Crane. And the two brothers cursed him: 'You go to Nubonga, you stay there!' Thus, they sent his spirit to remain at that place, near the South Alligator River [Gureneneri remained at Galabiri.]

The two brothers put their fish trap into the water at Galabiri and continued making long lengths of string. That trap floated away, disappearing into the water: 'It is the same as *namereidjul* [Gagadju] or *ngalyod*, Rainbow, that basket net moved to sunset way.' The older brother called out, 'You try to pull out that net, measure it to see what's in it. The younger brother went down to the water; he tried to pull it out, but there was nothing. 'It's gone!' he called to his brother. They felt all around in the discoloured water, feeling with their hands. They came to where there was a large Leichhardt fig tree at Galaigiri. 'We've come a long way,' they said. 'The water is dirty here: maybe we'll find the net here!' All along they had followed the grass that the Ngalyod [the net basket] had dragged out as it swam along. 'Brother,' the younger asked, 'Shall we put our footprint here?' And they did so, on the rocks there 'for people to see our tracks' at Anbereimadamana ('putting footprints') in Gagadju country.

They continued to Mageram-mageri billabong on the eastern side of the South Alligator toward the East Alligator, following along to Gwoiwengulu, going east and reaching Nyuminububu swamp. From there they went to Anangaragaba swamp, where there is a deep hole. Nearby they saw a clump of *banadbi* screw palms that emus eat, growing in a swamp at Djingu-banadbi [its name referring to these palms]. From here they went down to Bubun-ginwarana and then on to Gurulwula [Gagadju country]. All the way past these watering places they followed the fish trap which had become a Ngalyod. Travelling along, they saw Ninggaruwul, Mud Fish, and they gave the name to the place where he lived: Madjaringninggaruwul [the name referring to a 'line' of these fish]. They went on to Ginin, a salt-water arm of the East Alligator. From there they saw the Ngalyod net. They ran along the top of the bank in order to meet it at the opening of the arm into the East Alligator, and tried to pull it out. But the basket said, 'Leave me lying here, let me stay down here in the water.' So the two men left it, walking away in sorrow.

As they went along, the younger brother said to the other, 'Brother, brother, look — there is a man there!' The elder brother asked, 'Where?' 'No it is only a pandanus tree.' 'Ah, I thought it was a man!' This occurred at Imbunandjil in Gagadju country. However, a large group of people had been here, including Gudjubu, a Blue Tongue Lizard woman [*yarigarngurg, ngalgangila*]: she had been dancing and singing.

The two brothers camped here, and next morning went on. Not far from Imbunandjil they saw a Goose and its nest. This is the Dreaming site of Goose at Guneimbulada, near Angmeridja. [Its nest and eggs are there, and the rock into which Goose 'made herself' indicates her red nose, her black neck, eyes, and so on.] The two men went past this place. Then they saw Ngalbedjeidji, Whistle Duck, and chased it from its nest. They named the place Djomulubari-ngalbedjeidji [referring to the country of this duck]. This is on the other side of the plain, and a rock is its Dreaming site.

They went on to Gubarbir, through bush country where there is a billabong: they washed themselves and went down to Midegeilil plain, on the western side of the East Alligator [at the other side, east, was later Doyle's camp; this is Gagadju country]. They decided to climb the high ridge at Djanma to look across at the rocky hills near Oenpelli. 'Shall we go there?' one brother asked the other. They agreed to do so. They went through the bush and came down to Ngadab [in Eri country]. 'Ah, which way will we go?' they asked. 'We will go directly to those hills. If it is a good place, we'll stay there!' they agreed. So they continued to Uguuningidj, high up on the East Alligator, near the Crossing, and on to Malananggir, which they named; there is a hill and rockhole there, in the bush. Continuing through the bush they came to Mewaniwendj creek, a salt arm of the river. Crossing over, they walked along the plain and found a long billabong, and named it Manbulnam. Nearby, at Djumbilm (or Wurumelengemb) lived an old *yarigarngurg, nagudjug* man [Eri language]. He had turned into a rock at Indjuwumbelengg Hill; on his stone head are *rabird* crane feathers, and the white ground nearby also represents these feathers. [The name of this Dreaming man is handed on from father to son, and Djumbilm is that name.]

They walked on and crossed a creek, and the place where they camped they called Namiyambyadbau. The hands of the two brothers were clenched, their thumbs extended at right angles. [This had been caused by their habitual task of making lengths of string and rolling it on their thighs.] At this place they prepared fibre string and doubling it up put it in a string dilly bag, which they hung on a tree. Later they removed it and went on to a place which they named Undjedber-wiandj. [This name refers to a flat stick that they used to catch lice: it still stands there as a long, narrow, flattened, upright stone.]

Carrying dilly bags over their shoulders they came to Maganbingg, where they made camp. They complained that they were hungry and would need to catch fish. So they removed fishing lines from their bags and attached small pieces of meat to them, catching many fish. But they also caught a large cat-fish, which was 'like' a Ngalyod. They pulled the line in, but it broke at Madjanganbali. The water here was clear and they could see the cat-fish [= Ngalyod]. The soles of the elder brother's feet were white after washing them. [He stood in the clear water, and the white marks can be seen there today.] Cat-fish dragged the line all the way along. The elder brother got hold of it [he was hanging on: his name now changes to Win — see at beginning of myth]. The younger brother saw what was happening and spoke to the elder brother's wife, Igalangai [who now reappears in the story]. They followed the other brother, who called out, 'What are you two doing? Come and hold my feet!' [that is, to stop him from being dragged along by the cat-fish]. They stayed there at Madjanganbali: 'We have to remain here, like a Ngalyod.' Those three spat: and as they did so they called the names of the first people associated with this area. 'For all those people, we put here: Inmalaga, an old Eri man and his five sons: Ngalgabulg, Ngalind, Badjabadj, Inbumam and Ngeiidj (or Neiidji): these are names that people always used in this place.

There is a big rock here in the water. If anyone inadvertently touches it when swimming, it will pull the swimmer down into deep water: it is that Ngalyod. There are plenty of trees along the bank, but no-one can cut them down: it would spoil the place. If anyone were to hit this rock, the country would be flooded. Those three, the two brothers and the woman, and the Cat-fish-Ngalyod, remain there — always!

This rather complex myth combines a number of incidents. The Dreaming characters are from the Daly River, spatially far distant from the people who occupied the buffalo plains to the west of the East Alligator River. However, as we saw in Chapter 2, it is not unusual for mythic beings to come from what would have been a relatively unknown place. Also, on arrival in that area they could well expect to find other Dreaming personages already there, especially the great Fertility Mother, Waramurunggoindji, who did not want them to settle near her and sent them packing.

While Ngamangmulg, Mubering-geyemuna and Igalangai were cannibals, a point emphasised in the unfortunate happenings at Anagana Creek, they were also responsible for placing people in particular areas. In other words, they were carrying out 'creative' acts and leaving the names, if not the first people themselves, for future generations, a role also undertaken by Waramurunggoindj. One interesting feature is their vomiting people they had eaten, at Gangala-nalarugidj; but at the next place they came to, Ganababalwul, they 'named' four brothers, 'naming' and 'putting' in this context being synonymous; no connection, however, is made between the vomiting and the naming, at least not in the myth. On the other hand, the wholesale destruction of the people and all their possessions at Anagana Creek, and the killing of Manumoguruguru, illustrate the 'dark side' of the main characters — the two brothers, the wife, and the sister. Balanced with the 'naming' of human beings as well as the places associated with particular Dreamings, the myth itself is speaking not only about land, but also about life-taking and life-giving.

There are some inconsistencies in the structure of the story: for instance, the disappearance of Igalangai and her replacement by the sister, then the sister's disappearance and replacement by the wife; also, the obtrusive erotic incident. Nevertheless, the plot is followed through with the fishing net basket that is identified as a Rainbow Snake. It is the brothers' ill-treatment of the basket, by using it as a vehicle in which to kill Manumoguruguru, that causes it to become a Rainbow Snake. That theme brings about the appearance of Cat-fish, who is also a Rainbow Snake. And that leads to the eventual transformation of the brothers and the wife as Rainbow Snakes.

The following story was told to C. Berndt in 1950 at Oenpelli.

177. LOGLOG LIZARD: KILLING AND TRANSFORMATION

Long ago, when the first people were making themselves, an old man met up with two youths. He knew who they were. He called them grandsons, and they called him grandfather, mother's father. Perhaps they thought there was a possibility that they might travel with him. They were coming from the east, and as he was looking about he saw them near his camp. They were hoping to get to the *ubar* rituals — which were taboo to them, something they were not allowed to see. So he was not prepared to let them continue their journey. He said, 'I won't say good-bye to you and let you go to that *ubar*: I don't want to do that. But you two come hunting with me and we'll look for those possums that live among the rocks. We'll kill them, and fill ourselves up!'

They went with him to find possums, and they got plenty. The old man stood outside and the two boys went into the caves where the possums lived. They got sticks and twisted them in the creatures' woolly fur, then came crawling toward the cave entrance with them and killed them. They threw the bodies to the old man waiting outside. When they had enough, they went back to their camp and cooked and ate them. It was getting dark. Night came, and they slept.

Early next morning they went possum-hunting again. The old grand-father stood outside and the two boys went into the caves, the deep caves where the possums lived. He asked them, 'Grandsons, have you gone a long way, to get those creatures?' They answered, 'Yes, we're already getting them, and then we'll kill them outside.' They brought them out, killed them and threw the bodies to him: he caught them. Then they went back inside. He asked them, 'Grandsons, have you gone a long way?' They called back, 'Yes, a long way!'

He went to get dry grass, and used it to close up the main entrance to the cave. Then he closed it up on each side, and especially on the east side. He looked for all the little caves and little holes, and filled them all up. The two boys couldn't see anything around them, in the deep cave where they had gone. They called to the old man, 'Grandpa, why did you close it up? The cave is getting dark where we are.' He said, 'Grandsons, it's rain that has made the cave dark for you.' That's what they thought, but he was the one who had got grass and closed up the cave for them. He went and got fire, he set it all alight with a fire-stick. They were sitting inside: they were burning in there. At last their breath stopped, there in the cave among the rocks. Then it was all over, the smoke and the flames, and the two boys lay dead. They couldn't have done anything to get out of that cave.

That old man, that grandfather, went inside, got their bodies, and brought them outside. They lay there, dead. He took the elder brother first, and made his body clean, so it lay there quite pale. He put it separately. Then he did the same to the younger brother. He left them lying there and went for firewood.

First he dug the ground, then he put in the firewood, and then the termite mound. He lit a fire in that oven, and while it was burning he went to get paperbark and brought it back to where they were lying. He broke leafy branches into small pieces and put the bodies on the leaves. Then he got his stone axe, to cut them up into joints. He cut one of them open, taking out the liver and heart, both kidneys, and lungs and eating them as a snack while he was watching the oven, waiting for the fire to die down. Then he got the other body, the younger brother's, and cut it up. Then he threw out the glowing sticks, and the termite mound. He went to get special leaves, *man-djanggurlg*, that we use to mix with kangaroo to give it a good sweet taste. He put them in the oven. Then he put the bodies in, taking a little bit of paperbark to hold them with and to cover them, and on top of all that he put termite mound. Then, more paperbark as a cover. He ran to get his digging stick, and dug the ground to get earth, burying them.

Well, they were cooking in the oven. He went and lay down, waiting for them. He lay there for a little while. 'I think I'll go and get some pandanus,' he said, 'so I can make a basket, a deep basket, to put their bones in.' He said this, thinking in his mind. He went and got pandanus, got string from the leaves and dried it, trying not to let it get too dry. At last he was starting on the basket, working upward from the bottom. He cut it, went to look for more string from a special plant, tore it into thin strips and dried it. He twisted it on his thigh, added the string to the basket framework, and hung it up on a tree.

He came and removed the paperbark from the two bodies. They were cooked at last. He pulled out the bones, quite clean, and packed them into his basket. He ate some of the meat. The rest he took with him to eat on the way. He was going east, to the place where the boys' mother and father were living, taking the boys' bones to them. He ate the meat as he went along, camping by night and setting off again at daybreak. For three days he went on, still travelling and camping alone. He went on, and on. At last he got there. As he went, he was dancing, making the boys' bones jump up and down in the basket. Some of the people there, and the boys' mother and father, said to one another, 'It must be a *wurbu* dancing man coming, to sing a ceremony for us?' That's what the boys' mother said. But he was carrying their sons' bones.

He said to them all, that man who had killed the two boys, 'Clear the ground!' They cleared the ground. Then he went close to where they were sitting [waiting for the ceremony], and poured out the boys' bones in front of them. They got axes and knives, men got their spear-throwers, and they were hitting themselves in grief for those boys, when they saw the bones. Men were getting their spears and spear-throwers, spearing that man, and cutting him with axes.

That dangerous man ran, and transformed himself into a creature. He ran, and got into a hole in a tree. He said, 'You're all spearing me, but you're not hitting me! You're not hurting me! I'm still alive. Here I am, look at me! My eyes are looking at you!' They kept on attacking him. They got a long stick and were pushing it into the hole. He jumped up, he was running, he went into another hole. Still they kept following him, they went on doing what they had done first. He was jumping around, jumping out again and running into another hole, in a hollow tree. He was saying, 'You didn't kill me. I'm here! Look at me! My eyes are looking at you!' He went into a big tree, that we call *mandjalag*. It stands by itself among the rocks, a strong tree, like ironwood. He went in there, and stayed for a long time. They got bark, and grass. At first they tried to cut the tree with an axe, but its cutting edge [its 'nose'] got broken. They couldn't cut the wood: it was too hard. That's why they put bark and grass right inside the hole: bark and grass and quick-burning things, little sticks, and small dry bundles of *man-garandalg* grass that grows among the rocks. Then they set fire to it all, in the tree.

At last he himself was burning, there in the tree. He was feeling the pain. They could hear him banging with his nose against the tree, trying to get out. They heard his breath getting shorter. They waited until the tree fell down, cut by the fire. They saw his bones, all burnt, very small pieces lying there. Then they got more wood and burnt up his bones almost completely, because he had been such a dangerous man. They said, 'He might kill us and eat us, so let's kill him thoroughly, to make sure he dies forever.' They destroyed his bones, and left the remains lying there. Then they went back to where they had come from. They said to each other, 'We won't collect his bones [for any mourning ritual], because he was so dangerous. He killed those two boys of ours,' they said. 'So, leave his bones lying there. We'll just take the bones of our two boys. And it's good that we killed him. If he had stayed alive, he would have killed us!' they said. They went back, and stayed in their own country.

But that old man, whose name in life was Na-djundjun, like the name of his own place in Dangbun country, had changed into a small, shiny skink, quite harmless.

In a different version from another narrator (Myth 114), Loglog comes from the north and before his transformation he appears in a less aggressive role. In this one he comes from the rocky country to the south, and speaks the Dangbun language. Nganalgindja, who told the story, did not know how close his relationship was to the boys; but he was of the same territorial group as their mother, Djarolam. (Through their father they belonged to a different territorial group, Bulaldja.) Didja was the elder brother, Wogi-wogi the younger. The implication in the story is that they were not going to the *ubar* rituals to see the public, open-sacred sequences, but hoped to find a way into the secret-sacred side.

Loglog himself, it seems, did not plan to attend the rituals, Nevertheless, he was concerned about 'policing' the rules. But if one message in the story is, 'Don't try to break the rules governing ritual inclusion/exclusion', another message could be, 'Discipline or punishment should be appropriate. Don't overdo it!' The boys were punished too severely for what was only an assumed intention, not a clear-cut action. And Loglog did more than simply kill them, even though that in itself could have been seen as too drastic. The story dwells on what he did with the bodies, including his preparations for eating them, and on the dramatic, almost macabre, way he conveyed the death message — to people who supposed he must be bringing a pleasurable and entertaining dance-and-song session. The story includes no verbal message about this: the sight of the bones appears to have been enough to identify them — and also him, as the person responsible for them. The whole affair was exacerbated by the fact that the main characters were not strangers to one another: they had a close enough kin relationship to ensure that, ideally, such overtly hostile actions would not be expected between them.

In the end, the mode of Loglog's death parallels what he inflicted on the boys: being killed by flames and smoke in a hollow aperture (deep, narrow cave; hole in hardwood tree), followed by special attention to the bones (but virtual destruction in his case, preservation in theirs). However, in his new physical manifestation he is distanced from human beings in two ways. It is not only that he is in non-human shape, differing from them in size as well as in appearance. Also, he is inedible. They don't eat him; and in his current form he doesn't try to eat them, or even to bite them, not being transformed, for instance, into a crocodile or shark, or even a wild dog.

In the telling of the story, the drama was heightened by a series of changes in tone. Periods of relative quiet or routine activity were punctuated by sudden bursts of heightened energy, where things happened quickly. But even such a mundane process as the preparation of pandanus leaf baskets, replete with small details (partly summarised in the story as set out here), was fraught with tension because of its setting, and the knowledge of the reason for the baskets being made. Nganal-gindja, the story-teller, made the most of all the dramatic devices available to a narrator dealing with such material. And, as usual, the printed word alone is quite inadequate to convey them successfully.

Compare this last story with the following one, from the mainland opposite the Goulburn Islands, told to R. Berndt at Oenpelli in 1950.

178. BAN-GIN AND HIS BAG OF BONES

Ban-gin, a *namadgu* man, accompanied two young *nangaraidgu* men, Djalawanbed the elder brother and Boiweg the younger one, from Croker Island. Ban-gin was their father's brother, and they spoke Marlgu. The older man was taking these young men for initiation. They crossed the strait and walked to Indjinaid Point, on the mainland, went on to Wangaran [Malay Bay: Maung-Yiwadja territory] where they camped, and then to Waag and east to Mayadag, Maldalgud and to the Umanaid creek. They followed the creek, on the top side, starting from the bottom, and came to Manangai-irewaid on the south. Leaving the creek, they walked on to Wuragag (Tor Rock) where they camped, and then went south to Wulilil. Next day they continued to Aguru, camped there, and went on to Angu [crossing the traditional route from Oenpelli to the Goulburn Islands]. Here they collected lily roots and made camp. 'Well, my sons,' said Ban-gin, 'we had better follow Cooper's Creek.' So they went on to Mamunmulg, Ilbun and to Iwaniwulu [on Cooper's Creek]. Next day they travelled on to Merang, where they ate *mandaneg* 'bitter' yams; then to Mebag, Gunwirug and Yindjan, camping at each. They reached Wudgayeimiri, where Dreaming spirit children were calling out. [The place name refers to this. They are *djang* spirits and live in the water at this place.]

Ban-gin was very hungry. His two 'sons' tried to find food, but could not. They went to Mabalnandi billabong [Gunwinggu territory], leaving Cooper's Creek behind, and travelled south-east. 'Well, sons, we can't go any further. I'm feeling very hungry. Can you find anything for me?' Ban-gin asked. They came to Mirang: they saw a rockhole by a cave, and slept outside. Ban-gin said, 'You go and find rock wallaby. Go inside the cave; maybe you'll find something there. I'm very hungry. If we go any farther, I'll die!' And he added, 'What about this hole? It's a good one, you'll find wallaby inside!'

The young men went into the cave. 'Go right inside so that you can find those wallabies!' Ban-gin told them. When they were inside, he collected dry grass and shut up the cave entrance with it. 'What's happened, father? It's dark inside!' they called. He pulled out the grass to let light come in. 'You go farther in!' he replied. So they went farther into the cave. Ban-gin put more grass at the cave entrance. He could not hear them talking. He set light to the grass, and those two inside were burnt, and died.

When the fire was out, the old man went into the cave and saw them lying there dead. He grabbed their legs and pulled them outside. He put them on a flat rock, cut them up and ate them. [He had re-cooked them. At first they had not really been burnt, but had been suffocated by the smoke.] Afterward he collected together all their bones. He picked some pandanus leaves, dried the strands and made a basket — the long variety used to carry the bones of dead relatives. He put the bones into this, and carried them along with him on his back. There were a lot of Winggu people living in these parts. All the way he was dancing the *wurbu* initiatory song series. He came close to where the people were camped, where the real father and mother of the two boys were living. Ban-gin came in with his bag of bones, and danced right up to where the two boys' parents were sitting, with all the other people, looking at him dancing. He came toward them, and faced them; he called the place names [invocations]: 'You from Gunimbalng; you from Gogalag!' Then he tipped out the bones in front of them.

The father and mother were crying. All the other people were angry and gathered together their spears and axes. They chased Ban-gin. They threw spears at him as he ran away, but missed him. He went into a hole under the ground. They began to dig him out, but he escaped behind them. They saw him, and continued throwing spears; they were running after him, but missed him every time. He went into a hollow trunk lying on the ground: they put grass at each end and set light to it, but he came out at one side and ran away. They chased him, but he went into the ground again. They were digging all round. He came out! They threw their spears, but they could not hit him. He went into a tree that had a hole in it. They chopped it down, but he came out at the top of the tree, going along a limb. They saw him, and chased him, throwing their spears, but missing him. The spears fell 'like rain', but he dodged them all. He went into a tough-bark *mandjalag* ironwood tree. 'We can't cut this!' they all said. So they got grass and arranged it all around the tree, and they made a fire. The tree burnt down. Ban-gin tried to jump sideways, but the fire burnt his testes and they exploded, and he died. They all threw spears at him and then chopped him up. They tore his body apart so that it was all in pieces and they burnt all of them.

This took place at Biriginyeng-binin [its name meaning 'where they cooked (burnt) that man']. Ban-gin had killed those two young men because he was hungry!

The case of a man killing and eating his own brother's sons, especially when he is entrusted to act as an initiatory guardian, is a shocking affair, compounded by Ban-gin's tipping out the bones publicly before their parents. The reason is not clear; hunger in itself is an insufficient one. It is however, thematically similar to the last myth (177) and to Myth 144 in Chapter 6, although these deal with partly different sets of mythic people. That Ban-gin brought back the bones without providing any explanation for what had happened, is tantamount to an admission of guilt, inviting punitive action against him.

On the other hand, this myth (178) refers to two young men being taken to their initiation. Ritually, each novice would be regarded as being symbolically 'dead' until the process was completed, when they were 're-born' as potential adults. However, there is no indication that this myth can be interpreted in that way. In the text, the initiation ritual referred to was said to be circumcision. But circumcision was not traditionally carried out in this socio-cultural area because Waramurunggoindji did attempt to introduce it, but each time she circumcised a novice, he died (see R. and C. Berndt 1985: 252).

The next myth was told to C. Berndt at Oenpelli in 1950.

179. WIRI-WIRIYAG: THE BOY WHO WANTED HIS SISTER

Before, long ago, when we were not here, only those first people were here, there were two men and one woman. One of the men was her husband. She called the other man by the term for potential 'son-in-law', and the arrangement was that, when she had a daughter, the girl would be his promised wife.

After a while, the woman bore a girl — the elder daughter. She gave her to him, in betrothal. She bore her second child, a boy. Then she bore another girl — the younger daughter. They were all travelling about together. That man was giving his mother-in-law many things, kangaroo meat and various creatures, and he would go running to chop out honey to give her. So, she was thinking to herself, 'Shall I give you the younger sister, to join the older sister?' She gave her to him. Now he had both girls as his wives.

The man's name was Gargain, Chicken-hawk. The girls' brother was Wiri-wiriyag (a kind of green parrot). One day the two of them set off together. Wiri-wiriyag's mother had said to him, 'Why don't you two keep the kangaroos you spear separate, and taboo to those girls — because they're not allowed to eat them, being your own sisters.' [She meant that it would be friendly for them to go hunting together. At the same time she was reminding him that he could share what he caught with his parents; Gargain could do the same, but he would also share it with his wives.] So she and her husband and the two girls and the elder girl's children stayed in camp that day, and left the hunting to the two brothers-in-law. Gargain was going on ahead. Wiri-wiriyag was a little way behind; he got a stick, put it between his big toe and second toe, and broke it. Then he sat down as if he were in pain, but he was only pretending. He said, 'I'm going to pause for a while because a stick has pierced my foot.' He pretended to be getting the stick out. But after Gargain left, Wiri-wiriyag didn't go looking for kangaroos. He followed Gargain.

Gargain had speared a kangaroo, and left it hanging up on a tree where they had agreed to meet for a lunch-camp. Wiri-wiriyag came along and saw it hanging there. He rubbed blood from it on his spear and spear-thrower, then speared the already-speared kangaroo! He broke up his spear and thrower, stole the kangaroo body and came back with it to the camp where they were living — his sisters, and his father and mother. The girls were keeping a look-out, and saw him coming. They told their mother, 'Our brother is bringing a kangaroo!' She said to her husband, 'My son speared a kangaroo! So I'll go and get firewood, for us to cook it.' She didn't know that her son had stolen it and that it was Gargain who had speared it first. She was praising him. 'My own son has speared a kangaroo for us! We two want to eat, and get full!' She was about to go after firewood, but her son said to her, 'Leave the firewood. Those two girls can get it, my two sisters. After that, I'll cook the kangaroos.' His sisters got firewood. Well, his mother stood up, and said to him, 'Are you going to eat this, when it's your sisters who got this firewood? If you are their brother, then you should keep it separate from them. You are taboo to them, your sisters, and it's wrong for them to eat it from you!' Well, they were all cooking it. And already he had given his sisters the liver and heart and two kidneys, the guts and the lungs. They were all eating.

While the main part of the meat was cooking, they were sitting down waiting for Gargain, looking about for him. He was coming, carrying a lot of cooked kangaroos. He put them down. The two girls had got up when they saw him, and they came over to him. They told him that their brother had speared a kangaroo. 'But we don't eat it, because it's taboo to us.' [That's what they said!] Gargain said, 'And where did that young fellow spear it?' 'Well, where his spear got broken.' '*He* didn't spear it,' said Gargain. 'I thought he had come back first. When we were going along, something went into his foot. I said to him, "Well, if you're sick, with a stick gone into your foot, you just go back." I thought he was coming back then. And that is the first kangaroo I speared. I hung it up raw, on a tree. It was mine. I speared it first. So perhaps he was spearing that raw meat, and he took that spear and spear-thrower in his hands and broke them up himself!' 'So *that's* it! We thought he had speared it himself, but he didn't. He stole it from you. It was yours, and he stole it!' That's what they said to him. So then they were all eating it.

Early next morning the same two went out again. They were going along, when suddenly Wiri-wiriyag began to scream. '*Aa, aa, aa, aa!*', as if a stick was piercing his foot. 'I have to wait, because a stick injured me!' he said, 'Did it really injure you much?' 'Yes, it really injured me. I'll have to wait here while I take out the stick. So you go on ahead!' he told Gargain. 'You go first and start that grass fire, for kangaroos, then I'll catch up with you there.' 'Yes, then you'll catch up with me there.' Gargain thought they would actually meet as they arranged, but something else was going on in Wiri-wiriyag's head, in his mind. He went back to camp, to his mother and father and his sisters. 'Where are you going?' they asked him. 'I came back because a stick pierced me. I've got a big sore there.' 'What about coming here so I can look at that sore where a stick pierced you?' said his mother. But Wiri-wiriyag's response was, 'My foot has gone soft. You all come here where I'm lying, and look at me.' They came, and saw him lying down. 'Show us, let's see your sore.' They tried to look at his foot. They were looking in vain. 'Maybe you haven't a sore there, you're only pretending!' 'This is the sore, a big one: it injured me. I'm sick, dying,' he said.

They thought he was still lying down, but he wasn't. He was calling out to his sisters, 'You two, get up, we'll go swimming!' The girls told their mother, 'He's trying to get us to go with him.' She said to him, 'What's eating your ears, that you're trying to get your sisters to go with you? You're taboo to them, you're a forbidden person to them!' Her son, their brother, came back at her, 'You, we've talked too much to you, you're too old! I was only trying to get those children of ours, so we could go swimming together!' They went off, he and his sisters. They put the children down, on the dry ground, and went swimming by themselves. The two girls were clinging to a pandanus palm, holding on to it, when he came 'running' under the water and was pinching and tickling them. They said, 'Who's tickling us, coming 'running' under the water? It's you, brother!' 'No, not me! Maybe a fish was biting you. That's what happens when people go swimming!' The baby, on the bank, was crying for milk, and his grandmother heard him. 'Where have you all gone? Come up, out of the water, and get him, so you can give him milk!' One of the girls came up, the elder sister, the children's mother. But the other girl, the one with no children, was swimming about with her brother. He wanted her very much — her full brother! Well, they were all swimming, and then they came out of the water to where they were camping.

Gargain was away hunting, where he was camping. His two wives were sleeping in the house they shared with him. Their brother was sleeping in his own place, near his mother and father. They were all asleep. It was the middle of the night. They had been watching for Gargain, but he was sleeping out, at his hunting camp. He couldn't carry all the kangaroos he had got. 'It's no good, there are too many for me to carry alone,' he was saying. So, the others were asleep. That brother got up. He went, moved the two girls apart, and lay down between them. But their mother got up, and was searching for him. 'Where did he go, that boy?' she said to her husband. 'I don't know, no idea! What about you going to look! Where could he have gone?' They got some paperbark and lit it, as a torch, and they saw him lying in between his two sisters. His mother started hitting him. 'You get up! Lying here with your sisters! Isn't it a wrong thing to do! Aren't you full siblings? And you went running to sleep in between them!' '*Aaah!*' he said. 'Wait a minute, bring me some water, so I can wash my eyes! I didn't know I had gone to sleep where my sisters were. Why didn't you wake me up before, so I could go away from them? In the morning, when I see them, I'll spear them both and hit them with my spear-thrower. And I'll spear you too, though you're my own mother!' Then his mother said, 'Shame on you, for talking about spearing me! But you have no shame, when you go and lie down with your sisters! Maybe you can't sleep by yourself in your own house: you just want to sleep with your sisters! You, standing there, you have no shame!' That's what she was saying to him.

In the morning the girls' husband came back. He gave them all kangaroos, and honey. They left the old kangaroo meat from before, to eat after they had slept, and ate the meat he had just brought back. Then the two girls went to get water. Gargain and his little daughter stayed in the camp. He asked her, as he held her in his arms, 'Did you see your uncle coming back? He just left me altogether!' She said, 'Yes, father, I'll tell you straight. That uncle of mine came here, and we were all sleeping together, with my two mothers, his sisters.'

Gargain would have liked to make trouble, to quarrel openly, but he just left it. They all slept. In the morning the two brothers-in-law got up. Gargain said he had seen signs of a bees' nest before. 'Let's go, we can chop out that honey. You're strong, but I've become weak after carrying all those kangaroos home!' That's what he kept saying to Wiri-wiriyag. At last they got their spears and spear-throwers and axes, and their tightly-plaited baskets for carrying honey. They went off, and saw the nest. Gargain climbed up, and was cutting it out from the branch. At last it fell down. Wiri-wiriyag was standing on the ground, waiting. He went running fast, grabbed the eggs from the honeycomb and just swallowed them all, whole. Gargain said, 'Don't eat that, it's taboo to you! As a father, I'm keeping it taboo, for them [the children]!' 'Ah! If you had told me before, I would have left it! I ate it in ignorance!' Gargain, the one who had found the honey, came down from the tree and was chopping out the honeycomb. They filled up their baskets. Gargain, the finder, licked honey from the hole, as much as he wanted, then went and sat down to rest. He called to Wiri-wiriyag, 'What about you having a turn, and eating some?' Wiri-wiriyag said, 'I don't want it, because it's taboo.' 'I've already said you can eat,' said Gargain. 'Come on, you eat!'

At last Wiri-wiriyag got up. He went, and sat down by the hole in the fallen branch where the liquid honey was lying. He was eating it all, that liquid honey. Meanwhile, Gargain was getting his axe ready. 'Lick there, inside the hole!' Wiri-wiriyag bent down, licking. He paused, he was about to get up again, to breathe. But Gargain had nearly finished tightening the string that bound his axe: he was nearly ready to use it. He urged him, 'Lick again!' He prepared to strike. Wiri-wiriyag was about to lick just once more before lifting up his head, when Gargain slashed his neck with the axe. Then he pulled the two pieces apart. The head lay on the ground, separately. The body, Gargain just left there, because that's what Wiri-wiriyag had been humbugging his sisters with, and that's what Gargain was opposed to. That's why he chopped the boy's neck across.

Then he got the honey-baskets and took them back to the camp. When he reached there, the elder sister asked him, 'My brother, who went with you?' 'He's coming that way: I left him coming behind.' She told her mother and father what Gargain had said. They were looking out for him, calling, and listening. His spirit called back to them both — his spirit, because his body was lying dead. The honey in the baskets was waiting there. Gargain gave it to his mother-in-law, through her daughters. But he didn't tell her what he had done: he was hiding the trouble between himself and her son.

They looked about. No, no sign of the boy. At last his mother lit a big fire, for her son who was killed. She poured out all the honey there, onto the fire, cooking it like plant food. Well, Gargain was preparing to take his two wives away, back to his country, but their mother wouldn't let them go. She insisted on keeping them both with her. And she kept crying, 'My son, my son! I have breasts for you, my son!' She was 'pulling out her breath' for him, crying all the time. They got their belongings together and set off in the darkness, that father and mother and the two sisters, and the two children. As for Gargain himself, they left him behind, because he had killed their brother. They went a long way south, by night.

Next morning Gargain did something wrong. He went, that first man, that Gargain, and broke wood to make a fire to burn them up, to burn up the place where they were travelling. They were all burning there. At last they began to change into birds. Feathers were coming out for them: Gargain himself was already growing feathers. All of them were beginning to fly like birds. And they were talking like birds, in real birds' language, whereas before they talked like people. But that was before. Now they fly high up, they have feathers, they have made themselves into birds. And as for Gargain himself, every day when people light big fires for hunting, that's where he goes, looking for kangaroos in the burnt-out grass. Before, when he was a man, he used to spear a variety of kangaroos. That's why he grew feathers like a bird, and why he keeps looking for kangaroos.

Their talking as people, in real speech, is finished: now they are talking in the tongue of birds. And when they like, they fly up into the sky. They are birds.

Nganalgindja, who told the story, said she remembered hearing it first from her mother and father when she was a young girl, before she went to live with her promised husband. She remembered the names of all the people in the story except Wiri-wiriyag's father. His mother's name was Djorn-djorn-dug, a green bird like a *djuri* parrot that nests on the ground, 'always calling her own name'. The elder sister was called Gwudu-dug, the younger Ngal-da-dubbi. Wiri-wiriyag is also green like a *djuri* parrot, but with some long feathers, a long tail and a white neck, living in trees and 'eating among the flowers', and talking like the sound of his own name. Gargain, chicken-hawk, is known as a tireless hunter. His daughter Miri-bumbum, was at the running-about stage; his baby son was called Goid-balmud ('Bald-head').

Although the characters have their own personal names and separate personal identities, they make up the same kind of basic grouping that appears so often in other stories from this region, and traditionally was quite common as well in everyday life. That is, it constitutes a small family-based group whose members travel about together and co-operate in everyday domestic tasks: a man and his wife, their children, a man who is, or wants to be married to one or more of their daughters, and the offspring of that union. Although so few characters are involved, they demonstrate a number of core relationships that are fraught with potential conflicts. Betrothal and marriage arrangements make up one set of issues, and many stories and songs focus on these. The Wiri-wiriyag story touches only briefly on the topic, and the girls' feelings in the matter are not mentioned. There is a minimum of reference to their personal marital life, which also applies to their parents. Their father is a shadowy figure, and unnamed in the story. He comes alive only in his comment on Wiri-wiriyag's nocturnal excursion: the expressions used imply not only 'Don't know!' but also 'Don't care!'

This story concentrates on one main facet of intra-family relationships, and secondarily on another. The story-plot hinges on Wiri-wiriyag's obsessive affection for the younger of his two sisters. The mother-son relationship comes into this, because he seems to count on her support. He is sometimes referred to in the story as a young initiand, *na-gomdudj*, suggesting that he was only a young adult, not yet mature. His mother, and perhaps his sisters, seem to have made allowances for him on that account. The girls' husband did not; to him, the boy was incorrigible, the problem could not be resolved while he lived — nor was it resolved by his death. The transformation of all the characters into birds offered no solution either. It is (or rather, was) only through discussion of such stories, and the precepts they illustrated, that answers were assumed to be possible, and that was an on-going process, because the problems were inherent or latent in such relationships.

Nganalgindja excelled in this kind of dramatic story-telling. The story itself was fairly well-known, but she brought to it her own vivid, expressive style. The actual words were only a scaffolding for the unfolding of the story through changing tones of voice, facial expressions and gestures. The characters became 'real': the 'mother's boy', sure that he could get away with any of his tricks, and not suspecting that he might get hurt; his indulgent mother; his sisters, ready to play with him in the water while the baby, left on the bank, was crying for milk; Gargain, getting the truth from his little daughter, but managing to restrain himself from retaliating immediately. In that context, it was a fine example of the 'art' of story-telling.

A shorter version told to C.H. Berndt at Oenpelli in 1966, when Nganalgindja was no longer there, omits some details while it includes others. When Wiri-wiriyag's mother awakens him as he lies between his two sisters, she sings a sad song about him. Gargain is described as an old man, much older than his two wives; his transformation into a bird came when an avenging party of men finished all their bundles of spears but couldn't kill him. He grew feathers and flew away. In this version Wiri-wiriyag's mother turned into a *gulubu* dove, and so did her daughters and the baby (only one child). The story-teller did not remember the names of the two daughters or the child (see also Myth 143).

The next story is a Ngulugwongga myth from the Daly River, told to R. Berndt in 1945.

---

180. HOW THE MILKY WAY WAS FORMED

Bindag-bindag, Crocodile man, was married to Balmadj, Whistle Duck, and they had two daughters. They lived at Wurung-gum, on Bomaiyalg billabong.

'We'll have fish tomorrow night,' the father said, 'I'll go out early in my bark canoe.' Next morning he set off, and his daughters went to collect swamp food. Balmadj also left the camp, making sure her daughters did not see her. The two sisters collected food and returned to the camp. The younger girl saw their father returning: 'Sister', she called, 'father is coming!' She called out to her father, 'Father, we'll come and collect the fish.' 'No', he replied, 'You sit down there, I want your elder sister to come. Tell her to come!' 'Sister, he doesn't want me,' the younger sister said, 'You go, he is calling out for you!' So the elder sister went down to her father, who had beached his canoe at the edge of the billabong. He told her to come out to unload the fish: when she came, he copulated with her. Her younger sister saw this, and so did Balmadj, who remained hidden, watching. With her father, the elder sister carried the fish in a basket on her head, bringing it to their camp. By this time the mother had returned. They cooked the fish, ate, and then went to sleep. Bindag-bindag told his wife he would be going out early again in the morning and would not return till late in the afternoon.

Next day he went out by canoe, fishing. The two sisters went out to collect swamp foods. They returned, and Balmadj told them to put all the food they had collected to one side. 'Why, mother?' 'We'll camp together,' she replied. 'Yes, mother, we have been walking about too much'. But Balmadj told them to go out again. 'Come on, sister, we'll go!' they called to each other.

Balmadj stayed in the camp, looking to see how far her daughters had gone. 'They've gone a long way,' she thought. So she went out and obtained *durldjed* grass and brought it back to the camp, where she sat down, drying the grass and watching out for the two girls. As they were not yet in sight, she commenced to roll the grass on her thigh in order to make a long grass rope. Keeping a watch for the girls, she at last saw them coming. So she quickly dug a hole and put the rope within it, covering it with a sheet of paperbark. She sat there on the bark, waiting for them. They returned and put their food away with the rest they had collected. They sat waiting for their father. 'Father, he comes!' the younger sister said. Bindag-bindag called out, 'Daughter.' 'Father, I am coming,' the younger answered. 'You sit down, I want the big girl to come,' her father replied, adding 'Come on!' 'Sister, father called out for you!' The elder sister went down to collect the fish: her father copulated with her. They brought the fish back to the camp, cooked and ate it. Bindag-bindag told his wife he would go out fishing early in the morning. They slept. Next day he went out. The two sisters also went out, telling their mother they would need to go farther afield for food.

Balmadj waited until they had disappeared from sight. She then uncovered the rope and continued twirling the grass, extending its length considerably. She looked up and saw the girls coming: she put her rope away, hiding it, and sat waiting. The girls brought baskets full of lily roots; they put them with the rest of the food they had collected. The younger sister saw their father coming. She called out as usual, but he wanted the elder sister, who went down to get the fish, and he copulated with her. They returned to the camp with the fish, cooked and ate them, and slept.

Bindag-bindag went out early the next day to a place some distance away. The two girls went out; their mother had told them to come back early. She watched them go, and when she could see them no longer she removed her rope, extending it still further, completing it. She sat waiting for her daughters to return. They reached the camp and put their food with the rest. The father, too, had returned, and again it was the elder sister who went down to collect the fish and be copulated with. The younger sister watched them together. They returned to the camp, cooked the fish and ate. 'I'll go out before dawn,' Bindag-bindag told Balmadj. 'I have to go a long way for the fish; I'll return late.'

Next morning, Bindag-bindag went out. When he had gone, Balmadj told her daughters to collect all the food together and put it into two large baskets. 'Now, you two go and pull out this banyan tree and bring it here,' she told them. 'Why, mother?' the younger sister asked. 'Bring it here and put it down here, that banyan shade!' she repeated. 'Mother, what are we going to do?' the younger sister asked. 'Your father keeps his eye on your big sister, he doesn't call out for me! He is always copulating with her,' her mother said.

'You stand together, you two sisters,' their mother told them. 'What are we going to do to father, who is always calling out for my elder sister?' the younger girl asked. 'You look at this Dreaming (*woni*),' the mother said. She removed the rope from under the paperbark: 'It is the Dreaming *mebu*, Milky Way rope!' Looking at it, the girls became giddy, their 'eyes went around' ['as if they were drunk']. When they had recovered, they collected the food they had hoarded and put it into the two baskets; they put them on their heads, and picked up that banyan tree shade. The mother tossed the rope up into the sky. The elder sister climbed up first, the younger sister was in the middle, and the mother came last. They climbed up the rope into the sky. There they sat down under their banyan tree, with their food, and they coiled up the rope to form the extent of the Milky Way.

Bindag-bindag returned. The two sisters saw him coming. The younger sister said, 'Father is coming!' He called out from his canoe, but no-one answered. He came to the billabong bank, and called — but no answer. He went to his camp; there was no one there — only the sound of crows, '*Waag! Waag! Waag!*' 'What has happened to those girls? Has someone abducted them? Has someone killed them? Has their mother taken them away?' he thought. He ran around the camp, searching. No-one! He called his wife's name. 'Which way did she go?' He saw only the tracks made by ants. He called out for Balmadj *now!* There was no-one at all. He walked down the track leading to the water, looking, calling out for his wife.

From the sky, the younger sister called out. 'Father, I'm here!' 'What will I do?' he asked. 'You go and pick up that fish and bring it up here,' Balmadj said. She let down the rope. Bindag-bindag took hold of it and began to climb. However, Balmadj had other intentions. The younger sister suspected what she would do. She watched her mother, who removed a mussel shell 'knife' and got ready to cut the rope. Her daughter grabbed the knife and hid it. [She did not want her father to fall.] Her mother had hidden a large mussel shell and a small one behind each ear. Her daughter saw the large one and took it, hiding it. But the mother quickly removed the small shell and cut the rope just as Bindag-bindag, carrying his fish, was close to the top; he fell back. And where he fell is his Dreaming place. He crawled along on his injured knees back to his canoe and went into, the salt water, where he became a crocodile. The others remained in the sky, in the Milky Way which is the grass rope Balmadj made.

It was said that the younger sister condoned her sister's intercourse with their father; but it was also noted that she told her mother — although that is not referred to in the text. When Balmadj took out her large mussel shell, her younger daughter grabbed it as she began to cut: but because she was so engrossed with hiding it she did not see her mother remove the smaller shell. The two shells symbolise the elder and younger sisters. Also, Bindag-bindag was of the *burldjag* moiety, Balmadj was *garg*; the two daughters were *burldjag*.

The myth itself is fairly well-organised, leading gradually to a climax. The daily repetition of Bindag-bindag's intercourse with the elder sister holds the attention of listeners, especially because incest is involved. Under such circumstances, his punishment would be regarded as inevitable.

The following is one of the great myths of western Arnhem Land: it is religious but not secret-sacred. This version was told to R. Berndt in Gunwinggu, at Oenpelli in 1950.

181. YIRAWADBAD: BETROTHAL, REJECTION, DEATH

Yirawadbad, Poison snake, a *yariburig* man, came from Munanga, Macassar. He went first to Wungug, Melville Island, and after camping there for a while came across the strait to Djamalinggi, Cape Don [Wurugu language]. He was a very big, old, and bald-headed man, his baldness ringed with hair. His potential mother-in-law [*ngalgurng*] was Indjimad [*yarigarngurg, ngalbangari*] and her daughter Yugal [*yarigarngurg, ngalgangila*]. Yugal had three younger sisters, but their names were not known. Yirawadbad already had a wife named Warawoiwi [*yarigarngurg, ngalgangila*] whose mother was a Melville Islander. They camped at Djamalinggi. Warawoiwi slept with Yirawadbad. Yugal had been betrothed to him by her father and mother, but she stayed with her mother and sisters.

They moved camp to Mareidbuldang [at what is now the old jetty Landing, east of Cape Don; Wurugu-Yiwadja languages]. They remained there for some little time and then went on to Umaridj (or Gumaridj), farther east near the sea coast. He put a creek across a promontory [probably between Trepang Bay and Port Essington, with the sea at each side]. They came down that creek to Ngodidjbibigi where they camped, and then went on to Alawalalgbalgban billabong and creek. They walked to Waruwi, situated in the bush but on the coast, and they put a creek there. Continuing, they reached Arabulyu or, more correctly, Bulgad-bulgad-arabulyu, where Yirawadbad made a creek and called the place name. The party went on to Uru, where they camped and ate long *garbara* yams and put a big jungle there [at 'Jack Farmer station']. They stayed here for a while but then travelled on to Wongalu, where they camped on the beach near a hill. Warawoiwi was by now pregnant. Yirawadbad's betrothed wife did not like him: she was frightened of him and moreover, she had a lover. They left Wongalu, but came along slowly because of Warawoiwi's pregnancy: 'We had better go farther on to find more food,' they agreed. They went to Wiregini, a long beach, and walking along this [over Wurugu-Yiwadja territory] they came to Naguri, also a long sandy beach: he called the name of the place 'early one morning'. They continued to Warielia (Yiwadja), where they camped. The mosquitoes were particularly bad there, so Yirawadbad built a large grass hut; his side of the camp he made well, with no holes; but the other side, where that young girl, her sisters and her mother would sleep he made 'a bit ugly', with some holes in it. However, they left that place and came to Guldangan, where he made another grass hut in the same way; they camped there, and continued along the cliffs to Amerunuwulg, where they stayed and then went on to Gunawan, where they camped for a few days. They continued on. They were carrying a lot of heavy things, a bed of *mangulaidj* nut-grass and many other things: it was a very heavy load. They came to Irugunmulg, where they camped. Because there were so many mosquitoes, at each place where they camped they made a grass hut; his end was 'good', their end was 'bad'. They walked farther east, inland, to Inbirgab (Yiwadja) and eventually reached Malwaidj ('Reuben Cooper's Landing'), where Yirawadbad made a little hill, and camped. He called the name of the country, and made the hill to enable him to look out across the Marganala plain. He saw the plain ahead and then looked back: 'I've left my country a long way behind!' He looked south and saw Namargun (the Thunder and Lightning man); and he called that place Ungandun [where the lightning was]. He named that place from where he stood on the hill at Malwaidj.

They continued on their way. He saw the salt water: 'I want to see the salt water. This is the last time I will look on salt water. From now on, I'll go inland!' It was from Mananga hill that he saw the coast: 'I have to go away from it. No sea!' he said to himself. The party went on to Maragin, a little inland, and camped there for a few days. They walked on to Ildadbang, coming on to the Marganala plain: a salt-water creek ran through this place [that is, Marganala Creek]. They continued to Mirimiri, where they camped. Again there were many mosquitoes, so Yirawadbad built a large grass hut. Leaving that place, they went on to Wulgarma, where there was a little creek, (Yiwadja) and then to Almaldangari where they camped. They found food on the plain and came to Mamirud, where they collected long yams that were growing in profusion. The women dug yams, and Yirawadbad went out to hunt goanna with his three dogs, named Bunggerelgun, Golgolruna and Imilgir. They camped at Mamirud and then went on to Nonambala, where he made another grass hut of the same kind. It was here that Warawoiwi's child was born.

They walked on to Adjerage, where they camped for a long time. Yirawadbad tried to persuade Yugal to sleep with him; but she remained 'frightened' of him, sometimes responding angrily, sometimes 'quietly'. Leaving Adjerage they went to Irialang, where they camped. There were plenty of goannas here, but they were *walgalg*, tree goanna, and when they heard the Yirawadbad party they went into the trees. Going on to Manggalwub, Yirawadbad built another large hut, as usual. They stayed here for only a short while and went on to Gominan-munang on the Marganala plain side (Yiwadja), where he built a large hut. They went on to Angbalgbarang, on the plain, and he built a further hut, but after a while they continued to Banibuli, and then to Nundalngudj.

Attached to their party was a young man named Bulogu, Water Snake. He had been playing with Yugal: 'That's why she didn't want Yira-wadbad. She had been with Bulogu, and Yirawadbad was watching them!' They travelled on to Unggud. Yirawadbad went out hunting goanna. He wanted to take Warawoiwi with him, but she did not accompany him: her child had died of mosquito bites, and so had one of their dogs. When Yirawadbad returned, she could not reply to him when he spoke to her: she was too weak, 'mosquitoes had drained her of blood, she was almost dead'. They went on to Indjinmul and there Warawoiwi died. They buried her and her dead child as well as the dog at this place. They left the place immediately and went to Indabuma. Yirawadbad washed himself ritually there [as after a death], and they moved camp to Arubalgban [on the Marganala plain, 'land side', Yiwadja]. 'It is better we move on,' Yirawadbad decided.

They continued to Inbaning and camped, and then went on to Dalgung. Yirawadbad had broken his tooth on the cone of a pandanus nut, and he pulled it out at Dalgung. They went on to Uwaidjug, where he put a jungle and *gaman* bitter yams that he had brought from a long way away. Then to Nalmunda, where they camped, and to Wariyad where he 'put' a *manboiberi* tree [a species of wild 'apple': there are now two trees of this kind on the banks of Gunbalanya billabong, Oenpelli]. They continued to Adbamugid, where they camped, and to Milag-bilag, where there is plenty of *milag* grass: he made a depression among this, and rested in it. They moved on to the 'top side', to Ingbalungbun where he put a *marun* wild cabbage palm [the centre of which is eaten] 'for the new generations'. He also made a ritual object, *ubar* and put it there. In doing so, he called the *ubar* invocations that are used in these rituals. They went on to Inbalumbun, where there were Yiwadja people living. Yirawadbad 'made himself clever': 'What am I going to do?' he wondered. But he went on to Angbaranbinman, where there is a big cave. Yirawadbad and others of his party lived there for a while, and he went out hunting goanna. On one occasion, when rolling human hair [which he had brought from Macassar] on his thigh to make a waist-band, his penis became erect; he was thinking how much he wanted Yugal. They went a little farther on to Ragan-mari, a place so named because he threw away his hair string. He was impatient; his penis was still erect, and he pushed it against a flat rock outside a cave at Inyang-ngalwiag. [It made a hole of about four inches in diameter in the rock, which can be seen today.]

They moved on to Inyum-bulagang, where Yirawadbad made a shelter, and on to Idbana, then to Angbidbarang where they camped in a cave, eventually reaching Iluwindjulil. At this place Yirawadbad went out by himself and turned himself into a snake, and again he pushed his erect penis through a rock; he was 'hungry' for Yugal. [The hole may still be seen there, high up among the rocks.] Back in his camp he resumed his normal shape as a man. He went on to Aman-gan, where he put bitter round yams. Also, he climbed up onto the rocks and 'put himself' there, 'making himself a picture' [an ochred painting]. 'He was Dreaming himself' [pre-conditioning himself to become Dreaming]; 'he made himself clever', and said to himself, 'I'm good [at it] now. I'm going to kill that girl!'

They went on walking to Gudmadbari: here he collected some faeces from Indjimad and Yugal and heated these over a fire in order to sorcerise the two of them [that is, make them vulnerable to a future misfortune]. Then he climbed up among the rocks, and putting his head on the 'ground' with his body upright, used his tail to hit the rocks: 'He was getting his body ready to kill those two women. He was a *margidbu*, making himself powerful.' [Presumably he was now in his snake form. The rocks where he carried out this 'exercise' are named Balem-gurmerin, meaning 'where he put himself, fat': he took fat out of his body.] 'I'm a clever man. I've got more power,' he said to himself. [The fat made itself into rock.] Then he went out to 'bite' a bird. [The two women could not see him, because he was now in his snake form.] He tried to bite a bird but missed it and, instead, bit the grass. The place where this occurred is Manilgbanbun [Yiwadja name] or Dalgdambun [Gunwinggu name].

Indjimad and Yugal left their camp at Iluwimdjulil and went on to Madbari, north of Tor Rock; then they walked east to Aranagi, where they camped. Yirawadbad followed them in his human form and found them asleep. 'What about my trying her now? She might be quiet,' he thought. But Yugal had awakened and was watching out for him. He jumped onto her and put his leg between hers. Yugal was frightened and drew away. 'If you're frightened of me, you will miss that ground!' [He meant that she would not reach the place they intended to find.] 'I'm a clever man now. I'm going to kill you!' Yirawadbad said, angry at being repulsed.

They went on to Mangaram, and climbed to the top of some rocks. When Yugal slept, Yirawadbad tried to open her legs, but she turned to one side, keeping her legs tightly together. 'All right,' said Yirawadbad. 'You don't want me! Sometime I'll kill you!' Next night at Malulangudj he tried again to copulate with her, but the same thing happened. On the following day the two women went out to find *manbaram* roots and brought them back to the camp. [This ground was occupied later by Yiwadja, Maung and Gunwinggu; it was said that Yirawadbad collected the languages and mixed them.] Next day Yirawadbad went out to get bamboo; he found a large one, cut and cleaned it and made it into a didjeridu. [Another part of this myth tells how he threw these didjeridus to different places.] One particular bamboo he cut for himself; it was a big bamboo like an *ubar* in size. He polished it so it became black, marking it with sweat from under his arm. This was at Gwiyugi. He 'hid' that bamboo in an open place.

The three younger sisters of Yugal remained at Malulangudj, where the roots were cooking in the coals. Yugal and her mother went out again and heard a bird calling. They made a fire because the weather was cold.

In the meantime, Yirawadbad had turned himself into a snake. ['He had finished with being a man'.] He went inside the large hollow bamboo, the special one he had blackened. While he was in that 'log' [bamboo] he called the names of different birds. They all came flying over the log and perched on it. Crow looked into the log and saw Yirawadbad in his snake manifestation; all the birds were looking at 'him'. 'Ah, daughter,' said Indjimad as she saw the birds. 'You go and look, maybe something is there!' [that is, food]. Yugal came close to the log, and all the birds flew away. She came up to it and looked through one end, but she saw nothing: that was because she 'looked through his eye'. Yirawadbad was thinking to himself: 'This is a good woman; she has plenty of hair; she is a very nice girl, but she is very wild.' [He was thinking about her, trying to decide whether to kill her.] Yugal called out to her mother, 'Mother, I looked right through, there's nothing there: no bandicoot, no goanna.' She went back to her mother. All the birds returned to the *ubar*, covering it. [Note: the hollow log is first referred to as a bamboo, then a didjeridu, and now an *ubar*.] 'Something *must* be there,' the mother said. 'What about going back again, to make sure? There might be something!' So Yugal went, looked through the *ubar*, but again saw nothing. 'Mother, there's nothing there!' She rejoined her mother. Again, all the birds came back and perched on the *ubar*. 'Perhaps you haven't looked properly. Perhaps there is a possum or bandicoot there. It looks like an old log!' [Yirawadbad had made it look old by blackening it, and ashes were scattered all around it.] 'A bandicoot could have got inside.'

Indjimad herself went to look. She squatted before the aperture at one end of the *ubar*, with her legs apart, and looked in. Yirawadbad closed his eyes; he was ashamed to look at his *ngalgurng's* [potential mother-in-law's] genitals. ['That is why we can't look at our *ngalgurng*,' the narrator commented.] She looked through the *ubar* and saw that it was dark inside. She called out to her daughter, 'There *is* something here: I looked through, and it's dark inside!' 'I did look properly,' Yugal said, as she came over to her mother, breaking off a stick on the way. 'Daughter, you sit at the other end.' They were squatting one at each end, with the *ubar* between their legs. Yirawadbad turned round. 'He didn't want to look at his *ngalgurng*; he wanted to look at his (betrothed) wife.' 'You poke with the stick, and I'll grab what comes out,' the mother said, and put both her hands into the *ubar*. Yugal poked with her stick, but lost her grip on it, and it went to the other side. 'Mother, there is nothing here!' she repeated. The mother looked through again. 'I can see something!' She grasped the stick that had come through, and pushed it in again. 'I'm touching something here!' She pushed strongly; her daughter was ready to grab what came out. Yirawadbad waited: 'I have to kill her,' he said. The mother pushed that stick 'so hard' that sweat poured from her. And Yirawadbad bit Yugal on the hand. 'Something has bitten me, mother — a goanna or a bandicoot. I'm feeling it; you push hard again.' So the mother poked with her stick, and Yirawadbad bit Yugal again. 'Quickly, mother, push the stick.' He bit Yugal again. [Apparently, on these three occasions Yirawadbad did not bite her properly.] The mother pushed the stick once more, so hard that the sweat poured from her 'as if she had just washed herself'. And Yirawadbad thought, 'I'll have to kill that girl, but I don't want to. When I tried to copulate with her, she didn't want me. I've got to kill her, and my *ngalgurng* too. I've got to kill both of them!' Then he bit Yugal's fingers again.

At this juncture the smallest of the three daughters at Malulangudj began crying for her mother's milk. Indjimad called out to her other two daughters to look after the child. 'We have to kill this creature first.' The two girls told their little sister, 'Maybe they are killing a goanna for us,' and the child was quiet.

The mother pushed her stick through the *ubar*. Yirawadbad was ready: 'I'm going to kill them!' He turned his body, rolling himself up to Indjimad's end, and grabbed her fingers. 'I've caught it now,' she called. He bit her! Yirawadbad turned his head and came back to where Yugal was: he bit her hand. Mother and daughter, both fell back, they were lying there. Yirawadbad came out from the *ubar*; he made himself into a man. He spoke to himself: 'I have to kill everyone now! I am a man, but even people of my own skin, and other creatures too, I must kill. My skin is *yariburig*. I'm Yirawadbad!' [These events took place at Wadbal, at the head of No. 1 Sandy Creek to Wadbal Hill, with Tor Rock a little south.]

Then those three children ran up to the *ubar*, having heard the cries of their mother and sister. They saw the log, they saw their mother and sister lying there. Yirawadbad 'jumped' and turned himself into a snake and then, when he walked away, he turned himself into a man. He made a noise when he saw the three daughters coming. However, he left that place and went on. The three girls cried: they did not know what to do; they left their dead mother and sister there. [The narrator added that the mother and her daughter did not revive; they set the pattern for human death.] They asked the youngest sister where they should go. She replied, 'Andalmula (Garei-andalmula).' They turned back, and commenced walking, crying all the way. Finally, they washed themselves [as after a death], and poked their ears to remove *mulgilag*, wax. They stayed there, Dreaming, swimming in the billabong.

As for Bulogu, Yugal's sweetheart, he was frightened of Yirawadbad. They had all been camping together. Yirawadbad became very jealous, and Bulogu ran away southward: his story was unknown.

[The myth continues] with Yirawadbad leaving Wadbal and going eastward to Aguru (Gunwinggu-Yiwadja) in his human manifestation. He continued to Indjambid creek where he made a stringybark hut. [It became a rock.] He walked on farther to Maniwugum where he put yellow ochre, followed the creek from the head of the King River and, going through the bush, crossed another creek at Igurana. [There is now a road from here to Barclay Point on the coast.] He followed that small creek to Man-gu: with the stringybark he was carrying, he made a hut for himself, and it, too, turned to rock. [It will be recalled that Yirawadbad cut bamboos near Malulangudj. When he stood on Wadbal hill, nearby, he threw bamboo spears eastward: he found some of these later during this part of his journey.] At Malimangainbaran he cut off his moustache. Crossing a small creek at Ilawalalg, he looked for a spear he had thrown from Wadbal. He turned around, passing a jungle, and walked farther up to where many bamboos were growing: he found his spear among them. Going on to Balem-gurmerin, he removed fat from his body as he had before, hitting his body on the rocks: the fat made itself into a round rock [as this place name, too, indicates]. He walked on to Man-golidulbul [bamboo name] where there are springs and bamboo growing [from his spears], with hills at each side. From there, he went goanna hunting with his remaining dog, Ilawalyag [not previously mentioned]: the country is also called after this dog.

He found goanna and walked to a billabong, located at the headwaters of the King River. He made camp beside this billabong, at Andanyadari-igban. There are caves here: he tried to make a good camp but his hut was constructed roughly, in haste: so he called this country Andanyadari-igban. While camping here, he walked up the creek and pulled out his snake-tooth, replacing it with human teeth [that is, his own teeth]. He put his snake-tooth in the creek at Geiig-medjadbi, and it turned into a rock, standing upright in the creek near the King River.

Yirawadbad went farther up, coming to Ilawalalg [variation of Ilawalyag, the name of his dog]: he was feeling tired [a 'bit lazy' was the English expression used]. He was thinking this way: 'I'm getting too old, I'm losing my power!' He slept there. 'What am I going to do?' He turned over and made himself into a snake. 'I'll leave a man [that is, himself as a human being] and that dog here, so people can see them!' he thought to himself. 'I'm going to walk up like a snake.' He climbed the big hill: 'I'll try this rock!' He went through that rock and left his skin behind, and moved all the way under the ground. There is a hole in this rock, near the ground, not very wide: his skin flew away. That dog, Ilawalyag, turned into a rock. Yirawadbad moved under the ground just like a snake. He went for a long way [for about twenty miles] and he stood up again, close to, but north of, Nimbuwa. He made a billabong; he made himself into a snake. The billabong's name is Yirwadbad-dolmeng. He walked along, eating, arriving at Gerul where he made a wide billabong by coiling himself within it. From here he looked up and saw a hill. 'I've got to go up there, the rain is coming!' he said. He left the billabong and climbed up the hill. There he found a good place, at Gabald-djeyu: he made his body wide, he made it big, and he made it into rock.

That wide rock body of his may be seen and touched by anyone. But Yirawadbad also made a thin body, 'his real body', close to the fat one; and that thin body is the important one — no-one may touch it. He is down there at the bottom of the cave, in the dry part of the hill. 'If the wind is blowing toward that cave, he can smell us if we are near; then he goes farther in, because he might see us. If we touched that stone, his thin body, a lot of *yirawadbad* snakes would come out!' This place is high up, farther from Nimbuwa (Gunwinggu, Maung and Yiwadja). He made an *ubar* at Ilawalalg, its big name being Gubidbu; he made another at Maramidbal; in all, he made five *ubar*. This story you have heard 'is the Yirawadbad for the outside': that is, as contrasted with the secret-sacred version.

There are several versions of this myth; some are mentioned in R. and C. Berndt (1970: 119–20 and, especially, 230–33). It is based on a relatively simple theme. A girl rejects her betrothed husband who is much older and, moreover, in this version, bald, in favour of a young man (Bald-headedness was regarded as ugliness in traditional Gunwinggu society.) She persists in her attitude, and he becomes angry; he vows to kill her and also his mother-in-law, who has not insisted that the girl must accept him. In this case, Yirawadbad's response was to devise a special method of killing them both, in his snake manifestation. It is around the hollow log that much of the religious *ubar* ritual is focused. The symbolic significance of this object has two sides: as a vehicle through which death is imposed, and as a life-giving uterus symbol relevant to the Fertility Mother.

That aside, since the second aspect is not discussed here, in causing the death of the two women, Yirawadbad exacts punishment as much as revenge. In doing this, through his shape-changing power, he fulfils his destiny in becoming, finally, an important, living Dreaming site.

Around this basic theme are interwoven many details. From an Aboriginal viewpoint the strong story-line, enhanced with so many details, combine to make it a great myth. There is a sequence of incidents that gradually unfold in an atmosphere of growing suspense, leading to a double climax: firstly, the killing of the mother and daughter and, secondly, his final transformation and metamorphosis. The whole account is intimately associated with the country, with things being 'made' and places being named to commemorate specific events mentioned in the myth. The myth itself, in its various versions, retains its basic plot and much of the elaborating detail; and it is subject to varying interpretations, ranging from straightforward statements about marriage rules and marital relationships to esoteric religious associations.

The next story, of Luma-luma the Whale, or Luma-luma as a Rainbow Snake, was told to C.H. Berndt at Oenpelli in 1950.

---

182. LUMA-LUMA

That one they call Luma-luma — well, long ago when he was a man he had two wives. They set off far away in the east, toward the sunrise, and as they came along they were speaking in their own language. Well, he was bringing the *mareiin* rituals and the *ubar* and the *lorgun*. Little biting-baskets too, to hold between his teeth in fighting. And that Creature, that Snake, from underneath the ground. So they were coming, speaking in their own tongue.

They would hear those others, those first people chopping out wild honey, and he would go running and declare that honey to be *mareiin*, sacred and taboo. Those people would just leave that honey, then, because he made it taboo to them. He was always doing that. When he heard women going along, getting long yams, very big ones, he would go to look at them. If the yams were really large, he would declare them to be *mareiin* so the women couldn't eat them. Then he himself would eat them, because he had made it taboo to all the others. He kept on doing that. When those other men were spearing kangaroos with good fat, and fish, and various creatures, he would go and look, and declare them taboo so nobody but himself could eat them. He always had plenty to eat.

At last they were arguing about him, talking among themselves, those various men and women. 'Today, now, we'll attack him and kill him, because he makes everything taboo to us — small creatures, kangaroos, plant foods, honey. He stops us from eating all these things, when we ourselves were the ones who found them!'

But he was still coming along. He would go and settle down where he found a place he wanted. There he would be clapping the special sticks for the *mareiin* rites he was bringing, and he would say, 'It's good, all of it!' He kept doing that. He was showing those two women, showing them for the first time.

Well, they were still coming this way, toward the west. They were going along, camping, eating meat and plant foods and fish. They would camp, and early in the morning he would start to clap those sticks they were bringing for that *mareiin*. He said to his two wives, 'We'll go and sit down in camp, and you two try that *madjidji* women's dancing and I'll make a men's *mareiin* sound.' He clapped the sticks and they danced the *madjidji*. It was good! But they didn't look when he himself went among the grasses, transforming himself, and calling out from high in a tree, as they do in the *mareiin*. That's what he was doing. He found it first, and then he showed those people, those men, who transform themselves in their shade. It was finished: it was good. They set off again, still speaking in their own language, coming this way.

He could hear them cutting trees, those first people. He was already running toward them. They were about to start eating, but he made their food taboo to them. So they just had to leave it: they didn't eat that honey they themselves had found. He looked at the smoke from the fires where women were cooking plant foods, and he went straight there. He watched them taking food from the coals. He left the small things for them to eat, but the big ones he made taboo to them, and he ate those himself. They left them for him because they were afraid, those women. They couldn't do anything about it, because the food had become no good to them: that *mareiin* taboo was too dangerous. He kept on doing the same thing, that man who found the *mareiin* for us men and women.

His wives scolded him, because he was making those people hungry. No, it was no use. He was looking at that *mareiin* in his head, all the time, wearing the *mareiin* basket hanging down on his chest. The two women went out looking for plant foods while he stayed in camp, dancing the *mareiin*. So then, when they brought back food they would put the small things there for him, but the big things they would hide from him. They knew already that he might make these taboo to them and they would be hungry. They had been looking when he declared such food taboo to others who had not known about it before. That's what he was always doing.

He was still going about clapping his *mareiin* sticks. When they heard him, those men and women would say, 'That's the man, that Luma-luma, he has the *mareiin*! So, quickly, all of you hide the cooked things: the kangaroos, the small creatures, and the plant foods! He's already getting close to us!' Well, they hid it all. That man, Luma-luma, called out to them. They went. He said to them, 'Go and make a shade, so that I can show you this *mareiin* I'm bringing, then you will always know it.' They all camped there, and the men went up to their sacred place. Luma-luma was wearing the *mareiin* he always carried, and he was their headman when they came down from the place. They kept doing that. In the late afternoon all the women were getting fires ready. One fire was burning for the *dua* moiety, another for the *yiridja* moiety, because he had already told his two wives about his *mareiin*. So when the men came down, the women were dancing, circling around the tree. The *dua* men came down first, and then the *yiridja*, because that *dua* man Luma-luma had the *mareiin* first. The women danced the *madjidji*, as Luma-luma went back to bring the *yiridja* men down. Then he finished it; they finished it all. He told them, 'That's what you are to do when I die, because this *mareiin* I'm bringing, you are all to have it, and you're to wear the *mareiin* basket like I'm doing.'

He was coming along, and he found the place he had been planning to reach, there in the east. Luma-luma wanted those children, children who had died and were put on mortuary platforms. He would go and get them, and eat them all. When those various people went to look at the platforms, they said, 'He's the one, Luma-luma — here are his tracks! He's eating our children, finishing them all. What are we going to do to him?', they said, those men and women.

He went on and was camping there in that country he had found. But they were getting ready for trouble when they made those things taboo, creatures and fish, those big ones, when he saw them and declared them to be *mareiin*. 'We'll kill him, or he might always eat our children!' They set off, ready for a fight. They came from Balbanara, and from Bendjuwi, and from Manawugan, with spears and sticks and spear-throwers, to kill him, because he was a big man, that Luma-luma.

Well, Luma-luma was going into the sea. He was transforming himself when he was eating fish, and then transforming himself to look like a man again when he went back to his wives. He kept on doing that. Those two women would go hunting, while he was making himself into a fish, under the water in the middle of the sea. Then at last he would come back to where they were camping, looking like a man. He was trying to change himself, out there in the sea.

At last all those men, speaking different languages, came sneaking up to him. They said, 'You might go and eat us all, finish us all up!' They were throwing spears at him, all over his body. He himself, that Luma-luma, was saying, 'Wait, spear me slowly, so I can show you that *ubar* — how to transform yourselves, you men, when you go to your sacred place. Well, women would have been the ones in charge of that *ubar*, but Garurgen Kangaroo-woman was no good at it when she tried first: she couldn't do it. She went among the grasses and tried, but she couldn't get it right. Then that man, Gulubar Kangaroo-man, tried that *ubar*, and he did it properly. Now the *ubar* is for men. So spear me slowly!' Well, they speared him slowly, biting him on the body with one spear after another. He was looking at them as they filled him with spears. He was saying, 'Don't use a lot of spears, in spearing me, so that I can show you the *lorgun*: then you can transform yourselves after I die!' He was showing them all, showing that sacred ritual. Well, then they were spearing him again, with a lot of spears. He was saying to them, 'Go slowly when you spear me, and wait while I give you that *gunabibi*, when you bring out that Snake from under the ground!' He was showing them all, and his wives were doing the same for the women. They were showing them, those first people, people like us, who made themselves *djang*. They were teaching them the words that they kept in their minds.

Well, they speared those two women a little, and at last both of them died. Only Luma-luma stayed alive for a while. But then he was a very big man: he didn't die quickly. He gave them all that sacred ritual. He asked them, 'Did you get it all, that sacred ritual? Did you get it all, that sacred information I gave you? Tell me!' And those people, those real people, answered him, 'We have it all. The *mareiin* you gave us, and those clapping-sticks of yours you were carrying, that you gave us, we'll keep always, so we ourselves can make a shade and complete it all properly ourselves.' Then they began to spear him again, because he had already given them his *mareiin* basket too — his very own basket, that he gave them. He said, 'Well, you spear me. I've already given you that *mareiin*, the basket too, and clapping-sticks, that you take for ever. And I'll die when you spear me.' They speared him once more. At last they saw that his breath was finished. They went, and put him there on the beach, to dry — seated against a tree, with a string tied round his neck to hold him there. They didn't bury him, or he might have died forever, but they put him near the sea.

He went on, and transformed himself into a creature. His body went into the sea, under the water, and then afterward he became a creature. He goes about there in the sea, where he transformed himself, that Luma-luma. But he didn't kill any of us, he only stole the bodies of those children who had died. Then he ate their bodies. So, it was good that they killed him. He went into the sea, he became like a creature, like a Rainbow Snake, when he goes about in the water — he went forever!

The story of Luma-luma is especially intriguing because of its apparent contradictions. The religious rituals he was bringing continue to be important, and in myth and in discussions their positive qualities are emphasised. In the Luma-luma account not much is said about any of them. He indicates that they are good, that they are significant, and people need to know about them and perpetuate them, and the story notes a few items connected with them. But this is not a religious myth in the sense of providing instruction or information about either content or performance. Even the reference to the respective roles of men and women in the *ubar* ritual is more like a sideways glance at it than a definitive statement about it. Mangurug, who gave this version, was one of the senior and most knowledgeable women in the area at that time; and in other contexts she emphasised a different reason for the division of labour between them. (Kangaroo Man couldn't perform properly what is now the women's dance pattern; so Kangaroo Woman said, 'All right, we'll change, and I'll do the women's dance.' And so on.) Mangurug also knew that the *ubar* rituals did not traditionally come from the east: they were regarded as a distinctively western Arnhem Land development. It was the *mareiin* in particular that was believed to have come from eastern Arnhem Land, more than the *lorgun*, whereas the *gunabibi* rites spread from the south and south-east.

Luma-luma as a character does not show up too well, despite his beneficent role as a ritual-bringer. People in the story accept him in that role, at least to the extent of participating in rites under his direction. But alongside their acceptance is an even more strongly explicit rejection, culminating in his death and the death of his two wives. It was not only that he was greedy and overbearing, commandeering (stealing) all the best food that people had worked hard to obtain. But he did this in the name of religion, using the most powerful sanction in the repertoire — a religiously-based taboo, with its threat of almost automatic retribution. So they did not dare to resist him openly, and the hiding of food came later. The intriguing point here is the almost cynical or sardonic reference to an established and important traditional custom — that is, compensatory payments for ritual revelations, payments that in the ordinary way cannot be evaded. The Luma-luma story is one of the very few examples of this in western Arnhem Land.

This next story centres on Mururuma. It is one of the great dramatic narratives of the north-eastern corner of Arnhem Land, associated with the Riradjingu dialect unit, and was told to R. Berndt at Yirrkalla in 1946.

183. THE VIOLENCE OF MURURUMA AND THE RESULTING FEUD

Mururuma, the Bremer Island Turtle Hunter [Riradjingu dialect] had two sons, Dangadjiana and Wural-wural. He also had a number of wives of the Wonguri, Lamamiri, Waramiri and Gumaidj dialect groups. They lived at Bremer Island, where he made turtle harpoon rope. One day he went out fishing with one of his wives, a young *yiridja* moiety Wonguri woman. She was continually 'worrying about' her relatives, her father, brothers and sisters who were at Dalin-ngura [near Cape Arnhem. It was also said that she would not sleep with Mururuma and had a matri-cross-cousin sweetheart: see later]. So Mururuma became angry and taking up a knife, threatened to slit her from vulva to throat. But he held his hand because they were out fishing and, instead, promised to take her back to her family 'after he had completed some dancing'.

They returned to Bremer Island, where Mururuma and members of his group had been camping. There was singing, and dancing. Unloading the canoe, they walked up to the others, but the young Wonguri wife kept on worrying about her people and her country. After the dancing, Mururuma took up his knife and killed her in the way he had threatened. The people left her lying there. Taking their canoes, they crossed over to the mainland and walked south to Cape Arnhem, where they hid in a jungle, awaiting the appearance of a *miringu*, revenge or fighting party.

Meanwhile, the dead Wonguri girl's father, brothers and sisters, along with her cross-cousin (father's sister's son), arrived at Bremer Island. They did not know she was dead. They looked round for Mururuma's camp and, coming into it, the cross-cousin saw her body lying there. Immediately he turned to her brothers and told them, 'Wait, there is something in that camp!' 'Can we look?' they asked. 'No, you shouldn't see it!' he replied. [A man should not touch or look at the body of his dead sister.] Her cross-cousin was angry and upset. Her brothers said, 'All right, cousin, go by yourself. We'll wait for you!' He collected paperbark and wrapped up the body, and summoned all the people. He told them that Mururuma was their 'enemy'. They danced and sang in her mortuary ritual, and then buried her. [Normally she would have been put on a mortuary platform.] Her brothers were asking each other what they should do. The cousin replied, 'We will follow their tracks and find where we can kill them [him].'

Mururuma kept watching. He knew that the dead girl's relatives had found her body; 'something had told him'. The *miringu* party, consisting of the dead girl's cousin, father, brothers and sisters, went past Cape

Arnhem. Some of the others came into Mururuma's camp at Cape Arnhem. He was surprised, because he had been expecting to see her immediate relatives. 'I know you lot,' he said. 'I see you very well, because I've done something to one of your women!' The others, however, went westward across country to Arnhem Bay. They had decided to wait for Mururuma until he came to Melville Bay: they would confront him there.

At Arnhem Bay they met the great *miringu* leader, Bugalaidjbi ['a very dangerous man'], a Waramiri dialect man whose home was at Melville Bay: he had taken *miringu* parties to Caledon and to Blue Mud Bays, to Port Bradshaw, and to the English Company Islands, and even as far as Milingimbi. The dead woman's relatives arranged with him to kill Mururuma. Eventually, Mururuma came to Melville Bay and Bugalaidjbi saw him out hunting for stingray and fish. Bugalaidjbi got together his *miringu* party and they hid in the bush, awaiting Mururuma's return from fishing. Bugalaidjbi told them to wait for him, and said that he would speak to Mururuma first — 'Then, when I call out, you can come out with your spears and spear him.' Bugalaidjbi met Mururuma and told him that a *miringu* was after him: 'Look, the enemy is coming from that way!' But Mururuma replied, 'I think you are tricking me!' And as he turned his back, Bugalaidjbi threw his carved spear, so that it entered Mururuma's chest and came out on the other side. As he did this, the other members of the *miringu* emerged from their hiding place and threw their spears at the fallen Mururuma; they killed him. They built a large fire and threw his body on it, burning him. Then they took all Mururuma's wives, who had been with him, away to Arnhem Bay, where they redistributed them to other men.

Mururuma's friends and relatives were camping at Cape Arnhem, but his two sons were at Bremer Island. The people at Cape Arnhem were worried: 'When is Mururuma coming back? We haven't seen him for a long time!' His mother, father, father's father, father's brother and brothers went from place to place looking for him. As soon as they reached the point near Bremer Island [visible from Yirrkalla], at a mangrove tree, the spirit (*birimbir*) of Mururuma appeared. They thought it was Mururuma himself; they did not know it was a spirit. They were happy to see him, but when they came closer the vision disappeared. Then they looked out to sea, to the Muruwiri Rocks, and there was the spirit of Mururuma. And there it remains.

When they saw the spirit, they talked among themselves: 'Perhaps he has been killed! We must return to Cape Arnhem and get together our *miringu*, and go to Arnhem Bay.' They set to work making spears. 'We must kill those people because of what they have done to Mururuma!' When they were ready they set off through the bush to Arnhem Bay and came close to the camp, where they saw all the people, and the women who had been Mururuma's wives. The leader of this revenge party was a

Lamamiri dialect man named Yumbulul. They asked him, 'What will we do? Shall we attack during the night or the day?' 'We'll go during the night.' he replied. 'If we go now, they'll see us. We'll hide ourselves and go sneaking to them at night.' They waited there until all the people in the camp were asleep. Then the Cape Arnhem party crawled through the bush; the others did not know they were coming. They speared them because they had killed Mururuma. They took back with them all the wives who had been Mururuma's, as well as two of Mururuma's daughters, Bereibi and Mawuruma, who were married to Bugalaidjbi. Bugalaidjbi, however, escaped. The revenge party returned to Cape Arnhem. One of its members went on, and crossed over to Bremer Island to take the news to Mururuma's two sons, Dangadjiana and Wural-wural; the first had seven wives, the second three. 'So you have no father,' the messenger told them. 'What happened?' they asked. 'Bugalaidjbi brought enemies!' he replied. 'We will keep watch. If he [they] comes here, we'll kill him [them].'

Those two brothers saw a fire on the immediate mainland. 'Where is that from?' The other replied, 'I know where they [those who made the fire] come from!' The elder brother agreed, 'We'll go across.' They got turtle meat and seagull eggs and went over to the mainland by canoe, to the billabong side, at Wirawa (or Wireiwa). There they met Damanbia, a Galbu headman, who was accompanied by his large group of wives [number not known]. They asked Damanbia where he was from, and Damanbia replied, 'I'm from Cape Wilberforce.' 'How did you come here? 'I walked along the beach,' Damanbia said. 'Where are your wives?' they asked. 'They're getting lily roots at the billabong,' he answered. Damanbia then asked them, 'Have you any turtle?' 'Yes, we have a lot here,' and then, 'You had better get your wives.' So Damanbia went to get his wives; he did not know about the death of the two brothers' father, Mururuma.

The two brothers commenced singing the songs their father had sung — the same ones he sang before he killed his Wonguri wife. When Damanbia returned, they speared him with their carved spears. As he lay there dying, they told him: 'Our father is dead now. Some people of the Arnhem Bay group have killed him — from that lot he died!' The two brothers had a big canoe [from the Macassans], and they took all Damanbia's wives back with them to Bremer Island. There they remained for a while. One woman [one of the abducted wives of Damanbia] went to Arnhem Bay and told the people camped there of her husband's killing.

In the meantime the two brothers, the sons of Mururuma, went by canoe to Gwoimungara in the English Company Islands group. They beached at Damadbi island, and were catching tortoises in the bush when, in the distance, on the mainland, they saw a fire. They did not know that Bugalaidjbi was there. However, on the island were two of their nephews,

Dagadjinga and Milidjunga. Their mothers were Bereibi and Mawu-
ruma, who had married Bugalaidjbi, but had been taken away by the
Cape Arnhem group who had gone to Arnhem Bay to avenge the death of
Mururuma. (They were Mururuma's daughters; and Dagadjinga and
Milidjunga were Bugalaidjbi's sons.) They told their uncles to come to the
mainland to participate in a *buyuguma* 'friendship' dance for the murdered
Damanbia. [But, it was added here, 'This was not really a friendship
dance; Bugalaidjbi intended to trick them; it was going to be a big fight.
Bugalaidjbi had been tracking those two brothers.']

Dangadjiana and Wural-wural went in their sisters' sons' canoe. When
they came close to land, they saw Bugalaidjbi, but they thought he was
friendly. They looked around and could see no *miringu*; Bugalaidjbi had
his men hidden. The two sisters' sons did not know either. Nor did their
mothers [who had returned to their husband]. When they beached their
canoe, Bugalaidjbi came forward and said, 'Where is this enemy from?'
and added, 'We must spear you!' The two brothers looked about them
and took up their carved spears. But Bugalaidjbi picked up his first, and
speared the elder brother, Dangadjiana, through the back. The younger
brother, Wural-wural, ran away, with the *miringu* party after him, but he
dodged their spears. They all tried to spear him, but missed. Soon their
supply of spears was exhausted.

Dagadjinga remained sitting in the canoe. Bugalaidjbi called out to
him: 'Please, my son, kill your uncle [mother's brother]: don't forgive
him, you can spear him!' Dagadjinga replied, 'I look after my uncle; I'm
not going to kill him. He's my real mother's brother, he and my mother
are from one father. If I kill him, my mother will make trouble for me. She
might get a knife and cut my throat!' He spoke that way. The other
brother, the younger one, Milidjunga, however, got a long thin *dalbalanga*
knife [a Macassan *djagin* kris. He was young and did not think!] That
young boy threw that knife at his mother's brother's ankle. Thus
wounded, he was vulnerable. Bugalaidjbi was able to kill him easily.

Before the two brothers came and were met by Bugalaidjbi, he sent
Bereibi and Mawuruma out to collect oysters. But he had tricked them
too; they thought their brothers had been invited to a 'friendship'
ceremony. After the killing of the two brothers, Dagadjinga came and told
his mothers what had happened: that both their brothers had been killed.
The two sisters left their oysters and clams and in great anger rushed to
get their Macassan knives. They threw themselves on Bugalaidjbi's group
[those who were involved in the killing], cutting them: 'they were grieving
for their two brothers!' They turned to Bugalaidjbi, ready to kill him.
'Don't kill me, leave me alive!' he cried. But those two women did not
heed his pleading. They took him by the arm, in the daytime, and
wounded him. Next night, Dagadjinga wounded his younger brother
Milidjunga. These events, after the killing of Mururuma's two sons,

caused a further revenge party to come to Arnhem Bay, from the Bralbral and Gabin dialect groups: some people escaped, some were killed . . .

While the story of Mururuma and his two sons is a mythological account, it conforms closely with reports of the traditional patterning of feuding in north-eastern Arnhem Land (see Warner 1937/1958, Chapter VI). From time to time, some attempt would be made to resolve a particular feud-sequence, at least temporarily. However, it could easily be reactivated and continue through several generations. Usually, they involved a fairly large number of persons. Men were even more vulnerable than women, since they played an active part in *miringu* expeditions. In this story there are undertones as well as overtones. One suggestion is that Mururuma's victim was a nagging wife who tried his patience too far. Another is that the real reason was that she wanted to rejoin her matri cross-cousin — a relationship that would not traditionally have had any sexual implications. As in this example, feuds could be triggered by the killing of a woman, and they could include the abduction of wives and daughters of defeated men. Because people had to marry outside their own language units, and because at any one time there were usually several powerful men, each with a number of wives drawn from several different inter-marrying units, a wide and interlocking network of kin was likely to be caught up in any particular feud sequence; and along with that, for both men and women, went the problem of conflicting loyalties. [For a summary of a different version, told to C.H. Berndt by women at Galiwinku, Elcho Island, see C.H. Berndt in R.M. Berndt and E.S. Phillips (1973: 85).]

The following myth was told to R. Berndt at Ooldea in 1941 by a Mara man, near the Mandjindji dialect group.

184. THE REVIVAL OF CROW'S SON

Two men, a father and son, who were Dreaming Gaan-ga (Crows) came to Buril rockhole. They stayed there until the rain came and then the son went out hunting kangaroos. On wet ground, their newly-made tracks were easy to follow. He speared one at Berili, camped there for a while, and continued hunting. As he moved across the country he came upon a young *mamu* girl [in human form; she was a transformation of a *mamu-ganba*, a malignant spirit snake]. She was sitting by a rat's burrow not far from Buril. In the hole lived Medika (Grey Rat). This *mamu* girl and her mother intended to kill all the *medika* rats in the area. Her mother had gone into the burrow and was killing any *medika* she found, then handing them up to her daughter, who removed their internal organs and cleaned the carcases. She kept watch over her fire-stick.

The Gaan-ga son thought the *mamu* girl was alone. While she was concentrating on cleaning a rat he stole her fire-stick, because he and his father had no fire. The *mamu* girl saw him running away with it. When her mother emerged from the hole she told her what had happened: that a stranger man had taken their fire. The *mamu* mother was angry. She set off in pursuit of Gaan-ga, and saw him cooking kangaroo at Berili. She crept up behind him, bit him, and killed him. Then she smoke-dried his body in the ashes of his own fire. A little later, following her mother's tracks, the daughter arrived carrying all the rats in a wooden dish. They were happy to have so much meat. First they ate the kangaroo meat that the Gaan-ga son had caught. Next morning they set off to where the father Gaan-ga lived at Buril, carrying the son's body and the rats. Before reaching his camp, they placed the body at the bottom of the large wooden dish, underneath the rats. Entering Gaan-ga's camp, they put the large dish on the ground and covered it with bushes. From a distance, father Gaan-ga could smell his dead son. He returned to his camp and sat with the *mamu*. The *mamu* mother gave him rat meat; he took it away and ate it. After a while he heard the *mamu* girl crying, asking her mother for a portion of the dead son's body to eat: 'Break off a hand, mother, and give it to me!' Her mother broke off an arm and gave it to her.

That night Gaan-ga took up a heavy *winda* spear, about two inches in diameter, with a sharp wooden blade at one end. Away from the rockhole, he cleared a space, removing all the grass and bushes, and in the centre he lodged his *winda* firmly in the ground with its point upward. Then he began to sing:

gadji windang woningu dildurung
winda spear throw down upon it.

As he sang, he made a willy-willy, a whirlwind (*gubi-gubi-walba*). It rose up in the air and then came down to pick up the *mamu* daughter and deposit her body, impaled on the *winda*. Then he made another willy-willy that caught up the *mamu* mother and impaled her, too, on the *winda*. He left them there, dead.

He went over to where his son lay, dead. Wailing, he put the body into a wooden dish. Carrying this in the crook of his arm, he went on to Gaan, crying all the way. He placed the dish on the ground and went in search of bushes to build a wind-break. Sitting before the corpse, he bent forward and applied his lips to various parts of his son's body, sucking out all the *yuna*, pus-like fluid. Next he smeared the body with pus and, using this as an adhesive, covered it entirely with *wamalu* eaglehawk down he had collected. The young crow did not move for some time: his father sat a little distance away and watched over him.

While this was happening, Weruweru (or Buningga; Grey-black 'rabbit' Hawk) came in large numbers; they had smelt the corpse from a distance. The Weruweru had been 'way up north' and they came down to Gaan, following the smell of meat. They saw old Gaan-ga and his son, and encircled them several times. Gaan-ga hunted them away: so the Buning (-ga) sat waiting a little way off at Gulgon. As he sat there on a rock, looking toward Gaan, Buning sang this song. [It is uncertain whether the whole 'mob' sang: the text refers to one Buning, the leader.]

> *buning-djalba ralwal-ralwal buning-djalwal-ralwal*
> Hawk, flapping wings.

Then Gaan-ga sang:

> *danda walung-gana*
> *wadi danbana liralira dandan-walung-gana*
> From that rock, watching [the corpse].
> All the threatening ones.

Again Gaan-ga sang:

> *mayi wanawana*
> *miniliri rianu*
> *yu gaan-ga dumba dai*
> *mayi wanawana*
> Following food [those hawks]
> Heat of the fire [reviving]
> Yes, Crow is a clever man.
> Following food . . .

Watching his son, Gaan-ga saw blood gradually coming to the surface of his body. As the blood oozed up, young Gaan-ga stirred a little, first moving his fingers, then gradually his limbs, then his whole body. He was becoming alive again!

On seeing this, the Buning flew back northward: they knew he would not be meat for them.

Young Gaan-ga sat up; then he began to walk; then he sat by his father. His father got food for him and kept him warm. After a while he regained his strength and became fully conscious. His father washed his body, removing the feather down and congealed pus; young Gaan-ga became as he was before. They slept, and next morning continued on their travels eastward.

Two of the characters in this story are of a kind we have met before: malignant *mamu* who are antithetical to human beings, whether or not they are of the Dreaming. The theft of a fire-stick was sufficient to arouse that antagonism, and the outcome is easily anticipated. However, the mundane nature of the plot is transformed and dramatised by two scenes — the magical impalement of the two *mamu* women, and the revival of Crow's son. (It is interesting that Crow used eaglehawk, not crow, feathers in the revival process.) The final scene provides a climax, not so much in relation to the revival, but in how it was done, under the keen eyes of the brooding Hawk men, watching from the rock: the threatening ones, waiting for the meal that escapes them!

The theme of physical revival after death appears in the mythology of several different areas — in, for example, Myths 185, 186b, 188, from Balgo, the Daly River and Oenpelli. It begs the question of 'What can we do about death?' While the answer is usually, 'Nothing', in some mythic situations revival is achieved, but mostly death 'catches up' with the individual concerned. That theme is primary in Yawalngura's voyage to the Land of the Dead (see Myths 190 and 191).

The next story, told to R. Berndt at Balgo in 1960, is included here as a brief comment on the theme of bodily revival after death.

185.   THE ALIVE-DEAD-PEOPLE

Nightbird, Curlew (Namawilu or Windu) was simultaneously a *djagamara* and a *djuburula* man [that is, he stood in relationship to himself as father and son]. He came to Dalgabalyu soak, where he picked up all the bones of dead people, putting them together to form skeletons, and he carried them on to Badida soak. His habit was to load himself up with bones from one place, and take them to another. When a person died, he always heard about it, and later went to pick up the bones. He took them back to either Dalgabalyu or Badida and put flesh on them — he made them alive again. He was a powerful *maban* man, and was able to do this.

Curlew was living there, at those two places, 'fixing up the dead people'; and he had been doing this for a long time, when the Two Men, the Wadi Gudjara arrived, during their travels through this part of the country. [The Wadi Gudjara were also *maban* men.] They asked Curlew, 'Why do you pick up all those bones? Why can't you leave them alone?'

And without waiting for an answer, they proceeded to re-kill all the 'alive-dead-people'. And they killed Curlew, too. At and between Dalgabalyu and Badida there are heaps of rocks which are the bones of the dead. Curlew is there also, turned into a rock.

After that the Two Men left these two places and walked on to Badugudjara, westward, Canning Stock Route way.

Curlew is often associated with death in Aboriginal mythology, but here he was preoccupied with bringing dead people back to life. The Two Men considered this to be contrary to the natural course of events that applied to all living creatures. In their view, dead people should be left dead, at least as far as their physical bodies are concerned.

The following mythic incidents are focused on a small area near and on the Daly River (Ngulugwongga and Madngala languages). Myths 121, 130, 152, 175 and 180 also concern places quite close together, as do the two parts below, which are in fact separate myths. They were told to R. Berndt in 1946.

186a. THE 'LEPER' GOOSE

Close to Djiramu billabong [Ngulugwongga and Madngala] is Ngulgulngulgul (Ngulgulugu) hill. This is the Dreaming place of the 'half-dead' people who lived at Wunungu nearby as well as in a jungle a little distance away. [That hill is a taboo place; if anyone were to touch it or trip over a rock here, he or she would become ill and die.]

Birid (Goose) did not know this country. He had been travelling for a long time, and he was carrying his *garamala* [Goose Egg initiation ritual] didjeridu and a banyan tree. He came to Ngunung, at one side of Gayil billabong: at Minyi he blew his didjeridu, and the sound made the big plain that is there today. He continued on until he reached a little jungle at Anggabi. Here a large group of goose people were encamped for a *garamala* ritual. They had painted their faces with white-ochre, across the brow and nose-ridge and down the forehead. They also had their *yinindjararei* goose feather *garamala* ornaments. Birid looked at Djiramu billabong and called its name: he decided to stay there, and planted his banyan tree.

Now Birid had sores, *lalalg* [or, as was noted, *mutuma-birid*, leprosy] all over his body and face: 'he had come a long way!' He wanted to join the others at Anggabi, so he invited them to his camp. He sat there with his goose-wing fan, keeping the flies from his sores. The others came and saw

him, and they smelt him — it was a bad smell. Leaving him, they took
their didjeridus and feathered ornaments and flew away to Galmamba in
Madngala country, dropping their didjeridus there, and then on to Danbi
billabong, where they left their feathered ornaments in its deep waters.
Finally they went on to the Moiil plain. Birid, the man with sores, went
on to Ganyin in the Walgminindji territory of the Madngala.

186b. THE 'HALF-DEAD' PEOPLE DREAMING

Wulgul, Owl, commissioned two Bulil (Beetle Men) brothers to carry out
sorcery [for reasons unknown to the story-teller], on a particular young
man whose relatives were camping at Yirelyi: they were Mayang Wallaby
people [of the same group as noted in Myth 152]. The Bulil were living
near Ngulgul-ngulgul hill [see above] where the Dreaming Ngilg-yurabel
(or Ngilguli), the 'half-dead' people, lived. During the day they were
'dead', but at dusk they became 'alive'. At night the elder Bulil went
'sneaking' [to perform sorcery]: but each time he did so the Ngilguli heard
and saw him. During the day he crept up to the camp of the 'half-dead'
people and saw them all dead, lying there covered with sheets of
paperbark. So the elder brother said to the younger: 'You are a little
fellow; you had better go out tonight because those Ngilguli have seen me.
I'm too big!' The younger Bulil went out at night and escaped their
attention. He sneaked up on his victim, removed his kidney fat and
returned to his brother, telling him of his success: they slept.

The young man who had been sorcerised died. His parents and
relatives placed him on a mortuary platform at one side of Ngulgul-
ngulgul hill. They returned, mourning, to their camp at Yirelyi. Wulgul
and his wife Nunandeleg were also camped there. Nunandeleg
said: 'Husband, when people die they go to Wunangul. Let us wait there.
When that dead man comes, he too will come out at Wunangul; he will
stay there one day and then go on to his own country.' [The hill at
Ngulgul-ngulgul, and Wunangul, are staging places on the way to Anmel,
the Land of the Dead.]

Wulgul and Nunandeleg went out to Ngulgul-ngulgul, where the corpse
of the dead man lay on its platform. Wulgul took off the dead man's skin
and hung it from a tree, 'just like a piece of cloth'. Then he put a 'new',
living skin on him. They painted him with red-ochre, and decorated him
with arm-bands and a seed necklet. They prepared his own hair by
waxing on to it hair from a living person, tied on a wide waist-band, and
painted his face with white pipe clay. Then they revived that dead man.

All those 'half-dead' people at Ngulgul-ngulgul saw him, and sent him on to Anmel. But he returned to Yirelyi, where the Mayang people were. They saw this supposedly 'dead man' coming into their camp. They were frightened. They all ran to Ngulgul-ngulgul hill, where those 'half-dead' people were. But that revived 'dead man' spoke to his mother: 'No, mother, you must leave me here [at Ngulgul-ngulgul]. I can't return; too much blood has come out [that is, during the removal of his kidney fat]. I will leave you!' His mother agreed. She returned to Yirelyi, but Wulgul and his wife carried her to the hill, where she turned to rock.

[When Nunandeleg suggested to her husband that he should revive the dead person by removing his skin and replacing it with a 'new' one, she made the point that, when people died in their country, they always came first to Ngulgul-ngulgul hill and waited there for one day before going on to Anmel. At that juncture, she suggested, they could revive people so that no-one died. In the text it notes, 'Nunandeleg talks that way — let them come out at that hill and we'll do them like that (that is, put new skin on); we'll make them alive.' Nunandeleg 'talked well', but Wulgul 'talked not so well'. Wulgul was opposed to their revival; he said, 'No matter, let them go!' It is not, therefore, clear that the 'procedure' for revival (as noted above) was in fact carried out — although the text says: 'Wulgul took off that dead man's skin and hung it up on a tree . . .' It should be remembered that Wulgul was responsible for the death of that particular man, through the Bulil man he commissioned to carry out sorcery on him. In any case, it is unlikely that revival would have been seen as practicable, since the dead person had had his kidney fat removed. When the dead man speaks to his mother, he says as much (reference to loss of blood). An additional commentary on the text notes that Wulgul himself is a sorcerer — he was the Dreaming person who introduced this form of *mururu* sorcery. It is because of such sorcery that people cannot be revived.]

Leaving his mother, that 'dead' person left his bones at Ngulgul-ngulgul — but not his skull. He, in spirit form, went with those 'half-dead' people to Duyu hill, which was a further staging place on the way to the Land of the Dead, passing through Bombaigina, high above the plain. Wulgul and his wife sat down at Ngulgul-ngulgul for a while, and then went on to a jungle between the hill and Beradjeli. [This was later cleared by European settlers in the area.]

After these events, all the people were frightened, and went to Beradjeli. Djedburu was their leader. He spoke to his group: 'I'll go and sit down ['make myself' rock] at Neliyara on the Daly River [above Dargie's camp]. However, all of you must go away!' So, the members of the group dispersed; Djedburu went to Neliyara.

The first part of this two-faceted story serves as a backdrop that is intended to introduce the existence of the 'home' (or 'staging place' on the journey of the dead to the land of the immortals) of the 'half-dead' people — actually, this is their Dreaming site, at Ngulgul-ngulgul hill. The story of the 'leper' Goose is really a digression, a segment of a much longer myth that concerns the Goose Egg initiation sequence, where a novice, sitting in the middle of heaped-up goose eggs, is a symbol of the goose egg season and of their increase.

The second part concerns the basic dilemma facing all creatures, including human beings. The theme is, the possibility of reviving a dead person: if only the formula were known! Wulgul and his wife held that key, but the Dreaming man was loath to use it. Persuaded by his wife to do so, he knows that it will not be effective: Wulgul 'talked not so well'; his wife 'talked well'. There is a contrast here between 'good' intentions and 'bad' intentions — and, in this case, it has to do with sorcery. The removal of the victim's internal organs (a form of relatively widespread sorcery) militated against reviving that person; and in speaking to his mother, he too realises that it is not possible for him to live again. Without sorcery, the myth contends, people could have been brought back to life.

In the myth, it will be recalled, the revived man first goes to Anmel, before returning to the main camp where his relatives and mother are living. The point that does not emerge is that he is not permitted to remain at Anmel because he had been revived, and was not really dead. However, when he leaves his mother, he goes to Ngulgul-ngulgul hill where he leaves his bones *as* a dead person — his spirit is then free to go to Anmel. This theme is taken up in the Yawalngura myth (190 and 191).

The following story was told to R. Berndt at Balgo in 1960; it originally concerned Ngadi and Gugadja speakers.

187. MOON MAN AND SUN WOMEN

Wadi Yagan, Moon Man, *djabangari* sub-section, went hunting, killing only small possum, but no large ones. He put these small creatures in his hair. Returning to his camp [unnamed], he found that Two Dreaming Men, the Wadi Gudjara, had arrived. They saw Moon's shelter, but no water place: Moon had covered this. However, he gave the Two Men a drink and asked them what their 'skins' [sub-sections] were: they replied that one was *djangala*, the other *djabanangga*. Leaving them there, Moon went out for firewood. The Two Men looked around but saw no meat and wondered why he had gone out for wood. On his return, Moon made a fire and built it up, then removed a small possum from his hair. Putting it into the fire, he sang and the possum grew large — there was plenty of meat to feed his visitors and himself. They made camp and lay down.

During the night they heard the young Sun Women (Djindu), of mixed sub-sections [all of the eight categories are represented among them], singing and dancing. Moon Man told his visitors they must leave early: 'You must go back along your track to your home. If you go in sun-time, you will get burnt!' They therefore left long before daybreak: but they did not take Moon's advice. Instead, they walked a little way and then sneaked back in the direction of the sound of the women. When they reached the Sun Women, they found most of them sleeping. The Two Men found two of them who were not asleep, and asked them to go away with them. The two girls agreed and they went away together; but it was not long before they made camp and the men were ready to copulate with them. However, when they touched those girls they got burnt. [Comment: 'It was like an electric shock!']

Moon, in his own camp some distance away, felt that something was wrong. He had gone out hunting for possum, but had caught none: it was from this that he knew something was wrong. He listened to the Sun Women dancing. He picked up his axe and water carrier, followed the tracks of the Two Men, and found them burnt to death; the two girls had returned to their companions. Moon was angry and decided to kill those Sun Women. He came to where they were dancing and set about cutting off their legs with his axe. As soon as he had cut off one lot, they rejoined themselves and continued dancing. Moon 'killed' them all, but they all came alive again, and continued dancing.

Moon returned to where he had left the two dead men. He picked them up, took them to a special rockhole and put them inside it. The Two Men remained there 'dead', in the water, for a long time. Moon went out hunting again for possum. When he returned, he found they had revived: the water in the rockhole had revived them. Moon cried with pleasure because the Two Men were now alive. He told them to go directly to their home 'or you will be killed again!' He gave them presents of possum meat, and the Two Men went on their way. The Sun Women continued dancing all day and slept at night; Moon went possum-hunting at night and rested during the day.

A version of this myth appears in R. Berndt (1973: 21–22). The events took place probably at Yiraribi or Mandabanda, south-east of Balgo. In this case, the water in Moon's rockhole is an 'elixir of life'. As we will see in the next myth, Moon was willing for people to live forever. An initial choice was made at the beginning of time, and for himself, Moon chose that he would return physically in a continuously renewable body.

The next myth was told to C. Berndt in 1950 at Oenpelli.

188. MOON AND THE COMING OF DEATH

Long ago, Moon and Djabo were coming from the north, from the salt-water coast. It was a long way, so they travelled for a long time. They were looking for a place, looking for a country. As they came they were camping, and putting place-names. 'Supposing we go south, to Djawun country and Mayali country, and put ourselves there,' they said to each other. They were coming, camping, eating various plant foods and creatures, and spearing kangaroos on the way. For a while they were talking Naragani and Maung. Already they had bypassed Wuragag, Tor Rock, and reached Mangarubu, Cooper's Creek. They came and stood there, and said to each other, 'Let's camp here for two days, because we're tired. Here we can eat fish and small creatures and plant foods.' That's what they did, and then they set off again.

They came to Dirrbiyag, and planted *mandem* water-lilies that are still there today. 'Let's keep going, and sleep at Yidjindi on the way.' They went, and put their belongings at Yidjindi. They got goose eggs, eating some, and carrying some in their baskets. Then they went on again, following a rocky path. They settled down for a while at Wulg, Red Lily. They were making places, making fish and red lilies and *mandem* lilies. For two nights they camped there. Then in the morning they set off, and settled at Galarabi-djogeng, where they put the place name. They put little place names as they went. They came to Madjinbari and camped there for a while, eating honey and plant foods and small creatures. They moved around making places, and plant foods and foliage and fish and pandanus palms. After three days they went on again. 'We'll go straight on, to where the spear-bamboos are growing,' they said. When they got there, they pulled out their whiskers and made those spear-plants, which still stand today. They put the place name there, Djim-djim (Jim Jim), and they made a big stretch of water, like the sea. Nobody goes there, and nobody uses fish hooks or throws them into the water, because that is taboo, Dreaming water. Those two made it taboo, dangerous, and it is still taboo and dangerous.

They went on for a while, making places, putting small place names, and coming to Yorge. Then on again, to reach that stretch of water, that place they were wanting. 'Which way are we going?' asked Djabo. Moon said, 'This is the big creek we'll follow. I've been looking carefully at this creek. It's in Mayali and Djawun country, and this is the one we'll follow!'

They were going along, camping where they saw very good, clean sand. And camping again to eat honey and small creatures and kangaroos, and spear and eat fish. Djabo covered himself with ant-bed [termite mound] 'clay' to get kangaroo for them, and brought it back cooked, in the afternoon. They kept on doing the same thing, camping where they saw a good place, following the sand along by the creek. Then they found themselves among rocks. They made their camp high up, at the head of the rocky hills. They would go hunting for a while, and Djabo would get honey while Moon went after kangaroos. They weren't dying of hunger; they were just replete.

As they went south, they were still making places. They were cutting bamboo for kangaroo-spears and for fishing-spears. They were making big *galai-djidji* bags and little *malaga* bags to fill up with their belongings. Hair-belts too, to put round them, and forehead-bands. They were carrying feathers. They were making boomerangs too, for fighting; or for beating or clapping together, ready for the ceremonies they thought might be arranged for them, because they were coming into Djawun country. They were carrying things for the *mamurng* exchange ceremony. And they were singing, up there at the head of the rocky hills where they had their camp. Those people came to see them, and gave them a *djamalag* ceremony, because Moon and Djabo had plenty of things to give them in return.

Both of them were talking Mayali and Djawun now. They had left Naragani and Maung behind when they were camping at Mangarubu, because they knew they would be going into Djawun and Mayali and Gundje'mi country. So they dropped their 'old' languages there, the languages 'from our mothers and our fathers', they said to each other. They were still living at that place high among the rocks, eating small creatures and kangaroos. Kangaroo bones were lying about there, where they were camping.

But at last those two were 'listening to themselves', feeling ill. A great sickness had come. They lay inside, they didn't go anywhere, didn't go hunting. It had struck them down completely. So then they ate vegetable foods and meat they had got before, because they were so sick: they were dying. ['It was like a very bad cold.'] They said. 'We'll just die here, our bodies will lie here in Djawun and Mayali country. We left our mothers and fathers far away, and our grandparents: it is as if we had forgotten them. We've lost touch with them. So, if we die, who will take the death message about us to them, to our mothers and fathers and grandparents and uncles?' they said, as they lay dying. They got green leaves to put on the fire and steam themselves, because they were so sick. They said to each other, 'If we die, then nobody will come up alive again!' Well, Djabo died first. But Moon went on breathing for a while, because he was a powerful man, a clever man, a *margidbu*. He said, 'I'll die, and then I'll come back again, in another body — but still *my* body! I'm a powerful man, a *margidbu*!' Djabo just lay dead. His body was dead for ever. Moon could have revived him, but Djabo didn't trust Moon. He thought it was a trick.

Well, Moon died. They could have followed him and done the same as he did, those first people, those others. They saw him come up as a new moon. When he was high up in the sky, men and women and children called out, happy to see him. 'Yes indeed!' they said. 'That Moon, he's the one, he's a *margidbu*. He rose up; he holds the sky. We look at him: he dies, and he puts himself as a new moon again!' They told each other about Moon. He alone, he 'wins' over us, when his spirit comes out alive. That Djabo, he just died forever; he lay there as a dead body. But Moon made himself alive. Every day we see him: his body dies for three days, and then we see him as a new moon. But then, he's just a real *margidbu*, that Moon. We men and women, we could have become like that, we could have done what Moon does. But Djabo made it go wrong for us, when he died forever. As for ourselves, when we die, then our bodies die forever, and they bury our bodies — just as Moon said.

A considerably shorter Maung version of the above myth from Goulburn Island was told to R. Berndt in 1947.

189. MOON AND BANDICOOT

Moon (Gurana) and Spotted Bandicoot (Indarlbu) were two men, the former *yariyaning* and the latter *yariwurig*. They were living at Yurnguriyurana, on the track to Oenpelli. One day they had an argument. Moon said, 'When I die, everybody will come back alive, just as I will.' But Bandicoot replied. 'No, when they die, they have to go like this!' [He would make a sign, raising his hands claw-like, like the hands of dead people.] 'No,' insisted Moon, 'They must follow me!' 'No,' said Bandicoot. 'They must follow me!' And so they argued, all the way along the track toward Oenpelli.

At last Moon got angry. He got a handful of dry clay and threw it at Bandicoot. The clay stuck to his body [and the spots on bandicoot can be seen today]. Then Moon said, 'You have won [our argument]. When people die, they will follow you! But when I die I will return, alive!' And that is why we die, and do not come back alive.

Moon is a popular death-and-revival symbol. In Aboriginal Australia alone, stories on this theme come from a number of widely-separated regions. They supply a mythic answer to the question, 'When human beings die, why don't they come back to life again in the same form, as Moon does? Why are human bodies not renewable as Moon's is?' The stories are quite varied in many respects, not only in style and setting, but also in secondary themes or activities, and in the identity of the character (or characters) who rejected Moon's offer and so deprived human beings of the possibility of eternal bodily renewal.

Although in the various versions of the myth, and frequently in discussions about it, this was presented as an important issue, it needs to be seen in perspective. Firstly, in traditional Aboriginal belief, spiritual continuity is mostly not in doubt: physical organisms decay, but the spirit or soul lives on, in one way or another (according to differing regional beliefs). There are exceptions to the rule of 'no bodily renewal for human beings'. Notably, in some accounts a dead baby is said to have 'come back' to the same mother to be born again as the 'same' child. These incidents do not seem to be mentioned in comments on the Moon myth. Nor is the question of reincarnation in relation to adults. Secondly, cycles of growth and decay, death and renewal in nature were traditionally acknowledged as a feature of the everyday scene, and of religious rituals designed to keep the systems going, to ensure that physical life and fertility and seasonal continuity were maintained. All physical organisms, all the natural species, all flora and fauna, were seen as being subject to this inevitable process. Thirdly, within that natural range, some creatures were recognised as being able to change their bodily shapes, over and above what happened in the ordinary course of ageing: shedding parts of their old bodies (snakes, for instance), or taking on an entirely different appearance (caterpillars, cicadas, dragonflies, and a host of others). But on the topic of death and survival, Moon attracted much more attention in myth and story than any of these. Perhaps this was because Moon is highly visible and distinctively identifiable as a single figure, despite periodic transformations (waxing and waning) and regular periods of invisibility (indicating Moon's 'death'). Through all of this, Moon remains Moon. It could be, then, that the main question is not one of human mortality in a general sense, but rather one of individual, personal survival after death. That topic comes up in other contexts: in regard to stories and statements about Lands of the Dead (as in the Yawalngura story), or even in regions and circumstances where Aboriginal people greeted European newcomers as their own relatives returning from the dead.

This first story about Moon and Djabo is rather longer than some versions. The narrator, Ngalmidul, wanted to bring in what she saw as the principal features of their journey before the final events came about. During that journey they both had the appearance of men, and behaved like men in their ordinary human activities of hunting and obtaining food, and preparing goods for ceremonial gift exchange. Their other qualities are noted, for instance, in regard to 'making' and naming places, but Moon's special powers are not much in evidence until the very end of the story. He did not (would not? could not?) escape the sickness that affected them both, or the prospect of dying — even though he did not expect that state to be permanent. Moon draws attention to his anticipated sequence of sickness-death-physical renewal, but in this version he does not add that in his transformed mythic manifestation he would be obliged to go through the same sequence, at regular intervals, forever. There is no reference to this as being the cost, to him, of perpetual physical renewal. (Nor is there any reference to what the night sky was like before Moon took his place there.)

This version is an amiable account, with no major incidents to disrupt it. The two travellers are on good terms. Moon is, marginally, the dominant character. Djabo is generally identified, in his non-human form, as spotted cat or bandicoot, or other small animal, but the word is used in some stories for an 'orphan' or a supposedly neglected child. In this case he is certainly not involved in any argument or open quarrel with Moon, as happens to him or his counterparts in some other versions (as in Myth 189). Yet when it comes to a final decision, he 'didn't trust Moon' — and that is why he, and the entire human population on whose behalf (in some unexplained way) he had to make that decision, lost their chance of physical immortality. In everyday circumstances as well as in this situation, traditionally, in western Arnhem Land, a *margidbu*, an Aboriginal doctor, claimed to be unable to heal or to cure a patient who did not have faith or did not trust him (rarely, her). The myth has a message on that score too.

In the next example we continue with the theme of death, and life after death. We have included two versions of what is sometimes regarded as the same story — or rather, as a constellation of stories based on a 'historically real' and very unusual journey. It is one of the few accounts of a living human being, not a mythic character from the creative era, visiting the Land of the Dead. Warner (1937/1958: 524–28) heard one version from men at Milingimbi in north-central Arnhem Land in the late 1920s. It is rather different from our first version here, which was told to R. Berndt by Mawulan at Yirrkalla in 1947. This one is particularly interesting because Mawulan himself illustrated it in a drawing (see Figure 8.1) that locates the main features: the numbers in this myth refer to these. The name of the principal character here was given as Yawalngura (or Yalngura).

This story, not myth, came, Mawulan said, from the old people, 'a very long way back, long before my father's father's father'.

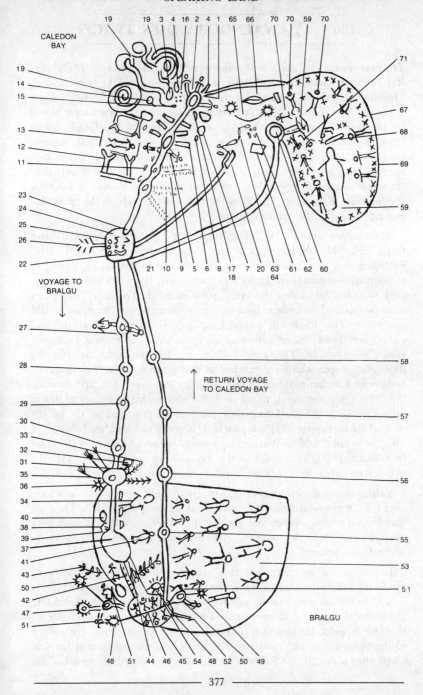

190. YAWALNGURA DIES TWICE?

The first events took place at Gumbu-gumbu, on the 'top side' of Caledon Bay, a cycad palm place (1). Spirit women [*mogwoi*; Wonguri dialect, Mandjigai clan, *yiridja* moiety] were collecting this cycad food (2). Their husband, Yawalngura [Duboingu dialect, *dua* moiety] saw ashes, blown by the wind from Bralgu, the *dua* moiety Land of the Dead, fall at Gumbu-gumbu. These ashes were black *gungoyu* 'dust' (3), near a paperbark tree (4). The two spirit women went on to Mulara (5) to soak their palm nuts: after a period of soaking [three to four days], they removed these and dried them, to grind them into a kind of flour for shaping into a damper (6); (7) is the flat stone on which the 'nuts' are ground, and (8) the grinding stone.

Yawalngura went out to collect turtle eggs: (9) and (10) are the two turtle nests. He ate the eggs at the place where he had found them, without giving any to his two wives. He returned to Mulara [5, above] — re his tracks — and there he lay down and died. His wives did not know; they were out preparing the cycad palm damper. The elder wife [they were two sisters] took some damper over to where he was lying, but he did not move. The other wife joined her. They removed the bark he had pulled over himself, and looked at his eyes: 'they had turned, as do the eyes of dead people'. They cried for him; they left him in the camp for one day. The people who were camped at this place painted Yawalngura's body with his clan patterning; they put him in a 'hut' (12), and there he lay (13). They cut wood, to get posts for making his mortuary platform [actually, 12 is the platform]; they put him on this, and all the people danced for this spirit. (14) is a yam leaf [in some versions; see below, and also the version told to Warner, a yam leaf is brought over on the wind from Bralgu]; (15) is the stick used to crack the cycad palm nuts; (16) the cycad palm nuts, and (17) the bark in which water is carried (also 18).

Yalngura saw the ashes drifting over. He thought he would make a long rope (19) in preparation for his visit to Bralgu, the spirit world. ['The rope was like an anchor. When you are out in a canoe, you drop it down into the sea in order to take a spell.' Actually, this took place later after he revived: see below.]

It was in the morning that they put Yawalngura on the mortuary platform, and in the afternoon that the people danced and sang for him. It was after the dancing that he jumped off his platform to the ground. He did not realise what had happened: 'Perhaps I died and they put me on this!' he thought. He looked at his body, and saw the painting. He walked to the main camp and saw that the people had moved from it [as was usual after a death]. He followed their tracks and heard the sound of the didjeridu and the singing, and women dancing and wailing. They did not see Yawalngura coming toward them. His two wives were watching and crying, and they saw him. They were frightened and tried not to look at him — they thought he was a spirit. He called out: 'I'm here, I'm alive! Why are you singing and dancing?' And all the people were happy that he had returned from the dead.

Next morning the women went out to collect and prepare palm nuts. Yawalngura, sitting in his camp by a hill at (5), saw ashes and a yam leaf, drifting from Bralgu, fall in front of him. He picked up some of the ash, examining it to see what kind of tree it came from; it appeared to have come from a pandanus palm. He picked up the yam leaf and brooded about it. He held it in his hand when the women returned. He showed them what he had found, which had come to him from Bralgu. He continued to brood about the leaf. A day or so afterward he got up early and went out to cut bark in order to construct a raft (20) — see his tracks. When it was completed, he joined together the lengths of rope (19). He slept at (5) for two days, and then loaded cycad bread onto the raft [sometimes referred to as a canoe], and he filled up the bark water buckets (17 and 18). He made everything ready.

Next morning he carried the raft/canoe down to the sea. He told all the other people, 'I want to go to the spirit country, to see what it's like.' Taking his two wives, he set off from (20) and paddled to Djilwanboi island, outside Caledon Bay. They slept there (21). He awoke before daylight and saw the Morning Star rising from Bralgu. (22) is a rock 'hut' [shelter], (23) fresh cliff water, and (24) his two wives with oyster shells (25), which they had collected, and thrown aside after eating the oysters; (26) is a shade, with *djadba* stingray meat and a fire. He left his two wives here while he went on to Bralgu. [It is not clear where he left his wives. In the drawing to which the numbers refer, Mawulan, the artist, put them by mistake in the wrong place (27); they should have been put on Djilwanboi island; (27) was merely where he anchored.] However, his wives were, apparently, left at Djilwanboi, and at (27) he simply anchored in the sea and went to sleep on his raft. Before daybreak he saw the Morning Star, which was guiding him. He went on to (28), where he anchored in the sea, and the next night at (29), using the Morning Star to guide him. He paddled on, and again anchored (30). He could see the Morning Star 'properly': it was large and brilliant. Next morning he went on and anchored at (31), Gei'au'gawuru, near Bralgu (Sandy Island): (32) is his canoe/raft. Yawalngura looked for turtle eggs: he thought he had found a turtle's nest (33). He put his stick in, to see whether any eggs were there, but the spirit of this turtle emerged and chased him; (34) are his tracks.

He reached Bralgu. He saw a large pandanus palm (35). It is from here that the Bralgu spirits hang the Morning Star (36) — this is as far as it will go. Yawalngura camped here: he saw that star, directly above his head. He walked on to (37) 'biggest Bralgu' and saw the guardian bird, Birg-birg (Pigmy Goose) (38) looking for the spirits of the newly dead who must pass through this entrance (39) into Bralgu. There is a small island sandbank where Balil-balil, the Turtle Man spirit, (41) stood guard. He sent Yawalngura to see two women: 'They will tell you where you can go!' The two women were Lialulgi and Yambu-yambu (42); the first has a number of alternative names; the second only one name, meaning 'yam'. These women were obtaining *ba-algu* or *galun* roots from a creeper (43), which was like a yam but tasted 'salty'. He went over to them and saw their yams (42). Balil-balil had hit his spear to warn the two women that Yawalngura was coming; and Yawalngura painted himself with ochre at (44). The two women, alerted by the noise of Balil-balil's spear, saw Yawalngura; they could not recognise him. One woman asked his name. 'I am Yawalngura; I am Gongbilma' [the singing stick he holds. He called all his names: not noted in this rendering of the story.] He called his names: and the two women knew him. They cried and held his arms and they felt his hands. They looked at each other: 'Ah,' they said, 'He is alive!' They felt his bones: and they knew.

He followed the two women to the place where the spirit people were dancing, and dust was rising from their dancing feet (45). Moving his dilly bag to his chest, Yawalngura danced the native companion (*djabiru* bird), coming down toward where they were. All the spirit people stopped their own dancing and watched him. [There is a detailed description of the dancing and the singing and who the spirit dancers were, which is not included here.]

The people were dancing at a special spring (46) at Bralgu, called Gwoyulung. [There are also many other names, as well as a number of alternative names for Bralgu and its environs.] Then the spirit people danced in the Morning Star ceremony, 'sending those star(s) out to us' (36); one went to Milingimbi (47); others went in different directions (48); and one to Galiwinku, Elcho Island (49). There were also dilly bags (50) in which these stars were kept before being sent out. Three young *dua* moiety girls sent out those stars, while the men danced. These young girls (51) were named Bereibi, Mawuruma, and Bereidnga: they were crying for that [those] Morning Star(s) because they wanted to keep them for themselves. But their father and brothers said, 'You must hurry and send them out, or all those people [who are alive] may die!' [That Morning Star is really made of the feathers of the land seagull, and the string which is attached to it is feathered.]

Yawalngura danced toward the spirit people and then spoke to them, asking them to give him their Law. They gave him the *gwoimali* spear-thrower (52) with the human hair attached at one end (the *muregu*). The spirit men held this object in their hands as they danced, but it was really the *gwoimali* of the Turtle Man spirit (41). They also gave him the

Morning Star emblem (a manifestation of the real Morning Star]. And
Yawalngura prepared to return home. But first the spirit people put the
yam creeper (43), the Morning Star emblem and the *gwoimali* into the
special spring or well (46); and taking them out again, gave them to him.
The yam was *mareiin* [sacred], and the spirit people gave it to Yawalnguru
so that it could be food for the living people. It belonged to the Djanggau.
The Djanggau had put all those things at Bralgu when they came through
that place on their epic journey to the Arnhem Land coast: all of those
things were their Dreaming.

Yawalngura took those things which were given to him. All the spirit
people danced at that special spring [well] (53), and they told Yawalngura that he had to return: 'You have to return, you're not dead properly;
you've still got bones. You can come back to us when you die properly.'

So the spirit people got his canoe/raft and put it at (54) with the things
they had given him. He paddled off to (55), where he anchored for the
night. He paddled on to (56) and anchored, then went on into the open
sea (57) where he anchored at sunset. Next morning he went on and
anchored at (58), from there he went on to Djilwanboi Island (21), where
he picked up his two wives. He showed them what the spirit people had
given him. Yawalngura (59) is depicted. They paddled on to Ngeidbi (60)
at the northern side of Caledon Bay; (61) is his canoe/raft, (62) his tracks,
(63) his dilly bag, (64) the dilly bag containing the Morning Star, (65) the
Morning Star *mareiin*, and (66) the string on which the Morning Star
feathered 'balls' are fastened. With his wives, he walked on to Mulara (5)
[in the drawing, actually 59]. There he met all the people: he showed
them what he had brought back from Bralgu and told them about what he
had seen, about the dancing and the songs. Two or three days afterward
he died. This time he died 'properly'!

All the people held a mortuary ceremony for him, dancing for him on
the top of the sandhill at this place (67). Their dancing and songs
replicated those of the spirit people at Bralgu when they sent out the
Morning Star: (68) is the didjeridu; (69) are bats encircling the dead body
of Yawalngura [the spirits of the Bralgu people manifested in that form].
(59) is the corpse of Yawalngura lying there, (70) the female mourners
painted with red-ochre, and (71) the two widows of Yawalngura.

The following version of a human man's journey to the island of the dead
was told to C. Berndt at Milingimbi in 1950. The main dialect of the
story-teller, an elderly *dua* moiety woman, was Djambarbingu; but
through her *yiridja* mother she spoke Gobubingu, the dialect her daughter
had been teaching to C. Berndt at Yirrkalla in 1946–47. So, she told this
in Gobubingu, the dialect she thought C. Berndt knew best. The
translation here keeps fairly close to the original. In this case there is no

initial dramatic death scene. The hint of impending drama comes with the yam leaf, blown (presumably, not by chance) in the wind from Bralgu. Before that happens, the traveller, Yawalngura, is introduced as an ordinary human person living in a quiet domestic environment with his family.

---

191. VOYAGE TO THE *DUA* MOIETY ISLAND OF THE DEAD

He was living at Balangara, an island place, with his children and his three wives. He slept, and at daybreak he set off. He saw a *lalai, gulaga* yam leaf, a special leaf. Hiding it behind his back, he came and sat down in his camp. 'Guess what I've found!' 'What did you see?' 'Guess!' 'What did you see? A turtle?' 'No!' 'What did you see? A *gulaga* yam leaf?' 'Yes. It's a yam leaf from Bralgu!'

'Hurry!' [he said to his wives.] 'Get food ready for me. Dig *gulaga* yams, *djidama* and *luwia* bitter yams, and *duwinga, ridja'ngu* and *baawang* roots. I'll prepare some twine.' 'Yes, all right!' They dug the roots for him. They soaked the *djidama* roots in water, and cooked in the coals the *gulaga* and *duwinga* and *ridja'ngu* roots. He made long lengths of twine, and rolled them up. Then he slept until daybreak. 'Hurry! Load up the canoe for me!' They put all the food into the canoe until it was full, with plenty of food and twenty paperbark baskets full of fresh water. He took with him only the youngest of his wives, an adolescent girl. All right. They set off. They went on, and came to an island. They saw many turtles, and they dug the ground. They came on the bones of a dead person! Again they dug the ground, and came on bones. 'Oh! What's this? It's bones of a dead person! Like turtle footprints! You stay here. Maybe I'll go into the jungle and look for that leaf.' He set off. He saw some leaves. 'These are all small leaves. *That* one was very big.' He kept looking about at the leaves, but all of them were small. 'Well! You stay here at this island place, at Bainyuwury, Darbainga. I'll go on.'

He went on. That evening the canoe landed at Wurubula. 'Well, maybe I'll go inland, into the jungle.' He went into the jungle, and looked about. The right kind of leaf wasn't there. All the leaves were small. He went back, got into the canoe, and set off. He went on, and landed at another island. He landed at Budadji-ngura. Off into the jungle! He saw that all the leaves were small. He set off again. He went on, went on, slept at sea, then went on. He was travelling on the water in daylight, he went on, it was night [he slept], and then daybreak. He set off again, going by day and then by night. He had light from the stars. He kept on. He saw the

Morning Star. 'Getting close!' He went on, following the stars at night, following the sun by day, going along on the water. He kept on. Night-time again. He heard a porpoise: '*Djuuu!*', like that! That porpoise, as if it came from land, from dry land! Daybreak. He went on in the sunlight, kept on, saw an island. He landed. He was at an island. He set off, going inland into the jungle, looking about for leaves, picking them up and checking them. They were all small. 'Maybe I'll go to that island over there and look.' He went in the canoe, landed there, at the island of Rurugun-ngura. After landing, he looked about. All the leaves were small.

There was a cliff-face of rock, over there. He set off in the canoe, went on, and landed. Bralgu! It was a little island [little Bralgu]. He went on and landed. He looked all around. The leaves were small. He dug some of the roots, cooked them and ate them. He was full. One lot he loaded into the canoe. Then he set off, he went, he went until daylight. Night came. At daylight he set off again, kept going until nightfall. He heard the sound of the Morning Star going up on its string: '*Dararar!*' Thus. He saw it, high up, on top. He went farther on, getting closer.

He climbed up, climbed until daylight. He drank water: it was almost fresh. Many porpoises were going along, in the fresh-and-salt water. He tasted the water again. It was a bit better. Then he tasted it again. It was good — fresh water! He heard water splashing at this place. He landed in the early morning, beaching the canoe, with his paddles. He saw a turtle, went and got it, cooked it in a shallow oven with termite mound. He ate the meat, with another turtle and a porpoise. He went on eating breakfast. Then, going inland, he saw black plums. He set off again, saw little red currants, ate some. He set off again, saw a variety of fruits [eighteen are named here].

He went on, moving quickly, and met two human beings, old men, of the Djarwarg clan: two brothers, Rabu-rabun and Biding-gura. 'You people!' they called out. 'A dead person, a dead person, is coming!' [Then they spoke to him.] 'Who are you? Are you a human soul?' 'No! I'm a human person, from over there. I came because of a *lalai* leaf.' 'Who are you?' 'I'm Yawalngura.' 'Oh yes, you're younger brother to me!' 'Where is your path?' 'This place is Bralgu. You follow this big path, this way. Don't turn aside and follow any other path, or follow any small path — only the big one.' 'I'll go straight along it, whether the yam is there, or not.' 'This *lalai* yam leaf is from there, from Bralgu!' [they said, calling the 'big names' for Bralgu.] '*Gumurur-ralgu-ngu, Djunu-mangbiri, Mangai-mangai-ngu, Galayin'boi!*' 'Yes, yes!' He set off, hurrying along. As he went, he heard the *gugug* bird calling: '*Kuuu!*' Then he sang, with stylised dance gestures, swinging his hands. [He did this so that the souls, or ghosts, would realise he was not a stranger.] He stopped, set off again, hurrying. Then he heard, '*Birg-birg-birg-birg!*': thus, the *birg-birg* bird calling. He danced with stylised gestures, singing. He set off again. Then he heard the spoonbill bird. He danced with stylised gestures. Then a long-nosed black bird, making a murmuring noise in its throat. He set off, going along, and saw the white *gururg* bird with long legs and wings, on a big swampy plain. 'You two sons, you look!' [the bird said]. The mother, the *birg-birg*, flew up, frightened of Yawalngura. The two sons were children, two boys. 'Father! This is father, he's come from over here!' Then he painted himself, painted his penis-symbol, his ceremonial spear-thrower, fringed with hair, and sat down. He put his long basket on the other side, with its string and also its fringe of human hair, and went hurrying, getting close. He saw a ghost, a human soul. 'No!' [said Rabu-rabun to the others]. 'This is a human person, from over there!' Then he went on, saw Buwa-buwayur [ghost, soul of a dead person] running. He hurried, sat down, then danced with stylised gestures. He went on, Yawalngura, and from there he danced with stylised gestures, getting close. He was swinging his hands, then stopped. 'That *wulambu* stick adorned with hair is yours, Rabu-rabun, and this one is mine!' [They exchanged them, as gifts.] 'This is what I came for, this *lalai* leaf, *gulaga* leaf! 'Yes, yes, younger brother! Then, you go on from there and meet our two sisters, half-way!'

He set off. He went on, half-way. Met them! 'Ah, brother!' Thus, Maalumbwoi and Yawalili. They had food cooking in a shallow oven with termite mound. 'Come, brother, hurry up, here's food!' 'First, you two, give me some water.' They hurried. 'Come on, drink this, with blood and with bones — yes, brother!' 'No! I can't drink this, I'm not dead! Be off with you! For me, give me good water!' 'Yes! What are you, a living person?' 'Yes, I'm a living human being, I'm not dead!' 'Good. This is clean water, good water.' He drank the water, set off, then paused and went back. 'Wait! First, a bag for food!' Those two moved aside the hot coals, and gave him food: Maalumbwoi gave him bad food. Yawalili gave him good food. He ate, he was full. He set off, with his long baskets hanging from his shoulders. He set off, going to the big place. He was hurrying, he got there, to Gurbulu. He heard '*Birg-birg-birg!*' Then he danced, with stylised gestures, hands moving. He stopped, set off again, getting close. He heard, '*Ngang!*', a goose calling. He began to sing, with stylised dancing. He set off, hurrying, getting close: '*Gu-gug! Gu-gug!*', a bird calling.

He saw a lot of people, women getting bulrush corms. 'Hurry, there are men here, people!' He hurried, getting close. They had come out from among the bulrushes, and they saw him. 'This is Yawalngura!' [they said]. One of them was Ngalabar, an old man. 'Ah! This is my son!' He hurried to meet him. 'What are you, are you dead?' 'No! I'm alive!' 'Yes, go on, you go first!' He hurried on, met a crowd of them, at Dauu-magarngu. It was afternoon when he met them, his hands moving in stylised dance, then stopping. 'What are you, are you dead?' 'No! I'm alive! I came for this leaf — *lalai* [and other names]!' He hurried on, paused, and sat down, and slept until daylight. Early morning! He set off, looking around as he went along. He saw a large leaf. 'This is what I came for, this leaf!' He rubbed it over himself. 'This is mine!' He showed it to his three local wives, his three dead spirit-wives. He slept until daylight. Again [one more night] he slept. They got for him *gulaga* yams, bulrush corms, *duwinga* roots, and fruit.

He set off early in the morning. He reached his canoe, pulled it out, and set off. 'I'm going in my own canoe, named Wunwun-mara!' He set off; he went early in the morning. He went on, until daylight. Darkness again. He set off again, going on. He landed. In the afternoon he landed at an island. He slept, and then went on by night, went on until daylight. He slept at sea, then set off in the early morning, going along in the sunlight. He kept going. Darkness! Travelling by night, until daylight. He landed at an island. He set off, landed slept in the sunlight at an island. Slept! Woke up! Afternoon! He set off, went on, then put up his pandanus palm sail. He went on by night, until daylight. He went on, then landed at an island. He didn't stay there. He set off, went on, slept at sea. He slept until daylight, then went on again. He went on by sunlight and by night. He kept on going, landed at an island. Got there!

His wife that he had left behind, was there. They set off, they went quickly, in the early morning, and landed in the afternoon. He ate plant foods, and turtle meat. He took it slowly, for a while, resting in his camp. Then, at night, he 'ate' one of his wives, the young adolescent girl. He died then: his penis died. 'Oh! He's dead!' They began to weep. They buried him in the ground. They left him there. That's all!

In both of these accounts, as in Warner's, the traveller who wanted to go to the island of the dead ends up by returning there, this time as a dead person himself. After his long journey to Bralgu and then back to his family, he was able to tell them briefly about his experiences before he left them again, suddenly. His post-mortem trip is not included in the story, partly because beliefs about the departure of a dead person's spirit, or soul, did not need to be outlined there, and partly because the focus is on what is presented as Yalngura's/Yawalngura's own perspective.

For the same reasons, the story does not provide a full picture of the Bralgu scene. The two versions here, and Warner's, cover different aspects, in different ways. They highlight the point that no single narrative or song can be understood in isolation. Their meanings depend, not only on the overall context in the community where they belong but also on other verbal and visual and aural sources of information on the same and related topics. In Danggoubwi's version, she takes it for granted that mentioning names and indicating, not describing, actions and incidents will be enough for her listeners, who can fill in the details from other sources if they do not already know them. For instance, apart from a preliminary reference to the Morning Star, she says nothing about what happens at Bralgu in relation to such stars — making them, sending them, where they go. During the period when this version was told, preparations were being made at Milingimbi for a Morning Star ceremony, which duly took place. Yet neither Danggoubwi herself nor any of the women listening to it mentioned that connection. It was a 'given', one of the unspoken items of information that help to make up 'the whole story'.

One more obscure or debatable aspect of the island of the dead issue was usually left rather vague, on the grounds (according to some people) that everyone would have a chance, eventually, to find out how it was resolved. Bralgu was a home for dead persons of the *dua* moiety, and after the death of such a person, the emphasis was on singing the special series of *dua* moiety songs to guide and help the soul on its way there. For dead of the *yiridja* moiety there was another island, to the north or north-east of the eastern Arnhem Land coast, variously named: Modilnga, for example, or Badu; and *yiridja* moiety dead were assisted to that place by different, *yiridja*, song series. But in life there are cross-linking ties between the two moieties. People take their primary moiety label from their fathers, but they have secondary rights and privileges in the moiety of their mothers — which must be different: a husband and wife must not be of the same moiety. Yawalngura was of the *dua* moiety, and could expect to go to Bralgu after his death. His wives at the beginning of the story, being *yiridja*, would not. But what about his three Bralgu wives? Or perhaps, as in so many myths dealing with the creative era, the everyday rules governing marriage and sexual relationships would not apply? Those questions aside, to expand on the items treated, and not treated, in these two versions (and Warner's), would involve not only reports of 'population and customs' at Braegu, and what the soul of a newly-dead person might encounter on the way and on arrival there. It would have to include also the relevant song cycles (mortuary sequences, and, especially, Morning Star), and the early stages of the Djanggau's journey (see Chapter 2). In effect, it would add up to a 'Bralgu book'. And that would be quite incomplete without its *yiridja* counterpart. As well, there are such considerations as the trickster spirit, the aspect which remains locality-bound after the death of its human body, and the animating spirit-children associated with conception and pregnancy, ritual affiliation and particular sites. The mortuary songs alone, in this region, include some of the most beautiful song-poetry in Aboriginal Australia; and the imagery that permeates the songs finds expression not only in story and myth but also in oratory, in fighting taunts and challenges, and even in everyday speech.

While the myths presented in this chapter have been selected for their dramatic qualities, it is clear that many others in this volume share some of these same features. Our method of selection would probably not be the same as those a traditionally-oriented Aboriginal might use in considering the matter of dramatic impact, which would vary according to the culture to which the myth series belonged, as well as according to the people concerned. On the other hand, each of these myths and stories attracted considerable interest and attention on the part of Aborigines who were listening at the time they were told to us. That was especially the case at particular stages of a plot's development, in regard to misadventure and misfortune. Listeners nearly always made appropriate exclamations and comments on such occasions.

In general terms, the identification and placing of mythic characters within their 'correct' mythological social and spatial slots were always important. Nevertheless, when it comes to dramatic action, it was not so much a question of 'who-done-it' — that is, *who* was responsible for particular actions. Rather, interest was focused on *what* they did, on what actually took place, and on how it happened, rather than on who made it happen. Concern for a person, as a relevant mythic being, was centred much more on his or her 'turning', 'making' or 'putting' — on the impact of that phenomenon on the natural (and social) environment. If he or she left a tangible 'reminder' within that context, through metamorphosis or some other form of transformation, then that *was* significant (see Chapter 2). And it was significant because, over and above serving as validation of the myth itself, it produced or resulted in something being left that had implications for human beings — whether that 'something' was a danger signal, or a species renewal centre, or simply an adjunct to the local landscape. Such memorials are/were living and active, possessing potential power that constituted a people's intellectual and practical resource supply. Many such centres, but by no means all of them, came into existence through some misfortune befalling a mythic character — some calamity brought about by himself or herself, or by another person interacting in conjunction with him or her. In such cases (see Chapter 2) a series of events, following one upon another, led inevitably to a finale, an end of one sort of physical existence, but also, through the act of transformation, marked the beginning of a different physical existence, according to some preordained scheme (the 'divine plan' syndrome).

Violence, or threat of violence, in one form or another, provides a range of pivotal features on which many of the myths are constructed. Scenes of murder, lust, theft, treachery, revenge, jealousy and fear stalk the stage-set upon which these mythic events are acted out. They are the themes that attract the attention of story-tellers, and appeal to listeners. And they are precisely, perhaps universally, the main elements of drama.

It has often been said that aspects of 'goodness' cannot be defined adequately unless they are contrasted with what could, in certain circumstances, be categorised as aspects of 'badness'. It is equally true that some aspects of 'badness', whether or not they are condemned by those persons who tell or listen to the stories about them, can be delineated in terms of personal and social upset or in their potential or actual propensity for destructiveness. In Aboriginal mythology, the 'good' (related to the smooth running of everyday affairs) serves as a backdrop to conceivably wrong actions. It represents the scenery or the stage props against which the 'story' can be worked out, and against which violence can be highlighted. In that sense, myth opens a door to vicarious excitement. That is not to say that excitement is manifested solely within the context of conflict. But it does imply that myth provides opportunities for people to experience incidents that can be savoured in a way which they cannot be in real-life situations where personal involvement and commitment intervene. In other words, mythic violence and aggression, potential or otherwise, provide a setting for the intellectualisation of emotional manifestations that are inherent in all human behaviour and social relations. In that respect, drama as expressed in Aboriginal mythology epitomises a people's demand for excitement, as a means (*one* means) of avoiding or escaping from boredom or emotional stagnation.

CHAPTER NINE

IN SEARCH OF MEANING

It is easy to say that there is more to myth than meets the eye — or the ear. The difficulty lies in trying to establish what that 'more' is, or might be, and how to get at it. Cassirer once wrote that the magic mirror of myth reflected the interests of people looking into that mirror rather than any intrinsic qualities in myth. In other words, the questions that are being asked help to shape the answer. Who is asking the questions — and what questions? Who is listening, or looking, or intervening, and maybe re-framing the answers as well? As myth-stories spread, other people become involved in the process. Students of myth come from widely divergent cultural backgrounds, and can suggest interpretations that amount to new versions or even new myths. On a smaller scale, change and variation are features of local situations, too.

'DIFFERENT, BUT A LITTLE BIT THE SAME' (LOCALLY SPEAKING)

In other chapters we have commented on the fact that even in a single region there can be different versions of what is regarded locally as the same story, or almost the same story. This is over and above the matter of 'layers of meaning' or degrees of complexity in interpreting symbolism, or esoteric allusions, in the sphere of sacred mythology.

Differences in personal style were taken very much for granted, though not always openly acknowledged. Other variations depended on circumstances. For some listeners there were things that might be elaborated, whereas for others they might be curtailed or even omitted: descriptions of terrain or vegetation, food collection or preparation, hunting sequences, or conversational material. Traditionally, stories were vehicles for providing practical information. They were teaching-and-learning devices as much as sources of entertainment. Techniques or processes merely noted in passing for adult listeners might be spelt out for children without disrupting the story line. Given the right audience, a story-teller could gloss over other items as well. When story-tellers and listeners share not only a range of information but also assumptions about such information, quite a lot can be left unspoken. A hint, a glance, a gesture, or even a pause may be enough. On that basis alone a story can take different shapes or be assembled in different ways — up to a point. One question then, is: When are two partly dissimilar stories regarded as the same? Or not the same?

In many cases the main criterion is a territorial one: linkage with specific sites or mythic tracks. Other items are important too: the names and attributes of the main characters, their actions, and the signs and instructions they left for posterity. But locality-centred questions are even more so. Where did it happen? Who lives there now, in spirit form and perhaps in some other manifestation as well? And, whose country is it? Which people belong to it and have special rights in it?

Nevertheless, there is no fixed rule that confines any one story to only one site or cluster of sites. Most mythic characters had associations of some kind with a larger span of territory in the course of their travels. There *are* site-specific incidents that are commemorated in topographical arrangements landscaped by mythic personages. From another perspective, locality-centred statements provide a coverage of the mythic population in a specific region, rather than following the physical life and exploits of particular characters, or as complementary to such sequential accounts. One example is the constellation of stories about 'what happened at Gogalag'. We have included a few excerpts from that constellation (Myths 54, 116, 122 and 157). Another western Arnhem Land illustration could come from Arguluk Hill near Oenpelli. Uluru, Ayers Rock in central Australia, is probably the most famous site (Mountford 1965), but there are many other places where a number of mythic characters live in close proximity. As against that, of course, there are the story-examples already noted where one or perhaps two mythic inhabitants discourage or actively oppose the intrusion of others.

Territorial anchors are a significant characteristic of most minor as well as major myths. As regards content, however, most of the human themes that the myth-stories deal with are certainly not localised, any more than many of the natural species are. Their relevance is very much wider. We have already mentioned the salience of such themes: jealousy, greed, hostility, resentment, suspicion, anger, hatred and dislike, as well as affection, friendship, co-operation, admiration, kindness and compassion. There are problems bound up with betrothal arrangements, or unhappy marriages: for example, a girl's resistance to a marriage that has been arranged for her by relatives, perhaps against her own personal preference for a young sweetheart. This theme appears in a great many myth-stories over the entire continent. It takes on local 'dress' and is treated in different ways, just as other human problems are. The wrappings and modes of expression that make a story familiar and understandable to people within one region can conceal its basic relevance or its basic appeal to listeners or readers outside that region, unless they can get through those wrappings to the nucleus of shared meanings. As against that, some aspects of the wrappings may not be all that different. Place-names aside, some of the same or similar themes or characters or action sequences appear over widely-separated regions. They are more noticeable, though, in areas where there is a fair amount of interaction among the people concerned even if they acknowledge that there are other cultural differences between them, including language differences.

SOME EXAMPLES FROM WESTERN ARNHEM LAND

There are, or were, probably thousands of myth-stories in western Arnhem Land alone. Over the years we have been told hundreds of them. Just to list them, let alone drawing comparisons between them, would be a rather lengthy procedure. As a matter of interest we note here a few examples, along with some from a volume compiled by Lazarus Lami-lami, an Aboriginal man from that region who was a long-standing friend of ours. We focus on Croker and Goulburn Islands and the adjacent mainland, and on people speaking Gunwinggu and Maung. Lamilami includes in his 1974 volume a number of stories that he knew personally. He wanted to provide a record of the Maung people, however, and not only an individual account, being a rather self-effacing person. Accordingly, he took his tape recorder around to various men on Croker and South Goulburn Islands to get their versions, and does not always specify in such cases who the speakers are.

Lamilami's version of Mayangaidj (Mayanaidj) and the giant (1974: 20–22) is almost identical, except for place-name details, with the one included here (Myth 88). So is the version told to C. Berndt by his sister Mondalmi early in 1964, except that in hers the giant died when Mayanaidj struck him on the penis. Lamilami's 'Wild dog and Kangaroo' (1974: 29–32) is very close to our 'Kangaroo's deceit' (Myth 93), except that in his version Dog killed and ate Kangaroo because he painted Dog's " 'lower part' [penis] under his belly". His 'Ambidj, the Rainbow Snake', named Inganar (pp. 34–38), is close to the Rainbow version set out in Myth 57. So is 'The Crocodile' (1974: 38–39), who was angry because people would not take him across a creek in the same bark canoe as themselves (see our Myth 145). His 'Moon-and-death' version (1974: 46–47) centres on a fight to the death between the two main characters, but not death for Moon (see our Myth 188). His version (1974: 47–49) of the *manya* (*mainya*) spirit and the man who was getting goose eggs, ends with the *mainya* getting the man's help to kill all the other *mainya*, including his dangerous wife; he himself had been kidnapped and was really a human man (see our Myth 72).

Lamilami's story of Wiri-wiriyag (1974: 60–64) is fairly short and concentrates on the final episode. Gargain urges the boy to put his hand into the hole in the tree to get honey. His hands gets stuck, he screams, and Gargain says, 'Now I'm going to cut your head off!' The boy's mother has been keeping some honey for him, but pours it all onto the fire when she learns of his death. This explains why wild honey in western Arnhem Land is to be found low down in the trees, whereas in eastern Arnhem Land is always higher up. (Compare with our Myth 179.)

In Lamilami's Yirawadbad story (1974: 66–69), when Mináliwu's mother urges the girl to go to her promised husband, the girl replies cheekily, 'Why don't *you* marry him?' Some other points differ too. Interestingly, there is no mention of the girl's father, and Yirawabad defers to his mother-in-law early in the story, when she chooses their travelling directions. (See our Myth 181.) In a version of Yirawadbad told to C. Berndt at Goulburn Island in 1964 by a young Maung woman, there are some differences in detail. One is that Mináliwu alone looks into the hollow bamboo (not log) where Yirawadbad is hiding in snake form. When she calls out, 'Mother, it bit me!' her mother comes running and is bitten too. They die; but Mináliwu calls out to warn her mother that a Rainbow is carrying her away. Mináliwu's little sister and baby brother also appear at the end of the story. And Yirawadbad, as in the majority of versions, turns into a venomous snake. The Yirawadbad myth was what could be called a popular story in western Arnhem Land. It was widely known, not only for its religious ritual consequences and implications, but also for its 'marriage problems' theme: problems in arranging marriages, as well as marital troubles between husband and wife.

Other stories told to C. Berndt in 1964 at Goulburn Island also show similarities and differences. The story of the two young men who turned into salt-water crocodiles, each killing the other's mother, is almost identical with Myth 126, except that the women 'bury' the fire so their sons can't cook the fish they insist on getting, and keep offering their sons *mandem* water-lily roots instead. Also, the place is different: Yandag-bu-ngulag, in Gunwinggu territory.

In a Guruweli story told by Meyaweidba, the younger of two sisters escapes because Guruweli's 'dog' (*djabo*, spotted cat) fails to keep watch; the elder girl, pregnant, is killed and eaten, but her relatives avenge her death and join all her bones together. Guruweli is killed at Proctor Point, Maligarang, and the long *garbara* yams associated with him became *djang* there. This is more like the stories associated with another malignant being, Biyu-biyu (see Myth 89 and 90); but in a Biyu-biyu story told to C. Berndt at Goulburn Island in 1964 by Ngalwalun, the two sisters escape and reach home unharmed. When Biyu-biyu, out collecting goose eggs, came back to his bark house because 'he had a feeling inside' that something was wrong, he found the girls there: they had come in to shelter from the rain. He says happily, 'You two have come, for me!' He asks whether they are hungry. 'Yes!' 'Eat these eggs, then!' They eat, and then say, 'We're going now.' He objects. 'You're my women, I'll marry you!' They run off, tell their parents, and urge them to send men to kill him. Biyu-biyu has dug a hole in the ground and made a fire inside. He is sitting nearby clapping his sticks (but no song is mentioned), and the men can hear the sound of a didjeridu. They attack him, pushing him closer and closer to the hole until he falls in: they burn him to death, and then bury him. He was the one who introduced the didjeridu. 'That's the reason boys and young men play the didjeridu. He started it.' ('But it was really his penis.')

In another Goulburn Island story, from 1964, Waibuma and Meyaweidba told about an old man who had been asked to mind the children while their parents went kangaroo hunting: 'We'll bring you some food, then.' He took the children up among the caves to get bats, blocked the cave entrance with grass, set it alight, cooked them, and ate them. One of the fathers came back with kangaroo, raised the alarm when the old man confessed ('I was hungry!'), and they finally killed him. This happened at Ganem-barbaga, in Gunwinggu country, and the old man's name was Gaburba. (Cf. Myth 144.) Later, a young Maung woman (Mamulaid) told a story of an old man who had been left to mind his little grandson, but instead caught him in a fish net and drowned him. When the child's parents returned and couldn't find him although all his relatives went searching, they attacked the old man with sticks and spears. Even his own daughter hit him. They dug a hole and buried him, at Marganala (Murganella).

Also at Goulburn Island in 1964, Lamilami's sister Mondalmi did not remember that she had told C. Berndt the story of Wurudja, Poison Island, in 1947. But this time she told it again, with Ngalwalun. It was very close indeed to the version we include as Myth 4. It started with a sorcery death at Marganala, and two men taking the death message to the dead boy's father. Again, there is no explanation for the man's being so thirsty. The two children who survived, at Croker Island, waited four moons before they emerged, after the ground had begun to get cool. And later, when *their* two children married, 'they made us': they were the ancestors of much of the population of that area.

In the same 1964 Goulburn Island bracket, Mamulaid's very short account of the husband who died while hunting (he wouldn't stop catching long-nosed crocodiles in a billabong, although his wife kept telling him they had enough), ends with his wife weeping over his bones (see our Myth 149). In Meyaweidba's version of Luma-luma (see Myth 182), he behaves like a Rainbow Snake and swallows many 'people, canoes, fishing lines, everything', out in the open sea. Only their bones were left, at Malagwiya island, the name of Meyaweidba's uncle (mother's brother) who had told her the story, and also the name of one of her sons. Luma-luma, she said, had first come from Milingimbi and from Cape Stewart, Minangandawa.

Meyaweidba and Mondalmi also told about Inganar, the Rainbow Snake, and an orphan boy being looked after by his mother's mother. He demanded one kind of food (sweet *yaldain* roots), although she said she had given him all there were. This version is very much like Lamilami's 'The Rainbow who swallowed the crying child', with everyone else nearby being eventually killed, though the young men who try to spear him are puzzled at first because the spears keep coming back to them. This version also identifies some of the people who are rescued alive when the Snake is cut open (see our Myth 55). An interesting variant of the Inganar story is included in a volume compiled by a number of young students who were then at Kormilda College, near Darwin (Bunug *et al.* 1974: 31–32). In Bunug's version of 'Inganarr, the Giant Serpent', spears and rocks had no effect on the snake, who had eaten all the people on North Goulburn Island. He swallowed his attackers too. Then he set off for eastern Arnhem Land. He felt tired and sick, and vomited out all of the people, who ran off to populate the country. That accounts for eastern Arnhem Land having more people than there are on the western side, and for North Goulburn Island having no permanent residents. An intriguing point in this version is that Bunug is one of Mondalmi's sons and Lamilami was his uncle.

Guwadu, an elderly Gunwinggu-speaker who had been living at Goulburn Island for many years, gave a version of the Nyalaidj dancers (see Myths 48, 49, 50) and an orphan boy whose crying brought the Rainbow. People teased him, offering him food but eating it themselves when he reached out to get it: this was at Gumara. Finally, the Rainbow ate the dancers and their dogs and the orphan: they went hard, like rock. The people who had been teasing him turned into birds — including *wiri-wiriyag* (or *biri-wiriyag*, where *biri-* is a third-person plural form with a 'past' aspect).

Guwadu also told about the honey-getting episode in the Wiri-wiriyag story where Gargain, married to the boy's two sisters, has gone hunting with him. Gargain cuts off the boy's head because he ate honey that was forbidden to him as a young initiate. This happened at Guguluwi, in Gumadir. Ngalwalun and Mamulaid had previously told a story very similar in some respects to Myth 179, except that the characters have different names. The boy, the young initiate, surreptitiously tickles his sisters as they bathe in the billabong, and deceives his brother-in-law, pretending to be lame, when they go hunting together. He denied eating the honey that his brother-in-law was keeping for something special, 'maybe for the *mareiin* rituals', but his mouth was so full of honey that his voice was inaudible. (A couple of the women who were listening added appropriate sounds at this point: '*Blp, blp, blp. . .*'). That was why his brother-in-law cut off his head. The story ends with the boy's spirit calling to his mother, and she calls back, wailing for him. Then she pours the basket full of honey on to the fire. Almost as in Lamilami's version 'now there is plenty of honey on small trees at that place, cooked; but everywhere else it is high up on the trees, raw'. This happened at Warawag, in Yiwadja country.

There are further stories from this series alone, apart from others, that could be cited for comparison. Instead, we turn to a different story, also told to C. Berndt at Goulburn Island in 1964, noted here in slightly abbreviated form.

192. CURLEW'S PUNISHMENT

A man and his wife set off to get honey, carrying their palm-leaf baskets. But she didn't like him: she wanted to be with other people and wouldn't go with him. She left him to go by himself. [The story continues with their getting and eating honey, separately.] 'What shall I do?' he asked himself. She wouldn't eat any of the honey he tried to give her, because she didn't like him. He took her climbing up among the rocks, pretending to be friendly. He cut down a couple of high trees to use as a ladder. 'Let's go up!' They climbed up and sat there, resting. She slept. He came down by himself, and threw down the tree-ladder. Next day, when she woke up, she looked about: 'He's left me, he's gone, he's thrown away the ladder! There's no way down! We could have gone down together! I've nothing to drink, nothing to eat! I'll die of hunger! He really disliked me! For ever!' She called out, wailing, and the sound of her song was like the cry of a curlew at night.

> *Gweeeelig-ba-ngaya! Eeeee!*
> *Nyalei ngangun? Eeeee!*
> *Nyalei ngangun? Eeeee!*
> *Burgyag rog!*
> *Burgyag nawu mandaneg ngangun,*
> *Burgyag mandjingmi ngangun!*
> *Djeega-bireen-bireen.*
> *Garad, ngabad, gundjeeega!*

[Sound of a curlew's call]
What [shall] I eat?
What [shall] I eat?
Nothing at all!
Not those bitter yams I [shall] eat!
Not those [other] bitter yams I [shall] eat!
[I used to drink from my mother's breast]
Mother, father, mother's breast!

Finally she died, and turned into a curlew. This was at Gundjumbur in Gumadir, in Gunwinggu territory.

Meyaweidba told this in Gunwinggu, her first husband's language. It was, she said, one of the stories he had told her about his own country. Curlew is *wila (weela)* in Gunwinggu, *gurwilu* in Maung, *wilu* in Yiwadja — a very widespread name for this bird, resembling its long-drawn-out cry. This story combines several themes. One centres on an unwilling wife and a rejected husband, an almost-certain setting for some kind of tragedy. Her punishment brings in another theme: a victim left stranded high in the rocky escarpment, foodless and waterless, unable to escape. This happened to the faithless wives (in Myth 147) whose husband was White Cockatoo man in C. Berndt's version. In this account, Curlew's husband leaves the story after he has removed the ladder, and nothing more is said about him. A third theme is included in the Curlew's song, as the last line. More usually, especially in Maung stories, it is the wailing cry or wailing song of two small children whose mother is being carried away out to sea by a Rainbow Snake or some other creature, or has been bitten by Yirawadbad, or otherwise lost to them. (The Gunwinggu word for breast or breast-milk, *gundjiga*, is spelt differently here to indicate the drawn-out cry in the song.)

Myth-stories are not water-tight packages. They draw on themes and episodes from a wider regional repertoire. That does not affect the linkage between stories and specific places, or the social and personal messages they convey. And, as in the case of Rainbow Snakes, mythic characters can exist in more than one manifestation. The repertoire of source-materials available in any region is enlarged through contact with others. This used to happen, and still does although in rather different circumstances, when people from neighbouring groups meet on ceremonial or ritual occasions, or for trading or gift-exchange, and so on. Also, people who had kinship or marriage ties with adjacent groups would pass on stories they had heard.

One such example comes, again, from Meyaweidba, who told it to C. Berndt at Goulburn Island in 1964. It was, she said, about a girl and a

maam spirit, or what Maung people called a *mainya*. She told it in
Gunwinggu. Because it is rather long we have summarised parts of it,
especially at the beginning.

193. A RUNAWAY WIFE
AND A *MAAM* SPIRIT

[The story opens with people setting off for the day, the men to spear fish
and the women to get *man-gulaidj* nuts. A mother and her elder daughter
are gathering nuts, when they are surprised to see the younger daughter
coming.]

'Why did you come back?' 'Because I'm hungry!' She had left her
husband behind, but they saw him coming after her. He was very angry,
and hit her with a stick. She was angry then, too. 'I'll go!' She got her
things, her digging stick, her fire-stick, her baskets, and she took spears as
well. 'He did wrong when he struck me! I'll go away, I'll hide from him.'
She set off, and came to a place where palm trees were growing and *man-
gindjeg* yams too. 'Oh! Yams for me!' I'll put my things down here, I'll
slice them and soak them for tomorrow. I'm hungry.' She sliced some
yams, got a sheet of bark and carried them back on her head. She cut
wood, dug the ground and put posts ready for making a bark hut. 'I'll stay
here, because now I've left my mother and father.'

A *maam* spirit smelled her. '*Mam, mam*,' he said to himself. 'A woman for
me!' He came hurrying in that direction, 'I'll go and look around for her!'
She was asleep inside the hut. He came closer, smashed a hole in the bark,
and put his head through. '*Wow*! Father, mother, child!' [*Djedje* is the
Gunwinggu term a woman uses for her children. Here she uses it in a
conventional exclamation.] But he said, 'Why are you frightened of me?
You thought of me, you had me in your mind, that's why I came. My
woman! You thought of me!' 'I don't want you. I'm going now!' 'No.
You'll stay.' He took hold of her. . .they slept.

Next morning she said, 'I'll go and get my *man-gindjeg* yams!' Instead,
she ran away, leaving her things, hurrying. He went after her, and
brought her back. They slept. Next morning, 'I'll go and get goose eggs!'
he said. She was already pregnant, heavy with babies inside: six of them.
They cooked the goose eggs in the hot ashes. She got up, took them out
and put them down, gave him some and ate some herself. They argued
about which of them should go to get more eggs, but he insisted that if she
went she might try to trick him again. He took his dilly bag, his bark raft-
canoe for putting goose eggs in, and his long turtle-spear to pole it with.
She waited until she thought he was a fair way off, out of sight of the hut:

'I'm going back to my mother and father!' She stood up, got the trunk of a pandanus palm and covered it with paperbark to deceive him, as if she were lying asleep there. Then she set off for the place where her parents were camping. She took her things, and went.

She went on, and half-way there she gave birth to a baby, a boy. She went on: a girl baby. A bit farther: a boy. A bit farther: a boy. Later, a girl. Later, a boy. That was all. She went on to where those people were getting *man-gulaidj* nuts. They looked round and saw her. She told them what had happened. 'I met a *maam* and he did wrong to me!' [He made me go wrong!] 'Good! You didn't want your husband!' ['Serve you right!'] They went on getting *man-gulaidj* nuts.

That *maam* came back, and saw that she had gone. He set off, running after her. He saw the first boy baby, hit him on the nose, killing him, and left him there. He did the same with the other five. Finished. Then he went on to where those people were camping. 'Here it is!' He went inside, and sat waiting.

At sunset the children came back to that place first. He didn't see them: his eyes were closed. Then he heard a voice. 'That's her talking!' She came running, and came inside. He opened his eyes. 'Oh! He's in there! Come, all of you, let's attack him! Come, all of you! That *maam* is here, the one who did wrong to me!' She kept calling to her mother and father, and the others. They got ready their spears, their sticks, their digging sticks, and went after him, pushing him outside the hut. They speared him all over with various spears, including spear-points of stingray-tail tips. They hit him on the head and back. He couldn't do anything. They pushed him into a big hole that they had dug ready for him, and buried him. This happened at Delegani, in Nagara-language country inland from Maningrida.

The women who had been sitting listening agreed, 'This is a new story to us!' And the resemblance to the 'Runaway wife meets a *mogwoi*' story (Myth 79) told to C. Berndt at Milingimbi in 1950 was heightened by the almost identical name of the girl in this 1964 version, Bowaliba.

SAME BUT DIFFERENT
(A DISTANT VIEW)

Although so many themes and motifs appear in stories throughout the continent, that does not necessarily make them the same story. They could be regarded as the same *kind* of story, when people meet and compare notes at traditional gatherings or, these days, at conferences. Quarrels about food or water or fire or marriage arrangements, for instance, belong within the range of commonly-recognised problems that are variously expressed in myth and story. And these common elements can serve as a basis for comparisons — for Aboriginal people discovering or building up a shared identity, or for students of myth or comparative literature who are intrigued by the whole question of similarities and divergencies in such material.

Widespread similarities in entire stories are more unusual, except in the directly religious sphere where travelling myth-ritual combinations are formally sponsored and spread among quite disparate groups. Even then, variations are inevitable, as these myths become adjusted or adapted to the myth-complexes already there, in the areas where they are being introduced.

One example of a myth-story, or a basic section of a myth-story that is on the fringe of more complex religious affairs, focuses on a group of sisters known by various names, such as Minmara and Gung-guranggara. (See Myths 16, 127, 159.) Women as well as men at Yalata tell this myth, or share parts of it (White 1975: 128–30). It extends throughout the Western Desert, from Ooldea, where we heard about them in 1941, to Balgo, where in 1986 a woman's open-sacred painting prepared for public exhibition shows seven girls running along a path pursued by two men. Mountford (1937), Tindale (1936, 1959) and Robinson (1966: 91–93) write about them. So did Kaberry (1939: 12) in the Kimberley area of Western Australia. Howitt (1904: 429–30, 489, n2, 787) notes several versions from southeastern Australia. In one, they are still being pursued in the sky by Native Cat man. In another, they had fire that was stolen from them by Crow. K. Llangloh Parker (1953: 105–09, also 125–27) gives a version in which the sisters, called Mayi-Mayi, are followed by a man who manages to get two of them as wives, but they escape up a high pine tree into the sky. (This is in the edition selected and edited by H. Drake-Brockman, where the illustrations are intended to provide an Aboriginal atmosphere. In the line drawing that introduces the story of 'Mayi-mayi the Seven Sisters' are seven figures, mostly based on wooden carvings from north-eastern Arnhem Land; a couple of them are male in their original forms, but here the illustrator has added breasts.) Mountford (1976a: 33–35) has condensed the Llangloh Parker stories into a romantic account that he calls 'The Pleiades and their lovers'. His more serious version (1976b: e.g. 460–80) (like others in that larger volume), is presented in more careful and unsensational detail. In most versions the core motif is the pursuit of unwilling or partly unwilling girls by a man, or a pair of men, who may be two manifestations of the same man; there are scenes of rape or attempted rape, the man may have an abnormally large penis, and in the final climax the girls are transformed into the star cluster known as the Pleiades, or

Seven Sisters, the form in which they can be seen now. Other groups of mythic women are not necessarily identified with these. For example, a Walbri party of Travelling Women chased by a man finally disappears into the earth (Meggitt 1966: 113–20).

In a different vein, a north Queensland story from the Endeavour River on Cape York Peninsula (Gordon and Haviland 1979: 9–11) is about a crocodile who wanted a human wife. He chose a young woman with a new baby, took her to his home and watched her jealously, but she managed to escape. On her way, she gave birth to crocodile eggs. The crocodile was never killed, though men tried to get him. From Rose River, on the western side of the Gulf of Carpentaria, Heath (1980: 235–40) sets out in vernacular text with linguistic annotations the story 'Crocodile steals woman'. A crocodile emerged from the water especially to catch a woman, took her to his home, and worked to catch fish for her. She gave birth to baby crocodiles, but at last managed to escape. He tracked her; she told her people to kill him, and they did. This is more like a version told to C. Berndt at Milingimbi in 1950 (noted in Chapter 10). That crocodile tried to be an affectionate and dutiful husband and father, and wept over each of the baby crocodiles she had given birth to along her escape route, but the union was wrong and therefore doomed from the start — and she already had a human husband. Some of the discussion centred on the importance of keeping to the accepted marriage rules and living a normal domestic life with people (characters) of the same kind as oneself.

Next: Emu, offspring, and trickery. K. Llangloh Parker published in 1896 (pages 1–5 in the 1953 edition) a New South Wales story of jealousy between emus and wild turkeys (Australian bustard, *Ardeotis australis*). Turkey woman tricked Emu woman into cutting off her wings. After that, Emu was unable to fly. In revenge, Emu hid all her own chicks except two. Then she told Turkey woman, who was feeding with her twelve chicks, that twelve were too many to feed properly — two were enough to rear. Turkey woman was worried about that, and killed all but two of her chicks. Emu reprimanded her again for being cruel and selfish, this time for killing her children. The outcome: emus today have no wings, and bush turkeys have only two eggs each in a season. Mountford (1976a: 49–51) gives a version in which the wing-cutting comes first and then the chick-killing, but says nothing about its location. In the end, the wild turkeys boast about being able to fly away out of reach of men and dogs, as emus cannot, but turkeys now have smaller families than emus do.

This story is widespread in the Western Desert. Some versions make use of one episode-cluster, not both, as in this account told to R. Berndt at Balgo in 1960. It begins with Emu woman coming with her chicks to live near Turkey woman, who had only two. Turkey hid her own chicks and went to visit Emu. She told Emu she had had to kill her children because there was no food anywhere around. Emu believed her, and killed her own children. Turkey thought this was a good joke. She called *her* children, who came running to her. Emu didn't know why Turkey had done this to her. She hit Turkey with sticks, but Turkey temporarily blinded her with wild tomato seeds, and went away. In the end, both women turned into birds, at Baniayindi in Gugada country but their spirits remain in the rockhole there. The moral is, 'Don't trust anyone, even someone who seems to be friendly, without being sure of the facts!'

A Jigalong version (Tonkinson 1974: 73–74) begins with the chick-killing: Emu made Turkey (Bustard) ashamed of having so many children and sorry for Emu herself who had (she said) killed all but two of hers. Turkey then killed all of hers except two. Later, in revenge, Turkey pretended she had cut off her wings because of her grief for her dead children. It was Emu's turn to feel ashamed and sorry: she cut her own wings. Then Turkey flew up, swooping and calling in triumph. Since that time, emus cannot fly and turkeys 'lay only one or two eggs'.

A Cape York story reported by McConnel (1958: 91–94) points out that there is always jealousy and rivalry between Emu and Native Companion. Emu husband and wife had only two surviving children: they had lost the others through neglect. The Native Companion pair 'had many children', and one day they asked the Emus to look after them; but the Emus hid them so that the Native Companions, returning from getting gum, could not find them. Later, they burnt the Emus with hot gum and the Emus retaliated. Now, native companions have 'only two chicks'. Also, a short version, 'The Brolga and the Emu', comes from Numbulwar in eastern Arnhem Land (Wingathana 1974: 38–40).

These stories combine explanations of bird behaviour with oblique allusions to human behaviour, as so many myth-stories do. Emus are more prominent in the world of myth and story, just as they are in everyday life, and their 'personal' characteristics receive more attention — vanity, greed and curiosity, for instance. But naturalists have reported at least two features that emus and turkeys/bustards have in common: only three toes on each foot and powerful legs for running: also, a turkey gorged with food (mice plagues and .ɔcust swarms) is likely to have trouble in flying.

In each set of examples the stories are similar, but not the same. The similarities and differences could serve as a starting point for a two-angled enquiry: locally specific, and ranging further afield. The Star Sisters' adventures lead into a symbolically complex and ramifying constellation of religious myth and ritual. The crocodile-and-woman stories, besides warning of physical dangers (salt-water crocodiles attack and eat people), deal with social and personal problems, too. The focus on Emu as a constant in the three last stories links up with other Emu stories, as the other birds do with their respective sequences in the same and different regions. Heath, for example, discusses the Nunggubuyu crocodile event along with a story told by the same man about a girl captured and raped by a buffalo. (In that case, the girl died.) The narrator said that both were stories about events in living human memory; they were not Dreaming myths, but were 'true' in a different sense.

A great deal could be said about all of these, and others, in regard to their local story connections alone. And they are *only* examples. It is true that over much of the continent a great deal has been 'lost' to posterity. Nevertheless, once the whole range of published and unpublished material becomes available, the resemblances as well as the differences in myth-stories will undoubtedly become more obvious. With the traditional lines of communication that linked so many communities through trade and through religious and ceremonial inter-relationships, it could hardly be otherwise. Apart from the well-known paths in the Centre and north along which myth-stories and songs could travel, the great river systems of the south-east provided ready-made routes for the spread of ideas as well as things. Even in the early days of European settlement, the Darling-Murray rivers constellation served as a major artery in the transmission of knowledge and information, including myths.

CONTINUITIES AND CHANGES

Most of the myth-stories we have discussed so far reveal little evidence of introduced elements in the course of the story-tellers' contact with Europeans. There are a few references, but with the kind we have selected, these are minimal. Under such circumstances we can regard them as being, in a sense, traditional statements. (Here we use the term 'traditional' to mean distinctively Aboriginal.) That does not mean they have remained the same over a period of time, or that they have survived unscathed during the many socio-cultural upsets that have befallen the several generations of story-tellers who have lived through these situations of radical change. Nevertheless, the nature of the mythology suggests that we are in the presence of a body of literature that is associated with a continuing tradition; that its narrative form and structure have persisted and been insulated to some extent from outside interference because of the high value Aborigines place on their heritage. It is clear, too, that people have to some extent separated more traditional myth-stories from those that relate to contact situations, and in doing so have given the opportunity for the traditional myths to retain their vital function of being interpreted, by their story-tellers and listeners, as time and occasion demand.

While we should not consider the content of such myths as exactly documenting social events, it is reasonable to believe that they say something about basic values and assumptions and that they are, or were, acceptable to the people concerned. Also, since many them are still being told, even though perhaps in different forms, and still hold the attention of many Aboriginal people, they are not outmoded.

Although we do not include here the mythology of ritual that substantiates or is otherwise relevant to religious performances, nevertheless most of the myth-stories we discuss involve mythic personages of the Dreaming, and so they, too, are religious in the broad meaning of that word. Moreover, many of the mythic beings we mention are also represented in the mythology of ritual: in a number of respects their stories are not all that different. However, the myths set out here are open-sacred, in contradistinction to closed- or secret-sacred in terms of knowledge and practice of men or women, separately or in collaboration. That the myths in this book retain their traditional quality has to do with three factors: they relate to mythic beings of the Dreaming; they are directly linked to specific stretches of land; and they deal with ongoing human concerns.

To appreciate the issue of mythological 'authenticity' it is necessary to keep in mind that virtually all such accounts were recorded by us directly from their narrators within a social context. There were always listeners present or nearby, who knew the stories and did not hesitate to comment on them or amend them when they were being told, or immediately afterward. We have drawn most heavily on myth-stories told to us prior to the 1960s, the bulk of them from six cultural groups. Ooldea was on the fringe of the Great Victoria Desert, part of what we now call the Western Desert. Balgo, on the edge of the Great Sandy Desert, is in the same broadly-defined desert area. In the Northern Territory there were north-eastern and western Arnhem Land, the 'buffalo-station' country west of the East Alligator River and the Daly River south-west of Darwin. Predominantly, the myths come from northern cultures, a lesser number from the central and southern parts of Aboriginal Australia. Those from Ooldea were told by people who in 1941 had only a passing acquaintance with Europeans. Some were still coming into the desert fringe settlements and were having their first glimpse of strangers. Balgo, which we initially visited early in 1958, was in almost the same position. The first waves of desert people came north, attracted to the Kimberley pastoral stations, late in the 1930s and into the 1940s, a few as late as the 1950s and 1960s. North-eastern Arnhem Land had considerable Indonesian and later Japanese and European contact. Nevertheless, as we have suggested elsewhere (R. and C. Berndt 1954: 14–31), the north-eastern Arnhem Landers were, without too much effort on their part, able to maintain their own socio-cultural perspective in a near-traditional form. Mainly, this was because at that time there were no permanent and large alien settlements in the area except for small-scale mission stations, and these had little direct influence on mainstream Aboriginal living patterns.

When we went to Ooldea, for the whole of the Western Desert there had been no systematic anthropological studies, except for a few isolated ones, that could have been utilised for comparative purposes. For north-eastern Arnhem Land the situation was different. Warner (1937/1958: 519–65) had carried out research at Milingimbi in north-central Arnhem Land in 1926–29. When we went to Yirrkalla in 1946, his work provided a basis for comparison with ours, particularly the mythology. Warner's versions of some of the myths we present here do differ in several respects, although there are some marked similarities. There is nothing unusual in that, considering that most myths have several versions. As we have seen, story-tellers project a personal component in the telling, emphasising particular features at the expense of others, or introducing additional details.

In western Arnhem Land, although our first exposure to the culture of that area was in 1945, on the Army Aboriginal settlements, and in 1947, at Oenpelli itself, we did not work consistently there until 1950. Because we concentrated on Gunwinggu, most of the myths were recorded in that language. Gunwinggu speakers were moving into the Oenpelli mission settlement — formerly a cattle station — from their home districts farther east, from the early 1930s. There seem to have been no Gunwinggu speakers at Oenpelli when Baldwin Spencer visited there in 1912. Included in this broad region were the Maung people, living on North and South Goulburn Islands as well as on the adjoining mainland. At the time of our research among the Maung, they were heavily influenced by the Gunwinggu and, as the myths note quite clearly, in some areas their territories overlapped. Otherwise they had no difficulty in identifying and separating out their own myths and linking them with others, if only because named mythic personages were concerned directly with particular local places and with the paths along which they travelled. In a sense, it was the land and the mythological substantiation of it that were of vital concern to the people, enabling the land to speak for itself.

West of the East Alligator River, a wide stretch of country reached almost to the outskirts of Darwin. The people who originally occupied it had been under devastating pressures from European and other outsiders. By the time we became interested in the area, in 1945, the population had been fragmented and dispersed. Some people were working on the buffalo stations; others in Darwin and elsewhere in the Northern Territory. However, there were some older people living at Oenpelli who belonged to these 'plains' cultures or had close associations with them and knew about the myths. Interestingly, and of importance comparatively, Spencer (1914: 290–318) had written down differing versions of some of those we were told so much later.

In the Daly River area, our main fieldwork was in 1945–46. The people with whom we talked had had intensive alien contact of a disastrous kind (see R. Berndt 1952b: 81–95, 188–92). Older local people still retained an excellent knowledge of their traditional society, but it was no longer a living reality. In any case, it had been heavily influenced by Wogaidj from the coast and the people living beyond the Moiil plain toward Port Keats, who in the mid-1940s were still traditionally-oriented, although the Wogaidj had experienced the spread of European settlement from Darwin. In the myths from the Daly and from the 'buffalo-station' country, some Aboriginal place-names are also given their European names. That practice is not so obtrusive in the mythology of the other cultural groups, although we have tried to indicate such names wherever that was possible.

Most of the myth-stories we include here, then, were told to us about forty or so years ago, and some only twenty years ago. We have chosen them rather than later versions, which we have also recorded up to quite recently, although we note a few of these. The point we make is that the greater number of the myths were set down in circumstances that approximated closely the near-traditional scene. Most of them had first been told to the story-tellers (they said) by their parents, uncles or aunts or grandparents, or other older people who would have had little or no contact with Europeans. This raises again the question often asked in this connection: to what extent does such a mythology mirror the kind of society or societies in which the people at that time lived? Partly, this is a question about what the people identify as being familiar and relevant to themselves.

The deities and other mythic characters, for instance, acted out their adventures against a natural environment that was already there but was also subject to their reshaping of it and, eventually, prepared for themselves to become part of it. While many of the resources were already available when they commenced their journeys and moved across large tracts of country, they were responsible, too, for leaving deposits of additional resources — not only what they carried and left at particular places, but also those that came about through their own transformation. They, too, became part of the local resources, of the actual landscape and what it contained. And they did this not just for themselves, or simply in fulfilling their destiny, but, as we are told, for human beings who were to come, those people who would constitute the 'new' generations for whom they were responsible — indeed, whom they had initially been responsible for creating, or causing to come into being. Wherever the mythic beings went or whatever they did, they left something of themselves within the environment, at particular places where their spiritual essence resided. There are, of course, exceptions to this; some disappeared, leaving not even a site to commemorate their presence in the land. Others of a different order continued to reappear in a visible or audible form — the Ngalyod and Wonambi Rainbow Snakes, for instance, and the *mamu, maam, mogwoi* and *mimi* and others. These characters were often credited with being in the land prior to, or at the same time as, the other mythic personages. Moreover, the character of all these mythic beings varied, and in so doing reflected the varied characterstics of human beings. It was, however, the 'speaking land', the context of the myths, the background against which they played out their pre-determined mythic roles that provided an atmosphere of verisimilitude. Traditionally, Aborigines were intimately acquainted with all the features within their own territories, and in that respect the myths speak quite plainly.

It is the content of social relations that are manifested in the myths against that background that is of special interest. One of the characteristics is that mythic personages have magical and supernatural powers. They are able to change their shape, transform themselves, and perform remarkable feats that are beyond the ability of ordinary human beings. In that respect, as in others, the world of the Dreaming is clearly distinguished from the world of everyday happenings; and that is true even though for certain purposes and especially in a ritual context, there are close linkages between them. However, in the ways that mythic beings behave — that is, in a mundane sense as contrasted with their supernatural actions — the fit between them becomes closer. It is with these that people may identify, at least partially. The deities and other mythic beings are, in terms of social relations, cut down to human, sometimes even less than human, size. Like humans themselves, they are motivated by passion, greed, anger and lust, contravening what are acknowledged as the 'rules' but also abiding by them. In a final sense, these mythic beings turn out to be characters of contradiction. Their patterns of social organisation do not appear to be all that different from what human beings themselves understand to have been the traditional or near-traditional modes of behaving and reasoning. Their ways of approaching diverse situations, their treatment of kin as against strangers, their expectations of how others should ideally behave toward them — all of these are found in the myths. And these, and others, are spelt out or indicated obliquely, although such recognition on the part of mythic beings or humans does not necessarily mean that they will be adhered to.

In considering differences between mythic and ordinary everyday events, it would appear that, with myth, they rest on the way the story-line is handled, on how the actions of the mythic personages are highlighted or emphasised in order to achieve a dramatic effect upon listeners, to enable them to identify with what is taking place in the story, to engender pleasure and satisfaction, or fear and abhorrence, depending on the plot. Conceivably, what people desire to hear about when told a myth are things that, given the circumstances, could, in all probability, actually take place; about something in which they could be involved.

In more general terms, any one myth is an abstraction of what purports to be a statement about something that actually happened. That is, at least, what most Aborigines with whom we have worked would say. Natural misfortunes are unpredictable; they do happen, and are beyond the control of human beings — and sometimes beyond the control of mythic ones. Ordinary misadventures within the context of social relations do take place, especially in conflict situations. These can, and do, get out of hand and are not easy to resolve. When everything is running smoothly, there is no real need to remark. Myths unerringly utilise 'trouble' cases, magnifying personal idiosyncrasies, indiscretions and malicious actions. They capitalise on the contravention of recognised expectations, glorying in the provocation of extreme reactions that inevitably lead to revenge, aggressive behaviour, sometimes to uncontrolled or mindless acts. In a sense, they epitomise the frailty of men and women, holding up a mirror, deliberately distorted, in order for them to see their own images — images of what they are themselves in terms of human possibilities.

It is not a matter of imagination on the part of the original 'recorders' of mythic events, or of the interpreters, the story-tellers. It is an issue of socio-cultural similitude, since myths are constructed and designed on the basis of aspects of reality. In that sense, mythology provides a perceptive glimpse of traditional living and thinking — a glimpse, perhaps, without suggesting that it is more than that. While myths are certainly guides to action, bad action as well as good, they also provide warnings for those who are prepared to listen.

CHAPTER TEN

OLD WORLD, NEW WORLD

The changes and transformations that were built into these myth-stories took place within a framework of more or less common understandings. The action-sequences that made up the 'story' part could be either low-key or dramatic, but all of them led up to some sort of climax, where the end was different from the beginning. They were all in the process of 'becoming', being transformed. The process did not stop with the conclusion of the verbal part of the story. The signs and landmarks and other 'memorials' continued the story in a different dimension. The mythic characters live on, in their relevance to human beings. It was not only the major mythic personages whose spiritual continuity was assured through religious ritual observances. Others also were at least latently active, potentially involved in the ongoing human situation. Within any region, interpretations also went on within a broadly-shared frame. Interaction between neighbours was on a relatively equal basis. It was quite unlike the tremendous discrepancy in power, as well as divergence in values and ideas, that marked their relations with Europeans.

INSIDE VIEWS, OUTSIDE VIEWS

The gulf between Aborigines and Europeans was even harder to bridge because Aborigines were non-literate. That alone was a great disadvantage to them in the new situation where their whole way of life was under threat. Their oral tradition served them well when they had control of their own affairs; but when their communication lines were blocked in almost every direction, they were in danger of losing their whole heritage, including their repertoires of myth and story.

In that predicament they began to rely on outsiders who were interested enough to record at least some of their traditions in writing. The usual problems of translation and interpretation were compounded in the rather inflexible circumstances of early colonial contact, and are still only partly resolved. For a very long time indeed, Aboriginal people who are fluent and articulate in their own languages but less so in English, have had to depend on intermediaries to record all kinds of material on their behalf.

'Inside views' (some writers prefer the expression 'emic' views), interpretations and symbolic allusions, and statements about meaning within even a small community, are never uniform. Age and sex (gender) distinctions alone contribute to this variability. As far as the myth-stories in this book are concerned, differences in story content between men and women do not seem to be obtrusive. We have not made a count of same-and-different items between story-tellers in this connection, but one factor here is the kind of answers women gave to the question, 'Where did you first hear this story?', or simply 'Who told you this story?' Women in western Arnhem Land, for instance, cited men (father, uncle, husband and so on) even more than women. In every case, though, the answers would have been different if we were dealing with strictly religious matters. It is in these that separateness and divergent interpretations are most noticeable. This is not a comment on equality or inequality in religious affairs, merely a statement about similarity and dissimilarity.

'Outside views', views from outside a society (some writers prefer the expression 'etic' views) are far more diverse than 'inside views'. The most obvious of them are usually quite easy to identify. Other cases are harder to detect, especially when outside views are put forward as inside ones, in terms of either interpretations or 'facts'. This is still an issue in respect of Aboriginal materials: Who is speaking or interpreting for, Aboriginal people? And what does this imply in the far-from-homogeneous Aboriginal context of today?

One view from 'far outside' looks at myths, tales, stories from a wider regional or global perspective, mapping uniformities and contrasts. The units of assessment vary according to the system that is adopted, but mostly they are smaller units such as motifs (as in the Aarne-Thompson Motif Index) and not complete tales. No such overview has yet been completed for Aboriginal Australia, although one is in the process of being compiled on the basis of published materials.

STRUCTURAL APPROACHES

Since the early 1960s there has been, and still is, a growing interest in another kind of outside view: structural analysis. A basic premiss is that the visible, audible material of myth (for instance) is only a screen, concealing its 'real' meaning. To get at that real meaning involves categorising, contrasting, comparing, taking all possible variants into account, and looking for fundamental oppositions, contradictions and mediators. There are echoes of Freud and Jung in the search for 'deep structures' and the significance of meanings that lie below the level of consciousness. Lévi-Strauss is its main exponent. His influence has been pervasive, even among people who do not wholly agree with his assumptions or his findings. As regards Australian Aboriginal myth, however, his analysis of the Wawalag myth in north-central Arnhem Land draws too heavily on Warner's interpretation. Maddock, in making a selection of emu myths to discuss what he calls 'the emu anomaly' (1975: 107–08), emphasises that there can never be a single correct or final structural analysis of any myth because there are always other possibilities. He has also (1970) attempted a comparative classification of 'Myths of the acquisition of fire in northern and eastern Australia'. Van der Leeden's analysis (1975) of a Nunggubuyu myth follows rather similar lines but in a single area. R. Berndt (1970) examines one set of Western Desert myths as expressions of traditional morality.

We include here, not a structural analysis of the Yirawadbad myth, but a suggestion about one way of looking at it. One of the positive advantages in structural analysis is that it need not imply total commitment to a single conceptual frame or a single set of procedures. It can stimulate a variety of approaches to mythic materials. Structural studies, including studies of social structure, have a long history in anthropology and the social sciences generally, as contrasted with the narrower and more controversial label 'structuralism'.

YIRAWADBAD

We will now comment on aspects of the *Yirawadbad* myth in summary, with some additional notes. In almost every case in western Arnhem Land where a narrative sequence is spelt out or implied, a final climax follows (comes as a result of) some action that is defined as wrong. This happens even in the case of characters who managed their own metamorphosis without the help of the Rainbow. Luma-luma's death was a direct consequence of wrongdoing. Yirawadbad killed his wife and her mother for the same reason — they did not conform with the rules. But most of the main characters in this area became *djang*; Luma-luma gave people the sacred *mareiin* and other rites; and Yirawadbad instituted the sacred *ubar* on the basis of the hollow log in which he hid before killing the women. In other words, out of the wrongdoing came good — the *djang* and the most sacred rites. There is no explicit statement that 'mythically speaking, wrongdoing is a necessary prelude to good', but the shape that dramatic conflict takes in Gunwinggu mythology emphasises, not 'bad from bad'

FIGURE 10.I

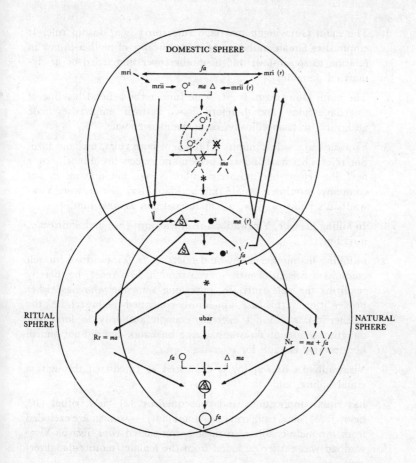

mri, mrii	= marriage rules	
fa	= emphasis on female authority	
ma	= emphasis on male authority	
(*r*)	= reaffirmed	
Rr	= ritual rule	
Nr	= natural rule	
○	= female	
△	= male	
△ʸ	= Yirawadbad	

○¹ = Yirawadbad's mother-in-law, living
●¹ = Yirawadbad's mother-in-law, dead
○² = Yirawadbad's wife, living
●² = Yirawadbad's wife, dead
⊿ˢ = (Yirawadbad as) snake
♀ = female as Mother
× ⋊ = rejection
* = breach
⌐⌐ = marriage

but '*good* from bad'. Pessimism is certainly the prevailing mood at the climax of the *djang* stories, but in the long term the outlook is optimistic.

Notes

1. The main Gunwinggu marriage rule (mri) is a kinship rule. It emphasises female authority (*fa*): specifically, of mother-in-law in relation to son-in-law, and of mother over unmarried or newly-married daughter.

2. The main Gunwinggu *marital* rule (under the general heading of 'marriage rules', and therefore shown as mrii) emphasises male authority (*ma*): specifically, of husband over wife.

3. Yirawadbad's wife commits a breach of both rules, mri and mrii. She rejects her husband as a person and rejects his authority over her. She rejects her mother's authority too, but remains in her company, forming a female (mother-daughter) pair or, from Yira-wadbad's point of view, a female coalition against him.

4. In killing his wife, Yirawadbad reaffirms mrii (*ma*) and, indirectly, mri; but,

5. in killing his mother-in-law and rejecting *fa*, Yirawadbad himself commits a breach of mri — even though, in a sense, he thereby reaffirms the rule (mri) by punishing someone who has either broken it or, in this case, apparently condoned the breach i.e., the mother-in-law did not exercise enough authority to force her daughter to accept Yirawadbad as a husband, and did not punish her severely enough for rejecting him.

6. Yirawadbad's breach (5) is expressed as (mediated through) a ritual killing, and

7. has ritual implications and consequences: (*a*) 'new' ritual (10, below); (*b*) 'new' ritual rule (*ma* dominant) — women are excluded from the male coalition in these secret-sacred rites, just as Yira-wadbad was earlier excluded from the female (mother-daughter) coalition.

8. Blame for (5) and for (4), above, as well as for (3), is ascribed to Yirawadbad's wife, not to Yirawadbad himself.

9. Retaliation for (8) is transferred from the purely human sphere to the sphere of man-in-nature (nature in relation to man): Yirawad-bad-as-snake, in the *natural* sphere, rejects *all* human authority (both *fa* and *ma*) and is hostile to human beings. (The sorcery aspect is relevant here, but we do not follow it up.)

10. Compensation for (4), (5) and (9) above is transferred to the sphere of sacred ritual: Yirawadbad as a symbolic snake in a ritual context

can bring benefits (life, not death) to human beings. In the human sphere, in his story, Yirawadbad's marital union was either uncon-summated or not satisfactorily consummated; and it was infertile. In the ritual sphere, he influences seasonal and natural (and human) fertility: (*a*) through symbolic union between male and female — snake in hollow log. (In the myth, Yirawadbad's wife and mother-in-law are both close kin to him, but in both cases the marriage/affinal link is emphasised.) And (*b*) through composite or merging or shifting sex identification, blurring or uniting male and female, *and* male and female authority — the *ubar* snake as Rainbow Snake (male and/or female); and the Ubar Woman as the mother of all human beings, but also described as the symbolic wife of male *ubar* participants, especially young initiands, on the secret-sacred ground — a combined kin (descent) and marital relationship of a sort that is quite outside the range of everyday acceptability.

Figure 10.1 could be set out a little differently in another diagram, not included here. The central theme, or core, begins with the action that precipitates the main sequence, the rejection of Yirawadbad by his promised wife. The union is incomplete and infertile: no new life results from it. At the same time, no offspring from it died or were killed, and so in that respect it could be described as entirely negative. The progression then, stated very briefly and without elaboration, is: (i) Yirawadbad kills his wife and mother-in-law — snake in hollow log brings death (to females); (ii) Yirawadbad retains his snake form in the natural sphere — snake in nature, alone and without log connection, brings death (to everyone, but 'especially hostile to girls'); (iii) Yirawadbad joins other males, asserting male control of secret-sacred ritual — snake in hollow log brings death (to females and to uninitiated males); (iv) Yirawadbad is partly identified with other mythical beings, including the Rainbow (male *and/or* female) and the Ubar Woman — snake in hollow log brings life and fertility (to everyone, male and female). And so on.

Finally: if Yirawadbad's wife was ultimately responsible, (8) above, for the train of events that followed her first 'offence', (3) above, this responsibility must extend to the ritual as well as to the natural sphere. In other words, as far as the Yirawadbad myth is concerned, without her action — specifically, without her rejection of her husband — there would have been no *ubar* ritual at all.

This brings us back to the Ubar *woman* as mother, not wife: in women's accounts, except for the human *ubar* participants, she has no husband. Whether or not we bring in the issue of matrilineal emphasis, this could be the beginning of a more complex analysis, but such an analysis would also have to include other versions of the *ubar* and related mythology, from both men's and women's points of view.

Discourse Analysis

This is another current preoccupation, one that tries to reconcile local (inside) perspectives with a wider (outside) vision that draws on comparative insights. The term 'discourse' is applied to a great variety of speech utterances. Consequently, a great variety of analyses goes under this heading. It is a particular concern of linguists; and again there is the issue of what the main unit of analysis should be: words or sentences, or some other unit (see, for example, Heath 1980, 1984). On the other hand, if mythic discourse is one form of discourse, we could also speak of kinds of 'sub-discourse' within that. Maranda (1978: 396) suggests that within semantic networks it is useful to speak of sub-discourse, which 'consists of the strings of high-probability associations that underlie speech acts in verbal discourses and out of which utterance discourses emerge'. 'Strings of meaning' can be a helpful device in considering the larger context within which myth-stories as 'packaged' narratives are set: the totality of utterances or references that relate to particular stories. We could see these, not as broken or incomplete strings, but rather as strings where not all of the connections are visible, or audible (for example, allusions at different times or in different places, and not necessarily to or by the same people). Whatever units are chosen and whatever procedures are adopted in examining them, Tyler (1969: 16) reminds us that such questions are not an end in themselves: 'Essentially, discourse analysis is one more aspect of the problem of context.'

In Australia, detailed analyses in a 'discourse' framework are just beginning to emerge. In regard to north-central Arnhem Land song-poetry, for instance, see Margaret Clunies Ross (1978); also her discussion (1983) of 'formal performance in societies without writing'.

Translating and Interpreting

Discourse analysis must take as its starting point the language in which utterances are made, basically in speech or secondarily in written form. Translation into another language has to depart from that basic source in varying degrees, according to the differences between the two languages, or even between two dialects. This is simply at the verbal level, without taking into account other aspects such as gestures and body movements that accompany speech. If translation is intended as a means of communication, dealing with the original source involves more than word-for-word 'transliteration', or a search for equivalents. Story-tellers in Aboriginal Australia have long recognised this fact, especially in regard to stories introduced from adjoining areas or other language groups. No story goes through that process completely unchanged. Something happens to it in the course of transmission. It moves into a different dimension, into other local idioms and styles.

The ideal way to explore that would be to look at (listen to) 'lines of transmission' through time, in the same and in different places. This is almost impossible, however. There is not enough evidence, because these processes have not been documented to any extent in live situations. Formal experiments in story-transmission do not serve this purpose, and are mostly focused on such issues as memory or communication or personal characteristics. For the real-life situation, what is available is a tantalising assortment of glimpses, at different time-points or at different places. Useful as these are, they do not reveal the intermediate links of narrators' (and listeners') versions, and circumstances that would help us to understand better the processes involved.

Rainbow Snake stories are particularly interesting in this respect, not only because they are so widespread but also because so many versions co-exist within fairly limited regions. So are 'Moon and death' stories. On a smaller and less ambitious scale, it would be an interesting exercise to compare Myth 193, the story of a runaway wife's encounter with a *maam* spirit told by a western Arnhem Land woman, with a very similar story told by a north-central Arnhem Land woman (Myth 79). Relevant points include personal styles and a fourteen-year gap between the dates of recording the two stories, at different places. Myth 193, told in Gun-winggu, resembles in general style other stories told in that language. No. 79, told in an eastern Arnhem Land dialect (Gobubingu) resembled other stories told in this and related dialects in that region. There are some common features but also some striking differences. We suggest these here and there in the translations, but what we have noted is no more than that. To stay closer to the originals would have called for more explanations, and not only of specific words or phrases and the conven-tionally-accepted modes of linking and separating (pausing between) them. The similarities between the two stories extend to some of the phrases in each of the respective languages that the narrators used. Overall, what this demonstrates is not a simple 'transfer' of a story-line, but a more complex constellation of factors than it appears to be on the surface.

Translating any myth-stories is, ideally, more than translating a story-line. It is like translating a culture. That is how such stories were used in traditional Aboriginal settings, with the expected end result that adults could 'read into' the stories information that was still in the process of being learnt by children. And what those adults already knew, or took for granted, is in some instances what students of myth from other areas or other cultures 'discover' in the course of their analysis. They put back into a myth-story some of the unspoken but essential items that were latent in it — or put back a few of the ingredients, perhaps inadequately interpreted or misunderstood. Of course, that is a feature of myth and story transmission everywhere.

In all of these approaches, and others, we come back to the same questions. Who is asking the questions about meaning in myth and myth-stories? Who is looking in the mirror? And interpreting the reflections?

Interpreting and reinterpreting myths and stories can be an intellectual and emotionally satisfying game. For anthropologists, examining them in their cultural contexts is an obligatory part of the exercise. The questions they ask do not necessarily anticipate the answers but can be straightforward lines of enquiry, open-ended about their potential findings. It is invidious to note only a few examples, among so many possibilities. Strehlow's monumental work on central Australia (1971) concentrates on song versions, but explores narrative myths as well, including vernacular renderings and detailed annotations. His earlier study (1947) has undertones of early mission bias, not in the myths he presents so compellingly, but in his discussions of their context — notably in regard to women, as contrasted with a rather more balanced approach in his 1971 study. In a more controversial interpretation of a range of myths from central Australia about relations, especially sexual relations, between men and women, White (1975) discusses the incidence of violence and 'frequently illicit' behaviour. She attempts to see these in the context of non-mythic life, but finally concludes (p. 140) that even 'women's own myths and rituals reflect and reinforce the female subservient role'. This is a highly debatable assertion. To counterbalance it, also in regard to central Australia, a useful contrast is Diane Bell's (1983) volume which accords a positive status to women in myth, ritual and 'real life' settings.

We have not discussed the major religious myths, including the pervasive theme that women in the early creative era had control of all the most secret rites, objects, and knowledge and that these were stolen or otherwise taken from them by men. This intriguing topic, and its implications, would lead us into another dimension of 'discourse'. So would other myth analyses that deal with religious matters. But we note in passing one reference to 'Swallowing and Regurgitation in Australian Myth and Rite' (Hiatt 1975) because it relates in part to one feature that is prominent in so many myths, and not only among Rainbow Snakes.

Interpretations of myths can in themselves develop new versions, or new myths, which become established in the literature and in new modes of oral transmission. Also, with the increasing absorption into a wider society of small communities that were once oriented most strongly toward their own regional traditions, distinctions between 'outside' and inside' perspectives are changing. They are not being blurred, so much as being reframed, or reshaped.

A CHANGING WORLD

That does not mean there was 'no change' before: the notion of 'before' is itself, of course, also flexible. Most myths tell of characters who came into a region from somewhere else, and many of them went on to other places, some also beyond the bounds of known territories. In north coastal areas the overseas places from which some of them came are specified. In western Arnhem Land, a number of famous mythic figures came from beyond Meville and Bathurst Islands — from Manggadjara, Macassar. On the eastern Arnhem Land side, the Djanggau came from an island in the Gulf of Carpentaria, or from another island beyond that, and their opposite moiety counterpart Laindjung emerged from the waters of that Gulf, in his own mythology. On Cape York Peninsula, influences from the Torres Straits and Papua New Guinea are also reflected in myths. Other characters came from inland places, but still as travellers. Relatively few, except in central Australian accounts, emerged and ended their physical life-stories in a single site or cluster of sites.

The notion of 'outsiders coming in', then, is mythically well-established. But because the Aborigines were for a long period more or less sheltered from the trauma of large-scale invasions by people of sharply different cultures, any small-scale incursions (shipwrecked voyagers, drifting canoes and the like) seem to have been absorbed: accommodated to the mythic reports of travellers, or helping to sustain them. In north-eastern Arnhem Land, north-east winds have often brought floating coconuts and large seed-pods as well as canoes at the end of the Wet season, and in the local culture there was a framework for dealing with such things. Everyone and everything belonged to one of two moieties, *dua* and *yiridja*. The *yiridja* moiety was concerned, among other things, with goods and ideas identified as being of alien origin. (A person belonged primarily to the same moiety as his or her father. Because no-one could marry within the same moiety, that meant that his or her mother would have to be of the opposite moiety, through *her* father. And so on.) So, narratives and songs about outsiders were told and sung predominantly by *yiridja* people, belonging to *yiridja* clans and dialect groups, although *dua* moiety people might have secondary rights in them, depending on their affiliations.

The next story is one of these, about contact with people from outside the range of normal local living.

194. DOG AND THE MACASSANS

He set off from Djiliwiri, that dog called Djuraindjura. He went on, and he made a stringybark canoe. He made it, lifted it upon his shoulder and went on farther. He went on, and when he was half-way there he put it down and rested. He carried it, he rested. He said, 'This canoe, it's my spirit, and it's like a tree standing in the bush with two legs.' [I'll leave it there.] He stood the canoe up, and left it. 'I heard movement, noise. Macassans, working on posts for a house. Who is doing it? Macassans, Balanda!' He trotted along on his paws, and stood up. 'Who are you?' asked the two Balanda. He said, that dog, 'I'm Djuraindjura!.' 'What place are you from?' 'I'm from Djiliwiri!' The Balanda went on making a house. Dog said, 'I want to come close to you, I want to see what kind of flesh you have' [what you look like from close-up]. He was carrying on his head a lot of fire-sticks, and little pegs or nails for joining bark canoes. The Balanda asked, 'What do you want? Do you want some of this cloth, or other things?' 'I don't want any of that!' said Dog. 'Do you want matches?' 'No! I've got fire-sticks!' 'How do you work them?' 'I do it like this.' [He showed them.] 'And what about your fire, how do you make it?' 'Like this.' 'Oh, that's good, your fire! My fire-sticks take longer,' said Dog. Then the Balanda said, 'I'm going away now.' 'Yes? Where is your country?' He looked at the fire burning; he called the names of various 'Macassan' places [as in songs that tell of Macassan visitors to this coast].

Those Balanda were getting ready to depart. They were pulling up the house-posts, taking them away. Dog asked again, 'Where is your country?' They called the names of other places, places on the Australian mainland and then their home places away to the north-west: 'the fires are burning there for my [our] grandparents, sons, elder brothers, mothers, at that place.' Then the Balanda asked, 'And you, where do you sleep?' 'I?', said Dog. 'Yes, over that way! I sleep in the grass. I'm going away now, back to my two elder brothers, Gwaidman and Bawal.' The Balanda put a mark on the rock, a footprint. [This was at Bam-balngur, on a great flat expanse of rock.] 'I put my foot here, like an anchor, the mark of an anchor. You'll be going trotting along on your paws? Look at my footmark, look at me. But I'm going away to Yumai-ngai, Naani-ngai, Dangaraburai, Nalgoi-ngai!' He went away then, Djuraindjura, and the Balanda went away. They went back, each of them, to their own countries.

[The story-teller gave that short account one morning. That afternoon, she and a couple of other women who had been present were discussing Dog's encounter and its implications, and she decided to amplify it a little. There was also the issue of whether, as some people said, Djuraindjura was a male or a female dog, or one or more manifestations. (The third-person singular pronoun, *ngai*, can be translated as either 'he' or 'she', or even as a collective form — as in the case of the Balanda.) But making and carrying canoes, even bark canoes, is usually regarded as a male occupation. In this next part of the story, then, Djuraindjura is noted as a female, but as having at least one brother.]

[The story continues, with a few extra comments on Dog's response to the Macassans.] Djuraindjura was sitting down. He asked, that Balanda, 'Do you want food? Rice?' 'No! No, I don't want that! I eat wallabies and goannas!' [naming various kinds] 'Yes, all right. But here's this different kind of food for you. I'll put it down here for you.' 'No! I don't want your food. I'm going away. I have plenty of meat foods. And in the waters and along the river banks there are plenty of geese and other birds for me to eat.' 'All right, you go. But you'll be sleeping without fire.' 'My fire, my light, is good!' That's what he said, her brother Bawal. He started off, going away. The spirit of that boat was moving, out on the sea, and from there the Balanda threw the anchor rope and was tying it up. Maybe it was trying to get away, pulling at the rope. But Djuraindjura was running off, into the bush, home to Djiliwiri.

The story-teller complained, 'That dog was no good! She/he refused matches, and food, and cloth! Now we people with dark skins are badly off!' The other women agreed. 'We could have had all those things!' And she added, 'If I had that dog here, now, I would beat it, strike it on the nose!' Danggoubwi in 1950 was small, lively and active, with several grandchildren. She was a superb story-teller, acknowledged as the most knowledgeable resource-woman in her community. This particular story was more sketchily told than any of her others, and she did not throw herself into it so dramatically. (One example, also in translation, tells of a girl who was kidnapped by a salt-water crocodile; see C. and R. Berndt 1982: 51–58.)

The Djuraindjura story is one of the few in traditional Aboriginal Australia that resembles the kind of 'cargo-cult' myths so common in Papua New Guinea, for instance. The visits of Indonesian traders to the northern Arnhem Land coast were discontinued in the first decade of this century, but in the 1940s and 1950s they were commemorated in long song-cycles that combine specific details with a wealth of poetic imagery. These traders were known by various names, but mostly as men who came from around the port of Macassar in the Celebes, 'Manggadjara'. Earlier versions spoke of a first category of visitors as Bayini, people with golden-brown skins, but later versions were beginning to merge the traders from 'Manggadjara' with the Japanese and the Europeans who came after them. In the first part of Danggoubwi's story they are called Balanda, but this is used more often for people of European descent —

probably from the name 'Hollander', referring to the Dutch who were in charge of the area of what was, for a long time, the Dutch East Indies. Dog was said to have skin the colour of ant-bed, termite mound, and when he wanted to come closer to the men who were building a house, in order to see their 'flesh', it was said to be their skin colour that interested him.

The time sequence in these two short statements is compressed, just as the rest of the content is. The 'Macassans' came and built houses, and later went away in their ships; and the song-cycles dwell on both these features, among many others. But the point of Danggoubwi's story, as in other similar versions along the north-eastern Arnhem Land coast, was the discrepancy in wealth between local Aborigines and outsiders —Macassan traders and, underlined in the use of the term Balanda, people of European descent. The two versions Warner (1937: 536–37) heard in the late 1920s make the same point.

A different kind of influence comes out quite clearly in another story. The first version was also told to C. Berndt in 1950 by Danggoubwi, with a small group of women who helped and added their comments. (We summarise it here, because a fuller version appears in R. and C. Berndt 1985: 397–99.)

195. MOON AND THE GREEDY CHILDREN

Moon was once a man, with two wives, and each of them had a son. The two women went away to collect water-lily roots and other foods while the boys stayed at home with their old father. He sat by the fire while they went a little way off to get fish, and then geese. But every time they ate these things themselves, and would not give him any. In the end, he prepared a large fish net, enticed them into it, then fastened it tightly and submerged it in the nearby billabong. They drowned. Late in the afternoon the two mothers came back, but no little boys ran out to greet them. The old man said they had gone off to spear birds. The women searched and called, searched and called. Nothing. Finally they went to the waterhole to drink. As the younger sister stooped down, something cut her mouth. They managed to lift out the heavy net. 'Here are our children!' They swore at their husband, while they dealt with the bodies and prepared a mortuary platform. Then, crying with grief and rage, they attacked him, beating him with great sticks. He fled from them, jumping aside, and climbing a high tree, higher and higher until he was out of reach of the sticks they kept throwing at him. At last he was far away, up in the sky. '*Wiribigili!*' he said. 'I'm Moon! All you men, you husbands . . .! You won't remain alive, you'll die! I'll die, but I'll come back, I'll come up again as a new moon!' Danggoubwi added that Moon had spoken the truth. 'Moon grows old, but he comes up new again in the sky; he shines as a new moon over the people of the western clans.' The place where this happened is Duldula, a Moon place-name, south-east of Milingimbi.

At the first National Aboriginal Writers' Conference, in 1983 in Perth, one of the speakers was a young woman who was involved in the literacy programme at Milingimbi. She told this same story, first in her own dialect (Ngeimil) and then in English. In substance, it is almost the same up to the point where the father gets the boys into the net. After that he ties the mouth of the net, fixes a rope and pulls them to the shore, puts them in a canoe, paddles out to sea and throws them overboard. The mothers, returning, cannot find their children. They are sure their husband has killed them. His first wife attacks him in the night. He climbs a tree to get away from them, while they sit waiting until he comes down. When he reaches the highest branch, he makes his pronouncement. In this case, however, '*Wiribigili*' is likened to the saying of Jesus on the cross: '*Elu Elu*', 'Father, forgive them . . .', and just as Jesus died and rose again, so Moon dies and comes back alive again.

The story-teller, Daphne Nimanydja, had not been born in 1950, when her mother and one of her mother's younger sisters were in the group of women with Danggoubwi, telling and listening to stories such as Moon. But although Milingimbi was a mission station then, Danggoubwi, in particular, was firm in her own traditional perspectives and tried (she said) not to let those 'new' influences affect them. In any case, the Methodist ideal at that time emphasised a tolerant approach to Aboriginal traditional culture. Now that Milingimbi is an Aboriginal community, however, analogies such as the death and renewal parallel at the climax of the story reflect the earlier mission concern with 'building on what is best in local Aboriginal culture'.

A short version of the 1950 story by Margaret Djuwandayngu Yunupingu from Yirrkalla appears in *Djugurba* (1974: 42–45); she was then a student at Kormilda College. Moon's two wives, unable to kill him, turned into brolgas to pursue him. Moon did not make his pronouncement about dying and returning as new for three days; that came in the following story. ('The Parrot Fish and the Moon', *Djugurba* 1974: 46). Roland Robinson (1966: 151–57) has a longer version: he calls Moon 'Nyalindee' (but the correct word is Ngalindi). In this, Moon's wives try to burn him to death for killing their sons, but he emerges in a new, resurrected body and eventually climbs up a high tree into the sky.

Mountford 1976a: 89–91, gives a rather similar account, but calls Moon 'Alinda'; he locates the story vaguely 'on the sea coast'.

Similar changes are taking place in other traditional myth-stories now, as they are re-told or re-interpreted for use in non-traditional or quasi-traditional settings. For instance, in schools or in literacy classes, they are arranged as children's stories, or simplified versions that can be used by adults learning to read and write, as well as by children. In some situations, adults perpetuate stories that they themselves learnt as children — *and* in the versions that they learnt then, because they did not proceed to learning adult versions and do not realise what these would have contained.

In other cases, younger people who have had some experience of European-style reading and writing feel uneasy about the more traditional ways in which their elders prefer to approach an informal story-telling situation. In western Arnhem Land, for example, a very prolonged account of the killing of a Rainbow Snake and salvaging and burying of human victims (Myth 56) illustrates one way of tackling an incident that, as the narrator explained, took a very long time. But there were also narrators, there and elsewhere, who skimmed over their subject matter more lightly, sketching in the main points and relying on gestures and discussion (audience intervention) to expand and embellish and add extra drama or humour. On some occasions, young women who had been to mission schools attempted to 'shape' such narratives, to make them more compact or less 'staccato' in style. European-based schooling can alter the content of such myth-stories indirectly by changing the preferred modes of telling them, as well as through more direct interference with the content itself.

Myth-stories of more or less traditional type continue to circulate through oral transmission, though more rapidly than they used to do when motor vehicles and radio and telephone contacts were not available. As well, accounts of relations between Aborigines and others, mostly Europeans, but also Indonesians, Japanese and Chinese, are coming to acquire an epic, almost mythic quality. The 'Captain Cook myth' has had wide currency throughout the Kimberley region of Western Australia (and not only there), as a focus for statements about colonial domination and relations between Aboriginal and non-Aboriginal people. In the same region, and spreading into the Northern Territory, is a constellation of songs and short narrative commentaries sometimes called the *djuluru*. They use mythic and other characters as a basis for an interesting ceremonial cult that is passed on from one group to another, much as other ceremonies are, but with secret aspects, and in various places having separate male and female leadership.

Myth as history, history as myth: these two dimensions are often identified, although various devices are used to make them seem distinct.

In the Aboriginal case, references to Dreaming personages and super-natural powers, or to the First People, or the early days of creation, are used to identify myths or myth-stories that have a special quality. It is not that 'supernatural' or unusual events, or spirit beings, and so on, are absent from the everyday world of human beings. (*Mamu, maam, mogwoi* and the like are living contemporaries of present-day people, as they are believed to have been since the beginning.) It is just that they are not a regular or consistent part of human life, on an everyday basis.

NEW TECHNIQUES, IN NEW SETTINGS

Myths and stories provide sets of alternative possibilities that *can* or may be translated into action if circumstances permit. These alternative possibilities include relations between people, and also appropriate behaviour between them. That was so traditionally, and continues to be so now. Traditionally, the range of possibilities was expanded when people met for ceremonial or religious ritual purposes, or for trade. But it has been extended enormously with the spread of pressures from the all-encompassing Australian society. Add to that the wakening of local Aboriginal authority (despite some apparent evidence to the contrary); opportunities for much greater mobility and continent-wide interaction with a great diversity of people, not only other Aboriginal people; last, not least, the growing impact of radio, films, television and video sets. There are more facilities for writing down and audio-tape-recording or even video-recording their own local traditions and their own personal and regional perspectives. But these are matched or overwhelmed by the inflow of information (and misinformation) about other traditions, other cultures, and other perspectives. Even in Aboriginal schools where 'Aboriginal culture' is taught by teachers who know something about it, or bilingual programmes (or English as a second language), pressures against the sustaining of local traditional or neo-traditional culture are almost irresistible.

Myth-stories were a resource in themselves. Collectively, they were a guide to topographic features and to natural and spiritual resources. They provided verbal pictures of the landscape, supplemented by other, non-verbal, records. As guides to action they were a store-house, an oral archive, of bad examples as well as good. They supplied information about life before birth and after death, and the human life-span in between. They contained all sorts of messages about what the world was like, what it ought to be like, and what people should do to keep it that way: no one myth or story could do that. In every region there was a corpus of myth-stories, all interconnected and interdependent. Each one existed within a context of stories, and a context of discussions and comments and activities that 'fed back' into them in a subtle blend of fantasy and 'fact'. This kind of context is no longer available, just as the traditional social context is no longer available. And an appropriate substitute in the current situation has yet to be worked out.

Earlier attempts to organise reading materials for schools using vernacular texts, interesting and innovative as they are, have had some initial problems. A north-eastern Arnhem Land 'story about the boy who became a sea-eagle' was told by one man in a *yiridja* moiety dialect, and translated first into a *dua* moiety one and then into English by a young woman who also illustrated the resultant booklet, *Djet* (Marawili and Wunungmurra 1977). But the story, the vernacular text and the translation are not entirely consistent. A collection of stories from the Warburton Ranges, *Tjuma. Stories from the Western Desert* (Glass and Newberry 1979), also includes vernacular renderings, but it underlines a major difference between traditional oral transmission and a product that can have a life of its own, away from the people who compiled it. The opening story focuses on Hawk-man and his mother-in-law, who had promised him her two teenage daughters in marriage. The girls didn't like him and went off with two young men. He speared them all to death, but took his mother-in-law safely back to another place. In the story, he and his mother-in-law speak directly to each other, with no reference to any special vocabulary — even though this is a relationship involving taboos and constraints. The 'bad example' of such behaviour would normally be commented on in discussions at the time of telling such a story, along with remarks on other facets of it. That could be done in a school environment, too. A book presentation alone, without such notes, makes no provision for that.

The use of vernacular texts is one aspect of the struggle to maintain local identity through a traditional resource, among people who speak their own languages and prefer to tell their stories through these rather than in English. Part of the opposition to this comes from exponents of Aboriginal English, who use the difficulties of translation as an excuse for avoiding it (Muecke 1983: iv). Where people choose to tell stories in Aboriginal English, that is the ideal course for them to follow. Where they choose to speak their own language, their choice should be respected, translation problems notwithstanding.

It is possible that material in English, or in Aboriginal English, will become dominant, *and* will come to be regarded by non-Aborigines (and by many urban Aborigines) as representative of Australian Aboriginal literature. A label often used these days is 'Black literature', produced by 'Black writers'. This submerges Aboriginal identity in a wider personal-social political identification: a 'Black Australian' is not necessarily an

Aboriginal Australian. Aboriginal poet and playwright Jack Davis (1985: 17) points to a trend which implies a considerable widening of the term 'Aboriginal': he cites a Commonwealth 'definition . . . that anyone is an Aboriginal if they like to define themselves as being one'. People of Aboriginal descent, especially those with rural and urban backgrounds, are writing and producing novels, plays, poetry, films, radio programmes, and so on, and making their voices heard more widely than Aborigines less fluent in English are able to do. And for many of them, out of their personal experiences and the oral history of their older Aboriginal relatives, based on the negative legal and other restrictions that applied to people defined as Aborigines, the myths and stories that interest them most fervently have strong political overtones.

One collection of narratives by Aboriginal speakers focuses on 'the general theme of contact with non-Aboriginals' (Hercus and Sutton 1986: 1). They are presented in the speakers' own Aboriginal languages, transcribed mostly from tape recordings (p. 10), with inter-linear as well as general translation and notes. The editors add (p. 10–11) their caution about the difficulties of conveying in written form the impact and the variability of stories told in the oral tradition, and their aim 'above all to do justice to the art of the storytellers'.

People from 'tribal' backgrounds are becoming closely involved in media programmes too, as well as in writing. The Central Australian Aboriginal Media Association has been prominent in this. And Walbri (Warlpiri) people are taking steps to produce, with technical guidance, their own video programmes to combat the influence of satellite-backed television material (not, however, to produce fictional programmes. According to Michaels and Kelly 1984: 27–28, 'fictional genres in the European sense are not apparent in the Warlpiri repertoire . . .').

New myth-symbols of Aboriginality are achieving an Australian-wide identification. Didjeridus and boomerangs, Wandjina mythic figures from the north-west coast, images of Uluru (Ayers Rock) and similar items serve in commercial advertising contexts as well. Some non-Aboriginal writers encourage the blurring and mixing of local Aboriginal identities. One example is a central Australian version of Lewis Carroll's *Alice in Wonderland*, *Alitji in the Dreamtime* (Sheppard 1975), where Wandjina characters, *mimi* figures from the caves of western Arnhem Land, and bark paintings from north-eastern Arnhem Land, are absorbed into a blend of general-Aboriginal culture, without discussion of the implications of this.

TALKING, LISTENING
TO THE LAND

Whether or not, or how far, we can contrast and compare Aboriginal traditional mythology with writing by people of Aboriginal descent today, is a difficult question. Differences between them are marked, not least in their views, emphases, directions and motivations. We have said that an appreciable amount of traditional Aboriginal mythology remains a living reality within its own social settings, despite changing features brought about through persistent Australian-European influences. However, notwithstanding its common human qualities, such land-based mythology is not necessarily amenable to being removed outside its own socio-topographic context.

Some Aboriginal writing today is preoccupied with reproducing what purports to be the 'old' mythology or developing a 'new' one — or both. In the process its writers can become engrossed with a past that went wrong through no fault of its own, or no fault of the victims, and the kind of navel-gazing that has resulted from that experience can perhaps be interpreted as therapeutically purging itself of, or perpetuating, its painful struggle with a dominant and unsympathetic invader. Making comparisons in that direction would enable us to see some interesting parallels between these two forms of literature — for example, in relation to western Arnhem Land mythology. There the concept of destiny that cannot be circumvented involves some mythic personages in situations from which they are unable to escape. Be that as it may, the nature of writing by many people of Aboriginal descent today, the kind of messages that are conveyed, how they are transmitted, and for whom, all pose issues that differ from those appearing in the traditional mythology, either today or in the past. They are really different dimensions of meaning and operating.

A theme of our volume, inspired by the traditional mythology itself, is of a land that is resonant with sound and presence — a land that is certainly not a passive or negative component. It constitutes a primary force in all the mythic accounts: it is a kind of common denominator. This is not just a matter of land in a generalised sense. The focus is almost always land-specific, on particular stretches of land that are associated mythically with particular people, at the mythic and human levels, in the past as in the present. That land speaks unequivocably, underlining what people imply is its concern for the affairs of human beings — even though it and what it contains act independently of them. The voice of this land is collectively that of the mythic personages, among whose many roles is that of interpreting what the land has to say of relevance to human beings. The messages conveyed, and the language in which they are couched, are for internal (local) consumption. They may be used for external purposes in connection with particular situations — to seek explanations for a changing world, to justify and validate a claim to Aboriginal land, and so forth. It is, however, essentially local-centred — even though what it has to say may well have wide implications, and not necessarily only in local contexts.

In the writing of Aborigines today, the voice of the speaking land, speaking in its diverse linguistic forms, has been muted. It can no longer, or only rarely, speak for itself through its own home-made media. Not only is its content radically different, so are its vocal expressions. Increasingly, it has slipped into an almost static, timeless entity, often with another language imposed upon it. It may also be regarded as something 'old', useful as a peg on which to hang an equally static and revamped Aboriginal heritage, designed for a purpose different from that it previously symbolised.

These changed circumstances point to a crucial difference between traditional and neo-Aboriginal socio-cultural situations. Traditionally, the land was/is an independent substance, with a life of its own — dynamic and constantly renewing itself as a natural phenomenon, with a voice of its own that had to be heard by those Aborigines who were entirely dependent on it, irrevocably linked to it. The neo-Aboriginal view is of a land subjugated to socio-economic and political ends.

The speaking land will probably continue to speak for some Aborigines and for some Aboriginal groups for some time yet. For many others, what it has to say will not be understood, or will be misinterpreted. However, whatever changes may take place within the structure of Aboriginal mythology, or whatever fortunes or misfortunes may befall Aborigines in the present or the future, the kind of mythology we have presented — whether it be in oral or written form — contains within it some eternal truths of social experience. These are manifested through the differing characters of mythic personages, and portray for our inspection their frailties and strengths. Across the mythic screen move the actors — some credulous, others perspicacious; some selfish, others generous; some treacherous, others straightforward.

Aboriginal mythology provides us with an immense mirror in which may be clearly viewed images that relate to the varied ways and means of mythic beings, that bear a striking resemblance to those of ordinary human beings in the course of their interaction with others. It is a mirror in which all of us may identify ourselves. In fact, that is probably the primary message that the speaking land has to offer, and, if that is the case, as it seems to us to be, its message is of universal appeal.

BIBLIOGRAPHY

Bell, D. (1983) *Daughters of the Dreaming*. McPhee Gribble, Allen and Unwin, Melbourne.

Bennell, E. and A. Thomas (1981) *Aboriginal legends from the Bibulmun tribe*. Rigby, Adelaide.

Berndt, C.H. (1970) 'Monsoon and honey wind' in J. Pouillon and P. Maranda (eds) *Échanges et communications: mélanges offerts á Claude Lévi-Strauss*. Mouton, Paris.

—— (1973) 'Oral literature' in R.M. Berndt and E.S. Phillips (eds) *The Australian Aboriginal heritage*. Ure Smith, Sydney.

—— (1978) 'Categorisation of, and in, oral literature' in L.R. Hiatt (ed.) *Australian Aboriginal concepts*. Australian Institute of Aboriginal Studies, Canberra.

—— Illustrator, D. Yunupingu (1979/1981) *Land of the Rainbow Snake*. Collins and John Ferguson, Sydney.

—— (1983) 'Traditional Aboriginal oral literature' in J. Davis and R. Hodge (eds) *Aboriginal writing today*. Australian Institute of Aboriginal Studies, Canberra.

—— and Berndt, R.M. (1982) 'Aboriginal Australia: literature in an oral tradition' in *Review of National Literatures* 11, Australia, special editor, L.A.C. Dobrez. Griffon House Publishing, New York.

—— and Berndt, R.M. (1983) *The Aboriginal Australians: the first pioneers*. Pitman, Melbourne.

Berndt, R.M. (1951) *Kunapipi*. Cheshire, Melbourne.

—— (1952a) *Djanggawul*. Routledge and Kegan Paul, London.

—— (1952b) 'Surviving influence of mission contact on the Daly River, Northern Territory of Australia' *Neue Zeitschrift für Missionswissenschaft*. VIII: 2/3.

—— (ed.) (1964/68) *Australian Aboriginal art*. Ure Smith, Sydney.

—— (1970) 'Traditional morality as expressed through the medium of an Australian Aboriginal religion' in R.M. Berndt (ed.) *Australian Aboriginal Anthropology*. University of Western Australia Press, Perth.

—— (1973) 'Mythic shapes of a desert culture' in K. Tauchmann (ed.) *H. Petri Festschrift*. Böhlau Verlag, Köln.

—— (1974) *Australian Aboriginal religion*. Brill, Leiden.

—— (1976) *Love songs of Arnhem Land*. Nelson, Melbourne.

Berndt, R.M. and Berndt, C.H. (1943) 'A preliminary report of field work in the Ooldea region, western South Australia' *Oceania* XIV: 1.

Berndt, R.M. and Berndt, C.H. (1944) 'A preliminary report of field work in the Ooldea region, western South Australia' *Oceania* XIV: 4.

Berndt, R.M. and Berndt, C.H. (1951) *Sexual behavior in western Arnhem Land*. Viking Fund Publications in Anthropology, No. 16, Wenner-Gren, New York.

Berndt, R.M. and Berndt, C.H. (1954) *Arnhem Land, its history and its people*. Cheshire, Melbourne.

Berndt, R.M. and Berndt, C.H. (1970) *Man, land and myth in North Australia: the Gunwinggu people*. Ure Smith, Sydney.

Berndt, R.M. and Berndt, C.H. (1964/1982/1985) *The world of the First Australians*. Rigby, Adelaide.

—— and Phillips, E.S. (eds) (1973) *The Australian Aboriginal heritage: an introduction through the arts*, 2 vols. Ure Smith (for the Australian Society for Education through the Arts), Sydney.

Blows, M. (1975) 'Eaglehawk and crow: birds, myths and moieties in south-east Australia' in L.R. Hiatt (ed.) *Australian Aboriginal mythology*. Australian Institute of Aboriginal Studies, Canberra.

Bunug *et al.* (1974) *Djugurba*. Australian National University Press, Canberra.

Cassirer, E. (1946) *The myth of the state*. Yale University Press, New Haven.

Chadwick, N.K. and Chadwick, H. (1932–40) *The growth of oral literature*, 3 vols. Cambridge University Press, Cambridge.

Clunies Ross, M. (1978) 'The structure of Arnhem Land song-poetry' *Oceania* XLIX: 2.

—— (1983) 'Modes of formal performance in societies without writing: the case of Aboriginal Australia' *Australian Aboriginal Studies 1*. Australian Institute of Aboriginal Studies, Canberra.

Davis, J. (1982) *Kullark — The Dreamers*. Currency Press, Sydney.

—— (1985) 'Aboriginal writing: a personal view' in J. Davis and R. Hodge (eds) *Aboriginal writing today*. Australian Institute of Aboriginal Studies, Canberra.

—— and Hodge R. (eds) (1985) *Aboriginal writing today*, Papers from the First National Conference of Aboriginal Writers held in Perth, WA, 1983. Australian Institute of Aboriginal Studies, Canberra.

Glass, A. and Newberry, D. (translators and eds) (1979) *Tjuma. Stories from the Western Desert*. Aboriginal Arts Board of The Australia Council for the Warburton Community Council Inc.

Gordon, T. and Haviland, J.B. (1979) *Milbi. Aboriginal tales from Queensland's Endeavour River*. Australian National University Press, Canberra.

Heath, J. (1980) *Nunggubuyu myths and ethnographic tests*. Australian Institute of Aboriginal Studies, Canberra.

—— (1984) *Functional grammar of Nunggubuyu*. Australian Institute of Aboriginal Studies, Canberra.

Hercus, L. and Sutton, P. (eds) (1986) *This is what happened*, Historical narratives by Aborigines. Australian Institute of Aboriginal Studies. Canberra.

Hiatt, L.R. (ed.) (1975) *Australian Aboriginal mythology*. Australian Institute of Aboriginal Studies, Canberra.

—— (ed.) (1978) *Australian Aboriginal concepts*. Australian Institute of Aboriginal Studies, Canberra.

Howitt, A.W. (1904) *The native tribes of south-east Australia*. Macmillan, London.

Kaberry, P.M. (1939) *Aboriginal woman, sacred and profane*. Routledge and Kegan Paul, London.

Lamilami, L. (1974) *Lamilami speaks. The cry went up. A story of the Goulburn Islands, North Australia*. Ure Smith, Sydney.

Leach, E.R. (1967) 'Genesis as myth' in *Myth and cosmos. Reading in mythology and symbolism*, American Museum Sourcebooks in Anthropology. The Natural History Press, Garden City, New York.

Lévi-Strauss, C. (1962) *La pensée sauvage*. Plon, Paris.

Lucich, P. (1969) *Children's stories from the Worora*. Australian Institute of Aboriginal Studies, Canberra.

McConnel, U.H. (1957) *Myths of the Mungkan*. Melbourne University Press, Melbourne.

Maddock K. (1970) 'The emu anomaly' in L.R. Hiatt (ed.) *Australian Aboriginal mythology*. Australian Institute of Aboriginal Studies, Canberra.

—— (1975) 'Myth of the acquisition of fire in northern and eastern Australia' in R.M. Berndt (ed.) *Australian Aboriginal Anthropology*. University of Western Australia Press, Perth.

Maranda, P. (1978) 'The popular subdiscourse: probabilistic semantic networks' *Current Anthropology*, 19: 2.

Marawili, W. and Wunungmurra, D. (1977) *Djet. A story from eastern Arnhem Land.* Nelson, Melbourne.

Marshall, A., Illustrator, M.-R. Ungunmerr (1952/1978) *People of the Dreamtime.* Hyland House, Melbourne.

Meggitt, M.J. (1966) 'Gadjari among the Walbiri Aborigines of Central Australia' *Oceania Monographs* 14 Sydney.

Michaels, E. and Kelly, F.J. 'The social organisation of an Aboriginal video workplace' *Australian Aboriginal Studies 1.* Australian Institute of Aboriginal Studies, Canberra.

Mountford, C.P. (1937) 'Aboriginal crayon drawings from the Warburton Ranges in Western Australia'. *Records of the South Australian Museum*, 61.

—— (1965) *Ayers Rock.* Angus and Robertson, Sydney.

—— (1976a) *Before time began.* Nelson, Melbourne.

—— (1976b) *Nomads of the Australian desert.* Rigby, Adelaide.

Muecke, S. (1983) 'Introduction' in P. Roe and S. Muecke *Gularabulu. Stories from the West Kimberley.* Fremantle Arts Centre Press, Fremantle.

Nangan, J. and Edwards, H. (1976) *Joe Nangan's Dreaming.* Nelson, Melbourne.

Nimanydja, D. (1983) 'A story about Moon, Ngalindi' in J. Davis and R. Hodge (eds) *Aboriginal writing today*, (also included in C.H. Berndt 1983). Australian Institute of Aboriginal Studies, Canberra.

Parker, K. Llangloh, Illustrator, E. Durack. (1896/1953) *Australian legendary tales*, selected by H. Drake-Brockman. Angus and Robertson, Sydney.

Robinson, R. (1965) *The man who sold his Dreaming.* Rigby, Adelaide.

—— (1966) *Aboriginal myths and legends.* Sun Books, Melbourne.

Roe, P. and Muecke, S. (1983) *Gularabulu. Stories from the West Kimberley.* Fremantle Arts Centre Press, Fremantle.

Sheppard, N., illustrator, B.S. Sewell; B.K. Wilson (ed.) (1975) *Alitjinya Ngura Tjukurtjarangka. Alitji in the Dreamtime*, Adapted and translated from *Alice's Adventure in Wonderland.* Department of Education, University of Adelaide.

Spencer, Baldwin (1914) *Native tribes of the Northern Territory of Australia.* Macmillan, London.

Strehlow, T.G.H. (1974) *Aranda traditions.* Melbourne University Press, Melbourne.

—— (1971) *Songs of Central Australia.* Angus and Robertson, Sydney.

Tindale, N.B. (1936) 'Legend of the Wati Kutjara, Warburton Range, Western Australia' *Oceania* VII: 2.

—— (1940) 'Results of the Harvard-Adelaide universities anthropological expedition, 1938–39: distribution of Australian Aboriginal tribes: a field survey' *Transactions of the Royal Society of South Australia* 64: 1.

—— (1959) 'Totemic beliefs in the Western Desert of Australia, Part 1: Women who became the Pleiades' *Records of the South Australian Museum* 13: 3.

Tonkinson, R. (1974) *The Jigalong mob: Aboriginal victors of the desert crusade.* Cummings, California.

Trezise, P. and Roughsey, D. (1980) *Banana bird and the snake men.* Collins, Sydney.

Tyler, S. (1969) 'Introduction' in S. Tyler (ed.) *Cognitive Anthropology.* Holt, Rinehart and Winston, New York.

Utemorrah, D. *et al.* (1980) *Vision of Mowanjum. Aboriginal writings from the Kimberley.* Rigby, Adelaide.

van der Leeden, A.C. (1975) 'Thundering gecko and emu: mythological structuring of Nunggubuyu patrimoieties' in L.R. Hiatt (ed.) *Australian Aboriginal mythology.* Australian Institute of Aboriginal Studies, Canberra.

Warner, W.L. (1937/1958) *A black civilization.* Harper, New York.

White, I.M. (1975) 'Sexual conquest and submission in the myths of central Australia' in L.R. Hiatt (ed.) *Australian Aboriginal mythology.* Australian Institute of Aboriginal Studies, Canberra.

Wingathana (1974) 'The brolga and the emu' in Bunug *et al.*, *Djugurba.* Australian National University Press, Canberra.

Yunupingu, M.D. (1974) 'The Moon and his family' in Bunug *et al.* (eds) *Djugurba.* Australian National University Press, Canberra.

INDEX

Since we have a separate list of the main story-tellers at the beginning of the book, we do not repeat their names here. Also, we have tried to keep references to our own names to a minimum. This applies to some other topics too, especially those dealing with land. ('Land' references appear on most pages of this book, in one way or another.) 'Shape-changing', 'Religion' and 'Myth' are also pervasive topics. With these we have noted examples, but not included every possible reference.

FOR THE BEST IN PAPERBACKS, LOOK FOR THE (🐧)

PENGUIN

Don't Take Your Love to Town
Ruby Langford

Ruby Langford and Susan Hampton worked together for two years on this book.

Ruby Langford is a remarkable woman whose sense of humour has endured through all the hardships she has experienced. Her autobiography is a book which cannot fail to move you.

'I felt like I was living tribal, but with no tribe around me, no close-knit family. The food gathering, the laws and songs were broken up, and my generation at this time wandered around as if we were tribal but in fact living worse than the poorest of poor whites, and in the case of women, living hard because it seemed like the men loved you for a while and then more kids came along and the men drank and gambled and disappeared. One day they'd had enough and they just didn't come back . . . my women friends all have similar stories.'

Born at Box Ridge Mission, Coraki, in the 30s, Ruby Langford's story is one of courage in the face of poverty and tragedy. She writes about the changing ways of life in Aboriginal communities—rural and urban; the disintegration of traditional lifestyles and the sustaining energy that has come from the renewal of Aboriginal culture in recent years.

The Law of the Land
Henry Reynolds

'I am at a loss to conceive by what tenure we hold this country, for it does not appear to be that we either hold it by conquest or by right of purchase.'
G. A. Robinson, 1832

In this readable and dramatic book, Henry Reynolds reassesses the legal and political arguments used to justify the European settlement of Australia.

His conclusions form a compelling case for the belief that the British government conceded land rights to the Aborigines early in the nineteenth century.

FOR THE BEST IN PAPERBACKS, LOOK FOR THE (🐧)

PENGUIN

BOOKS BY KEVIN GILBERT IN PENGUIN

Living Black
Blacks Talk to Kevin Gilbert

National Book Council Award for Australian Literature, 1978

'Aboriginal Australia underwent a rape of the soul so profound that the blight continues in the minds of most blacks today.'

Kevin Gilbert has talked with his people and taped their story—in the bush, in small country towns, and in the black ghettos of Sydney and Melbourne.

'What emerges is a damning indictment of the white man for his despicable discrimination, his injustice and intolerance, his ignorance and, above all, his failure to recognise the Aboriginal as a fellow human being—a human being with a deep sense of pride, a history as old as time and an affinity with his land that the white man will never understand.'

Herald

'A frank and compelling social document which exposes themes and issues important in the everyday lives of Aboriginal Australians. Its criticisms and lessons should not be ignored.'

Neville Perkins
Australian

Inside Black Australia
Kevin Gilbert

From the campfires and 'reserves' of the desert, from riverbanks and prison cells, from universities and urban ghettoes come the inside voices of Australia.

These are tough poems that resist the silence of genocide and the destruction of culture. The collection is an angry call for justice and the restoration of the land and the Dreaming. The Aboriginal lives glimpsed give white Australians a hint of the deep possibilities of belonging in this land.

Forty voices are heard in this first anthology of Aboriginal poetry.

FOR THE BEST IN PAPERBACKS, LOOK FOR THE 🐧

PENGUIN

BOOKS BY THEA ASTLEY IN PENGUIN

Hunting the Wild Pineapple

Leverson the narrator, at the centre of these stories, calls himself a 'people freak'. Seduced by North Queensland's sultry beauty and unique strangeness, he is as fascinated by the invading hordes of misfits from the south as by the old-established Queenslanders.

Leverson's ironical yet compassionate view makes every story, every incident, a pointed example of human weakness—or strength.

Beachmasters

The central government in Trinitas can't control the outer island. But then neither can the British and French masters.

The natives of Kristi, supported and abetted by some of the *hapkas* and *colons* of two nationalities, make a grab for independence from the rest of their Pacific island group. On their tiny island, where blood and tradition are as mixed as loyalties and interests, their revolution is short-lived. Yet it swallows the lives of a number of inhabitants—from the old-time planters Salway and Duchard, to the opportunist Bonser, and the once mighty *yeremanu*, Tommy Narota himself.

Salway's grandson Gavi unwittingly gets caught up in Bonser's plans and, in a test of identity too risky for one so young, forfeits his own peace.

FOR THE BEST IN PAPERBACKS, LOOK FOR THE (🐧)

PENGUIN

An Item From the Late News

Wafer, who saw his father blown apart by a bomb in the second world war, and who grew up under the shadow of the nuclear bomb, seeks to spend his middle years in a place of solitude where he can prepare for the inevitable . . .

Allbut, scarcely a dot on the map in the vast Queensland outback, seems to be that perfect place.

But Wafer's peace-loving ways are not understood by the clean and decent locals and when it comes, the final blast is not the one he expected.

It's Raining in Mango

Sometimes history repeats itself.

One family traced from the 1860s to the 1980s: from Cornelius to Connie to Reever, who was last seen heading north.

Cornelius Laffey, an Irish born journalist, wrests his family from the easy living of nineteenth-century Sydney and takes them to Cooktown in northern Queensland where thousands of diggers are searching for gold in the mud.

The family confront the horror of Aboriginal dispossession—Cornelius is sacked for reporting the slaughter. His daughter, Nadine, joins the singing whore on the barge and goes upstream, only to be washed out to sea.

The cycles of generations turn, one over the other. Only some things change. That world and this world both have their Catholic priests, their bigots, their radicals. Full of powerful and independent characters, this is an unforgettable tale of the other side of Australia's heritage.

FOR THE BEST IN PAPERBACKS, LOOK FOR THE

PENGUIN

BOOKS BY JESSICA ANDERSON IN PENGUIN

Tirra Lirra by the River

A beautifully written novel of a woman's seventy-year search to find a place where she truly belongs.

For Nora Porteous, life is a series of escapes. To escape her tightly knit small-town family, she marries, only to find herself confined again, this time in a stifling Sydney suburb with a selfish, sanctimonious husband. With a courage born of desperation and sustained by a spirited sense of humour, Nora travels to London, and it is there that she becomes the woman she wants to be. Or does she?

Winner of the Miles Franklin Award.

Stories From the Warm Zone and Sydney Stories

Jessica Anderson's evocative stories recreate, through the eyes of a child, the atmosphere of Australia between the wars. A stammer becomes a blessing in disguise; the prospect of a middle name converts a reluctant child to baptism. These autobiographical stories of a Brisbane childhood glow with the warmth of memory.

The formless sprawl of Sydney in the 1980s is a very different world. Here the lives of other characters are changed by the uncertainties of divorce, chance meetings and the disintegration and generation of relationships.

Winner of the Age Book of the Year Award.

Last Man's Head

Detective Alec Probyn has his enemies too. His recent stand on police violence has led to his being suspended from duty. He has a growing suspicion that a vicious crime is about to be committed. All the more disturbing as the suspect and the victim are both members of his own family.

How can Probyn prevent this crime and its shattering consequences? In the savage resolution he discovers that his anti-violent stand has not magically cancelled out the violence in himself.

FOR THE BEST IN PAPERBACKS, LOOK FOR THE

PENGUIN

Series Editor: Dale Spender

The Penguin Australian Women's Library will make available to readers a wealth of information through the work of women writers of our past. It will include the classic to the freshly re-discovered, individual reprints to new anthologies, as well as up-to-date critical re-appraisals of their work and lives as writers.

The Penguin Anthology of Australian Women's Writing
Edited by Dale Spender

'Only when all the women writers of Australia are brought together is it possible to identify . . . a distinctive female literary tradition.'

Australia has a rich tradition of women writers. In 1790 Elizabeth Macarthur wrote letters home while she travelled to Australia; in 1970 Germaine Greer published *The Female Eunuch*. Thirty-seven writers—working in every genre—are included in this landmark anthology.

Margaret Catchpole	Mary Grant Bruce
Elizabeth Macarthur	Miles Franklin
Georgiana McCrae	Dymphna Cusack
Louisa Ann Meredith	Katharine Susannah Prichard
Catherine Helen Spence	Nettie Palmer
Ellen Clacy	Marjorie Barnard
Mary Fortune (Waif Wander)	Eleanor Dark
Ada Cambridge	Dorothy Cottrell
Louisa Lawson	Christina Stead
Jessie Couvreur (Tasma)	Sarah Campion
Rosa Praed	Kylie Tennant
Catherine Langloh Parker	Nancy Cato
Barbara Baynton	Faith Bandler
Mary Gaunt	Nene Gare
Mary Gilmour	Olga Masters
Henry Handel Richardson	Oriel Gray
Ethel Turner	Antigone Kefala
G. B. Lancaster	Germaine Greer
Mollie Skinner	

Mr Hogarth's Will
by Catherine Helen Spence

Jane and Alice Melville have been disinherited by their uncle, who believes that a 'boys' education will serve them better than an inheritance.

The sisters struggle for independence and fulfilment takes them from Scotland to Australia and a new vision of their lives.

First published in 1867.

FOR THE BEST IN PAPERBACKS, LOOK FOR THE

PENGUIN

Kirkham's Find
by Mary Gaunt

Phoebe Marsden wants a place of her own. At twenty-four she refuses to compromise her ideals and marry for expediency. Her younger sister Nancy does not share her ideals. Against everyone's advice Phoebe decides to set up on her own and keep bees.

Phoebe is one of the first Australian heroines to choose between marriage and a career. Her choice has unexpected ramifications for another sister, Lydia.

First published in 1897.

The Peaceful Army
Edited by Flora Eldershaw

In 1938, at the time of Australia's 150th Anniversary, this collection was published in honour of women's contribution. The list of contributors is a veritable 'who's who' of women in Australian cultural life. They include: Margaret Preston, Marjorie Barnard, Miles Franklin, Dymphna Cusack and a young Kylie Tennant. They write about Elizabeth Macarthur, Caroline Chisholm, Rose Scott and early women writers and artists.

In 1938 Kylie Tennant concludes the volume. Just before her death in 1988 she reflected on the intervening fifty years.

FOR THE BEST IN PAPERBACKS, LOOK FOR THE (penguin logo)

PENGUIN

Her Selection: Writings by Nineteenth-Century Australian Women
Edited by Lynne Spender

Nineteenth-century Australian women writers were published widely in magazines, newspapers and books in Australia and abroad. Their writings provide an insight into the lives of women, the opportunities and obstacles, the hardships and the successes. This lively collection brings together works that have been unavailable for many years.

Included are works by: Georgiana Molloy, Louisa Lawson, Annabella Boswell, Mary Fortune and 'Tasma'.

A Bright and Fiery Troop: Australian Women Writers of the Nineteenth Century
Edited by Debra Adelaide

Who was the most popular detective story writer of the nineteenth century? A woman, Mary Fortune.

Who was the internationally famous botanist and artist who also wrote novels? A woman, Louisa Atkinson.

Who wrote the first convict novel? A woman, Caroline Leakey.

Who wrote the first novel with an Aboriginal protagonist? A woman, Catherine Martin.

This book opens up the hidden history of Australian literature and is the first crictical appraisal of the major Australian women writers of the nineteenth century.

The book includes photographs.